A Monastery in Time

FRONTISPIECE Chogchin and Maidar Temples of Mergen Monastery, 2007. (Hürelbaatar Ujeed)

A Monastery in Time

The Making of Mongolian Buddhism

CAROLINE HUMPHREY
AND HÜRELBAATAR UJEED

The University of Chicago Press Chicago and London

CAROLINE HUMPHREY is professor emerita and director of the Mongolian and Inner Asia Studies Unit at the University of Cambridge. She is the author or coauthor of twenty previous books, most recently *Urban Life in Post-Soviet Central Asia*.

HÜRELBAATAR UJEED founded the Hürelbaatar Institute for Mongolian Studies at the Inner Mongolia Normal University and is senior research associate in the Mongolian and Inner Asia Studies Unit at the University of Cambridge.

The University of Chicago Press, Chicago 60637
The University of Chicago Press, Ltd., London

Printed in the United States of America

22 21 20 19 18 17 16 15 14 13   1 2 3 4 5

ISBN-13: 978-0-226-03187-3 (cloth)
ISBN-13: 978-0-226-03190-3 (paper)
ISBN-13: 978-0-226-03206-1 (e-book)

A CIP record for this title is available at the Library of Congress.

♾ The paper meets the requirements of ANSI/NISO Z39.48-1992 (Permanence of Paper).

Contents

Transliteration

For Mongolian terms we have given the written form used in Inner Mongolia, since the spoken form differs from place to place and introduces ambiguities. We have employed the spelling in Lessing's dictionary (1960) with some simplifications: г and G are both represented by "g"; K and X are both represented by "h"; and the diphthongs *ayi, oyi,* and *eyi* are rendered as *ai, oi,* and *ei*. Detached letters at the end of words, usually hyphenated, have been attached (e.g., *süme,* not *süm-e*), but hyphens have been retained for case suffixes. Some of Lessing's transliterations have been changed to make the letter as it is pronounced more recognizable by readers unfamiliar with his conventions: thus for "ø" we write "ö"; for "y" we write "ü"; for "č" we write "ch"; for "j" we write "y"; for "ǰ" we write "z"; for "z" we write "j." The Mongolian letter "sh" and "s" before "i" are both rendered as "sh." Readers should note, however, that the spoken form often differs considerably from the written; thus, for example, "Muna" (dictionary spelling) is pronounced locally "Mon."

For some words from Mongolian and other languages that have entered the English-language academic literature we have departed from the usage noted above and kept now familiar spellings (e.g., Khan, Shambhala, Sumeru, Panchen Lama, Dalai Lama, and *oboo* instead of *obuga*). Likewise, we have spelled certain place names according to modern renderings, for example, Bayannuur, Beijing, Darhan Muuminggan, Höhnuur, Höhhot, Lhasa, and Ulaanchab. For personal names we have followed the usual practice in Inner Mongolia of joining the elements into one word; the exception is names where the first element ends in a consonant and the second begins with a vowel, and in these cases the elements are separated by a hyphen (e.g., Minggan-agula). On pages 100–101 we have followed the published transliteration of Mergen Gegen's poem.

For Mongolian titles published in Cyrillic we have used the Library of Congress system. Chinese names and words have been transcribed according to the Pinyin and Tibetan according to the Wylie systems.

Acknowledgments and a Note on the Writing of This Book

Acknowledgments

Our greatest debt is to the lamas of Mergen Monastery, most especially to the Chorji Lama Mönghebatu, who was our host during the years of our fieldwork from 1995 to 2007. Without his welcoming us to his monastery, the numerous arrangements he made for our benefit, and his generosity and forbearance we could not possibly have accomplished our study. We owe more than we can say to the understanding that Chorji brought to our project, his sharing of problems with us, and his own honesty and patience during countless hours of conversations. We are also immensely grateful to Lubsansengge Lama, now sadly deceased. Sengge Lama gave tirelessly and generously of his wide knowledge. In a friendly sprit he patiently explained endless points of doctrine, local practice, and regional mythology. His restraint, humor, modesty, and devotion to others were vivid lessons in the life of a Buddhist monk in difficult circumstances. We would like to give special thanks also to Minggan-agula Lama and his family, who unstintingly gave us their time and attention in rituals, interviews and everyday conversations. We greatly appreciate the many paintings Minggan Lama made for us that depict his artistic vision and understanding of the deities and landscape of Mergen Monastery.

Other lamas of Mergen and the Mongolian chanting tradition were also most helpful and we would like to record our thanks to them: the Baragun Da reincarnation, Boruheshig Lama, Galluu Lama, Heshigdalai Lama, Heshigbayar Lama, Arbinjargal reincarnation, Dalantai Lama, Bayanbilig Lama, Nasansed Lama, Nasundalai Lama, Norbuu Lama, Lubsangshirab Lama, Ünenbat Lama, Sodnomjamsu Lama, Samtan Lama, Dampil Lama, Jongrai Lama, Altanbagana Lama, Tumenjirgal Lama, and Darja Lama. We would also like to thank Ganbaatar Lama and Bayanchimeg, who are located in Ulaanbaatar.

Our sincere appreciation goes also to many people of the lay community around Mergen, most especially to Dr. Dalantai, and also to Erhimbayar, Shirüngerel, Udbalchecheg, Chasuchihir, Sechin Teacher, Lubsangshirab, and Batuchilagu. This book owes enormously to the sincerity and generosity with which they shared information and sometimes painful memories, with us. We are especially grateful to the members of Chorji's family circle for their hospitality and friendly welcome: Ulagangerel, Navchingerel, Chinggelbatu, and Erdenibatu.

Our research would not have been possible without the long-term support of Inner Mongolia Normal University. We are most grateful to President and later Party Secretary Chen Zhongyong and to current President Yang Yijiang for their unfailing support. Over the years Chen Yue, Director of the Foreign Affairs Office and Head of the International Exchange College, coordinated the administrative aspect of our research, and became a good friend in the process. The university generously provided us with accommodation, transportation, and guidance through many years of work. We would also like to acknowledge the support of Inner Mongolia University and many colleagues from its faculty.

Numerous scholars from Inner Mongolia helped us with invaluable insights and provided a wider perspective from which to understand the Mergen tradition. We would like to thank especially Professor Ü. Naranbatu and Professor Ba. Mönghe whose long experience, expert advice and patient help with our questions on Buddhism and Urad history and culture have been of crucial value to this book. We hope we have correctly rendered the essential import of their advice, even if we were not able to include all the points of detail. Dr. Mönghebuyan provided friendly and energetic devotion to the research and carried out many interviews for us, and for this we are also very grateful. We would also like to thank specially Professor Nasunbayar, who joined us in exploring the Muna mountains and conversing with local people and throughout the project gave us the benefit of his comparative anthropological perspective. From Inner Mongolia Normal University, Professors Chen Shan, Ochi, Jaggar, and Qi Bagatur generously shared their knowledge of regional culture with us. Inner Mongolia University Professors Chimiddorji, Rashisürüng, Bayarmendü, Erhimbayar, and Erdenibayar gave us insight into historical and linguistic matters. All of these people were most hospitable to us in Höhhot, and we have warm memories of more generous banquets and informal dinners than we can count.

For the field visit of 1998 we would like to acknowledge the valuable research investigations of Mönghebuyan, Nasunbayar, Gai Shanlin, Gai Zhiyi, Temüchine, and Balzhan Zhimbiev. In later visits we were joined by James Laidlaw, Chris Evans, and Jonathan Mair and we thank them for their intellectual insights and companionship.

Very many scholars have provided invaluable help in composing this book. We are especially grateful to Christopher Atwood for his detailed advice, generous support and exceptional historical understanding, and to Johan Elverskog for his invaluable orientation in comparative Mongolian history. We thank Donald Lopez for giving generously of his time to caste a rigorous eye over a version of the first chapters. Hildegard Diemberger, who contributed her deep knowledge of Tibetan culture, has been a wonderful colleague. The following people have commented on draft chapters and/or helped with fieldwork, translations, and interpretations, and we sincerely thank all of them: Aitoro Telenged, Michael Banner; Uradyn Bulag, Matei Candea, Isabelle Charleux, Chuluun, Chuluunbat, Joanna Cook, Pamela Crossley, Baasanjav Dune, Chris Evans, Biancamaria Fontana, Roberte Hamayon, Richard Koeck, James Laidlaw, Lu Hui, Jonathan Mair, Ulrich Pagels, Morten Pedersen, Tatiana Skrynnikova, David Sneath, Justin Tighe, Tsymzhit Vanchikova, Piers Vitebsky, Balzhan Zhimbiev. While we were writing our book, Uranchimeg Borjigin Ujeed was writing a PhD on the liturgical works of the 3rd Mergen Gegen. This book owes enormously to her expertise and collaboration.

The research for this book was financed by grants from the British Academy; King's College, Cambridge; McDonald Institute for Archaeological Research, Cambridge; and the Mongolia and Inner Asia Studies Unit, University of Cambridge. We are thankful to these institutions for their support.

We are most grateful to Libby Peachey for her miraculously effective administrative help over the years, to Lefkos Kiryakis for the maps, to Mary-Elizabeth Cox for her devoted help in preparing the book for publication, and to Tom Hughes for his splendid copyediting of the final text.

A Note on the Writing of this Book

This book is the result of collaborative research and authorship. The initial visit to Mergen Monastery was made by Hürelbaatar is 1992 and he was joined by Caroline Humphrey in 1995, whereupon we conceived the idea of writing a book together. Our first interest was in the monastery as a Buddhist focus in a historical landscape, in the palimpsest of overlaid economic, military, and sacred sites that surround Mergen and the reflections on these in contemporary oral narratives. Accordingly, in 1998 and 2000 we revisited the area with a team including regional archaeologists, anthropologists, a linguistics scholar, and an architectural historian. Our appreciation of the archaeological depth of the landscape was greatly enriched by the presence of archaeologist Chris Evans during our visit in 2000. This period of fieldwork resulted in an unpublished report and five publications (Humphrey 2001; Evans and Humphrey 2002 and 2003; Hürelbaatar 2006; Humphrey and Laidlaw 2007).

At the same time, our attention could not but turn to the religious vitality of the monastery itself. This became the focus of our succeeding visits in 2002, 2005, 2007, and 2009 (joined by anthropologists James Laidlaw in 2000 and 2002 and Jonathan Mair in 2005). As the lamas talked to us about their tradition, it became obvious that the history of the monastery and its liturgical culture were essential themes, and we worked in Cambridge on translating three main bodies of texts: the writings of the 3rd Mergen Gegen, the history written by Duke Galsangwangchugdorji, and the contemporary work of Inner Mongolian scholars. A chapter on the exceptionally turbulent history of the 1920s to the late 1940s was omitted for reasons of space, and we hope to publish on this period later. Meanwhile, our successive visits to Inner Mongolia contributed to our gradually deeper understanding of the conceptual world of Mergen people and their rituals and everyday practices. Since the ethnography of current activity was the basis on which we tried to work out the nature of the monastery as an institution, the ongoing events at Mergen became part of the content of the book. Each year we expected a resolution into some more or less steady state (upon which we could come to an idea of the overall shape of the book)—

only to find that events overtook our previous conclusions. The result is the account that follows, which acknowledges in the Epilogue that the story of the monastery does not have an ending and that "the tradition" has to be understood in the light of these changes. We have tried to do justice to the character of these events while taking great care over the representation of the leading characters at Mergen to whom we owe so much. Some names have been changed, but as the book concerns a historically well-known monastery we judged it necessary to retain many of our respondents' identities. Any faults in representation are our responsibility and we know that inevitably there must be different views of some of the incidents we have described here. We sincerely hope that the people who have maintained the Mergen tradition in the contemporary world will find their portraits here to be just and sympathetic. We have done our best to describe the challenges they have faced and their courageous responses to them.

Introduction

One day in October 1992 Hürelbaatar Ujeed hitched a ride on the mudguard of a tractor to an abandoned Chinese army base. When he reached the officers' mess he saw sloped tiled roofs behind—for here a monastery was concealed, the remains of Mergen, once a great Buddhist foundation and head of a constellation of many smaller monasteries scattered across the region of Urad in Inner Mongolia. They professed a unique kind of "Mongolian Buddhism," using texts written in the Mongolian language. A conical peak glinted in the mountains just behind Mergen. This was the summit of Muna Mountain, where the monks climbed each year to chant for sacrifices.

What does it mean to be a Buddhist in a Mongolian way? While virtually all Mongols, including the monks at Mergen, are adherents of Mahayana Buddhism and the Gelug order dominant in Tibet, this monastery was exceptional—rebellious even—in rejecting the Tibetan liturgy used across Inner Asia and insisting on its own vernacular rites. What cultural sources flowed into this particular idiom of Buddhism, which we call "Mongolian Buddhism," and how does its particular perspective on the world create certain dispositions in the monks and lay people of the vicinity? How did the monks sustain this religious aesthetic of the Mongol liturgy when it was abandoned elsewhere? And what does this localized form mean *now*, in these western regions of China, a country in which the state has constantly sought to regulate religion and yet seems to be changing faster at present than at any time in its history? The Cultural Revolution shattered not just buildings and religious services but also the lives of the monks, so much so that the revived Buddhism of today cannot be practiced in the same fashion it was only a generation ago; and if that is true, then what does it mean to say these people uphold a tradition? Our research revealed that the monastery had a turbulent earlier history: it was sacked or burned several times; once abandoned by all the monks; and splits, quarrels, and expulsions seemed to be endemic. We began to ask ourselves how it ever stayed together, and what it means for any institution to be "a whole"? These questions came to preoccupy us during some fifteen years of research at Mergen Monastery in Urad. We hope this book will provide coherent answers to them.

But in truth those questions were not the reasons we began our extensive research at the monastery. These arose in 1992 from Hürelbaatar's perception of a rare magnetism at Mergen, a time when most Mongols in Inner Mongolia were still wary of all religion. There was a subdued fervor about the place, and on his first visit Hürelbaatar sensed that the religious activities there distilled something precious to the people. It was as if they had awoken from a blurry sleep and could hardly believe that these unfamiliar actions they were undertaking in the ruins of the monastery—acts which only a few years ago would still have been unthinkably dangerous—were indeed the prayers and rites they grew up with. Soon Hürelbaatar encouraged Caroline to join him on a longer investigation with a simple aim: to discover what kind of Buddhism there was in this place. In this age of the anthropology of airport lounges and internet sociality, we were convinced that prolonged study of a particular site had value in revealing general—possibly universal— predicaments out of particularities.[1] That was why Mergen Monastery—an obscure structure in a backwater of an undeveloped part of China mattered. It allowed us to extend our imaginations to the utterly specific in order to focus on what essential element in human interactions would enable a group of people to impose their own direction and sustain a particular ethical-aesthetic form of life.

In 1995, when Caroline joined Hürelbaatar at Mergen, a wary joy was still apparent, seeping through the throngs of people at the monastery. It was infectious—a ray of affect that was shed from smiles and glances onto us. This affinity was not just a current running through people, it

1. Mergen Monastery was thus an "arbitrary fieldsite" in the sense that it bore no necessary relation to the general questions about tradition we were asking (Candea 2007, 180). Yet from another perspective it was a fundamentally non-arbitrary site, since it was the only monastery that created, and insisted on maintaining through history, Mongolian-language Buddhism.

was also in the "things" of the place: the temples whose scars seemed to make them animated, traumatic; the dark loft, ankle-deep in bats' droppings, from which one could glimpse the Buddha's face; the paths, worn by steps that seemed to point in a mysterious direction. All the things of one kind at Mergen were embedded in another kind of thing; they each contained their own meanings as we encountered them, and yet also hid other meanings as yet unknown to us. If we visitors felt the allure recessed within these objects, still more it seemed did the local people who meandered around. In those times of our first visits, laypeople would just stand "aimlessly," or sit on some brick corner, drab figures in worn communist-era clothes, maybe chatting, maybe not, but mainly just savoring the energy of the place itself.

It is because this atmosphere changed and darkened after only a year or two of our visits that we became aware of the historicity of religious life, its propensity to transform even while ostensibly staying the same. By fits and starts, since we did not live constantly in the monastery but visited every two years or so from 1992 onward, we realized that "things were different from last time." Even such relatively short gaps were enough to make us realize that it was impossible to write about the monastery and the relations between the monks living there simply as a system or a culture. We had to start thinking about what was the same about an institution that was constantly *happening*, and about the difference between processes of continuous transformation and discontinuous events.

Concerns about time have largely structured the shape of this book. Its main framework follows our eight successive visits to the monastery between 1992 and 2009. On each occasion we were brought into contact with another way that religion is manifest there. But at the same time we were told of scenarios in the monastery's past, for the lamas[2] see themselves as part of a continuing tradition, and they constantly referred to historical people, events, and ways of doing things. The ensuing chapters therefore follow our visits in sequence, but also try to do justice to what the lamas thought was important by presenting substantial historical material. As far as possible, we attempt to describe this in conventional chronological order and to relate the stories we were told to other kinds of information—though because almost all

2. We follow local practice in using the respectful term "lama" for all men who had taken vows, whether or not they were monks living in the monastery and irrespective of religious status.

the monastery's historical documents were destroyed or lost there are unavoidable gaps.

Thus, woven together in the book are two time frameworks. The longer historical one concerns the "Mergen tradition." That is the creation, renaissance, travails, ruin, revival, and trauma of a specifically Mongolian way of practicing Buddhism from the early eighteenth century to the present. The other time series concerns the fine grain of the seventeen years of our fieldwork. Even during this relatively brief period some startling and bitter events took place. We were brought face to face with ruptures, alterations, inventions, and breakdowns, some of these apparently brought about by changes washing in to this remote spot from transformations in China, while others seemed locally produced, the result of sharp clashes of personalities and significant decisions that had to be made. We hasten to add that neither of the time frameworks used to organize this book corresponds to a Mongolian understanding of the past. It is not that the people we met at Mergen would have any specific disagreement with these chronologies, but left to themselves they tend not to think in these ways. They conceptualize past times, sequences, epochs and events according to particular cultural genres—not one but several such modes of "historicity" (Hirsch and Stewart 2005). One of the aims of this book is to explore these modes as people actually use them.

The Question of Tradition

The confrontational dramas of events in the monastery made us see that we could not approach "tradition" in the same way that the lamas did. For them the Mergen tradition was a matter of pedigree: about what came first, what was genuine, who taught whom, which activities or beliefs had been faithfully transmitted and which had not. We felt, on the other hand, that we had to operate with an anthropological idea whereby tradition involves not just the deliberate and self-conscious transmission of a body of religious teaching and ethical practice, but a repeated mediation, whereby each generation of Mergen lamas works *on* as well as *in* that tradition, constantly selecting what they take to be most valuable in it and discarding certain elements along the way. As James Laidlaw writes about the religious tradition of the Jains: "Its relative coherence and partial systematicity are their ongoing and never-completed achievement" (2010, 121–22). Further, we follow Alasdair MacIntyre in his understanding that any historically embedded tradition must involve internal dissent. "A tradition," he says, "is an argument extended through time in which certain fundamental agreements are defined and redefined in terms of two kinds of conflict: those with critics and enemies external to the tradition . . . and those internal, interpretive debates . . . by whose progress a tradition is constituted" (1988, 12).[3] Tradition, as Dreyfus aptly remarks about Tibetan monastic education, has its intellectuals. Any view that characterizes tradition by its static antiqueness, contrasting it to modernity and innovation, deprives such cultures of their intellectual content and drive (2003, 9).

Saba Mahmood's discussion of Islamic pedagogy (2005) provides a most thoughtful account of tradition. Viewing it as a discursive formation, an idea whose genealogy reaches back through Asad (1986) to Foucault ([1972] 2002), she contrasts such a concept with the notion of "invented tradition," a set of idioms about the past that justify present practices (Hobsbawm 1983). Rather than the latter perspective, which privileges a body of overseers, Mahmood prefers the generative openness of a conception of tradition as a field of statements and practices (2005, 115). Seen in this light, one effect of an Islamic discursive engagement with sacred texts is the creation of sensibilities and embodied capacities (of reason, affect, and volition) that in turn are the condition for the tradition's reproduction. Such an approach "does not assume all-powerful voluntary subjects who manipulate the tradition for their own ends, but enquires into those conditions of discursive formation that require and produce the kind of subjects who may speak in its name" (ibid, 115–16).

Although we share this perspective, the notion of "a discursive formation" still seems to imply the presence of something unproven—a mysterious totality within which are accommodated the people who make this tradition. But our ethnography resounds with the presence and mediating agency of particular personalities. Traversed by diverse possibilities these people became active subjects, crystallizing a facet of themselves, in connection with events and decisions (Humphrey 2008). This does not mean that we resort to a presentist "invention of tradition" perspective; but rather, while agreeing with Mahmood that "the past is the very ground through which the subjectivity and self-understanding of a tradition's adherents are constituted" (2005, 115),

3. A tradition would nevertheless differ from what Bruno Latour has called "matters of concern," the exposure of disputed issues around which assemblages of facts, opinions, and pressure groups gather (Latour 2005a, 114). The latter are potentially endlessly extensive networks, whereas a tradition implies some sense of closure, or a turning inward of the debates to a core of issues.

we see the fragile reproduction of tradition in the ability of individuals to play or refuse to play, to divert performances in their own diverse ways, to pluralize pasts, and to interfere with others on behalf of what they take to be the ensemble.

In our case, a "tradition" is what is held (in different ways) to be a corpus by people attached to an institution, the monastery—yet "institution" is another concept that needs to be queried. If we agree that an institution is not a superordinate master structure, is nothing beyond the ideas and practices that make it up, then Bruno Latour's analogy with orchestral performance is illuminating. Latour insists that the magic of musical harmony is not achieved, as is commonly assumed, by each musician sticking closely and correctly only to their own part given by a superior order. On the contrary, it comes about by attending *beyond one's part* to all the others, knowing when to listen and when and how to play. Each instrument thus has to do with all others, but in extremely varied ways, and it is from these positions that each has its own conception of the whole. The conductor and the score, with its last minute penciled in additions, do not "represent the totality" so much as provide the temporary material whereby the acute attentiveness of each to all the others can be achieved. Not only is success not guaranteed, but lack of harmony is a normal condition—and chaos is an intensification and dramatization of it (Latour 2010, 4–6).

It is in this sense that we see the fragility of the Mergen tradition. Several times during the fieldwork we left Inner Mongolia wondering whether the monastery would still be in existence on our return. It might seem obvious, looking at the broad sweep of history, that the force of recent events in China—the cumulative onslaught of mass Han immigration into Inner Mongolia, the Cultural Revolution, the oppressive political control of religion, the loss of Mongol language among many in the young generation, and the capitalist, globalizing transformation of the economy—must have thrust the Urad Mongols into something like the doomed state of the Crow culture in nineteenth-century America (Lear 2006), leaving their regional and idiosyncratic "Mongolian Buddhism" a meaningless irrelevance in more ways than one. But, as we record in this book, for most of the Mongols living around Mergen that is not the case. For them innumerable elements of the patchwork of "Mongolian Buddhism" remain deeply significant—though increasingly they are overgrown, like some fragile flower species scattered in a forest of rampant trees. We came to realize that religion can flow into new contexts and is not dovetailed to a particular economic way of life. The main problem for the people of Mergen is a different though related one: gathering and sustaining an assemblage of people who care enough about religion, and about one another, for them even to bother with disagreements or debates in the tradition.

In any case, "Mergen Monastery" could not be just assumed as a lasting, self-cohering "social unity," even though the local Mongols speak about it in this way. Pursuing as far as we could the scanty historical documents, we discovered the lineaments of a different—molecular, as it were—formation, scattered, sometimes cohering, but constantly splitting, spreading, and contracting (Chapter 3). In tension and mutual attraction with the lay political leaders of Urad, the monastic formation was impelled in various directions by particular personalities and the decisions they took.

The most prominent of these were the reincarnate lamas (*hubilgan*) of Mergen. They were monks of extraordinary sanctity, as their "souls'" (*sünesü*) were believed to be those of previous holy bearers going back to the deity originating the given line. The reincarnations also had a certain political legitimacy, as they could not take office unless recognized by the government of the day. Among the great lamas of Mergen the supreme figure in the monastery's history was the eighteenth-century Lubsangdambijalsan, who was the 3rd in the reincarnation line of the Mergen Gegen ("Wise Radiance"). He is the linchpin of the tradition because he was its greatest cultural innovator. As liturgist, poet, translator, composer of music, and controversial historian, he almost completely reconstituted the "Mongolian Buddhism" previously practiced at Mergen, and thus set in train the tradition recognized today. Lamas constantly spoke of things they happened to do—even if they hotly disagreed with one another—as having been laid down by the great 3rd Mergen Gegen.

1992–A Great Reincarnate Lama Comes to Mergen

Hürelbaatar's 1992 fieldwork coincided with what everyone at Mergen felt was a momentous happening. The occasion was the consecration ritual of a gigantic statue of the Maidar (S. Maitreya) Buddha, the Buddha to appear on earth in the coming epoch. The rite was conducted by the most senior reincarnation in the whole of Inner Mongolia, Ulagan Gegen,[4] who traveled to Mergen from the capital city of Höhhot

4. Ulagan Gegen ("Red Radiance," 1920–2004) was a Mongolian born in Ordos. He took *gelüng* vows and studied at the great Tibetan-language monastery at Kumbum, where he received

for the purpose. We begin the book with this sequence of events partly because they were the baseline for the time series of our fieldwork, a point of departure for changes we observed; the main reason for introducing them here is that they reveal some key aspects of the "way of being" of Mongolian Buddhists. These interrelated themes are: the central importance of making "will-vows" (*irügel*, pronounced *yörööl*) as an intentional form of self-transformation; the ways people talk, and do not talk, about religion; the heterogeneity of Mongol frameworks of time; and the embedding of religion in everyday life.

First, however, we should provide some context of a conventional historical kind to explain why this particular event was so important in the history of Mergen.

Before the Communist government came to power in 1949, there were still hundreds of monasteries in Inner Mongolia, and Buddhism remained an important, though much contested, social force. During the 1950s and early 1960s, relentless pressure was put on the lamas to leave the monasteries, take up a productive occupation, marry, and abandon "useless" and "harmful" beliefs in religion. By 1966 and 1967, the outbreak of the Cultural Revolution, most small monasteries had already closed and only a handful of monks were left in those like Mergen that remained open. Now these monasteries too were sacked and shut down, and the residual lamas were accused and humiliated, tortured, and in some cases killed. Following this trauma, a further campaign against the (in fact defunct) Inner Mongolian Peoples' Party (*Nei Ren Dang*) attacked local officials—and indeed anyone imagined to sympathize with traditional Mongolian culture—tracked them down, and accused, insulted, beat, imprisoned, and executed them. This second terrible campaign had more victims than the Cultural Revolution. Meanwhile, Chinese workers and farmers poured into the region in greater numbers than ever before, leaving the Mongols even in a mostly rural area like Urad as only a small minority of the population. At party meetings, in workplaces, in the press and in schools and universities, religion was declared a harmful remnant of the past, unworthy of the attention of a decent, forward-looking person. There was a political rationale for the oppression of Buddhism in Inner Mongolia too. In the context of China's constant fear of disintegration and its attempt to transform a former sprawling empire and forge a nation state,

the Gabju (T. *dka-bcu*) degree and rose to become Tsanid Hambo and hold the highest seat. A renowned expert in philosophical debate, he returned to Inner Mongolia in 1958 and remained there for the rest of his life.

the religion was seen as a possible rallying point for "splitists" and disaffected ethnic minorities. For this reason, even after attitudes toward religion in general became more benign in the mid-1980s, the central government forbade the recognition of any new Buddhist reincarnations in Inner Mongolia, for fear they would become leaders and rallying points.[5]

Yet this multiple onslaught did not bring about a radical break in Buddhist life, or at least not directly. For a fair number of Buddhist lamas did survive these terrible years. They were people who had lived in monasteries from early childhood through their early adulthood and who simply would not, or could not, metamorphose themselves into atheist communist subjects. They, together with devout laypeople living near the monastery, reestablished worship at Mergen in the 1980s (Chapter 1).

The construction of the Maidar statue had its own history. All sacred representations at Mergen, including the previous giant statue of the Buddha-to-Come, had been destroyed—yet the lamas needed objects of worship. The lofty hall of the Maidar Temple held only the shattered base of the earlier statue. When government attitudes toward religion softened around 1990, the lamas were able to request a state grant for restoration of buildings, but they were told that no new statue could be built. How to get around the ban? What followed was an entirely traditional procedure. The manager of the monastery, whose lay name is Mönghebatu, had been recognized as a reincarnation in the Chorji line when he was a young boy in the 1950s, before the prohibition on recognizing new reincarnations. Though he had only recently returned to the monastery from his lay life as a teacher, he soon assumed unquestioned authority as "master of the monastery" at Mergen. On his own initiative he sent the lamas out on an alms-collecting round (*badar*, from S. *pātra*) to raise income to construct a statue. Two by two, they traveled all over the county (called the Banner) and to neighboring regions. The Mongols living hereabouts are mostly herders, and they gave generously: money, and also hundreds of sheep and goats, flour, butter, and other products. With these contributions pouring in, Mönghebatu was able to go back to the government officials, saying, "We have to build a new statue because the masses want it. This is the

5. The state allowed the recognition of reincarnations in the Tibetan Autonomous Region. This different policy is attributed by officials to the more developed, secularized society of Inner Mongolia as compared with Tibet ("they no longer need these backward religious figures"), but ordinary Mongols tend to point to age-old Chinese fear of Mongol political clout and the consequent tighter control of Mongol regions.

people's demand." To this socialist phrasing the officials had no reply and they agreed. Permission also had to be granted by Ulagan Gegen as head of the Buddhist establishment in Inner Mongolia, and he too gave the go-ahead, though being part of the Tibetan-language orthodoxy he tried to insist that a Tibetan sculptor be employed rather than the Mongolian artist suggested by Mönghebatu. In the end the combined income of the government grant and the *badar* was used to commission a giant gold-painted statue from the Mongolian master, and to provide a lavish feast for the thousands of people who would come to the enlivening ceremony.

Still, not all of the sheep and goats could be consumed in one meal. Mergen monastery no longer owns pasture lands as it had in the past, and we enquired what happened to these animals. The solution again was a long-standing Mongol practice—the extra livestock were given out to poor herding families in the area to look after. This procedure, whereby wealthy individuals acquired religious merit by donating herds to monasteries, which then allocated them widely among dependent households, can be seen from an economic point of view as a distribution mechanism that dealt with problems of unpredictable climate disaster on the one hand and local oversupply of animals on the other (Humphrey 1978). However, in this particular case there was a twist to the tale. For in 1995 we were told that these sheep and goats had not flourished in their new households. The reason given was one that will be encountered frequently in this book: the animals had languished because of the sins of the people and their neglect of religious observance. Nevertheless, one way or another, practically all Mongol households in a wide region were involved with the new Maidar statue.

Hürelbaatar arrived as preparations were under way for the great ceremony. The mountains rose starkly above the rock-strewn plateau; the whole escarpment was bare, devoid of the stupas that had formerly decorated it. But the monastery at its foot was bustling with activity. Thirty-two lamas were staying there, most of them old hands from pre-Revolutionary times but also including some young men. Three dusky yellow prayer temples had survived, along with some of the now shaky, half-bricked up, tile-roofed, and ancient-seeming courtyards of the reincarnations of past days. The monks were living in barracks built by the People's Liberation Army of China. In one such grimy dwelling lamas were chatting as they prepared dough offerings. Above the doorway of the main *Chogchin* temple laypeople from a neighboring district had hung a large homemade banner. It depicted a galloping horse with the inscription, "The silver gray horse dances in the cosmos, Let us raise the Wind-Horse Genius (*hei mori sülde*) of the Mongolian people." The wind-horse and a battle-standard embodying the *sülde* (genius, inspiration), as we were later to discover, were of the utmost importance to the people in the monastery (Chapter 5).

The huge new Maidar statue loomed expectant and unvisited in its dark temple, for as yet it had no power. The walls on either side were covered in a thousand empty niches, waiting for small Buddha statues to be placed in them at some future time. A light bulb dangled from a wire, and when this was lit it could be seen that someone must have climbed over the pedestal, onto the knee and up the bulging arm to the shoulder of the Maidar to tie a red cloth across the eyes. This would be removed when the statue was consecrated, "enlivened" as the Mongols express it. Everyone knew the figures down pat: the statue was eighty cubits (about 160 feet) high, and three hundred *jin* (330 pounds) of holy texts (sutras) had been placed in its stomach. All this was satisfactory—everything was ready.

Soon more and more people began to arrive—most walked from the nearest main road and railway station, but some came on horseback, bicycle, and motorbike. A strip of red carpet was laid out at the end of the track that wound outside the army wall to the monastery entrance. Ulagan Gegen's car was due to arrive by mid-morning, since any enlivening ritual should take place as the sun is still rising (the radiance of new godly power should parallel the ascent of the sun). Patiently the crowd waited, but Gegen did not come. They continued to wait. Everyone knew that because he was a high government official as well as a lama his every move was controlled by state authorities,[6] and as the morning turned into afternoon people began to suspect that the delay was a tactic of officials to spoil the ritual. At last, puffs of dust in the distance announced his approach. Two Mongol riders galloped down the road to welcome him.

Ulagan Gegen stepped with an abstracted air towards the temple, hidden behind dark glasses, protected by a wavering silk canopy held over him by the lamas, jostled by thousands of people. We would never again see such a throng at Mergen. Why did so many come from far and wide? The main reasons were, as people said, to receive the blessing of Ulagan Gegen and to worship Maidar, for whose statue so many contributions had been made. These answers already point to the as-

6. Ulaan Gegen was director of the Buddhist Association and Vice Chair of the Political Consultative Committee (PCC) of Inner Mongolia, and he was also a member of the PCC of China. All this gave him little overt political power but very high status.

pects of Buddhism that ordinary Mongolians greatly value: personal contact between the faithful individual and the powerful lama on the one hand, and the wish to attain future enlightenment on the other.

The advent of Ulagan Gegen was highly unusual for Mergen. As will be later explained, the monastery's tradition had come to stand for a different, more demotic, sensibility than that represented by this Tibetan-educated high prelate. It is useful nevertheless to describe his stately visit, since it is an example of the kind of relationship between lama and laity that previously obtained in the monastery (Chapter 3) and has come to be prevalent again, in the capital city of Höhhot and elsewhere in Inner Mongolia (Mair 2007). Ulagan Gegen was seated on the main throne in the large temple. In the dim light his presence gleamed, as he was dressed not in the dark red of a lama's clothing but in the golden gown prescribed by his high rank. Crowds waited patiently to prostrate before him one by one. Each layperson laid down a small money donation, after which Ulagan Gegen brushed their heads with a holy text in a gesture of blessing. Still wearing dark glasses, he moved his hand wearily and did not even look at the people as they humbly bowed in their hundreds. When the lamas filed past he touched their heads with his hand. When it was the turn of the extremely holy Danzan Gegen, a reincarnation who had come all the way from Ordos and who was so aged he had to be supported by two people as he moved through the temple, he stood up respectfully and the two lamas touched their foreheads together.

The name of this ritual, *mörgül talbihu,*[7] is an example of the concreteness of the language of Mongolian Buddhists. For "mörgül," often translated as "worship," literally means the butting of animals, knocking the forehead against something, extending to bowing or a full-body prostration. Ulagan Gegen said nothing during the entire procedure and preserved a sacrosanct distance. But it would be mistaken, in our view, to interpret this abstraction "socially" or "politically" as his tactic to maintain his own mysterious sanctity, for that was not necessary. Ulagan Gegen, this gracious, enigmatic old man, *was* the emanation of a god,[8] and furthermore, because of his advanced prac-

7. The rite is differentiated by the kind of contact made: if the lama touches the worshipper's head with his hand this is known as *motor talbihu* (motor being the respectful term for hand). If he touches with a holy sutra the expression is *sudur talbihu,* and if he gives a small portion to eat or drink this is known as *adis oghu.*

8. The Ulagan Gegen, like the Dalai Lama, is an emanation of the thousand-armed Avalokiteśvara; the visiting Ulagan Gegen was the 11th in this particular reincarnation line of the deity.

tice, was held to command tantric ability that infused his blessing with the power to transform the receiver. Also incorrect would be a common type of anthropological explanation for the giving of money succeeded by the blessing gesture, i.e., to interpret it as an exchange. The money, or any other tiny gift a person had to offer, was not given *for* the blessing but was a token of sincerity, a sign that this individual was actively and intentionally entering a relation with the lama. Accepting the commitment to act in this ritual way, each person undertook to present him- or herself as a needy worshipper (*mörgülchin*) and submitted to the hope that the actions, the bow, and the gesture, would subtly transform them and take them one tiny step closer to enlightenment. We never again witnessed such a hierarchical benediction; the lamas of Mergen could not—or would not—perform it.

The Procession of Maidar Buddha and "Willing"

The enlivening ritual at Mergen was carried out by means of a fairly brief chanted text. After this the eye-coverings on the Buddha were removed, as the statue was now "alive" and could see and interact with people. Ulagan Gegen chanted the text in Tibetan, which he did alone in a quavering voice, for the Mergen lamas, whose own consecration texts are in Mongolian, could not accompany him. Some laypeople now came forward to prostrate full length before the Buddha. But the main event as far as the laity was concerned was to happen later. This was the procession of the Maidar Buddha round the perimeter of the monastery, followed by adoring crowds. One of the most important festivals of the Buddhist year, this ceremony is carried out annually in all larger Mongolian and Buryat monasteries, often at great expense (Jagchid 1979, 126–27; Hyer and Jagchid 1983, 86; Borjigin 2006, 45–47). In Halha (Outer Mongolia) at the end of the nineteenth century, thousands of lamas and even greater numbers of laity would attend Maidar processions (Pozdneev 1887, 384–92). At Mergen a small statue of Maidar is mounted in an elaborately carved, brilliantly painted shrine-palanquin. This is born aloft on the shoulders of several lamas, and carried out of the temple and around the monastery in a slow sunwise circumambulation. Music accompanies it—a monks' orchestra of conch shells, wind instruments, large drums, bells, and cymbals—along with cheerful conversation and laughter of the lamas, men, women, and children following. As the palanquin sways over the grassy slopes a

1 A lama preparing to duck under the Maidar Shrine, 2005. (Hürelbaatar Ujeed)

queue also forms in front of it. Each person, from the aged to small children, takes part in the rite by ducking under the palanquin as it moves forward. Amid jostling and friendly boosts to the slow, each person silently makes a "will" or "vow" (*irügel*), and as they do so they reach a hand upward and deposit some money in the shrine. Lamas remove the money as it piles up and the procedure is repeated until everyone has had a chance to crawl under the image as it passes over their heads. An explanation of the procession was only given by the more communicative of the lamas when we asked them: the territorial circle, as well as the cyclical repetition each year, signifies the belief that the future Buddha, Maidar, will turn the Wheel of the Sacred Law in the future, just as it had been turned by Shakyamuni (Gautama), the Buddha of the current epoch (see also Hyer and Jagchid 1983, 86). As for the silent making of a will, this is something ordinary people are ready to talk about. There are many occasions in Buddhist life when people make wish-vows of diverse kinds, but at this time everyone makes at least one main will—that they individually will be reborn in this world as a human being in the Maidar epoch.

Talking about Religion and "Talking Religion"

Moving to the question of the ways that Urad Mongols talk about religion, we should mention their laconic indirectness—a way of talking between people who *already know* and understand a great deal that need not be mentioned. One of the advantages of joint fieldwork by a Mongolian and a European anthropologist is that what is strange for the latter is often part of the tacit knowledge of the former.

Caroline once asked a group of laypeople why this particular Buddha was so immensely respected at Mergen—what was the meaning of Maidar?

A man replied, "The meaning is—it is eighty cubits high."

"No, I mean, what idea lies behind this Buddha, as distinct from other gods you might have chosen to worship?"

"The idea is—it is huge, as I just said."

"Ah . . ."

For this Urad layman, one word—"huge"—is what he was prepared to say and it was enough, because religion for most people is not conducted in explanatory propositions. Much of lay Buddhism at Mergen today is distant indeed from one key aspect of the recent "protestant" trend in Buddhism found elsewhere in the world, the clear verbal formulations that are the heart of egalitarian lay religious understanding (Gombrich and Obeyesekere 1988; Clarke 2006, 266–69.) Here what is immediate is nonverbal: the visual presence of the looming statue, the glittering of the small statue in its palanquin, the actions of bowing, crouching, and laying money, the sensation of being touched, of joining a walking crowd, of having people breathing down one's neck. Lyotard distinguishes between "figure," a field of affective intensity, and "discourse," which strives for linguistic-philosophical closure and is limited to what can be read and given meaning within a closed linguistic system. "Figure" refers not to a realm of decidable meanings, but a zone where "intensities are felt" (1973, 9–23). With this idea we can see that the main "intensity" Urad people feel in the presence of Maidar is of their own "smallness," an effectual positioning that they also perform by crouching down and crawling under the god.

An implication of restricted use is that language objects in Mongolian (words, expressions, sentences) can on such occasions be likened to visual objects (images, statues) in the sense that one tends to read into them meanings learned "by other means" (Pinney 2005, 260, citing Ginsburg 1989, 35), such as the surrounding context, implicit shared knowledge, or previous discussions. Our fieldwork was full of conversations like the one above concerning Maidar, when Caroline would have been none the wiser had it not been for Hürelbaatar, who, having been brought up as a Buddhist in Inner Mongolia, was usually able to tap into, or supply himself, with due caution, what was known "by other means," i.e., the meanings that were not in what people actually said.

Talking *about* religion, which the Urad Mongols do rather rarely (unless pressed by anthropologists) is not the same as *talking religion*, where "talking"—chanting, praying, willing, confessing, conjuring, etc.—forms a series with actions, performances, and silent intentions. Everyday talk about a matter is after all intended to convey some information, however cryptically, but language, when it is used in religious ritual, has a main purpose not to instruct or inform but to generate a new state, perhaps a renewed sense of a religious perspective on everything else, by its strange and artificial ways of talking. That is it fundamentally aims to redirect the attention of people and produce an effect in them (Latour 2005b). Language in this sense—its liturgy—is the great pride of Mergen Monastery and it is why the 3rd Mergen Gegen's composition of a new poeticized corpus was so important (Chapter 2). This then is another way in which religious talk (prayers, chants, supplications, spells) is like religious iconography (statues, paintings), for both are designed to shake and destabilize ordinary modes, to seize people in complex and subtle ways. Mergen Gegen wrote in Mongolian with the idea that the native language would be more direct and effective than Tibetan in address to the Buddhas. In Chapter 7 we discuss the question of understanding the texts and we introduce a lama who was able to bridge between "knowledge" of Buddhism and the mute effect of much of religious activity.

Maidar and Time(s)

Hürelbaatar explained the layman's cryptic reply to Caroline, saying that any Mongol with the barest knowledge of Buddhism would know the following: Shakyamuni Buddha—the one known generally as "the Buddha"—compassionately deigned to return to this world to help living beings toward enlightenment, a task to be performed in his own vast eon (M. *galab*, S. *kalpa*). Maidar Buddha also has his own epoch, the eon to come. In each eon, Buddhism rises and declines, until a new eon results in a new rise and fall, and so on endlessly. The problem with the present eon, Shakyamuni's, is that he chose to appear on earth at a time of relative degeneration, when the life span of a human being was a maximum of around a hundred years, a pitifully short time that allows hardly anyone to achieve enlightenment. When Buddhism is strong, people live for thousands of years and thus almost all of them can become enlightened beings and escape the sufferings of this world into Nirvana. The great attribute of Maidar Buddha is that he will appear during his eon at just this apex time of supreme possibilities. This is why the Mongols worship Maidar so fervently. His great size is a way of representing the idea of great longevity. By worshipping him now, people can somehow participate in this future blessed state, devoutly willing that their souls will be reborn at the time of Maidar and enlightenment become possible. In fact, Hürelbaatar continued, when you consider these matters more deeply as a Buddhist, the difference between past, present, and future is annulled. What happened in the past is contained in the present, and what is being done right now determines the future. Believing this, as many Mongols fervently do, death is not a bad thing, something to be dreaded; it is not the end for a person, just a small gap separating one life from another life, an indeterminate liminal period the Mongols call *jaguradu*.[9]

With Maidar people imagine an "epoch"—a "self-defined piece of time" that we can think of as a "stoppage" (Wagner 1986, 85) amid great expanses of endless time, and another dimension as it were from the practical duration of everyday activities. A corollary is that, from a Maidar perspective, a human life—this current life—becomes infinites-

9. No one said so to us explicitly, but given the idea that immense material size stands for great age, an analogous translation of physical movement into time could also work for the act of "crawling under." Ducking into and reappearing out of the tunnel formed by the lamas upholding the palanquin may be a way of enacting the idea of death-rebirth. Such actions are very widespread in folk as well as Indo-originated religions in Asia.

imally small (a moment *agshan*, from S. *kshana*). One way to picture this instant, at least for a European reader, is to contrast it with a completely different European way of using momentariness to destabilize ordinary temporality, moments that Kracauer referred to as "time atoms." He was referring to Marcel Proust's great work which radically deemphasizes chronology and turns the spotlight instead on discontinuous "time atoms" touched off by accidental bodily sensations, these are "memory images of incidents so short-lived that time has no time to mold them. He restores these microscopic units to their true position by presenting huge enlargements of them. Each such "close-up" consists of a texture of reflections, analogies, reminiscences, etc. which . . . serve to disclose the essential meanings of the incident from which they radiate and towards which they converge" (Kracauer [1969] 1995, 161–62). The Buddhist idea of *agshan* seems like a mirror opposite of this: in the Mongol case the person's life is shut down into an instant, and the sensations that are so essential to Proust are revealed to be not true but illusions. Such ideas are conveyed among Urad Mongols by parables. One, for example, concerns a man who was skeptical about a great lama, Dawasangbuu, with magical powers.

One day the man went out of his yurt to defecate. He was squatting down, when Dawasangbuu Lama appeared, pointed and said, "There is a black horse, ride that horse." The man thought he could easily do that, mounted the horse, galloped off, but actually he couldn't control it, and willy-nilly found himself far away on an island in the sea. He couldn't leave, so he married, settled down, had children, and they grew up. Years went by. Suddenly, one day the island was flooded, his wife and family were swept away by the waves. They drowned. He was crying, "I have lost my whole life . . . my son . . . my household." His wife wondered if he was still defecating, looked out of the yurt, and saw him sitting crying. He returned to consciousness and realized that all those years were an illusion. In all those years he had lived through, the sun's ray had moved only the width of his fingernail. This showed him that the long time he thought he had experienced was an instant (*agshan*). A whole human life is like this, in reality.

So in this teaching your merely human confidence in your own ability to understand what is true is deluded, and holy magic has the purpose of demonstrating your limitations.

But there is another side to this view of time that a whole life is reducible to a micro-second, and this is the idea that however tiny it is in the great scheme of things, a human life is quite extraordinarily precious. Because only in human life with its unique combination of pleasure and pain, not in any paradise or heaven, is it possible to develop virtue and wisdom to the degree necessary to set one free from the entire cycle of rebirths. "It is difficult to attain a human body," goes one of Mergen Gegen's religious songs. "It is difficult to take part in Buddha's religion; it is difficult to confront a previous *irügel*; it is difficult to forget the results of actions [karma]" (Mönghe 2010, 100). A Mongolian version of an ancient Buddhist tale concerns the extreme improbability of human life—and hence the need to value it. A hibernating sea-creature sleeps on the ocean bed and comes up for air once every sixty years. It looks around and goes back down again. Imagine you have a ring made of willow branches and throw it randomly across the sea. Your chance of being born a human is as unlikely as the chance of your ring catching on the creature's snout.

The teaching of the extreme rareness of human life is a central tenet of Buddhism (Lopez 2009, 317), but these images are peculiar, maybe particularly for Mongols, who know neither the ocean nor the animals that live in it. Surely the strangeness is deliberate, working as a reminder, a jolt out of the day-to-day sense of time that is given by simply living it. The same has to be true of the Maidar statue. For its hugeness is not just a simple index, "huge = impressive = long-lived," but is also designed carefully to destabilize ordinary ideas of size, space, and proportion.[10] The giant Maidar, first constructed by the 8th Mergen Gegen in the 1920s and recently (that is, in 2008) fully restored, is a complex structure. It consists of an apse, in which the main god looming on its plinth is accompanied on both sides by ranks of a thousand tiny identical Buddhas. Far larger than human size, far smaller than human size—entering this space puts into question what is absent here, the proportion of the human being. The structure deliberately breaks the habitual gaze of the viewer so as to attract attention to his *present* state, the only one that can be said to offer salvation. The Maidar temple at Mergen demands of the worshipper "What size are you now?"—where your equivocal physical size stands for the abstract calibration of one's self in the religious dimension of liberation from this world. The temple asks the question—it does not provide an answer.

Let us think further about the statue itself, for Buddhist transcendentalism may not be the only kind of time implied by its presence. Christopher Pinney in a seminal paper (2005) on materiality asks,

10. See the discussion by Doreen Massey of the idea of "relative space," whereby space (and time) are understood as dimensions that are defined by the entities that inhabit them and not vice versa (1999, 262). In this sense Maidar could be seen as creating its own space-time.

"From which moment does that object come?" He argues that objects in themselves have their own times, which in principle are separate from the period of the context used to interpret that object. Most important, if anthropologists assume that changes in representation of a god can only be understood as a visual representation of a historical change in ideology, they cannot catch hold of "how the materiality of representation" creates its own force field (ibid, 261). The dynamics in the aesthetics of god-making obey their own movement, not that of contemporary society, and can even be at odds with it. In other words, objects may sometimes be "unrevealing" of their cultural-political context; they may belong to a different, non-contemporary time. Pinney asks, "What if we start looking for these disjunctions, and all those objects and images whose evidence appears to be deceptive and whose times do not appear to be 'our time'?" (2005, 263). The new giant statue of Maidar was evidently a disjunctive object in relation to its general contemporary context, being reconstructed in the China of the early 1990s for neither a socialist nor a commercial purpose. It can however be interpreted in a different way, by referring not to its date but to what Pinney calls its "age," meaning its position in the sequence to which it belongs. Such sequences have time schedules all their own (ibid, 264).

This insight enables us to see the statue of Maidar made in 1992 as one in a sequence of images of this god made over the millennia in Asia. In religious art there is a certain recursive quality, since each artist goes back to his own previously learned repertoire of proportions, colors, decorative elements, etc., and yet inevitably makes things in his own way. Each image is designed *yet again* to spur people, to transcend, distort, and opacify the visible world. In our immediate case, the 1992 statue was the second in a series of three giant Maidar statues at Mergen. The first, built in the 1920s, was attacked several times and finally destroyed by the army in the 1960s. The second, whose consecration in 1992 we described earlier, was damaged by an earthquake in the mid-1990s: an ear and an arm broke off. But perhaps the earthquake was not an accident, people began to think, maybe there was something wrong about the statue, the reason it could not survive. It was at this point that people began to talk about its appearance: they remembered that Ulagan Gegen had been not altogether happy with it, saying that its face had the wrong proportions and was "too Chinese-looking." It was subsequently decided not to restore the damaged statue but to make a new one on its base, inviting on this occasion not the previous sculptor but Tibetan artists from the great Kumbum monastery. This necessitated a new expensive "enlivening" ceremony in 1999, but the worshippers were now happy that their god fitted their canonical understanding of Maidar's appearance. It is our view that despite the ethnic jousting the discomfort about the "Chinese face" was primarily an aesthetic judgment. It was not so much a disparagement of the qualities of being Chinese, as the diagnosis of a misfit, referring to the sequence of god images in which this statue belonged.

We have now sketched several disparate time frameworks associated with Maidar: notably, the epoch, the instant, the succession of vast, cyclical eons, and the recursive sequence of statue images. These kinds of time are unlike one another, and they are also different from other kinds of time used by Urad laypeople, for example when they milk their livestock, glance at their watches, or visit an astrologer. We are faced therefore with the coexistence of multiplicity and difference. This is to concur with the argument made by Kracauer against the conventional historians' assumption of "Time as One Great River." Instead, time consists of many "cataracts," each pursuing their own trajectories.[11] In this respect, the unity of the "historical period" may disappear before our eyes (see discussion in Pinney 2005, 264), or at least may be much less useful in explaining why people do things than is often imagined.[12] In this book we cannot dispense with ordinary linear history, but we do try to reveal at several points in the chapters that follow how disparate cultural phenomena may inhabit a given era and yet not be each other's contemporaries.

Willing, Death-Rebirth and Mongol Family Life

Of course we do not wish to make the argument that religion as a whole is an archaic incubus in present-day society. The same statue that has its own "age" in the sequence of Maidar images is also a contemporary object of current wrangling (like the disagreement about who the sculptor should be). In some important nexuses the connections are more than sheer adjacency in time: they inflect one another. Here we

11. In making this point, we insist that multiple and diverse ways of reckoning and experiencing time are present in all societies, not particularly in non-Western ones. Therefore we distance ourselves from what Fabian (1983) calls "chronopolitics," where the society under anthropological study is portrayed as occupying a kind of time different from that of the anthropologist.

12. The "historical period" here refers to periods constructed by historians and should not be confused with what Hirsch and Stewart, following Roy Wagner (1986), call the "epoch" (2005, 270–71). The latter refers to an indigenous sense of the presence of time, as opposed to its passage, an organic sense of simultaneity that makes sense of events occurring within the contours of the "now" of the epoch.

point to some relations that cross a distinction sometimes made in the anthropology of Buddhism (e.g., Tambiah 1970; Southwold 1983) between properly religious goals and the practices of everyday life (see also Chapter 1). We show how "willing" is a practice that permeates both spheres and creates connections between them.

It will be remembered that when people "crawl under Maidar" they make a will to be reborn as his disciple, i.e., as his subject in the great apex time of his epoch. This idea of the will (*irügel*) is integral to Buddhist life. In its most general sense it implies intention, without which any action, however good in its effects, cannot be counted as a truly virtuous act. *Irügel* can be translated as "wish" or "aspiration," but more strongly implies "vow" or "resolution," not just wanting something to happen but an active force in the willing that makes it happen. The elder who "blesses" (*irügehü*) a young person is willing the flowering of auspiciousness in them. This generative aspect of Mongol thinking is evident when people say they "put" (*talbihu*) a will, a verb that means not just starting something but allowing it (in its fullness) to happen.[13]

The devout will exists both as a silent resolution and in verbal forms, such as an openly stated intention, as well as in written texts or oral poetic improvisations. Existing in many ways, the idea of the devout will is also central to the Mergen monastic tradition. The great founder, the 3rd Mergen Gegen, wrote *irügel* texts for many different deities, expressing the desire that those gods' qualities (wisdom, compassion, repelling evil, etc.) should come to fruition, and these texts are scattered through diverse services during the year.[14] Besides this, a special service called *irügel* is held once a year in honor of Shakyamuni Buddha, when laypeople come with efficacious wishes for deceased souls written on scraps of paper, which they hand to the lamas to mention during their chanting. Now along with his liturgical texts, the Mergen Gegen also wrote will-benedictions for seemingly nonreligious objects, like the yurt (to be pronounced when establishing a new dwelling) and for fire, while he composed others for a range of ritual, yet not specifically Buddhist, occasions such as obtaining fortune (*heshig*) or desiring happiness (*öljei*). The idea of "willing" is thus manifested in a field that is far broader than Buddhism—among the Mongol people there are also *irügel* as oral poetic improvisations for bringing in a new daughter-

13. Thus the expression *jam talbihu* (literally "road put") can mean "build a road" but also, and more commonly, "give way for someone," "enable something to happen."

14. The religious act of wishing is found not only in texts explicitly called *irügel* but also in *jalbaril* (prayer conjurations) and *magtagal* (eulogies), which often contain passages that are in effect wishes.

in-law, for felt-making, for arrow-making, for fermenting alcohol, for milking mares, for wishing the rebirth of an animal one has killed in a hunt, etc. (Gaadamba and Tserensodnom 1967, 105–13)—but the central concept remains the same and it is focused on the effectiveness of beneficent intention.

We do not wish to overstate the importance of either Maidar Buddha or *irügel* in Mongolian Buddhism. As later chapters will show, there are several other deities, standing for different spiritual qualities, which are worshipped just as sincerely at Mergen. The *irügel* is only one of many liturgical genres chanted at services, and indeed the more religiously ambitious monks regard practices of "willing" as inferior to meditation or tantric initiations that more directly move the lama's progress along the path to enlightenment. Nevertheless, we have introduced our book with these two topics because they show how Buddhism, as a distinct ensemble of beliefs and practices, while it cannot be *explained* by given social practices, is nevertheless inflected by them—and vice versa. It is because of these links and parallels, understated or even unvoiced as they often are, that we can think of the phenomenon of *Mongolian* Buddhism. Vowing to be reborn in the epoch of Maidar, while it may be common across the Buddhist world, is at the same time shadowed or underpinned by distinctive cultural practices deeply embedded in ordinary human relations.

Like will-wishes, the idea of rebirth is not limited to religious contexts. People hold that—and this is a lay matter, separate from the elevated reincarnation of sacred souls in lines of high lamas—a baby may be the rebirth of a deceased relative, usually someone quite close and known to the child's parents. A newborn child's body is scrutinized for birthmarks or other physical signs that would indicate that it is "really," say, a grandfather who has reappeared in this form. We do not dwell here on the complex psychological pressure this puts on the child as it grows up (Empson 2007), but focus on the conjoining of these two ideas, the willing to be reborn, amid the everyday tangles of kinship relations. Let us give an example, a domestic history told by Hürelbaatar.

In the 1920s, to everyone's joy a boy was born in a rich family where several babies had earlier died. To save the child's life from the misfortune hanging over its birth family, the boy was given away immediately, to be brought up in an auspicious household with many thriving children. These were very poor people, but the ruse was successful, and the boy grew up strong and healthy till he had passed the time of danger, when he was around twelve. The poor family returned him.

But almost immediately they asked for his older sister in marriage. The rich family was aghast—how could they give their beautiful well-to-do daughter to live in wretched conditions with a man she did not like?—but they could not refuse because of the beneficial deed (*achi*) the neighbors had done for them. The girl was duly married, was very unhappy, fell seriously ill, and came back home. Wasting away, she asked her younger brother—the "cause" of her ill-fated marriage—to look after her. He tended her hand and foot, for after all she had paid for his life. She knew she was going to die, and at this point she made a will (*irügel*) to repay her brother, saying to him many times: "I will be reborn as a son to you." The family was again torn. They condemned the will—not for the change of sex, not for the imposition of an unhappy identity on a yet-to-be born child, and certainly not for the sister's pious intention—but because the brother was as yet only fourteen. He would not marry and have a son for years. This meant that the sister's precious soul would languish and suffer before it could reappear on this earth. "Don't make this will," said the mother. "I must," the sister replied.[15]

Now willing to be reborn in your own family is not a very Buddhist ambition (for such wishes are entangled in emotional attachments and disengagement from attachments is the teaching). But nevertheless it can be seen that this kind of *irügel* and the wish to be reborn as a disciple of Maidar are congruent, adjacent kinds of ethical practices that people can maintain, and ultimately they are not even at odds with one another, since every person is destined to be reborn countless times in any case.

We have mentioned the woman who willed to be reborn as her brother's son to show that people are serious about these matters: the life after this life is an object of preoccupations, repaying debts, projections into the immediate future of a known world. But what kind of imagination is involved with the idea of being reborn as a disciple of Maidar? We do not deal fully with this question here, but make the point (which will be developed more fully in later chapters) that for the contemporary Urad Mongols at least, such outward, ultimate images are ways of thinking that annul the gulf of death, or rather transcend it in virtue of a higher good, and that this propensity toward the defiantly heroic is also to be found in non-Buddhist contexts (Chapter 5).

15. In the event, so strong was the family's rejection of this *irügel* that when the sister died they had an especially powerful death ritual performed to lead her soul down a different path, and thereafter they believed that she had been reborn in paradise. So later, the child who was eventually born, the brother's son, does not think that he is a rebirth of his father's sister.

Such a multivalent, visionary orientation is characteristic of Mongols in general—at any rate, of many Mongols of diverse backgrounds—and is not the preserve of Buddhist monks.

Let us look more closely at the imagination of Maidar. He "descends" to earth from his special paradise out of compassion for living beings, but still the imagery is airy and cosmic. Mergen Gegen's praise poem for Maidar, which is still chanted in the monastery, reads:

[You] have light like the rays of the sun
[You] are clear and transparent like the moon
Looking at [you], [people] feel the helpful energy of your body
[We] pray at your feet, O compassionate one. [. . .]
For the sake of becoming a compassionate Buddha (*burhan*)
I will first become your companion;
Tasting the holy water of doctrine,
May [I] reach the extreme end of the land path (*gajar mör*)
(Galluu and Jirantai 1986, 434)

The strength of such beyond-this-world vision for ordinary people gives a different emphasis from that described for Southeast Asian countries, at least by certain anthropologists. Southwold, for example, describes Sri Lankan villagers and their local priestlike Buddhist monks as preoccupied with merit making, with the easier, more understandable aim of securing a prosperous future life in the current world as we know it (Southwold 1983, 102–04). At Mergen, to the contrary, it is not just the lamas but all those laypeople who "crawl under" Maidar who participate individually in the desire ultimately to transcend this ordinary world. For them, being reborn in this present world—and remember that Maidar's epoch is *this* world transformed—is not disjunctive from that distant goal. Rather it is, at the least, the next step on the long path toward ultimate liberation.

ONE

Buddhist Life at Mergen

Let us now meet our main characters, the lamas who bear the Mergen tradition, in the midst of a rite-cum-festivity they held in summer 1995. This event revealed far-branching temporal and spatial networks in which the lamas were involved. If a tradition is a recursive assemblage of people, ideas, and objects, each element of which has myriad links elsewhere, it will be appreciated that these elements are in fact *more* complex than the single "whole" (the tradition), to which people only ever lend, temporarily, some facets of themselves (Latour 2010, 7). The chapter broaches in this way its main goals: first of all to present certain individual people and through them begin to indicate some of the complexity of the contemporary monks' lives, the variety of ties they each maintain, and what holds them together as a group. Second, to provide the minimal historical information about the Urad Mongols and Buddhism in Mongolia necessary for readers to understand the major ideas and practices called on by lamas today.

The ceremony in 1995 brought home to us how mistaken would be a description of Mergen as an inward-looking community dwelling in its landscape, even if the lamas often promote that very impression. Doreen Massey's idea of place as meeting place, which she developed into the concept of sites as open and changeable "happenings"—of place as provocation—is far more apt here (2006, 34–36; see also Massey 1999, 262).

1995–A Multiple Celebration

Soon after we arrived that year, a crowd of monks and laypeople poured out of the main temple and followed an elderly lama up the hill to the perimeter wall. A boy lama, his face grave and angelic, handed a bow and arrow to the old monk. His trembling hands barely managed to draw back the string—he was aiming at an unlit bonfire below the army wall. The crowd pressed forward on all sides, some praying and some with cameras at the ready. A tall, ill-shaven lama in a crested hat rudely pushed them back. Now the elderly lama stirred himself into a strained hopping dance, his face raised to the sky and his eyes obscured by the black fringe of his headgear. He drew back his arm, but the arrow plopped disappointingly short. No matter—other ochre-robed lamas now rushed forward, lit the fire and threw onto it a large pyramidal wooden structure carved as tongues of flame. Inside we caught sight of an unidentifiable glistening red pointed object. With smiles and laughter, and without waiting to see whether these things burned properly or not, the whole crowd rapidly dispersed and clambered down the hill back to the monastery.

The occasion was the casting out of the sins of the previous year, these having been transferred into the pyramid (M. *sor*, T. *zor*). Earlier that day we had seen the pyramid taken out of the temple and held aloft by four lamas while hundreds of people pushed and shoved into a queue that ducked under it. As with the Maidar circumambulation described in the Introduction, they were making silent vow-wishes, on this occasion for the expulsion into the *sor* of their own particular misfortunes and ill consequences of bad deeds. We knew by now that the frail old lama was the Western Great (*Baragun* [pron. *Baruun*] *Da*) Reincarnation, and that the scowling tall lama was Jongrai, the manager of the monastery's practical affairs. Soon we learned that the small boy had come with his older brother from far away in Horchin, in northeast Inner Mongolia, to become pupil lamas at Mergen.

But it took some time before we began to think that the description above should perhaps be phrased in a different way. Were these people "lamas" or could it be more accurate to call them "people acting as lamas"?

For only eight years earlier Mergen Monastery had been closed and empty, its remaining temples and ruins inhabited by bats, snakes, and scorpions, the lamas sent away in the 1960s to prison or hard-labor jobs in the communist economy. Even now the busy monastic scene we observed was episodic. For periods of the year most of the thirty or so lamas who gathered for important ceremonies would scatter back to their homes in surrounding villages. Only a few lived at Mergen permanently, and these lamas invariably had wives and families living nearby. In other words, all of the lamas had renounced their vows and led radically different lives before they returned to the monastery when it reopened in 1987. When they decided to come back and retake their vows, this did not mean forsaking those lay ties, though certain vows—notably celibacy— would mean changing the character of the relationships. What kind of monk did this history make them?

Martin Mills has argued that even in regions of Asia with unbroken monastic traditions, such as Ladakh, most Buddhist monks continue to be supported economically and emotionally by households, while older family members tend toward religious goals and take simple vows. Thus monastic inmates should be seen on a scale of Buddhist virtue—they are "incomplete renouncers" (2003, 69). Rather than entirely eradicating all domestic ties and local spirit agencies, they work religiously to overmaster them. Human wealth and fertility, and the chthonic forces in the landscape become objects of ritual attention: they become "'fuel for the fire'" of Buddhist self-transformation (2003, 258–62). In our case most Mergen lamas took only *ubashi* vows when they returned to the monastery, i.e., those earlier regarded as those suitable for devout laypeople, and although a few took the stricter *getsül* vows, there were no monks who aspired to full *gelüng* vows.[1] Yet unlike in their youth, when they had been sent to the monastery as young children by their families, now they had consciously decided to return. In this wider context it is fair to conclude that the Mergen clergy *were* monks, but they were post-communist monks, people marked and colored by experiences not only outside religion but antithetical to Buddhist beliefs.

On the day after the expulsion of sins, a different throng took over the square in front of the main temple. Sitting behind a long table on the temple veranda were government officials and professors, dapper in suits and ties. On the table were piles of newly printed books. Above stretched a banner celebrating in Mongolian and Chinese "the achievements of Mergen Gegen Studies." Mergen Gegen is the famous eighteenth-century reincarnation mentioned in the Introduction, and

1. The *getsül* (T. *dge tshul*) vows include refraining from sexual intercourse, but apart from this acknowledged restriction, the content of vows was rarely discussed and left as a matter of tacit understanding. It was known that there are 253 *gelüng* (T. *dge slong*) vows, but no one could explain what these were. See Sneath (2000, 32–33) for a description of the local interpretation of vows in northeast Inner Mongolia in the 1990s.

the studies a corpus of books published on his work, its influence, and its relation to the local Urad culture. Some of yesterday's lay worshippers had returned dressed in festive Mongolian national dress, which, unlike in 1992, was now deemed appropriate for such a public occasion. There were also numerous newly arrived journalists, writers, publishers, teachers, artists, and students. Naranbatu, an Urad Mongol who had been a lama in his youth and was now a university professor in the capital Höhhot, was senior among these intellectuals. Meanwhile, the Western Great Reincarnation, Jongrai, and the solemn boy were nowhere to be seen. Indeed, few lamas were present, but one now took center stage. This was a strongly built man of middle age, wearing an open-necked shirt, dark glasses and a straw fedora hat. He was the Chorji Lama, a reincarnation at least as senior as the Western Great Lama, but he was presenting himself today as Mönghebatu (his lay name), one of the lay officials. As host to the assembled dignitaries, he wielded the microphone with aplomb in a welcoming speech. The orations told us that the Mergen Monastery was home to a special and wonderful Buddhist tradition, with its own cultural history, something that makes it worthy of academic study. But the whole occasion said something more, for the officials, it was whispered, were no mere locals, but included the vice chairman of the Inner Mongolia Autonomous Region (IMAR), the vice chairman of the Regional Political Consultative Committee, and the director of the Inner Mongolia Cultural Press. The IMAR forms a vast swathe of northern China. What could have brought such important people to this obscure monastery? The names of the officials were all Mongolian, so the conclusion was inescapable. The Mergen tradition, whatever that was, must be of national as well as Urad ethnic importance *and* it must be something approved by the Chinese authorities at a high level.

The speeches were lengthy and no more interesting than such speeches usually are. As they wore on, an elderly and yet wirily muscular man in Buddhist robes came out of the temple. Curious locals detached themselves from the audience to see what he was doing. He was carrying a long blue silk scarf he had just been given by a herder, which he unwound and held up to show what he had written on it on behalf of the giver. The inscription started with a Sanskrit mantra and proceeded in Mongolian: *Om–a-a-hum. Om-a–a-a-hum. Om–a-a-hum. Reliance. [I] bow down, raise thoughts, confess sins. Mention it happily and pray. However small the merit [I have] accumulated, I devote it to achieving bodhisattva-hood. May the life of my family and my own body be lengthened and may demons and ghosts be cleansed away.*

This lama was Sengge,[2] whose hard-bitten air and strikingly intense manner we would come to know well. The herder had given him the scarf to hang on a strange object of worship, the Urad ancestor Jirgal Bagatur's battle standard, which was kept in the Temple of Fierce Deities. This was puzzling enough, and the character of the prayer was also unfamiliar: it took the form called "reliance" *(dagatgal,* pron. *daatgal*), which we learned was an entrustment placed with a sacred power to fulfill the herder's wishes. The lay participants evidently took this Buddhist prayer to the spirit of a battle standard entirely for granted and, when it turned out that Sengge Lama was processing a heap of such scarves, we realized that what looked at first sight an odd unsanctioned activity was in fact the form taken by a mainstream popular religious activity (Chapter 5). The lay devotion to the battle standard was channeled almost entirely through Sengge Lama—and ignored by Mönghebatu.

Soon the officials and academics, including us but not the lamas or local people, were invited to a banquet. This introduced us to another contradictory aspect of what happens at Mergen: on occasion, the religious nature of the monastery is eclipsed and it is given the persona of institutional host-proprietor in an ongoing relation with the officials representing wider society. The feast was held in the palace of the reincarnation line of Mergen Gegens. In its lofty hall people were carefully seated according to rank, with the officials at a high table and the junior teachers around the walls. There was a long wait, during which alcohol was served in tiny glasses and cigarettes handed round. Sharp knives were issued to each person. Finally, steaming sides and haunches of boiled mutton were brought in on platters and carved into hunks. Each person then wielded his own knife, with officials courteously cutting off juicy and fatty pieces to offer one another. Toast followed toast, drunk in sharply powerful alcohol; replete, the diners sat back. A group of local people appeared and began to sing; the songs were from the "'eighty-one poems" of Mergen Gegen. These are lyrical and ethical pieces that have become folksongs handed down among Urad people. Singers, men and women, stationed themselves before each guest, offering a song, to which the correct response was drinking yet another cup of alcohol. The Chorji Lama Mönghebatu was the only lama present, and he was soon engaged in offering yellow silk scarves and bowls of drink to the singers. Each person took the proffered bowl and with

2. His full name was Lubsangsengge, but as he was popularly known as Sengge Lama we have adopted the shorter form in this book.

an airy gesture flicked drops three times with the fourth finger of the right hand—these were offerings to the sky, the earth, and the ancestors—took a sip and then returned the bowl to Chorji to be filled once again to the brim. We were hazily aware that these drinking rituals followed the pattern of host-guest relations observed throughout Mongol lands in worldly situations—Chorji was offering respect to his guests; but, we wondered, would Mergen Gegen have been happy for his sacred poems to be used in this way? Coherent thought was now lost in a swelling of general singing. The high guests threw off their jackets and joined in. It grew darker outside as passionate songs filled the hall. Professor Naranbatu, doyen of Mergen Gegen studies, offered solos of wonderful precision and expression. Some lyrics were witty, with fast, syncopated rhythms. Other songs were a ragged, deeply felt, roaring of the whole hall. Eventually, everyone stumbled to the doors—rain was slashing into the mud outside, people sheltered by the red pillars of the veranda , wind tore at the branches of the trees. Rain! In parched Inner Mongolia, this was a sign that the occasion was blessed.

Different publics were "provoked" into existence and separated out by these various events: The Chinese journalists attending the "expulsion of sins" took notes in bemused curiosity, while locals and lamas were not invited to the main banquet and feasted separately. The city intellectuals had specially chosen the occasion of the ritual to celebrate the publication of their books, knowing that hundreds of local people would be present. The mass turnout then validated the appearance of the politicians. On all sides the wariness Hürelbaatar had sensed in 1992 was gone. There was a brief happy coincidence of diverse interests. Mongolian high officials, who are sidelined to a great extent from hard power spheres, have made the politics of culture their arena of expertise. What could be better than to celebrate a *Mongolian cultural* form of Buddhism, separated as it were by Mergen Gegen's use of the vernacular from the dangerous alignment with renegade Tibet? As for the Urad intellectuals now working in the capital city, they could safely promote the uniqueness of Mergen Gegen and his embracing of Urad cultural customs: academic employment, publications, research projects, students, all looked set to flow; nostalgic memories could be brought to life; and obsessions with identity explored. The lamas, furthermore, could bask in a new sense of their own importance as bearers of something now officially labeled a tradition (*ulamjilal*). This sense of pride also extended to some of the local inhabitants. Most turned up simply to worship, enjoy themselves, and exchange news, but some had participated in providing information for the books and could now see themselves as the carriers of a specific Urad culture. They included local party stalwarts such as Shirüngerel and Erhimbayar, both owners of large herds, who despite being loyal communists did not hesitate to take part zealously in the "expulsion of sins" rite.

True, at Mergen ruins were everywhere, the yards were full of weeds and the temples empty of ancient statues. But in 1995 this was also an institution resplendent in confident activity. The enthusiastic throngs of worshippers and sympathizers seemed to ensure support for the future. We had earlier visited other monasteries of Inner Mongolia, all of them using a Tibetan liturgy and, apart from the urban precincts of Yehe Juu in Höhhot, the main monastery of the capital city, most of them were bereft. Their abandonment was eloquent evidence of the scorn in which religion was still mostly held in public life. Official attitudes were changing and Buddhism was coming to be acceptable as part of "ethnic culture," but religion *per se* was ignored, suspect, unvalued. Shiregetü Juu in Höhhot was huge but empty; Usutu-yin Juu at the edge of the city was dank and ruined, with no monks in sight; Shira Mören in the mountains to the north was little more than a scenic adjunct to a tourist camp; Maidar Juu to the west was restored as a museum—its multistoried temples were impressive in their flourishing gardens—but not a single monk was there and hardly any visitors were prepared to pay the entrance fee; Höndülen was a gaunt shell inhabited by a handful of defensive monks, hemmed in by the smokestacks and factories of Baotou (M. *Bogutu*) city.[3] Mergen in 1995 was an astonishing contrast to all this. At its prayer services two banks of lamas sat bent over their sutras, chanting squarely in unison, sounding their drums, wind-instruments, and bells with practiced ease.

Lamas' lives and the community of monks

The unity of the lamas, the sense that this was a community with its own order and spirit, was an ephemeral enchantment. Even after two days we knew that it could not be the whole story. Each of the monks had taken a decision to come here from some other place and another kind of life: all suffered traumatically, in different ways, during the Cultural Revolution, which pushed them apart. These different histories affected—were part of—what each of them was *as a lama*. Thus we could not write about Mergen Monastery in generalities as though

3. For a survey of contemporary Inner Mongolian monasteries, see Charleux 2006.

there was a typical lama. The occasions when these people came together and formed a corpus would have to be explained; just as important, we would have to do justice to their individuality.

The complex singularity of each person was intricately interwoven with the sociality of Mergen. This was borne in on us when we wandered outside the precincts one hot day. Just outside the main gates was a little two-roomed house selling sweets, buns, beers, and a few ritual items like prayer beads and packets of juniper powder incense for the laity coming to services. A young woman was selling these things, her baby son at her side, and sitting in another part of the room, as though in a world of his own, was a young man painting a Buddhist deity at an easel. This was gentle, hollow-cheeked Minggan-Agula (henceforth Minggan), whose name means "Thousand Hills." He had recently become a lama at Mergen, having been expelled from the nearby monastery of Badgar for having flouted the rule of celibacy by having a love affair. Badgar, which we had not yet visited, is the monastery most famous in Inner Mongolia for the learning and high standards of its monks. Minggan had been accepted at Mergen and allowed to live there with his partner, but only after some controversy; in recognition of the desirability of celibacy the couple was allotted this little house *outside the gates*. The other lamas at Mergen all had wives, but their households were decently distant in villages round about, and if the very elderly monks were allowed resident wives to take care of them it was on the understanding that their relations would be celibate. Dreamy Minggan seemed to care little about his marginal status; but we saw from the slight disdain with which he was treated by some other lamas that, very simply, these people would intervene in one another's lives on behalf of what they took to be an ensemble and that such acts, in effect, constituted the institution of the monastery. Work of discussion and controversy went into maintaining these mutual interferences, and such internal agreements continued to be applied even in the confusing situation where religious ideas conflicted with Chinese civil law—because according to the latter, of course, there could be no discrimination on the grounds of living with a spouse.

The monks in the monasteries of Inner Mongolia largely go their own ways in such matters. Provided they can appear to conform to the law of the land, no one examines too closely how they arrange their affairs, and monasteries vary widely in how lamas are recruited, ranked, paid, and educated (Chapters 3 and 11). If the situation assigned to

Minggan provided a clue as to how the monastery worked, another incident indicated to us how an individual decision taken "inside" could involve a more subtle interplay with external social relations than one might imagine and indeed affect the aggregate of the institution. The Chorji Lama Mönghebatu told us that while having two daughters—a family he maintained in the city of Baotou—he now wanted to adopt as his son, and keep in the monastery the younger, angel-faced boy lama from Horchin. This would have been impossible according to earlier rules, for all ambitious monks took vows of celibacy at an early age and were debarred from forming their own families. An older lama could have a disciple; he could not have a son. However, times were different now after the era of high communism, and Chorji had an extraordinarily powerful dual status as a reincarnate lama and government official (Chapter 9). So no one openly raised an objection to the plan—except, it seems, other members of Chorji's family. At this point, the boy's older brother fell very seriously ill and Chorji felt he had to allow both of the young lamas to go home; it would be unethical to keep the younger boy and leave his family only with a son who was on the point of death. So for several reasons the adoption did not go ahead. When we returned in 1998, the boy lamas had both vanished and they will not return to the pages of this book, though Chorji continued to mourn the absence of this boy with whom he lost touch. We see here that the "causes" for a decision may lie in networks of relationships outside the self (Strathern 1995, 69–86) and that the deciding self in Mongolia is not "private," but open to and inclusive of such relations. Furthermore, such decisions affect the relational conglomerate we have called the monastery. If Chorji had had his way, if he had acquired an heir, a young lama trained in the liturgical discipline of Mergen and furthermore someone he could have cared for, the sad events we shall later describe would almost certainly have been very different. Indeed, the whole character of the monastery, the relationships that made up the actuality of its working, would have been subtly altered. These are some of the reasons why our book is a study of the quality of institutional relations not as a pre-given structure, but as created by particular people in diverse interactions with one another.

The lamas were people drawn from a local environment. They were almost all Urad Mongols, while much of the religion they professed was shared with Buddhists far and wide. So let us now proceed to explain what this means. We shall use conventional historical terms, leaving most of our discussion of the lamas' own understandings to later chapters.

The Urad Mongols and Mergen Monastery

Mergen Monastery is located in a region of southwestern Inner Mongolia commonly known as Urad, on the north side of the bend in the Yellow River (M. *Hatun Goul* "Queen River," C. *Huanghe*). It has a beautiful, auspicious site according to Mongol views, with mountains towering behind, the Mergen River trickling alongside, and a view over the plains to the gleaming waters of the great river.

The band of territory along the Yellow River including the Muna Mountain range (C. Wulashan), has been the territory of the Urad Mongols since the seventeenth century. Earlier, the Urads lived far to the north in the present-day Hulun Buir region bordering on Siberia. They were the people (*ulus*) ruled by a single noble family tracing its ancestry back to the twelfth century, to Hasar, younger brother of Chinggis Khan.[4] In the seventeenth century, earlier than most other Mongol groups, the Urad decided to align themselves with the Manchus, who were in the process of taking over China. Shortly after establishing their Qing dynasty in 1644, the Manchus dispatched the Urad from the north to act as guards of the empire against still unconquered Mongols. When they arrived in their present lands in the 1640s–1650s, the Urad leaders with their followers had already formed into Banners (*hoshigu*, pronounced *hoshuu*), the new military groupings set up by the Manchus to take the place of earlier Mongol political formations. The three Urad Banners, called the West, Middle, and East Banners, [5] consisting of a number of subordinate units called *sumu*, were allocated territories. The three were ruled by two brothers and a cousin from the Urad

4. For discussion of "tribe" and "clan" as used in Western scholarship, see Sneath (2007). When they were living in Hulun Buir the Urad seem to have been linked by patrilineal kinship only at the level of the nobles, who traced their ancestry to Hasar. The common people were divided into groups of one a hundred households (*jagutan*), notionally providing one a hundred soldiers), and these were associated either with territory, a specific function, (or both). So the Maltagur Jagutan dug fortifications, the Dagutan Jagutan were singers, the Haranuud Jagutan provided black horses, etc. When the Manchu Qing applied the Banner system to the Urad, the *jagutan* were reorganized into groups called *sumu*, and these were allowed to choose which Banner to join. Most *sumu* decided to join the Urad West Banner, attracted by a brilliant military hero at the time, called named Üben. The West Banner thus acquired twelve *sumu*, the Middle Banner six, and the North Banner also six. When the Qing sent the Urad from Hulun Buir to their present region at the Muna Mountains, the West Banner moved first and therefore took up the western end of the range, the Middle Banner followed, acquiring the eastern end, and the Northern Banner arrived in the rear, taking land to the north of the mountains. (Buyanbadarahu 1987, 35–42).

5. Some authors such as Atwood (2002) refer to Urad Right and Left Banners, rather than West and East; right/west and left/east are the same words in Mongol.

noble family, each now dignified by the title of Duke (*güng*) bestowed by the Manchus. It is important to realize that the Urad arrived in their present lands as an army, expelling or suppressing whoever lived there before: The idea of victorious emplacement has been central to their narratives ever since. Along with two other Banners formed by armies also from the north (and also said to be descended from Hasar), the Urads were to make up the Ulanchab League, a broad grouping headed by one or another of the Banner rulers. It was the Banners, however, more than the Leagues that were the practical, operative political units of the Manchu system.[6] Mergen Monastery, founded at the beginning of the eighteenth century, became the official monastery of the West Duke Banner, which was the senior of the three Urad groups as its first Duke had been genealogically senior to the two other leaders.

In practice the old Mongol idea of the *ulus* (a people, a nation) did not disappear. The Urad commoners, mobile pastoralists, were free to migrate across the lands of all three Banners, though they were taxed according to their Banner registration.[7] Meanwhile, the three lines of Dukes maintained a single patrilineal genealogy right up to 1949, when they ceded power to the Communists (Buyanbadarhu 1987, 16–30). Thus although each Banner was a separate political entity according to the Manchu administration, there was a sense in which the Urads continued to think of themselves as one people, later called the Urad *aimag* (Bühechilagu 2007, 1). Within the Banners, the *sumu* units increasingly came to resemble clans (membership by descent from father, common rituals, mostly exogamous), and today the Urad use the terms *sumu* and *obug* (clan) interchangeably for these units .

The economy of the Urads was based on herding sheep, goats, horses, camels, and, to a lesser extent, cattle. From the mid–nineteenth century, Chinese settler-farmers began to occupy in significant numbers the fertile lands around the Yellow River, which consequently reduced the pasture available. Many Mongols were forced to retreat northward into the Muna Mountains and the sandy plains beyond. Mergen Monastery, however, held on to an extensive territory south of the moun-

6. The "autonomous Banners," like the Urad West Banner, were different from the Banners in the "eight Banner" system. The former was an administrative unit of civil population, while the latter was an organization of military reservists subject to call-up by the Qing armies (Atwood 2004, 30–31).

7. Early twentieth-century Mongol society can be categorized into three main groups: nobles (*taijinar*, the descendants of Chinggis Khan and his brothers); lamas; and laity (*harachu arad*). The laity was subdivided into service households (*albatu*) or (*hariyatu*), monastic serf households (*hara shabi*); households on relay service duty, and male and female slave-servants (*bogul*) (Altanorgil 1998, vol. 3, 22).

tains until the mid–twentieth century. Its large horse herds, which had been a prestige item, were greatly reduced after the Communist takeover, and subsequently all herds were decimated during the turmoil and hunger of the late 1950s and early 1960s. By this time, many more Chinese farmers had been drafted into the territory, until nearly all the land up to the foot of the mountains was occupied. After the Cultural Revolution, when the communes were closed and households began to herd their own flocks again, the Urads turned mainly to goats, the only animals capable of finding fodder in the craggy mountains. By 1995, with practically all pasture south of the mountains gone, goats kept for cashmere sales were the mainstay of the herders. The diverse and self-sufficient household economies that were still remembered by elderly Urads were transformed by dependency on world markets. Luckily for the Urads, they happened upon good times with the goats: prices for cashmere rose dramatically during the 1980s and 1990s. By then the herders had abandoned the felt tents (yurts) that were still common in the 1940s (Camman 1951, 99) and moved to Chinese-style mud-brick houses. Recently many have been able to build large comfortable new houses. They have even started to employ Chinese to do the hard herding work for them in the mountains.

But prices rise and fall. Reliance on external markets brought uncertainty and anxiety. Furthermore, by the late 1990s, a terminal crisis loomed: the environmental degradation of the mountains threatened to end the pastoral way of life of the Urads altogether (see Epilogue).

Mergen Monastery suffered greatly during the wars of the twentieth century. Sacked in 1913, in the following decades it was at various times set on fire and ransacked; parts of it were destroyed. During the Cultural Revolution, Mergen only escaped total ruin because it had been occupied by the People's Liberation Army (PLA) and turned into a forward military base directed towards the Soviet threat.[8] In 1987 (after a miraculous event described in Chapter 7), some former lamas stormed the monastery and began to worship again. The army was still in occupation, however, and a wall was built to separate the military and the religious parts of the site. The troops left a few years later, but the army retained ownership of the land and buildings. This jarring mix of the military and the religious in one site seems at first an unlikely coincidence. Thought about more broadly, though, it soon be-

8. From the early 1960s onward, China's relations with the USSR deteriorated sharply. Large Soviet armies were stationed in Mongolia, whose border lies not far to the north from Urad lands. But by the late 1980s relations had improved, and the PLA was withdrawn from Mergen.

comes clear that this was not a matter of chance, either geographically or historically.

If you stand with your back to the bend in the Yellow River and face northward, the jagged Muna Mountains extend from left to right as far as the eye can see. Behind them lies the high plateau of dry windswept lands of the nomads. In the eighteenth century the Mongols built a series of Buddhist monasteries along the foothills of these mountains facing south, one for each valley. They look down on the quite different activities of the Chinese in the plains below: irrigated agriculture, busy trading villages, a mainline railway, highway, factories, and the steelmaking city of Baotou. This has always been boundary territory: the crumbling line of one of the ancient Great Walls of China snakes along here, and the valleys emerging from the mountains are met with a line of ruined forts said to have been built in the Han Dynasty. The impression that this is a militarized landscape is strengthened when one sees the remains of Japanese gun emplacements from the Second World War and the glimpse of a PLA radar station on one of the mountain peaks. This is frontier country, no doubt about it. But it is a frontier between two such different entities that one side, that of the Mongols, seems evanescent. They built nothing much here except the monasteries—and most of them were destroyed in the Cultural Revolution.

Should we then see the monasteries as outposts of Mongol civilization, like the edges of an indistinct, ebbing and flowing sea-like culture that spread all the way back into the vast steppes and deserts of inner Asia? This book will suggest the contrary: that these monasteries were not the peripheries of a larger entity, but were themselves centers and focal points of distinct political groupings, in lands that the Mongols once controlled but no longer do. They were centers of a curious kind, generated by mobile, nomadic people. For centuries, the Mongol way, if we see it at its most abstract, had been to organize society around a moveable fulcrum in an expanse considered otherwise to be a void. This created a place—and always the same kind of place—at each time of stopping and settling somewhere (Humphrey 1995; Pedersen 2007). Mongols were initially suspicious of cities and walled housing, seeing them as entrapments potentially fatal to their strategic advantage of mobility. Even when they engaged artisans to build settlements, Mongols historically tended toward temporary or mobile usage of them. Rulers might settle subordinates and captives in cities for various functional reasons; but they themselves did not often live in them, preferring seasonal camps and life in tents. Such cities, or, more correctly, towns, were relatively easily abandoned and replaced by settlements in other regions. Out in the grasslands the social principle of leaders who gathered followers around them in greater or lesser numbers, taking their centers with them as it were, continued throughout the vicissitudes of conquest and decline, a pattern found in many states and empires founded by nomads across Asia (Sneath 2006, 20).

There was a change, however, in the sixteenth and seventeenth centuries, when the Mongols (re)converted rapidly en masse to Buddhism. The most powerful Mongol Khans began to build temples and monasteries as monuments to their munificence as religious donors. Isabelle Charleux observes that while distant steppe Mongols were still mostly content with temples in yurts, the Eastern Mongols were already acquainted with Chinese architecture and found it more practical and prestigious to build in bricks and stones. Rich donors required secure places for their precious gifts. In particular, large statues could hardly be relocated with each nomadic movement and were often the original reason for the building of a settled temple. Indeed, the characteristically multi-meaningful Mongol word *juu* means statue of Buddha, monastery, temple, and Lhasa (called "Western Juu," Charleux 2006, 195). Ih Juu ("Great Juu"), the largest and earliest monastery in Höhhot, was built from 1579 to 1580.

Buddhist monasteries were built on a wide scale in the early eighteenth century when the relatively peaceful conditions brought about by the Qing had already taken hold. The local political leaders—princes and dukes—continued to live a mobile existence in felt tents, but monasteries were now being built to last. Often sited deliberately far away from centers of Chinese population, they became repositories of wealth, learning, art, music, and medicine. They were significant marks and validations of the presence of a group in a territory (Charleux 2006, 26), as well as being the crucibles of spiritual endeavor for the benefit of all sentient beings in the vicinity. As larger proportions of the male population entered the monkhood, monasteries expanded and proliferated, developing into key economic as well as religious centers. There were very few properly Mongol towns; most urban settlements were accretions around Chinese trading posts or large monasteries, or a combination of the two. Thus, right up to the end of the Second World War, the governing Duke of the Urad West Banner lived in a mobile manner, though now with a modest palace and a small office as well as tented encampments. The monasteries of his domain, which were by far the most solid structures around, were incomparably more impressive. Unfortunately for the monks, the wars of the twentieth century made the monasteries targets; they were sources of booty, refuges for people in flight, and frequently the temporary quarters of passing armies. As a result, many monasteries, including Mergen, set up their own militias. The appropriation of Mergen Monastery in the 1960s as a base for the PLA looks less strange in the light of this history. But what was the religion of which it was a part?

Buddhism in Mongol Lands: A Historical Outline

The Mongols were aware of Buddhism from the earliest period of their history. Prior to the emergence of the Mongols as a strong political entity in the twelfth century, the first Türk Empire (552–695) had made Buddhism the court religion, and the succeeding Uighurs retained it along with Manichaeism. The Uighurs were to be a strong cultural influence on the early Mongols. However, the people of the steppes who took the name Mongol were not Buddhists. They worshipped the deified Sky (*tngri, tenggri, tengri,* "Heaven," "God") and the Earth (*gajar*); carried out rituals for ancestors and spirits; venerated fire, mountains and rivers; and had religious specialists the academic literature describes as "shamans." But the Mongols were generally curious, open to outside religious influences, including Buddhism, Daoism, Nestorian Christianity, and Confucian teachings, and later in western regions also Islam (Jagchid 1988, 83–120). Diverse Buddhist influences came to them from various quarters. It is evident from their religious vocabulary that the Mongols must have known about the basic ideas of Buddhism before they were influenced by the Tibetan form (Stebetak 2003, 163).[9]

Although Tibetan Buddhism eclipsed the Chinese variant among the Tangut,[10] the Mongols were at first more taken with Chinese Chan Buddhism that had flourished during the Jin Dynasty (1115–1234). Under Chinggis Khan, officials who followed Chan masters achieved high rank in imperial service and persuaded the emperor to agree to privileged status for Buddhist monks. Chinggis himself later wavered in favor of Daoism, but his successor, Emperor Ögedei, preferred Buddhism. Before long Tibetan and Kashmiri Buddhism gained imperial favor, following renewed links with the Tanguts (now part of the Mon-

9. For example, the terms for the central notion of the "three refuges" (Buddha, Dharma, and Community of Monks) are old words of probable Uighur, Sogdian, and Greek origin: *burhan, nom,* and *huwarag.*

10. Tanguts founded a kingdom known as Xia (1032–1227) in the region between Tibetan- and Mongolian-dominated areas, and they maintained close ties with the Tibetans.

gol Empire) and the Tibetans (Atwood 2004, 48). Tibet was shortly annexed to the empire, much of it under indirect rule through the leaders of the Sakya (T. *Sa skya*) order, whose prelates had impressed the Mongols with their learning and magical healing powers. In 1253 Emperor Hubilai (Khubilai) summoned the Sakya leader's nephew, the famous 'Phags-pa Lama, to his capital. The lama conferred on the emperor the initiation of the Tantric Buddha Hevajra. Such initiations and the institution of Tibetan preceptors became regular at the Mongol court (Atwood 2004, 48–49).

The Mongols remained open to other religious teachings, however. They held public debates between different religions and between diverse schools of Buddhism; Nestorians remained in certain families, and shamans, fortune-tellers, and ritual specialists carried on at the court and throughout the land. The domination of Tibetan Buddhism in court circles is widely ascribed to Hubilai's promotion of 'Phags-pa to imperial preceptor and the creation under him of a Supreme Control Commission to administer the affairs of Chinese and Tibetan monks (Atwood 2004, 49). Thereafter the Indo-Tibetan textual tradition, under Mongol patronage, came to influence the earlier Chinese and Uighur ones and acquire its own status as part of established Buddhism in China. The Mongols had taken their cursive script from the Uighurs, who remained active interpreters and translators at court, but they were now joined by Mongol scholars, who translated from Tibetan and other languages and also wrote sutras, hymns, biographies, and scholarly works in Tibetan (Bira 1994, 347–50; Atwood 2004, 49–50). Thus the Mongol imperial court was not simply a place of crude xenophobic authoritarianism and rapacious fiscal appropriation, as is sometimes portrayed by historians taking a Sino-centric point of view, nor did it "acquire civilization" just from China (Gernet 1982, 372). This was a cosmopolitan multilingual environment, with diverse influences from Tibet, Central Asia, India, and Kashmir.

Along with this, the Mongols never gave up the worship of the Sky/God, which has remained to this day the center of domestic lunar New Year rites from the most elevated rulers to the ordinary people (Heissig 1980, 48). The notion of "destiny" (*jayaga*) given by Heaven was a very old idea, traceable to the pre-Mongol imperial steppe traditions (Bira 1994, 374) and linked especially to political power. After the death of Chinggis Khan the spirit of the great Mongol Emperor became an object of worship, not only among his own descendants but far more widely. Since he was the preeminent ruler who had been "destined by Heaven" to rule, it was held that only with proper worship of both Heaven and Chinggis Khan could legitimate government be reproduced (Elverskog 2006, 48–50). However, the Chinggisid religious-political rites for the installation of Khans were on the wane even before the Mongols accepted Manchu rule, and as an idea for legitimacy they were then transformed in various ways. As for the old notion of Sky and Earth as active principles of cosmological order, it was increasingly sidelined by Buddhism and excluded from the strict definition of "religion" (*shashin*). But it continued everywhere in families, local communities, and princely courts, which continued to hold regular rites to venerate and propitiate the power, agency, or anger of Sky/Heaven. This idea is particularly prominent in works of the 3rd Mergen Gegen. One of his poems celebrating his homeland culminates in no Buddhist formula but in these words:

May all best things be completed
That have been made to prosper by Heaven and Earth;
May there be the good fortune
Of even, peaceful happiness
(Galluu and Jirantai, eds. 1986, 638).

As we shall describe in later chapters, Mergen Gegen was exceptional in continuing to draw together in his works what Elverskog has called the "bifurcated system of legitimacy" (2006, 45), the pre-Manchu coexistence among the Mongols of two sources of religious power, that of God/Heaven and that of Buddhist institutions.

Let us now track back in history to the emergence of the institution of the Reincarnate Lama (*hubilgan*), which is so important at Mergen Monastery. Mongols themselves often speak of these holy figures as though they had been there since the dawn of time, and it is true that the idea of *incarnation* (a human body as the vessel for the emanation of a Buddha or bodhisattva) emerged in the ancient period of Mahayana Buddhism. But *reincarnation* (rebirth of this emanation soon after the death of the previous incarnation in a line of holy figures) is late in origin, dating from the twelfth-thirteenth century in Tibet (van der Kuijp 2005, 28–29). In a situation of competition for power, the advantage of the concept of reincarnation is that it confers extra sanctity on the holder and at the same time, by transmitting authority from one sacred leader to another in perpetuity, trumps the kin-based rivalry found in ruling lineages. A reincarnated lama—as a monk ideally committed to monastic vows of poverty and liberated from of familial ties—could wield a different kind of power and, in principle, would not seek to build kin-based political and economic clout with which to foment rebellion (Wylie 1978, 584). However, as McCleary and van der Kuijp describe (2010, 156–70), the various schools of Buddhism in fifteenth- and sixteenth-century Tibet competed fiercely for novices and lay adherents, not to speak of powerful patrons, wealth, and land; in all of this the reincarnate lamas were the fulcrums.

The Mongol Yuan Dynasty in China fell in 1368, and retreating from China, the Mongols are widely supposed to have "'reverted to shamanism" (Heissig 1980, 25), but evidence suggests that the nobles maintained a variety of religious practices, including Buddhism (Serruys 1963; Jagchid 1988, 121–30; Charleux 2006, 26). It can be said then that a certain element of choice was present for Mongols with regard to religion, or rather that they maintained a polity in which religious variety was a value. The aristocratic culture in general was one that encouraged independent decision-making, whether or not the subject was part of an imperial structure (Sneath 2006, 8). When, in the sixteenth and seventeenth centuries, the "'second conversion" of the Mongols to Buddhism occurred on a mass basis, the "shamanism" that the common people practiced was itself also a mixture of disparate practices (Heissig 1980, 6–23).

The princes were converted first. They again made close links with Tibet, and again decisions had to be made about which Buddhist order to support. Elverskog has argued (2007, 64–69) that the now accepted story, that the Mongol rulers gratefully accepted the tutelage of the Gelug school, masks what was at first multiple patronage of diverse religious specialists, notably under the great Altan Khan (1508–1592). Still, after Altan Khan initiated the reincarnation line of the Dalai Lamas by conferring this title on the eminent Gelug prelate Sönam Gyatso in 1578, the Gelug–Mongol relation was to prevail.[11] The Gelug, which Mongols call the "Yellow Hat" order, had been instituted according to the teachings of the great philosopher and Tantric master Tsongkhapa (M. Dzongkaba; 1357–1419), who criticized degenerate magical rituals and advocated a celibate monastic life for monks, with lengthy training and discipline. The dominance of this order in Tibet was due in part to its mass character and success in maintaining doctrinal orthodoxy, but also to the military backing given by Mongols. To this day commoner Mongols maintain a mythicized version of these struggles, according to which a Mongol hero, Dugar Jaisang, "'cleansed" Tibet of corrupt prac-

11. According to Shen Weirong (2010, 33), the reincarnation line already existed and it was merely the title of Dalai Lama that was retrospectively granted to the two earlier incarnations.

tices (Humphrey 2007). Those were the practices of the Bön religion and all of the other non-Gelug schools that the Mongols lump together as "Red Hat" orders. In those groups, great respect was given to Padmasambhava (T. *pad ma 'byung gnas*, Guru Rinpoche; M. Badamsamba, Lobonchimbu, or Badmajüngnei), the semi-mythical Indian Yogi of the eighth century, who is said to have tamed the malevolent local gods and spirits of Tibetan lands (Charleux 2002). Many of their specialists led non-monastic, non-celibate lives and upheld mystical and tantric practices. But in both Tibet and Mongolia these orders were sidelined by the increasing dominance of the Gelug-pa. So revered is the Gelug founder Tsongkhapa by the Mongols that he is known as "'the second victor," the first being Shakyamuni Buddha.

Mergen Monastery, like almost all Mongolian monasteries, belongs to the Gelug order, which in theory excludes any other kind of Buddhist presence. Even so, there are traces of Red Hat influences today: links are maintained with the Nyingma monastery of Agu-yin Süme lying not far away to the west, and some of the Mergen lamas worship Padmasambhava privately.[12] The next section provides some brief but essential information about the contours of Tibeto-Mongolian Buddhism in contrast to Chinese Chan Buddhism. The Mergen monks see themselves unequivocally as upholding the former and having little in common with the latter. However, Chan is relevant to our book in several ways. In the mountains near Mergen there is a cave where a Chan adept meditated not so long ago (Crane 2001) and his memory is venerated by Mongols and Chinese of the area. Furthermore, in the last year or two, the Chorji Lama—to the discomfiture of many—invited Chan Buddhists to reside and take part in activities at Mergen (Chapter 9).

Tibeto-Mongolian Buddhism

a. Central ideas and how they are understood

Tibeto-Mongolian Buddhism centers on the goal of enlightenment or Buddhahood (M. *bodi* from S. *bodhi; bodi sedhil*), the aim of personal or collective salvation from the desires and suffering of the ordinary world (M. *sansar*, from S. *samsāra*). Enlightenment entails the realiza-

12. See Charleux 2002. Hamid Sardar mentions links between the poet Danzan Ravjaa (1803–1857), renowned for his attraction to "red" practices and the Mergen tradition. Sardar also describes how powerful "red" tantric rites were maintained secretly by some of the highest Gelug reincarnations, hidden from the abbots and monks of their monasteries (2007, 270).

tion that the self is essentially an illusion: that the grasping at self lies at the root of our world-bound existence, and that negation of the self therefore lies at the heart of the path to liberation (Jinpa 2002, 70). Now even uneducated Mongol Buddhists know about this theory, but they operate for the most part with the idea that there is a self akin to a "soul" (*sünesü*), which transmigrates from one life form to another over countless generations. All living beings are subject to the causative and ethical principle of *karma*, which is the result of their actions (M. *üile-yin üre*, the fruit-seeds of deeds). According to the balance of good and bad deeds built up over this and previous lives, a soul acquires merit (M. *buyan* from S. *puṇya*) and is able to take rebirth after death in a better (human or god) or worse (animal, insect, etc.) form. While the Theravada path, found mostly in Southeast Asia, gave emphasis to ethical and karmic considerations, including the goal of Nirvana, the ultimate state of selfless bliss beyond this world, the Mahayana path, prevalent in China, Tibet, Mongolia, and Japan, came to focus more on achieving enlightenment in this world.[13]

A principal Mahayana teaching concerns the bodhisattva, a person who having achieved enlightenment and thus also being able to enter Nirvana, nevertheless chooses compassionately to return to the world to help bring salvation to other beings. In Mongolian this is expressed as the "will" (*irügel*) of the bodhisattva, who may choose to return in any form, even a monkey or an insect. So greatly is this ideal of compassion admired that there is even a prayer *not* to enter Nirvana.[14] In general the Mahayana use of Sanskrit (as opposed to Pali), its involvement in arguments with varieties of Hindu and Jain thought, and its greater cultural incorporation than Theravada traditions gave it a different "flavor" and aesthetic (Collins 1982, 23–25). Tibetans, to a much greater extent than Chinese Buddhists, took up an inflow of Vajrayana,[15] also known as tantric, teachings from the eighth century onward and they were later

13. Mahayana, the "Great Vehicle," contrasts itself with Hinayana, the "Lesser Vehicle," of which the Theravada tradition is the only one to have survived. For excellent accounts of Theravada Buddhism and a deeper discussion of doctrinal issues concerning the self than we have been able to include here, see Collins 1982 and Cook 2010. See Pei-ye Wu 1990, 71–76, on the Chan doctrine of sudden enlightenment and its influence on the emergence of autobiography among Chinese Buddhists.

14. *Nirvan ülü bolhui-dur jalbarimoi*: "I pray not to become Nirvana." Differentiating Nirvana, in which one no longer exists in any conventional sense, from enlightenment, ordinary people in both Buryatia and Inner Mongolia read this prayer after a ritualized confession of sins. Their aim instead is to generate an altruistic *bodi sedhil* (enlightened mind).

15. The Sanskrit term *vajra* refers to the thunderbolt or diamond, symbolizing the indestructibility that can pierce any obstacle. In Mongolian, Vajrayana is known as the vehicle or path (*hölgen*) of the thunderbolt (*wachir, ochir*).

transferred to the Mongols. Vajrayana uses secret mantras and complex ritual techniques as means toward the ultimate goal of enlightenment. Instead of reaching enlightenment through gradual and long accumulation of virtues, tantra enables a faster attainment, even in this current lifetime.[16] A first stage is silent recitation and meditation on powerful words and syllables capable of spiritual effect, called by Mongols *tarni*, (S. *dhāraṇī*) and often referred to in English as mantras.[17] An initiated person engages in self- transformation first by visualizing the body of his personal tutelary Buddhist deity (M. *yidam*, T. *yi-dam*) and identifying with it; then, if a higher stage has been reached, by "becoming" this very body himself. The ritual environment becomes the perfected realm, represented by the mandala diagram, controlled by the deity / self. By this means "one gains power over beings in other spheres of existence, either dominating them, so that they may do one's will, or identifying oneself with them, so that one may enjoy their higher states of existence" (Snellgrove 2004, 130). This process is aided by yogic practices aimed at manipulating and controlling subtle physical energies to produce liminal states of awareness. However, abuses of power developed in many places under the guise of tantric rites. Tsongkhapa did not reject tantra, but he maintained that it should be practiced only after undertaking extensive preliminary training and understanding of the sutras (M. *nom* "book, doctrine, dharma") laying out the fundamental principles of Buddhism and the ethical framework within which tantra should be understood. According to Mongols, he wrote his teachings at three levels in accordance with the three levels of innate ability of religious practitioners (*gurban törülhiten*), some more apt for advancement than others. Only those born into the highest level could achieve enlightenment in this life (see Nietupski 2011, 39 and Dreyfus 2003, 340 for alternative Tibetan understandings). Strict orthodoxy in this matter has always been challenged by the tendency of all kinds of people to grasp the magic-mystic aspects of tantra as quickly as possible.

Lamas we knew at Mergen saw tantra as the supreme path of a totality. Sengge Lama characterized the paths by their "refuges" (sacred founts of trust or faith, M. *itegel*). He said that Theravada has three refuges (*Burhan* [Buddha], *Nom* [doctrine] and *Huwarag* [the community of monks]), Mahayana has four (*Lama, Burhan, Nom, Huwarag*), while

16. See Dreyfus 2003 and Gyatso 1998 for an extended discussion of tantric practice by Tibetan monks.

17. We use the word mantra, since it is relatively well known in English, interchangeably with *tarni*. See Gyatso 1992c, 198, on the use of mantra and *dhāraṇī* in scholarly literature.

tantra has five refuges (*Lama, Yidam, Buddha, Nom, Huwarag*). Mergen monastery once had a range of services, among which tantric texts invoking the *yidam* Yamantaka (S. Yamāntaka) had pride of place (see Chapter 2; for details, Ujeed 2009, 178–86). Contemporary Mergen monks say they adhere to the Gelug teachings about the necessity for long training before engaging in tantra, and no monk currently at the monastery thought himself sufficiently adept to undertake advanced esoteric meditation. But in practice they carry out several rituals that can be considered tantric in a broad sense.

b. Buddhism in the Mongolian context

Popularly, the deep insight obtained through tantric initiations is often said to be evident by the ability to perform miracles; the laity living around Mergen love stories of this kind. Now certain historians have poured scorn on the Mongols for turning their backs on Chinese Buddhism, their "indifference to philosophical questions, their weakness for magic and their belief in miracles" (Gernet 1982, 383). However, miracles, as discussed in Chapter 3, do not represent a degeneration of Buddhism, but a certain aesthetic, or mode of evidential demonstration within it. The disdainful attitude is reminiscent of earlier Orientalist approaches to Buddhism, where a contrast was drawn between "true Buddhism as taught by its founder" and folk "corruptions" found in later times. Various scholarly approaches proposed correctives to this bald view, in particular to argue that: 1) a space for popular concerns can be discerned in the Buddha's original teaching (Gombrich 1971); 2) that the Pali canon itself contains different philosophical and practical strains that look contradictory when analyzed abstractly (Spiro 1971, 144–47, 258–73); 3) to propose that spirit worship and other village practices formed a structurally integrated whole with Buddhism (Tambiah 1970); 4) conversely, to suggest that true Buddhism was the way of life lived by ordinary people as distinct from that of monks (Southwold 1983); 5) to argue for a ritual syncretism between Buddhism, shamanism, and sacrificial cults (Holmberg 1989); or 6) to cut across the "great"/"little" divide by categorizing Mahayana Buddhism into three "systems" oriented towards Nirvanic salvation, karmic morality, and worldly welfare (Samuel 1993; for further discussion, see Collins 1982, 13–15).

We do not argue that there are no fractures in Urad Mongols' thinking about religious life, but that they do not generally correspond with the divisions mentioned above. One reason for this is that Buddhism arrived in Mongolian regions in several different and indistinct waves. As Christopher Atwood rightly observed, the Buddhism the Mongols received was already a complex mixture from Tibet, and ultimately from India, a prior interlacing of elements that runs against "the old two-tier model with its predictable picture of the clerical figure forced to make concessions to popular superstition" (1996, 139). In other words, there was no "pure Buddhism" to start with. Nevertheless, the lamas of Mergen do make certain discriminations. Our task is to chart these as best we can, while at the same time acknowledging our outside, inevitably partial, view that allows us to abstract the main tenor of these accounts from hundreds of observations and conversations.

Contemporary Mongols have a category they call religion (M. *shashin*, from S. *śāsana*), by default the Buddhist faith, and scholars have more problems than they do in conceptualizing what it comprises. If "religion" included, when it arrived, a range of practices not thought of as Buddhist by scholars, such as pacifying demons, divination, or fire worship, a complication is that when Tibetan missionaries came to Mongolia in the seventeenth century they met a new host of sacral and occult activities, analogous to but in many ways different from the popular practices of Tibet, i.e., worship of the Sky/Heaven, ancestors, mountains and trees, sacrifices, consecrations of animals, shamanism, spirit possession, and so forth. The distinctive Mongolian cosmology, in other words their concepts of the diverse forces at work in nature (*baigal*, "what exists"), constitutes a realm of action. Lamas' prayers are effective in speeding "souls" to rebirth, so why not also to diverting other energies to beneficent ends? Many of these countless forces tend to be reified as *tngri* ("skies" or "gods") of one kind or another: fate *tngri*, enemy *tngri*, fire *tngri*, fortune *tngri*, lightning *tngri*, even jealousy, egg, and cuckoo *tngris* (Heissig 1980, 50–53). A pervasive sky-god idiom, appearing in prayers chanted by lamas, differentiates Mongolian practices from those of Tibet.

The salient characteristic of the Mergen tradition is that it came to absorb a large range of these popular ritual activities, transforming them from elements in mere coexistence with one another into conceptually lower levels of the Buddhist ensemble. Shamanism, however, was not included. It is therefore important to correct the earlier blanket description of *all* these folk practices as "shamanic" by writers such as Bawden (1968) and Heissig (1980). In much of Mongolia, properly shamanic rites, i.e., those involving shamans and their *onggud* spirits, were virtually eliminated by ardent Buddhist missionaries and princely edicts during the seventeenth century, but many other folk cults conducted by elders of the community survived. So today there are no shamans in Urad, but rituals for mountain, tree, and water spirits, fire deities, sacrificial and ancestor cults, consecrated animals, etc., are alive and well. The significant fact is that they were incorporated into the practice of "the Mergen tradition" through the texts written by Mergen Gegen, though not in such a way as to completely eradicate their non-Buddhist characteristics.

This Mergen incorporation was significantly different from what happened in other Mongol regions that used the Tibetan liturgy. There, standard Tibetan prayers were imported for local cults of mountains, the worshipped peaks were renamed, and the previous local spirits were replaced by well-known Buddhist deities. This "lamaization" of rites was resisted in some areas and never entirely completed, but nevertheless it is discernible that the general import of the process was to engulf and digest the local cults, dissolving their originality into preexisting categories brought by Tibetan masters. It is at least arguable that in Mergen Gegen's case the effect was the *converse*. So large and vivid was the place given to these cults in his writings, and in the regular rituals of the monks, that they could be said to pervade the character of his Buddhism—lending it a particular local color and aesthetic (see also Atwood 1996, 135).

One way we can perceive coherence in "religion" (*shashin*) is through the techniques of rationalization people use to relate its various parts. Definition (e.g., of types or characteristics of gods) is one such technique. Numbering classes of things is another (the "five consecration-giving gods," the "eight offerings," and a host of others). Another technique is hierarchization: the ranking of types of objects of worship and practices. At Mergen, the main spine of precedence is approximately as follows: after the five "refuges" (*Lama, Yidam, Buddha, Nom, Huwarag*) there follow: *arhat*, enlightened disciples of Buddha; *choijong*, higher protector deity; *sahiusu* (*sahigulsun*), lower protector deity, of which there are several subtypes; *gajar-un ejen*, land god, along with *sabdag*: land/tree spirit and *luus*; water spirits; *chitgür*, ghost; *sholum-shimnu*, demon. Various sky gods are accommodated among the middling ranks. Because these rationalizing techniques exist, the monks are able to create topologies of diverse elements and chart meaningful maps within them.

Individual lamas differ in how they fit gods into such schemes, yet we did not find conflict among them about these matters, though they were often in hot disagreement about practical concerns. One reason for their acquiescence in shifting sacred hierarchies and ritual arrangements can be explained by a significant observation made by Dreyfus about the character of definition in Asian traditions. He notes that definition in the Tibetan Buddhist knowledge system is not essentialist. Unlike Western traditions derived from Plato that see definition as accounting for the essential being of phenomena, in Indian and Tibetan thought definition is only concerned with a salient property that unambiguously points to the object. "Hence, definition is intended to enable an object to be properly identified within a certain context, not to provide a final statement on it" (Dreyfus 2003, 308–09). This is in accord with the general anti-substantialism of the Buddhist religious philosophy. Dreyfus notes a tendency in Tibetan monasteries, nevertheless, for methods of teaching to essentialize definitions, leading to bitter disputes between monks defending them. We saw little of this tendency in Mergen, however, perhaps in part because the monastery has no philosophical debating tradition (*choira*); but perhaps derived more from the general notion that for Buddhists, "gods," etc., are appearances, a manifestation of something else, or a form taken from a particular point of view; thus "one" can flow into, or be part of, "another." Each lama, however definite he was about his opinion, somehow implied by his manner that this was the way *he* defined the world, not how it was in an absolute sense. A certain ontological modesty prevailed.

Perhaps most important "holding together" practice at Mergen was the general assumption that things may be done at different levels (*jerge*) of expertise and profundity. This is expressed by adjectives such as "high-level" (*degere*), "deep" (*gün*) or "precise" (*narin*), which were contrasted with "simple" (*eng-ün, yerü-yin*), and "low-level" (*doura*) performances. The distinction does not lie in the complexity of the act—it is a didactic point made in many stories that the most "simple" action can be "deep" when it is properly, devotedly done. There is a saying: "There is no difference between sweeping the ground and achieving enlightenment" (*gajar shügürdehü burhan bolhu ilgaga baihu ügei*). The religious quality of an act is emergent from the frame of mind, the intention, and moral qualities of the actor. At Mergen there is a vast central swathe of practice, which under *the same name,* can be performed in different ways.

c. "Transmutable keys"

We suggest the term "transmutable key" for such operations. They are ways of saying or doing things that are "the same" and yet, as performed by diverse people, have very different intentionality. They may be found elsewhere in the Buddhist world, but in the Mongolian case they can be related to the "non-fit" of language mentioned in the Introduction. People can say they are doing X when the semantic diapason of X is wide-ranging, to the extent that radically alternative things are meant by the same expression. What is important about this is that it enables people to "talk the same language," to interact with one another's worlds, to construct metonymical parallels between actions of different quality. The most spiritually advanced lamas are thus linked with the ordinary lay people and thus a sense of a Buddhist community is produced. We give two important examples of such "keys," though there are many others.[18]

First is the use of the word *burhan*, which is commonly used for a wide range of religious entities: Buddhas, bodhisattvas, all deitylike emanations of these, heavenly and land gods, and even for certain famous historical figures like Tsongkhapa. To "become *burhan*" is also the term most widely used for achieving enlightenment. The same phrase is used euphemistically for "to die," since the pious hope is that good people become gods (*burhan*) in heaven or the "pure land" (*sugavadi*, from S. *sukhāvatī*) after death. Thus the same expression is commonly used for achieving a range of different states, such as being reborn as a bodhisattva, being reborn in the "pure land," or becoming enlightened in this life. Furthermore, "enlightenment" is not seen as one state but has several varieties, and these in principle are a progress through many levels.[19] Along the way, one stage, as Mongols often say, is "finding the seed and path" (*ür-e mör-i olhu*), which means a state of imminent potentiality, the seed of Buddhahood, and from this one cannot be reborn in a lower state. This is the first of five bodhisattva paths, the path of accumulation. Higher still, there are ten places (*arban gajar* or *orun*) through which bodhisattvas pass. "Become *burhan*" might refer to any of these possibilities. Only the context enables people to understand which meaning is intended. But often an amiable and convenient vagueness prevails. The effect of this is to elide categories and mist over

18. Atwood (1996, 124–31) provides an example in his description of the fire ritual in Mongolia. It is integrated into Buddhism, and yet exists in three varieties: a lay form (a household offering rite to male and female deities), a tantric form (a professional lamas' rite involving dissolving the conventional world into emptiness and visualization of the deity of fire using Sanskrit mantras), and a third form somewhere between these two, created by Mergen Gegen.

19. Buddhists, including Mongols, say there are eighty-four thousand methods of achieving enlightenment. Lamas specify that whatever means is chosen, the practitioner has to achieve completion (M. *baramid*, S. *pāramitā*) in six virtues: compassion, insight, energy, forebearing, alms-giving, and clerical discipline. This list differs according to region (Lessing 1960, 1162).

discriminations that would expose hierarchical differences between speakers and their understandings. We commented in the Introduction on the general Mongolian language ideology, the assumption that one is among people who will catch a precise meaning, even if the words do not actually say it. To "become *burhan*" has this quality; as Webb Keane notes, some religious speech is effective precisely because it can support ambivalent or even contradictory beliefs (1997, 65). *Burhan* allows the humblest practitioner to ignore "levels" and suture practical aims or personal imagination onto the great endeavor.

The most common method of meditation[20] is another "transmutable key" and a prime example of something that can be done with different degrees of mastery, faith, and understanding. This meditative practice is called "counting mantras" (*tarni togalahu*) and it can be done in an extraordinarily wide range of ways, from a central element in a strict devotional exercise of a tantric adept that can take years to accomplish, to an activity—sometimes seeming almost mindless—that devout laypeople undertake in their spare time.

The *tarni* (mantra) handed down from guru to disciple through the ages—a set of syllables, Sanskrit words or sometimes sounds without meaning—is the mark on which the mind is focused. A *tarni* (mantra) is an extreme condensation of a complex teaching, such as impermanence or no-self, or of the qualities of a deity (Gyatso 1992c, 174). As described to us, "'counting mantras" does not mean simply keeping the mark at the center of attention, but pronouncing it repeatedly it, often silently to oneself, but distinctly so each syllable is apparent. Track is kept of repetitions by rolling the beads of a rosary (M. *erihe*), hence the expression "counting mantras." In popular speech among both lamas and laypeople, the phrase "counting mantras" may stand not only for repeating sounds, but also for the whole series of properly tantric practices (visualization, offering, contemplation, manipulation of body energies, etc.) in lengthy courses of meditation. Mergen folk greatly admire the few exceptional people who have been able to accomplish (*bütegühü*) such a demanding course, and they reverently showed us a cave in the next valley where a lama had achieved this goal.

Meditation ("counting *tarni*") done by laypeople ideally involves developing insight that will cleanse the "soul" by the technique of noting, counting, and regretting recent sins of body, speech, and mind,

20. Europeans may have a mistaken image of "meditation" as being simply a mental state. Manuals for practitioners show that meditation (M. *bishilgal*) refers not simply to states of mind but to highly formalized procedures in which all aspects of the actor's physical regimen and deportment are prescribed in detail (Sharf 2005, 260).

but sometimes it is done for aims in this present world such as averting anticipated misfortune (see pp//). For some elderly people, whose economic, sexual, nurturing, etc., tasks are over, meditation can almost become their whole life. They may spend hours gazing unseeingly into space, their lips moving, their fingers twisting. Occasionally, though, their eyes dart around and it is evident that the *tarni* counter's attention has been caught by what is happening round about. But the numbers of told beads keep piling up; something is being achieved. It is in the huge area of ambiguity of meditation across the range from the solitary adept in the cave to the old man listening in to family conversations that counting *tarni* acts as a transmutable key.

We would like to draw attention, however, to what Mongols value here, which is not simply a matter of high ascetic discipline as against humdrum routine, but the crucial matter of religious purity of mind. This precious quality may exist—or not exist—in either the "high" or the "low" forms of meditation, and to explain the point we provide one of several stories that circulate as moral guidance on this point.

A smart daughter-in-law learned the *mani* mantra, "On Ma Ni Pad Me Hum," from a lama, and she started practicing it and making nice offerings. Her mother-in-law, a simple, illiterate woman, asked, "What are you doing?"

"I'm chanting *mani.*"

"Oh, please teach me those words you are mumbling."

Smart daughter-in-law threw out, "OK, it's *mohur olugaitu, teneg türgüü* (useless appendix, stupid head)."

Mother gladly accepted these words and faithfully chanted them.

Later, Burhan Bagshi (Buddha) was passing by their house and saw the bodhisattva Ariyabalo hovering over the roof [a sign something there was blessed]. He told his disciple, "Go and see what is there." The monk went and found the mother chanting.

"What are you chanting?"

"*Mani.*"

"That is not right," and he taught her the mantra Om Ma Ni Pad Me Hum.

Sometime later, Buddha with his disciples again passed by the house. But Ariyabalo had disappeared.

"Go again and see what has happened."

The monk went and found the mother chanting both mantras, but she was distracted, asking each time, "Is the one taught by my daughter-in-law right, or the one taught by the lama right?"

The disciple reported this to Buddha, who said, "Go and tell her to chant, 'Useless appendix, stupid head,' I was wrong before."

This story is told to teach that it is sincerity and clarity of purpose that are most important. There are many such stories that serve to hold open the possibility of miraculously special attainment even for stupid and sinful people. And the stories are funny or shocking. But even now some people in Urad believe that such stories are not instructive fictions, but contain a reality that pertains to them—in something like the way certain devout Christians approach stories in the Bible. This is one reason why even the humblest meditation is personal and somewhat secret. "Count your mantras so even your top button can't hear," the Mongols say. To be too open might invite ridicule ("What have you got to do with such high matters?"), and in this situation people hold that the scorn itself may become an occult thing, an impediment (*harshi* or *barchid*) that will harm the striving for enlightenment. It is in this sense, the illusoriness of appearances and never being quite sure of the spiritual purity of another person—or oneself for that matter—that counting *tarni* provides a bridge between different realms of religious experience.

d. Fierce deities

Mergen Monastery today has two main temples, the lofty Maidar Temple (which is joined to the main hall for services called Chogchin Dugan) and the separate small Temple of the Fierce Gods. The latter, in which Mergen Gegen took a particular interest in the eighteenth century, is a place of particular potency. It is now time to introduce the Fierce Gods (M *dogshid,* T. *drag gched* "terrible executioners") and explain why they are so important in religious life.

Janet Gyatso observed about meditation that "insight . . . performs the critical function of destroying the defilements, . . . and destruction is synonymous with enlightenment" (1992b, 5). This idea of destruction is crucial to understand a main doctrinal significance of the chief Fierce Gods, the emanations of bodhisattvas and other deities taking wrathful forms. When a fierce form of such a god is chosen as one's *yidam* (personal tutelary deity), visualizing and assuming in oneself his or her power is a means of counteracting and destroying not only external impediments but also the *inner* defilements of the person. This teaching is made available to all, even though rather few people practice the cultivation of a personal *yidam*. The three intertwined sources of defilement are ignorance (*munghag,* represented by a pig),[21] anger

21. This source of defilement is conventionally known as ignorance, but we were told that *munghag* has the meaning also of stupidity (*teneg*), covetousness (*hobdug*) and not wanting to

(*urin*, represented by a snake), and lust (*tachiyanggui*, represented by a chicken).[22] A depiction of their consequences for a person's life and future, the Wheel of Samsara (the benighted cycle of birth, death and rebirth, *sansar-un hürdü*) is painted in practically all Mongolian monasteries, including Mergen. Three fierce protector *yidam*s were most frequently chosen at Mergen: Yamantaka, Mahakala, and the goddess Öhin Tngri ("Girl Sky Deity," T. Palden Lhamo), as we describe in later chapters. Other *yidams*, best known in their peaceful forms, such as Avalokiteśvara (associated with compassion), Tara (enlightened activity) and Manjusri (wisdom) were less frequently taken, although they are popular in other Mongolian regions. By adopting one of the *yidam*s as a personal deity one enters the philosophical and yogic path signified by that god and enters into the complex symbolism of the legends associated with it. *Yidam*s are chosen according to one's own nature, with the guidance of one's guru teacher from among the lamas. Thus the practice offers a personal path through a spectrum of cosmological alternatives, and the choice of a wrathful form is to take a stance both toward oneself and the world around.

The *yidam* is not a category of deities but those among various types adopted to serve an individual's practice of self-transformation. On our visits in 1995–1998 the small Temple of Fierce Gods contained a disparate array of paintings, photographs, and statues, including the higher deities usually chosen as *yidam*s, but also some fierce gods called Protectors of the Faith (*choijong*, T. *chos skyong*). These repel external threats—for a person, a monastery, or the religion as a whole. Lamas described shifting sets of four, eight, alternatively ten, of these—the precise composition of this class depended on which lama one was speaking to. Some of such deities are understood to be masters of the land and to have come from a non-Buddhist existence, and as Mills writes of the Dharma Protectors in Ladakh, "they do not so much represent a static class of deity as the results of a certain cosmological dynamic with reference to the Buddhist doctrine. In principle at least, any numen can be a *chos skyong*, although in practice most such deities need to have been of such power as to warrant the attention of a Buddha-figure to "bind them to the doctrine" (2003, 186). In Mergen, as well as in the monastery studied by Mills, the class of fierce "Protectors of the Faith"

know. It is the opposite of *mergen* (wise). A very educated or powerful person can be *munghag*. A former lama gave the example of someone who, knowing they must die, devotes him or herself to building a hundred houses.

22. Anger incorporates the idea of passion or fury; lust refers to base attachments, including sexual desire but also greed for any attractive object.

crosscuts what was philosophically speaking a significant distinction and incorporated both the supra-worldly emanations as well as locally originated deities. Among such Fierce Gods worshipped at Mergen, some, like Erlig Khan, King of the Underworld,[23] are known all over Inner Asia; while one, Muna Khan, spirit ruler of Yellow Peak, the highest mountain of the locality, is little known outside Urad.

In the Temple of Fierce Gods, paintings of several deities depict them in sexual congress—and lamas are well aware that the esoteric, symbolic tantric significance of the act is lost on most viewers, who take it literally.[24] These deities may appear in animal form, have multiple limbs, blood-dripping fangs, or hermaphrodite sexual organs; they ride strange beasts, trample on living beings, or dangle flayed human skins. . . . All of these appearances have meanings to be decoded, but they are at the same time simply very frightening images. As Mongols say: "Poison [has to be destroyed] by poison" (*hor-i hor-iyer*). Thus, along with the ideas of terrible purification of spiritual impediments and repulse of external demonic attacks, Fierce Gods invoke "in your face" powerful human urges—to which the monks have ambivalent attitudes. Further, through the dynamic of local incorporation, these gods also represent autochthonous, natural energies of the land. The complex combination of ideas associated with the Fierce Gods makes them ambiguous beings, powerful but potentially dangerous, requiring diligent and constant care.

Worship of Fierce Deities is a main difference Mergen lamas see between their kind of Buddhism and that of the Chinese. Sengge Lama used to tell us that Mongolian Buddhism has four central tasks (*üile*): peace and joy (*amurlinggui*), expansion or increase (*delgerenggüi*), control or mastery (*erheshinggüi*), and ferocity against impediments (*dogshiranggui*). The Chinese, he said, uphold only the first two of these. As we shall see in later chapters, the word *dogshin*—wild, ferocious, ruthless, violent, raging—has a tremendous salience at Mergen and is not confined to the sphere of religion. Even in religious texts there can also lurk a political impulse. The chanting texts for the fierce gods

23. Erlig Khan is a *choijong* and seen as lower than his suppressor Yamantaka, a ferocious form of the bodhisattva Manjushiri.

24. In Gelug teaching the tantric practitioner may use the image of sexual congress for visualization and meditation, but unlike in some of the older orders of Tibetan Buddhism, such as Nyingma, should not practice sexual yoga with a real partner. Mills argues for Ladakh (2003, 125–26) that these tantric images symbolize reproduction. Since sexual desire is not in most regards conceptually distinct from householder life it is not, as in the West, divorced from reproduction. The tantric imagery mirrors, and in some senses is an alternative to, household relations.

emphasize "suppressing" and "repelling," and many of them cite not only the personal impediments of greed, cruelty, etc., but also a range of more everyday ills, such as storms, droughts, epidemics, bandits, and enemies. In Mergen we heard of the existence of one text in this "driving-off" genre called "Repelling the Black Chinese" (*Hara Hitad-un Hariulga*). Obviously problematic in contemporary China, people mention this prayer only in whispers.

Person, Self, and Sociality in a Buddhist Pastoral Society

We do not see Mongolian culture as extraordinary in any broad human dimension. We want to suggest, nevertheless, that their way of life has enabled Mongols—and specifically the lamas of Mergen Monastery—to be highly independent, self-willed, and idiosyncratic people. We shall argue that they have been so in historically specific ways for many centuries despite the absence of any of the props or causative influences commonly brought forward to explain individualism in the West—such as Protestant Christianity, the concept of private property, the Enlightenment, Romanticism, or a capitalist industrial and post-industrial work ethic.

Anyone familiar with Mongolian history will know of the several archetypal occasions on which wise and great people (usually women) extolled the virtues of social unity. Mongols have a saying, "A single person is not a person" (*gagcha hün hün bish*). It might mistakenly be concluded that Mongolian society is one of those pervasively relational, transpersonal environments anthropologists have so often described. And it is true that these "historical" maxims about solidarity are popular today. In Höhhot we visited the elegantly laid-back Urad artist Togtanbilig who had been at the Mergen celebrations in 1995. We found him in his city studio, its walls hung with stylish Mongol calligraphy, most of it being exhortations to unity attributed to Chinggis Khan and designed for sale. Togtanbilig's sideline was engraving personal seals for individual people to distinguish their identity and property. We would argue, in fact, that it is because Mongols have tended *not* to be unified that the maxims are seen to be so necessary and so wise. Hürelbaatar once joked about what it feels like to live in Mongolian society: "Of course, every society must have structures. But if we compare . . . the Mongolians, we are like matches in a box. While the Chinese, they are something like . . . honey in a pot." This kind of statement suggests one particularly conscious positioning of "a Mongol person"—seeing it not on its own, but in contrast to the Chinese, which must be related to centuries of experience in not becoming one of them.

Many Mongolian ideas relevant to selfhood are quite different from the Buddhist teachings, most noticeably the tendency to emphasis what a person *is*, rather than what they should be aiming to become. This includes ideas about descent (a person is the outcome of descent from the father and mother), about personality (for example, someone is, or is not, a secure, reliable, centered *labdagun* kind of person), and about their intrinsic vital force (*sülde*).[25] However, what may have been indigenous ideas associated with individuality merge with Buddhist teleological concerns: for example, the unique combination of astrological elements for each human birth as auspicious /inauspicious, and the idea that each person has innate inclinations or talents inherited from previous lives (*abiyas*).[26] Each child is born with its own predisposition deriving from the character of its "soul," which had previous (but unknown) lives. Putting all this together, most Mongols consider three components to be fundamental: descent from the mother's side, through blood; descent from the father's side, through bone; and elements brought forward from earlier lives (*abiyas*), including *irügel* of a personal kind, such as willing to become a merciful person in one's next life. Babies have indistinct personalities, and the parents try to discover what their child's innate propensity might be by observation, for this will give them a guide about how to bring it up. In Hürelbaatar's region when the child is around one year of age, a test is arranged: various objects such as a bridle, a musical instrument, a sutra, or a pen are laid out on a table and the parents watch to see which one the child points to or picks up. Then it is known that this child, unconscious as it is of this fact, will be talented at singing, or sewing, or recognizing the faces of animals, or have some other vocation, and the parents can adapt the education accordingly.

If this idea of innate propensity seems to point forward from the simple existence of personal characteristics to some kind of future perfection of them, another idea that seems to combine a Buddhist flavor with an indigenous concept is the accepted right of each person to

25. In the thirteenth-century *Secret History of the Mongols*, *sülde* (*sülder*) is referred to as a quality of both a clan and an individual (Rachewiltz 2004, 328, 904).

26. This word derives from Sanskrit *abhyāasa* ("practice"), but the Mongols have given the term a different meaning. In everyday contexts Urads speak of "birth ability" (*törülhei abiyas*), in more religion ones of "gift of wisdom" (*abiyas bilig*). A former lama told us that such abilities are singular, not describable except in relation to individuals. If karma is like "seed," before planting, *abiyas* is more like the fruit (of deeds in a previous life).

make a will (*irügel*). Lamas teach that your devout wish will be fulfilled sooner or later, but when that happens (it could be in your next life) depends on how accomplished you are spiritually. But can one ever know about this? This question leads directly to Buddhist ideas about the self.

It certainly would not be correct, though the people of Urad generally say they are Buddhists, to assume that their ideas coincide with orthodox Gelug teaching. Rather, we have to deal with several inconsistent sources of ideas, including the Mongol practical life experience, local interpretations of Buddhist theories, Marxist ideology, recent Chinese exhortations about "human quality," entrepreneurship, etc. And amid all this, the best one can say about the doctrine of the sutras is that it is something many people hope to understand. Nevertheless, since our book is about Buddhist lamas their goals have to be important; so here we briefly describe the central Gelug doctrines of the self and the person and explain how Urad ideas relate to them. How does the insistence that the self is an illusion square with the robust individual agency that we claim for the Mongols?

The Gelug-pa founder Tsongkhapa upheld the ancient Indian idea that the human being is made up of five transient aggregates (S. *skandha*)—physical attributes, feelings, perceptions, mental formations, and consciousness. He insisted that there is no self that exists either among the aggregates or separate from them. In this he was arguing against non-Buddhist philosophers who upheld the idea that each person has a permanent, unitary, and independent self or "soul" (S. *atman*)[27] and that the constituent components dissolve at death, whereas the pure *atman* (the true self) of the individual continues to survive. Tsongkhapa's argument against this position was complex: it revolved around the logical impossibility of explaining any meaningful relation between the self and his or her physical and mental attributes (aggregates) if an independent true self is posited. People identify intuitively with their body or mind: when my arm is injured, I instinctively think, "I am injured." This does not imply that I am identical with my arm, but Tsongkhapa uses the argument to demonstrate that in our natural conceptions of self we do not have a notion of an entity separate from the mind/body aggregate (Jinpa 2002, 82–85). One might then conclude that perhaps the self is identical with the aggregates. However, this is an argument Tsongkhapa also refutes, on the grounds that those

27. In non-Buddhist "Hindu" thought, the transcendent essence of the self, the *atman*, is merged with the Ultimate Reality of the Universe (Brahman).

who hold it have a mistaken underlying assumption that the person is reducible to the real existence of physical and mental states (Jinpa 2002, 86–87). Thus, having argued that neither a self, which is ontologically distinct from the aggregates, nor a self that is identifiable with them, exist, Tsongkhapa argues that "identity and existence can only be maintained as thoroughly contingent and in some profound sense 'unreal'" (Jinpa 2002, 104–06).

Among laypeople today such ideas are salted down into a commonsense refutation of the ultimate existence of the self. We are made up of aggregates, they say, so imagine these being taken away one by one. What happens if you lose an arm? If you go blind? If you can no longer think? In the end, the self is nowhere to be found. Where am I?—In the whole body, in the head, and if I die, in my soul or in my body? However, the tradition at Mergen was not set up to answer such a conundrum: Mergen Gegen was not a philosopher, but rather he was a moralist. His teachings for laity (*surgal*) proceed on the basis of Tsongkhapa's constructive theory of the person (S. *pudgala*, M. *bodgali*) as distinct from self[28] and the crucial importance of one's present intentions and actions for the fate of this person through many lifetimes.

The person is not the self but exists rather as the conventional designation for a unique "aggregated" individual subject to moral (karmic) accountability (Pietz 2005, 197). Tsongkhapa's theory of the person assumes (karmic) causation and its never-ending continuity—this is simply the way the universe works. He argues for the presence of a neutral "basic mind" that retains its continuity through sleep, coma, and even death, and it is this that persists from one life to another. This is the repository for karmic imprints, the results of previous actions. Fundamentally, it is the karmic process and its resulting imprinted patterns that maintain the aggregates as a temporary unity and perpetuates the individual's continuity of existence (Jinpa 2002, 137; see also Collins 1982, 229). This process is described as a circular chain of twelve links

28. Tsongkhapa takes seriously the Buddha's statement that he does not have any argument with the conventions of the world and hence argues that the person is one such convention. We should not seek to go beyond this to some essence (either of consciousness or the aggregates), but we can, on the other hand, retain our deeply ingrained, prelinguistic *belief in our own existence*. This innate I-consciousness he calls the "mere I." Instead of subverting such a belief, as some Buddhist schools did when they argued that the self is nothing but the aggregates, Tsongkhapa maintains that we should retain belief in ourselves as a self-sufficient and substantial reality, so it can be used in our striving toward enlightenment (Jinpa 2002, 112–15; Collins 1982, 73). This idea of the "mere I" allows Tsongkhapa to explain memory experiences, which are difficult for Buddhists of other schools to square with the central theory of no-self (Gyatso 1992, 11). Recollection necessarily occurs from an I-perspective, even if that person is nominal, conventional, and relative.

of dependent origination: initial ignorance gives rise to heedless acts that imprint the consciousness; this state of mind gives rise to further wrongful behavior, and so on. Soon emotions like grasping and craving arise. In this context, Jinpa writes, "craving is principally a thirst for existence. Therefore, the process of life as an unenlightened being is said to be a product of karma and delusions" (2002, 137).

At Mergen the chain of twelve links of dependent origination[29] is illustrated in the painting of the Wheel of Samsara by the doors of the main temple. The series of pictures begins with a blind woman and ends with people mourning at a mountainside. We often saw children looking at this painting, being instructed in its meaning by elders. So lay worshippers know some version of the above theories, but they interpret them in their own ways. One of these paintings represents an empty house, which in doctrine represents the six senses (a human is like an empty house, with doors and windows through which sensations enter). Minggan Lama gave this an intentional twist: if you are like a house, anyone can live in it, anything can take it over—a ghost, Buddha, a deity, and so forth. If you choose to take Buddha as your guest, you can let Buddha occupy you. The individuality of moral agency is central to all Indic traditions and is so for Mergen Gegen too. The Wheel of Samsara spins as fast as the wind, he writes, so we must act now. His teachings are concrete and he uses himself as an example:

> [I] have oppressed young, old, bad and good
> By relying on the government of ruling nobles and officials.
> That may be the karma of fate.
> [But] by acting, will [I] not get some kind of merit for correcting [my faults]?
> [I] am speaking and confessing my difficulties of this life and later lives. [. . .]
> [I] became a man through ancient merit [of previous lives].
> If we are careful and [act] well in this life
> How can the fortune of the next life not be increased?
> (*S2*: 3r-3v).

Lamas told us that the human person is composed of the body (*beye*), speech (*hele*), and mind-emotion (*sedhil*), a theory they attributed to the Buddha. The "soul" (*sünesü*—a pre-Buddhist term), however, is conceived in various ways that resemble neither the eternal and cosmic

29. The twelve links are: ignorance, action, consciousness, name and form, contact (through the six senses and their objects: visible form, sound, smell, taste, touch and thought), awareness, craving, grasping, becoming, birth, old age, and death (Sodubilig 1996, 21).

atman nor the neutral "basic mind." Most commonly, it has its own naturalistic features, being revealed in a way of talking, a clumsiness of movement, or a quality of temperament that re-occur in successive lives. Confusingly, the lamas, like Mongols in general, also hold that a person has more than one "soul." Most people agree that there are three and that they have different fates after someone dies, but people have different ideas about the components. According to one old lama the *beye* soul of the body resides in the bones and in the end decays into the earth; the *jarlig* (honorific "speech") soul of the mind goes straight to heaven or hell; the *sedhil* soul of feeling or conscience has a varied fate depending on the person's actions. Thus for this monk the divisible "soul" more or less mirrors the Buddhist notion of the three elements of the living human being. The idea is also reminiscent of a range of five deities described by Mergen Gegen as having been placed in the temple of Fierce Gods in his lifetime: the King of Deeds, the King of Speech, the King of Wisdom, the King of the Body, and the King of Feeling/Conscience (*BJ* 1780–1783: vol. 1, text 14). From this we see that there is a historically long-lasting imaginative mode, which is subject to internal variation that divides the human spirit into elements. These are not identical with the aggregates, but reified attributes with intention and potency.

There is another idea current today, however, whereby there is just one "soul," also called *sünesü*, but it migrates from limb to limb, organ to organ. This vagrant soul may escape or be enticed away from the body, leaving the person weak, disoriented, and dispirited. Normally, however, it moves around the body, its position depending on a time schedule determined astrologically according to the birth date and time. Let us say one day your soul is in your right ear—you must avoid any actions that might harm your ear for fear the soul will also be attacked. When someone goes into hospital for an operation, they take care to find out from a lama where their soul is, so as to schedule any operation at a time when their soul is not in that part of the body. One day in every twelve, the ox day, the soul is in the whole body—older people know which day this is and avoid having even a haircut or dental work that day.

Little effort is devoted to establishing a consistent and mutually agreed upon set of relations among the various elements we have mentioned here: and in fact that would be virtually impossible. We referred earlier to fractures in the thinking of Mongolian Buddhists and it is here, most importantly in notions about the person, that we find they exist. The karmic imprint of acts in previous lives, the causal force of wills/vows, the illusory nature of self, the varied souls, and the idea of innate propensities are not logically consistent. The gaps between them do not stem from a division between pure Buddhism and the "corruption" of local thought, but from the different ontological and epistemological nature of the questions Buddhists are required to answer. These questions belong to different domains of discourse and are brought up in different contexts. The inconsistency of the answers provided by Mergen monks is not different in kind (though far less sophisticated) from the disagreements found in the classics of Buddhist thought, and about which sharp and endless debates have raged over the centuries. As Jinpa observes (2002, 141–42), the great master Tsongkhapa himself recognized that the notion of personal identity is in the final analysis non-analyzable and perhaps best apprehended by poetic metaphor. Nevertheless, if we think of the various "answers" as (inconsistent) resources an individual might call upon in trying to lead a good life, they can coexist quite happily, for few people try to answer two questions at the same time.

It is now time to move on to the first of the personalities of this book, Lubsangdambijalsan, the famous 3rd Mergen Gegen. The monks' most immediate contact with the great man was through the prayers he had composed, which they chanted for hours every day. Soon after we arrived in 1998 the senior lamas drew us aside for a conclave. They told us gravely that the great treasury of Mergen Gegen's collected liturgy, which the lamas call *bum jarlig* (*BJ*, literally "hundred thousand ordinance,"), had been printed using wooden blocks in Peking in 1780–1783, and that the monastery's copy had been destroyed. All the monks had for their chanting were texts gathered from here and there after the Cultural Revolution, written down by memory or hand-copied from aged lamas now dead. The only place in the whole world where the original block prints are to be found, they said pointedly, is in your British Library! Delicately, they hinted that they would not accuse the British of imperialist plunder. But they wanted access to these volumes. Now, via a roundabout route involving a graduate student who obtained photographs of the British Library volumes and sent them to Japan, from where his teacher sent them to a professor in Inner Mongolia, the *Bum Jarlig* had just been reprinted in facsimile in Höhhot (*BJ* 1998). But, and this is what the lamas emphasized, three important prayers were missing and had not been included in the reprint. They must have them. Full of guilt for the misdeeds of imperial ancestors, Caroline promised to locate the books and send a copy of the missing texts. That was not enough. The lamas said they wanted to go to England and see and touch the originals; they wanted to make obeisance and pray to them. Caroline also promised to see if she could arrange this, and we take up further episodes in the labyrinthine story of the missing texts in later chapters. This event in the early part of our research opened our eyes to the centrality of texts.

TWO

Mergen Gegen and the Arts of Language

Mergen Gegen was something like a Mongolian renaissance man. Apart from his strictly liturgical work he wrote an idiosyncratic history of the Mongols, treatises on ethics and medicine, language primers, poems, and songs for which he composed the music. He choreographed two "Mongolian" versions of the Tibetan ritual dance *cham*, translated the collection of parables *Subashita*,[1] and created a great diversity of ritual texts—for the *sülde* (spirit of vitality and might), Shambhala the kingdom of the righteous, worship of fire, making rain, the ritual cairn, battle standards, Chinggis Khan, the local mountain god Muna Khan, and a deity called White Old Man (Futaki 1997; Heissig 2000). Many of his poems, songs, and ritual texts praise the landscape around Mergen, a region he calls the "country" (*orun*) of Muna Khan. Lamas told us proudly that his works are known all over Mongolia—and it is true that some of them were hand-copied and have been found as far away as Halh Mongolia, and Buryatia, in Russia.

The monks at the monastery speak about Mergen Gegen quite familiarly, almost as though they knew him. He was impressive if prickly (*amar ügei*) they say, but he was also was romantic (*hwartai*), and he did contrary things. For example, lamas claim he asked to be buried upside

1. The "Teaching of Aphoristic Jewels" (S. *Subhasitaratnanidhi*) written by Sa skya Pandita in Tibetan in 1251 was very popular among Mongols, and many translations were made from early times. A copy of Mergen Gegen's translation is in the British Library.

down under the threshold of the main temple when he died.[2] They say that Mergen Gegen's disciples could not bring themselves to follow this impossible request ("How could we allow everyone to walk over his sacred remains?"). The great lama's will was like an ominous founding event, since the fact that his wish was not carried out was one of their explanations for the misfortunes that dogged the monastery ever after. The lamas credit Mergen Gegen not only with composing the supremely artistic form of the Mongolian liturgy, but also with a range of other abilities and accomplishments, including being able to see with his "third eye," magical feats, establishing the "order of services and rules of monks" conduct, introducing wonderful objects of worship, and moral instruction for the laity. "Mergen Gegen opened up a new universe," they say.

In this chapter we show how Mergen Gegen laid the ground for a new subjectivity among his followers, with both aesthetic and political dimensions. This was a constituting move, an event in something like the terms suggested by Badiou (2001).[3] The subject of such an event both constitutes and comes to know a new state, both turns inward to perceive himself and at the same time, since what is offered is a perspective, addresses himself outward to newly envisioned contours of the world. The kind of perspective proposed by Mergen Gegen is unfamiliar to Western commonsense. For different reasons it was new in eighteenth-century Inner Mongolia too, in this case being not so much alien as simply not thought of in this aesthetic form before. An analogy is Haydn's musical architectonics, which was not dreamed of in baroque music until he wrote them (Badiou 2001, 68–69).

We need to deal with a few issues before getting to grips with Mergen Gegen's ideas and achievements. First is the question, Who was he? On what basis can we talk about "him" at all?

The 3rd Mergen Gegen and "Mergen Gegen"

The key actor in this story, Lubsangdambijalsan, the 3rd Mergen Gegen (1717–1766), presents particular challenges for the idea of the individual. For a start, he was the third in a line of reincarnations, all supposed at core to be the same person. He also poses a different kind

2. There is no written evidence that Mergen Gegen actually made this will.

3. According to Badiou the event establishes a new truth, a way of understanding the world unavailable in previous systems of knowledge, sustained by new subjects who decide upon this as against other possible paths, and then hold to that truth (see discussion in Humphrey 2008).

of question because of the nature of the oral and written accounts whereby he is presented to us. From a conventional historical point of view, the man who lived in the eighteenth century is almost a cipher. No biography (*namtar*) survives, there is no description or painting of him in life, and as far as we know almost no Chinese materials of the period provide outside information on his activities. Perhaps because of his unorthodox stance, even compendious histories of Buddhism written later by lamas are mostly silent about him.[4] Nor did Mergen Gegen write an autobiography, and so we have nothing as revealing as the subtle self-absorption characteristic of Tibetan visionaries who wrote "secret autobiographies" (Gyatso 1998). All that exists is what he let slip about himself in his writings on other matters, the works attributed to him locally, and the often fantastical stories told about him by various people of later generations. These limited sources present rather different persons.

Focusing on Mergen Gegen's own writings, we can say that if authored narratives are a means that define an individual's social territory and the author's singular identity within that grouping, they can also indicate how that person constructs a self (Nair 2002, 18–19). Yet in some ways Mergen Gegen protects rather than reveals himself in his last and most personal text, his history *Altan Tobchi* (hereafter *AT*), for it was political dynamite. The book was written in response to, or at least in the same intellectual field as, other histories written by Buddhist lamas and Mongol scholars in the seventeenth and eighteenth centuries. Mergen Gegen's concern was thus with the broad sweep of origins, peoples, politics, and morality, and much less with the kind of personal adventures that form the basis of the stories about him. Yet if we see a contrast between the critical, tactical Mergen Gegen as author and the brilliant, high-handed, magical lama of the legends, this is absolutely not because the former was "rational" (in a Buddhist kind of way) while the latter was invented by irrational folk thinkers. On the contrary, we suggest that Mergen Gegen and the lamas of later generations, until approximately the 1920s, broadly inhabited the same mental world. Indeed, the commonality of outlook may be more than that, for in a twist to our tale we shall see that the lamas and laypeople of Urad participated in the works of "Mergen Gegen."

Let us consider for a moment how we know anything about the 3rd Mergen Gegen. The bare bones of his life are found in our most reliable

4. Mergen Gegen is not mentioned by Dharmatala ([1889] 1987) nor by Erdenipel ([1920s–1930s] 2005).

source in a conventional historical sense, the memoirs of a duke of the West Banner, Galdanwangchugdorji (hereafter Duke Galdan), written in 1846, some eighty years after the Gegen's death. A hyper-anxious person, the Duke evidently put great store on accuracy, as he repeatedly legitimates his account by referring to records kept in his office and Mergen Monastery. According him, the 3rd Mergen Gegen was the son of Lubsang from the Urad Middle Banner, was invited to the monastery as a reincarnation by the then Duke in 1721, studied under the learned Chorji Lama of the time, wished to take his vows (*gelüng sahil*) from the great Jangjiya Gegen but not finding him took them instead from Rakuwa Gegen at Dolonnuur. The 3rd Gegen died in 1766, whereupon his remains (*sharil*), as a whole corpse, were invited into a copper coffin and placed in a silver pagoda. A special temple with a courtyard was built for it (Galdanwangchugdorji [1846] 1994, 180–81). Today, a *sharil* temple survives at that spot but the remains of Mergen Gegen have disappeared.

A fuller account[5] appears in a work that has a different character, the two-volume compendium about Mergen Monastery, its history and rituals, written by a former Mergen lama called Galluu, who will be mentioned often in this book (Galluu 2003, vols. 1 and 2). Galluu also pays attention to his sources, notably oral accounts from senior lamas like the 8th Mergen Gegen and Oruwa Lama, all of whom have now died, and extensive notes he claims to have taken from two internal histories of Mergen Monastery called the Yellow Book (*Shira Debter*) and the Brown History (*Hüreng Teühe*)—now both lost. The result is a mixture, inextricably entangled with lamas' stories and Galluu's own memories. Inner Mongolian scholars criticize Galluu's work, especially the dates therein, and say that some of it may be pure invention, but they admit that it also contains much valuable material. Meanwhile, the contemporary monks, who were already estranged from Galluu by the beginning of the 1990s, also disparage his writing—although its hybrid character and virtually all of its materials are, as far as we could judge,

5. According to Galluu, the 3rd Mergen Gegen was born in the family of Lubsang on the eighth of the first summer month of 1716 in Urad Middle Banner, in Bayan Hadai village of Aru Horchin Sum. His childhood nickname was "Mergen Baatar." His father and mother were prosperous, having herds of five kinds of livestock filling the steppes. They were sincere believers in Buddhism and were patrons (*öglige-yin ejen*) who made charitable donations to the people (*arad*). Both parents took lay *ubashi* vows. The family was high ranking, literate, and cultured. Lubsang knew Tibetan, Manchu, and Chinese as well as Mongolian, and was head of the secretariat of the Banner office. Mergen Gegen was the youngest son in the family of three sons and two daughters (Galluu 2003, 86).

similar to their own ideas. At the very least, Galluu tells us what a contemporary lama thinks Mergen Gegen's life should have been.

Galluu describes many elements of the 3rd Mergen Gegen's achievements, his meditations, his lengthy sojourns in Tibet and holy India, the *bandida* [pandit] title he was awarded there, his great learning and knowledge of many languages—some of this almost certainly invented—as a repetition of the activities of the 1st Mergen Gegen. Also somehow standardized is Galluu's account of how the 3rd Mergen Gegen was discovered as a child, which we mention, as it is relevant to how the personhood of the great lama is conceived. After the death of the 2nd incarnation, a delegation of Urad Banner officials and high lamas from Mergen was sent to Tibet to obtain indications about his rebirth.

> They asked the 5th Dalai Lama and the 4th Panchen Lama to make a careful investigation. [The two lamas] made a very strict magical examination and found out that the reincarnation of Mergen Gegen would be born in Urad Middle Banner in the family of Lubsang and they revealed his appearance (*dürsü*), and the ten people [of the delegation] saw it in the mirror and admired it. Immediately, they asked the Dalai and Panchen Lamas to give a vow name and a prayer. Following the tradition the great Lamas gave the vow name Lubsangdambijalsan, made up of elements of their own names,[6] and they offered a will-poem (*irügel-ün shüleg*) as a chanting text. (Galluu 2003, 88)

The religious identity of the 3rd Mergen Gegen was thus indexed to the names of the greatest Tibetan reincarnations. Meanwhile, the will-poem singles out the new Mergen Gegen as the only one among the lamas (who are often called "relatives of merit" *buyan-u sadun*) with an immeasurable fate (the word *hubi* means fate, share, and fortune).

> May the Decoration of Doctrine [the 3rd Mergen Gegen]
> Who has become the single relative [*gagcha sadun*] with an immeasurable fate (*hubi*),
> Who is decorated with [the abilities of] listening, making heard, and meditating,
> And the smiling blessing of Muna, music, religion, and the lotus,
> Smile graciously in the world.
> (Galluu 2003, 90)

6. The 5th Dalai Lama's name was Agwanglubsangjamsu and 4th Panchen's was Lubsangchoijijalsan (Galluu 2003, 89).

Galluu then describes the celebration when the boy was invited to the monastery, his throne with three dragon heads, the writing of his vow name in gold on a silver plate, and the Mongol manly games that were subsequently held. During this festival, "five-colored clouds appeared every day in the sky and occasional soft rain. Flowers blossomed in the countryside. Each morning a seven-colored rainbow appeared from the west; in the afternoon, there appeared a double rainbow from the east. Visitors, dressed in their finest clothes and decorations, saw countless beauties in this land" (2003, 92). Though Galluu writes that these and other details were "excellently described in the Yellow Book of Mergen Monastery," we have no way of knowing if this was the case, nor what kind of text the Yellow Book was. The salient point is that realist accuracy is not a concern for the lamas (though it is to professional scholars). In this respect, the 3rd Mergen Gegen is not a historical figure in the European sense at all, but a culture hero and "fount" (*egüshel; ug*). He appears in this account as already godlike, associated with music, communication, meditation, and fortune, and, readers should note, that he is blessed by the local mountain deity, Muna, both of them smiling in the blessed landscape.

Turning now to Mergen Gegen's works, which present considerable complexities, the texts in his collected liturgy (*BJ*)—some lacking an author's colophon and others providing a variety of authorial names[7]—were gathered and printed in 1780 through 1783 by a committee of lamas in Beijing,[8] some seventeen years after his death. There was considerable political jousting over the membership of such committees, which opens the possibility of manipulation of the contents and the inclusion of jointly authored works.[9] These texts are also full of uncertain readings, as we discovered when poring over them in Cambridge. Though supervised by Mongols, the wood blocks were carved by Chinese craftsmen who did not know Mongolian, and they contain strangely shaped letters, incomplete words, and so forth. These printed texts are not used by the lamas, who instead use their own handwrit-

7. Uranchimeg Ujeed has established that the various names can be understood as alternative or disguised names for Mergen Gegen (Ujeed 2009, 121–22).

8. One print is held in the British Library and two in the St. Petersburg State University Library. The Höhhot reprint in 1998 also includes a fifth volume containing additional texts for lay rituals, other circulating manuscripts the editors consider to be reliable, and four cassettes of chanting.

9. See the interesting discussion by Nietupski (2011, 27–29) of the production of works by the 3rd Gungtang lama (1762–1823) of Labrang. This shows that a distinction was made between composing (orally providing the outline and sequence of ideas and citations) and writing (done by scribes).

ten manuscripts. Although they claim faultless copying of the latter, these are likely to have changed over two and a half centuries; indeed Sengge Lama told us that each successive Mergen Gegen liked to make tiny additions to the chanting texts. If there are these uncertainties to the religious texts, we need to be even more careful about Mergen Gegen's other works. His history *Altan Tobchi* (1765) has survived in only four known manuscripts, and it is unlikely that any of them is the original (handwritten by the great lama himself).[10] One version (printed in typescript in 1942, republished 1998) indeed includes the names of people who lived long after the Gegen died and so clearly was subject to supplementation. From the genealogies at the end of the history it is evident that the numerous small changes and some additions in this version were made in the mid–nineteenth century. An even more equivocal status clings to Mergen Gegen's other works, the hundreds of prayers, grammatical works, songs, and poems gathered in a volume known as *Gbum Jarlig* (Galluu and Jirantai 1986) from manuscripts kept by local people and songs sung by them. They may contain circulating folk material later attributed to Mergen Gegen as well as altered or jumbled versions of his works (Naranbatu in Galluu 2003, 22; Kripolska 2003, 243).[11] Finally there is the collection of "eighty-one original songs," which are folk songs of the Urad people attributed to Mergen Gegen (Mönghe 2010).

The ordinary lamas of the 1990s had no access to the eighteenth-century liturgy or the history, and few if any of them purchased the expensive recent reprints. Instead, they operated with handed-down

10. One manuscript (khul 101) held in the library of St. Petersburg University is *Yeke Monggul ulus-un ündüsün altan tobchi tuguji orusibai* (Golden Summary History of the Origin of the Great Mongol People/Nation). It was collected by Pozdneev in the late nineteenth century from northern Mongolia, partially published by him, and later published in full facsimile of the handwritten text in Mongolian with translation into Russian and extensive notes by Baldanzhapov (1970). Another version of this manuscript was discovered in 1967 in the State Library of the Mongolian People's Republic but has now disappeared. Two other manuscripts are known from Inner Mongolia, the "Golden Summary composed by Mergen Gegen" *(Mergen gegenten-ü johiyagsan altan tobchi)* and the "First and Second Books of the Golden Summary" (*Altan tobchi-yin terigün hoyadugar debter*). The former was found in Gegen Süm Monastery and the latter, found in Ordos, is a copy of it. One of these manuscripts was the basis for a publication in 1942 (republished in 1998 edited by Chimeddorji et al.). Baldanzhapov's detailed comparison of the St. Petersburg manuscript and the 1942 publication shows conclusively that the former is earlier ([1765] 1970, 16–24), and our own examination of the latter revealed data added to the genealogical chapters after Mergen Gegen's death. The St. Petersburg manuscript has been republished in Ulaanbaatar in Cyrillic rendering, with notes and genealogical tables (Mergen Gegeen Lubsandambiizhaltsan [1765] 2006).

11. We acquired a manuscript of Mergen Gegen's moral teachings that was circulating in Mongolia in 2006; the colophon states that it was copied by hand from a published edition of fifteen hundred made by the Mongol State Literary Academy in the twelfth year of Elevated by All (1923).

materials, the mélange of faithful hand-copies of chanting texts, oral stories, and songs, all reproduced by themselves and local believers, and they are convinced of its genuineness. This corpus was taught them by respected teachers, they say, therefore it *is* the tradition of Mergen Monastery—an attitude that was not held in such a trusting way by the 3rd Mergen Gegen himself. He also used both written and oral materials when writing his chronicle (*AT*), but he was critical of confusions over dating, misinterpretations, wrong evaluations, and particularly over certain stories he judged to be malicious, politically motivated gossip (Baldanzhapov 1970, 35).

In short, the lamas and people of Mergen have participated in the authorship of Mergen Gegen's works, not just as the listeners/validators for whom they were created (Nair 2002, 21–22) but even more directly as subjects of the tradition who added to, changed, or shortened some of "his" texts. Even so, it is possible to distinguish the 3rd Mergen Gegen as an individual author from the "Mergen Gegen" participated in by later generations, and both are interesting figures. As for the former, it is not so difficult to see what he most reliably can be said to have authored, based on a 1774 collection of his liturgy,[12] the 1780–1783 *Bum Jarlig* and the earliest manuscript of the history, since each later change in the latter was painstakingly noted by Baldanzhapov (1970, 370–400). A characteristic style—caustic, word conscious, and passionate—appears in these texts. As for the collective author "Mergen Gegen," one might be tempted to distinguish two strands—a solemn moralistic person and a wayward magical one—were it not that the lamas recognize no difference between them (Chapter 3).

Laying these complexities aside for the time being, let us now address the broad historical framework in which Mergen Gegen's achievements and political stance can be interpreted.

The Imperial Polity

The cultivation of a particular localized sensibility within the Manchu Qing Empire (1644–1911) in the mid-eighteenth century has to be considered in relation to its political culture and the complex interrelationships within it. Then at the zenith of their power and prosperity,

12. A collection of Mergen Gegen's works assigned by him for Öljei Badaragsan Monastery was printed in 1774, containing eighty works, of which forty-seven were among the 129 works in the *BJ* (Ayusheeva 2005, 105).

the Manchus presided over a vast multiethnic, multilingual, and multi-religious realm. Yet they were a tiny minority. As recent scholarship has brought into focus, one key to Qing success lay in its ability to implement flexible policies directed towards the main non-Han peoples inhabiting the outer parts of the empire (Rawski 1998, 7).

Among these peoples, the Mongols were probably the most important. The Manchus' rise to power in the early seventeenth century had owed much to precedents they saw in the earlier Mongol Empire. The Mongols were the major source for early Qing political structures, military organization, legal institutions, and writing system (Elverskog 2006a, 15).[13] However, by this time the Mongols had become shifting, warring groupings inhabiting vast territories. The Qing policy towards the Mongols thus became a dual one: to uphold certain imperially generated unifying stereotypes of ancient Mongol history and culture, while at the same time keeping the contemporary Mongols disunited in economic and political weakness. Pamela Crossley describes this as a two-vector plan: taxonomic unity combined with extreme political fragmentation (1999, 324).

We mentioned earlier how the region now called "Inner Mongolia" had become by the eighteenth century a string of dozens of Mongol Banners, mostly allowed to rule themselves,[14] provided their leaders acknowledged the paramount status of the emperor. The Banner leaders and highest lamas were required every few years to attend the imperial court in Peking to present themselves to the emperor, offer obeisance, and receive his "grace" (M. *heshig*). The prevailing idiom was the subjects' unworthiness, and their striving to repay the supreme benediction of imperial grace and the laws and benevolent instructions bestowed upon them. These quasi-personal ritualized relations between local rulers and the sovereign created a rhetorically dominant centripetal structure focused on the emperor, which applied across the empire to Chinese as well as Mongol and Tibetan subjects (Atwood 2000, 91–130). In policy more broadly considered, the emperor was the embodiment of imperial universalism, a multiple person, adopting a different face for each of the various recognized constituencies in his realm—he absorbed the recognized distinctive strains of the empire into his person (Farquhar 1978, 33–34; Crossley 1999, 223–46; Krahl 2005, 242–43). Thus he could appear variously as generalissimo, law-

13. See, however, Martynov and Pang 2003, which argues for the strong influence of Chinese ideas of government from the very beginning of the Qing.

14. An exception was the system of the Chahar Banners, ruled by Manchu officials, this being a formation that had resisted Manchu rule in the seventeenth century.

maker, Son of Heaven, Buddhist incarnation of Manjushiri, leader of the hunt, disciple of a lama teacher, Confucian elder, and so forth.[15] This transformability of the face of the emperor correlated with differential policy with regard to the constituencies of the empire (Rawski 1998, 17). Thus, "the Mongols" were treated differently with regard to administration, economics, religious policy, and military affairs from the Chinese, Tibetans, Uighurs, and Manchus, and even on some issues from one another. Universalism combined with selective policies. If the metaphor of the wheel is appropriate to the Manchu empire, the governmental spokes were of different kinds.

Elverskog's *Our Great Qing* (2006a) has radically reformulated the prevalent interpretation, according to which the Manchus "conquered" the Mongols in the early to mid–seventeenth century, pacified and controlled them by means of Buddhism, and instantaneously converted their previous social organization into the Qing system of Banners. He shows that the early relations between Mongol groups and the Manchus were mostly negotiations, not conquests, that they were conducted in the pre-Buddhist religious idiom of Heaven (*tngri*), and that the formation of Banners was not instantaneous but a lengthy process (2006a, 24). The Mongols' own earlier political concepts were only gradually replaced by the consciousness of imperial Qing subjects. As the two major Mongolian concepts of *ulus* (people, nation, community) and *törü* (principles of righteous rule, later the state or government) occur frequently in Mergen Gegen's writings, it is worth briefly discussing them here.

Elverskog's analysis shows that *ulus* was a term that could be applied in the widest sense, for example for "the Mongol people" of Chinggis Khan's empire, but also for sub-groupings that were distinct political entities. An *ulus* was ruled by a *törü*, but the crucial idea was that it retained its coherence as a distinctive community having its own customs whatever government was present. This idea allowed a rebellious prince to split from a confederation with one *törü*, establish his *ulus* as a separate political entity, and then set up his own *törü* government. Conversely, several *ulus* could decide to join together under one state. The *ulus-törü* system made possible the fragmentation and terrible civil wars among the Mongols in the fifteenth through seventeenth centuries. Indeed, Elverskog suggests that many Mongol groups accepted

15. In terms that echo Marshall Sahlins' heroic model of the person, Crossley observes ". . . one finds imperial ideology tending towards a universality of representation that depended not upon all-as-one (as many modern republican ideologies have done) but upon one-as-all, that 'one' being the emperor" (1999, 33).

the *törü* of the Manchus because the military power of the Qing could provide protection against attacks by other Mongols (2006a, 20–24). Far from "submitting" to the Manchus in the early 1600s, the alliance could be understood as one between equals, as many Mongols themselves still maintain. In this light we can see the Urad not as a "tribe" but as an *ulus*, and, as will become clear, the 3rd Mergen Gegen did his best to foster the traces of this consciousness even when Banners had become the reality of government in the eighteenth century.

The Urads, distinctive both because they were Hasarid incomers and by their early loyalty to the Manchu state, were bordered on either side by Mongol *ulus* of more independent ilk, the Chinggisid Tümed to the east and the Alasha to the west.[16] But this made little difference to the spread of Buddhism in the region. There was a sustained surge of enthusiasm, which, although it was supported by the Manchus, was by no means simply an imperial project (Elverskog 2007, 59–75).[17] By the mid–eighteenth century there were hundreds of monasteries in southern (Inner) Mongolia. It is estimated that by the mid– nineteenth century between thirty and sixty percent of men in Inner Mongolia were monks (Miller 1959, 27; Charleux 2006, 126–27).

Duke Darmashiri,[18] who founded Mergen, was typical of the Mongol nobles who initiated this remarkable process of construction, and we now consider the local polities they ruled in more detail.

The measures taken by the Qing included mapping each Banner, tax registers, prohibition of population movement between legislative areas, and surveillance against plots and disloyal communications. Nevertheless, Qing rule was far from hegemonic and involved clear recognition of the subject power of the subordinate polities. The encompassed lords had to appear at imperial audiences, but the emperor also had to "present" himself before the lords, resulting in complex dialogues

16. The Chinggisid Mongols, who held out longest against the Manchus and saw alliance as capitulation, retained a grudge against groups like the Urad. The delivery of the great seal of the Yuan (Mongol) Dynasty into the hands of the Manchu emperor, and his recognition in 1636 as the new sovereign of the southern Mongols (Miller 1959, 3), was later elaborated into a folk legend whereby the Urads handed over a precious Buddha statue to the emperor. With this relinquishment of powerful items, it is lamented, Mongol resistance crumbled.

17. The Manchus supported the spread of Buddhism by exempting lamas from taxes, state duties, and military service; by building and certifying certain establishments as Imperial Monasteries, some of which provided salaries and fuel allowances; and by the emperor's direct patronage of certain reincarnations, sacred sites, and publications. The support was not unconditional, however, and the government attempted to limit the number of lamas by instituting a system of registration. The number of monasteries, and of lamas attached to them, by far exceeded the officially recognized limits (Miller 1959, 69–85; Rawski 1998, 253–54).

18. Duke Darmashiri, who ruled between 1689 and 1725, was the 7th duke in the line of succession from Üben and led the Urad to their present lands (Buyanbadarhu 1987, 22).

wherein substantive claims were addressed (Hevia 1995, 55–56). Back in the Banners, the princes and dukes had almost unlimited power over their subjects. In the eighteenth century, Chinese high officials were rare visitors to Mongol regions, which they regarded as wild and strange lands "beyond the wall" (Popov 1875, 153–65).

Great public ceremonies were occasions for the local polity to reveal itself. Bulag has suggested that such occasions created a "ritual community," whose character changed historically according to the strategy of the Qing in governing its Mongolian and Tibetan colonial subjects (2002b, 41). In Höhnuur (Höhenagur, Kökönuur), where there had been an Oirad Mongol rebellion against the Qing in 1723–1724 (more on this later) the conquered Mongols and Tibetans were ruled by a Chinese governor, who supervised the annual ritual assembly at Lake Höhnuur (2002b, 37). In Urad, by contrast, the Mongol Banner dukes were legitimated to convoke the rituals, which took place at sacred cairns called *oboo* (written form, *obuga*), see Chapter 5. The three Urad Banners held the rituals separately, on three summits of the Muna mountain range and also at *oboos* located more conveniently in lowland areas. At the great fairs and games that followed such occasions, nobles, lamas, and their lay followers gathered together, discussed matters of concern and adjudicated disputes, a pattern common throughout the Mongol lands. Mergen Gegen took care to reform these *oboo* rites, and he composed the texts that are currently chanted at them.

Besides these annual ceremonies, Mergen, as the official "Banner Monastery," held regular Buddhist services for the prosperity of the West Banner polity. Meanwhile most of the monasteries in the East and Middle Urad Banners kept the Tibetan liturgy and never took up Mergen's Mongolian one. Why was Mergen's example not followed in the whole political territory of Urad, if a certain *ulus* consciousness was still present, as we have suggested? The answer to this must be that the Banner system, by the mid–eighteenth century when Mergen Gegen was active, had become the practically operative political reality (Elverskog 2006a, 37). Mergen Gegen's history provides a fervent appeal for wider unities, but clearly he was not in a position to bring them about.

Mergen Monastery was the heart of a *religious* domain. It was without precise boundaries, an archipelago of fluctuating extent, consisting of sacred sites extending from the Yellow River northward across the Muna mountains to the plain beyond, with a few subject monasteries located in the Middle and East Banners, and at least one far away, in Eastern Inner Mongolia, in Horchin. Although this was Mergen Gegen's base and it was to become the "place" (*orun*) of his tradition, he had different—more expansive, transcendent and imaginative—entities in mind when he wrote his *Altan Tobchi* history. Here he wields the word *ulus* at different scales—the supreme one being the Mongol people as a whole, the "Great Mongol Ulus" in the full title of his book.

It was not a propitious time to advocate Mongolian culture. The pluralistic rule of the Mongolian *uluses* characteristic of the sixteenth and seventeenth centuries had featured translation projects into Mongolian, use of the vernacular in some services, reincarnations recognized among local nobility, and flirtations with non-Gelug sects and Chinese Daoism. But this had been swept away by the firm alliance between the early Qing court and the Dalai Lama, in which orthodoxy and use of Tibetan liturgy was central. The pact was confirmed in the meeting between the Shunzhi Emperor and the 5th Dalai Lama in 1652 (Elverskog 2006a, 104–07; see also Nietupski 2011, 6–8). Thus by Mergen Gegen's time Mongolian language Buddhism had long since been relegated to regressive, inferior status. In practical usage for services, Tibetan had ousted it almost everywhere—this was the language of imperial loyalty.

In such a situation, the obstinate and quirky Mongolian Buddhism of Mergen Gegen a century later looks contentious, even mutinous, and indeed an anthropological interpretation in terms of resistance would be the usual response. Furthermore, it is easily dismissed as the failure of a relatively minor figure in the Buddhist hierarchy—Mergen Gegen was "not a success" (Atwood 1996, 139) and had "no lasting impact" (Elverskog 2006a, 121). However, as Atwood and Elverskog also hint, such an interpretation misses the point by adopting a narrowly political criterion of success. Mergen Gegen was engaged in a different endeavor, involved with power in a broad sense but not *Realpolitik*, as we attempt to show. In some senses he was clearly a success, if only because he established a distinctive vision that has survived to the present day.

Non-Imperial Imagination from Inside Empire

In the anthropological literature on colonial empires, the "tensions of empire," with good reason, tend to be conceived dualistically: they arise between rulers and ruled, exploiters and exploited, or the privileged and the subalterns. The geography is that of metropolis and periphery, the politics is that of conquest/domination and resistance; the chronology, the impact of modernity on a preexisting space-time seen as premodern. Even works that seek to destabilize these categories, like Chakrabarty's *Provincializing Europe* (2000), which questions not only the direction of agency in colonial situations, but also the conventional analyses of what counts as agency if an Indian point of view is taken, as well as the historicism of earlier interpretations, are nevertheless still preoccupied with dualistic relations. There are some studies, notably Fred Cooper's *Colonialism in Question* (2005), that broaden the vision—he discusses connections and imaginations within, across, and against empire—and work on Chinese history has done the same, querying boundaries and ethnic categories erected by the state (Struve 2004; Purdue 2005). But these tend to be magisterial overviews, taking a perspective from away and above, and we feel that something remains to be investigated if we try to situate ourselves *inside*. In other words, if we think about what might be the horizons of people living right there in the middle of an empire. At one level this concerns the Mongols' cosmological ideas on how they occupy land and on another, their imagination of realms, sovereignties, and jurisdictions around them.

In mainland Asia, even in a centripetal empire like the Qing, interior-located subjects are never only related to the center, but have coexisting attachments to other far-flung constituencies (ethnic, religious, or economic) in realms and sites outside the empire. For a lama like the 3rd Mergen Gegen, the vast expanse of Buddhism, stretching from India to distant regions in Mongolia and China, was the primary attachment. Such an imperial subject is engaged not in dual but in tripartite or multiple relations. We are reminded of Georg Simmel's analysis, in which he argues that relations between three are inherently different from those between two (1950, 146–62), if only because the capacity of any two of the three to enter an alliance against the third tends to create an unstable inequality (see Bulag 2010, 10–11).

As we have mentioned, the "big picture" of such triangular relations in eighteenth- century China was that the Qing rulers aligned with the Tibetan Buddhist hierarchs to squeeze out the Mongols, subordinating them both religiously and politically. Yet that overarching axis did not prevent a certain local agency, and we suggest that this operated in great part through the bringing into play of yet other relations and cultural resources at the disposal of the subjects. in the case of the Mongols including pre-Buddhist political loyalties, genealogically imagined relations with outlying Mongol groups, and heterodox religious links. It would be mistaken to align such subtleties with the reduced perspectives (self-interest and power hunger) of the logic known as *Realpolitik*. Since the days of Simmel, anthropology has largely abandoned his kind of psychological sociology and brought different analytical objects to the table—representations, identities, material objects, imaginations, affects, phenomenal experiences, to name but some. Looking at matters in this way enables us to do two things: first, we can question the extent to which *Realpolitik* (or anything in Mergen Gegen's activity we might identify as such) was fundamental or even a guiding motive at all for him, and second, we can enlarge the range of imaginative objects he drew into the array of relations he created. In particular we shall show that genealogies and geographies could be objectified elements for him, wielded in relational scenarios to produce alliances and separations—and indeed, vast time-space frameworks in which ethnic identities could be spun, and separate (non-imperial) visions cultivated.

Vernacularization

The realm of Buddhism in Mergen's time was in most respects a quite different kind from the imperial domain. For while it was true that certain high lamas were recognized as having political roles, both independently and as allies and official preceptors of the Qing emperors, and many monasteries were wealthy and powerful, the Buddhist religion prescribed a clear hierarchy of values in which worldly matters were subordinate. The priority given to meditation and tantric practices, the charisma of worshipped personages, the chanciness of marvelous events, visions, discovery of treasures, pilgrimages, and great rituals, all made the sphere of Buddhism a world of its own. This world had no unified political rule, no geographical boundary, no enumeration of adherents, no administrative regulation throughout the whole, no judicial system, no overall unequivocal hierarchy of ranks, and no center. Lhasa was the seat of the Dalai Lamas, but cosmologically the center was the mythic Mount Sumeru, and there were many Mount Sumerus in places of sanctified concentration in the landscape—indeed Mergen Gegen was to acclaim his own Muna Mountain as one of them.

It was in this boundary-less Buddhist world that Mergen Gegen wanted to make his mark. His lifetime endeavor was the transformation of the disregarded Mongolian liturgy into something grand and beautiful, in the face of the dominance of the Tibetan. This brings to attention the relation between the cosmopolitan and the vernacular.

It is significant that by the eighteenth century the cosmopolitan language for much of Inner Asia was not the political language of the imperial rulers, Manchu—for there was no single language of superscription in the Qing Empire—but the language of the religious authorities, Tibetan. For Mongolians this was the preeminent language not only of the Buddhist liturgy but also of philosophy, history, literature, geography, medicine, and astrology. It was used by educated people of other ethnic backgrounds, and it cut a lateral swathe across Asia extending into both the Qing and the Russian empires.

In many ways, therefore, the cultural role of Tibetan in the mid-Qing dynasty was similar to that of Sanskrit in the first millennium. Sheldon Pollock (1998, 2000, 2006) has described Sanskrit as forming a "cosmopolitan world," in which across South and Southeast Asia all high-status communications in religion, politics, law, literature, and philosophy was conducted, Sanskrit being gradually displaced during the second millennium by various vernaculars. Now this process was not just an *analogy* to the much later and more limited replacement of Tibetan by Mongolian in our case, for Sanskrit itself was directly relevant to Mergen Gegen, as we shall describe below. First, however, we briefly outline the arguments made by Pollock with regard to South Asia, to pinpoint the relation so crucial to Mergen Gegen, that between language and a moral vision.

In Pollock's view, there was a parallel macrohistorical move in South Asia and Europe, when in the same general period (the eighth through sixteenth centuries) the cosmopolitan language of Latin was challenged by vernaculars in Europe, and Sanskrit was replaced in literary culture by various regional languages in India and Southeast Asia. Vernacularization in both cases was accompanied by changes in political-cultural practices. The central difference between Europe and South Asia was that in the former Latin was generally imposed, being the language of conquest, whereas Sanskrit was a language of cultural affiliation, and we can say the same about Tibetan in North Asia. In Europe the displacement of Latin presaged the emergence of nationalism and the nation state, but in South Asia, vernacularization produced political entities of a very different kind, so differently conceived that they are difficult for Euro-American historians to understand. The usual assumption that vernacularization must be a form of political resistance, must come "from below," and therefore be a form of vindication, does not work in these Asian cases.

With vernacularization, Pollock writes, the literary function, "whereby power constructed for itself, its origins, grandeur, beauty, perdurance, and which can perhaps therefore be characterized as the function of interpreting the world and supplementing reality," was no longer the work exclusively of Sanskrit poetry (1998, 11). Pollock argues that using your own vernacular in this way is a conscious choice: people are *deciding* no longer to prioritize the uncentered cosmopolitan culture that transcends existing polities, and instead to focus on their own region, knowing full well that in using the local language they will be doing something less prestigious and addressing only the limited category of people who can understand that language. The very sense of the world around is altered, shifting from images of universality to those of a more finite space, such as "the cultivated land of Kannada" or "Beautiful Lady Lanka" (2000, 608). Vernacularization is, Pollock argues, the creation of "Place" (*deshi*) as distinct from the dominant trope of the cosmopolitan, which is the "Way" (*marga*). Let us briefly examine this set of ideas, to ask whether they apply in the Mongolian case, and if so what kind of "place" is created, to ask how it might relate to regional polity and what the nature of that formation might be.

Thinking about what such a cultural locale might have looked like in the Mergen case we have to stand back not only from the assumptions generated in Euro-American scholarship, but also from those of twentieth-century Mongolian historians. For example, there is a "nationalist" reading imposed on the eighteenth century, namely that the Manchu Qing government was trying to control the Mongols by using Tibetan Buddhism to tame them, and hence the Mongolian liturgy was a kind of national contestation of imperial policy (Galluu 2003, 707). Alternatively, there are the suppositions generated by Marxist education, expressed in terms of "class struggle" by some Inner Mongolian scholars. Thus, Mergen Gegen had his lamas chant in Mongolian because the "mass of the people" wanted to understand the ideas and philosophy of Buddhism (which, of course, they could not do if the chanting was in Tibetan). This socialist version suggests that Mergen Gegen was someone like Wycliffe, whose translation of the Bible into English was a task heroically done to satisfy the spiritual needs of working people. We shall argue that these answers, however plausible, are nevertheless anachronistic, and that something more interesting and unexpected was going on.

First we need to see where Megen Gegen was coming from. What was the line of Mergen Gegens in which he was the 3rd, and what did it stand for? In the next section we describe how this line of reincarnations inherited inspiration from a remarkable wandering missionary lama of earlier times, Neichi Toin [Neyichi Toyin] (1557–1653). The link is that one of Neichi Toin's closest disciples, known as Mergen Diyanchi Dinuwa ("Wise Meditator Dinuwa") became the 1st Mergen Gegen. Considerably more is known about the 1st Neichi Toin than about any of the early Mergen Gegens because his biography was written. This work—written in 1739 by an eminent Urad, Güüshi Lama Biligundalai—can tell us about views on the great missionary at just the period when the 3rd Mergen Gegen was active.[19] In this work Neichi Toin appears as original and self-willed, forging his own path at a tangent to the developing power structures of the Manchus. At the same time, he is celebrated as an earthy character, deeply Mongolian in his attitudes and habits.

The inspiration of the wandering lama

In the sixteenth century a young prince called Abida of the Torgud (this was a branch of the Oirad federation of western Mongols) was out hunting. He shot a pregnant female wild horse and slit open its belly. When he saw the dying animal turn round to lick its crying baby, he was so affected by the pathos that he swore to renounce the material world. With this moment of truth, he gave up his wife and young son to become a monk (Purbueva 1984, 49, fol. 6r). Following the pages of his sacred book fluttering in the wind, he ran away to Tibet for instruction. There he learned the two methods of *sutra* and *tantra*, and when he said he would like to go to another country for meditation he was told to go the East (i.e., Mongolia). He became the Neichi Toin, an extraordinarily successful missionary of Inner Mongolia. Looking at his life enables us to perceive the kind of inspiration he provided, as well as some of the parameters of Buddhism's advent and consolidation in the region.

The Holy Toin pursued the path of Buddhist asceticism; he was an itinerant *lama* (spiritual guide), but not a monk living in a monastery. He lived in personal poverty, demonstratively refused rich apparel and other comforts offered to him—he traveled covered by an old felt, with a sheep's shoulder blade as his drum, a cow's horn as his bell, and a

19. The biography used the writings and memories of disciples of Neichi Toin as its chief sources, among them the Mergen Diyanchi Dinuwa. "Prajna Sagara," author of the 1739 work, was not an eastern Mongol as has been supposed, but the distinguished Urad, Biligündalai, who had been a disciple of the 2nd Neichi Toin, before he moved to work in Peking (Ujeed 2009, 74–75, 84). Many other versions of the biography exist (see details in Heissig 1954; Purbueva 1984, 17–21).

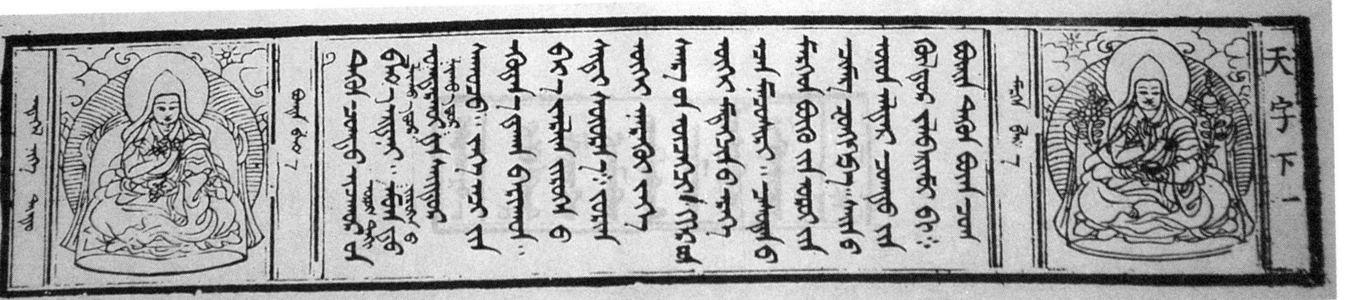

2 Neichi Toin (left) and Mergen Gegen (right). (From Bum Jarlig, 1780–1783)

human skull as his bowl. He proselytized in Mongolian. He spent years meditating in caves in severe mortification, and never stayed for long in the main monastery built for him, Bayan Hoshigu in Horchin. His magic feats became legendary, such as melting, through the heat generated by his spiritual power, the ice surrounding him on a winter meditation in the open steppe; or providing great storms of rain; or children for infertile couples. He moved from place to place in the wildest ranges of Inner Mongolia to spread the dharma (*nom*) and demonstrate his tantric mastery, and thus convert the Mongols of remote regions from shamanism to Buddhism.

Neichi Toin's early life is reminiscent in some ways of well-known Buddhist images, of charismatic "forest Monks" (Tambiah 1984), cave-dwelling yogic poets like Milarepa, or traveler holy men who brought back and spread the scriptures like the Tang Dynasty Monk Xuangzang (Atwood [1992] 2006, 3–5). Several of the stories about Neichi Toin describe his rough behavior, humor, and magic power. Once Neichi Toin happened on a wedding being held by a Mongolian khan, who offered him a whole cow's head as food. The lama had no dish, so he put the head on the earth to eat it. Amazed at his simplicity, the khan's brother then offered him an old, lame, white stallion. Neichi Toin was not to be put down, and responded, "I am a fat one among lamas, and you are fat among princes—so do we have something in common? Let me tell you, there is meaning in this gift of yours: the stallion means the spread of male descendants from the father, the white color indicates the spread of religion, and that it is an old horse means the long life of religion. Just its lameness is not so good." Following this, the khan and his brother became devotees of Neichi Toin (Purbueva 1984, 70, fol. 46r).

Neichi Toin appears in the biography as comparable to the exemplary Padmasambhava, the semi-mythic yogin credited with converting Tibet to Buddhism in the eighth century. Padmasambhava had traveled through Tibet using his tantric powers to defeat the local chthonic gods, binding them to renounce blood sacrifices and forcing them to accept Buddhism (Mills 2003, 15). However, the holy Toin's emphasis was different. He allowed a fearsome mountain god to remain rampant, praying only not to fall under its power,[20] but he set out to eradi-

20. While Neichi Toin was meditating on Chogtu Sümber Mountain, a huge figure dressed in armor and with a head the size of a cauldron appeared to his disciple. "Where is the lama?" he asked. The disciple nearly fainted away, but managed to reply, "He has taken a vow of retreat and will not lift it soon." "Ha, Ha," laughed the giant and went away. When Neichi Toin reappeared

cate shamans and *onggod*, the spirits of unquiet human ancestors.[21] He was bent on total subjugation rather than negotiation with shamans.[22] He insisted, often against pathetic objections, that shamanist fetishes must be burned.

Almost everywhere, Neichi Toin was extraordinarily successful.[23] People had resented the demands for offerings made by the *onggod*, and now they felt emboldened to reject these spirits by virtue of the magical powers granted them through his tantric spells and initiations. Princes, dukes, and their wives fell over themselves to offer him lavish donations, all of which were given out again to followers and converts (Purbueva 1984, 45). Neichi Toin held rituals for great gatherings of people of all ranks, and he agreed to the construction of magnificent monasteries. Centuries later the Urad region at least bears the mark of his activities: shamans have practically disappeared, while the mountain gods—more or less loyal to Buddhism—continue to be worshipped.

Neichi Toin is particularly significant to us, as it is from this fervent line of tantric Buddhism that the Mergen tradition originated. Not only was the Toin's disciple to become the 1st Mergen Gegen but a century later the 3rd Mergen Gegen kept his marvelous accomplishments alive by composing a short hagiography (*BJ* vol. 1, text 37) and prayers addressed to the holy missionary and his successive incarnations (*BJ* vol. 1, texts 36, 38; Galluu and Jirantai 1986, 464, 457–73), while virtually the entire second volume of his collected works is devoted to Yamantaka, Neichi Toin's chief tantric inspiration.[24] Mergen Gegen may have seen Neichi Toin as a concentration of diverse strands of Buddhism, since he compared him with "Red Hat" Padmasambhava, but most prominently he extolled Neichi Toin as the Second Tsongkhapa, founder of the "Yellow Hat" Gelug order. The very appellation "Second Tsongkhapa" indicates that Mergen was making links in a chain extending beyond the Toin himself and in this way asserting the doctrinal legitimacy of his own inspiration (Ujeed 2009, 94). Today, the

from his yogic retreat, he prayed to Yamantaka not to fall under the power of this mountain god (Purbueva 1984, 61, fol. 26r).

21. *Onggon* (pl. *onggod*) means literally "vessel," but the term is used for the spirits themselves as well as the fetish-like material vessels they inhabit.

22. For details, see Heissig 1992 and Purbueva 1984, 65, fol. 40r.

23. Neichi Toin was far from alone in converting the Inner Mongols, as many princes invited lamas from Tibet to spread the doctrine, but he is acknowledged by southern Mongols as the most active, successful, and charismatic missionary of his time (Darmatala 1987, 426–39).

24. Ujeed (2009, 178–86) discusses these Yamantaka (Vajrabhairava) texts, emphasizing the information Mergen provides on teaching and initiation lineages and his desire to maintain in his own monastery the pure tradition handed down from Tsongkhapa, without admixture of synthetic texts from other sources.

lamas at Mergen frequently mention Neichi Toin as a brilliant star, the origin of their tradition. They proudly recall their links with his later reincarnations, such as the 6th Neichi Toin, whose mummified corpse was worshipped in nearby Güng Monastery, and with the 9th (and last) Neichi Toin, who was killed in a road accident in 1980. However, the original Neichi Toin was to be suppressed by the Qing court, and we now explore the reason for this—the dangerous volatility and sense of empowerment given by the religious movement he created.

In the early seventeenth century when the Neichi Toin was active, many Mongols were illiterate and what the missionary offered them to replace the shamanic fetishes was: prayers (*jalbaril*) in Mongolian which they were to learn by heart, powerful mantras (*tarni*), the sage's own generative religious power (*ubadis*), magic (*shidi*),[25] miracles, and, most significantly, initiations (*abishig*) into "secret" practices of the faith (Ujeed 2011). These included an unorthodox tantric procedure he invented for originating and substantiating the fearsome bull-headed Yamantaka (Heissig 1992, 125) and the invocation of "Nuuch Huriang-gui" (lit. "secret concentration"). What particularly affronted the authorities was that he intended to teach these methods to everyone.

It would be mistaken to assume that Neichi Toin succeeded so well because of a similarity between tantric practice and the shamanic procedure of "trance" and mastery of spirits. The visualization of the form or body of a *yidam* involves something different, the dissolving of the conventional world into emptiness, and the perception—and even realization—of a state of enlightenment (Mills 2003, 92–93; see comparison of shamanism and tantra in Samuel 1993; Atwood 1996, 128–39). But how to attract laypeople to such ideas? Neichi Toin used the donations given him by nobles to pay a sum in gold, silver, horses, or sheep to people who learned by heart elements of the Yamantaka prayer, or who took initiation to acquire the *tarni* of this god (Heissig [1953] 1992, 125). However, what the cynical might see as a bribe the biography records as a double gift from the missionary: the inner gift of the teachings of Buddha and the outer gift of valuable capabilities (Purbueva 1984, 45, fol. 74r). The ordinary people thus initiated would acquire the power (*chadal*) of this most powerful god, at once a source for spiritual liberation and at the same time, since this is a fierce and violent deity, the means to vanquish demons, misfortune, and enemies.

25. *Shidi* (from Sanskrit *siddhi*) is a term used both for the "realization" of enlightenment and for the evocation of supernormal powers (Mills 2003, 12), see discussion in Chapter 3.

All this was seen as a threat to the Manchus' central control of Buddhism in Mongolia. The biography notes that Neichi Toin had refused to be the emperor's lama, then to hold a service to cure his illness, and finally to give him tantric initiation (Ujeed 2009, 79). It was the teaching of precious *tarni* to uninitiated laypeople that provided the excuse for his suppression. Jealous prelates accused him of making open and widespread that which should have been kept holy and secret. "The Neichi Toin lama wandering among the Northern Mongols conducts himself like a Buddha [. . .]. He lets everybody, from the carriers of cattle troughs to the dung-collectors, who are not able to distinguish the good from the bad, recite the Yamantaka and other prayers, and acquire the most profound of the Buddhas and the most secret and specialized of the Vajra doctrine" (Heissig [1953] 1992, 126). On the authority of the Dalai Lama, the Toin was banished from the capital and sent to Höhhot, where he would be confined in surroundings dominated by Tibetan orthodoxy. Most of his follower lamas were dispersed, and shortly thereafter he died.

Neichi Toin's disciple, Mergen Diyanchi Dinuwa, who became the founder of the Mergen reincarnation line, is a rather mysterious figure, as his biography has not survived.[26] His name, "Wise Meditator Dinuwa," indicates that he engaged in lengthy meditation, but he was not a missionary, nor was he known for magical demonstrations to the laity. If this makes him a different kind of figure from Neichi Toin, so were the achievements attributed to him by recent lamas, scholarly learning, and his massive work of translation from Tibetan into Mongolian (Galluu 2003, 31–47). Here we can see a trace of the well-known distinction in Tibetan Buddhism between *adepts* (of techniques of liberation) and *clerics*, the masters of branches of learning (Kapstein 2000, 19). It is clear that Neichi Toin represents the former, while the 1st Mergen Gegen is held to represent the combination of both kinds of mastery. In fact, however, the 1st Mergen incarnation must have been a very old man when he was invited to Urad lands by Duke Nomun, and it was the 2nd Mergen Gegen who is attested to have been a fine scholar and translator and upholder of Neichi Toin's Mongolian language tradition (Ujeed 2009, 104–05).

Despite the accumulation of similar achievements ascribed retro-

26. Despite confusion in the scholarly literature between several lamas entitled Mergen ("wise") who were disciples of either the 1st or 2nd Neichi Toin, Ujeed clarifies that Mergen Diyanchi Dinuwa was the founder of the line at Mergen monastery (2009, 96–104).

spectively to the early Mergen Gegens by the present-day lama Galluu, we should point out that a Buddhist tradition cannot in fact be carried by a single line of reincarnations for the simple reason that one incarnation is born after the death of his predecessor and therefore cannot receive teaching or *tarnis* directly from him. The teachings have to zigzag via other high lamas, and these gurus also form disciple lineages that branch backwards. As for the 3rd Mergen Gegen, while he worshipped Tsongkhapa and Neichi Toin as his inspiration, his teacher guru was Ögligündalai, a disciple of the 2nd Mergen Gegen. These predecessors were respected resources. Yet the 3rd Mergen Gegen created something beyond any of them, which reminds us that innovation (contrary to the dialecticians) does not always have to emerge from conflict and struggle.

Mergen Gegen's Social World

Nomun, the 5th Duke of the West Banner, had been one of those nobles bowled over by the renown of Neichi Toin, and it was his descendant Duke Darmashiri who was to build the first monastery in the West Banner (next chapter). The dukes called the lamas "meritorious relatives" *lama buyan sadun*, and this was literally true in some cases, for the majority of the reincarnations in Mergen were scions of the noble family.

The intricate involvement of the dukes and high lamas goes against the foundational Gelug ideal of the separation of monks from familial ties. It can be related, however, to central arguments made by Pollock. He writes that in the case of Sanskrit, vernacularization was not inspired by religious innovation. It was not provoked by internal schisms, nor was it generated by the rise of popular devotionalism. Thus, in general terms, it was unlike the rise of Protestantism in Europe. Pollock argues instead for the crucial role of the court in the vernacular turn. "It is cosmopolitan elites—men like Pampa fully in command of Sanskrit and enjoying rank and status, paid by the king for his work [. . .], writing courtly poetry for their peers, who first turned Kannada [. . .] into an instrument for literary and political expressivity. What we need to understand . . . is what this courtly literature meant for the self-understanding of polity and why it came into existence when it did" (1998, 31).

Our case may have been similar, suggesting that the vernacular turn by the educated Urad elite, the nobles, and high lamas was taken on behalf of a conceptual unity—our people (*ulus*) or our land (*orun*)—

that included, but did not coincide with, "the masses." One of the 3rd Mergen's prayers to Neichi Toin praises him for not giving way to discrimination (*alagchilal*) between different kinds of people, and describes him as having a supreme destiny corresponding to the entire Mongol people,[27] and the two lamas were both insistent that the teachings should be understandable. Yet for Mergen Gegen, more than Neichi Toin, the lower people (*dooradus*) were included in social unities not as a separate constituency to which particular attention should be paid, but as followers and serfs. His history follows Sanskrit texts in describing the appearance of four "castes" (M. *ijagur*) following the downfall of perfect human beings and the emergence of desire, sexuality, biological birth, diseases, kinship, and political organization. The four *ijagur* are those of the Brahmans, the kings, the people who live by laws, and the "black caste" of killers and meat eaters (*AT1* 1970, 273–74, fol. 6v and 7r). Many passages mention the dangers of elevating the lower people (*AT1* 1970, 306, 316–18, 328, fol. 23r, 28r, 29v, 34r, etc.). They should follow the higher people (*degedüs*, pronounced *deedüs*, which also means "ancestors") as a matter of course. The upper people, for their part, had a responsibility to rule justly and live their lives by "the book" (*nom*, doctrine, morality, sacred texts). It was because the higher people were destined to lead others that it was so crucial that they be morally upright. The failure of the nobles of Mergen's time in this respect was the subject of several angry passages in the *AT2* (e.g., 1998b, fol. 34r).

In this vision of the social world, although the roles of lama and lay ruler were conceptually distinct, it would be incorrect to see the dukes as "secular." Indeed, such an idea—of a kind of life altogether without what we would call "religion"—did not exist. In both Mongol and Manchu cultures, rulers dealt with gods and spirits. The Urad *oboo* sacrifices mentioned earlier can be seen as a merging of Mongol customs with official Qing practices throughout the empire. As Kuhn has written about eighteenth-century China:

> The commoner's daily battle against evil spirits was mirrored, at the very top of society, by the concerns of the imperial state. [. . .] On every level of officialdom, from the imperial palace to the dustiest country *yamun*, agents of the state were intermediaries between man and the spirits. Their role marks them, in a sense, as

27. "[We] pray to you, who were worshipped even by the sky-gods and the eight species of dragons; at that time, your supreme destiny corresponded completely to the entire Mongol people, who worshipped the lotus of your feet, you brilliant one. Please bless us" (Mergen Gegen, *Neichi Toin hutugtu-yin chadig magtagal*, verses 19–22, in Galluu and Jirantai 1986, 461–62).

priests: communicating with the gods on behalf of mankind to ensure the proper ordering of worldly events, primarily good conditions for agriculture and peace for the realm. (1990, 107)

It is in this context—the concern of rulers for flourishing and righteous social order—that we can begin to perceive the existence of a common culture shared by the Mongol nobles with the high lamas.

By the 3rd Mergen Gegen's time, along with the sophisticated Tibetan texts produced in monasteries, there was also a literary culture among the aristocracy that was not simply religious in the narrowly Buddhist sense. This is seen not only in the requests by nobles for texts of lay rituals to be written by lamas,[28] but in the numerous histories written in Mongolian by educated laypeople in the sixteenth through eighteenth centuries, which are concerned precisely with the destiny and achievements of kings (khans), their responsibilities, and the moral qualities they inherit. An example is "The Flow of the Ganges" (*Ganga-yin Urusgal*, 1725), written by Gombojab, a learned Chinggisid noble who was expert in four languages.[29] The flow of the Ganges is a metaphor for the continuous descent of the "Golden Lineage" of Chinggis Khan. Many such Mongols from prosperous families were educated in Manchu, Chinese, orthography, and calligraphy at Banner schools, after which a career in officialdom awaited them, while others studied for a time in monasteries. Women too could receive education at domestic schools, and the colophons of many manuscripts record the names of women called *nomchi* (learned, religiously literate) who sponsored these texts. Because the Mongols were excluded from the Chinese examination system and were left to their own devices educationally, cultural elements trickled in from many sources. The resulting literary-religious-historical culture continued until the end of the Qing in 1911 (and beyond, in many regions). This, we suggest, was the sponsoring environment for the 3rd Mergen Gegen's vernacularization. A century earlier Neichi Toin's goal had been to convey Buddhist powers and understandings to the Mongol people; Mergen Gegen's concern was to encompass the culture of that community and elevate it.

28. Many of Mergen Gegen's works have colophons stating the names of the noble patrons who asked him to write them.

29. Gombojab wrote in Tibetan a *History of Buddhism in China*, translated sacred texts from Tibetan into Mongolian, wrote Tibetan-Mongol dictionaries, translated a treatise on sculpture from Tibetan into Chinese, and wrote a comparative analysis of vowels and consonants in Sanskrit, Tibetan, and Mongolian (Puchkovskii 1960, 7–12).

"Auspiciousness of the Ancient Root"— The Crafting of Genealogical Identity

It is significant that Mergen Gegen's last major work, *Altan Tobchi*, envisaged the history of the "great Mongol people *(ulus)*" as a genealogy, albeit one much enlivened by events. It creates a vast network in time and space, linking the Urad Dukes to the very origins of the universe. In such works the imaginary and the conceptual have a reality of their own, for, as Pollock writes, "epic representations provided a template for structuring real political aspirations, or, what amounts to the same thing, the discursive understanding of political aspirations" (2006, 237). Genealogy for Mergen Gegen was little concerned with the preoccupations anthropologists have usually assigned to it, property and legitimate succession, but instead it created a framework through time for a moral world. What then was the shape of Mergen Gegen's *AT*, and how was that space related to the eighteenth-century Qing Empire in which real hard power was exercised?

Curiously, for a text written by a lama, the history has relatively little to say about Buddhism, while many pages are devoted to the wars, internecine struggles, and above all the genealogy of the Urad ancestors. Mergen indeed describes his genealogy (*üye-yin bichig*) as a fruit tree, in which his words are silk-like flowers and leaves. He has written the book to explain how:

> The peoples and countries, all of them,
> Appeared [on earth] from the will-prayer of blessed Sumeru [Mountain],
> The seed of the seed of the rulers and khans
> Filled with the light of the sun and moon and stars;
> Branching off from them [there appeared] the early descendants of previous years;
> Their descent was suffused with the summer air of cause and reason.
> (*AT1* 1970, 263, fol. 1v)

Mergen Gegen used sources originally written in Sanskrit, Mongolian, Chinese, Persian, and Tibetan, and the first cosmological section is based on the *Abhidharma-kośa* and other Sanskrit texts, apparently bypassing Tibetan translations (Baldanzhapov 1970, 29, 66–74).[30] But

30. Mergen Gegen knew Mongolian, Chinese, Tibetan, and some Sanskrit. With regard to the latter, it seems that he used some earlier Mongol translations directly from Sanskrit rather than through Tibetan (Baldanzhapov 1970, 29).

Mergen Gegen's history does not copy anything. Frequently at odds with earlier accounts, it challenges the idea that the sacred teachings came only through Tibet. Instead, Mergen insists on the importance of the works of Chinese Buddhists, accuses a Tibetan king of wrongfully rejecting them during the Tang Dynasty, and criticizes contemporary Mongol nobles for despising all sacred texts except the Tibetan (*AT1* 1970, 130, 142, fols. 14r, 20r and v).

Mergen Gegen's history is above all a confrontation with the conventional Mongolian elevation of Chinggis Khan. It praises instead the author's own ancestor Hasar—who is depicted as a holy (*bogda*), brilliant, and righteous hero, and attributed with many of the achievements of his older brother Chinggis (*AT1* 1970, 333–34, fol. 36v and 37r). Mergen mentions his local Muna Mountains, but omits their Chinggisid associations found in earlier histories, where they appear as a sacred territory for preserving the cult of the great emperor, "a refuge for a broken state (*törü*) and a home pasture for a peaceful state," as well as being the scene for an affecting speech to Chinggis's spirit.[31] Instead he makes Muna Mountains the scene of Hasar's achievements. Hasar is described with unblinking approval saving the Mongol army by annihilating an "evil Tangut" [Tibetan[32]] and making a sacrifice of his victim's heart to a mountain (*AT1* 1970, 337, fol. 38v). By elevating his own ancestor Hasar and linking him with the Urad lands, Mergen Gegen was engaged in a certain kind of territorialization; but this should not be confused with the "localization" that Elverskog describes as a characteristic of the late-nineteenth century, when Qing Banners became sources of identity (2006b, 127). Mergen Gegen ignores the Banner. His territory (*orun*) is defined, at various scales, by the genealogical edifice headed by Hasar.

Mergen Gegen's first step was subtly to query the convention established by his time of attributing the Mongol rulers (both Chinggisid and Hasarid) with direct descent from the ancient kings of Tibet. Questioning, without specifically denying, the idea that the ancestor of the Mongol rulers, Börte Chino, was Mukarijambu, a son of the Tibetan king, he instead links Börte Chino to the Mongol idea of Heaven (*tngri*). He notes sarcastically, for example, that identifying Börte Chino

31. These words are found the early seventeenth century anonymous *Altan Tobchi* (Bawden 1955, 137). For discussion of this Chinggisid vision of Muna Mountain and the cult of Chinggis Khan, see Elverskog (2006b, 99–102).

32. Eighteenth-century Mongolian writers often used the term Tangut (M. *Tanggud*) as a synonym for Tibetan, though the Tanguts were properly a different people that assimilated into other groups after their conquest by Chinggis Khan.

with Mukarijambu arose from a mistake in the Mongol spelling of the Tibetan name (they are so different we can interpret this as an indirect denial of the identity), and he writes: "I have described above the history of India and Tibet. Although that may seem not very necessary for our Mongols, I have written it in order for people to know whose son Börte Chino was—the son of Heaven" (*AT1* 1970, 309, fol. 24r).[33] The idiom of "son of *tngri*" is similar to the Chinese notion "Son of Heaven," but more likely here stems directly from Mongol folk thought, whereby significant ancestors (i.e., those designated the founders of social groups) are singled out from the human stream by being fathered by rays of light or other heavenly signs.[34] Saying this openly would have struck a bold note to Mergen's readers, already accustomed to Tibetan ascendancy and numerous chronicles attributing the Mongol emperors with Tibetan ancestry (e.g., Sagang Sechen [1662] 1996, 23r; Darma Güüshi [1739] 2000, 50).[35]

The form of Mergen Gegen's history is not dissimilar to other chronicles.[36] It is the content, perspective, and iconoclasm that is unusual. First of all, genealogy is used to define and bring into the open a hitherto more or less invisible grouping. Within "our Mongols," Mergen singled out the descendants of Hasar as a united ("full") clan (*bürin obug*). Vast, dispersed, and politically unrecognized in his day,[37] this grouping had earlier been unified for centuries, according to Mergen Gegen, but then regrettably split into four during the Mongol civil wars of the

33. In other chapters, repeating that Börte Chino was the son of Heaven, Mergen ignores Tibet, linking the Mongol ancestor only to the original king of India, Mahasammadi, a reincarnation of Manjushiri. Börte Chino was descended from Mahasammadi, he writes with characteristic imaginative exactitude, in the 1,121,565th generation (*AT1* 1970, 262, 310, fol. 1r and fol. 25r).

34. Such incidents are found in the iconic Mongol historical source, the thirteenth century *Secret History of the Mongols* (Onon 2001, 37, SH §1, §21, §59). Although it is unlikely that Mergen Gegen had read the *Secret History* (Atwood 2006, 398–410), the idiom linking the birth of extraordinary leaders to Heaven was a commonplace of folk thinking.

35. Two other chronicles called *Altan Tobchi* (*Golden Summary*) exist, one by an anonymous author and one written by Lubsandanzan, both of which title themselves as histories of kings.

36. Other Mongolian works of the period have a similar genealogical framework, owing much to Tibetan styles of history writing, but with different content and emphasis. *Erten-ü Monggul-un had-un ündüsün-ü yeke shir-a tuguji orusiba*, for example, cuts short the cosmology, dwells greatly on the deeds of Chinggis Khan, and focuses at the end on Chinggisid noble genealogy (Shastina 1957).

37. These descendants included the rulers of the Horchin, Gorlos, Jalaid, Urad, the ten Dörbed Banners, Muuminggan, Aru-Horchin, and Dörben Hüühed Mongols, and also six subject Banners of Tibetans. Mergen Gegen carefully says that "he heard" these sixteen Banners, plus the Ööled and Torgud of Höhnuur, were all one clan (*obug*) (*AT2* 1998, fol. 26v). A modern Inner Mongolian scholar summarizes the present understanding of the descendants of Hasar in a very similar list (Saijirahu Bao 1999, 197–202). The Oirad was a complex federation of groups, including some Ööled and Torgud, changing in its components over the centuries, but having in common that its rulers were not of Chinggisid descent (Atwood 2004b, 420–22)

sixteenth century and "started to take wives from one another." These "indecent relations" continued until the Manchus forbade marriage between kin in 1634 (Baldanzhapov 1970, 103; *AT2* 1998, fol. 26v). Mergen Gegen thus saw the descendants of Hasar—scattered though they were over thousands of miles—as a lineage-defined entity within the Mongol *ulus*, while the final chapters, which consist almost entirely of a name-by-name genealogy of all three branches of the Urad nobles, show that he imagined them as a similar (sub)unity.

Evidently, Mergen Gegen approved of the early Qing (ineffectual) efforts to rationalize administration of the Mongols by corralling them into groups as patrilineal clans (Sneath 2007, 96), but what he was doing was something greater: the large imaginative entities he evokes, "the Mongols" and the "descendants of Hasar," were precisely the kind of threatening federations the Manchus wanted to eliminate when they divided Mongols into small Banners. For Mergen Gegen the "descendants of Hasar" included the Oirad rulers of the refractory Ögeled and Torgud of Höhnuur,[38] whose rebellion against the Qing was not defeated until 1724, while other, even more marginal, Torguds fled backwards and forwards between the Qing and the Russian Empires into 1770s. Let us recall also that Neichi Toin was not only an Oirad (a Torgud) but had also been suppressed by the Emperor—Mergen Gegen carefully notes his genealogical position and that of his next two incarnations, all of them being included among the "descendants of Hasar." The sprawling geopolitical image Mergen Gegen evokes is provocative indeed. Perhaps it is because he was aware of the political objections his history might arouse that he did not openly declare his authorship and hid his name in a play on words in the first paragraph.[39]

To return to the "triangular" relations of empire mentioned earlier, Mergen Gegen's general strategy was to pay exaggerated homage to the Qing state and emperor in order to get the leverage to extract himself from cultural domination by the Qing's Tibetan allies. But he can be seen to take a number of (not always consistent) positions. In the triad Mongol-Tibet-India he denies Tibet in order to link with India. In relations between Mongol-Tibet-China he pointedly supports Chinese

38. Most of the Oirad of Höhnuur were subjects of Güüshi Khan, who was a descendant of Hasar.

39. He uses the expression *gegen mergen* (enlightened wise), though as an attribute rather than a name, (see discussion in Baldanzhapov 1970, 8). Mergen Gegen does not refer to himself in the genealogies, and the earliest version of his *AT1* (1970) also omits the names of the two Dukes of the West Banner of his generation. The Mergen Gegen referred to in the 1998 publication is the 4th, not the 3rd, Mergen Gegen.

Buddhists against those who respect only Tibetan Buddhism. In the confrontation of Hasarids with Chinggisids he identifies of course with the former, but he also wrote two prayers to Chinggis (see Chapter 7).[40] And on another occasion he scorns the Oirads, who were so frightened of the Chinggisids they even lost consciousness in battle and trembled "as if their lungs fell out of their mouths" (*AT1* 1970, 341, fol. 40 v). Now such criticism of the Oirads would be fully in line with Qing rhetoric at the time, for the empire had not yet succeeded in fully quashing them. Mergen Gegen writes about "our state" (*manu törü*), meaning the Qing, and unlike many other Mongolian historians he uses Chinese dynastic reigns for dating. Yet Mergen is by no means unequivocally a Qing loyalist. He excoriates those Mongols who "under the excuse of observing the rules of ceremony bow their heads to officials. . . . who fill the vessel of suffering with violence and unfairness" (*AT1* 1970, 367, fol. 53v). One of Mergen's great genealogical lists ends with the imprecation: "Excellent and holy Hasar's [greatness] has continued through all generations up to the present without break. You who support the Dai Qing rule [only] have the chance obtain the title of "noble." Do not forget the fortune (*öljei*) of your ancient [Hasarid] root. Remember this!" (*AT1* 1970, 361, fol. 50v). What these various positions more profoundly imply is that the subjects of empire do not hold a single political vision that could be rendered as inevitable ("in *his* position he would see matters like this"). It is necessary to appreciate that there are *visions* rather than a vision, that the very shape of each of them is contorted by the presence of the others in the relational field, and that the carving out of heterodox spaces was experienced as strain.

Mergen's words about Qing rule were bold, even treasonous in an empire ruled by Manchu-Chinese colonial power. "I am old, ill, and useless," wrote Mergen at the end of his history. And he continues ironically, "With regard to that, a writer of a genealogical book [in this time of decline] is like a two-legged inhabitant of Dzoada—not a human at all.[41] However, a person cannot stay silent, just as a drum must give out a sound if it is beaten with a stick" (*AT2* 1998b, 93, fol. 53v).

The attempt to construct a common identity amid the shouldering

40. It is odd that Mergen Gegen did not write a prayer to Hasar, as far as we know. An explanation for this may be that no high noble asked him to write such a prayer, and this is perhaps due to the fact that the Hasar memorial shrine was maintained by a senior branch of the descendants, who supported Tibetan liturgy.

41. Dzoada is a country in Indian mythology where the inhabitants have only one leg, according Gerel, the translator of *AT2* into Chinese (Chimeddorji 1998b, 274). A two-legged person arriving in Dzoada is not counted as a human being.

bulks of others, and to frame this identity genealogically as something inherited and hence given, was not of course political nationhood in the modern sense. Rather, Mergen's vocabulary, *hubi* (fate, destiny), *ug* (base, stump, root, origin), *ündüsün* (root, beginning, origin, principle, principal*), ijagur* (origin, genesis, species, "caste," type of rebirth), *gol* (aorta, center, fount), and *ishi* (stem) shows that he was operating with a notion of cosmological-biological reproduction, where the heroic righteous ancestors (*degedüs*) were linguistically identified with the "high ones" (*degedüs*) of his day. The vision of virtuousness pouring down from the past, the unfolding of rightful destiny, had been compromised, however, by Mongol divisiveness and even as he wrote was spoiled by the violent and selfish behavior of his contemporaries. Certainly, there is evocation of the Buddhist notion of the epoch of universal moral decline here,[42] but Mergen is more concerned with the unique situation of the Mongols, and he repeatedly mentions that they risk punishment by sky gods and devils, rather than consequences expressed in a more Buddhist idiom (*AT2* 1998b, fol. 27v). "What is needed [now]," he writes at the end of his book, "is those weighty words, rituals, and laws which held sway in ancient times when our people flourished under the name of the 'four hundred thousand Mongols' . . . and the descendants of Holy Hasar ruled their *ulus*" (*AT2* 1998b, fol. 33r). The gold and silver of patrilineal descent should not be sullied by elevating the iron and copper of relations through wives. "In the epoch of decline, debauchery of mind causes mad darkness. Only the genealogical book, mounted on the wind horse (*salhi-iin morin*), is able to dispel and drive away this darkness. It should shine like the rays of the sun's aura. Only then will the lotus flower of the eight powers of the Sky and Earth happily flourish and spread" (*AT2* 1998b, fol. 33v). We are left with an idea of unfolding, of a sense of "the Mongols" as a moral-cultural category reproduced through time, whose ancestral destiny should be manifest in any political circumstances. Mergen Gegen groans at the difficulty of rendering this adequately in writing: "Just as a mosquito, fluttering and hemmed in, [cannot follow] the track of the eagle soaring and swooping above, [I] also flutter when [I] cannot reach the quality of the literature previously written for the root [of the ancestors]" (*AT1* 1970, 368, fol. 54r).

Possibly, since the "root of the ancestors" could be understood as the Indian kings, Mergen Gegen is comparing his feeble efforts with

42. The present epoch is described as the "time of calamities" *chöb chag* (*AT* 1998b, 92). For an illuminating comparison with the tropes of Tibetan history writing, see Bjerken (2002, 200–203).

the achievements of Sanskrit authors. It was conventional in Buddhist autobiographical writings to affect such a studied modesty (Gyatso 1998, 105), but Mergen's imagery has a freshness and immediacy rarely found in chronicles of his time.

Mergen was certainly more aware than most high lamas of his time of the religious participation of the laity and desired to reach out to it,[43] but he knew that by the mid–eighteenth century there was no longer any need to engage in missionizing, for Buddhism was in unquestioned ascendancy. So in thinking about what Mergen Gegen's real contribution was, we should note that he in fact broke with Neichi Toin's fierce proselytizing style, though he continued to offer homage to it.[44] Leaving behind lone asceticism, what Mergen was striving for was to create a generative vision of the past that would create a people—an inclusive moral community that did not yet exist. Mergen endorsed the idea of different levels of practice (Chapter 1), and central to his endeavor throughout was his artistry; he decreed strictly defined poetic styles appropriate to the relevant genre. The same disciplining move meant that the *tantras* also were not to be performed according to will and available to all, as they had been under Neichi Toin, but only to be done by the initiated within ritual. Music was essential to the great majority of his work. He is credited with composing the melodies not only for the religious folk songs of "Mergen Gegen" but also for the central liturgy chanted by the monks; this includes tunes for several Yamantaka tantric invocations,[45] for which he also specified the appropriate symbolic hand gestures.[46] Monotonous prayers were thus elevated into powerful and beautiful performances of superlative religious efficacy.

43. The fact that he wrote primers for learning the Mongol alphabet is some evidence for this. Mergen's attitude to the laity is seen in one address he made to his lamas: "You are living depending on the monastery's power, and if you don't think about the well-being of the people who have done good [to you] how can you be different from the laypeople who are settled here? Even laypeople think about their father's good deeds and benefits handed down by masters, and they act lawfully by thinking of the power of the customs of their homeland. So there is no need to mention monks [i.e., they should do better]. Therefore let us be aware of the rules and favors that each of our gurus taught us, from the Sakyamuni Buddha's religion to the religion of the second Tsongkhapa—the religion of the Holy Toin [Neichi Toin]" (*BJ* [1780–1783] 1998, vol. 1, p 23f).

44. In his prayers to Neichi Toin, Mergen Gegen hardly mentions the missionary's years of meditation in caves, but rather stresses his this-worldly activities, wisdom, compassion, teaching of doctrine, and even his institution-building role at the Baga Juu Monastery, in Höhhot (Galluu and Jirantai 1986, 462).

45. Mergen wrote seven melodies for Yamantaka texts and a further eleven melodies for chanting in the *Yamantaka-yin Wang*, the main invocation and initiation service for this deity (Mergen Gegen 1784, vol. 5, pp 16f.-18.f.; 41b.- 44b.). Dharmatala, eclipsing Mergen Gegen, wrongly attributes these musical and poetic achievements to Neichi Toin ([1889] 1987, 357).

46. Mongols use the term "hand seal" (*gar-un tamga*) or the Tibetan word *shagjiya* for these hand movements (S. *mudra*). They have the meaning and power of symbolic acts, which help save

The Arts of Language

Mergen Gegen's texts contain two kinds of linguistic objects, mantras (*tarnis*) and discursive texts (prayers, instructions, eulogies, etc.). The former are syllables without propositional meaning but powerful *as sounds* handed down from ancient times, and they normally begin each text as well as being scattered throughout. We discuss the mantras in later chapters, and here we describe the texts themselves.

Although discursive, they are not straightforward communications. Monks' chanting can be very fast, intoned in a way different from speech, and often drowned by loud music, and so even in Mongolian it is not easy to understand by lay listeners. Obviously Mergen Gegen was opposed to the obfuscation of sense through the use of Tibetan, the kind of holy mystification that some anthropologists have seen as maintaining priestly power (Bloch 1989, 37). But the main aim of his reformed liturgy was not to convey complex theology to the lamas or laity. Rather, Mergen Gegen's efforts were devoted to establishing elevated and *effective performance* of prayer and ritual. In order for this to happen it was necessary to make the liturgy—which was mostly not an exposition of ideas but aimed rather at efficacious engagement with the deities—follow poetic forms, be grammatically correct, and beautiful—and in this way also to make it more apt for chanting, easily learned, and memorable by the monks.

Central to this task was the question of how language could render the authenticity of religious endeavor. The high-ranking Jangjiya Gegen had validated the vernacular chanted liturgy, saying that that the Mongolian language was "fated" for the Urad country, but he nevertheless decreed that Tsongkhapa's central sutra, called "Stages of the Path" (*mör-ün jerge*, T. *Lam-Rim*), should be studied in Tibetan at Güng, one of the monasteries in the Mergen system that had set up a college especially for this purpose (Galdanwangchugdorji [1846] 1994, 37). Thus, paradoxically, the Güng monks were to study the key text of philosophical explanation in Tibetan—but chant the prayers to achieve religious efficacy in Mongolian. The Jangjiya's pronouncement fits with the idea that it would be authentic to study the *Lam-Rim* in the language it was

---

the six types of sentient beings by circling the golden wheel of doctrine in the ten directions. There are hundreds of such gestures, which lamas categorize into four types: doctrine, vow, great, and karmic (Galluu 2003, 376).

written in, whereas the liturgy, which was Sanskrit in origin, could as well be chanted in Mongolian as in Tibetan. The point may seem scholastic, but it reaches to the heart of what the 3rd Mergen did. In fact, he himself made the argument more strongly when he wrote that translating via a third language risked introducing "changes again and again" into the sacred texts (*BJ* [1780–1783] 1998, vol. 1, p 20r). "If we search for purity, there is nothing better than the Sanskrit fount (*gol*). If that cannot be done, it is beautiful to compose [it] yourself in your own language" (*BJ* [1780–1783] 1998, vol. 1, p 84r)

The background to this statement is that translations from Sanskrit to Tibetan were very different from translations from Tibetan to Mongolian. For when Sanskrit was translated into Tibetan (from the seventh century onward), Buddhism was under threat in northern India. Tibet became the place of refuge for the holy scriptures, and extraordinary effort was devoted to rendering them perfectly (Kapstein 2000; Bira 1994, 264–65). The work was done over centuries of close collaboration between Tibetan scholars and Indian pandits, resulting in an accurate and subtle rendering of the meaning of the texts. In the case of Mongols, while the very earliest Buddhist texts had reached them via Uighur, and with the help of Uighur scholars (Bira 1994, 262), thereafter virtually all sutras were translated from Tibetan rather than Sanskrit, even if the lama-translators knew the Sanskrit language. Such was the veneration of the Tibetan texts as linguistic objects that they were translated into Mongolian word by word.[47] Often the result, since Tibetan belongs to a quite different language family from Mongolian, was awkward and contorted language, in which the meaning was faithfully transmitted but so mechanical in execution that it could become difficult to understand (Bira 1994, 232, 266). These plain translations, which existed in great numbers, though they mostly languished in monastic libraries, are what Mergen Gegen set out to transform.

Mergen Gegen commented that the lamas today, when confronted with such Mongolian texts, do not care about the meaning and norms of doctrine but only peer at the letters on the page as if they were account books. They follow Tibetan rhythms in chanting with the result that "the soul of the previous syllable is erased by the tone of the subse-

47. Even for mantras (*tarni*), where Mongols tried to retain the sound of the Sanskrit words, transcriptions were often via Tibetan rather than directly from Sanskrit. Silent (unpronounced) letters in Tibetan were often retained in Mongol transcriptions, such as *Gbum*, where Tibetans and Mongolians actually say "*Bum*."

quent word." In written texts the syllables of one Mongolian word are divided,[48] the monks get tired and suffer, pronunciation is difficult and punctuation is wrong. The translators had violated the Mongolian art of harmonious writing (*üg nairal*) and tone (*ayalgu*) of translation. The resulting mess should be transformed, he wrote, by the use of "regularized poetry" (*nigedgegsen silüg*) in accordance with the ancient rules [of poetics] (*BJ* [1780–1783] 1998, vol. 1, text 12, p 20r; p 83v-84r). The key here is Mergen's use of meter/stress (*shad*). The lamas can instantaneously tell if a text is an "old Mongolian" version, or one that was "*shad*-ized" by Mergen Gegen, and they love to sing out these transformed texts, pinpointing the accentuated syllables.

Perhaps only native speakers of Mongolian can truly appreciate the aesthetics of Mergen Gegen's work. "What shows Mergen Gegen's great talent is that, using meter, each line of the poem is folded by syllable and thus fitted for chanting with melody; he beautifully joined the meaning with the art of writing" (Tserensodnom 1997, 121). His poetry and songs are tightly organized not only by meter, but also by parallelism and rhymes that occur at the beginning of lines according to Mongolian stylistics. This can be seen visually on the page in the following example of one of the eighty-one songs (Mönghe 2010, 298).

Cag-a-yin üre tungalag bolju	[In] the clarification of the fruits of boiled sour milk
Cag-tagan neyilekü jirum-tai.	There is a law [of nature] that corresponds with time.
Saragul tungalag uqagan-tai kümün-dü	To a person whose intelligence is clear as moonlight
Sanagsan kelegsen cöm-iyer qubi-tai.	[His] thoughts and instructions are completely predestined.
Qabur-tagan urgugsan nailjagur-un nabci-ni	The leaves of the branch that grows in its spring
Qamug suqai-dayan üjemji bolun-a.	Will be the (beautiful) vision of the entire tamarisk [tree].
Uqagaragulju kelegsen kümün-ü üge-ni	A person's words spoken to enlighten [people]

48. This problem occurred because Tibetan is written laterally and Mongolian vertically, and dual-language texts gave precedence to Tibetan.

Uqagan-tai kümün-degen ugtumji bolon-a.	Will be a foretelling to an intelligent person.
Namur-tagan idegesigsen nabci-yin üres-ni Neyite tümen-degen tejigel bolun-a.	The fruits of the leafy plants which ripened in autumn Will become the sustenance of their whole community.
Nasutan ebüged-ün kelegsen üg-e-ni Nilq-a kümün-degen surgal bolun-a.	The words spoken by the aged elders Will become teaching for immature people.

Mergen Gegen's desire to make Mongolian memorable and beautiful forced him often to press the language to its limits, to force rhymes out of it, and create new word forms (Tserensodnom 1997, 122).

Yet, in his concern for perfection in such matters, Mergen Gegen surely must have been influenced by Tibetan disciplines (for all his attempts to distance himself from Tibet). Metrics are the "very backbone of Tibetan verse" (Sujata 2004, 112), involving not only the number of syllables per line, but also making subdivisions linking groups within a line, such as in a line of eight, the three first syllables, the three last syllables, with the middle two syllables as a pair. Such numeration had to be calibrated with stress and rules about repetition (Sujata 2004, 112–17; 140–41). We are not competent to assess Mergen Gegen's metrics in any systematic way, but the whole idea of *shad*, so beloved of the lamas, shows that he too was concerned with such features of verse. At the same time, his use of poetic figures (simile, metaphor, and other rhetorical devices) was influenced by the seventh-century Sanskrit classic of poetics, Dandin's *Kāvyādarśa* (*Mirror of Literature*).[49] This had been translated into Tibetan in the thirteenth century at the behest of 'Phags-pa lama and hence was accessible to educated Mongols from that date. Numerous commentaries on Dandin's work were written by Mongolians from the seventeenth century onward, and *Kāvyādarśa* has exerted an influence in learned circles ever since (Bira 1994, 229–31).[50]

49. The 3rd Mergen Gegen's poetry sometimes employs a technique directly borrowed from Dandin, the *terigülegchi bey-e* ("leading person"), which uses the first person as a kind of declarative rhetoric (Ba Mönghe 2004, 389). The first person is normally avoided in Mongolian speech and writing.

50. Danda (1759–1842), a monk from Alasha, the region bordering Urad to the west, wrote a "Description of Language Adornments" and a book on the theory of poetry, *Suvdan Erihe* (Pearl Rosary),

Interestingly, Pollock also writes of the influence of Dandin's treatise elsewhere in Asia. For example, it played, a defining role in the creating of Thai poetry at the Ayutthaya court in the seventeenth century. "It is instances such as these that help us gauge the extraordinary importance that the instruments of Sanskrit cultural virtuosity possessed for intellectuals and their masters throughout Asia" (1998, 14).

What the Mergen Gegen was accomplishing then was not a simple vernacularization—a rendering of Buddhist thought in Mongolian. That had been done in the awkward translations of earlier generations. Here there was a simultaneous re-cosmopolitization. If we remember that Mergen's liturgical texts were created for chanting and the important cultural role of his songs, his role seems more like that of Alexander Pope for English, in the words of Samuel Johnson's remark on Pope's *Iliad*—"His version may be said to have tuned the English tongue, for since its appearance no writer, however deficient in other powers, has wanted melody" (quoted in Barnstone 1993, 219). Such a translator is engaged in something more than a literal rendering—rather, this is a creative transposition where the spirit or tone of the original is recreated in another context. If there are two responsibilities here, one to the original and another to the receivers in the second language, Mergen Gegen was preoccupied with both. He was taking the existing Tibetan and Mongolian translations and aligning them with widely admired Sanskritic norms of verbal sophistication.

And in composing melodies for chanting and songs, he dedicated himself (or at least the lamas today say he dedicated himself) to Egeshig-ün Öhin Tngri, the Goddess of Music, the Mongolian version of the Indian Sarasvati.[51] This "musicalization" of language, using local Urad melodies but in the spirit of a Sanskritic goddess, was akin to his move in the creation of a landscape through ritual, where the world is narrowed down to the particularity of the Muna Mountains and its spirits—and is simultaneously expanded again by imagining their transmogrification into great Buddhist deities through the mental actions of believers (Chapter 5). Such forms assert at once the regionality and the supraregionality of place (cf. Pollock 1998, 28).

---

both evidently influenced by the *Kāvyādarśa* (Stebetak 2003, 159). See also Erdenibayar (2007, 311) on the studies of Dandin by Ishibaljur, Mergen's great contemporary from the Höhnuur region.

51. Sarasvati is goddess of learning and the arts. In Mongolian regions the benign form devoted to music and learning is much more rarely found than the fierce form of Ökin Tngri, (T. Baldan Lhamo) (Syrtypova 2003, 82–86). Mergen Gegen was therefore unusual in his choice of personal deity. Later generations of his lineage did not forget his preference, as can be seen by the brightly painted dancing figures of the musical Ökin Tngri carved along the base of the massive Maidar statue.

Mergen Gegen was familiar with the technique of classical Sanskrit philosophers that used simile and metaphor to link familiar and emotionally meaningful images to religious narrative literature. This form of intertextuality has been called "mythic allusion" (Kragh 2010, 479), and it relies on creating relations between the newly written text and the listener's familiarity with ancient Buddhist stories popular across Asia. But Mergen Gegen's quirky spirit seems to have been more at home with literary shock tactics—to make the most homely objects the bearers of Buddhist ideas. In the poem above he plays with the similarity of *chag-a* (boiled sour milk) and *chag* (time). With his deliberately bizarre expression the "fruits of boiled sour milk" he is not afraid to index the "fruits of deeds" (*karma*), a link that is further implied by the explanatory reflections on the fruition of wisdom over time that interrupt the expected poetic parallels (spring/autumn) of plant life. The tamarisk that appears in his poem is a native of the semi deserts around Mergen and is credited by locals with the magical power to dispel evil spirits (Chapter 6). Here it appears as a metaphor for the gradual flowering of words spoken to enlighten people.

Cosmopolitan Choices in Imperial Space

How should we think about Mergen Gegen's achievements in relation to the imperial realm of Manchu China? Mergen Gegen was not—like so many poets confined inside empires of the early twentieth century—reaching for external revolutionary ideas with which to confront state-led injustice. His focus was inward: the people who should be reformed were not the Qing officials but his own disunited Mongol contemporaries, especially those local lords who were consumed with anger (*urin*) and pride (*omug*), such that they altogether forgot the magnanimity of the ancient khans (*AT1* 1970, 294, 341, fols. 17r and 40v). He was not, however, seeking to resurrect any Ashokan ideal of kingship. Rather—as we have seen—he combines two strange bedfellows, genealogy and Buddhist elevated liturgy, to provide a vision of a bracketed off space-time in the context of the Qing Empire.

It is significant that Mergen Gegen, like the other Mongol historians, does not dwell on the feature of Buddhism that had so frequently disturbed the Chinese state: its alternative vision of community. This consisted in principle of four groups, monks, nuns, with laymen and laywomen to provide (and provide for) them. From its first penetration of China, Buddhist monasticism had offended Confucian thought: the prioritizing of celibacy cut across the assumed integration of family/clan and the court, the homology of virtue whereby filial piety was applicable in both the personal and public spheres. Buddhist individualism, its ideas of charitable giving beyond kin, of encouraging women to religious goals rather than bearing sons, or forbidding clerics to bow to elder lay kin after ordination—all were anathema (Lu 2005, 97–100). Perhaps Mergen Gegen, surrounded by monks, thought that the idea of such a community did not require further advocacy; or perhaps he did not want to raise specters of the state's persecution of Buddhists in earlier dynasties. Whatever the reason, he praises patrilineal kinship in a way that could—just—be aligned with Confucian modes, but his real aim was quite different. It did not map the family onto the state. We argue that, although he could not ignore the politics of the empire, Mergen Gegen was engaged in an endeavor that was tangential to questions of government, for his goal was not power in the sense of *Realpolitik*, but cultural and moral autonomy.

Still, what made even this kind of autonomy a politically sensitive endeavor was, first, the fact that even the mighty Qing could never achieve blanket hegemony over Chinese society—the Qianlong emperor was apprehensive precisely over spiritual currents that might conceal treasonous thoughts. His policy encouraged Buddhism, the Tibetan variant especially, but at the same time he was suspicious and contemptuous of many actual monks (lazy, pretentious, sexually dubious), particularly the hordes of unofficial, nonregistered lamas. Anxiety about marginality was an important reason for Qianlong's insistence on regulation and inspection of monasteries and licensing of monks. In the 1760s, just as Mergen Gegen was writing his history, the emperor was presiding over a campaign to root out members of a secret Chinese messianic sect, suspected of being inspired by Buddhists and Daoists, that had, (in his mind) crept insidiously across the empire to reach close to Inner Mongolia. These "soul-stealers" were allegedly taking power from living people by clipping a little hair from their braids and then using it in paper fetishes to wreak harm (Kuhn 1990, 107–11). Local officials were ordered to discover miscreants—and some were punished with death. In such an atmosphere, all deviations from orthodox practice were noticed, including it seems at Mergen.[52]

A second danger in view of Mergen Gegen's glorification of the no-

52. Galluu (2003, 47–48) recounts an elaborate story of an imperial inspection of Mergen monastery in the fourteenth year of Eyeber Jasagchi [Shunzhi].

tional Hasarid confederation was the Oirad rebellion that had broken out in 1722–1724 in Höhnuur during his youth,[53] while far-flung military campaigns were still being launched to tie down the Zunghars (also Oirad) from 1733 to 1771 (Perdue 2005, 256–92). It was in this situation, where the splendid extravagant dynasty was presiding over inner dissension, as well as near and distant wars, that the Mongols—to all outward appearances fervently loyal—generated a literary renaissance. As our anthropological instincts tell us, Mergen could not have been absolutely alone; it is just that his contemporaries chose other solutions. A brief look at them is instructive.

In eighteenth-century Inner Mongolia there were at least two other literary giants among the lamas. One was Lubsangchültüm (1740–1810), known as the Chahar Gebshi, who wrote on philosophy, ethics, linguistics, law, history, biography, and medicine. His collected works are in Tibetan, but a few Mongol texts have survived too, among them prayers to local deities. Lubsangchültüm's monastery is known to have conducted certain prayers in Mongolian. The explanation was that a valuable text in Mongolian, the *Yüm*, had been brought to the monastery by an early reincarnation, and it was thought that disaster would ensue if it were not chanted. But it was relegated to services chanted by laymen (*hara bagshi*), while the main services were conducted in Tibetan. And although the *Yüm* was thought somehow to be necessary, conservative lamas criticized the practice, saying "Doctrine chanted by lay people brings no benefit," and this caused conflict with the laity (Lubsangchültüm 1983, 11). It is not known how long this dual chanting lasted, but it did not survive into the twentieth century. This is the classic case of superscription by the dominant language, along with relegation of the vernacular to the untended and unvalued. As with the services, Chahar Gebshi's most prestigious writing was in Tibetan. These were fully cosmopolitan works, broader in scope than those of Mergen Gegen, including a life of Tsongkhapa and historical studies on Tibetan monasteries and the Oirad conquests.

The second great Mongolian writer, Ishibaljur (T. Ye shes dpal 'byor), a reincarnation of Sumpa Khenpo (M. Sumba Hambo, T. Sumpa mKhan po, 1704–1788) did not write in Mongolian at all.[54] His works

53. A Mongol leader, Lubsangdanjin, angered that the Manchus did not ratify his control of the government in Lhasa, had revoked the use of Qing titles and declared himself Thunderbolt King (Wachir Khan) (Bulag 2002b, 32; Nietupski 2011, 9).

54. Ishibaljur was descended from a ruling family of the Baatud people, a section of the Oirads, and he lived in the Höhnuur region (Erdenibayar 2007, 304). People from this area, in-

include history, philosophy, medicine, mathematics, astronomy, geography, and ethnography, as well as important studies of Dandin's poetics, and he also left an unfinished autobiography on his death (Bira 1970, 14–32; Erdenibayar 2007). Ishibaljur wrote one of the first historiographical works by a Mongolian, containing a critique of sources and chronological systems, and an assessment of received ways of writing history (Bira 1970, 20–23). His description of the world[55] is exceptionally far-ranging, including places of pilgrimage in India, regions of China, Manchuria, Korea, Japan, elaborate descriptions of Bukhara, Samarkand, the Russian arctic, Sweden, and the mythic land of Shambhala. He even engages in discussions of economic life in Turkey and the advantages of Islam over having "no belief at all" (Bira 1970, 28–30; 1994: 195; Kapstein 2011). Ishibaljur's work is quintessentially cosmopolitan, striving as it does to accomplish its goals in high literary mode "pleasing to the ear and collated with the most authoritative works" (Bira 1970, 20). As an old man he wrote a history of Höhnuur, the lake of his homeland. This work emotionally describes the beauties of the region, its mountains, rivers, pools, and plants. It contains a long section about the unsuccessful Oirad uprising in 1722–1724 and provides details of the cruelty of the consequent repression, when six thousand people were killed, seventeen villages burned to the ground, and the great monastery of Gunlun, with twenty-five hundred lamas, completely destroyed (Bira 1970, 27). Ishibaljur's work was daring in a different way from Mergen's. By writing in Tibetan, he like Lubsangchültem conceded to the prevailing Lhasa-Qing axis, but he was also able to express his lack of subservience and give visibility to victims of state power (Erdenibayar 2007, 308).

Mergen Gegen, who wrote in Mongolian, does not mention the Oirad revolt at all. Evidently, there is also a politics of language here. For one thing, all three learned lamas avoid use of Chinese. The Mongolian scholar Bira provides an explanation: colonial subjection to the Qing Dynasty did not result in Mongolian cultural incorporation into the Manchu-Chinese world. Instead it drove them to look outward to the alternative religious authority of Tibet (Bira 1994, 269–70). Which-

cluding the Monguor, a small group with a distinctive dialect living in predominantly Tibetan cultural surroundings, often had an interlocutory role, and it was probably no accident that several of the eighteenth century's most distinguished multiculturalists were Monguor, including the famous Jangjia Gegen Rolpa Dorji (Rolbidorji) 1717–1786).

55. *General Description of the World ('Dzam-gling spyi-bshad)*, written in 1777 (Kapstein 2011, 342).

ever way we assess this opinion,[56] use of Tibetan implied a cosmopolitan scope, both in the wider geography the Mongols invoked and the transnational elite they addressed. But this is exactly the vision Mergen Gegen ignores. He is simply not interested in routes to foreign places or distant capital cities. His invocation of the *ulus*, at different scales, chooses "place" rather than "path" (Pollock 2000), and from the vast entity of the descendants of Hasar he homes in on (re-territorializes) the community at Urad. Rather than depict it as the benighted site of colonial suppression, he elevates it as a blessed, powerful place.

Comparing the works of these lamas, it is apparent that the choices they made among the tripartite-quadripartite relations of empire profoundly altered the character of the entity (or assemblage) they constituted as "Mongol." For Lubsangchültüm, the most orthodox of the three, the practice of superscription—the use of language politics to assign rank— relegated Mongolness to a lowly, local, and essentially lay sphere, while Tibetan was maintained for higher, spiritual and cosmopolitan relations. Ishibaljur, on the other hand, by using only the one (Tibetan) language was able to present a "horizontal" trans-local landscape, in which the mixed community of Höhnuur appears as a small place in the vast geography of the world. Warning his readers against seeing their own home as better than anywhere else, he is able to provide a realistic description of the terrible harm done it in war. Mergen Gegen adopts neither of these stances. His picture of Urad, if we take all of his works into account, involves both a loving embrace of particularities of place and an attempt to elevate them inspirationally to merge with the highest ideals of Buddhism. In all three writers we see different variants of what Bruno Latour has called the globalization of the local, where the macro should not be seen "as a *wider* or *larger* site, in which the micro would be embedded like a Russian matryoshka doll, but as another, equally local, equally micro place, which is *connected* to many others through some medium transporting specific types of traces" (2005a, 176–77). In Ishibaljur's geography this medium of the macro is his rendering of cities, routes, and distances. For Mergen Gegen, it is a kind of fractal cosmology that enables him to identify the local as an instance of centering.

56. Elverskog and Kapstein see little consciousness of colonial oppression among the Mongols and describe their political allegiance to the Manchu court as completely tied up with religious commitment to Tibetan Buddhism, since the court mandated such religious adherence (Elverskog 2006a, 124; Kapstein 2011, 342). Bira is correct that Mongols turned their backs on much of Chinese culture, but fails to take account of the numerous ways they were also excluded from it, most notably by being shut out of the examination system and hence from higher educational accomplishments in Chinese style.

"Fabulation" of a People to Come

Mergen Gegen saw all action as conditioned by precedents and understood his own creation as the fruit of the blessed Neichi Toin, whom he called the 2nd Tsongkhapa, the great initiator who of course also had precursors. Such a vision does not refer to the past as something that is over, but instead fashions it as a propulsive process towards what has yet to happen. We can refer here to Deleuze's discussion of the relationship of art with politics in his reflection on the "creation of a people"—the artist has a deep need of a people, but the collectivity invoked does not yet exist. Artists cannot themselves create a people, but–"When a people is created [*se crée*, 'creates itself'], it does so through its own means, but in a way that rejoins something in art. . . . or in such a way that art rejoins that which it lacks. Utopia is not a good concept: rather, there is a 'fabulation' common to the people and to art" (Deleuze, interview in 1990, quoted in Bogue 2007, 91). Deleuze's fabulation—the co-creation of haunting images that imitate perception and thereby induce action—is a productive idea; and in our case it can apply to the works of "Mergen Gegen," especially if we remember their jointly created character mentioned at the beginning of this chapter.

So how was Mergen Gegen engaged in the fabulation of a people yet to come? The specific traces of *derivation* are the first of his tools. The idea that source was a necessary condition for the result, had priority, and thus was seen as better and more sacred, was common to all Mongol writing of his time.[57] Chronicles, genealogies, religious biographies all recorded the seniority of ancestors over descendants, early saints over present-day ones, teachers over disciples, fathers over sons, older brothers over younger. Key concepts of ancestry (such as origin, birth, root, stem, and genesis) crossed over into the religious domain such that they also become a foundational ontology for gods, spells, and great lamas. Thus we find the notions of the root (*ündüsün*) lama, "mother" (*eh*) texts, kin-origin (*ug*) mantras, and "mother" and "father" gods. Mergen Gegen in his history of the world describes birth-by-reincarnation (*hubilugad törübei*) as superior and happening first, later giving way to birth-through-

57. Gombojab's *Flow of the Ganges* ([1725] 1960) and Lomi's *History of the Mongol Borjigin Lineage* (1732–1733) create a similar "genealogical" effect to Mergen's, but concern the Chinggisids rather than the Hasarids. However, we should beware of assuming uniformity. The Urad lama Dambadorji's history *Crystal Mirror* (1835–1838) eschews genealogy and instead he devotes the great majority of his book to a racy account of events, intrigues, and battles (Zheleznyakov and Tsendina 2005, 62–154).

human wombs (*umai-eche törübei*), but the important point is that they are both conceptualized through the word *törühü*—to originate or be born (*AT1* 1970, 271, fol. 5v). Such ideas give meaning to any position in a vast scenario of before and after and, furthermore, color any particular point with the notion of incompletion—for in the Buddhistic imagination any action tends teleologically towards an *as yet unrealized fulfillment*.

Another of Mergen Gegen's techniques was *directional spatialization* based on the perspective of "I/we." The grand finale of *Altan Tobchi* integrates human geographies in cosmographical schema. He used an idea found in many Mongol chronicles from the sixteenth century onward expressed by the formula "the five coloreds and the four foreign." This denoted, it seems, the five peoples closely integrated into the Mongol Empire and the four outside peoples with whom they had relations. Much ink has been spilled over the question of exactly what the phrase refers to, but a widespread view is that the "five coloreds" are the Mongols (blue), the Chinese (red), the Sartaul (Central Asian Muslims, yellow), the Koreans (white), and the Tibetans (black), while the "four foreign" have more varied ethnic constituents (Baldanzhapov and Vanchikova 2001, 85).[58] What Mergen Gegen did was to take this ethnic geography and transform it into a grand multidimensional schema that is at once a politics, a moral cosmology, and a specification of who "we" are. In *AT1* 1970, 365, fol. 52v, the five coloreds are clearly meant as peoples, since Mergen writes that, united under one government (*törü*), they require works on military arts and religious learning. Later, he says that these same five coloreds "are" the five moral qualities of compassion (*örüsiyel*), order (*jirum*), customary law (*yosu*), wisdom (*mergen*), and firmness (*batu*). Next he takes the macro-micro step, declaring that if the expression "five colored and four foreign" is taken in its wide sense it refers to the structure of all and every world (*hamug ele yirtinchü-yin togtagal*), and if it is taken in its narrow sense it means the qualities of one human body (*nigen bey-e-yin ahu chinar*).[59] He then ties the "five moral qualities" to the schema of "elements" (M. *mahabud*)[60],

58. Ishibaljur uses a similar scheme of four directions (Tibet and India to the south, China to the east, a country called Tazig to the west, and the land of Gesar to the north) surrounding his own Oirad parentage in the center (Erdenibayar 2007, 304–05).

59. Mergen adds that if this expression is related to the direction of the state (*törü-yin jüg*), then it means the simultaneous mastery of military affairs and writing, and if it relates to the direction of doctrine (*nom-un jüg*) then it means the study of holy books and mantras (*AT1* 1970, 366, 53r).

60. From the Sanskrit *mahābhūta*, the "four great elements" (water, fire, earth, and air), or the body conceived as an aggregate of elements. The "five elements" (*wu-xing*) occur in Chinese philosophy and astrology, being metal, water, fire, wood, and earth.

well known all over Asia from ancient times as water, wood, fire, iron, and earth. Now these "five elements" are also directional, water being in the North, wood in the East, fire in the South, iron in the West, and earth in the center. Mongols, who know this last scheme backwards even today,[61] would instantly see that the Mergen Gegen's construction would identify the Mongols with "blue" and "earth." Finally, Mergen lines up the elements with the moral qualities and describes their interrelations: wood (compassion, the World Tree) is soft and gives way to iron (custom), which is hard; fire (order or rule) being hot is opposed by water (wisdom), which is cold,[62] and he emphasizes that only *one* element, earth (firmness, honesty, strength, loyalty *batu*) is useful to all and has no opponents (*hari ügei*) (*AT1* 1970, 366, fol. 53r). He does not say, but his readers would easily conclude that this is what he means, that the Mongols with their quality of *batu* stand in this central integrating position. At the same time, taking the micro-position where the schema stands for the human body, he is saying that *batu* is the supreme moral quality for each person—perhaps not the most Buddhist thought, but one which recurs frequently in Mergen's songs. Now the various systems employed here are each separately well known in Mongol culture, but this dense concatenation of peoples, directions, physical elements, and moral qualities is Mergen's own. It is he also who ties this complex structure, itself timeless, to *derivation-production*. For he stresses that each of the moral qualities is a type of wisdom (*belge bilig*) that was taught by great (magically empowered, marvelous) people of the past, whom he and everyone else should seek to emulate.

It is significant that the very last paragraph of the 1942 [1998b, 187] edition of *Altan Tobchi*, a section added in the nineteenth century after Mergen's death, continues this thought but with a more clearly "national" cast than his own writing. "Mergen Gegen" here calls for the "extraordinary Mongol religion" to spread at all times—a most provocative expression, for the Mongols were not supposed to have their own religion separate from the Tibetans.

61. Mongols literally know the scheme of elements backward, counting it on their fingers, since it is very popularly used in divination, where it is elaborated into a scheme of the "eight seats" of the eight cardinal directions to predict people's fortune according to their birth date. Boys are born in the Fire Seat and count clockwise year by year to reckon their seats over the next seven years, while girls are born in the Water Seat and then count backwards (counter-clockwise). In this operation an individual's "good" and "bad" directions change year by year, until they reprise the sequence after eight years.

62. Mergen calls these four mutually oppositional elements the "four foreign (*dörben hari*)," and comments that when they are matched in strength the result is *arga bilig* (the interdependence of contradictory forces, literally "means and intellect," Ch. *yin yang*), (*AT1* 1970, 366, fol. 53r).

Nineteenth-century scribes may have strengthened the national cast of Mergen's book, but his own view was already Mongol-centric and we can now relate it to our earlier discussion of empire. His scheme was a daring response both to Mongol non-integration and to the political culture that faced him—the colossal, thousand-year-old centricity of the Chinese state, *zhong guo*—the Middle Kingdom. We are reminded here of Daniel Richter's *Facing East from Indian Country* (2001), in which the hegemonic white-settler gaze directed to the west is reversed, to provide a perspective from alterity, through a native-based history of early America. Mergen's vision, however, shows that alterity need not be imagined in binary terms: there can be a construction that asserts autonomy without proposing one single alter. Mergen proposes a centric model that addressed eight directions (i.e., all directions) and in this he was following Sanskritic prototypes, for the formal numerical topology of five and four employed by Mergen Gegen associates his scheme with the ancient Asian *mandala*, the concentric diagram that establishes sacred space, or acts as the emplacement for a god or king.[63]

Mergen's densely-correlated scheme is always more than a political claim. His vision of community consisted both of *essence*, where his writing of derivation and genealogy created the parameters for an inherited identity, and of *exposure*, the reactive turning outward to the other. In this sense he is playing not only with macro and micro (the universe and the human body) but also with community defined as interiority and opened out as externality. We see this "opening out" in the idea that the defining element—earth in the case of the Mongols—is conceived as only one of the substances of the world, intrinsically related to, exposed to, and interacting with other such elements. Because the idea of the five elements, like so many of the schemes he takes up, can operate in a fractal way at different scales, Mergen Gegen can also say that each individual Mongol person (and "the Mongols") is not

63. It is well known that north Asian polities in general, including the Manchu Empire itself, have constantly called upon the *mandala* as a model of centric rule (Geertz 1980; Tambiah 1976; Hevia 1995) and Buddhist ritual agency over land (Makley 2007, 63–67). Recent work on Mongolia has pointed out that the *mandala* is not just a retrospective claim. The *mandala* can be deployed and *planted* anywhere. Thus, it can have an innovative political character as a religious paradigm to situate arriving communities within new territorial domains or to map out a Buddhist landscape in a wilderness (Pedersen 2007). Elverskog has argued that already in the sixteenth century Altan Khan had used the *mandala* as a technique in the Buddhist conversion of the Mongols, it being "the mesocosmic template between real landscapes, both geographical and political." He suggests that mandalization not only helped to reformulate the Mongol Ulus into competing smaller *ulus* units, but also erased earlier Chinggisid legends and cults of the land (2006b, 113–14). Mergen Gegen, by contrast, embraced his own interpretation of local legends and cults into the scheme; see Chapter 3.

just identified with one element but should have all five moral qualities (implicitly, so should all human beings, *AT1* 1970,170, fol. 52r). In sum, he was drawing together various cultural strands into a transformational system of *truth creation* for his people. Very different from Confucian family-state models, this was a vision that was at once open and finite, that by its mandala-like structure harkened to tantric techniques of self-awakening[64] and at the same time proposed the idea of a specifically Mongol ethic in which it was possible to be a morally aware subject. It was up to each individual to enact this truth: "Uprightness was firmly founded on [the basis of] the order, custom and wisdom established by the supreme root. Know about this! [But] what any epoch becomes is up to the present inclination (*ayas*) of that time. Although they say it is the result of people's previous deeds, surely it is explained logically by what kind of thing a person does [now]" (*AT1* 1970, 170, fol. 53v). The last sentence of the book (1998 edition) ends with a vow-wish, as it were to bring into existence "we Mongols," calling on them to: ". . . change behavior, which has been so terrible and beset with bad omens. May each individual (*bodgali*) with the help of writing [i.e., this book] be confirmed in modesty-shame (*ichil*) and becomes the solid container of truth and integrity" (*AT2* 1998b, 94).

The Mongol language and indeed the arts of language were necessary to such an endeavor: one can do ritual in a language that is not one's own, one can pray to gods, call down rain and ward off evil spirits. But it is not possible to inspire a moral regeneration without the resonant words that speak to people of the "good" and "bad" things they heard about in childhood and know in themselves. The arts of language were techniques that linked these ordinary Mongol words in formal ways and impelled people to think of their relations with one another. In effect Mergen Gegen was a creative sculptor of words and maker of a new meaningful cultural space. His creation—in complex ways and notwithstanding its vulnerability—is still crucially important to the lamas of the monastery.

Present-Day Lamas Inhabit Mergen Gegen's Vision

We end this chapter by trying to explain how contemporary monks can be invested in Mergen Gegen's vision, or to put it in another way,

64. For an excellent discussion of "regimes of truth" in relation to tantric practice and the particular technique of the *mandala*, see Mills 2003, 107–24.

can be the subjects of its truth perspective. These are the people who take part in re-producing the songs, poems, rites, and stories attributed to the great lama. Roland Bogue's essay on Deleuze's idea of fabulation describes how, according to his collaborator Guattari, the "group subject" (unlike the "subjected group," which receives its identity from outside and struggles against such inscriptions) forms itself from inside and keeps itself open: "All investment of desire is social and . . . always concerns a social historical field. The desiring subject here passes through a series of intensive states and identifies the "names of history" with those states: *"All the names of history are me"* (Bogue 2007, 97, quoting *Anti-Oedipus* 1977, 21). Deleuze's idea of the hallucinating, fabulation-creating subject "who raves universal history" is too tempting to ignore. So we finish this chapter by describing a "history" (fabulation) told us by the monks, which places them within the world of Mergen Gegen. If the lamas of today are not "the people to come" dreamed of by the eighteenth-century Mergen Gegen, they are nevertheless his people by virtue of—to the extent that—they identity with the vision of the world they attribute to the great founder.

Sometime in the early 1990s Sengge Lama and a respected local herder called Shiraotgun rolled with some effort a large round stone several hundred yards from near the gate of the army compound to a prominent spot in the square in front of the Fierce Deity Temple. [65] It should be remembered that the monastery faces south, looking over the great highway (the "south road") running east to west, from Beijing to Tibet. In Sengge Lama's words:

That round stone lying in front of the Fierce Deity Temple, it arrived by means of a curse (*hariyal*) from the Western Land [Tibet]. One day our 3rd Mergen Gegen Lubsangdambijalsan was sitting in his palace and he told his fierce oracle (*dogshin gürtüm*) to go into a trance. The prayer was chanted for the oracle to become mad (*galjagu*). "Go quick, on the south road there is a stone rolling along, hit it and take it!" said Mergen Gegen. The oracle was in a trance and rushed there, along with one person beating the drum and one the cymbals, but he ran so fast they couldn't catch up with him. The road was not a highway like it is today, but just an ox cart road. Along it the round stone was bowling fast towards the east, all by itself. It was bringing disaster. The oracle chopped it with his sword and made a mark on its side. That mark was very clear in the past, but now it is getting worn. Our teachers told me that the stone was caught then, and brought back to the monastery by beating

65. This story was related to us several times. Other versions are found in Mönghe 1996, 124–27 and Galluu 2003, 741–44.

it. Our Oracle Temple used to stand over there, southeast of the building where you are living. The oracle brought the round stone to the door, and ordered, "You sit here!" and that way he made it stay and it couldn't move. Where was the round stone going? A lama from the east (Inner Mongolia) had gone to Lhasa to study and debate doctrine—and he silenced the Tibetans monks. They couldn't answer him in the debates. That's why they made a curse-stone. They sent it at the time of the 3rd Mergen Gegen to punish the people of the east [i.e., the Mongols].

It stayed put until the Cultural Revolution—and then the stone started to move again. It went into the courtyard and rolled here and there. It was so frightening. Where would it go? In the end, it stopped to the west just inside the army gate. But people didn't recognize it among all the other stones and rubble. Later, when the lamas took back the monastery, people remembered it and asked where it was, and someone told them it was there. Then Shiraotgun and I brought it back by rolling it, and put it beside the censer in front of the Fierce Deity Temple.

When you looked at it by day, it was there. But one day an oracle from another monastery came and said, "Your stone is rolling around the monastery." When I looked again I saw it had moved to the south. It was evading us! Luckily, our lamas, there were about thirty of them then, found the invocation for the oracle's guardian deity (*sahigusu*). They chanted that book and since then the stone has stayed still. It has become peaceable (*nomuhan*). If you go and look you'll see the mark of the sword. That mark is there. This is not a lie. That is not a stone from around here. It came from the land of Black Tibet. Yes.

It is difficult to deny a certain hallucinatory quality to this narrative. Yet it makes sense as soon as one pictures its positional features: located in the middle, between the west land (Tibet) and the east land (eastern Inner Mongolia), the Mergen Gegen and his fierce *gürtüm* heroically stop the dangerous curse sent by the Tibetans to punish the Mongols. Threat and foreboding are embodied in the stone. It is subdued, but starts its disturbances again during the Cultural Revolution, when the Mongols are again under attack. But in the end it is once again pacified, this time by means of the monks' chanting. It had to be moved from its dangerously marginal place by the gate to the very center of the precinct under the eye of the Fierce Gods to be kept under control—and by this action, Sengge gave us to understand, the monks of Mergen are bravely saving the other Mongols. They are doing exactly what Mergen Gegen did (stopping the stone), taking history upon themselves (as he did), and in effect they are *living-acting* as subjects of his world.

THREE

Mergen Monastery and Its Landscape

The Mongolian monastery was rarely a place of ancient permanence and seclusion. Often it was a hub, a crossroads and an exchange for the surrounding life—that of scattered herders, farmers, officials, and traders—and in the process functions were added or subtracted and layouts changed. A monastery was a crucible for the preoccupations of these people as well as the lamas. Particularly important in a mobile society was "gathering"—bringing together reincarnations and disciples, but also rents and taxes, lay worshippers, flocks, grains, donations, trade and festivity. The very word for a religious service, *hural*, means assembled gathering.

Another key idea is "sheltering" (encircling, protecting) something or someone precious. One of the words for monastery in Mongolian is *hüriye* (enclosure, precinct). The built form can be seen as a vessel, and the temples, pagodas, shrines, etc., of a monastery as the housing of sacred items. In monasteries we also find a sense of the holy that arises from a hiatus or still point in movements and practical engagements (Humphrey 1995). The sacred in this sense could only be groped for and half-contained, and it drove certain ineluctable, unpredictable orientations. So what we shall attempt to describe here is the monastery as an ongoing, unfinished product that embodies a tension between the processes generated by a way of life in given historical circumstances, and certain orientations towards transcendence that would point beyond those processes and might disrupt them.

When we arrived at Mergen in 1998 there were gaping vacancies in the administrative structure of the monastery—there was no abbot (Da Lama) and only two of the seven reincarnations were filled. The lamas seemed to be dwelling haphazardly among the many empty or semi-ruined buildings. This was a peaceful year, when the monks were in good accord and the regular summer rituals took place according to schedule. Jongrai Lama, the bursar, chugged on his motorbike between the monastery and the straggling village of Two Wells to buy provisions. Herders came to collect Sengge Lama for rituals at their homes, and he would flash by riding pillion, with a brilliant smile and wave of the hand. In fact our first agreeable impression of the casualness of monastic life was not correct. We learned that what the lamas did, and how and where they lived was carefully considered. To understand why the monks held such firm ideas about their place in the scheme of things it first has to be understood that the main subjects of "gathering" and "sheltering" were the lamas themselves, considered not just as people engaged in religious activities but also—especially the reincarnations—as sacred objects of worship.

Since the lamas were primary in the entire complex of people, buildings, sacred mountain, springs, worshipped objects, pagodas, and so forth that made up the monastery, we first outline their changeable matrix of relations. Subsequently, we describe the founding and history of Mergen, which will illuminate the processes of gathering, housing, and dispersal and also lead to observations about Mongolian understandings of monastic life. The second half of the chapter deals with the local sense of sacred and occult forces, and the way in which the monastery is held to be a subject of fortune caught amongst them.

The Monastery as a Complex of Relations

Among the monks there are two vital streams of relationships, the teaching of the doctrines, prayers, and communal rituals, all of which link guru and disciple monks in face-to-face contact, and the lines of reincarnations (*hubilgan*), in which the incumbents succeed one another without ever meeting.

Until the mid-nineteenth century there were seven reincarnation lines at the monastery—Mergen Gegen, Baragun Da (Western Great),

Chorji, Güüshi, Emchi, Hubilgan Lamahai and Shirege[1]—and most of these lineages persisted into modern times. Dominant over any other lamas, their coexistence was at once necessary to the reproduction of the tradition and a source of instability. Each was distinctively charismatic, and each line maintained its own establishment distinct from the management of the monastery as a whole. At no point were the *hubilgans* imagined as a collectivity and they were rarely all present at the same time. Yet each of them was more religiously powerful than any monastery official, such as the abbot, and this gave the institution as a whole a curiously contingent character, dependent on the variable spiritual and human relations among these people. In addition there was until the 1930s an oracle-magician (*gürtüm*) at Mergen, an ambiguous figure, not considered to be a true lama, who could become possessed by a *choijong* deity and utter predictions while in a trance. The *gürtüm*'s prophecies and miracles can be seen as an attempt to penetrate, pin down, and direct the numerous uncertainties and dangers affecting the monastery and its clientele.[2]

The 3rd Mergen Gegen wrote five texts concerning the "management of inner harmony" in the monastery. These include statutes defining ranks and offices, an exacting list of services to be performed (Chapter 11), the seating at services that would mark precedence, and the rights, duties, and punishments of the lamas. Yet the total effect was far from systematic. He mentions a reincarnation only once, and his codes therefore do not deal with the main cause of instability. There are two

1. An eighth lineage, the Rasang Lama line, is described by Galdanwangchugdorji ([1846] 1994, 208) but this did not survive into the twentieth century.

2. Old lamas at Mergen said they saw with their own eyes how the *gürtüm* conducted healing rituals using a sword. He first made an offering to a fierce deity, which was done by slitting his tongue with the sword, receiving grains of millet or rice from an assistant, blowing blood onto the grains in his palm, and throwing them toward the god. After this, the lamas would chant a text that brought the *gürtüm* into full trance, his tongue would become whole again, and in this state he conducted skillful operations on patients—cutting them, then blowing on the wound, which would then heal. The patients were too terrified to feel pain. The *gürtüm* also helped in the "throwing the *sor*" rites, by going first to the place and "taming" the *sor* before a lama threw it. He also did this while in trance, stabbing the *sor* repeatedly with his sword. Lama maintained the *gürtüm* in trance by beating drums and cymbals and by chanting, imploring the deity to stay in possession of the oracle. The *gürtüm* performed divinations, following which he would instruct patients to undertake reparative rites, such the "washing the face," repelling evil, or making a reliance-promise (*dagatgal*) to a Buddha. The *gürtüm* of Dabaga monastery was a rather foolish man, and certainly not learned in Buddhism, we were told, but when he was in trance what he said was "very special, always correct." During the 1930s civil war, the nobles would frequently ask him to divine from which direction and at what time an enemy would come; about that year's rains, and coming disasters for livestock and people. After this *gürtüm* was killed, no further oracle was appointed in the area.

points to be made here: first, that the existence of statutes contributed to the sense in which the monastery was a "society," providing reference points about conduct to which lamas could refer based on Mergen Gegen's version of the ancient Indian Vinaya code for monastic communities. Second, however, that the codes radically underdetermined the actual social dynamics. As was the case elsewhere in the Mahayana world (Mills 2003, 25), the *combination* of "clerical" statute-based Buddhism with the inspirational effects of tantric practices, not to speak of the wayward personal charisma of the reincarnations, was inherently heterogeneous and changeful. In the proverbial phrase, "gathering" here must have been something like herding cats.

For one thing, the monks, especially the reincarnations, were highly mobile. Lamas spent much of their time visiting other monasteries, sometimes for years. Some prominent reincarnations had establishments in more than one monastery, they readily accepted calls to conduct rituals in other seats of religion, and they seem to have enjoyed chances to travel and give blessings to new groups of people. Invitations from shifting herding populations afforded the high lamas an ever-present field of possibility. One outcome was the propagation by Mergen Monastery of numerous small "subject" (*hariyatu*) monasteries. People told us, in that systematizing way of speaking that so easily misleads the unwary, that there had been twenty-four of them and that they comprised all the monasteries of the Urad West Banner. Actually the situation was more patchy and fluid. At one time or another there were at least thirty subject monasteries, including some located outside the Banner, in one case hundreds of miles away. Mergen reincarnations and lamas maintained links with these outliers,[3] gathered monks from them for important ceremonies, and could also move there if they so wanted.

For such reasons, in the prayer halls of Inner Mongolia there is the phenomenon of the "empty chair," the seat waiting for its incumbent and perhaps unused for decades. Thus, temples often have an expectant—or a bereft—quality, depending on one's point of view. They were marked by absence, being places from which someone had gone, or to which someone might be coming back, but still imbued with something of that person's sanctity. Rebecca Empson's research on householder life among herding people shows that this tension between absence and presence is characteristic of Mongolian life more generally.

3. The *hariyatu* monasteries were subject to one or another reincarnation's establishment rather than to the monastery as a whole.

Indeed, she discusses (2007) a kinship based on separation and notes how a positive tie of absence affects many aspects of social life. Certainly such distance-spanning relations at Mergen were resilient, and the lamas did not cease to be "Mergen lamas" just because they were not there.

The monastic complex was made up, however, not just of lamas, but also of the buildings, lay serfs, economically useful land, statues, pagodas (stupas) and relics, meditation caves, and the sacred sites that dotted the landscape. To set up auspicious conditions for using land, for example for grazing, taking wood or water, burying someone, or building a house, people take account of the lay of the land and make offerings to land gods, which are seen as powerful and willful. The main land deity for the Mergen area was Muna Khan, lord of the mountains, and we explain the monastery's relations with this deity in Chapter 5. Here we note only that Muna Mountain had a double presence: it was conceptualized both as the protector deity (*sahius*) of the monastery in a local geography, a source of (non-Buddhist) fortune, and it was also seen in the image of Mount Sümer [S. *sumeru*], the eternal cosmic center of the world. The monastery had a similar dual existence: as a large user of land it had to engage in local relations with both mundane and land-god powers and at the same time being a Buddhist institution housing many emanations of holiness, it can be understood as a cosmological subject in relation to the general conditions of auspiciousness and inauspiciousness obtaining at given times.

It is in this context that we discuss the foundation of the monastery, which is directly related to the kind of institution people thought it was. There are two quite different versions of its origin. They can be seen as figure-ground reversals, each supplying a radically alternative view of the monastery as a relational object. The starting date, place, and founder(s)—are all open to question. This is not only a disagreement over the facts of what happened, but also a question of what counts as a place of origin or a founder according to different viewpoints—indeed a question of what the monastery is.

The Implications of Foundation Stories

According to Inner Mongolian historians, the very first Mergen monastery was an establishment at Hairatu, by the Yellow River, built in 1677 by Duke Nomun, who had been converted to Buddhism by the Neichi Toin. This monastery was built for the 1st Mergen Gegen, and called "Mergen" after him. From 1701 to1703, Nomun's grandson Darmashiri, the 7th Duke and descendant in the 24th generation from Hasar, built a larger and more glorious monastery at the present site. He invited the 2nd Mergen Gegen to take up residence in the new establishment, which consequently became known as Mergen Monastery and received a title from the Manchu emperor.[4] The old monastery at Hairatu became the personal worshipping place of the dukes and was renamed Güng-ün Süme, "monastery of the dukes," (Buyanbadarahu 1987, 20–22; Mönghe 1995, 91–94; Ujeed 2009, 96–97) Mergen grew is size and importance. In 1772 the Manchu administration undertook its support and over one hundred officially registered lamas began to receive an allowance from the court. In this lay-written history, it was dukes, princes, and emperors who built monasteries, found lamas to occupy them, and then with plentiful detail about the amount of silver, etc., involved, financed the provision of deity statues, pagodas, monks' salaries, and *oboo* shrines.

The lamas of Mergen, however, have a quite different version according to which it is monks and the land, with its mysterious presences, that have priority. Dukes are not mentioned. Three holy lamas, Chorji (Master of the Law), Baragun Da (West Great), and Lamahai (Respected Lama), it is said, were wandering near the Muna Mountains looking for an auspicious site. They made offerings to the ten directions, dug a hole, and buried a golden offering cup. Continuously chanting prayers, they waited for a sign. Out of the pastures there appeared an old herding couple, the husband called Mergen (Wise) and the wife called Egeshig (Melody). These people made an offering of milk to the ten directions, bowed to the lamas, and received blessing from them. The lamas asked, "What is the respected elder's name? How old are you?" The old man said, "My name is Wise and this year I am a hundred and eight years old." Hearing this, the lamas were very pleased, and said this was a good omen for the development of Buddhism and benefit to all sentient beings. Explaining their idea to found a monastery, they proposed, "Let's together examine and find the good place." The couple went back home happily, and the old man gave a single chopstick to his wife and said, "Examine the place where it would be fortunate to build a monastery." Old Woman Melody went out to the pasture and stuck the chopstick in the ground—and it was the very place where the

4. In the forty-first year of Kangxi (1702) the Qing court offered Mergen the title *Guangfa Si* (*Shajin-i Badaragulugchi Heid* "Spreading Religion Monastery") (Choiji 1994, 62; Zhang Mu ([1867] 1982).

golden cup was buried. Joyfully, the three lamas decided to found a monastery there. They built the monastery and gave it the name "Mergen" (Galluu 2003, 19–20).

Several people told us versions of this story, and for them it was not just a legend, but true and consequential. The Mergen monks, we were told, later examined the old couple and divined that the man was one of the emanations (*hubilgan düri*) of Manjushiri and the woman was an emanation of the Goddess of Melody, Egeshig-ün Öhin Tngri. Nevertheless, they were members of society too. Old Man Mergen belonged to the aristocratic Haranuud clan. His descendant Batutai had no sons, and this made the monks anxious. Why? Because in synchronistic thinking the fate of the descent-line of Old Man Mergen was assumed to parallel that of the monastery: if one died out, the other would too. So an adopted son, Ulagan, was found for Batutai. Today Ulagan's grandson is a poor herder named Shirahulu living in East Debeseg village. Shirahulu's wife told us that lamas often come to visit to exhort him to worship at the monastery, because it was his ancestor who had divined the site. This whole line of reasoning shows that people can imagine Old Man Mergen as a real person whose spiritual force lingers on through his descendants.[5]

This is why the pointing to the *auspicious place*, with its mysterious deities who are at the same time elderly married herders, is the key to this perspective. This story reverses the scene of the historical account, whereby monasteries are meritorious good works which can only be kept going by the devotion of wealthy lay patrons. Here it is the three holy lamas who are the initiators, while the old couple are not patrons but deities of the blessed place. The herder who points with her chopstick is like an index of the pastoral household stopping its movement and making a camp—a camp whose fire becomes the singular sacred point linked to Sky/Heaven by the vertical of smoke and prayers (Humphrey 1995). The story foregrounds the happy conjunction of the lamas' choice of such a spot and the old woman's pointing. As if only by being sited here, the monastery houses and protects auspiciousness and becomes an holy place.

It is intriguing that this story also grounds an ongoing social division among the reincarnations. Lamas told us that within living memory the monastery was divided into two notional precincts (*hüriye*),

5. The deeper tension revealed by this legend relates to a theme common in the Mahayana world: the monks cannot found the monastery on their own, they require the validation of the married couple to locate the sacred space, and yet such a couple cannot reside there (see Mills 2003, 278–79).

the East and the West. The compounds of the three founding lamas, each of whom was to initiate a reincarnation line, formed the East section, while Mergen and the other three reincarnations constituted the senior Western part. Furthermore, Galluu's account attributes an ethnic distinction to the three founders: they were not Urads but Tümed Mongols and, significantly, their patrons and worshippers came from Tümed lands. Although many subsequent reincarnations in these lineages were Urads, the attribution of an original difference is significant. There is considerable mutual suspicion between people of different ethnic-regional groups in Inner Mongolia, and we shall see that external, non-Urad support for certain reincarnations (but not others) has been a factor in splits within the monastery throughout its history.

Galluu's account of how Mergen Gegen was invited to the monastery is also instructive, since it suggests an endemic disorder among the monks that only a paramount leader could overcome. "The three holy lamas through their merit in founding a monastery received Buddha's sanctity (*burhan-u hutug*) meaning that they had entered the path to enlightenment and therefore would be reincarnated. However, though they tried hard, the activities of the monastery were not successful. They acquired many disciples, but Mergen was not a monastery just a monastic meeting-place. Many monks, if they came to a service, would not come again. Some of the disciples, expecting good fortune and being overeager, crowded and pulled and pushed one another. In the end, the situation was understood—they were lacking a wise central leader of the monastery, a decoration of the Wachirdara peak, a Gegen with high merit. The mass of monks agreed to invite such a Gegen, sent an appeal with a gift to Neichi Toin, and he allocated the first Mergen Dinuwa" (Galluu 2003, 23–24). Gegen ("light, splendor, brilliance") is a title equivalent to "Serene Holiness," accorded only to the highest incarnations.

The 3rd Mergen Gegen's own description of the founding integrates these accounts and shows considerable political astuteness. "In the land subject to Muna Mountain," he wrote, "before building the well-known Mergen Monastery, [there was] the sign of the existence of Merged (wise people), in that a person called Mergen made [this land] his home." Next he describes the religious feeling (*süsüg sedhil*) of Duke Darmashiri, who founded the monastery. It is interesting that he also gives a political reason for that act, which was aimed "especially to promote the Manjushiri Bogd Ejen's [the Manchu Emperor's] ten thousand good fortunes." Although in his account it is the duke and not the three lamas who was the founder, the Gegen makes a point of tactfully

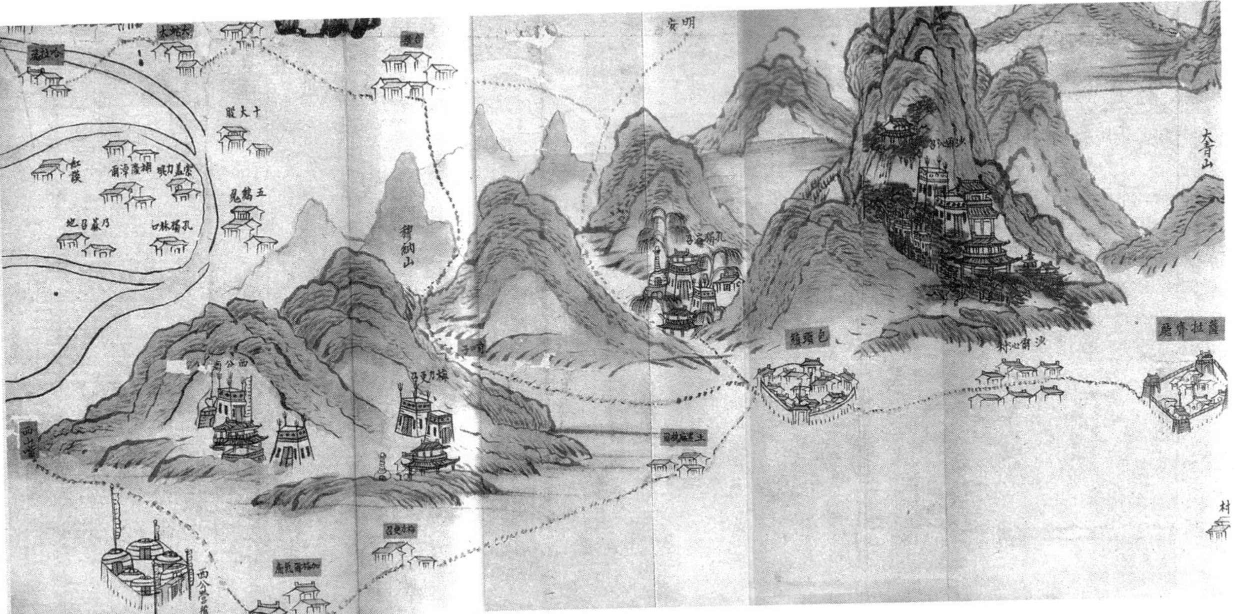

3 Eighteenth-century map of the Urad area showing the Muna Mountains. The camp of the Duke of the West Banner is located at bottom left. The monasteries, from left to right, are: Güng Monastery, Mergen Monastery, Hündülen Monastery in the mountains, and the large Sarchin Monastery to the right. To the far left is a mark indicating the town of Qianqi (C. Xishanzui). The walled city of Baotou lies in front, between Hündülnen and Sarchin Monasteries. Shar Oroi (C. Muna Shan) Mountain is shown clearly behind Mergen.

praising the leadership of the learned and wise first Chorji, who was his own teacher (*BJ* [1780–1783] 1998, vol. 1, text 14). This account, we can now see, covers all the bases. It is significant, however, that he starts with an idea that comes right out of the pastoral nomadic culture, the auspicious land subject to the mountain (*muna agula-yin hariyatu gajar*).

The Organization and Economy of the Monastery

Historians agree that the monastery was at its strongest in the mid-eighteenth century during the heyday of the 3rd Mergen Gegen. At its most prosperous it had around five hundred lamas, of which approximately a hundred had official registration with the Qing administration (Choiji 1994, 62), though Galluu writes, based on the Brown Book, that there were around fifteen hundred monks in Mergen in the mid-eighteenth century (2003, 1074). If the latter figure is correct, Mergen would have been a large monastery by Inner Mongolian standards, though by no means the largest, and considerably smaller than several monasteries in Tibet.[6] By "Liberation" in 1949, Mergen had only around sixty lamas.

The 3rd Mergen Gegen's internal regulations[7] were written at the request of senior lamas and seem to have been independent of any other authority. According to them, the whole jurisdiction under Mergen Monastery was divided into four sections called *aimag*, each with its own administrative hierarchy, and all monks belonged to one of these.[8] But the four sections, if they were ever implemented, did not survive and were supplanted by the division into the two camps of the reincarnations' more anarchic establishments mentioned earlier (which suggests that the lamas' story of the founding may be a late version). What follows, is a description of the situation in the early nineteenth century and thereafter.

The singularity of each monastery in Mongol realms makes them confusing places to study, because each deployed its own hierarchical

6. Miller (1959, 15–16) classifies "very small" monasteries as having up to a hundred lamas, "small" ones 100–299 lamas, "medium ones" 300–670 lamas, and "large" ones having numbers up to a thousand and beyond. By contrast, Drepung Monastery near Lhasa had around ten thousand monks just before the Communist takeover (Goldstein 1998, 24).

7. *BJ* 1780–1783, vol. 1: 21r-25r and 53r-76v.

8. This organization was similar to that of certain other great Mongol monasteries (Pozdneyev [1892] 1971, 303).

arrangement of a number of commonly known offices (Miller 1959, 50–63). In nineteenth century Mergen the hierarchy of offices for the monastery, apart from the reincarnations, comprised the Da Lama, who was the overall administrator; the chair lama (*Shirege Lama*), who supervised religious services; the senior and junior proctors (*Gebhüi*[9]), responsible for discipline of the monks; and the leader of chanting (*Umjad*). The common monastery treasuries and the seven reincarnations' estates each had one or two bursars (*Demchi*), an accountant (*Nirba*), and a negotiator (*Ombu*) to count herds, collect taxes, and buy and sell goods.

This may seem straightforward, but the articulation of the communal posts with the reincarnations is anything but. The names of the reincarnations are surely significant. Two of the reincarnations were called by the same words (Da and Shirege) as administrative posts, two by titles (Chorji, "Master of Religious Law" and Hubilgan Lamahai, "Respected Teacher Reincarnation"), while the others were named by monastic specializations (Güüshi, "translator," and Emchi "doctor"). Now it is clear that by the nineteenth century the reincarnation lines were separate from such posts, titles, or specializations. Thus the position of chair lama (*Shirege Lama*) was often held by a monk who was not the Shirege reincarnation, while the post of Chorji[10] ceased to exist at Mergen, although the Chorji reincarnation was continuous. The later Güüshi and Emchi reincarnations were not translators or doctors. It looks as though historically the first holders of certain senior and specialist positions in the eighteenth century were simply declared to be incarnations, thus giving rise to reincarnation lineages with the name of that office. The names, approximate dates, and families of origin of all the lives of each of the reincarnations are known (Mönghe 1996, 50–76) and all of them originated during the lifetime of the 3rd Mergen Gegen. This suggests that the great Gegen, who was attempting to rationalize the monastery into a coherent institution, himself endorsed a transformation of his officers into incarnations.

The *cluster* of high lamas at Mergen was crucial in enabling the tradition to survive. Uranchimeg Ujeed makes an important point when she explains that, since each reincarnation line had to survive long years of childhood in each generation, the presence of gurus and disciples from the other lines was an essential source of continuity, given that Mergen had to supply its own teaching environment (2009, 136).

9. *Gesgüi* in Miller (1959, 50), pronounced locally "*gewhüi*."

10. T. *Chos rje*. In many other Mongolian monasteries *Chorji* was both a post, assistant to the abbot, as well as a title, meaning master of the (religious) law (Miller 1959, 51).

The long-lived 1st Choriji, Ögligündalai, who was a disciple of the 2nd Mergen Gegen and the main guru of the 3rd and 4th Mergen Gegens, is a case in point. Yet while the other reincarnation lines added to the luster of the monastery, their loyalty to the Mergen Gegens could not be guaranteed.

The potential for competition was underpinned by the fact that the reincarnations headed separate economic establishments (*sang*) with their own subjects (lamas and serfs families), property and premises. Unlike the monastery as a whole, the *sangs* were walled compounds, locked at night.[11] All of the monks at Mergen belonged to one or another of the seven reincarnations' *sang*, being recruited in childhood as pupils of the relevant lama (though in practice young monks might have other lama-teachers too). They remained members of their *sang* till death, whereupon the *sang* was responsible for conducting their funeral rites. Each *sang* compound had its own deity for worship (*shitügen* pron. *shüteen*), altar and prayer hall. On the nineteenth of the fifth month, lamas from each establishment set out to worship separately at their *sang*'s sacred spring (Galluu 2003, 703–05). Further, each reincarnation had his own religious staff; for example, a lama was appointed annually in each *sang* to "wash the face" of the reincarnation with holy water, that is to cleanse him of the sins of the previous year. The most overt competition between the *sangs* took the form of wrestling bouts. Each establishment had its own lama wrestlers, some of them well-known semi-professional sportsmen, and the long-term effects of one particularly ill-natured bout between the Mergen Gegen and Chorji *sangs* in the 1940s are still evident today (Chapter 10).

The treasury (*jisa* or *jiba*) of a given *sang* covered the cost of around half the living expenses of each monk on its rolls. The other half, including the means to build a house, yard, and fence, as well as clothing, books, and other items needed for the religious services were provided by the monk's family or from his own earnings, though the guru teacher might help if he was wealthy (Galluu 2003, 1070). Some men never became fully ordained monks, and maintained wives and households in nearby villages. When a new reincarnation was found, the *sang* also paid the "price" to the family for acquiring one of its members (see below).

The study of Buddhist disciplines and techniques was divided into

11. The *sangs* were all constructed on the same principle, with a worshipping hall to the north and living quarters for the incarnation to east and west. A gate to the south led to the lower courtyard containing housing for the *sang*'s officials, visitors, and stabling.

ten schools or faculties (*rasang*). What is complicated about this—but understandable given the dominance of the reincarnations—is that in Mergen by the nineteenth century, unlike in many Mongolian monasteries, the *rasang* were managed by the *sang*.[12] These faculties are not mentioned by Mergen Gegen (they must have arisen after his death), seem to have been weak, and perhaps indeed were no more than retrospective wishful thinking. The lamas we knew told us that Mergen Monastery was unable to grant higher Buddhist degrees. A reason for this is that translation of Tibetan texts into Mongolian was extensive but never sufficient to encompass the vast range of works necessary for producing the higher specialists. It is clear that whatever scholastic faculties had been founded in Mergen's history—schools that might have formed the basis of a monastery of the clerical type—were swamped, or rather divided up and taken over by the reincarnations.

The income of the monastery was derived from several sources: the taxes and services provided by the lay serf families (*albatu* or *hariyatu shabi*), most of whom were attached to each *sang*, registered monks' salaries from the state, allocations from the Banner, and donations from wealthy benefactors. Grain came from Chinese farmers to whom the monastery rented land. Lamas would also go out to beg for donations to fund particularly large rituals. The monastic serfs and the monastery as a whole were exempt from taxes to the Banner, though transport taxes were paid. Apart from the monastery's three treasuries that financed its communal services, the other treasuries were those of the reincarnations. In 1750 the Mergen Gegen *sang* had five thousand horses, which were dispersed in herds across the monastery's lands. Hubilgan (Lamahai) *sang* had nearly three thousand camels. Baragun Da had fifty-two hundred sheep and goats. Shirege had three thousand cattle. Chorji and Güüshi each had two thousand sheep and goats. These were herded by a total of around two hundred lay families (Galluu 2003, 1074). In principle the monks of a given *sang* would live off its resources, some therefore having a richer lifestyle than others, but

12. The Mergen Gegen's *sang* managed the four faculties of Lam-rim, musical art and ritual dance (*cham*), doctrine (*choira*), and history and literature; the Hubilgan Lama's *sang* ran the faculty of fasting (*Nungnai*); the Baragun Da managed the faculty of sutra and mantra (T. *Jodba*); the Chorji Lama managed the faculty of the Wheel of Time (*Düinghör*); the Shirege Bagshi ran the two faculties of yoga and meditation (*Yarnai* and *Naljirwa*); the Emchi Lama managed the faculty of medicine (*Mamba*), and the Güüshi Bagshi *sang* held the two faculties of translation (*Güüshi*) and sculpture and painting (Mönghe 1996, 47; Galluu 2003, chapter 15; Charleux 2006, 113–14). Many Inner Mongolian monasteries, even large ones such as Dolonnuur, had no scholastic faculties. Dolonnuur was directly under Manchu administration and was the residence of reincarnations recognized by the emperor for their services to the state (Miller 1959, 61).

the livestock specialization of the *sangs* at Mergen suggests that sharing of produce must also have taken place.

Mergen monastery had around twenty square kilometers of land in each direction. With wars and banditry plaguing the monastery from the beginning of the twentieth century, income fell across the board. In 1913 large sections of the monastery were burned down in a raid by Chinese forces, suspecting it (rightly) of sympathy with the declaration of independence by Mongolia in 1911. In the 1920s the astute 8th Mergen Gegen decided on a solution, to raise a lump sum by leasing out land, over and above the already rented out area.[13] This would provide for rebuilding as well as a regular income. No doubt the new land leased to Chinese entrepreneurs for farming reduced the available pasture and was a factor in loss of livestock by the 1940s. In fact, incoming settlers, taking land from Mongols, had long been one of the most bitter of Mongol complaints; yet the fact that a large alienation of land was carried out by the saintly Mergen Gegen is passed over in silence by the lamas today. The temples were beautifully rebuilt and added to, but after decades of civil war and the abandonment of the monastery for a period in the 1930s, much of the precinct was in poor shape and the herds were decimated.[14] By "Liberation" in 1949, each reincarnation's *sang* had only around ten serf families attached to it, a total of fifty to sixty for the monastery as a whole.

Map 1 shows the extent of the devastation wrought on the monastery in the 1960s and later. This included demolition of the outlying Gembi-yin Süme, a hermitage high in the mountains used by Mergen lamas for meditation, and within the precinct the destruction of flower gardens, orchards, and groves of pine trees and the filling in of a lake. Known as Lake of All *Sangs*, it was quite deep, edged by a stone path and trees, and fed by a stream. Monks used to take walks around it. They worshipped a god, Yellow Jambal riding on a lion,[15] whose brass statue was mounted on a stone pillar in the center of the water. The Otochi

13. In the 1920s eight hundred hectares were rented to Chinese farmers, the produce being divided in: 8/10 to the monastery and the producer. Three threshing floors were provided. In the autumn the incoming grain rent was divided up between the five *sangs* (the Emchi and Hubilgan Lamahai establishments had ceased to exist by this time) and the monastery's common treasuries. The farmers also supplied vegetables and potatoes for winter and spring, with the result that the lamas were well fed even in hard times (Galluu 2003, 1072).

14. The herds were reduced to two hundred sheep and goats, ten cows and fifty horses in the Mergen Gegen *sang*; seven hundred sheep and goats in Baragun Da Bagshi's *sang*; around 120 horses and cattle in Shirege Bagsi's *sang*; thirty sheep and goats in Chorji Bagshi's *sang*, and about forty sheep and goats in Güüshi's *sang* (Galluu 2003, 1071).

15. Jambal is a deity with many forms, a *yidam*, and a helpful protector.

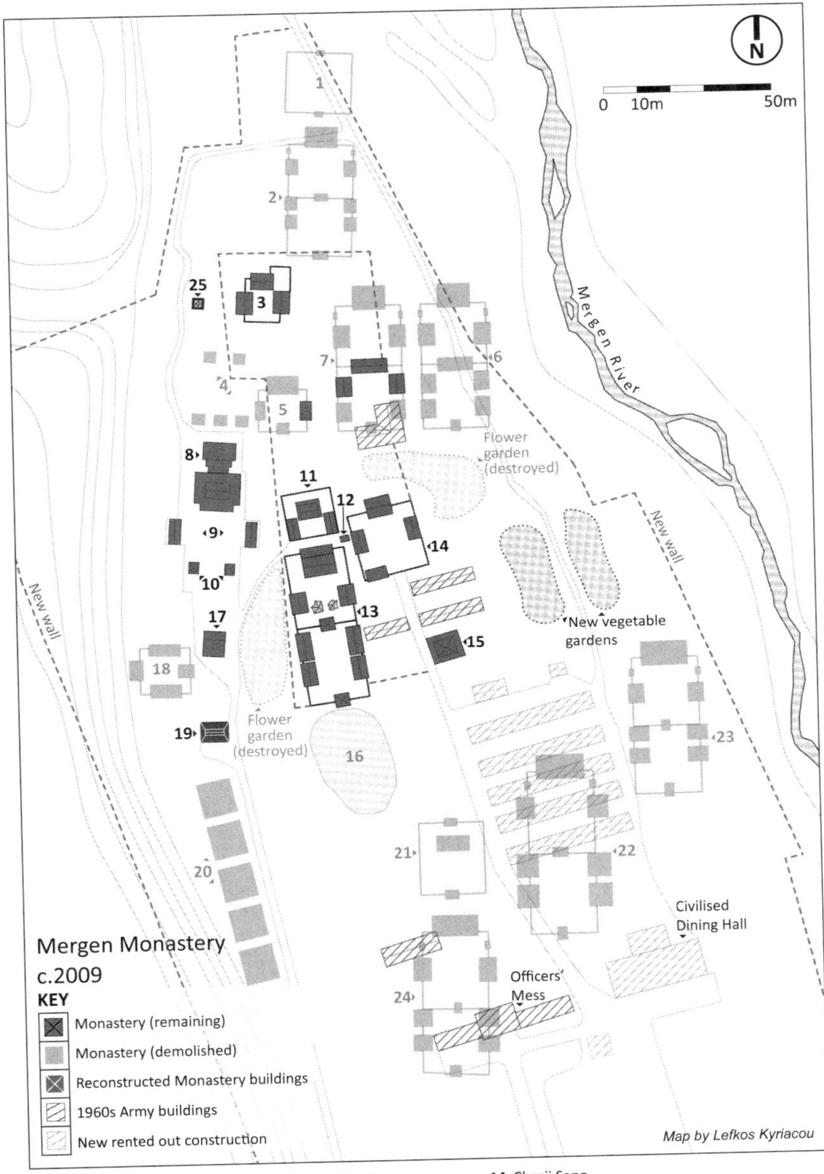

1 Otachi Süme. Temple of the Doctor. (demolished)
2 Shirege Lama Sang. Double Yard Sang. (demolished)
3 Baragun Da Bagshi-yin Sang.
4 Five white pagodas (*suburgan*). (demolished)
5 Ih Jaba. (partly demolished)
6 Güüshi Sang. Two story building. (demolished)
7 Güüshi Sang's Palace for Buddha worship. (partly demolished)
8 Chogchin Dugan. The main hall for worship (includes the Maidar Temple).
9 Two small buildings for storage.
10 Two newly built pagodas.
11 Temple of Relics (*sharil*).
12 Residence (*labrang*) of 8th Mergen Gegen.
13 Mergen Gegen Sang (large double courtyard with two trees).
14 Chorji Sang.
15 White pagoda.
16 Sang Dalai (a lake). (destroyed)
17 Temple of Fierce Deities (Janhan Süme).
18 Maidar Treasury (*jaba*). (demolished)
19 Maharanz Temple. (demolished, rebuilt in 2004)
20 Tibetan-style houses for lamas. (demolished)
21 Temple of the Stone. One room temple, with fence and two gates. (demolished)
22 Hubilgan Lamahai Sang. (demolished)
23 Emchi Lama Sang. (demolished)
24 Mani Treasury (*jaba*). (demolished)
25 Baragun Da Lama's *suburgan*.

Map 1 Map of existing and demolished buildings at Mergen Monastery.

temple,[16] Emchi *sang*, Hubilgan Lamahai's *sang*, Shirege Lama's *sang*, and most of Güüshi Lama's *sang* were demolished, as were the separate living quarters for the monks, some of which were stone Tibetan-style houses. Several other buildings seen in Map 1 have vanished, such as the Maidar Jiba, a courtyard housing the supplies for services at the Maidar Temple, the Yehe Jiba, a similar treasury for the main Chogchin Temple, and the Mani or Nyungnai Jiba, the treasury for maintaining constant chanting of the *mani* prayers. Five large pagodas (*suburga*) protecting the Chogchin Temple were also demolished.

Overall, the picture is of a highly complex institution in which the component parts had their own income streams, and this applied to all levels, from the subject monasteries to the great temples inside Mergen to individual monks. The disciples of the Mergen Gegen, for example, would be part of his establishment (*sang*), but they also had income of their own from their families and lay devotees. The whole agglomerate was held together by the overall religious preeminence of the Mergen Gegen. We suggested reasons why this situation was precarious, but let us now look at the uniting and dividing processes in more detail.

Inside the Monastery: A Kinshiplike Sociality

Sergei Oushakine (Ushakin 2004, 21) describes two ways of thinking about kinship: the first is as a process of creating and relinquishing relations (some evident and some latent or hidden); the second is to conceive kinship as the formation of *what members see as organic wholes*, such as families, households, clans, etc., in response to groups perceived as outside them. The latter kind of formation, he writes, can only exist on the basis of a system of signs that allows the unitary body to appear whole and seem, somehow, to have its own continuity. The intersection of these two perspectives makes an entity such as "a family" a social space in which it is possible to take up incompatible positions. This argument is not inconsistent with the idea, mentioned earlier, of society being produced by each person encroaching on the others, to correct their comportment in accordance with the (different) sense each has of the ensemble (Latour 2010, 4). Mergen monastery was, and is, "kinship-like" in these ways. In the following section we

16. Otochi is the deity for physicians and herbalists. No mention was made of this temple during our fieldwork, and it may have fallen into disuse following the demise of the Emchi ("doctor") Lama lineage in the 1930s.

describe various links, splits, and suspensions in relations. But first it is worth reconsidering briefly some of the signs by which the monks could imagine the monastery as a whole entity.

We have already mentioned some key features: Mergen Gegen's list of communal services and his rules for monks, the notion of the reincarnation as religious leader, and the idea of the blessed site subject to the mountain. A guardian deity (*sahius*) protected an area around the monastery within which hunting and agriculture were forbidden, and inside this a notional path (*goriya*) encircled the precinct itself. The *goriya* was an invisible boundary within which the rules of monastic propriety were upheld, and monks required permission to go outside it. The rules included obedience to seniors, not quarrelling, fighting, or thieving, and refraining from sexual relations.[17] No animal was to be killed unless for eating, no alcohol was to be kept, and no women were allowed within the *goriya* after nightfall. Sexuality of all kinds was in principle disapproved, but in practice it was relations with women that were disbarred,[18] and this meant that if monks were to sin they had to go outside the *goriya* (an important point, as we shall see). Curiously, donkeys were also not allowed inside the *goriya* although horses could enter. The reason for this, as we were told, was that donkeys were considered impure because of their large sexual organs, and because they were owned by Chinese and contrasted with the horses used by Mongols.

The idea of a whole entity can also be seen from the punishments decreed by Mergen Gegen for those who disobeyed his rules. Unruly monks could be chastised, fined, or beaten by the proctor of their section, but supernatural punishment also awaited them from deities watching over the whole monastery. "People who do wrongful things, I do not consider them human beings," he wrote. "If you do not respect the rules, the Root Sky-God (*ündüsün Tngri*) will be angry. If you young lamas are not trustworthy, your Life Force God (*sülde Tngri*) will decline. You will be given up by the Guardian Deity of the monastery" (*BJ* [1780–1783] 1998, vol. 1, text 9, 65v).[19]

17. Defecating and urinating within the *goriya* were not allowed, though very elderly monks were excused obedience to this rule.

18. Homosexuality was common in Mongolian monasteries in the early twentieth century and was not taken so seriously as a sin because it did not involve procreation (bringing new beings into the world of suffering). Indeed, a common term for homosexuality was *bandila* ("to *bandi*," from the word for boy lamas [*bandi*], Baasanjav, pers. comm.). The lamas at Mergen avoided talking to us about sexuality of any kind.

19. The Guardian Deity (*sahius*) was different from the god that was the object of worship (*shitügen*). At Mergen the former was Muna Khan, while the main common *shitügen* was Maidar.

The track of the *goriya* could change somewhat from time to time, but—wherever the monks decided it lay—it came into prominence at the important rite of the circumambulation of the coming Buddha Maidar described in the Introduction.[20] On this occasion the *goriya* became a path marking the inside/outside of the community to be blessed. Inside, the main buildings were added on an approximately north-south axis, which entailed commonly accepted spatial notions of seniority: north was "above" south, and west was senior to east. Buildings were sited in relation to the idea that visitors would enter from the south and proceed via the Temple of the Guardian King Deities, *Maharanza* (S. *Mahārāja*) Süme, to the holier shrines. The existence of this accepted structure meant that meanings could be read into the grouping of buildings. For example, the compounds of the three founding reincarnations, linked as the "east" alliance, were sited in a line that did not fit the north-south orientation, but lamas felt it to be special: it was aligned, they said, with the three stars of the tail of the Mechid constellation (Pleiades), which are worshipped by Mongols.

The importance of such spatial techniques today will be discussed in Chapter 9, but meanwhile let us comment on the ways in which the relations of the monastery resembled kinship in Oushakine's account. We have already noted that all monks were recruited to the *sang* of one or another reincarnation, that each *sang* had its own compound and property, and that when a child was found as the next reincarnation the relevant *sang* would pay his family to transfer membership from the lay grouping to the religious one. This payment was explicitly likened to the brideprice paid at marriage and the same word (*törhüm*) is used for the birth family of an incoming bride and for the birth family of a reincarnation. If the guru's *sang* was like the kin-group of an ordinary monk, in the case of the 3rd Mergen Gegen, the whole monastery became his new "family":

> The Banner and monastery prepared a great expenditure to invite the 3rd Mergen Gegen. Inviting a reincarnation is like inviting a bride and involves discussing the livestock and money to be given to the mother and father to return the benefit of the white milk [they gave to the child in rearing it]. Especially when inviting a Gegen and Bogd they [the monastery officials] give the fortune-merit of "nine whites," the nine kinds of treasure, the five types of livestock, and gold and silver. They pre-

See Hyer and Jagchid 1983, 94, for the Kanjurwa Gegen's views on the originally "evil" character of guardian deities.

20. In most monasteries the sacred Tibetan Ganjur texts were also carried round the *goriya* at an annual ritual.

pare all these very well. They invited the 3rd Mergen Gegen when he was aged five in 1721. (Galluu 2003, 89)

Naming practices were another series of accepted signs that created sociality within monasteries. Young lamas entering the monastery were given a vow name that contained part of the name of his lama patron/teacher. The practice is continued today, so the young lamas recruited in 2004 by Chorji, whose vow name is Ishiperenleijamsu, each contain part of this name (Ishichimed, Ishidawa, etc.). This establishes a branching set of relations, linking the pupils by an element of common identity with their teacher (an element that may or may not be carried into a further generation). This is not unlike the common familial practice in Mongolia whereby birth siblings may be given an overlapping series of names, each containing a common element as well as other different elements. Such practices—if we use the metaphor of space—provide a perspective on the "landscape" of the socialized domain in which names are given, and furthermore they localize the "I" by placing the name of the subject relationally.

A reincarnation has three names: the name title of his line, the vow name given to him as a monk, and the lay name given him at birth. He uses exactly the same name title as his predecessor, being in a sense the same person. He does not, however, consistently take part of the vow name of the previous incarnation; rather, these vow names are given by famous ordination lamas who may enjoy giving part of their own name—as the Dalai and Panchen Lamas are said to have done for the 3rd Mergen Gegen (see p 69)—a custom that reflects the wider religious terrain reincarnations belong to. Nevertheless, the pragmatics of naming high lamas also recalls kinship practice. Like the elders in a family, a reincarnation in the monastery is seldom if ever called by any name, and in reference it is respectful to use the title rather than the vow name (Humphrey 2006b). In any case, the kin-term or title that is actually used is minimally specific as a personal designation. This is indeed confusing to an outsider. For example, several reincarnations in different monasteries in the Urad region were (and are) called "West Lama," and this laconic practice assumes—like "granddad"' in an intimate domestic group—that *who* this refers to is already known.

Today at Mergen it is also possible to flip into secular ("socialist") mode, to put aside religious sociality altogether and call lamas by their lay birth names. If everyone present does this, including the lamas, then the practice can be simply familiar and democratizing. At times we observed everyone talking as though the monastic world had evaporated (or been put off to another occasion). But in most contexts, when other lamas are being called by their titles, referring to someone by their lay name implies insultingly that this person is not a real lama. This situation in which everyone has at least two names allows for highly nuanced interactions. Polite smiles prevail, but everyone understands exactly what the naming signs imply.

The Reincarnations: Appearing, Splitting, New Foundations

Here we describe some of the dynamic processes associated with the reincarnations. How, for example, did they originate, how did they deal with social class and non-reincarnate lamas, and how did they relate to one another? We end the section with the pivotal history of the "cursing proctor," an event that illustrates the politics of clashing personalities, and also shows how new monasteries have sometimes been founded—by exclusion.

a. The emergence of incarnate lamas

In principle, reincarnation lines do not start from nothing, as the first embodiment is held to be the emanation of a bodhisattva who lived in a remote era. The Mergen Gegen line, for example, is said to have derived from Manjushiri (Galluu 2003, 77). Now the initiation of a lineage is retrospective, since it is not evident that one has been started until the first *rebirth* has been recognized, but nevertheless there must be something truly exceptional in the original person that indicates he is no ordinary human being. Such "bodhisattva-like" features can be highly varied. They may be tantric and meditational achievements, deep knowledge of the scriptures, or meritorious acts, and in any of these cases the exceptional quality is also made evident by magical ability. What is problematic is when the evidence of divinity, whatever that happens to be, is tangled up with the social origins, activities, and personality of this first person. It is significant that Mongolian vocabulary systematically occludes divine and human origins, for one word, *törül*, is used for both human physical birth/descent and incarnation/reincarnation. Such an entanglement can cause upsets for generations in the monastery. An example is the reincarnation line of the West Lama of Güng Monastery, as recounted by Duke Galdan: in Duke Darmashiri's time, a *gelüng* lama got sacred power (*ubadis*) from Mergen Gegen and, in a double confirmation of sanctity, he was also an emanation of the bodhisattva Ariyabalo. He could fly using his cloak as wings, and he did not use a boat to cross the Yellow River but walked over it. When people looked at the hem of his garment they saw it was only wet the width of two fingers and they knew he had magical power (*shidi*). The nobles recognized him as their lama and worshipped him (Galdanwangchugdorji [1846] 1994, 6).

So far so good, but now the story gets stranger. After the *gelüng* lama died, his body was put (literally "invited") into the Yellow River. Meanwhile, a Chinese farmer called Lao Sang had built a beautiful temple on the riverbank devoted to the worship of Sky and Water Spirits. Lao Sang was a good man who lived by Mongol customs and he married a Mongol girl, the daughter of an Urad noble. One day she went to the river to get water and found a pole lasso floating in the water. She took it and that night she received a sign (*temdeg*) and became pregnant. When her son was born, his first words were, "Mother, I came to you sitting on the point of that pole." People were amazed and concluded that he was the reincarnation of the lama who had been interned in the river. But Lao Sang was not happy with this idea and he took his son away to the Inner Land (China) where he taught him magical games (*ilbi-yin nagadum*) (Galdanwangchugdorji [1846] 1994, 7–8).

Note that this story parallels *pre-Buddhist* Mongolian accounts of the birth of the progenitors of ruling lineages, where the biological father is replaced by a supernatural vital force, thus singling out the origin hero from the ranks of ordinary ancestors (see p 93). Not all supernatural powers are equal, however, and the duke's text differentiates between different kinds of magic, the sacred *ubadis* given by Mergen Gegen, the wider magic *shidi* of the *gelüng* lama, and the unholy and trivial *ilbi* taught by Lao Sang. The story proceeds that the nobles chased after the runaway father, negotiated to get the precious boy back, and sent him to Lhasa for Buddhist instruction. There he pleased the Jangjiya Gegen, the state preceptor, who gave him the vow name Lubsangshirab. Lubsangshirab Lama then came back to Urad and asked the Mergen Gegen to compose a Buddhist text for worship in his Chinese father's temple for the Sky and Water Spirits (a text still used to this day). Still, he did not have a proper Buddhist monastery of his own. The 3rd Mergen Gegen died, and Lubsangshirab was invited to be Shirege Lama of Mergen and to manage the internal and external affairs of the monastery (Galdanwangchugdorji [1846] 1994, 9).

However, Lubsangshirab had a difficult time: he was meanly housed in the lower courtyard of the Mergen Gegen *sang*, the monks insulted him by calling him "Lao Sang reincarnation" (recalling his lowly Chinese father rather than recognizing his sacred origin from the *gelüng* Lama), and they grumbled that he was throwing his weight around like an Ombu, the negotiator involved with property and mundane management. Complaints about him were made to a Banner official, who happened to be the head of the 3rd Mergen Gegen's birth family. Lubsangshirab reacted to this by leaving: he invited his beloved and aristocratic young disciple Wangdui Toin to take over as Shirege Lama in Mergen, while he had a small monastery built for himself at Tariyan Tühüm. When he was old, he remarked wryly, "I understand that it would have been necessary to have high birth to support Buddhism. As the son of a Chinese, I was looked down on. So I made a hard resolution (*hatagu irügel*) before a Buddha statue that I would be reborn next in a "high root and thus be able to do helpful things for religion" (ibid, 11–14). His next incarnation, Lama Ariyabalo, who was invited to be the 3rd West Lama of Güng Monastery, was indeed the brother of the ruling duke, a complex psychological situation that we discuss in the next chapter.

b. Acquiring learning, succeeding to high office

The entanglement of birth status and fitness for office was even more marked in the succession to the post of Da Lama at Mergen. This was an appointed position and the nobles were directly involved in choosing the incumbents. It was not magic ability that was required so much as knowledge of the scriptures and liturgy. Through the late eighteenth and early nineteenth centuries the post was given to various aristocratic lamas, including the Hubilgan and Chorji reincarnations. At one point a West Lama reincarnation of the Güng Monastery was asked to stand, but he demurred, saying that while it was wrong that the abbots were often chosen for their noble birth, he himself was also not suitable as he had spent much time away from Mergen, did not know its liturgy or rules, and had no deep knowledge of Buddhism. So the post was given to the Western Great reincarnation of Mergen, but he rapidly asked for leave and went away to Amdo. At this point the officials had trouble finding anyone learned enough to take the position. The West Lama of Güng was asked again and refused. In the end he agreed to become advisor to a number of short-lived or very young holders of the abbot post (ibid, 192–224).

The problem at Mergen was that after the demise of a generation of brilliant lamas at the time of the 3rd Mergen Gegen, ability and scholarship seem to have fallen away. And so whatever higher learning talented lamas acquired had to be found at considerable expense[21] outside Mergen, which meant in Tibetan language monasteries, and therefore at a remove from the regular liturgy. The Mergen Gegen reincarnations at this period were either children, or seem to have become more detached artistic figures.[22] The dukes too were caught in this dilemma. They wished to maintain the independent Mongolian tradition of Mergen and at the same time have renowned and highly learned lamas in charge of their monasteries. The office of abbot, although it did not have a *sang* attached to it, was a powerful executive position, entitled to receive high visitors and donations on behalf of the monastery and to regulate and punish all lamas. So, while not always highly learned the Da Lama remained a key political actor, deeply involved with the Banner aristocracy right up to modern times.

c. A "subordinate" monastery

If any of the reincarnations had exceptional ability, they were liable to found their own separate monastery even if they held office at Mergen and they were also susceptible to being invited away to other regions. The first Güüshi ("Translator") Lama, Nomundalai, is a clear example of the able, supra-institutional Lama who floated from place to place. Nomundalai was a famous and highly respected translator of sacred texts, a doctor, and author of the biography of the 2nd Neichi Toin. Apart from his seat at Mergen, he had a temple built for him in "the city" (probably Höhhot). He was also invited to preside far away to the north at Bayan Hoshigu, in Horchin, the monastery that had been built much earlier for the 1st Neichi Toin.[23] This was the principal monastery of several in the region that continued to use the Mongolian language in the eighteenth century (Dharmatala 1987, 357). Possibly, one reason why the Güüshi Lama maintained separate bases away from Mergen was rivalry with the 3rd Mergen Gegen, for the Güüshi's translations were in the old style that had been displaced by the Ge-

21. Duke Galdan frequently mentions the gifts of silver, horses, and other precious items given to eminent gurus when lamas achieved advancement (such as taking higher vows, receiving titles, or obtaining empowerments to engage in tantric activities).

22. Little is known about the 4th Mergen Gegen. The 5th was a poet and songwriter, and the 6th died in early childhood, his father having refused to give him up to the monastery because he was a noble heir.

23. Bayan Hoshigu, along with Debeseg, Güng, and others, was a subject monastery of Mergen, according to the Mergen monks. The statement is not uncontested; the scholar Rashisereng told us that Mergen monastery in Urad was named after the older Mergen Monastery (i.e., Bayan Hoshigu) in eastern Inner Mongolia. Essentially the argument hinges on whether the tradition is held to have started, with the "root lama" Neichi Toin or with the Mergen Gegens.

gen's new harmonized liturgy. However, Bayan Hoshigu monastery too brought in the new liturgy, and Mergen Gegen is recorded as having specially designed a set of texts in order to have "the line of my religion established" there.[24] Further, the first Güüshi had brought a separate group of monk disciples to Mergen to perform his own version of the *cham* dance, which perhaps was in competition with the Mergen Gegen's choreography (Galdanwangchugdorji [1846] 1994, 203), while the 2nd Güüshi spent long periods in Tibet and at Badgar Monastery.

The strong external support for the Güüshi reincarnations resulted in a flow of donations to Mergen. The Güüshi *sang* came to be the largest in the monastery. With two double courtyards, it was twice the size of Mergen's establishment and was the only one to have a two-storied temple as well as a separate temple for the Arhats (lay disciples who found enlightenment). The blue-roofed dragon-decorated palace, built by the dukes at the very beginning of the monastery's history, was sold by the 1st Hubilgan Lamahai incarnation and then moved into the Güüshi *sang*. From this we see that built structures were arranged and shifted to suit relations between the lamas at particular times. The later Güüshi reincarnations spent most of their time away from Mergen. The PLA destroyed the Güüshi *sang* almost completely, maybe because it contained very old buildings or ruins that were not suitable for military use (see Figure 1).

d. Tournaments of magic and miracles

Relations between reincarnations depended on their personalities,[25] but when conflict arose the institution could split, or sections of it could atrophy. The American soldier Schuyler Cammann wrote about one Urad monastery in the 1940s:

> Ch'ien-li Temple formerly had had two Living Buddhas, both important incarnations. The jealousy between them was intense, and each had ultimately retired to one half of the monastery, which was divided into two sections by a small gully. Not only was the whole monastery torn by their intrigues but it was an expensive proposition maintaining two princes of the Church in the style to which they were

24. Colophon to the three volumes of wooden block prints by Mergen Gegen made in Beijing in 1774 designed for the services at Öljei Badaragsan Süme (Bayan Hoshigu). In living memory Shiraotgon Lama from Mergen used to go periodically to Bayan Hoshigu to examine the monks there on their knowledge and competence in chanting.

25. For studies of the coexistence of reincarnations, see Lattimore and Isono 1982, Hyer and Jagchid 1983, and Nietupski 2011.

accustomed. The problem was finally settled many years ago by a wise abbot. One of the incarnations died, and the abbot saw to it that they could never locate the body into which his soul had been reborn, so he was quietly forgotten. His half of the monastery decreased in importance and was ultimately abandoned to crumble into ruins (1951, 90).

Avoiding such closeted enmity, most of the reincarnations at Mergen founded alternative small monasteries to which they could retreat (Galdanwangchugdorji [1846] 1994, 180, 184, 190).[26] Within the monastery, the 3rd Mergen Gegen had paid attention to issues of precedence, evidently anticipating tensions,[27] but as we have noted his rules did not refer to reincarnations. Duke Galdan's memoirs are no better guide, as he was so respectful of lamas that quarrels are hardly mentioned or described in such roundabout and apologetic terms it is impossible to understand them. All we have to go on is the imagination of the lamas and laypeople in recent times. Here, interestingly, the relations between reincarnations have the same "substance" as their own supra-natural existence—they take the form of competitive magic and miracles.

Magic here is a relational discourse, a public act, and one of the techniques whereby supremacy over others is demonstrated. In appearance such lamas' magic has parallels with power tournaments between shamans, where one feat succeeds another in escalating ferocity.[28] But while shamanic magic has been frequently discussed, that of Buddhist lamas has been largely ignored, perhaps because scholars have seen it as an unworthy addendum to a serious religion. We argue, however, that magic is central to the Mongolian practice of Buddhism, and that—despite a superficial similarity—is understood to be quite different from shamanic magic. Two things need to be remembered here: first, that lamas' magic takes place in *their* landscape, in which as we noted earlier the ontological status of the monastery is that of a subject of fortune, gathering, and dispensing occult forces, both good and bad, in a cosmology of astrologically set signs. Magic is one kind of *evidence*

26. The first Hubilgan incarnation, for example, had the separate Chagaan Hot Monastery built, and often went to live there. The lamas of this monastery, which remained the alternative seat of the Hubilgan reincarnations, were folded back into Mergen in 1939, after raids by Chinese Republican soldiers had made it uninhabitable (Galluu 2003, 815).

27. Mergen wrote that in academic situations the senior lama is the one with the greatest knowledge. In making regular decisions, authority depends on the functional position of the lama. On all other occasions, seniority is decided by the level of the vow taken by the given lama and previously established precedents (*BJ* [1780–1783] 1998, vol. 1, 54v).

28. It is not unknown for lamas to use "conquering" (*darlag*) magic that hurts enemies, but this always has to be justified by the idea that the enemy would create greater sin than the sin of suppressing him.

in this fortune-pervaded world. Second, and differently, Mongolians see lama's magic as an almost incidental outcome of exceptional (Buddhist) insight, and therefore quite other to the spirit-produced magic of shamans. More profoundly the two are not commensurable, since they are formed in different perspectives on the world with different existential components. In fact, the word "magic" covers several different Mongolian activities and concepts, and we focus here on *shidi* (supernatural power), originally a Sanskritic notion that does not exist in the indigenous shamanic cosmology. In principle *shidi* is simply a result of enlightenment, what an enlightened lama is able to perceive and do, rather than a technique for obtaining worldly ends. Reincarnations have this ability by definition, and since there are many more reincarnations than people who have achieved enlightenment by meditation, in popular talk, magic usually appears as a "natural" ability, rather than one acquired by effort. It fits with this that the idiom of magic at Mergen is often joyous, even playful.

An example is a legendary contest between the Mergen Gegen and Lubsangshirab, the West reincarnation of the Güng Monastery mentioned earlier. When the West Lama was invited in to be the Ombu (financial manager) of Mergen Gegen's *sang,* he became rather powerful and the Gegen decided to test him. The two lamas went out to the Jewel Oboo in the grassy plains and threw their handkerchiefs in the air—each one turned into a hare and ran away. Mergen was surprised when he saw the Ombu's ability and said, "Go and catch those two hares!" The Ombu ran crazily hither and thither but could not catch them. Mergen Gegen smiled, took out another handkerchief, made a knot and threw it up and it turned into an eagle—which immediately caught the hares. So the Ombu knew he was beaten and began to behave more respectfully and modestly (Mönghe 1996, 121).

What is the quality of humor one senses here? It is not ironic, presenting the holy figures engaged in ludicrous pursuits and thus trying to make a point. Somehow in Mergen it is possible for the reincarnations to be immensely respected and at the same time sources of amusement—as though the wondrous and the funny are entirely compatible. One of the Shirege Lama reincarnations had "no nose," i.e., a very flat face. He wore a ragged mantle and was always drunk and gave no sign of being a reincarnation at all. But in reality he was a *hubilgan* with completed sacred power (*ubadis*). Along the main road running east to west in front of Mergen (the same traversed by the Rolling Stone, see pp 113–14) there lies the ramshackle settlement of Two Wells. In a story about the No-Nose Reincarnation it is recounted that Two Wells ran out of water whenever there was a drought. Only a few households lived there in those days, but they invited the incarnation to conjure up water. No-Nose arrived and they were disappointed when he chanted no sacred text at all, but just ate his fill of meat and drank alcohol till he fell asleep. "We invited a real bag of food," people said. At midnight, No-Nose Reincarnation stumbled out to urinate. His hosts were worried—after all he was a reincarnation and was drunk, perhaps they had better follow him quietly to see he came to no harm. To their horror they saw him go straight to the double well and urinate into it. "Respected Lama, what are you doing? That is a well. . . ." No-Nose was angry and said, "Be silent!" He pulled up his trousers and went back to Mergen. The next morning there was overflowing water in the wells (Mönghe 1996, 116–17).

With such stories, Mergen and its surroundings becomes the scene of amazing events, and the 3rd Mergen Gegen was the top wonder maker. Such discourse of magic should not be seen as a creation of the laity separate from the religious life of the monks (e.g., Heissig 1980). Nor are there grounds to see it as a displacement, an imaginative play hiding "the real" (underlying tensions). Rather, this kind of story is one means by which people represent the direct access to power of the tantric adept or the reincarnation. The use of Sanskrit terms indicates that Mongols see the idea as belonging to an ancient practice. Note the wide range of meanings of the important term *ubadis* [S. *upadeśa*]—"teaching, religious instruction, magic, supernatural power, and sorcery" (Lessing 1960, 858). In the stories quoted *ubadis*, like *shidi*, is demonstrated both by the mocking magic of turning piss into water and the overcoming of human limitations by the miracle of walking over the Yellow River, as well as by the tantric ability of adepts who have trained for years. *Shidi* can even be used in the sphere of higher learning—Duke Galdan wrote that "increasing [one's] knowledge of theory (*onul*) is *shidi*" ([1846] 1994, 39). These are examples of what we called "transmutable keys." There is no good reason to separate these usages into "Buddhist" on the one hand and "non-Buddhist," or "folk" on the other, and every reason to recognize the fact of elision and multilevel understandings.

For many of these acts, the word miracle is more appropriate than magic, miracle being definable as an instantaneous switch into a natural "eternal" causation that is hidden by the durational causality of conventional, transient reality (Bauman 2008, 217). The miracle as transformation-in-a-flash is an event that manifests the quality of the instant over process, and thereby makes the framework of convention irrelevant. Now one aim of meditation and tantra, as mentioned earlier, is revelation of the illusory nature of conventional knowledge. Thus effects we might describe as "magical /miraculous," denoted by Mongolian terms such as *ubadis* and *shidi*, are not just an incidental part of the Buddhist religion practiced in these parts—they are essential to it. And this has an implication—what laypeople see as extraordinary is not so for the religious adept. For him what he reveals is the faultiness of appearances—and his ability to do this is the coincidental effect of who he (really) is.

Such a view on the world is often evoked poetically in the writings of "Mergen Gegen," for example in a poem about the monastery, where he declares that even the Manchu state (*törü*) is supported by "the Ones with Magic" (*shidi-tan*). He then disturbs the assumption that they can only be elevated lamas by saying they can also be the flowers on the mountainside:

At the support-providing Muna Mountain
Is the roundly completed Mergen Monastery.
This is the universally illuminating mountain
Of the ones with magic who protect the state.
In the bosom of Muna Mountain
There are dazzling colorful flowers;
Bestowing a thousand magic powers
[They] illuminate ignorance and darkness.
(Galluu and Jirantai 1986, 71–72)

Shidi here can be translated as "magic," but it is also a way of expressing the luminescence glowing from places of religious sanctity (see below).

In the present time, Urad people say that concentrated tantric meditation creates magical ability and they unhesitatingly endorse it as a wonderful faculty.[29] Mantras (*tarni*) inherited from famous lamas of the past can be employed as spells. Minggan Lama, for example, "tied down" a huge boulder teetering on a hill above his house by engraving

29. However, well-educated Buddhists in Inner Mongolia, aware of Tsongkhapa's reforms, tend to be circumspect about magic. They maintain that highly adept monks are able to do it but should restrain themselves, for magic in the end is worldly—it impresses people, but it does not itself help in gaining salvation. In some Buryat monasteries, monks were expelled for demonstrating magic. This suspicion of magic as a self-indulgence is not shared at Mergen however—most people admire it.

it with a *tarni*. This, it was said, would not only protect his family but also stop dangerous landslides in the whole surrounding area.

Finally, we give a fairly recent example that links together several themes of this chapter and in particular shows how talk about supernatural power (*chidal*) forms relations among people at Mergen. When the last Shirege Reincarnation died in 1957, his remains were cremated on the feather-grass plain behind the Lamahai Oboo to the north of the monastery. Old woman Rulmajid happened to be passing at the foot of Darchug Hill. The smoke from the cremation formed a stream that went straight to her. Observing this, respected Boroheshig Lama laughed, "Old Rulmajid has born no child in her whole life, perhaps she'll bear a reincarnation now!" Next morning, when the lamas went to collect the sacred relics of the Shirege Lama from the pyre, it was found that Shirahulu, who was the married-in son-in-law of Rulmajid's adopted daughter, had appeared out of the blue to help with his cart and horse. Nine months later, a son was born to Shirahulu, and everyone—the lamas and the laypeople, began to call the baby Shirege Lama. The local savant Mönghe, who recounts this "real information," writes that people drew this conclusion about the reincarnation because "the beginning and the end of the line of the clues to the real events were connected" (1996, 115). The line consists of the previous Shirege incarnation—his body—the smoke—Boroheshig's joke—Rulmajid—her son-in-law—the powerful relics—the baby boy. The clue-like reasoning of such accounts, similar to that recounted by Duke Galdan about the origin of the Güng reincarnation line, is how people try to apprehend what might lie behind the surface. The idea that something (or someone) might really be something else fits with the presence of so many reincarnations. It matches their form of existence (a reincarnation is *hubilgan*—from *hubilahu* to transform), and it supplies unearthly links relating them to one another.

e. The Cursing Gebhüi*—dispersing and gathering*

In 1998 several lamas told us about the dramatic confrontation between 3rd Mergen Gegen and the Cursing Proctor (*hariyalchi gebhüi*)—the *gebhüi* being the official responsible for discipline among the lamas. This story demonstrates in sharp relief the potential conflict between the monastic rules and the magical power of the reincarnations, and it shows how the narrative of events mapped a sacred landscape. Above all, it is a prime example of the different kinds of "interference" by one person in the affairs of the other in the name of an imagined entity (the monastery) that Latour sees as constituting the institution (2010, 7).

So resonant was this event, legendary or not, that it continued to be a cause of ritual creativity during our fieldwork (see Chapter 9). Rather than see such recurrent dramas as "cultural schemas" reflecting cultural contradictions (Ortner 1989, 14), we prefer instead to see the drama of the Cursing Proctor as an exemplar, an idea of a past event that is kept alive and elevated as a guide for future relationships and subsequently followed in one's own way (Humphrey 1997a, 25–47; Bulag 2002b, 183–206)—these "ways" always being implicated in the current personal, historical, and political situation. In reading the following account, readers should remember that the narratives are those of contemporary people, for whom the story presents contrasting values.

Sengge Lama told us: one day, Mergen Gegen arrived very late for a service and it was noticed that he did not sleep in his quarters the previous night. He must have gone outside the *goriya*. He was a young Gegen who liked to visit people at night, our Mergen Gegen! During the service, the proctor dared to stand up before all the monks, took off his hat, bowed, and criticized ("cursed") Mergen Gegen to his face. "You composed the rules, and now where did you go?" The Gegen had nothing to say. He returned to his palace, crying. "I was wrong," he said to his *ombu*, "the proctor's criticism was right. And because I have been shamed in front of all the disciples, I must leave my monastery now." When the *ombu* told the proctor about Mergen Gegen's unhappiness, the proctor replied, "The Gegen of our monastery must not leave. I'll go instead." He walked away in the southwest direction. At the hill where the *oboo* now stands he turned to look back at the monastery and two tears dropped from his eyes. He went further to a distant place, where he could only just see the pinnacle on the Chogchin temple, sat down, and cried. Mergen Gegen knew the tears were the sign of a misfortune-causing curse and so he built a shrine to deflect the curse from the monastery. Nevertheless, dissension continued among the monks and many followed the proctor. To deal with this Mergen Gegen constructed a "Cairn of the Community of Monks" (*Olan Huwarag-un Oboo*) on the hill where the proctor's tears fell. People say that if regular offerings are not made, discord will constantly arise among the monks.

Told this way, the proctor was in the right and Mergen Gegen was conscious of his fault. Note that Sengge, the teller of this story, was not a reincarnation, spent his life in posts such as proctor or *umjad* (master of chanting), and often held forth on how good strict rules have regrettably lapsed at Mergen.

Galluu, however, provides a pro-Mergen account, which is interesting for several reasons. Mergen Gegen was absent from his palace and late for the service because he was checking whether anyone among the monks had his heavenly eye (*tngri-yin nidü*) opened by completing doctrine and knowledge of Bodhisattva.[30] When the proctor came to the Gegen's house to fetch him for the New Year's *irügel* service, he could not find him, but when the first part of the service was ending, the Gegen was sitting on his chair in the temple wearing a long green gown, a golden-edged red-silk mantle, and a five-pointed mountain hat.[31] How could the proctor, whose heavenly eyes were not opened, understand this appearance? He was following a different logic, namely the rules of the monastery. He railed:

"So your great temple can't hold you? So the high chair of eighty-one yogi-masters is too low for you, you green *damshig* (unreliable person)?"

After the service, Mergen called in the proctor:

"Couldn't you see that I was showing my magic powers (*ridi-shidi*) [acquired by] completing the Green Yamantaka meditation, and that I had transformed into a green body? Why was your heavenly eye not opened even though you completed the Yamantaka meditation many times? Last night I went to the thirty-three sky-gods and I met the Emperor of Heaven (*Hormusta-yin Hagan*). We discussed many things for the benefit of all sentient beings. I came back on the Morning Star, and I performed the completion [of the tantric magic action]. You didn't see me, though I was there finishing up and you left. I went after you, but then I sat in the service with a peaceful mind. Why do you blindly and stupidly talk this way? You leave now, you with your confused mind, and go to a remote mountain and do very hard meditation to open your heavenly eye" (Galluu 2003, 730).

This account shows the Mergen Gegen, faced with opposition, ignoring the monastic regulations he himself had composed in favor of magic power acquired through tantric practice (completing the Green Yamantaka meditation). For good measure he adds his own even more startlingly direct access to divinity, the cosmic journey to the thirty-three sky gods. Individual charisma is given decisive priority over monastic duty. Interestingly, the next part of the story shows that even the proctor was caught up in the same tantric logic.

30. This expression may be imported by modern lamas from the Chinese concept of *tian mu* ("heavenly eye") used in *qi gong* practice. Mongols normally talk of opening *bilig-ün nidü*, "wisdom eye," a stage of Buddhist enlightenment.

31. Tantric-rite headgear with five upright pointed plates painted with deities.

"Now the Proctor understood, bowed to his teacher, and went away to the wilds of Tamarisk Steppe. He gathered lamas for the *mani* prayers and he himself became a tutelary deity by completing the envisioning of Ariyabalo *yidam*. He also gathered fifteen women lay believers and held Mani services for them. After all this, he moved to Debeseg Mountain and there he built the Debeseg Monastery and developed Buddhism. He accomplished merciful deeds and got the bodhisattva path (*bodi mör*) and later the Mergen Gegen recognized his reincarnation" (Galluu 2003, 730–31).

In 2005 we visited Debeseg Monastery, a gaunt shell in a windswept valley high in the Muna Mountains, the remains of a much larger establishment. Here the one remaining lama, the West Reincarnation Arbinjargal, told us that the cursing proctor was indeed the founder of the monastery. But Debeseg was not to be a haven of clerical discipline—the fever for reincarnations was strong there too. Arbinjargal filled in the story. Following his expulsion from Mergen, the proctor had prayed in the steppe, had meritoriously gathered "seventy pieces of stuff" (*dalan heseg yum*) and sent them to Mergen Gegen to return the favor of giving him an education and a high post, and then set out for the mountains to found a monastery. He located a rich patron who provided the funding. Before long, not only was the proctor recognized as an incarnation, but the patron was too. Indeed Arbinjargal himself was the reincarnated "descendant" of this patron: "When this monastery was built in the eighteenth century I was a layperson," he told us.[32]

The Cursing Proctor stories bring to the fore the idea of "gathering"—the banished proctor assembled lamas and laypeople in the wilderness and he "gathered seventy pieces of stuff" to send to Mergen Gegen. The idea of collecting together is a positive one in Mongol thought, being a foundational idea in both politics (the leader gathers his followers) and economic life (the herdsman gathers his flocks). Yet gathering is not uniting (*neilehü*). The component parts scatter again after they have been brought together. But it is contrasted with the negative acts of breaking up (*hagachahu*) or splitting and annihilating (*butarahu*). Behind these stories is the idea that the proctor could redeem his destructive act of dividing of the monastery by devoting himself to "gathering," and Mergen Gegen could counteract the curse and the tears by

32. In more prosperous times Debeseg had three reincarnation lines. At present the line of the Cursing Proctor is in abeyance, as is that of the third *hubilgan*, the East Reincarnation. The originator of the latter line had arrived at the monastery as a wandering alms-seeking monk (*badarchin*), but he was clever and good at chanting, so they asked him to stay.

constructing an *oboo*—a piling together of stones and branches symbolizing a collectivity of people.

Monasteries in the Wrong Place, the Wrong Time

This leads us back to the monastery as a subject in a spatial and temporal landscape. As mentioned, the present monastery of Mergen was built in a place people agreed was auspicious. From this spot it would exude a blessing to other beings in the landscape. But Mergen had to be protected—from the tears of the proctor, for example. We soon discovered that although it was in the right place, it had been built at the wrong time, setting in train various ill consequences. Monasteries and their surroundings constitute fields of events in which time as well as space give rise to intersecting positive and negative vectors.

The story of Güng Monastery shows that auspiciousness of place is always provisional. As Duke Galdan recounts, the first Güng building at Hairatu was on the bank of the Yellow River, which flooded in 1785. It was agreed to move it, and a spot was proposed at the foot of the mountains where someone had seen a snake biting a mouse. The chair lama of Mergen intervened, however, arguing that this did not fit his idea of a good omen,[33] and he made a report to this effect to the highest authorities. Nevertheless, the monastery was rebuilt at this place. To validate the choice, a drawing was carefully made of the surrounding mountains and shown to a high reincarnation, the Ganjurwa Gegen. He opined that the supporting mountain had the shape of a heavenly letter[34] and that this must be a mark of auspiciousness and the spreading of doctrine. Against this, a Chinese land surveyor was also suspicious of the snake with the mouse omen and made his opinions known. People were unhappy at the lack of agreement, but by then the monastery had been built (Galdanwangchugdorji [1846] 1994, 11). Güng Monastery remained under the pall of being in the wrong place. It had to be moved twice subsequently, and in the Cultural Revolution it was wiped from the face of the earth.

33. The sign is ambiguous: it could be positive if the mouse is seen as an ordinary house mouse and the snake is seen as a *lus*, an auspicious spirit, but negative if the mouse is interpreted as the wealth-bearing mongoose and an ordinary snake is biting it. *Lus* are underground and water-living creatures, such as snakes, lizards, and fish, who belong to eight types. They are said to bring clouds and rain. The Green Lus are the most respected as they are also held to bring wealth. The Sky Lus is called *luu* (dragon), a complex idea associated with the Chinese (dragon *long*), the Tibetan (dragon, serpent, *klu*), and the Sanskrit (*naga*).

34. This was Hormusta's (Indra's) letter, *Ha-sam-lau-rig-ja*.

Attempts were made to predict and pin down auspiciousness. Manuscripts circulated in Mongol lands with illustrations of the "shape" of mountains in swirls and coils, indicating the cosmological quality of that type of mountain. Such divination books were used to decide on the right places to build houses, tombs, and monasteries. They attributed mountains with vitality and depicted, for example, "Mountain like a sick dragon" or "Mountain like a mounted ancestor." The texts accompanying the illustrations can be extraordinarily opaque, conflating place and time and attributing directions with fortune and/or moral qualities.[35] The strange mixture of elements conveys the idea of a mystical conjunction that we might describe as a meeting of ontologically incompatible existences. In the curvaceous calligraphic depictions of mountains described as producing various fates, we find the kind of "thinking the real through transformation" alluded to by Jullien when he writes of "l'efficacité qui n'a pas son origine dans l'initiative humaine, mais résulte de la disposition des choses" (1992, 13). Solid things, or even artifacts, have an inherent change-producing vitality. Mergen Gegen described his monastery as "the dance of a phoenix," an example admiringly quoted by the contemporary local writer Mönghe (1996,10), which suggests a similar "ambivalence . . . qui . . . trouble insidieusement les antitheses" (Jullien 1992, 12).

In divination texts "place" (*orun*) can refer to an astrological time as well as a site. The lamas decided that Mergen Monastery was built at the wrong time in this sense. After the 3rd Mergen Gegen was installed "the affairs of the monastery were not so prosperous. The reason was that its date of building was incorrect, the twenty-ninth day of the second month in the Blue Female Hare year. Although this was a lucky day (*tangsag*), it also turned out to be the Iron Sky Day of Death, the day the Sky Demon (*tngri-yin shimnu*) creates chaos and obstacles. When Mergen Gegen discovered this, he went into ritual overdrive for damage limitation: he made a suppression spell (*dom darulga*) and a ritual for Erlig Nomon Khan, the king of the underworld, he threw out the *sor*, and created the Lingka ritual dance (Galluu 2003, 28).[36]

The building of the monastery on the wrong date had endless consequences. For not only was it necessary constantly to repeat the throwing of the *sor* rite, but correcting the problem also required the hold-

35. *Gajar-un shinji*, nineteenth or early twentieth century anonymous manuscript from Inner Mongolia, p 10.

36. The local savant Mönghe explained the inauspiciousness of the date differently: the Female Hare is problematic in that it suggests that believers will run away like hares in the face of enemies (Mönghe 1996, 37).

ing of a particularly magnificent ritual dance, the Lingka Cham, every twelve years in the Hare Year. This, along with the Maidar Cham,[37] was one of the two ritual dances choreographed by the 3rd Mergen Gegen.[38] In the Lingka dance the lamas, after completing the full tantric Yamantaka visualization, don huge papier-mâché masks, and enact the appearance of a fearsome deer, which draws out a huge hideous demon from the Lingka, an edifice constructed to look like a trap or prison. On the order of protector deities, the body of the demon is cut into pieces. Not only is it killed in this way, but in an excess of anti-demonic rites, the *sor* is also thrown and a "suppression spell" is chanted. It seems that demons do not really die, but reappear and have to be killed each twelve years. Mergen Monastery is therefore fated to conduct this dance throughout cyclical time.

So central is this dance to Mergen's identity that the monastery is sometimes known as Hare Year Temple (Galluu 2003, 29–30). Today the misfortune of the wrong time is far from forgotten. Despite the difficulties of bringing in lamas, costumes, and reconstructing the dance, the Chorji told us that he had managed to hold a Lingka Cham at the appropriate time, in the first month of the Hare Year in 1999. In this way, Mergen Monastery can be seen as a subject of fortune constituted by the actualization of a happenstance of time (Da Col 2007, 229), a subject which swings into focus, as it were, each twelve-year cycle, reminding people to take action.

Monastery Rites, Personal Rites

We have met the *sor* before in this book (see Introduction). To remind readers, the *sor* is a wooden or papier-mâché pyramid containing a red shape made of dough inside, topped by a tiny human skull, and framed by painted tongues of fire. We now discovered that the *sor* had a different meaning in the context of the Lingka as distinct from the Maidar

37. The Maidar *cham* for the coming Buddha was performed at Mergen on the fifteenth of the first month of the New Year to commemorate the defeat of six demons by Shakyamuni Buddha and to welcome the coming Buddha, Maidar (Mönghe 1996, 37).

38. Lamas told us that Mergen Gegen wanted to get the *cham* from Tibet. He went to Lavrang Monastery, but the monks there were jealous and did not allow him inside the curtain they had hung around the dance floor. There was just a little space between the bottom of the curtain and the ground. Mergen peered under and observed how the feet moved. He copied these steps when he came home, but had to invent everything that happened above the feet (the arm movements and some of the dramatic roles). This is why Mergen dances are said to be different from those in Tibet, to be especially fast, sharp, and clever—even proud, as a soldier on the march.

rituals. In the latter, described earlier, the *sor* was seen as a depository of sins and misfortunes and therefore it had to be "'thrown out," whereas in the Lingka context the *sor* was a weapon, which is ritually "thrown at" the demonic enemies. In other words, the same object and gesture are constituted as different actants /actions in the two cases. Lay Mongols have no problem in accommodating both ideas as the same time, and there is even a third understanding of the *sor*. Its heart consists of a vertical object made of red dough, and thus it can be seen as a fierce variety of *baling*, the mysterious dough shapes with multiple meanings used in many offering rituals (sometimes called "offering cakes" in Tibetan, *torma*, Mills 2003, 122). Seen in this light the *sor* is a food offering, thrown to the demons to satisfy them and keep them at bay.

No attempt is made by lamas to separate out the ideas, no neat division between the Lingka and Maidar dances; rather, a number of meanings are left available for the same actions. We do not think this is a result of contemporary mixing up of formerly separate rituals, nor of sheer carelessness. Rather, the co-activation of ill-assorted meanings is done consistently, not only at public rituals but also in domestic settings. The face-washing ritual is a good example of how such a doubling works. This is done not only as an annual ritual for high lamas, but also by ordinary laypeople when they feel they are polluted (*bujar*), for example, by ill luck, bad dreams, depression, or attending a funeral. First the lama creates sanctified water (*rashiyan*) by infusing it with medical herbs and blowing mantras over the pot. A few drops of *rashiyan* then purifies a large bowl of clean water, and an assistant dips into it to rinse the mouth, face, and hands of the polluted person. A special basin is placed to collect the now dirty water as it falls from the washing—a basin already containing food leftovers and tea leaves. The whole mixture is thrown to the spirits—with the double (almost incompatible) meanings: first, "let us get rid of our polluted water" and second, "here is food for you, so be satisfied and do not attack us."

Similarly, items like the *sor*, which seem the archetypal esoteric implements of monkish ritual, can be part of everyday practice. People friendly with an able lama may ask him to wield a small *sor* on their behalf in order to harm a personal enemy. This kind of request was prevalent during the Cultural Revolution and later political campaigns, as revenge for the many cases of malicious accusations against innocent people. A *sor* cannot work against an unknown enemy, but if people knew that someone had used a political movement to mask a personal vendetta, they might secretly approach a lama to help exact vengeance or at least ward off the harm.[39] We have tried to show in this section that public rituals are not divorced from ordinary people's lives. The monastery as ritual subject has an affinity with, or appears in parallel with, individual subjects, who use some of the same techniques for their own reasons.

"Temptation" and the Magical Operator

The monastery finds itself in a land already teeming with forces in which Mergen Gegen is held to be the chief operator. The monastery could be seen as a localized interaction consisting of all the *other* local interactions distributed elsewhere in time and space, which have been brought to bear on the scene through the relays of various nonhuman actors (Latour 2005a, 194). But although there are interactions among such mediators—the ruins, the stony ground, the sparse rain, the electricity cable, the birds that arrive in spring, and so forth—it would not do justice to Mongol understandings to eliminate intention, passion, and assumptions about causality. Rain occurring at a certain time to the benefit of a certain place is very often seen not as water drops randomly falling from clouds, but as the "provision of rain" for a given place/subject/ego. It is as though the Mongols pay particular attention to the "sensible," i.e., to the *felt* relation between the thing and "I."[40]

It was understood that occult forces in the land were set going into the indefinite future by the acts of particular individuals. If chief among these was the 3rd Mergen Gegen, he should perhaps be understood in these contemporary narratives not so much as the handed-down image

39. Hürelbaatar remembers that one evening in deep winter during the Cultural Revolution a *sor* was found in a field outside the village. It was frozen hard and half-buried in snow, otherwise it would have been eaten by animals. The find caused great turmoil. At one of the constant political meetings, it was announced that an ideologically forbidden object had been found and it was imperative to find out who was the guilty person who had made it. Everyone knew that only lamas made such things. There were only three former lamas left in the village. People tried to deflect enquiries to the neighboring settlements. In the end no one admitted responsibility and the affair died down, but Hürelbaatar's grandfather knew that only one of the lamas had to the ability to conduct such a "hard" ritual. "Throwing a *sor*" was secret not only for political reasons, but also because good lamas should not do such harmful things.

40. As Quentin Meillassoux has written: "Without the *perception* of redness, there is no red thing [. . .]. Whether it be affective or perceptual, the sensible only exists as a *relation*: a relation between the world and the living creature I am. In actuality, the sensible is neither simply 'in me' in the manner of a dream, nor simply 'in the thing' in the manner of an intrinsic property: it is in the very relation between the thing and I" (2008, 2).

of a historical person, but rather as the present-day representation of what "our tradition" stands for and the way it reacts.

In a standard Buddhist account, the interactions of a lama with the powers of the land could be seen as "temptations"—in the sense of an external agency that arouses one's desire (*hüsel*), creates a sensual attachment (*tachiyanggui*), and thus hinders the search for the higher goal of enlightenment. One's duty is to resist and exclude them, especially if one has taken vows. But Mergen Gegen did not exclude these encounters. This means that the tradition has established its chief creator as a "tempted" person—in other words, dealing with "temptation" is a resource of the tradition. What is significant about Mergen Gegen is that these external encounters are not seen as necessarily negative. Most importantly, they are not interpreted as a moral downfall (*doruital*) even if they seem to be precisely that—because there always must be some truer vision at issue. Rather than being seen as an inward fall from grace, the temptation-encounter is here addressed outward as positive action, "dealing with" it in ways that could end up for good or ill.

This seems different from the typical Buddhist intervention in the land in many Tibetan traditions: notably the ancient scenario of quelling a monstrous and malevolent female being associated with snake-like creatures (*klu*) thrashing in a watery underground by means of erecting stupas and monasteries to pin down her limbs—a scene reinforced by stories about Padmasambhava's defeat of land gods. Makley argues for Tibet that "mandalization" was the main framework for constructing authoritative male subjectivity in unequivocal domination over the female.[41] In Mongol lands, however, lamas we spoke to disclaimed knowledge of an underground demoness, while the *mandala*, which we discussed earlier in the case of Mergen Gegen's *Altan Tobchi*, is not primarily, if at all, tied to gender constructions. In the Mergen environment, gender relations are often framed in the more complex structure of what we have called temptation. Here as we shall see, transgressive desires can lead to positive outcomes if the encounter is managed skillfully.

The first of the resonant legends told to us concerns the malevolent danger of the Human Rock (*Hümün Chilagu*). This is a case where Mer-

41. Writing of the great Labrang monastery in the Tibetan frontier region of Amdo, Makley argues that mandalization was based on indigenous understandings of masculine efficacy as the taming of the wildness and femaleness embodied by capricious non-Buddhist deities (2007, 53). Taming rituals, including the *cham* dance-dramas, were forms of violent space making that arbitrated hierarchical arrangements of humans and deities, and imposed material and organizational requirements on people (2007, 54).

gen Gegen slipped up—to the detriment of successive generations. Human Rock is a pinnacle on the mountain ridge to the northwest of the monastery. It was Shirüngerel, a prosperous herdswoman living in the hamlet of West Plateau (*Baragun Debeseg*), who first pointed it out to us. "Can't you see how that man rock stares down at us?" she had asked. We could not see a rock of particularly human appearance among the many jagged peaks on the horizon. She thought our eyesight was maybe not so good and lent us a pair of binoculars. Only after discussion did we clarify that it was the slightly bent finger-like pinnacle that she had in mind. The malevolent gaze of this rock falls diagonally on the northwest corner of the monastery. To bar its way, Mergen Gegen had erected a ritual flag (*darchug*) on an intervening hill to inspire the monastery's wind-horse spirit (*hei-mori*) and vital force (*sülde*). This hill is still known as Darchug Hill, though the flag itself was dismantled in the Cultural Revolution. And the 3rd Mergen Gegen had done further protective work by building a row of five *sach* (shrines) between the flag and the corner of the monastery. His *sach* are now a row of tumbled heaps of stone.

Why was this double defense needed? The story is that the Human Rock is the [spirit] master of the rocks and forest, the guardian of a treasure of silver, which was secreted in a deep hole under the waterfall in the Valley of Birds. Mergen Gegen quite simply was tempted and greedy. Several stories recount how he made efforts to get the silver. This angered the spirit master, who constantly created troubles for the monastery. Mergen Gegen then sent a Chinese stonemason to cut down the Human Rock. The mason climbed up the mountains, reached the White Yidam Peak by evening, and then started to chop at the stone man on the western ridge. Blood spurted out from the body without stopping. Terrified, the mason tumbled back down to the monastery. From that time, the Human Rock caused even more misfortune, which is why Mergen Gegen set up his double defenses. But evidently they were not totally effective, for Galluu writes that more is needed. He provides five Sanskrit mantras and tells his readers: "If you lay disciples of the world do not know these mantras, every morning when you get up you should point to the Rock Person and curse it, saying, 'May your crimes and deeds of anger be smashed by Heaven and eliminated by Earth'" (Galluu 2003, 746).

It seems there is in fact no silver ore in the Muna Mountains, though there is gold, which is the target of semi-undercover gold-digging expeditions, and they are full of other valuable resources: wood for building, medicinal herbs that can be sold at market, fruits, and wild animals that can be hunted for various purposes. Perhaps "silver" stands for all those precious attributes of the mountains that properly belong to its guardian spirit. In fact, depredations of the mountains have been a constant theme in the history of Mergen, starting with a petition by Duke Darmaridi to the Qing authorities against Chinese woodcutters—a protest that was endorsed by Mergen Gegen, who wrote a strongly worded poem to this effect. Yet in these narratives of the Human Rock, it was Mergen Gegen himself who started the damaging series of misfortunes by his desire to appropriate the silver. Perhaps Mergen Gegen here represents a certain high-handed willfulness of reincarnations, which is not seen as triumphant, for misfortune continued to dog the monastery. In 1998, it is true that no one cared enough to repair the flag or *sach* shrines, but some elderly people implied that such neglect would have a bad outcome.

The 3rd Mergen Gegen was also the initiator in positive relational energies in the landscape. If the Darchug Hill lies to the northwest of the precinct, there is another hill of similar height standing to the northeast. On this hill the Goddess of Melody (Egeshig-ün Öhin Tngri) appeared in a revelatory vision to Mergen Gegen. He made her thereafter his personal deity, and also invited her to be the protector god of the Mergen Gegen *sang*. This is the same deity who appeared as the old shepherdess whose prodding with a chopstick divined the auspicious place for the monastery, but on this occasion she took the form of an attractive young woman. The lama invited her to his realm from her homeland (*nutug*) in the northeast continent of Mount Sümber (Sumeru) and built a memorial stupa (*suburgan*) for her on the shoulder of the northeastern hill. People remember this pagoda as beautiful and painted brilliant white, with a shrine housing a *hot mandal* for the deity alongside.[42] Öhin Tngri is the tantric consort of Manjushiri, and two forms of the deity were worshipped here, the gentle music goddess and the fierce defender form, Tegüs Chogtu Öhin Tngri, suppressor of demons amid a blood sea. Mergen Gegen used to meditate on both forms, and he is said to have hidden his ritual vase (*bumba*) and his Manjushiri "'wisdom sword" (*bilig-ün ildü*), both integral to the relevant tantric rites, at this site. On auspicious dates, Galluu writes, a seven-colored rainbow would gleam from Öhin Tngri's stupa in the

42. To invite and visualize a *yidam* deity it is necessary to construct a place or palace (*hota*) in which to invite him or her. The *mandala* is a stylized plan of such a divine pavilion (see Chapters 2 and 6). The *choyag* (caretaker) lama responsible for the Sharil Temple where the sacred remains of the Mergen Gegens were kept would come to this spot on the first, eighth, and fifteenth of each month in the evening to make lamp and incense offerings (Galluu 2003, 750).

daytime and the ray of Manjushiri's pure wisdom would shine out in the evening. "Anyone who understands the magic (*ridi-shidi*) light emanating from this stupa, if he or she worships with true trust will have his wisdom eye opened and his mind cleared. If he has any illness, especially if he cannot talk properly, that problem will be cleansed" (Galluu 2003, 750).

Öhin Tngri Hill was a prime site of "mandalization, but unlike in the Tibetan model described by Makley, here there is no idea of suppressing the female. The protective, purifying deity at Mergen is feminine and both of her forms, gentle and fierce, are seen as strong and helpful to the people of Mergen. We have mentioned that Mergen Gegen's main liturgical theme was Yamantaka, who is a wrathful form of Manjushiri, but these stories prioritize Manjushiri as the god of transcendent wisdom, and his tantric consort, the goddess of music, poetry and sacred speech. There could be no more perfect construct for lamas trying to maintain the Mergen tradition.

We were taken to see the Music Goddess's stupa almost as soon as we arrived in Mergen, as it was regarded as one of the most important sites in the vicinity. The pagoda had been demolished in the Cultural Revolution,[43] but the foundations were visible, including a hole some four feet deep. These ruins are on the shoulder of the hill. On the peak there had been a stone fort, with slits for firing. When this fort was demolished a woman's helmet was found underneath it. People say that many ancient objects must have been stolen from this hill, and only *Hitad-Mitad* (Chinese) gold prospectors could have been rash enough to do it. The Öhin Tngri hill is even now sacred ground. Children are not allowed to play there and older people say they can see its former white pagoda gleaming in their mind's eye. It was conch-like in its beauty and "'like an inlaid pearl seen from a distance" (Mönghe 1996, 92).

Thus, Mergen Monastery found itself at the intersection of three powerful invisible currents: from the southwest the curse and the tears of the Proctor, from the northwest the malevolent stare of the Human Rock, and from the northeast the beneficial gleam of the Goddess of Melody. Each of these forces was initiated, or brought into play, by actions of the 3rd Mergen Gegen.

Note that these are occult points that linked together powerful diagonal *directions,* slicing across the square north-south orientation of

43. We were told that this pagoda was used as a target by soldiers practicing during the occupation of the monastery by the army. Local people were outraged and said that this sin caused rain to stop falling.

the monastery. Mongols are highly aware of direction and always construct sacred buildings facing the south, or front. The diagonal lines of occult influence therefore reach the monastery at its corners—and corners are regarded as points of vulnerability in many everyday situations in herders' lives.[44] Sengge Lama told us that the benign energy of the Goddess of Music (northeast) forms "one thread" (*nige utasu*) passing through the main door of the Chogchin Temple to reach the *oboo* (southwest) where the proctor shed his tears. Then he mentioned that the line extends further, to another monument in the northeast direction, beyond the Öhin Tngri Hill.

Several people told us the story about this site, Öhin Jilaga ("Girl Gulley"), a steep cleft in the mountains beside the road on the east side up the Mergen Valley. What happened was that a young girl fell in love with a lama in the monastery, but in this situation of temptation the relationship could not be consummated because of the lama's vow of celibacy. In despair the girl killed herself and her spirit began to haunt the gulley. The unhappy spirit took revenge by attacking the penises of men passing by, causing them to have painful erections. Mergen Gegen took pity on this girl and built a monumental stone penis facing toward the gulley "to satisfy her." After that, the spirit was calmed and men could pass the spot without problems. However, during the PLA occupation in the 1960s this phallic edifice was blasted into pieces to provide building materials and widen the road. During our fieldwork, the recent deaths of two young people who fell when wandering into the nearby waterfall gulley were tentatively attributed to the anger of the spirit at this destruction. Logically, the girl's spirit should still haunt the area. But no rituals are now carried out to appease her. Our explanation for this is that the original situation—the presence of a large number of monks sworn to celibacy—does not exist these days, and furthermore the area is no longer part of the lived landscape. It was taken over by the army and no herders live in this desolated place. Since the road was widened, a weapons store was built nearby, and only occasional tourist buses churn up and down to a recently built camp in the mountains. Thus certain powerful mythic accounts recede from people's preoccupations, without however completely disappearing.

Sexual and vagina-related interpretations of caves and rock clefts are

44. For example, when people sit round a square table no one should sit at a corner. A person at the corner will have misfortune; for example he or she will be wronged/criticized by others. Winds that blow diagonally (southwest, northeast, etc.) are often said to be inauspicious, bringing illness, etc.

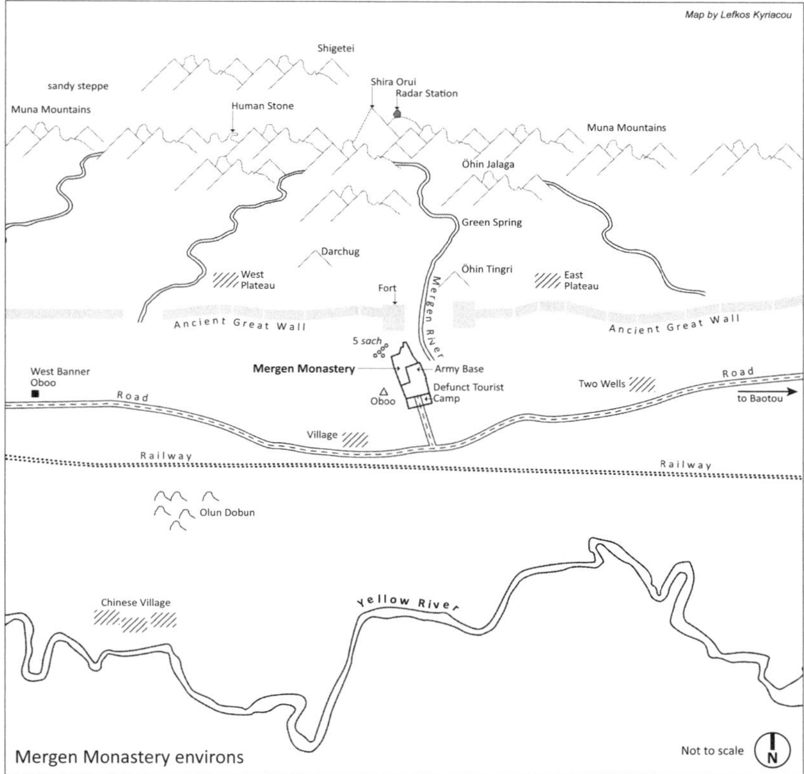

Map 2 Sketch map of the Mergen Monastery.

found all over Inner Asia. Essentially non-Buddhist in inspiration, they are associated with female fertility and also—by ritualized squeezing through the cleft—with accumulation of merit (Lessing 1957, 95–99; Charleux 2002, 81–83). Mergen Gegen's construction of a phallus facing the cave is certainly not unique (see Humphrey 1995, 15, for an example in a shamanic context). What is significant is the positive understanding of sexuality and fertility generated by rituals at such places. We draw attention here, moreover, to the position of Girl Gulley, given that the Muna Mountains are full of similar ravines. For it makes up a line from northeast to southwest whereby scenes of high emotion associated with temptation—sexual yearning, and the sadness of being expelled for upright objections to misdemeanors of the night—pass through the monastery. As Galluu's story of the cursing proctor shows, however, a Buddhist understanding relegates such preoccupations to the worldly superficiality that overlies a deeper reality, as our final narrative also indicates.

Given the Mongol predilection for symmetry, one might expect to find an occult current also emanating from the fourth direction, the southeast, and indeed we discovered this to be the case. Down in the bed of the Mergen River there was a sacred pool, the Green Spring (*Nogugan Bulag*), which used to provide water for the entire monastery. Often covered with bright green weeds, this pond was watered by three sources and until recently stood in a grove of trees. At various times small shrine-temples had been built beside it.[45] Mergen lamas, especially those of the Chorji *sang*, used to conduct annual rituals there, with sacrifice of a castrated goat in the fifth month to give thanks and request rain. The last shrine was razed to the ground in the Cultural Revolution and the pond was dug out to make a well. But it dried up, and the trees have been cut down. Now the site is just a dry, boulder-strewn bend in the riverbed and rituals are no longer held there. Shirüngerel was bitter as she told us this history.

In Shirüngerel's story, a huge green snake (*mogoi*)[46] came wriggling up the valley from the southeast and stopped for a rest at the Green Spring. Let us, however, take up the more detailed version in her son's book (Mönghe 1996, 99–103). One day, Mergen Gegen told his *ombu* and other officials to prepare for an important guest coming from the southeast direction—"Set up a decorated Mongolian yurt with tea, food, lamps, and incense to welcome the guest." The disciples prepared all this and looked out, but no one like a distinguished guest appeared. Late in the afternoon, at the time of releasing mares, two strange figures came into view, a beautiful young beggar woman in a worn-out green robe, a torn vest with red brocade border, and carrying a white particolored bag, and a man in helmet and armor with a red-brown face, leading a blue horse. "We have come to meet the Mergen Gegen," they said. When the lamas reported that two shabby-looking people had arrived, the Gegen said, "These are just the honored guests expected," and he ordered yogurt made from three kinds of milk, tasty fruits, rice

45. One of these temples was built in the 1940s by a herder called Gombu from Baragun Debeseg. He moved a stone that looked like a sitting man from a place in the plain and made it into a deity (*burhan*), which the Mongols called "Geser," said to be the Mongol equivalent of the Chinese warrior-hero Guandi. This temple was ruined in a flood. Another shrine was built by a local Chinese man, who called it *Long Wang Miao* (Dragon Prince Temple) (Mönghe 1996, 190).

46. Sometimes dignified as *lus-un sabdag*, a Tibetan-derived term for a water deity, in written versions of the legend.

cooked in butter, and other dishes to be prepared. After the meal, the warrior-like guest said it was time for him to go. He mounted his blue horse and set off into the mountains. Mergen Gegen entertained the young woman alone in his palace, lighting lamps for her and talking pleasantly the whole night long.

A temple-keeper lama (*nirba*) had a wrong thought: "Why is our Gegen so keen on this strange woman?" He licked his finger, quietly poked a hole in the paper window and peered in. He saw a monstrously big (*aburgu*) green snake lying coiled on the left side of the bed, with Mergen Gegen sitting alongside, talking animatedly, smiling, and counting his prayer beads. The next morning the lama had gone completely blind.

After entertaining the respected guest, the Mergen Gegen saw her off from the Green Spring. She went up the valley to Kidney Spring, where she took a rest, and then crossed the mountains to an area of moving sand dunes. These were destructive, suffocating shifting sands, sent by a curse to spread from west to east and ruin the Harachin grasslands. Traveling constantly in a southeast to northwest direction, the green snake stopped the sands at a place called Güyüg Oasis, stayed there for a night, and then went on to Shitügen (also called Shigetei), a subject monastery of Mergen, in the hills north of the plain, and there she settled down.

Mönghe's comment is that this snake woman was none other than the Green Master Spirit (*ejen*) of Water, come to fulfill the task of managing water in the era of decline for the benefit of religion and living beings. The Master of the Mountains, Muna Khan with his blue horse, led her to Mergen Gegen, and the Gegen entertained her and discussed how to supply inexhaustible water to the area. After their agreement, a green spring gushed out at the place where she stopped, a kidney-shaped spring emerged where she took rest, and leafy oases were created in the desert where she stayed the night (1996, 103). Galluu also gives an entirely positive account of the Green Snake Woman: "Mergen Gegen wanted to worship her and give her the Shitügen Mountain as her home, in order to keep this Green *Lus* in his land (*nutug*) forever" (Galluu 2003, 729). These stories indicate that the idiom of the relation between lamas and female spirits was not so much subjugation as "agreement" (*tohiral*), a distinctive shift in emphasis as compared with Tibet. They also show how the geography of the region was imagined—the blowing desert sands of the upland steppe and the leafy mountains with their trickling springs, so well documented by travelers in the nineteenth century (Przheval'skii [1875] 1946, 122–25; Obruchev 1950, 86–95).[47] Natural processes in this environment are not seen as independent of human activity but interactive with it—indeed in this case by means of a deceptively teasing scenario of temptation. If a woman, this person should not have stayed overnight within the *goriya*. But if a she were a wonder-working snake . . . ?

The 3rd Mergen Gegen appears as a cosmic player, initiating and countering energies in the surrounding lands for the protection and succor of his monastery. There is a cautionary note to these narratives, however, if we take them together. Even the greatest lama has to operate skillfully, respectfully, flexibly—in a word, he must be an *argachin*, he must *argadahu* (coax matters along). If he fails to do this, as when he decided brutally to cut down the Human Stone, matters end badly. If he hosts and appeases local deities like the water-bringing green snake all is well. Everyone told us that although the Urad lands in general are regularly drought stricken, Mergen Monastery has never lacked for water. Note that *arga* (ways, means, methods, steps, trick, scheme) has philosophical connotations, as it is the "male," "light," and "positive" pair to the term *bilig* (talent, gift, intelligence, endowment, wisdom), which is the "female," "negative" principle. *Arga-bilig* is the translation for the religious pairing of "skillful means" and "wisdom," the two qualities possessed by the Buddha (S. *upāya-prajñā*). It applies to the tantric pairing of Manjushiri and Öhin Tngri, and to the Chinese *yin-yang*. At the same time, *arga-bilig* is the basic principle of all generative processes, both human and non-human.

This chapter has illustrated some of the complexities—indeed contradictions—of the Mongolian monastery as an object of thought. It can be seen as the victorious *mandala*, set down in some spot to purify and rule it. Yet for some reason this cannot be an autocratic act: it requires the blessing of an autochthonous power (here, a married couple of elderly lay herders) before the site can be known. Buddhist triumphalism can be undone in other ways—a fortunate place may be admirable in every way, but the whole enterprise may be subverted by the inauspicious date chosen for the founding. Further, the pristine, symmetrical *mandala*, as soon as it is embodied as buildings in a landscape, is subject to the constant processes of human intervention, shifting, demolition, addition and rebuilding, gathering and dispersal, such that

47. Przheval'skii's account, deriving from his travels in the 1870s, enables us to estimate the lifespan of some of these legends about the Mergen landscape. Some that he mentions are no longer current, while others, such as the story of the silver, are still popular.

the original plan becomes barely discernible in the village-like reality. This in turn is punctured by pure sanctity: the temple is the housing for the statue, relic, or reincarnation—all of these "alive" and in some sense unpredictable (see Chapter 7). Here and there around the monastery are constellations of other vital points that the lamas say are necessary to its survival. These are places of events, affect-laden springs, rocks, protective shrines, cremation sites, and so forth. The residents today, both lay herders and monks, see Mergen Gegen as the prime cosmic initiator and manager of relations with the energies of these objects. Above all, he can see things for what they really are. Nevertheless, there are ways in which he is not imagined as unambiguously all-powerful or perfectly virtuous. Stories are repeatedly told—and salted into folklore—of his possibly irregular relations, and in such contexts he has to be an *argachin*, here not so much in the philosophical sense as in the worldly idea of a skillful operator. This indicates that the Mongols exercise their imagination about the play between levels of reality, and repeatedly bring to the fore the conventional actuality in which Buddhism is not all-powerful, but has its place in a wider scene.

Where then does this leave the dukes and politicians, the other serious powers in this world?

FOUR

Duke Galdan, Perspectives on the Self in the Qing Era

Professor Naranbatu described to us in loving detail the temples at Güng Monastery where he had been a lama as a boy. He wanted to tell us about a fateful day during the Cultural Revolution. One cold winter's night in 1966 everyone was wearing thick coats, padded inside with fur. Güng Monastery had been demolished and all of the sacred texts removed; they were left in a shed awaiting transport to the Baotou paper mill for recycling. A former Mergen lama, Huashang, now a schoolteacher, noticed the guard was momentarily absent. He darted inside the shed and grabbed a particular bundle of manuscripts—the historical memoirs of Duke Galdanwangchugdorji—put it inside his coat and ran out. There was an aim to his raid: as a teacher Huashang knew that not only religious texts were being destroyed but evidence of Urad history too. Later, when it became possible after 1984, Naranbatu and others started scouring the countryside for any remnants. He visited a distant relative and explained his task. She turned to her husband, Huashang, and said, "That book you have been hiding, isn't that just the kind of thing our cousin is searching for?" Huashang did not look up. His wife pressed him again. Huashang went out silently and eventually came back and put a bundle wrapped in cloth on the table. Naranbatuu was overjoyed. No other historical account had survived. "Everything we know is in Ga Güng's history—without it we'd know nothing," he told us.

Besides historical information, Duke Galdan's text provides an internal view of the moral predicaments of a ruling lord (*jasag noyan*) of his time (he ruled Urad West Banner from 1834 to 1854). One of the texts in the manuscript is his autobiography, which may be among the first by a layman in Mongolian literature.[1] His melancholy account, haunted by self-reproaches, represents an experiment in a radically interiorizing act—the writer depicts not just what he sees happening around him but what he sees within himself. The other items in the bundle of papers include a history of Güng and Mergen monasteries and three long poems.[2] The latter are "verses of contrition" (*gemshil shilüg*), expressing deep regret for being the kind of person he was—a noble and not a lama. The duke's writings are evidence of a sensibility that up to now has been unsuspected—or at least unstudied—among the pre-modern Mongols. The early appearance of the genre of "words of regret" (*gemshihü üge*) shows that from the thirteenth through fourteenth centuries a consciousness of self had appeared in writing by Mongols. "Agent regret" involves seeing oneself doing something and feeling that action to be wrong (Humphrey and Hürelbaatar 2005, 3–5). The early examples show people disputing and agonizing over what was right or wrongful action in a period of radical political change. They did not, however, take the further step of reflecting on the different kinds of self proposed by distinctive ethical systems and how one might consciously transform oneself in the light of such a system (Laidlaw 2002), let alone attempt to escape or transcend such schemes.

In the nineteenth century, however, distinctive moral orders were not just present but long since firmed up by the presence of specifically Buddhist education, as well as the Qing imperial code (which was allied with more distant Confucian prescriptions), both of which coexisted in tension with the continued transmission of indigenous Mongol kingly-heroic ethics. It is exactly the consciousness of such alternatives that

1. Mongolian authors wrote Buddhist biographies-hagiographies (*namtar*) in both Mongolian and Tibetan, but few examples are known of autobiographies. Several distinct and brilliant traditions of autobiography emerged in Tibet from the fifteenth century onward (Gyatso 1998; Diemberger 2007b). But the genre did not spread to Mongolia, perhaps because it arose mostly in non-Gelugpa sects, whereas the Mongols were rather solidly Gelugpa from the sixteenth century on. Duke Galdan's writing is idiosyncratic; it does not have the Nyingma fascination with mystical visions (Gyatso 1998, 266), nor does it seem influenced by Chinese Chan Buddhist revelation, Confucian autobiography (Wu 1990), or Chinese narratives of the self in dramatic historical events (Struve 2004). Its layman's outlook and ethical preoccupations also differentiate it from the earlier autobiography of the lama Ishibaljur (see Chapter 2 and Erdenibayar 2007).

2. The history, autobiography, three poems, and some Banner correspondence were published in Naranbatu and Mönghe 1997, but a further manuscript from the bundle, giving details of economic transactions, has not yet been published.

besets Duke Galdan. They can be seen as forming three pressing, overlapping, and yet basically contrasting "apparatuses," which Foucault called *dispositifs* (Gordon 1980, 194–228), a *dispositif* being a strategic yet heterogeneous arrangement of discourse, institutions, architectural forms, social arrangements, laws, or moral propositions. Such an ensemble is experienced as coming from outside, like a commandment. Giorgio Agamben (2007, 28) takes this idea further by investigating how a *dispositif* produces a characteristic subjectivity ("subjectivation") by engendering, controlling and orienting ". . . the comportment, gestures and the thoughts of men." While any individual person may "host" several such subjectivities, in each case they take the form of an implicit agreement to the terms created by this particular apparatus (2007, 13). We use this idea to show how it provides the parameters for contrasting kinds of historical subjectivity that may coexist for an individual person. Duke Galdan was not the first of the Urad dukes, nor was he the last, to have been pulled in two or three directions. Galdan's father's brother, Duke Jigmiddorji (ruled 1779–1791), was torn by the same issues, and so, at a much later period, was Duke Shirabdorji (ruled 1931–1936), although neither of them left written records. Duke Galdan, who wrote poetically and at length about his feelings, could be seen as exemplifying what seems to have been, in some ways, a repeated dilemma in the lives of Mongol local rulers.

The background to Duke Galdan's life in broad terms is as follows: the loss of sovereignty by the ruling nobles under the Qing gave rise to doubt about the value of ancestral Mongolian aristocratic ideals and practices; or perhaps it would be more accurate to say that they were made latent, shifted to a pool of ideas that could be called upon, but separated from practical government. Nevertheless, the dukes inherited a set of Mongolian martial ideas and inspirational practices that they did not allow to die out completely. Indeed, these were some of the indigenous themes most promoted by Mergen Gegen, and after his lifetime the main elements, such as the sacrificial cult of *sülde* (vital force) and the Battle Standard, found their way into the annual cycle of services at Mergen Monastery. With the end of the Qing in 1911, these martial rites of glorification of rule, which were sponsored by dukes and other leaders, came to the fore during political crises (Chapter 5). It is significant that, even though the dukes themselves as a political institution were abolished after "Liberation" in 1949, the cults went on being performed for some years and indeed were revived in the 1980s. This indicates that the set of ideas with which the nobles were especially associated did not in fact belong just to them, but was—and still is—something of value to many Mongols. As we shall see in the case of Duke Galdan, he associated his position as ruling noble with both Manchu Qing militarism (Waley-Cohen 1996) and with the Mongol aristocratic-martial way of life, and both caused him agonies of self-recrimination. The duke could not make himself an actor unselfconsciously at ease in either of the major lay *dispositifs* appropriate for his position. But nor could he assimilate to the Buddhist world, for although he had spent time in a monastery in his youth and tried hard (on and off) to uphold religious ideals, he was cast into despair by the presence right beside him of his older brother, a reincarnate lama with a halo of brilliance like all incarnations. Duke Galdan described himself as a stumbling practitioner of the 3rd Mergen Gegen's teachings, and he also evidently saw himself as an emulator in questions of aesthetics and poetics. On the face of it, the duke's writing is obsessed with the question: Why have I not been able to make myself the kind of person I hold to be most morally admirable?

But what are we to make of the "I" which occurs so often in Galdan's writings? Agamben's theory of subjectivity (subjectivation) proposes a de-anchored, "social" subject, one who may be envisaged as lurching between different *dispositifs*. We note, however, this interstitial, imprinted, blank cannot account for a given person's character, or in William James's term, their temperament. This chapter, based on a close reading of Galdan, suggests that anthropologists need to develop ways of incorporating a "nonsociological" (Anderson 2006, 6) understanding of individual character, which can be seen as whatever, at a given time, a person *trusts* within himself and "loads the evidence for him one way or the other" (James 1975, 11). Duke Galdan is one of several people in this book for whom we have found that their particular temperament steered their actions, and hence had effect in the wider direction of events at Mergen.

The Donator-Preceptor Relation and the "Two Orders"

There is another problem with the *dispositif* idea—proposing itself as theory it does not allow for theorizing by the people living within it. Yet already in early Indian and Tibetan thought Buddhists were theorizing the rightful relation between kings and religious leaders. In the famous "patron-priest" paradigm, or "two orders" (*hoyar yosu*) as it came to be known in Mongolia, the lay ruler supports the spiritual authority of the religious leader, who in turn recognizes the ruler as protector of religion. Thus a ready-made slot was available for the duke, and indeed he refers to the model, naming his own lineage as merit-making patrons of the Urad monasteries and detailing the gifts they supplied. However, even a brief account of how the "patron-priest" idea came to be received by Mongols and its political fate by the nineteenth century will show why someone like the Duke could find it less than inspiring.

Seyfort Ruegg has argued that the translation "patron-priest" is misleading and that the Tibetan term *yon mchod* should be translated as "donor-preceptor," signaling the honorable teaching role of the lama recipient (1997, 857–58). It is true that this compound term is best known in reference to the relationship between the Mongolian Emperor Qubilai and the Tibetan 'Phags pa lama (1997, 860), but it is relevant that the Mongols' operation of similar-sounding concepts was open to significantly different understandings from the Tibetan. The Mongolians' unique political history, their world-scale Empire and repeated attempts to reconstitute it, or something like it, gave an edge to the imperial side not present in Tibet. Concomitant with this is the relative downplaying of the idea that the lay ruler is to be seen primarily as a donor. In the White History (*Chagan Teühe*), a key sixteenth-century Mongol text of political philosophy, the Buddhist Chakravartin king dominates over both orders.[3] The temporal side is identified with a sanctified and universal ruler, who himself spreads doctrine, while the idea of the king as donor does not appear. At the end of the text the ruler is extolled in expressions that seem hardly Buddhist at all. The great deeds of Qubilai Khan were achieved, "Through the power of the eternal Sky (*tngri*), by the rays of the great genius, and in the things handed down by his divine majesty Chinggis" (ibid, 99). Thus inserted into an important text that seemingly only reproduces the standard "donor-preceptor" theory is something rather different: the insistence, within an overall Buddhist idiom, on the Mongol idea of an independent source of supreme kingly power.

As Elverskog convincingly argues, the later orthodoxy—identifying the patron-ruler as a Buddhist devotee and providing him with a tacked-on bodhisattva status in the case of the Manchu Emperor[4]—became a ruling ideology of the Qing, and this not only obscured the

3. "The person who carries out the worldly order, rolling a thousand golden wheels among the living beings suffering in the dark night, the one who spreads the doctrinal principles (*nom-un törü*) and *tarni* without mixing them, that person is called the True High Chakravartin Emperor" (Liu 1981, 80).

4. The Qianlong Emperor (1736–1796) adopted the role of universal ruler, portraying himself, especially for Tibetan and Mongolian audiences, as an incarnation of Manjushiri.

actual plurality and dynamics of Mongol religiosity but also skewed the writing of history. Because many Mongol chronicles were written within the framework of this ideology most European accounts follow it too, doing "epistemic violence" to the Mongols by depicting them as "Tibetan Buddhists" (2007, 63). Mergen Gegen, however, was one of several Mongolian Buddhist leaders to question the orthodoxy—and Duke Galdan, educated in this tradition, would have been aware of alternative visions.

The great king who is dignified as Chakravartin or bodhisattva is different from the reincarnation who assumes ruling power (Ruegg 1997, 864). Tibetans turned to the Buddhist reincarnation as ruler, while the Mongols from early times went for the king with religious pretensions.[5] Though they seem like parallels, what is crucial is the ontological difference in the sources of their power. This is exactly what is revealed in the story of the Mergen Gegen's meeting with the Manchu emperor, which we shall shortly discuss. But the problem for a minor ruler, such as the duke, was that the Mongol Chakravartin role was long since defunct. The Manchus adopted and saturated the Mongol tradition of declaring the emperor as bodhisattva, disallowing any rivals, and they dampened the pretensions of subordinate rulers in other ways too. A concomitant of the bestowal of imperial "grace" (M. *heshig*, grace, fortune, bounty, translating the Chinese *en* "sovereign grace") was its co-product—the sense of obligation, self-abegnation, and guilt of the recipients for falling short in repaying the benefit (Atwood 2000, 112). At the same time, Confucian ideals of obligatory political loyalty sutured to filial piety, spread widely to the Mongols through oral narratives, imperial edicts and translations of Chinese novels (Atwood 2000, 125). Thus, while both dukes and high reincarnate lamas went to the Qing court to present their credentials and receive grace, it is not surprising that the meetings of the former seem to have resulted in something of an imaginative blank. The lamas' encounters with the emperor, on the other hand, are the subject of amazing legends, and these miraculous episodes, at least in Mergen accounts, are wildly at odds with Buddhist Qing orthodoxy. It is not difficult to see the reason for the difference. The lamas' ability to confront the emperor derived from their "other" nature, whose spiritual superiority was at least spo-

5. All of the Mongol Yuan Emperors after Qubilai proclaimed themselves to be incarnations of one or another deity or bodhisattva. Mongol historians from the seventeenth century onward also credit Qubilai with having taken the Tantric consecration of Mahakala, which was thought to endow him with the deity's marvelous "three-fold" intellect and consequently great ability to govern (Grupper 1980, 52–60).

radically acknowledged by the emperor, whereas the Mongol nobles had nothing much to offer amid the oppressive context of ranks and hierarchies in Beijing.

All that was left for the Mongol prince was to deploy his inheritance of the ancient Mongol notions of valor attached to great leaders such as Chinggis Khan and Hasar back at home in his Banner. The all-Mongol ritual sites for worshipping these great warriors had been isolated, pacified, and localized. The cult of Chinggis was particularly Buddhisized, shrunk from its earlier manifestation as the ritual center of the Mongol nation (*ulus*) (Elverskog 2006a, 115–16), its celebration of military victory sidelined by the Manchus' promotion of their own martial success (Grupper 1980; Waley-Cohen 1996). In this situation the more abstract, depersonalized ideas associated with these great heroes, in particular the notion of *sülde* (vital power, might, inspiration), were diffused away from the cults and became omnipresent, available for appropriation by diverse people. For some Mongol nobles such ideas might gleam bright and large, but for others like Duke Galdan they seem to have been eclipsed by the heavy weight of actual governmental duties, and they surfaced in his narratives only in the form of (morally problematic) martial pastimes. For him there was an alternative, but unattainable, source of prowess and inspiration: the Buddhist incarnation, who escaped institutionalized clerical hierarchies and took part in unpredictable adventures. Most remarkable is that the incarnate lama did not reject the aristocratic Mongol male--militant culture. Rather, he appropriated and mastered it, building it into his vision of religious achievement.

The Incarnate Lama as the "One Who Can Do" (*Chadagchin*)

In one sense the supreme effectiveness attributed the incarnate lama can be understood in relation to the "donator/preceptor model." For by donating to and protecting the incarnation the patron enabled him to take action. In the canonical vocabulary the duke and his family were "masters of donations" (M. *öglige-yin ejen*), while the Urad monasteries and incarnate lamas were "sites of worship" (M. *tahil-un orun*). What are the implications? One side repeatedly, devotedly gave, in the hope of adding to his or her intangible tally of merit, while the other side graciously accepted—land, serfs, supplies of useful products, building materials, silver, and livestock. These donations supported monastic services, repairing buildings, and so forth, but they also set the great lamas free to act, to orchestrate impressive rituals, travel with suites of servants, and engage in the higher pursuits of education and enlightenment. To live in acceptance of this scheme meant that the role of the prince was to give, that of the Lama to *do*: to meditate, but also pray, demonstrate magic, educate, know languages and translate, to dispense blessings by rituals and pilgrimages, to cure disease, and cleanse pollution. Indeed, for Urad people the imaginary of the incarnate lama in the geography of Asia was one of freedom—sometimes a boundless willful excess of cosmogenic freedom.[6] In stories of confrontation with the Emperor, the lama is not just the skillful operator in the locality, as described in the last chapter regarding the 3rd Mergen Gegen, but can also become the supreme achiever, the "one who can do" (*chadagchin*).[7]

Let us examine a story about Mergen Gegen and the emperor provided by Galluu (2003). Although the tale is a twentieth-century account, it comes from inside the Mergen tradition and we may suppose that Duke Galdan would have been familiar with very similar, if not the same, stories. This legend goes beyond the standard genres known in Sanskrit and Tibetan literature (Robinson 1996, 57–69) because it specifically deploys the Mongolian military-heroic culture and indigenous genealogical-hierarchical notions.

Galluu's account starts with a long preamble in which he provides his (a former lama's) view of imperial politics. He writes that the Manchu emperors were determined to tame and weaken the Mongols, to eliminate their culture and replace it with Tibetan. Most Mongols were meekly unsuspicious of Enghe Amugulang Emperor (Kangxi), because "he is our sister's son (*jige*) and how can a mother's brother (*nagachu*) doubt his nephew?"[8] The Oirads, however, saw through this "poisonous policy" and rebelled; but the only result was that the Kangxi Emperor killed eight hundred thousand of them (Galluu 2003, 708). The story then begins: it was the 1st Mergen Gegen's turn to go to Beijing

6. See the story recounted to Przheval'skii by Mongols in the Mergen region about a reincarnation who led a drunken life in Beijing. Angry at being reprimanded, the lama had the capital city tipped on its side, and then he stormed off to Inner Asia where he fetched a mountain range from the Altai and dumped it the wrong way round near the Yellow River: this became the Muna Mountains (Przheval'skii 1946, 122–23). Such worldly freedom is at odds with the Sanskritic model, which developed in a different direction in India, certainly among the Jains. There, gift giving to monks is a morally perilous activity, and its best aim is to enable the renouncer *not* to take action in this world, to allow him to retreat to stillness and contemplation (Laidlaw 1995, 302–14).

7. See the stories about the high reincarnations of Outer Mongolia published by Charles R. Bawden in *The Jebtsundamba Khutukhtus of Urga*, 1961.

8. The thinking behind this familial appropriation of the Qing emperor was that the mother of the Kangxi emperor was a Horchin Mongol.

on duty.[9] When he arrived, the emperor immediately recognized his brilliance, and made Mergen Gegen his "worshipping lama"' (*tahil-un lama*). Soon he offered him a highly adorned horse and also handed over a gold ring gifted by his daughter. One day Chinese, Manchu, Mongolian, and Tibetan religious specialists were called in to perform the fire-worshipping ritual. But none of them dared to do it—they said they would have to go back to collect their texts. The emperor was angry. "You can't do that. I invited you as specialists, paying a high salary and feeding you. How come you can't conduct the ritual for the fire which raises my vital force (*sülde*)?" All silently kneeled waiting for words of condemnation. The emperor was worried. "In my great Manchu Dai Qing Dynasty, are there are no real experts?" He watched them and saw there was one person standing, not kneeling, and was pleased. He went to this lama and saw that it was his own *tahil-un lama*, Mergen Gegen. What was the emperor thinking? He suddenly laughed loudly and sat on his throne. Mergen Gegen was angry inside, but appeared calm, and he walked in front of the emperor and kneeled, lit a lamp, and made an incense offering. In his mind he secretly prayed to his monastery and made three bows in the direction of his birthplace. Without any explanation he chanted the fire incense offering prayer (*sang*) by heart, composing it together with the *irügel, tahilga* (offering), and *öljei oroshil* (introduction of happiness). In this way he completed all parts of the fire worship for the emperor, which had previously been performed only with the invocation *(irügel)*.[10] Everyone was delighted with this complete version and gave respect to Mergen Gegen, and his fame flourished (2003, 709–10).

Mergen Gegen wrote a poem honoring Kangxi as the reincarnation of Manjushiri and this made the Emperor want to keep him longer. But the Lama was longing to return to his monastery to spread Bud-

9. Galluu systematically attributes to the 1st Mergen Gegen achievements others describe for the 3rd. As the 1st Mergen Gegen was not recognized as a reincarnation during his lifetime, and did not have a monastery, he would not have been subject to imperial duty under Kangxi (1662–1722).

10. These four prayers comprise Mergen Gegen's fire worship service published by Galluu and Jirantai, 1986, 372–87. The text invokes *sülde* (militant vitality) at several points. Mergen Gegen stresses the Indian origin of fire worship and its spread through many nations (see also the Kanjurwa Gegen's view on the pre-Buddhist origin of fire worship and the object of the rite to purify the participants, Hyer and Jagchid 1983, 75). Atwood 1996 analyses Mergen Gegen's fire worship texts and his role in reproducing the "non-Buddhist" ingredients of many Buddhist rituals, showing how Mergen Gegen's fire prayer contrasts with a radically different, tantric version. The latter belongs to the world of a technician operating by written instructions, whereas our story confirms that Mergen Gegen was understood by the lamas in his tradition to cap such a method by virtue of his interior knowledge that meant he could recite "by heart."

dhism in Mongolian. He thought of a way to escape: he left the city on his new horse, saying "Today I am going outside to rest and play." But the emperor was suspicious and ordered his servants, "Don't let him run away. Bring him back without harming him." The servants caught up with Mergen when he was a short distance from Beijing. They told him what the emperor had said, but Mergen Gegen had decided to go home and he thought of a means (*arga*). He gave his beautiful horse to the soldiers and he sang a song to them. The soldiers listened and were moved. They took the horse and went back to the Emperor and told him what happened. When Kangxi asked, "What did the Lama sing?" they replied:

> The *biligtü* [wise] yellow-brown [horse's] pasture is in the uplands west of Beijing city,
> [But] a turquoise and silver bridle is on the head of the wise yellow-brown [horse],
> Even if it is close by, it is difficult to pass the obstacle of the hollow place,
> Even if the state edict (*törü-yin üge*) is shortened, it is difficult to gainsay it.

Hearing this the emperor was very angry and asked his soldiers to capture the lama and bring him back to Beijing. Meanwhile, the Gegen was travelling through the mountains on foot. When he reached Datong, in Shanxi province, it was the time of the annual *nagadum* (pronounced *naadam*) fair when men compete in the manly games: wrestling, archery, and horse racing. Mergen Gegen put on a disguise of lay clothes to pass through the town gate, but he was captured and taken to the Mongolian general in charge of the place. Although the general guessed he was Mergen Gegen, he did not give him up to the emperor, but said quietly, "If you really are a layman, you wrestle as my subject. I will let you go if you win as my champion." Mergen Gegen agreed, fought bravely, won the championship, and was set free. When he reached the gate, the emperor's soldiers would not let him pass a second time. He was taken back to the Mongol general, who again tried to find a way out. He said, "A lama can wrestle, but I haven't heard that they can shoot, so if he wins the archery competition he must be a layman and I'll let him go. If he fails, you can take him to the emperor." Mergen Gegen agreed to shoot in the fair, but he was worried, because lamas must not kill and he had not learnt to use a bow and arrow. That night he made a confession of sins (*namanchilal*) in the direction of Mergen Monastery. With an incense offering, he prayed to the local spirits of the homeland, the tutelary guardians of the monastery, and to the previous generations of lama teachers, and he immediately composed a song. The next day he went to the archery field, fitted an arrow in his bow, and sang his song, praying silently as he drew the bow:

By skillfully and beautifully opening the bow of intellect,
And fortunately setting the arrow of wisdom (*bilig*),
Hit the center of the target in the south direction.
For boastful chattering people
Hitting the target coin is just a matter of [getting] money.
But for fast, clever and proud minded people
It is the clear, beautiful [realization] of nirvana.
The (wooden) stem [of the arrow] and the skill, a pair,
Are flying powerfully and perfectly.
And [even if I am] stuck in this bad forested place,
Where stupid wrestlers are making throws,
[I can still] ride the fast horse [of]
Sharp mind and intelligence.
By means of my fearless wisdom
Slowly let [me] release [the arrow]
To reach successfully and beautifully the distant target.

His arrow flew with the wind, went through the hole in the backbone of a horse, and speeding two hundred paces through and beyond the target, broke the golden coin behind it. At this achievement, the assembly was amazed and overjoyed. The search party of soldiers had nothing to say, and Mergen Gegen was allowed to pass through the gate.

The news reached the Manchu emperor's ear. He was surprised and frightened. He did not say anything and let it pass. But he took Mergen Gegen's name off the committee of translation and publication of the Ganjur-Danjur and replaced him with another Urad monk, Biligündalai. After he got back to his monastery, Mergen Gegen systematically translated Buddhist doctrine into Mongolian, revived Mongolian chanting, and made it flourish (Galluu 2003, 707–15).

This is not a naïve "folk story" but a complex narrative that can be related to coexisting pools of different cultural elements. For a start, from early in Mongol imperial history, the *nagadum* games were organized by leaders at all levels of society to celebrate a military victory or a successful hunt, to eliminate a rival, to pit kin groups against one another, to conclude marriage agreements, and demonstrate virility (Lacaze 2006, 96). At all periods up to the present, the state, including socialist and communist governments, have used the *nagadum* as a public scenario of power, something that would be understood by any listener to the story of Mergen Gegen's exploits. Furthermore, archery, the skill in which Mergen Gegen showed himself to be supreme, was not only the main attribute of the duke's primordial ancestor Hasar but was also—in the form of hunting—more than a mere sport for the Mongols; success raised the hunter's spirit (*hei mori*).

Then what were the two songs the Mergen Gegen sang, the first to the soldiers and the second to himself, as he drew his bow? They are among his works handed down locally, and we cannot know whether the story was elaborated to make sense of them or whether the songs did arise from some eventful sojourn of the Gegen in Beijing. Certainly, it is clear that Mergen Gegen did on occasion compose poems as indignant commentaries on contemporary political events. The second song, however, has a metaphorical, religious character. It is a play on the analogy between archery, intelligence, and the "distant target," where the worldly military skills are appropriated, successfully mastered, and mentally transformed into facilities for religious attainments. It thus can be seen as an example of the Tibetan genre of "songs of experience" of the kind made famous by Milarepa, poetic celebrations of personal spiritual achievement (Jackson 1996, 380–81). However, if we look at the story as lay people might have understood it, the main point is surely to show Mergen demonstrating his supremacy over the emperor, his ability to elude control, his capacity for spiritually powerful composition (and the need for this shown by the ruling powers), and above all his mastery of Mongolian manly abilities—where along with wrestling and archery, we should not forget success in attracting women and the gold ring given by the emperor's daughter. This gold ring is a real object that will appear again in Chapter 6.

Lamas and Dukes in Local Conditions of the Early Nineteenth Century

In terms of control over people, resources, and arms, the duke unquestionably held greater political power than even a high incarnate Lama. He was salaried from the central government, allocated thirty personal servant families, and commanded an elaborate hierarchy of officials whom he had the right to appoint and dismiss. The duke had his own office (*yamun*), militia, and treasury (*sang*) as well as having overall charge of those of the Banner (Buyanbadarahu 1987, 44–48). In the late eighteenth century, the Urad West Banner had a military corps and a lay population of around forty-five hundred (Tighe 2005, 41–42), made up of twelve mobile divisions of herders (*sumu*). By contrast, Mergen monastery never seems to have had more than fifteen hundred lamas and two hundred subject families at most, and these, as we have seen, were divided and under the control of several reincarnations. The West Banner ruled by the duke was the senior in the well-established local polity of Urad. A Qing map of the empire of around 1820 clearly shows the combined banners of Urad (C. Wulate) as a significant entity, equal to Ordos, Halha Right Wing, Muuminggan, and others (Tighe 2005, 26–27). When the French naturalist and missionary, Armand David, visited the area in 1866, he described Urad as "a kingdom divided into three principalities," although he remarked sourly that he had been wrongly told by the Chinese in Beijing that it was marvelous—when it was not (1868, vol. 1, 43; vol. 2, 4).

Yet the crucial fact about the monasteries was their de facto independence and, for the larger ones, their wide-ranging membership and cross-Asian relations.[11] The Qing state was not against limited independence for the monasteries, and sometimes prevented attempts by ruling nobles to get control over them (a part of their "divide and rule" strategy).[12] Indeed, in a few places scattered across Mongol lands, the incarnation presiding over a monastery was given princely ruling status (*lama wang*).[13] The Qing, however, did not want this kind of theocratic mini-polity to develop on a general scale in Mongol lands: in principle, incarnations were to be valid only if recognized by the state and normally they were maintained as separate institutions from the abbots of monasteries. In particular, apart from a very few exceptions, it was not allowed to be an incarnate lama and a ruling noble at the same time. Yet there was widespread local manipulation of these rules. How were

11. In 1799 the exceptionally well-connected Badgar Monastery had 1,268 monks coming from forty-five Banners and other administrative units across Inner and Outer Mongolia, as well as one Tibetan lama (fifty-two of the monks came from the Urad West Banner) Altanorgil 1998–1999, vol. 1, 221.

12. In the late eighteenth century the ruling prince of the Urad East Banner competed with Muuminggan Banner to get control of Badgar Monastery, which formed an enclave between their lands. However a commission from Beijing decided that it should continue to be a separate entity not included in any Banner, but overseen in religious matters by the Janggiya Gegen (Altanorgil 1998–1999, vol. 5, 276–92).

13. A well-known case was the Hüriye Banner, in Eastern Inner Mongolia, where it seems that from an early time (before the Qing edicts forbidding finding reincarnations in ruling families) a system was established whereby the in principle celibate lama prince was succeeded by his nephew from within the same noble family. Owen Lattimore sees this lama prince as the head of a "pseudo tribe, with its monks forming its ecclesiastical corporation, and yet with a kind of tribal aspect because of its territorial possessions and the laymen inhabiting them" (1934, 255–56).

dukes and reincarnations related, when the attraction of keeping the two kinds of power in one family was so evident?

In the first half of the eighteenth century, the Urad West Banner was ruled by Dukes Darmadai (ruled 1689–1725), Darmagarudi (1725–1751), and Darmariddi (1751–1764), whose names indicate the Buddhist inclination of the noble family. The 3rd Mergen Gegen came from a prosperous and educated, though not aristocratic, family, and it was not until the 4th that the tendency became established for the main reincarnations to be found in the noble lineage—they tended to be younger brothers and cousins of the heir to the dukedom. Evidently this was a situation of negotiation, ambiguity, and confrontation on several levels. First, we should not discount the possibility that the system for "discovering" a child as a reincarnation did in fact allow for randomness on occasion. But even if the system of choice was manipulated, the outcome was not certain. The duke's family in several documented cases refused to give their son up as a reincarnation, even to be the Mergen Gegen, and the line continued only because this boy (the 6th Mergen Gegen) died suddenly and the "soul" was soon discovered in another child (Mönghe 1996, 112). In the early twentieth century the Hubilgan Lama reincarnation line was extinguished when the recognized boy was held back because he was a potential heir to the dukedom (Galluu 2003, 161). What lay behind such reluctance was not only that the first heir could die of accident or disease, but also that a father might not know which son would become duke (the system of succession to the dukedom allowed for the most able among the potential heirs to be the one selected). If a boy had become a lama, it seems that his accession to high political position had precedence over his religious vow. The pious Wangdui Toin, younger brother of the heir, was forced much to his regret to give up his holy calling as a monk to become Duke Jigmiddorji when his older brother died (Galdanwangchugdorji [1846] 1994, 14).

Duke Galdan was born into a particularly intense thicket of religious-political relations. Not only was he the nephew of Wangdui Toin/Duke Jigmiddorji, a thwarted reincarnation, but his father and mother, Duke Batuwachir and his consort, were deeply religious. Furthermore his older brother was revealed to be the 3rd West Reincarnation of the Güng monastery. The previous (2nd) reincarnation, it may be remembered, suffering from taunts about his Chinese birth father, had made a wish-will (*irügel*) that his next reincarnation would be born in a "high root." This high person was Duke Galdan's brother, who became known by his incarnation name of Lama Ariyabalo.

Perhaps it was because of the *irügel* that an eldest son, otherwise usually designated as heir, was given up to the monastery. Evidently the siblings, one a reincarnation the other a lay heir, did not have easy relations. Galdan was a younger brother and in Mongolian family custom was due to accord unquestioned respect to his senior. Even so his memoirs record his reluctance to fully accept his older brother's teachings when the latter set off to study in Lhasa. Perhaps it is necessary to recall the economic situation here.

Documents published together with the duke's memoirs show that the noble family under Duke Batuwachir, religious though they wanted to appear, were not happy to support even their own Güng monastery from their family treasury, and attempted to shift the payments to the Banner treasury. Since the lamas chanted for the benefit of all people of the Banner, why should they not pay for it (Mönghe and Naranbatu 1994, 241)? Such reluctance to adopt the role of "master of donations" extended to funding reincarnations. Duke Batuwachir had blocked the attendance of the 5th Mergen Gegen at the Qing court on the grounds that earlier visits "had wasted thousands of langs of silver from the Banner and monastery treasuries," and Duke Galdan remarks that since the economic situation was getting tighter he had not paid for attendance by the Western Great incarnation; and since this nonattendance had become customary it "would not be appropriate" for other high lamas to go (1994, 183–84). But counterbalancing this reluctance to support the political-economic aspect of the reincarnations was their undisputed religious sanctity. Lama Ariyabalo, because he was the reincarnation of the wonder-working lama who walked on water, who in turn had acquired his sacred power from the *ubadis* of Mergen Gegen, could not be questioned. This was the situation Galdan struggled with.

Galdan grew up as the third son of powerful Duke Batuwachir. He was taught to read by a military man, Deputy Lieutenant Shangdashi, but because of his disobedience was then sent for intensive education by lamas from Mergen and Güng Monasteries. When his older brother was already enthroned as 3rd West Lama of Güng Monastery, the parents instructed that Galdan was to be treated no differently from any young lama, so Galdan suffered from cold and lack of proper food. His mother died of illness and was replaced by a stepmother. When he was nineteen, Galdan took up the post of scribe at the Banner office and got married. At twenty-four he was given an *abishig jinang* consecration[14] and took vows as a lay devotee (*ubashi sanwar*), and he continued to

14. This is an empowerment or permission to read certain sacred texts or partake in rituals.

receive Buddhist teachings and study literature. Galdan was appointed to the dukedom at the age of thirty-four, after the sudden death of his father, his other older brother having been mentally ill for over twenty years. He took two more wives. When he was forty-six he contracted a serious stomach illness, from which he never fully recovered, and after that he ceased to pay much attention to government duties. He mainly stayed at home resting, reading books, and writing poetry and literature (Bühechilagu 2007, 894–95). Below we translate the prose version of his autobiography, abbreviated for reasons of space. The half-oppressive, half-inspirational older brother incarnation is a constant presence, somehow closing off the options.

Duke Galdan's Autobiographical Sketch

I the Duke have written this account for my lay and lama sons to understand the old custom and rules of Mergen Monastery and Baragun [Güng] Monastery [. . .].

I (lit. my body *minu biye*) was born ignorant and stupid, fierce and thoughtless, and because I did not listen to the teachings of my father and mother, they criticized [me] for being stupid and acting according to my own wishes.

Always, since [I] was aged ten [I] liked killing and smashing things, and loved using traps, lassoes, slings, and sticks, and wandering in hummocks of thick grass, killing any baby animals which were bigger than rats or mice and sparrows. [I] roasted goose eggs on fires, and [I] made baby hares my food, and in this way [I] grew up making all those activities like games. From the age of fifteen, [I] went hunting on horseback, using a gun or a bow and arrows on the northern and the southern side of the mountains. [I] forced yellow and black people [lamas and lay serfs] to serve me, and in this way [I] made people fed up with me, but [I] did not know fear or shame, and [I] did not notice how my father and mother were worried about my acting like this, and I went on acting like an animal (*adugusun mal*).

In the Ox Year, when Lama Ariyabalo went to Juu [Lhasa], I was seventeen years old. He graciously gave me his counting beads, saying "Venerate father and mother," and he was crying when he taught me this way. That was the rosary that he held in his own hand. And [I] did not care. [I] shed a few tears, just as a custom for seeing someone off, and I went back.

Later, when [I] was twenty years old, Galsan the Senior Proctor of Mergen came, and he advised me privately. "Your father and mother are worrying about you always hunting; you may fall in water, a hole in the ice, or a deep valley while you are out hunting. At least, stop using a gun. I am asking for this as an old man." When [I] heard about the worried mind of my father and mother I melted a little. I replied to the Senior Proctor that I would stop carrying a gun.

In the year of the Snake, [I] went to the north for hunting. When [I] heard lamas were passing [I] hid [my] bow and arrows and dogs and brought several of the huntsmen to meet them. [I] bowed [to the lamas] in the place called Mangnai-yin Dabusun.

In the spring of the Horse Year or Sheep Year, [I] heard the Meritorious Relative Lama [his older brother Ariyabalo] saying to Gunga Norbu Rabjimba, "Following the order of Jalsarai Gegen, [I am] preparing to go to Potala." He went out and said to his close accompanying disciples, "Now we are going to depart. We don't want to stay here." The Gegen had ordained this kind of determination necessary for a man who is going to study the scriptures. "We should not stay here–[we] will always die and death might arrive any time. Only if this idea is kept firmly in mind will the idea of making *dharma* be firmly born," the Lama said. [I] took what this lama and Jalsarai Gegen said as a magically powerful teaching (*ubadis*). But [I] understood only weakly, "Yes, what they are saying is aimed to teach me," and I couldn't completely give up hunting.

In the Monkey Year, the Bogda Jangjiya Erdeni came to Jibhulangtu. My body got an illness of the back and leg. [I] sat in warm spring water. [I] went to Jibhulangtu to bow to him and stayed for over a month because of my illness, and during this time the Düinghor Gegen gave the teaching of eight blessings [. . .] in which it is said that to respect karma [one] must always think about death and remember that you are mortal, not eternal, and that you must take care to pay back the favor of your father and mother. [My] feelings (*setgel*) were a little softened, especially by the inevitable sufferings of householders and by the detailed teaching about the great beneficial help of the noble lamas who have certainly gone out and renounced [householder life]. Then [I] requested a worshipping object from the Gegen who was giving this teaching, and [I] promised to Meritorious Lama Relative that [I] will stop hunting. [I] also made a strong vow to leave my family, which is most important. Then, in front of the worshipping object (*sitügen*) and Meritorious Lama Relative [I] made a confession (*namanchilan*) for the cleansing of my sin, and was blessed with the religious power (*ubadis*) of the confession having been received. [. . .]

Later, when [my] Holy Father was head of the League, when the lamas from Halha Darhan Beile Monastery came and accused Jargal Lama in their quarrel, Lama Ariyabalo said to me, "You have a look at the texts of the internal rules for lamas by Mergen Gegen. If a person who has no belief reads that text he will always reveal the lamas' mistakes (*gem*) and then he himself will accumulate [sin] and fall. This is why this writing is kept secret by calling it the 'internal agreement' (*dotogadu üye*)."

In the 18 useful teachings in the works of Jangjiya Gegen, it is clear that, [if you] to refuse to say bad things about any lama group, if you give all kinds of help, and care about the completion [of meditation] by the renouncer monks and respect them rather than criticizing them, this can be considered a pure phenomenon. [I] listened to this teaching and I thought that if [my] believing mind has been corrected a little, then it would not be sinful for me take and read the internal rules. He [Ariyabalo] gave this permission. Therefore, when there was something that needed to be seen to, occasionally [I] read them and [I] prayed while thinking of what the lama had said. Trying to avoid observing the mistakes and quarrels of monks, [I] tried to refuse to do the things that are obstacles to the ethical teaching of having faith (*itegel*). [But] even if [I] was careful about trying to avoid such deeds, and even if [I] read the magically powerful teaching of the 7th Dalai Lama, [I] spent most of the daytime sitting in vain, gossiping, passing the night by half-sleeping, and [my] mind got blurred, and the time of thinking by the rule of pure doctrine was just a microsecond. The heart word of the teaching is: reflect on yourself critically [literally, analyzing yourself hit the target]. Like this, if [I] observe my own mind/feelings according to the ideas taught by Meritorious Lama Relative, it is truly difficult to annihilate one's own mind and doctrine.[15] I was originally an ordinary layman. It seems it is a therefore a great disgrace for me to write this [high] level of words, but by always thinking of how Lama Ariyabalo Gegen pulled me in the direction of religion and because he gave individual me—living like an animal, bad me—teachings from childhood to now, and by observing my own mind by myself in its degree of attentiveness [I] clarified [my] own faults, [I] write this by the way of mentioning the Lama's favor [to me]. Furthermore, when my body reached 46 years old in the Horse Year [I] lamented (*gemshijü*) about my previous [deeds]. Meanwhile, by the order of Bogda Jiramba Lama [I was] reading the Ganjur and praying and circumambulating.

In the Horse Year I succeeded to the power [of the Dukedom]. Starting from the assembly in the next Sheep Year, making the excuse of old custom and [telling myself] that war and hunting are matters of government and the imperial state of the Holy Master [the Manchu Emperor] [I] went again for hunting. [To me] going on campaigns and hunting were pleasure (*jirgal*). [I] did not pay attention to the moral sins [*niswanis*] as enemies,[16] [I] was cheating myself and that was really disgusting. [I] was really stupid, that's the right name for me, an animal person with a human form. Thinking about this now [I] have been suffering-regretting (*gemshihü*) it." (Galdanwangchugdorji in Mönghe and Naranbatu [1846] 1994, 195–278).

Here, very unusually for Mongolian literature at this period, we find someone analyzing his own conflicts, his personality, and the people who influenced him. All of the duke's writings are remarkably honest,

15. Galdan seems to have in mind here that to reach true enlightenment, one has to eliminate not only one's own thoughts but also the doctrines—the latter are just a means to reach the ultimate goal.

16. *Niswanis*, from a Uighur translation of S. *kleca*, defilement, vice, sin. Galluu writes that the *niswanis* contain the "three great poisons of the world": attachment, anger, and ignorance (2003, 885).

in the sense that they are not just conventional declarations of having committed typological sins. His various accounts concern everyday life, specific dates and real people. He documents, for example, the time and place of his making an "irreversible vow" to leave his family—a vow he did not keep, and indeed he married two further wives. In some ways the catalogue of faults makes his memoir seem familiar, even "modern," and likewise the duke's dwelling on his backsliding, his difficulty in controlling his greed, his ability to put on a false façade for others and to deceive himself also seems to recall European autobiographies where the authors also reveal their inadequacies. But the duke's writings are in fact completely unlike modern European autobiographical writing in one respect: they do not use the idea of the self to query the status quo. Duke Galdan is caught up by the two main *dispositifs* of his time, that of Buddhism and that of the Manchu state. Indeed, at times he identifies with each of them, and because he is a thoughtful man, he is caught by contradictions between them. Yet he criticizes only himself. Clearly, however, he does not have the romantic belief that he is an individual whose life task it is to be true to his own autonomous personality, which Karl Weintraub has seen as the hallmark of the European modern sense of self that emerged at the end of the eighteenth century with Goethe (1978, xi). There is no hint that one should search for such an authentic self, nor, that having found it, its specific quirks and sensitivities should be cultivated. On the contrary, the Duke seeks to acquire teachings about an ideal model of human behavior, in which personal idiosyncratic variations would be irrelevant at best.

One could say that the duke—who has been educated in the Mergen tradition—saw himself as trying to carry out the classic Buddhist renunciation, that of the wealthy prince who rejects his family and his inheritance, along the lines of Neichi Toin (or even the Buddha himself). The reiteration in his poems of the necessity to remember that death may happen any time refers, likewise, to a fundamental teaching of Tsongkhapa: in which such mindfulness is the technique whereby to relegate the purposes of this life in favor of those of a future more enlightened one (Lopez 2009, 316–67), and the Duke's preoccupation also has a flavor of Stoic ethics, where awareness of death frees the subject to be the kind of person he wants to be, the one who "makes dharma."

Galdan's negative, abjected "me," to judge from his repeated self-description as *munghag* (stupid/ignorant)—"I was an animal in human form"—does appear to be a standard idea, and one might then ask whether the duke has a sense of his singular self at all. Here, however, it is useful to think about the point from which a retrospective autobiography is written: that is when an author looks back on his cumulative experience and puts a particular interpretation on his past (Weintraub 1978, xviii). The duke by this time had swung definitively in favor of the Buddhist apparatus, which influenced his vocabulary and colored the interpretation he presumably expected readers to make of his accounts. Thus, another episode of backsliding is summed up in the following humorless way: my illness was caused by my fault in drinking too much alcohol (fermented mare's milk), but "there was no way out and I had to start drinking spirits again as a medicine." One could imagine Mongolians laughing at this. But the duke is determined to make didactic points from his faults. So he does not shirk recalling the earlier times when he would not have held the same perspective, when he was enjoying hunting and drinking, particularly just after he became duke and completely forgot about karma, mindfulness of death, and so forth. By the time he was writing he could not depict himself as identifying with the aristocratic lifestyle, even though Mergen Gegen's more frisky songs would have given him a fine rationale for doing so. So nowhere does he mention the great lama's light-hearted toasting song presumably written for lay officials like himself that praises strong liquor as "'god's gift (*tngri-yin heshig*) to humans'" (Mönghe 2010, 166). Instead, the duke mournfully recalls dragging his official duties as if pulling a plough, and looking only for an easy life, "lying down like a cow" (Mönghe and Naranbatu [1846] 1994, 263).

However, there are passages in the poems suggesting that the duke did not just see himself as a succession of conventional inadequacies, nor yet as an undifferentiated person striving for an abstract ideal. An almost unacknowledged sense of self is revealed by the fact that he is able to describe incompatible socio-religious orders (*jirum*) rather than just being in one of them. This is the self who has to discipline himself not to criticize the lamas, and who watches himself engaging in deception. Most of the time there is no hint that Galdan has anything but contempt for himself in such situations. In episode after episode, readers are invited to join Galdan in condemning an earlier self he now despises, such as the boy who barely pretended to cry when his brother left for Lhasa; or "cheated himself" when he had just become duke by citing the state order (*jirum*) as a justification for taking up campaigning and hunting again. But we can nevertheless sense in all of this a concern for the continuing "I"; there is one passage in which the duke refers to his "intrinsic character" and takes a pride in it.

One day he came across Deputy Lieutenant Shangdashi, his old teacher, seeming to be drunk and sitting on the grass by his horse. The teacher said, "You princely heir, if you are really my disciple, you should hand my foot into the stirrup. I'll get going if you see me off by taking my blessing (*adis*)." This was deeply insulting, because a noble did not touch the foot of a lower official, and it was unthinkable that a lieutenant could give a blessing to a member of the ruling house, which would involve that high person bowing to him. The duke wrote, "Although he [Shangdashi] was acting in this aggressive way, [I] because of the strength of my innate nature (*abiyas-un erhe*) was not angry or resentful at all, and I sent my helpful teacher on his way as he requested. After that event, I never was jealous, suspicious, or without faith in lama teachers." And further on the same page, as if to demonstrate again his equable character, he says that when he was accused of usurping his elder brother's position as duke, "I took [these accusations] as my karma, and I sat there like a queen piece on a chessboard, experiencing the taste of my karmic deeds" (ibid, 261–62).

Perhaps in this way, between his professions of humble devotion to Buddhist ideals on the one hand and loyal upholding of the emperor's government on the other, the duke indicated that he had a sense of self that was independent of either *dispositif.* There was no great event or shattering conceptual innovation in his life. But at his period the very fact of recording the faltering trajectory of a layman's life was new. He tried to see this life as part of an ongoing reproduction of the Mergen tradition that merged the transmission of tantric initiations with noble genealogy. Recalling that the 7th Dalai Lama had given the *lung jinang* initiation to Mergen Gegen, and how the latter had given it to him (Galdan), the duke writes that the "root lamas" of Mergen had been endlessly helpful to him, and not only to him but to his grandfather, great-grandfather and other ancestors of his family (ibid, 261). It seems that such a feeling of being part of a hereditary tradition gave Galdan a certain confidence in the value of his experience and his opinion. That is why he wrote his history—to teach others. We can consequently make sense of an episode mentioned by Galluu. A senior aged lama recalled to Galluu that Duke Galdan had told the 7th Mergen Gegen of his intention to write a history of Mergen Monastery. The reincarnation replied that a lay disciple who does not understand the meaning of doctrine cannot write a history of Buddhism, and the two men quarreled (Galluu 2003, 77).[17] If this incident happened, the duke must

17. Galluu, a disciple of the 8th Mergen Gegen, may have been trying to justify his own position as an ex-lama writer of voluminous historical works on Mergen. The episode cannot have happened quite like this, since the 7th Mergen Gegen was only a young boy when Duke Galdan died. Perhaps the quarrel was with other senior lamas.

have believed sufficiently in his own judgment to stand up to the lamas (he did after all write the only history now in existence). The issue was crucial—the right to write the history and thus to define the qualities of the Mergen Mongolian Buddhist tradition.

Redemption by Writing

Duke Galdan read Mergen Gegen's works and took them ultra-seriously, as one of his poems indicates:

Having read on occasion the decree of Mergen Gegen called "Adistad-un Duradhal" (Reminder of the Blessing Givers),
[I] found and read again this decree in the first volume of his collected works;
Having read it, I myself was immediately very disgusted with myself [lit. body];
The disgust came about only due to the Holy Mergen Gegen's teaching.
(Mönghe and Naranbatu [1846] 1994, 256)

Dashiram-dur üjegseger Mergen Gegen tan-u adistad-un duradhal hemegsen jarlig
Jarlig tegün-i sumbum-un terigün boti-eche nemen olju üjeged
Üjegsen darui öber-un beye-anu beyen-ece-ben mashi jigshiged
Jigshigsen tere anu gagchahu Bogda Mergen Gegen-u surgal-ece bolbai.

We have introduced a few lines of Mongolian here because we wish to argue that, if the content of Mergen Gegen's teachings made the duke despair, the great Gegen's arts of poetry were what gave him heart. For the duke's poetry is exceptionally highly wrought, using Mergen Gegen's techniques and others original to himself. In the poem above the last word of each line is repeated to start the next line, which has the effect of emphasizing these words: decree; read; become ashamed. He employs the *shad* metrical system, making his verse suitable for oral rendition. He combines attention to the sound of words with links made purely by semantics. The grammar and orthography are correct, and the whole impresses Mongol readers as eloquent, skillfully done, and beautiful (Ba. Mönghe 2004, 249). Galdan's use of "linked heads" (*tolugai holbuhu*), whereby words at the beginning of each line are rhymed, is a tour de force. Most Mongol authors usually link a verse of four lines or so, Galdan links page after page. In one long passage, he starts every line with words rhymed to begin with *ge-* and repeatedly throws in the words *ger* (home, household, felt tent) and *gem* (sin, fault), so the reader or listener could not avoid the association *ger / gem, ger / gem* . . .

Simultaneously, he ends each line in this passage with a trope based on the meaning, not the sound of the word: all of these ending words are first person pronouns in one grammatical form or another ("I," "to you," "from us," etc.). Galdan's second long autobiographical poem is quite astounding from this point of view: every single line begins with rhymes on the letter "a" and practically every line ends with "I" (*bi*) or "to me" (*nadur*). (Mönghe and Naranbatu [1846] 1994, 257–65). The duke went much further than the great lama in his use of the first person. Although Mergen Gegen may have deployed a Sanskrit first person model on occasion (Mönghe 2004, 389), his works contain nothing like the duke's insistent—almost indecent—drumming with the word "*bi*" ("I").

The duke's poems can be arresting:

For ten months I lay in my mother's womb, and with that favor
I went out, opening my mother's door and shouting;
I was aimlessly gesturing, like a red hairless baby rat;
I was struggling to move, I could only move my skin and flesh.
From that very time, I softly set off in the direction of death.
(Mönghe and Naranbatu [1846] 1994, 265)

There was a point to such vivid writing: the Duke intended his books to teach the young. "The reason for giving names to each poem and writing them as three books is to teach them separately to children, or whoever wants to learn letters, that is what I was thinking" (ibid, 247). So perhaps after all there was a comeback against the incarnate lama. The duke could appropriate Mergen Gegen's legendary power of poetry as well as moralistic teaching. However, this still left somewhere adrift the ancestral past, the half-eclipsed *dispositif* of the Mongol nobility, with its apparatus of sacrifices, swords and flags, *oboo* rituals, armor, and battle standards. Duke Galdan simply leaves all this out of his writing. As we shall show in the next chapter, however, it had not disappeared from Mongol life.

FIVE

Sülde: The "Spirit of Invincibility," Its Multiplicity and Its Secrets

It comes as no surprise that the Mongols, who once conquered a vast area of Asia, should cultivate a spirit of invincibility, triumph, and vital force (*sülde*). But what would come of such notions after the end of the Mongol Empire and once the Mongols had been divided and colonized—and indeed more recently during China's revolutionary and modernizing twentieth century? During our visits to Mergen in the 1990s we found a sacrificial cult of *sülde* to be flourishing, both within the monastery and at numerous other ritual sites in the region. The most prominent of these was at the highest summit of the Muna range, the sacred Yellow Peak (*Shira Orui*), whose master deity Muna Khan was implored in prayers composed by Mergen Gegen to "become our *sülde* without leaving us." This chapter explores an important but little studied theme for religion in Mongolia: the implicit politics of the cult of *sülde*, its replication over time and space, the moral contradictions it generates in a Buddhist context, and the combination of public exultation and hidden anxieties that we discovered in its ritual topology.

One of the most important ideas for Urad people, *sülde* is also one of the most elusive and difficult to grasp. Today it not only has a range of meanings ("might," "sovereignty," "majesty," "inspiration," "life force," "spirit of victory," "glory," "guardianship"), but can also take diverse forms and manifest itself in various sites. The most unmistakable is the battle standard (*tug* or *tug sülde*). This is a pole topped by a metal trident or spearhead, to which is attached a ring dangling long tufts of hair. But *sülde* also appears in the spirits of mountains, ritual cairns (*oboo*), ancestor and hero spirits, sacred flags (*darchug*), and flying canopies (*labari*). It is imagined as a deity (*Sülde Tngri*). It is also a kind of life force in each individual living person. The idea of *sülde* is found early in Mongolian history in pre-Buddhist contexts, and in Mongol lands to this day *sülde* is generally not celebrated in Buddhist temples and is counted a "lay people's object of worship" (Sodubilig 1996, 287). The 3rd Mergen Gegen, however, wrote many invocations to *sülde*, both for use in his officially mandated calendar of monastic services (*BJ*, 1780–1783, vol. 1, text 9) and for rituals held outside for laypeople. *Sülde*, we shall suggest, was the spirit at the heart of the ancestral-aristocratic notion of "country" (*orun*) whose construction we outlined in Chapter 2.

We first describe the present-day invocation of *sülde* at the sacrifice to the mountain deity Muna Khan and examine how this particular cult is constituted amid a plethora of alternative narratives about the god. This opens into a discussion of the cult's internal complexity, notably the secrecy or interdiction (*chegerlehü*) that is engendered within it by its close relation to death and associated taboos. From early times *sülde* in the form of a battle standard had incorporated a duality that Mongols have found inherent in military victory. The triumph of establishing a powerful government, represented by a white standard, was distinguished from the violent destruction of an enemy, indicated by a black standard.[1] In some ritual sites, however, the two notions coexist as the two aspects of a single worshipped entity. It will be argued that the killing of enemies—and even more so the physical death of one's own ancestors—was both horrifying and productively energy giving; this generated a moral ambivalence that buried unmistakable reminders of death beneath the acclamation of life force that formed the main thrust of the ritual invocation of *sülde*, whether in non-Buddhist or Buddhisized form. The cult of victory had to suppress the viewpoint of the defeated; these were people who had been beaten, raped, or killed, but who were feared nevertheless to be ultimately unconquerable and whose vengeful anger undermined the glory of triumph and

1. Chinggis Khan set up the "nine-legged" white battle standard (*tug*) in 1206 to mark the establishment of his state after victory over the peoples of the steppe (*Secret History*, paragraph 202, Eldengtei and Ardajab 1986, 660). The distinction between the black and white standards was well established by the sixteenth century in rituals (Liu Jinsuo 1981, 85).

could never be entirely dispelled. Furthermore, in the changing forms it took over the centuries, the cult had to adapt to—or somehow deal with—the fact that the great Mongol empire itself had been overcome, had lost control of China, and been divided. All of this generated various jarring, "minoritarian" and half-suppressed discourses that sabotaged the very idea of victory. We hope to show, in what is necessarily a complex account, how the dominating discourses and rituals not only produced visions of an inspired and divinized Mongolian polity (while at the same time pushing alternatives into realms of silence, rumor, or disdained legend), but also performatively brought into being a psychic experience of the power they extolled.

The 3rd Mergen Gegen was the prime agent of a dominant ordering when he composed Buddhist-tempered texts for the local *sülde* cults. But his context of writing did not last: the broad religious and political relations he had envisaged in the mid-eighteenth century (Chapter 2) shrank into more local concerns during the nineteenth century (Chapter 4, see also Elverskog 2006a, 127–65). By the first half of the twentieth century, even though the leading characters—the dukes and lamas—remained in place, the cults were challenged (though not eradicated) by revolutionary ideologies, civil wars, and various kinds of modernization sweeping in from China, Japan, Russia, and Mongolia. After the devastations of the early Communist campaigns and the Cultural Revolution the cults were celebrated publicly again, but in a completely transformed political situation. Nevertheless when we reached Mergen in the 1990s the lamas were in no doubt that a thread of "tradition" had been reproduced through these times, an assumption we attempt to analyze. By interleaving discussions of the ritual in the 1940s, our experience in the 1990s, and analysis of the content of the texts, we hope both to document the Urad version of the cult of *sülde* and to illuminate the question of its replication or reenactment.

This, however, will not be a history of *sülde* cults but rather an anthropological account. *Sülde* as Sky God or inspiring spirit is imagined as a multitude counted as one (see p 219) and likewise it manifests itself in assemblages of various items for worship that are also thought to form wholes. Yet these collocations turn out not to be mere jumbles but arrangements, and they have distinctive relational forms. Toward the end of the chapter we contrast the different ritual assemblages associated with Muna Khan, Chinggis Khan, and Hasar, and we argue that they are indicative of coexisting but divergent indigenous concepts of political order.

Since our ability to produce an ethnographic understanding of these cults was conditioned by having taken part in them, we begin with the contemporary sacrifice to Muna Khan and the invocation of *sülde*.

Toward the Mountain God

In summer 1998 lamas were drifting in for the great Mani gathering to bring blessings to all participants. Leisurely preparations were also under way for another ritual, the sacrifice to the battle standard (*tug sülde*) of an Urad ancestor called Jirgal Bagatur Jahirugchi ("Joy Hero Adjutant"),[2] which was kept in the Temple of Fierce Deities along with his armor, clothing, and weapons. It was during a lull before these two great monastic rituals that Chorji Lama suggested we should see with our own eyes the sacrifice to Muna Khan. Knowing that the annual ritual had already been performed that year, we were doubtful about participating in a sacrifice put on for our benefit. But Chorji was persuasive. This celebration on Yellow Peak is so important, he said, it is the culmination of all the small Muna rituals held in the area, it raises the spirit of the whole region and the deity would certainly be happy to be given another offering and worship. Our objections—the short time available, the fact that the main path to the summit was closed by Chinese troops, the prohibition on women taking part—were swept aside. We could take a short cut up a side valley, they said, all we have to do is to find a guide. As for the ban on women, it is true that a few years ago, when an official took dancing girls with him to enjoy the sacrificial feast he ran into all kinds of problems (including with his wife) as punishment from the mountain god. But these days China has become a society of equality and female participants regularly attend the sacrifice at Yellow Peak with no sign of anger from the deity.

In the back of our minds was a legend, declaring the truly cosmological significance of Yellow Peak:

In ancient times, Hormusda Tngri[3] and Burhan Bodhisattva created the three worlds—the upper Sky Land, the middle world of Jambutib, and the underworld of the Eight

2. The top officials of the Banner under the duke (*jasag noyon*, ruling lord) were the east and west administrators (*tusalagchi*) and under them the two adjutants (*jahirugchi*) each of whom had charge of six sections (*sumu*).

3. The name derives from the Zoroastrian god Ormuzd (Ahuramazda) and seems to have reached the Mongols in pre-Buddhist times (Banzarov [1846] 1955, 60). Later, Buddhist translators from Sanskrit and Tibetan used the name Hormusda to render the Hindu god Indra into Mongolian (Heissig 1980, 49).

Dragon (*Lus*) Kings. They sent mountains from the Sky to the middle world, leaving only Muna Stake Mountain in the Sky. Since all the mountains fell from the Sky at once like hail, and the middle world was full of oceans, the seas burst into floods, and nothing could be firmly established—from east to west, everything was churning. Khan Hormusta couldn't find a way to settle them and was afraid. Then Chinggis Khan, who at that time was living in the Sky as the Flourishing White Sülde Sky-God, advised Khan Hormusda, "It will be difficult to establish those mountains firmly if you don't send a mountain which can act as a tying-up stake (*argamji gadasu*) to control them." Hormusda asked which mountain should be sent. Flourishing White Sülde Sky-God said, "Send golden-yellow peaked Muna Mountain to the very navel of the Höndelen Mountain range. I'll live on that mountain when I go down to pacify the earth." So Hormusda sent Muna Mountain to a place centrally located between the Hinggan and the Altai mountain ranges. Then all the mountains were fixed where they were, as if they had been hammered in by a *muna* (pestle or mallet). Muna Khan Mountain got its name because it was the golden mallet of Khan Hormusda (Jirantai in Compilation Committee of Inner Mongolia, vol. 1, 2000, 408–09).

Here Yellow Peak is the crucial stabilizing point of the middle world. The story links the name "Muna," a somewhat archaic term for a mallet, with the stake (*gadasu*) which also appears in cosmology as the name of the Pole Star ("Golden Stake," *Altan Gadasu*), the fixed point Mongols refer to when traveling in the steppes at night. It associates the mountain's appearance in the world with Chinggis Khan in his manifestation as Sülde Tngri. Such a notion of centricity, both geographical and political, is extremely powerful. The whole legend is hardly Buddhist save for the fringe appearance of Burhan Bodhisattva, nor does it conform to the primary Tibetan Buddhist notions of the sacred mountain.[4] Yet the Buddhist lamas were planning to go to considerable trouble to worship the mountain a second time in one summer. Faced with such an interesting paradox we could hardly refuse to go.

So it was settled. Caroline would be the patron of the sacrifice.[5]

4. Karmay (1996, 59–60) points out that there are two different notions of the sacred mountain in Tibet. The primary one is the holy mountain in a Buddhist sense, a place where a sacred person lived, blessed by divinity, or where sutras or other sacred objects have been found or remain still hidden. These mountains are the object of pilgrimage from far around. The less revered type of sacred mountain is the dwelling place of a local deity, worshipped for mundane purposes by local people. The latter cult is kept distinct from the monastic establishment in Tibet. The Mergen tradition, where Buddhist lamas take part in sacrificial blood offerings to the local mountain deity, would be regarded with horror in most parts of Tibet. See Diemberger 1997 and 1998.

5. The lay patron provides the expenses of the sacrificial animal and feast, the monastery provides the ritual offerings.

Sengge Lama would bring young Minggan Lama and his own grandson to perform the chanting and music, while Chorji and some friends would officiate at the raising of the *sülde* flag on the peak. Otgon, an elderly herdsman, was recruited to be the guide and he said we could stay overnight in his *otur* (hut on distant pastures) near the summit. We would have to find donkeys, as horses cannot manage the steep rocky climb. These would be necessary to carry the materials for the sacrifice and also, the lamas said persuasively, we would be able to ride them if we got tired on the way. Looking at the craggy looming peak, this seemed like a good idea. We were to start early, attain the summit in one day, stay overnight in the hut, and return the next day.

On the appointed morning, the assembled donkeys were restive, and it took some time to load them with the sacred texts, the picture of Muna Khan,[6] the great drum, cymbals, and so forth, as well as food and many bottles of alcohol for the sacrifice. In the end we ambled out from Baragun Debeseg rather late and wound our way up the dry bed of the Ündür-ün Goul River, the beginning of the short cut to the summit. Grassy areas on the banks, with occasional shepherds' huts, soon gave way to steep-sided rocks and crevices. Vultures circled overhead. The donkeys were skittish and any idea of riding them was abandoned when they began to dash under low-hanging branches. At one point, the edifice of sacred objects on one donkey's back was swept to the ground, breaking the glass on the picture of Muna Khan. No one took this as a bad omen; we reloaded and set off again, slipping and stumbling on the loose shale. Otgon told us legends about the rocks and caves we passed.

Yellow Peak is the highest of three worshipped mountains in the Muna range, we learned. They are called the "Three Oboos" and "older and younger brothers" (*aha-degü*) and they are: Yellow Peak, worshipped by the West Banner, the senior of the three Urad Banners; the Pagoda Stone Mountain (*Suburgan Chilagu*),[7] worshipped by the Middle Banner; and the Box-Chest Stone Mountain (*Abdar Chilagu*) worshipped by the East Banner.[8] Erhimbayar, an elder of Baragun Debeseg, had insisted that women were not allowed to venture onto these peaks dur-

6. This was a large framed color photograph of a painting of the deity.

7. The Pagoda Mountain is worshipped annually on the thirteenth of the fifth month, with chanting provided by lamas from Höndelen Monastery. Individuals also make separate offerings there, like herder Altansumbur who told us he keeps up the ritual because families who do so are successful and wolves do not attack their flocks.

8. The people of the East Banner no longer travel to worship the Box-Chest Mountain; they took a piece of stone from it to worship locally.

ing sacrifices, or indeed to attend any *oboo* ritual. Why? Because *oboos* are like the tombs of ancestor heroes and women would pollute them. We know, he explained, that our ancestral kinship (*udum törül*) derives from Hasar, who had three sons. His eldest son became the forefather of the West Banner, the middle son that of the Middle Banner, and the youngest son of the East Banner. Now this information cannot possibly be correct, as Hasar lived in the thirteenth century, long before the Banners were formed in the seventeenth century. But the picture given by Erhimbayar, and repeated by Otgon, was perfect: the entire polity of Urads, divided into three banners, was made to coincide neatly with the patriarchal concept of the ancestor with three sons, and in turn with the three prominent peaks in the mountain range. The aged lama Boroheshig told us of another way these three mountains provide reference points for a holistic view of the world: they represent the three central categories through which human conduct is judged—physical action, intention, and speech. The Yellow Peak is body (*beye*); the Pagoda Mountain is mind/heart (*sedhil-jirühe*); and the Box-Chest Mountain is tongue (*hele*). As the Buddha is known to have achieved perfection in these three aspects, we had the impression that Boroheshig was reading the three aspects of Buddha's person onto the mountain range. Yet, as we shall see later, this unifying homology of patrilineal genealogy, geography, and religion faces some internal challenges.

The three mountains can only be seen together from far away; close up they are concealed by other peaks. Indeed Shira Orui only became visible to us once we had toiled up near-vertical cliffs to reach the first ridge, descended into a leafy valley, and made our way to a second higher ridge. Pines sprang from rocks over empty space, as if designed for a Chinese painting. The shimmering Yellow River was visible far below, and in the other direction loomed the bare conical peak of Shira Orui. Behind it on a slightly lower mountain was the white globe of a radar station built in the late 1960s. Many Urad people told us the history of the station, which had been set up to counter the Soviet threat. Initially, the PLA had intended to build it on Shira Orui and had set about dynamiting its pointed summit to provide a level platform. But suddenly several soldiers died—punishment from the mountain for the damage done to it. The army was forced to transfer the radar installation to the other, flat-topped mountain. This history was told to convince us of the power of the mountain.

Traversing beyond the second ridge and another hill, a pastoral scene opened up—perhaps the very prelapsarian idyll that had so overjoyed European explorers of these mountains in the nineteenth century (David 1868, 35–40; Przheval'skii [1875] 1946, 124–45). In the center of a glade was Otgon's shepherd's hut, on one side ran a clear stream, and on the other was an empty goat pen woven from branches. It was almost dark when we arrived. We would sleep the night in the hut, it was decided, and conduct the sacrifice right here during the next day. A large bedlike slab of rock would be convenient for laying out the offerings—this spot was often used to spare aged lamas the extra climb to the summit. After a cold night huddled in the hut, the ritual began at dawn: the lamas laid out ritual offerings[9] on the rock, hooked the portrait of Muna Khan to an overhanging branch, and began to chant. Otgon's shepherd boy meanwhile called in the goats. They had been more or less invisible among the rocks, but as he called white heads appeared here and there till a teeming flow of white goats come down to the glade. Strangely docile, they trotted obediently into the pen. Now all the laymen in the party took an interest in the judicious choice of the right goat for the sacrifice. Muna Khan is an angry (*dogshin*) deity, it was explained, and he must be presented with the blood, meat and life organs (*jüldü*)[10] of a fine male goat if he is not to be offended. A large energetic goat was caught by a hind leg and the others were let out to graze. There was now an interval, to the continued sound of Sengge Lama's chanting and cymbals, while we waited for the arrival of the man assigned to kill the goat. Chorji Lama had invited him to attend. For not only is killing an animal in principle a sin which most people try to avoid, but in the Mergen area this man was the only specialist in the art of preparing the *jüldü* for sacrifice.[11]

Erhimbilig killed the goat ritually by tearing its aorta and then carefully prepared the elaborate arrangement to be offered to Muna Khan as well as the sections of meat to be allocated to the various people

9. The ritual items consisted of numerous small cups of water and rice; juniper powder; dough figures; matches; sacred water in a special bronze pot; butter lamps; and a large bottle of strong alcohol. After the animal had been killed, a pot of fresh blood and a large platter of cooked meat were added to the stone altar.

10. The *jüldü* consists of the organs (heart, lungs, and windpipe) that represent the life of the animal and can be considered the "sacrifice" proper. Sengge Lama instructed that a pot of blood and some additional meat should also be laid out before the deity, while most of the meat is set aside for consumption by the participants. The same life organs of the sacrificed animal, under different names, appear in rituals across north Asia, from Yakutia to the Altai (Dmitriev 2001, 25).

11. Normally communities in Mongolia assign the duty of killing animals to a low-status man, who is paid for the task. In this case however, Erhimbilig, the man usually invited throughout the Mergen area, is a respected doctor and seer (*üjegechi*), both professions contributing to his ability to prepare the *jüldü*.

present in their particular social roles. The *jüldü* was arranged exactly as Sengge Lama described for the 1940s and as we saw later in the sacrifice for the battle standard in the monastery, with the organs wrapped in the skin, and slits made so that the goat's eyes would look toward the picture of the deity (for details see Humphrey and Laidlaw 2007, 264–71).

Experiencing *Sülde*: An Extension of Self

We first realized that *sülde* was integral to the Yellow Peak sacrifice when we asked Sengge Lama which texts he would chant for Muna Khan. The evening before, well prepared as always, he gave the list of twelve prayers, all written by Mergen Gegen, which would take five or six hours to chant in total. They included along with the texts for the five "angry" (*dogshid*) Buddhist deities, the extended version of the Muna Khan incense offering prayer (*sang*, T. *bsangs*), which begs him to "become our *sülde*," and another very similar text called simply *sülde*.[12]

The importance of *sülde* became more evident the next morning. Leaving Sengge and Minggan Lamas chanting, Chorji Lama took charge of a group to raise the sacred flag on the summit of Yellow Peak, a rite called Erecting the *Sülde*. Setting out before dawn, Chorji, Hürelbaatar, and four other people clambered over jagged rocks to reach the summit (Caroline conscious of the gender prohibition did not go and stayed to watch the preparation of the *jüldü*). At the peak, the old path, a stone altar, and a nearby tree had been blasted away by the army. A ten-meter high metal pole topped by a trident now stands there, with the ragged remnants of the canopy flag (*labari chimeg*) erected at the last ritual fluttering from it. The pole was taken down, and a new sail-like canopy consisting of a long tube of red, blue, white, yellow, and green nylon cloth was fitted over rings the length of the pole. Against a fierce wind, the pole was then re-erected and fastened with three metal lines to the rock. Chorji put on in his yellow lama's robes and made liba-

12. The texts in order of reading were: Ochirvani (eight pages), Erlig Khan (sixty pages), Jamsaran (forty pages), Tabun Khan (forty pages), Damjin (twenty pages), these being the five Dogshid. This was followed by Chagan Eserün Doorma (two pages, the rest being lost), Ündes-ün Sang ("root purification" prayer (fifty pages) a standard text), Sülde (twenty pages), and Muna Khan (thirty pages). After this, the Uhiyal Ergühü ("offering washing [the face of the deities]") text was read, followed by the Achilahu Nom (a prayer thanking the deity for its help). Finally, Dalalga ("beckoning blessing/merit") was read.

tions, throwing alcohol onto the flag. Then each person took a bundle of wind horse (*hei mori*) papers to a high rock and flung them as far as possible into the abyss toward the southeast.[13] The idea is for the papers to fly as high and far as possible, thus raising each person's *sülde hei mori*. Facing out over the distance with the wind rushing from below up the face of the mountain, the papers flew far and circled—as if they were not carried by gusts of air but flying by themselves like birds. No one could see them landing. This "raising" is exhilarating, wonderful, Hürelbaatar says; it boosts one's fortune and likelihood to be lucky. The feeling of swooping and fluttering with the paper wind horse was an extension of self—the self which is identified with the *sülde* "valorous spirit" and *hei mori* "vital energy" in each man.[14] Finally, as a separate rite, each person sipped a little alcohol from tiny silver cups, thereby receiving the fortune blessing (*heshig*) of Muna Khan.

The group then descended to the site of the sacrifice by the shepherd's hut, where the prayers to Muna Khan were reaching a culmination. The religious part of the ritual was concluded by the receiving of *dalalga*, a rite to beckon merit blessing (*buyan heshig*), which is incorporated as the ending section of numerous Mongolian ceremonies including all *oboo* rituals (Chabros 1992). Accompanied by chanting of the relevant text, Caroline, as patron of the sacrifice, took *dalalga* by holding up a pot containing a cooked front leg of the goat. Each time Sengge Lama chanted about various kinds of *heshig* (of happiness, immortality, wish-fulfillment, complete wisdom, etc.) and called "Come in!" (*"Hurai!"*), Caroline repeated *"Hurai, hurai, hurai!,"* circled the pot clockwise in the air, and thereby beckoned the grace into the meat, and the rite was then repeated by others present. Such *dalalga* meat should always be eaten on the spot or taken home, and not given away to outside people.

Why would people take part in this rite when they had just been spiritually invigorated with fortune by the raising of *sülde* and the wind-horse? It seems that *dalalga* invokes a somewhat different idea of fortune: the flying of the canopy and the open gesture of throw-

13. The papers in different colors, about ten centimeters square, were printed in Mergen Monastery with the sign of two crossed thunderbolts (*wachir*). Although people invoked *hei mori* by calling *"Sülde hei mori degjee!"* when throwing them, the papers were not in fact printed with a wind-horse image.

14. Women are not supposed by Urads to have wind-horse energy, though they may have *sülde*. For further discussion of this ritual and the acquisition of fortune, see Humphrey and Ujeed 2012.

ing the papers are an extension outwards into an airy and limitless space, whereas *dalalga* is a drawing inward of a different, more storable, "countable" kind of fortune (*heshig*). The beckoning rite is a necessary component and completion of any significant act of giving away, such as a sacrifice (Chabros 1992).

As the closing texts were being chanted, clouds suddenly covered the sky and rain started. This turned into a downpour. Sengge Lama after battling with gusts and fluttering pages gave up chanting and everyone took shelter in the hut. People looked in dismay at the slashing water threatening to extinguish the fire outside on which the pot of meat for the sacrificial meal was boiling. Clouds filled the valleys below us. Chorji gloomily said there would be a flood, it would be dangerous, and we would never get down the mountain today. Suddenly everyone remembered that rain is a good thing; that the prayer to Muna Khan actually asks for rain, and this must have been a successful sacrifice. Buyan then recalled that he had had this experience three times—sudden rain as soon as a sacrifice ended. No sooner was this relatively cheerful conversation under way than the clouds swept away as quickly as they had arrived. The sun came out. We feasted on the goat meat and the plentiful strong alcohol. And soon set off, somewhat drunkenly, down the tortuous mountainside.

The rite we participated in was an impoverished version of the ritual as it used to be performed before the advent of the Communists. The present-day ritual omits many actions and at least one long text formerly chanted. The political aspect has also changed. Today regional Communist officials make an effort to attend when they decide, or have been instructed from above, to support "minority culture"; but the main impetus comes from the local lamas and residents who not only depend on the mountain spirit for prosperity but also are concerned to assert publicly the sacred character of this land in the face of its potential alienation (see Chapter 10). This is very different from the situation in the first half of the twentieth century, when the rites at Shira Orui and Banner *oboos* were important occasions for the reaffirmation of the sacred-political power of the Duke and his officials.

Sülde can be seen as an aspect (and affect) of power. *Sülde* has always been associated with *törü* (the state, principles of government), a relation that was renewed by Prince Demchügdongrub [De Wang, Prince De] when he set up an autonomous government in Inner Mongolia in the 1940s. He displayed two massive battle standards (*tug sülde*) at his headquarters. In such a context *sülde* becomes a sign of sovereignty.

But what is a battle standard? It is above all a rallying point, but also a mobile vanguard—soldiers make it the prong of an attack, fighting outwards. The *tug sülde* is a point of shifting vantage, from which distant goals can be envisaged, and its implications are centrifugal, the radial extension of rule to outer regions. The political idea can be seen in Mergen Gegen's praise of Hasar in *Altan Tobchi*:

> To sum up, Holy Hasar did right in every direction: he subjected the four foreign peoples under his authority, he eliminated the cruel ones, he gave happiness to those who followed the law, he made the hundred tribes (*aimag*) and many clans (*obug*) peaceful and harmonious. The source of the great power for founding the Yuan Dynasty (*törü*) derived from Holy Hasar. Therefore Hasar's beneficial deeds are as high as the Sky and as wide as the Earth.
> (Quoted in Ba. Mönghe 1997, 216–17)

Sengge described in detail how the rite was performed in his youth (early 1940s). It is clear from this account that the 8th Mergen Gegen had charge of the spiritual transformation (the raising of the *sülde*), while the lay leaders made the energizing this-worldly offerings (including the blood and the *jüldü*). Each *sumu* was required to send representatives, bringing numerous fatty rumps of sheep (*ugucha*) for the offering. The duke and his officials initiated the rite, sending envoys to beg the honored lamas to attend, and during the ceremony they prostrated even to the youngest monks. However, seeing the event as a whole, it looks as though this humbleness of the lay leaders before religion was a stage in the circulation of acclamation within a wider rationale, where it was the political order the nobles and *sülde* stood for that dictated what the whole event was actually about. This became clear in what Sengge Lama said next.

Sengge clearly saw the Shira Orui ritual as part of a regionally dispersed cult that included Jirgal Bagatur's battle standard kept in the monastery, the celebrations at the West Banner *oboo*, and rituals held at various private Muna shrines in the area. The Banner *oboo* is located amid fields some eight miles from Mergen, and it consists of an impressive three-tiered cairn with a central pole-trident and numerous willow branches stuck into the top (Chapters 6 and 10; see also Humphrey and Evans, 2002). It was linked to Shira Orui by a line of smaller cairns extending from the main *oboo* in a northwest direction, "pointing to the mountain," as people told us. Sengge confirmed the non-Buddhist nature of the rites:

If we talk about the *oboo* sacrifice, it was a ritual that happened before people came to have a religious attitude (*shashin üjel*). It is a thing of Chinggis Khan's time. Chinggis' generals went from place to place fighting battles, and this sacrifice was to celebrate their victories. "Celebrating" in modern words is a memorial, so the sacrifice was to commemorate victories. They killed livestock. What kind? They killed the father animals—bull, ram, stallion. Because if there are no males the herds cannot be increased. They killed the males of all five kinds of livestock and offered the testicles to the *oboo*. After killing the bull its testicles are thrown on the *oboo* and the head too.

After making this association between victory in war and male procreation, Sengge Lama's next remark shows how this theme linked to the social hierarchy. "The willows on the *oboo*, they are put on by a noble ranked person. If there is no noble (*taiji*), ordinary people can't step up to the *oboo*."

Mönghebuyan, a Urad teacher from the Middle Banner, joined in, "Who are nobles? Let me tell you. They are the true descendants (*udum*) of Chinggis." "Yes," agreed Sengge, and there was then some discussion about Chinggis's younger brother Hasar, during which it was agreed that direct patrilineal descendants of Hasar are also nobles.[15] Sengge called the original ancestor of the West Banner *Burhan Noyon* ("holy lord"). He also mentioned several times that while he himself is a commoner, Chorji Lama has aristocratic birth. Evidently, the social preoccupations that so exercised Mergen Gegen had not been entirely forgotten. Mönghebuyan continued, "In Mongolian society . . . if there is no noble, the society cannot be formed—it cannot become one thing. Our Mongols have Banners and *Sumus* and their leaders are always nobles. If there is no noble, your *Sumu* cannot be formed. Ordinary people are just the providers of labor service (*albatu*)." Both were excited now, for the topic was forbidden until recently, and Sengge warmly agreed: "Yes, yes, all commoners are servants of the governing order (*jirum-un albatu*). If you are a noble and I am your *albatu* in one year I must do so many days work unpaid for you. This was decided from ancient times and practiced until Liberation." This conversation made clear to us that

15. The *taijis* were first only the descendants of Chinggis Khan's descendant Batu-Mönghe Dayan Khan (1480–1517), but with the Qing organization of society into Banners the term was extended to local leaders claiming descent from Chinggis's brothers. The Qing later organized what became a numerous class of *taijis* into four ranks, with salaries paid from the state (Atwood 2004b, 225–26). This enabled the Qing to extend their state-managed ranking system to virtually all leaders in Inner Mongolia.

the Shira Orui sacrifice, and indeed the entire "*sülde* complex," was understood to replenish the spiritual vitality of society organized around the nobles, without whom there would be no society (see Sneath 2007, 163–67).

Hürelbaatar then asked why lamas were allowed to carry knives to the *oboo* ritual.

"I just told you," said Sengge. "Our religion commemorates war victory at Chinggis's time, wrongful (*yalatu*) as it was. And although it's called an *oboo* offering, actually it is also a gathering of laypeople where they make appointments and conduct business. The rites are to symbolize their unity and show heroic majesty. They used to hang up a bow and arrow, which was their main weapon, in remembrance. That is why lamas carry knives when they conduct the *oboo* offering. In religious life a lama doesn't kill livestock or carry knives, but in the case of *oboo* they can, because this is the tradition of commemorating the Master, Lord Chinggis."[16]

Sengge's certainty hides the starkness of the opposition, so ancient in Asia. In fact, acrimonious disagreement about animal sacrifice at *oboos* arose in the monastery from time to time (see Chapter 10) because the bloody variant of the rite went against the explicit instructions of the 3rd Mergen Gegen. In a well-known text he had set out a model for the *oboo* ritual that did not involve killing animals:

> If we kill an animal we do sin and we will break the virtue of offerings at once, just as hail slashes down and ruins the crops. I think it is a mistake to slaughter rams, male goats, and bulls, to offer *jüldü* and heart like [those of] a vanquished enemy, to let them bleed, and to take out the fat, and wrap the whole thing up with cut wet skin. What is the use of such dirty and sinful offerings? It would be virtuous and magnificent only if we offered plain offerings (*BJ* 1998 [1780–1783], vol. 4, text 16, 4r).

In a political context Mergen Gegen's rejection of blood sacrifice recalls what Heesterman has called "the inner conflict of tradition" of ancient Indic culture: "To turn power into authority, the king must ally himself with the Brahmin, but the Brahmin must reject the alliance in order to safeguard the authority for which the alliance was sought. While the king stands for the order of conflict, the Brahmin's order is absolute,

16. The Kanjurwa Gegen likewise recalls wearing lay clothes and attaching a knife to his belt to attend *oboo* rites in the 1920s and 1930s "inasmuch as this was not a Buddhist ceremony" (Jagchild and Hyer 1979, 89). At the Shira Orui rite all participants wore lay clothes most of the time, but Sengge Lama put on his lama clothes for chanting and Chorji donned his for erecting the *sülde*.

negating all conflict. The one's order is the other's disorder" (Heesterman 1985, 7). In the same impasse the Mergen monks have swung between alternative modes. It is very possible that while Mergen Gegen was in charge the Muna Khan offering rite was conducted without blood sacrifice. But his rejection would have been seen as detrimental to the order of the nobles, which as Duke Galdan testified (Chapter 4) celebrated, symbolically and in actuality, legitimate conflict, warrior ancestors, and the joy of hunting. The 3rd Mergen Gegen was credited, in Galluu's legend (Chapter 4), with transcending the impasse by flaunting militant abilities, which however only disguised the superiority of his "real" (absolute) nature. But such virtuosity was regarded as a singularity. After his lifetime, evidently the pendulum swung the other way, to the side of the aristocratic order, and many lamas adapted by slipping temporarily into lay guise. Urad people had a fatalistic explanation of this turn; they told us that blood sacrifice is the sign of an epoch when the local land gods are in ascendancy and the Buddhist ones in decline (cf. Mills 2003, 320). This discussion indicates that any analysis would have to take account of two variables complicating the picture given so far: a) historical shifts in which version of the rite is enacted and which relegated to the background; and b) the mottled stream of narratives, at any given time, consisting of those exposed in bright light and those hidden in the shadows.

The Deity as Line of Continuous Variation

So far we have argued that *sülde* is associated with a radial vision of military power, with light and air, and with the aristocracy as the integrating skeleton of society. The primary local vessel for *sülde* is "Muna Khan," a term that can refer to the mountain Shira Orui itself but more usually to the deity who guards the whole range. Muna Khan is a Land Master (*gajar-un ejen*), a deity enjoined to protect Buddhism (*choijong*), and he is also worshipped at a series of lesser shrines (called "Muna") set up in the valleys closer to people's homes. It turned out that this kind of god is no simple object: the more we heard about Muna Khan, the more mysterious and multi-natured he seemed to be.

The picture of Muna Khan we were carrying up the mountain was of a military hero in armor, with a red angry face, mounted on a pale blue horse, brandishing weapons. This is a variant on the standard pictorial image of the local militant deity, master of the land, which is known throughout Buddhist Inner Asia, from Tibet to Buryatia (Zhukovskaya 1977; Heissig 1980, 89; Diemberger 1998; Karmay 2005; Berounsky 2006). The horse always gallops toward the left, the hero wearing armor always turns to face the viewer; surrounded by flames, he waves a weapon in his right hand, holds a treasure by his chest in his left hand, the sun and moon are in the sky. Commenting on the painting of Muna Khan, Galluu writes: "His mount, called Cloudy Blue, has its tail and mane standing up. Marvelous Mon Khan distributed the wonderful *sülde* of the victorious hero, full majestic light (*sür gerel tegüs*), with ten colors, five rays, and seven rainbows" (Galluu 2003, 651). The pictorial image thus personified is quite different from that of the myth in which Muna is not humanlike but a mountain sent to fix and stabilize the world. The mounted hero, on the other hand, fits with the cross-Asian idea of the fearsome autochthonous Land Master tamed by the power of a great religious adept.[17] If Padmasambhava was bent on total subjugation of such masters and Neichi Toin warily left them alone (Chapter 2), Mergen Gegen adopted a different strategy, for in his texts Muna Khan is transformed and elevated to a more marvelous and godlike being. This Buddhisized mounted warrior is what we call the dominant or majoritarian object of worship at the Shira Orui *Oboo*.

Yet this was far from the only view. In the story most frequently told to us, Muna Khan is a mundane figure, namely the kitchen fuel manager of a great monastery in Lhasa. Each year he flies to Muna Mountains with its plentiful trees in order to supply Lhasa with wood for cooking. The annual ritual on Yellow Peak is to welcome his seasonal visit. At first this story is puzzling, for Muna Khan the magical fuel manager must be depleting the mountain range of its precious trees, the very treasure that the 3rd Mergen Gegen and Duke Darmashiri petitioned Beijing to preserve, and in principle one of the main resources the Land Master is supposed to protect. Local people made this association when they joked, 'These days we have a new Muna Khan, the Forest Protection Agency!' But Buddhist thinking perhaps explains the paradox. Donating to a holy cause, such as lamas in a monastery, is a meritorious act of giving that rebounds positively on the donor. So in this view, if we ask why the Muna Mountains are so abundant in trees, the answer is: because their master Muna Khan gives for a religious cause he gathers merit and therefore his trees multiply and flourish.

17. Very similar pictorial images of land masters have long been common in Tibet (Diemberger 1997), not to mention much earlier martial gods in India (Pollock 1993). Such cults may have spread from India to China, where from the fourth century both Buddhists and Taoists bound warrior folk deities into subordinate positions in their pantheons; from the ninth–tenth centuries such deities were being made into monastic guardians (Hansen 1993, 76).

The popularity of this story today may be related to the actual threat to forest resources that preoccupies local people (Chapter 10).

Another tale about Muna Khan is definitely less than heroic. Muna Khan is a soldier in Chinggis Khan's army, left behind when his horse stopped to piss. Proceeding westward, the army had to travel fast through the thickly forested mountains; in such terrain even a short stop for a horse to relieve itself could result in a soldier getting lost. Normally in this situation, Boroheshig Lama told us, the soldier would tap his horse's hoof with his whip, meaning "Please wait for me, I'm here." But in this case the army in their rush could not hear the soldier and he was abandoned. He became the Land Master of Muna Mountains. This story must refer in a roundabout way to the fact that the Mongol Empire was defeated in China, and the last emperor with his armies had to leave the capital and retreat to the steppes. What does "traveling fast in a westward direction" imply but the very opposite of victory—something more like hasty retreat? The abandoned soldier story is a disturbing reminder, a talisman of a dread episode in history not forgotten by local people. As Elverskog has pointed out (2006b, 100) in several sixteenth and seventeenth century Mongolian chronicles the Muna Mountains are sanctified by words attributed to Chinggis Khan, they are "a good pastureland for a peaceful state, a fine place of refuge for a shattered state." In other words the great emperor was predicting the region to which the defeated Mongols should retire. Mergen Gegen too writes in a poem of the country of Muna Khan as a land that provides treasures for the state in peaceful times and a place of refuge for men (literally "male bodies") in times of disaster (Mönghe 2010, 231). But the story of the soldier is surely the product of a more mournful and workaday imagination, in which the idea is less that of secure refuge than abandonment by the army/state.

Then there was the puzzling and highly popular story of Muna Khan and the 9th Panchen Lama. This Panchen Lama (1883–1937), who had quarreled with the Dalai Lama, left Tibet and traveled all over Inner Mongolia. On this occasion he was on his way to visit Prince De, who was planning to build a temple for him in Sönid. On the seventeenth day of the seventh month of the Yellow Mouse Year (1933), when the great lama was passing near Güng Monastery, his car suddenly stopped.[18] Muna Khan had appeared on the northwest mountain. The chauffeur was terrified. No matter how they tried, the car would

18. On the pan-Asian motif of stopping of the chariot of the holy personage, which only starts again with supernatural impetus, see Humphrey (1991, 208) and Elverskog (2006b, 99).

not start again. The Panchen Lama told his disciples to run quickly to Güng Monastery and chant the prayer to Mahakala a thousand times. As soon as they had finished, Muna Khan disappeared and the car started. Ever since this time, people have prayed strongly to Mahakala (see Epilogue). This story illustrates the power of the Land Master as opposed to that of the Buddhist incarnation. No one ever made clear to us whether Muna Khan was stopping the Panchen Lama to welcome him or obstruct him. But in any case the story depicts Muna Khan as an imperious autochthonous spirit intervening when the great Buddhist prelate traverses his territory, ultimately allowing him to leave only when the even more powerful Mahakala is invoked.

How can we deal with the wayward heterogeneity of such materials? Surely the idea of the lost soldier, even a soldier of Chinggis Khan, is not compatible with the mountain that centers and stabilizes the world, and the traveling fuel manager, however amazing his magic, is distinctly at odds with the blazing source of *sülde*. No one ever tried to link these stories.

In fact, the proliferation of deity is a general phenomenon in Mongolian religious culture. We should distinguish, however, between multiplications that represent categorization or the elevation of number itself (e.g., the nine *sülde* deities, the seventy-five versions of Mahakala, etc.) and the production of several unlike images as in the case of Muna Khan. Any "one deity" can be subject to both of these different multiplication processes (see Humphrey 1997 concerning the multiplicity of the goddess Tara). The "21 Tara goddesses" is an attempt to systematize ideas of pattern and numerousness—such numbers seems to suggest an idea of filling out space-time by the given deity. But this grid of near-identical Taras coexists with another kind of multiplicity—inventiveness with no number and the folk identification of Tara with living and historical figures. Anthropologically, if we consider this latter kind of productivity, there is no ground to establish any of the cases as *the* correct one. The same point can be made even more forcefully of Muna Khan, where the pictorial image, the warrior horseman, is like a template that could represent the spirit master of almost any mountain in Mongolian lands, and yet it coexists with heterogeneous narrative alternatives. Although in theory the various stories might be assigned to some date or some social group, in practice this is neither possible nor appropriate because everyone we met knew all of these narratives.[19]

19. The exception was the legend of the Mountain Stake, which was recorded by Jirantai in the Urad region but not mentioned to us in the field.

They were recounted to us always as if they were each the truth, even though they were quite different from one another and people were aware of the alternatives.

All of this indicates that we need a way of conceptualizing such multifarious associations. Deleuze and Guattari's idea of the "line of continuous variation" in language may provide a useful insight. They argue for the primacy of the pragmatics of language, as distinct from its informational, signifying, or communicative function. Language is a way of doing things. Thus, looking at the different ways an expression like "I swear" appears, we are not dealing with "variants," a term which suggests there is one central meaningful term from which the others diverge. Deleuze and Guattari argue that each of the heterogeneous pronunciations of "swear" is an actualization in what they call an immanent line of continuous variation. The idea applies not only to phonemic, but also to grammatical, syntactical, and semantic situations. Thus in the case of semantics, "I swear" pronounced before a judge in a court, in a business deal, in taking political allegiance, or declaring love, should not be seen as having a single denotative core of meaning utilized in diverse contexts, but rather as different actualizations of contextually embedded speech distributed along a virtual line. Each "I swear" presupposes associated patterns of actions and topics that comprise its context, a collective assemblage of enunciation, as well as nondiscursive entities (bodies, practices) (Deleuze and Guattari 1998, 94).

Authoritative Intersection of the Line

There is no reason to suppose that the heterogeneity of local stories was any less in Mergen Gegen's time than our own. We argued in Chapter 2 that language was the great lama's main means to establish his particular order. Here Deleuze and Guattari again become relevant. They insist that, "Language is made not to be believed but to be obeyed, and to compel obedience" (1998, 76). One might not agree entirely with that statement, but it is certainly the case that to learn a language is to learn a host of categories, logical relations, associations, and so forth, whereby the world is given a certain coherence. It follows that the order imposed by language is far from neutral; it is part of the complex network of practices, institutions, goods, tools, and people implicated in relations of power, and is thus central to what we called earlier a *dispositif*. Lines of continuous variation are subject to the same conditions of order (or disorder) as language in general, and Deleuze and Guattari suggest they can be engaged with into two basic ways. They can be constructed, regulated, and disciplined, or they can be set in oscillation, intensified, amplified, and ramified (Bogue 2003, 117–19). These alternatives are related to "major" and "minor" usages of language: in the former mode they can be standardized in such a way as to restrict variation and regularize relations of power; but in the hands of minors (minorities) they can also diversify usages, destabilize linguistic regularities and, intensify lines of variation.

The discontinuous semantic chain of Muna Khan that we found in the Mergen area suggests that it is the product of just such minoritarian imagination. The prayer-writing endeavor of the 3rd Mergen Gegen, on the other hand, seems to have been aimed at creating a majoritarian usage at the behest of the Dukes.[20] In appropriating the cult of the mountain he transmogrified the warrior horseman into a Buddhism-supporting deity capable of gathering and dispensing *sülde*, and by institutionalizing the *oboo* cult he territorialized the worship to his own Urad domain. This accomplishment was a superscription over the earlier cults of Land Masters that associated them with origin-creating ancestors who wandered from place to place (Elverskog 2006b, 99–106).

Mergen Gegen wrote several texts in honor of Muna Khan and *sülde*. Some of these are complex works in several voices, employing a Buddhist idiom and structure,[21] including instructions to the lamas as well as invocations, eulogies, vows, imprecations, and confessions. In other words, they contain a certain reflexive and didactic recognition that sutras are part of larger actions (Keane 1997, 51). There are also several poems about Muna Khan, which are more lyrical and political. Nevertheless, a standard image of the cosmic, magical, and powerful Muna Khan/Sülde Tngri is conveyed, a uniformity of vision that required Mergen Gegen to cut across the line of variation by ignoring other images and known legends. In fact, Mergen Gegen takes simplification to

20. The colophon to Mergen Gegen's extended *sülde* text states that it was written at the request of the duke: "The custom of erecting the *sülde* is called 'the Sun which spreads the light of Benefit and Happiness.' This text is written by humble Lama bStan rKiyan [presumably Mergen Gegen] on the order of the State Supporting Duke Dha [presumably Darmashiri] of Urad, who has complete and wide-ranging knowledge of how to make the ancestors prosperous, and of discussing and studying genealogy, clans, belief and praise" (*BJ* 1780–1783, vol. 4, text 12, 8v).

21. One *sülde* text (*BJ* 1780–1783, vol. 4, text 14) has the following structure: preparation of ritual space/instruments; *yidam* evocation; invitation of Buddhist deities to descend; taking refuge and confession of sins; gratifying (*hanggal*) the *sülde*; offerings to *sülde*; golden libation to Buddhist deities and *sülde*; raising the *sülde*; glorification (*magtagal*); binding the *sülde* to provide support (*dagatgal*); receiving blessings (*dalalga*). This is similar in structure to the texts composed in Tibetan for the worship of local deities in Buryat lands (Berounsky 2006).

its limit, since he provides no narrative of Muna Khan—in his works the deity is a god with attributes, but without a story.

Replication, Disguise, Suppression

We can contrast two processes: replication and diversification. Mergen Gegen's *Sülde* and Muna Khan texts contain many near-identical passages, and evidently his attempt to stipulate the ritual form of the *oboo* also involves the idea that the same items, proportions, and actions be replicated year after year. Here *sülde* can be interestingly contrasted with *Tngri* (Sky, Heaven, God). For whereas *sülde* has been reproduced as a relatively constant set of ideas through Mongol history, *Tngri* splintered to a much greater extent into countless particular varieties, many almost losing any association with the sky (Heissig 1980, 50–59). The decentering of *Tngri* parallels the disaggregation of the Mongol state into numberless principalities and their morphological shift into the Manchu Banner system. As for *sülde*, it is true that it accreted new adjectives after the thirteenth century, especially to do with light (Skrynnikova 1992/3, 58) and was later Buddhisized in the hands of Mergen Gegen. It is also the case that the political rituals associated with it have waxed and waned, ceasing altogether in some regions and times (cf. Pollock 1993)[22], so *sülde* came to mean something like an individual's virile spirit in some parts of Mongolia,[23] while in others the association with the *oboo*, flags and standards, is the preoccupation only of a few politicians.[24] But where they surfaced, *sülde* cults replicated at different scales a recognizably similar set of ideas and rituals. This is perhaps explainable by the fact that lineages of hereditary guardians were established at key *sülde* cults, such as those of Chinggis Khan and Hasar, precisely to ensure that prayers and rituals were strictly followed.

Replication itself is not simple, however. As Bruno Latour reminds

22. Sheldon Pollock (1993) points out mythical figures like the warrior Rama have moved into and out of cult status in Indian history. Far from having always been a god, as present devotees claim, Rama was first known as a central figure in a sacred narrative, the Ramayana. He only started to be extensively worshipped around the eleventh–twelfth century, during the same period that Muslim peoples began to invade India. Pollock argues that Rama began to be worshipped in temples at this time because his deified warrior image was apt, first, to legitimate Hindu rulers, and, second, to vilify enemies as Other, i.e., not to be accommodated but to be defeated or annihilated.

23. Bernard Charlier, pers. com., concerning Mongols in far western Mongolia in 2007. See also *sülde* as life force among Buryat shamanists (Manzhigeev 1978, 94–95).

24. Rebecca Empson, pers. com., concerning Buryats in north east Mongolia in 1990s.

us, following Wittgenstein, people never follow rules; they just "embroider" on the pattern these provide (2003, 10). More precisely, repetition involves two acts separated in time, though both are present in the mind of the actor, and it is constituted not directly *from* one to the other but *between* two co-present series (those thought to belong to "then" and "now") in function of a virtual object (the idea x) in question. This imagined object is constantly in movement, "always displaced in relation to itself," and therefore it affects the terms and relations of the two psychically actual series of actions. This displacement of the virtual object is the principle through which, in actuality, repetition is necessarily disguised (Deleuze 1994, 104–05). Strict as the guardians may be, with an inevitably wavering idea of *sülde* there can be no identity of successive enactments, and yet because of the notion that there is "strictness" it is exactly this displacement that is obscured.

This disguised dynamic of replication should not be confused, however, with the suppression, which also occurs in the imposition of an authoritative version, of the other diverse potential ideas and actions that are held to be "different" and not integral to "the tradition." Mergen's writings contain evidence of suppression of stories felt to be radically offensive to the majoritarian vision of the gods and heroes who manifested *sülde*. Such attempts to define a cult inevitably create exclusions and secrets. In his day there probably were stories in circulation specifically about Muna Khan that Mergen Gegen desired to brush aside, though we have no sources to indicate what they were. But that he wanted to keep the lid on some other local narratives is clear. We briefly discuss the two most important of these, concerning Chinggis and Hasar. In each case Mergen Gegen laid out in his *Altan Tobchi* what he thought was right, as distinct from the "shameful gossip of stupid Mongols" (Baldanzhapov 1970, 154). That his attempt was unsuccessful is obvious from the fact that the stories are still circulating in Inner Mongolia two and a half centuries later.

The Lizard Beauty and the Queen River

A great deal of this chapter has been about means of exerting authority in different ways, by writing texts that dictate the meaning of rites or by actions that bring about sensations of personal dominance. The idea of *sülde* runs through these various actions, being the very "order word" through which a regime of dominance is manifested. However, the triumph of *sülde* in the land is no less problematic than that of the

Buddhist *mandala* discussed in Chapter 3. It is dogged by an insidious subversion, a "rumor" so magnetic and recurrent that most chroniclers from the early seventeenth century onward felt they had to rewrite it in a sanitized version (e.g., Bawden 1955, 140–41). The louche version is thus found virtually only in oral form[25] and it is still regarded as deeply improper. It gains its subversive attraction, we think, from the linking of sexual antagonism and the defeated enemy.

The "rumor" concerns the death of Chinggis Khan, who is the archetypal fount of *sülde*. The conventional story, repeated in many chronicles, is that he died as a result of an illness contracted after he fell from his horse while he was hunting (e.g., Onon 2001, 257–58). The indecent story was told us by the irrepressible Buyan: while Chinggis was campaigning against the Tangut, who were led by the upright Shidurgu Khan, his attention was caught by a patch of white snow mixed with red blood. "What is that?" he asked. He was told it represented the most beautiful woman, Shidurgu's wife, Gürbeljin Gowa (Lizard Beauty).[26] He was determined to acquire her, so he had Shidurgu Khan put to death, and forced Gürbeljin, who was also called the Red Queen, to become his consort. She made a knife with a sharpened coin and kept it hidden in her hand. At night, when the Khan had come to her bed, she cut off his genitals and threw them away. She then ran off and jumped into the Yellow River and drowned. Ever since, the Mongols have called the river Red Queen River (*Ulagan Hatun Goul*) or simply Queen River (*Hatun Goul*), because her spirit haunts it. Chinggis died as a result of his wound and his organs then become a plant called *goyo*, this being a potato-like vegetable that grows well in desert conditions. It can be eaten and is very nutritious, and is also used to make alcohol, cigarettes, and medicines.

This story must be anathema to the whole glorification of Chinggis Khan, in particular to the male pride manifested in the *sülde* cult. At one level it is "secret" because even to tell it aloud offends all decency (the genitals are commonly known in Mongolian as "secret place"). At the same time, telling it is dangerous. Even today some country people are wary of possible retribution from Chinggis's spirit.[27] Why does it

25. Several travelers such as Potanin (1883, 804), Przheval'skii ([1875] 1946, 138), and Lattimore (1942, 36) were told the story.

26. The lizard is among the creatures like fish, frogs, snakes, and worms that Mongols group in the category of water creatures (*lus*).

27. A similar attitude is found with regard to the story about Mergen Gegen's night time meeting with the Green Snake Woman (Chapter 3). People find it quite understandable that the lama whose curiosity led him to spy on this encounter was then blinded.

persist? A broad reason is the configuration of the landscape, which consists essentially of a long mountain range facing a great river. It could not be the case that, when so much is made of mountains, nothing at all would be said about the wide and dangerous river flowing alongside. Poems about the Urad landscape regularly contrast these two as a pair structured as male/female, high/low, north/south, beneficent/harmful. The Yellow River was prone to massive changes of its course, sudden surges, and floods. Areas near Mergen could be flooded for miles, or destroyed by bogs and sands in which people could be sucked to their deaths (De Lesdain 1906, 60).

Whether Lizard Beauty was imagined in one of the more proper versions of the story or not, in her capacity as the spirit of Queen River she was a power to be reckoned with. Mergen Gegen wrote a prayer for worship of the Queen River, and readers may not be surprised to know that it is curt, being only forty-five words long, and makes no reference whatsoever to the narratives about the Lizard Queen: "We pray to you, May you cleanse misfortunes and hindrances. May you increase merit (*buyan*) and glory (*chog*). May you gather the goods [we] desire. May you do away with vengeful war. May you complete [our] affairs and deeds quickly, easily, safely, and without obstacles' (*BJ* 1780–1783, vol. 1, text 63). So generic is this majoritarian text that it could not possibly cope with the multifarious urgency of misfortunes for which the river was held responsible.

In fact the great river was the subject of regular rituals conducted by all the nearby monasteries. Sengge Lama was fourteen in 1944 when he last took part. If the main seasonal ritual was done in spring to avert floods, the river was also worshipped to bring rain.[28] And Sengge also remembered another occasion. "Why did our monastery worship Queen River? Older Brother Lama went to Badgar Monastery. He found fevers and infectious diseases spread there. Our Chorji's previous incarnation was asked for *abural* (salvation) and he suggested conducting the Queen River propitiation. These diseases come from distant places, flowing with the river. To cleanse them you must do the Queen River offering." Evidently, Mergen Gegen's brief text would not suffice for such a serious undertaking. Naranbatu notes that the lamas had to use many other powerful sutras at the propitiation of the Queen River.[29]

28. A text by Mergen Gegen called *Hura Orugulhu Jida-yin Ubadis Hemegdehü Orusiba* (Sutra Called Magic Power of the Stone for Bringing Rain) was chanted while 108 sacred pills (*rilü*) were put into the Yellow River (Naranbatu footnotes in *BJ* ([1780–1783] 1998, vol. 5, p 29–30).

29. The *Lus-un Sang, Altangerel, Yehe Sang,* and *Arigun (Namdag) Sang* sutras were chanted. Further, a lama threw 108 dough shapes into the river chanting a text called *Lus-un Baling* (ibid, vol. 5, fol. 9).

Hasar and the Black Cursing Woman

If the river was one unpredictable counter to the great *sülde* of the mountain, the landscape contained other scattered reminders that military valor was not invincible. Further semi-suppressed stories were encoded in the valleys around Mergen that depicted the might of ancestor Hasar in decidedly ambiguous light. Urad chronicles relate that Hasar angered Chinggis during the same campaign against the Tanguts. They were camped on a promontory of the Muna Mountains and an owl hooted in daytime, a bad omen. Chinggis ordered Hasar to shoot it, but instead he killed a "good-tongued" magpie, which happened to fly across the path of his arrow (Jimbadorji [1849] 1984, 417). Hasar was punished, put in a well and left there for months, where he became ill. Meanwhile, a Black Cursing Woman (*hara hariyalchi emegen*) belonging to the Tangut Shidurgu Khan, appeared out of the mists on Muna Mountain, cursed the Mongols, raised a demon and caused a terrible snowstorm. Chinggis' troops began to fall ill and die. Chinggis ordered Hasar to be brought out of the well to shoot this woman. He shot her, but weakened by his sufferings hit her only in the kneecap. As she fell dying, she cursed: "May the male descendants of Hasar die of wounds/May his female descendants be abandoned by their husbands!" (Bawden 1955, 140). Buyan embellished the bald accounts of the chronicles with local lore: Hasar, having been in the well for over a hundred days needed to eat the soup and meat of a hundred black goats in order to regain his strength. After he recovered, he stood on the peak of Shira Orui and shot the Black Cursing Woman just as she was making an offering of tea to the Sky. Falling, she threw her offering ladle to one side and she caught at a tuft of *hamhuul* (tumbleweed) with her other hand. The place where her ladle fell is called Ladle Mountain, which is behind Shira Orui. When Hasar shot her, his arrow cut through the mountains at a place called Debeseg, and that place still has a runnel through it. Black Cursing Woman shouted as she died:

> Your black goats won't reach a hundred!
> May Hasar's descendants be broken!
> May the *hamhuul* grow with no roots!

Buyan told us that because of this curse tumbleweed is ruining our Urad pasture. It's useless for animals—it grows up in spring, but because it has such shallow roots it dries out and turns into a ball of fluff.

In Mergen Gegen's version of this story, the curser is a Tangut man, who was living with a lone widow. Hasar killed the man with one shot, took out his heart, and made a sacrifice of it to the mountain. He also killed the widow and cut her body into large and small pieces. Mergen Gegen adds, "This cannot be discussed" (Baldanzhapov 1970, 152). Yet still today people explain certain place names by where the "large and small pieces" fell—the Heart Oboo, the Hip Ridge, and so forth. By such stories the people of Urad and Ordos have made the land around them a constant reminder. Since the curse (*hariyal*) is the negative equivalent of the will-wish (*irügel*), discussed in the Introduction, it is effective—in other words it is a performative—and the names refer to an ongoing potential for misfortune for the people.

Lizard Queen and Black Cursing Woman are figures projecting the very opposite of everything prayed for in the cults of Chinggis and Hasar: they are female, non-fertile, and enemies (Tanguts). With regard to gender, it is not, however, women as such, nor female sexuality, which is seen as antithetical here—remember the celebration of the Green Snake Woman described in Chapter 3. Rather, the stories reveal that the violation (stealing, rape, killing) of women belonging to the enemy is the black and dangerous side of war, for the fact that these women are physically weak does not mean that they lack loyalty or power of spirit.

The after-effects of their deaths bring poverty of herds, lack of descendants, disease, or weed-infested land.

Evidently both of the legendary women lurked in Mergen Gegen's consciousness, as his *Altan Tobchi* takes the trouble to denigrate the Lizard Queen story and declares that Hasar's killing of the cursing Tangut and the widow must not be discussed. Later historians such as Jimbadorji and Rashipungsug had similar views. Both were of the opinion that proper Mongols could not have come up with such calumnies. But all the evidence is that these were Mongol stories that refused to disappear. Their fundamental, semi-repressed message is that victory creates defeated enemies, who take revenge even after their death. You can cut them apart or shoot them to pieces, but still their dying curses bear fruit.

Two Ancestral Shrines: Patterns of Concealment and Political Visions

Nearby to Urad were two founts of *sülde*, the shrines of Chinggis Khan in Ordos and Hasar in Muuminggan Banner. They illustrate in different ways the complex layering of things kept hidden and they also point to two indigenous configurations of power. Examining these cults, however briefly, enables us to see the historical contingency of many politically associated majoritarian practices, including Buddhisization, and how the secrets so created were interwoven with the long standing, indigenous concealing of sensitive and sacred matters connected with death and mourning, sexuality, and supernatural retribution.

In effect what we have to consider is the political and subjective implications of what we have described as the interventions—the order-words and authoritarian statements—issuing from the works of Mergen Gegen, who wrote important prayers used in both cults to this day. The public Buddhisization of both cults always concealed other concerns not easily expressible in standard public texts. The idea we adopted from Deleuze and Guattari—the "line of continuous variation" cut across by the "order word"—can now be seen to apply to an external analytical point of view. For someone inside, what is before them is not like a line of alternative equally weighted narratives, but could be imagined as a number of planes superimposed on one other, any of which may be moved to the foreground in given circumstances. This situation can be related to a kind of subjectivity characteristic of the "minor" actor. The distinctive and alternative stories he or she knows that explain a particular aspect of the world are not completely separate from one another. They are co-present and attached, even if some are occluded. For this reason even the word "alternative" may be misleading, for in a person's mind one image, let us say a despised or forbidden image, is also a datum attached to another, say a public image of the same object. And vice versa. Someone in such a situation is not merely the site of a conjunction of separate elements, since the constant process of objectifying, foregrounding, and evaluating elements, while relegating others, is a linked-up mental activity, sometimes consciously so. It is for this reason, we think, that in a situation of power encompassment like that of the Mongols, the shifting, sorting, and burying of cultural elements—and the production of "secrets" (*nigucha*)—was a constant preoccupation of many people. A frequent reshuffling of stories in relation to political situations would be a natural tactic of the minoritarian. A majoritarian perspective, on the other hand, would also produce secrets, but they would be elements excluded from a stable and normalized vision (even perhaps hidden from the majoritarian subject itself rather than from some external power).

Looking beyond Mergen Gegen to the broad context of China, there were wider political factors that reinforced the tendency to remain silent (or hide) divergent views. One was the long-standing practice of secrecy/censorship, alternating with periods of relative disclosure, among China's rulers themselves (Spence 1999, 2001). If we think about the Urad Mongols today, their practices of "hiding away" may to some extent be a reaction to, or mimicry of, the Communist regime, brutal and secretive as that has been. But it would also be a practice honed by long historical experience of living with multifaceted domination. Not only were all Mongolians long *used to* engaging with powers, to presenting a blameless face in several different directions at once, meanwhile shifting earlier/alternative political and religious notions to some hidden space, but in the unprecedentedly dangerous and chaotic twentieth century their lives depended on the stance they took.

Mongolian worship of heroic ancestors begins, however, with an internally generated blotting out: from the time of his death Chinggis Khan was worshipped by Mongols, but the imperial burial ground, known from Chinese sources to be located somewhere in northern (Outer) Mongolia, was deliberately made invisible. No trace of burial would remain, the ground was not to be entered, or the place spoken about. And so effective were these prescriptions that the imperial burial ground has never been discovered, despite several foreign archaeological expeditions to find it. Practices of occlusion associated with death are generated by a certain Mongol public position: the physical decease of our worshipped ancestors is different from the case of defeated enemies. Those, as we have seen, raise the issue for ego of having killed and therefore facing retribution, but here it is the grief of bereavement that is concealed from the "us" who are celebrating the normalized life that attempts to continue what has gone. *Sülde* is aligned with this public attitude, and the ancestor's spiritual energy that transcends death is sometimes called *sülde*.[30] The complex Chinggis and Hasar shrines enfold both of these concerns, revealing diverse aspects in rites at different times.

The cult of Chinggis Khan in Ordos has been well studied (Mostaert 1935–1936; Lattimore 1942; Chiodo 1993; Bürintegüs1999; Sainjirgal and Sharaldai 1983; Hurcha 1999; Atwood 2004) and we do not attempt a description here. We point out only some salient facts concerning the kind of indigenous polity celebrated and why such a polity might have need of *sülde*. The cult has been maintained over the centuries by hereditary guardian priests, the Darhad, whose most important

30. Horchin Mongols invoke the spirit of their ancestors, *Degedüs-ün sülde aburala!* May the ancestors' *sülde* save us!

duties are eternal mourning for Holy Chinggis, maintaining the four seasonal sacrifices each year, and the great sacrifice for his black battle standard (*sülde*) in the dragon year in each twelve-year animal cycle. It was the rites for *sülde* that were conducted in public, with massive expense and participation of officials from far and near. The battle standard was first taken round many districts for worship and to gather in the offerings. The rite of "fiercening the Black *Sülde*," to embolden the participants for fighting, was said to have involved sacrifice of a human enemy. By the nineteenth century this was substituted by an animal sacrifice, a goat that had to be stolen in a raid conducted by appointed "heroes." The blood was drunk and spattered on the standard. After the rite held in Jun Wang Banner of Ordos in 1905 the participants set out on (possibly ritualized) raids, in remembrance of the fact that Chinggis Khan had embarked on war just after offering to his standard (Bürintegüs1999, 1048–60).

By contrast, the secret rites, called *garil*, were for mourning at the death of the great ancestor. They involved the invitation of the "soul" (*sünesü*) of Chinggis, its propitiation and sending away, together with a "beckoning fortune" (*dalalga*) ritual. There were songs expressing grieving with accompanying music. At some historical point ". . . when the Lord's worshipped things were made secret and the color of the secret was deepened, the words of the songs were changed so that people could not understand them" (Bürintegüs1999, 214). These "changed" songs are chanted in the language of the gods (*tngri-yin hele*), consisting of repetitious incomprehensible syllables.[31] Nevertheless they had to be sung in such a way as to express pain, bitterness, sadness, and longing (*gashigudahu*).

Let us now consider the political form being celebrated here. The mausoleum complex consisted of a number of yurts ("palaces")—stabilized by the eighteenth century as the Eight White Yurts—which for most of the year moved nomadically around the Ordos and neighboring regions and gathered together only for the great spring sacrifice. The shrine was the fount of Mongol kingship and it was where great khans had been enthroned in the fifteenth through seventeenth centuries. The cult objects, collectively called *onggud* ("vessels" for spiritual power), consisted of the casket of Chinggis and his principal wife, Börte, in one specially extended yurt, the caskets of two other wives each in their own yurts, and distributed in the other five yurts Ching-

31. Some of these hymns in the language of the gods, collected in Ordos in 1957, have been published (Rintchen 1959, 109–13).

gis' milk pail, his arrows and quivers, his reins and saddles, his tethering post, tethering rope, and his treasury containing old writings and precious items. Attached to this complex were other sacred items such as Chinggis' battle standard, his white horse, and his special cart pulled by white camels (Atwood 2004, 161–62).

What is the concept of the great emperor envisioned at this shrine? Chinggis is known as *Ejen Hagan* (Master Emperor) and here we draw attention to the notion of *ejen*, which refers to the master and ruler of a domain at either imperial or household scale. Both the public Eight White Yurts and the secret *garil* rites presented notions of family or household. At various periods Chinggis' mother—and most of his wives, brothers, and sons—seem to have had yurts set up in their honor at the shrine. Even the mythical Lizard Queen was honored, displacing the wives Yisui and Yisügen in the seventeenth century (Atwood 2004, 163–64). Given the fact that Chinggis' and Börte's relics are said to be present in the same casket, that he also had a presence in the yurts of his other wives (but no yurt has ever been designated as his alone), and that other family members, along with his horse and camp equipment, have also been elements of the shrine, it is apparent that Chinggis is not imagined as a lone object of worship. Furthermore, many *kinds* of sacred presence are gathered here: the "absent presence" of Chinggis, the utensils, the holy books, the horse, etc. As Hürelbaatar suggests, Mongols intuitively feel all of these have to be worshipped because *they actually existed* and played their parts. Taken as an ensemble, we suggest that what is being elevated by worship is the complex intimate domain of an emperor imagined as the master of a divine "economy," as we discuss further below.

Let us now consider the different political idea represented by Hasar. For some reason, Hasar is remembered but not worshipped in the Urad region.[32] However, not far away, in Darhan Muuminggan Banner, there is a temple shrine for Hasar. It was first set up in a yurt-palace when the Muuminggan people arrived from the north in 1633. The shrine was destroyed in the Cultural Revolution, but was rebuilt as a brick temple in 1988. Before that it had been moved four times and the sites give some clues as to its historical role. With the gradual relaxation of the Qing policy of not allowing cultivation of Mongol lands, settlers moved

32. Why Mergen Gegen wrote a prayer for Chinggis but none for Hasar, even though his history *Altan Tobchi* is a paean of praise for the great warrior, is unclear. Perhaps one reason was that a "land" could have no more than one supreme spirit master, and that fount of *sülde* for Urad was Muna Khan. Also, the Urads as a junior branch in the Hasarid grouping were not the line entitled to maintain the shrine.

in to the vicinity of cities. The shrine was moved in the opposite direction, first in 1710 away from Baotou, then in 1872, and again in 1888, on each occasion away from incoming Chinese. It was moved a fourth time in 1917, together with the center of the Banner government, to a remote area (Mönghedelger 1998, 81–83). This line of movement suggests the shrine was connected with a notion of Mongol defiance and separateness. Hasar's temple today is a complete contrast to the Chinggis memorial site. If the latter is visible from afar, is widely publicized, and draws thousands of Chinese and international tourists, the former is located in distant pastures, down a lonely road. One could easily pass by without noticing the cleft in some hills that leads via a twisting path to an inner hollow where the temple stands. It is as if the shrine itself is a secret.

Before the Cultural Revolution there were three cult objects here: a painting of Hasar, the Black Sülde Battle Standard, and a deity called Dür Shod Dagbuu. Only male nobles (*taiji*) were allowed to enter and prostrate to the spirit; women and Chinese were strictly forbidden from the entire precinct. Lay hereditary guardians called *Höhe* read the four main prayer texts in Mongolian, including the Black *Sülde Sang* and the Mergen Gegen's Lord Chinggis *Sang*, and there was also a song known to local herdsmen calling upon Hasar's *sülde* to bring success and defeat enemies (rites of shooting arrows had the same purpose). At some unspecified date, lamas took over the worship; they got rid of the warlike Black *Sülde* text and started to read in Tibetan. But no one forgot Hasar's association with military prowess: he is habitually referred to as Habutu (skilled in using weaponry) Hasar. Hasar was depicted on two sides of a single piece of silk. On the front was painted the peaceful (*amurlinggui*) aspect of Hasar, but on the back was the angry, fearsome (*dogshin*) face. Illustrations in a local booklet show that the peaceful side was a naturalistic portrait, the head and shoulders of a bearded warrior with helmet, bow and arrow. The fearsome face on the hidden side was huge, black, and round, thickly daubed in primitive style, with two staring eyes and a small grinning mouth just visible. It was painted, people said, with the painfully extracted black heart blood of Hasar (Mönghedelger 1998, 100–101).

Dür Shod Dagbuu is the secret Tibetan name for a god whose "open" name was Sanwan Idshinorbu. According to local Mongols, the secret name means "Master of Corpses" and the public one "Jewel Fulfiller of Desires." The deity originated with a man who was wrongly accused of carrying out a robbery and was skinned alive in punishment. Realizing that "a thief is a person with extremely bad karma," he made a vow to discover and point out robbers and bandits after his death, and the booklet notes that he is worshipped at Hasar's shrine because the great warrior was also famous for suppressing thieves. The dual-named god was worshipped in the form of this man's bones, his complete skeleton (Mönghedelger 1998, 88, 98). But surely we can also see in this object of worship a moral concern with fulfilling desire. For the man was punished for the very same profitable and even glorious crime (raiding, armed robbery) that made Hasar himself infamous. The entanglement of two ideas in one deity seems to lay before us the dread thought that "fulfilling desires" in this way cannot but create the corpses of the innocent, as does the harsh punishment of people unjustly accused of being robbers. At the shrine it was Hasar's benign face that was shown to the public, but Dagbuu/Idshinorbu was worshipped openly as a skeleton and so it seems that the latter was introduced as a second object of worship in order to remind people of the "secret" second name, "Master of Corpses." The Hasar shrine thus housed a quite different set of open and hidden elements from the Chinggis one. By the 1950s, however, under the influence of lamas, it underwent a similar cosmetic makeover: the worshipped form of Dagbuu was no longer an actual skeleton but a standard Buddhist painting of Chitipati, two dancing skeleton deities, male and female, with hands and legs intertwined (ibid, 98).[33]

Today the shrine has been rebuilt in a more complex form. It consists of three rooms. The middle one is open for worship of a plain white bust of the benign version of Hasar, with a bow and arrows and a sword, and an altar for offerings. The right-hand room is the most sacred; it is kept locked and contains a closed felt tent. The guardian unlocked it for us revealing an altar opposite the door with new versions of the peaceful and fierce Hasar portraits, the Dagbuu/Chitipati dancing skeletons, butter lamps, and a large conch shell.[34] The black *sülde* standard and a quiver with arrows stand beside the altar. The left-hand room contains numerous recent paintings of ancestors, including Chinggis and his two brothers, Belgüdei and Hasar, as well as three lengthy genealogies of the leaders of Hasarid tribes. Also attached to the shrine is its consecrated horse (*setertei mori*), kept as a mount for

33. This is the well-known Tantric Buddhist image of Chitipati representing two enlightened deities, emanations of Chakrasamvara, employed to bring wealth and also to protect against thieves.

34. In Indian epics each hero carried a mighty white conch shell, its triumphant blast intended to bring terror to the enemy. The conch shell was retained in Buddhism as a symbol of power, authority, and sovereignty, and also to represent Buddha's resonant voice with which he called people to the path of *dharma*.

Hasar.[35] We were told of plans to build four "palaces" at the shrine in which worshippers could come to stay, one for each of the main Hasarid tribes, but so far the plans were unrealized in this modest, difficult-to-find place.

No less than the Chinggis mausoleum, the Hasar shrine is a "society" of things. The unifying idea in the Chinggis case is the familial grouping or household, while in Hasar's shrine it is the patrilineal descent group of warriors (complicated by the presence of Hasar's alter ego among the gods, the "master of corpses" Dagbuu). In each case the worshipped ancestor is imagined as the fount of a great political grouping. But what understandings of the political life would account for these strange multiples?

The Circulation of *Sülde* to the Polity

In these shrines we see an ordering of multiplicity different from those of number/category or the more open folk diversity of Muna Khan stories mentioned earlier. The functional and conceptual relations between the elements in these shrines suggest that these multiplicities can be seen as something like what Agamben (2008a, 2011) has called an "economic theology." He was referring by this term to the dynamics of the *oikonomia* of the Holy Trinity (God the Father, the Holy Spirit, and Jesus). Agamben argues that early Christian theology gave rise to two contrasting paradigms that applied in both divine and human life, both of which have influenced European political thought: ". . . the political theology, which founds the transcendence of sovereign power on a unique God, and the economic theology, which substitutes the idea of an *oikonomia* conceived as an immanent order and which is domestic and non-political in the strict sense" (our translation, 2008a, 17).

Too much attention has been paid, Agamben argues, to developing the former idea, for example in the work of Karl Schmitt and his followers, and not enough to the latter. Agamben's theory is that when a polity is conceived as an *oikonomia*, where its head is essentially the manager, sovereign rule can be conceived, contra Schmitt, separately from government—"the do-nothing king who reigns but does not gov-

35. The Höhe guardian was very proud of this beautiful white horse, which was let free and captured once a year for re-consecration. In this rite a lama was invited to chant while milk was put on the horse's back and it was stroked till it shivered, whereupon it was set free again.

ern" (2008a, 115–34; 137). Yet real power, whether divine or human, must hold these two poles (of reign and government) together. This is brought about by the effective procedures of Glory. "Why," asks Agamben, "does power need glory? If it is essentially the force and capacity for action and government, why does it need to assume the rigid, onerous and 'glorious' form of ceremony, acclamations, and protocols?" (2008a, 14). His answer is that when politics is conceived in this governmental-economic way—and here Agamben quotes from medieval theologians—two things are needed in the world: order, and the grace by virtue of which order exists (2008a, 137). For such a concept, which is both political and metaphysical, to be actualized requires the ritual actions of Glory—acclamations, gestures, insignia, avowals, in which religion and politics cannot be distinguished. The ceremonial here is constitutive, the liturgies are speech-acts, the gestures are performatives, all of which invokes the divine grace and at the same time confers publicly recognized juridical force on the acts of acclamation, and thus *constitutes* the power of the king (2008a, 288–94; 2011, 170–71). These ideas, although Agamben refers strictly to Christian history and political theory, are very illuminating when we consider Mongolian political ideas. For, as Mergen Gegen writes, at the very beginning of history, when it was not possible to establish government of human beings through skill, wisdom, charity, reasonableness, or law, there had to be a leader "raised by all" (*olana ergüdegsen*) (Baldanzhapov 1970, 114)—a phrase that remained in the Mongolian political vocabulary into the twentieth century. What is this "raising by all" but the common acclamation that had the juridical function of constituting the sovereign?

The *sülde* rituals are about reenacting this moment of conferring sovereignty and grace to the societies of people and things that are multiple yet conceived as one. To be more precise, what can be seen in the rites is a movement of glory/acclamation, which is first produced by gestures and offerings made to elevate the deity and then brought radiating and circling back to "us" in the form of *sülde* spirit—and "us" in the context of these rites is the ruling duke, officials and other nobles, and the representatives of the *sumus*—in other words, the managers-masters of the realm.

Mergen Gegen's *sülde* text ends, "Pronounce [this text] with faith without discriminating origin (*ijagur*) or clan (*obog*)" (*BJ* 1780–1783, vol. 4, text 12, 8r). The notion of the polity was thus not limited to the nobles. But the "original democracy" that Karl Schmitt saw in such forms of acclamation (Agamben 2008a, 263) was not of course all-embracing in the Mongol case. For even though the "economy" of the Eight White Yurts comprised a recognizably familial and inclusive, if fluctuating, set of people and things, such plurality was not replicated in the worshipping congregation. The principles of inclusion were different. The *worshipped* multiple comprised anything or anyone that existed and mattered, powerful entities, whereas the *worshippers* were the limited set of the proper representatives of the polis. Women, slaves, and foreigners were excluded, and anyone polluted by birth, menstruation, death, or sin was forbidden to attend. Only in the contemporary period have these restrictions partially been lifted.

Yet the polity to be invigorated was nevertheless imagined as a vast radial extension of those actually present, and in this context it is significant that the divine *sülde* was conceived as a cosmic assemblage. This can be seen from Mergen Gegen's texts, where, having fortified themselves by calling down and visualizing themselves as a *yidam* tutelary deity,[36] the lamas are empowered to call upon the god *Sülde* Tngri. The latter is already numerically multiple—*Sülde* Tngri is another way of talking about the Nine *Sülde* Tngris—but it is also plural in an "economic theology" sense, i.e., implying a praxis among its diverse elements. Imagined here is a divine military assembly: the nine are "fully armed older and younger brothers" and come with their companions (*nöhörselte*), servants, sky gods, water gods, horses, an eagle floating above, a black bear stepping in front, hunting dogs running behind, and an army of magical soldiers (*hubilgan aimag cherig*) (*BJ* 1780–1783, vol. 4, text 12, 3r–3v). Invited to descend and sit firmly, the *sülde* gods are then offered—provided with—the glories of a kingdom—a beautiful palace, flowers, food, drink, agricultural products, flags, weapons, horses, skins of game animals . . . (ibid, 4r–4v). Implored in a series of poetic metaphors to "become our *sülde* without separating from us," the gods are extravagantly praised and acclaimed: "You were raised as the body of the Great *Sülde* Tngri in the universe, I praise you! You were very angered, but you have a smiling face, I praise you! . . ." (ibid, 6v). The god is enjoined to "Make very firm the following": "The extra victorious decoration of religion and state (*nom ba törü*), the top beauty of the treasure of fame and name; make amazing deeds as many as countless seeds and have them blow in the wind to the ten directions. May you increase the happiness of living beings and make the lotus of re-

36. An orthodox tantric understanding of the invocation of *yidam* at the beginning of the *sülde* text chanted at Shira Orui would be that the ritual is divided into two parts, first, higher activities for enlightenment and, second, the invocation and propitiation of Muna Khan/*sülde* (see Klein and Sangpo on such a structure for hail protection rites in Tibet, 2009, 401).

ligion and doctrine greatly blossom out. Spread the thousand lights of [the ruler's] orders and suggestions. Purify the darkness of [people] who do not have custom (*yosu*)" (ibid, 7r–7v). The Complete (*tegüs*) Great Sülde—the nine brothers with their retinue—is begged to "look after us all three times a day, pay attention to us and correct us three times every night, see us off when we go away, take care of our welcome when we return, . . . take care always to be our beloved friend (*hani nöhür*) forever" (ibid, 7r).

The ferocious Black *Sülde* version of the rite—abhorred by many lamas—was done to charge up the government of the *oikonomia* for war. This is where we can most clearly see the difference between the concepts of the Hasarid and the Chinggisid polities. For Hasar did not govern a people but an army; he was only ever a war general and thus the Black *Sülde* was a permanent fixture of the rites at his shrine (though the lamas banned it for a time). The "economic theology" here concerns relations between triumphant legitimate victory, morally suspect ferocity, and death. The Black Standard represented a force singled out periodically to strengthen people for battle, to boost the life energies into an implacable power by "fiercening" (*dogshiragulahu*) the standard—surely a transformation of a governmental politics into the agonistic one emphasized by Schmitt. It seems no accident that, through the Qing into the present day, the recalcitrant militarism and ethical self-questioning prominent in the Hasar cult should have become recessive and hidden away. Chinggis, on the other hand, was the governor of an empire, and his much richer commemorative site included White and Varicolored Battle Standards and diverse rituals. Mergen Gegen's writings in praise of Chinggis stress happiness, merit (*buyan*), intelligence, law, and strength (*batu*) far more than warlike qualities (Mönghe 2010, 68). The four-legged[37] Black *Sülde* seems to have become a separate item, brought to the Chinggis memorial site for worship only at intervals. In 1935 it was kept some thirteen miles from the Ejen Horuga familial sanctuary (Lattimore 1942, 59). In those times it was clear from the prayers who were the enemies that the fearsome *sülde* was directed against (Bürintegüs 1999, 1050). Mongols told Owen Lattimore that in ancient times there was a powerful Irgen Bagatur (Chinese Hero), and he constantly threatens to rise and overthrow the Mongols. The parading of the black standard of Chinggis every twelve years was to keep him suppressed (Lattimore 1942, 59). The concern of the main shrine

37. The four legs represented the kings of the four conquered directions, the Chinese, the Tangut, the Sartaul (Central Asian), and the Solunggus (Korean).

by contrast was concerned with constant commemoration of the familial nexus at the heart of an empire.

This chapter has described three sites—the Shira Orui *Oboo* of Muna Khan, the Chinggis sanctuary, and Hasar shrine—where *sülde* was (and is) invoked, each of them representing a different religious-political constellation. Each enfolded suppressed or secret aspects that reveal local awareness of the moral ambiguities that attend contemplation of Mongolian history. The main axis, in a concept of political order that was manifest in reality until the mid-twentieth century, was a distinction that was never entirely complete between the benign *sülde* that channeled the glory of sovereignty to a government (of both "household" and "ancestral lineage" kinds) and the black version of *sülde* through which flowed the ferocious power to suppress and kill. The invocation of the special spiritual fervor required to kill human beings was no mere fantasy. In the wars of the twentieth century the Mongols found themselves fighting other Mongols. The Urads splintered into many changing factions—revolutionaries, reactionaries, followers of Chiang Kai-shek and the Chinese Republic, clients of the Japanese invaders, and supporters of Prince De and the Mongol nationalists. On particularly terrible occasions, soldiers had to be "charged up" in order to kill their own neighbors. Thus it was that two sites for invocation of *sülde* that we have been able to mention only briefly, the battle standard of Joy Hero Adjutant and the Banner *oboo*, were given sacrifices in the 1920s and again in the 1940s. On these dire and eventual occasions, it was hinted to us as a secret, the intention was to make the most powerful sacrifice—of a human not an animal victim.[38]

It has only been possible to discuss three main sites here, but there are countless others in southwest Inner Mongolia. Some are the *oboos* that are said to have the remains of famous warriors/ancestors buried beneath, while others are local and household Muna and *sülde* shrines. From this, and from the fact that each individual is held to have *sülde* spirit as part of his/her make-up, it can be seen how multi-scaled and pervasive are the ideas we have tried to analyze here. By the time of our fieldwork, war was no longer in the cards: the PLA had moved its base elsewhere, the model of the border-area fortifications disappeared from the Officer's Mess, and the radar station on the nearby mountain was moldering to a ruin. But the people living near Muna Khan Mountain

38. We intend to describe these dramatic events in a different publication. Several elderly people maintained that the first sacrifice to the Banner *oboo* had been a human one and that this man's remains were buried so deep under the cairn that they were unaffected by the depredations of the Cultural Revolution.

kept the worship of *sülde* alive. As we shall describe in later chapters, versions of the ideas that link religion and power would surface in a different form even in peaceable times. Next we turn to the dramatic life (and after-death) story of the 8th and last Mergen Gegen. This eminent lama had been a dignified conductor of the *sülde* rites, as Sengge told us, but his many activities were to open up the monastery to different, modern concerns.

SIX

The Afterlife of the 8th Mergen Gegen

Introduction 2000

In 2000 we were allowed to stay in the Mergen Gegen's *sang*, the most spacious and elegant of the remaining compounds of the reincarnate lamas. At the northern end of the courtyard is the Gegen's temple, locked, empty, the haunt of swooping bats. The eastern house, where we slept, was divided into four dusty rooms, each opening onto the courtyard, while the western side was used for storage of flour, butter, oil, and other items used in offerings. One pine tree was all that remained of the garden the 8th Gegen had cultivated before his death in 1972. To the south is a gatehouse leading to the second courtyard of the *sang*. Various people lived in this lower yard from time to time, lamas coming to attend services and a devout elderly woman, the companion of Galsangochir Lama.

After a few days we made an acquaintance who put our living in the Gegen *sang* into sharp relief. This was a new arrival, Sodnomjamsu Lama (henceforth Sodnom), who, people whispered, was said to be the reincarnation of Mergen Gegen. We were taken aback. How had we not known about this before? And why was *he* not living in the Gegen *sang*? Sodnom was the nephew of Galluu, the former Mergen lama whose books we have cited. Energetic and articulate, he had a comprehensive knowledge of the liturgy and evident mastery of the complex hand gestures that accompany many chants. "You can see he must be the reincarnation," a layman said, "from the way he holds himself, his amazing fluency, as if he knows the doctrine with no need to be taught." We knew that the government had refused to recognize any new reincarnations, so officially Sodnom could not be the 9th Mergen Gegen. But why was there a polite but firm absence of enthusiasm from the monastery lamas? Surely they should welcome the reappearance of the great leader of their tradition. The reasons for their reluctance will become evident over the coming chapters, and meanwhile we note that Sodnom never reappeared at Mergen after that summer. At the monastery it was accepted that the 8th Mergen Gegen would not be reincarnated in human form in the foreseeable future. His physical absence put into question the alternative agentive means by which a *hubilgan* may have a continued presence.

Living in this deserted courtyard, one could not but try to imagine the life of the last Mergen Gegen whose official residence this was.[1] As we gradually discovered, his actions had in some ways followed the example of his predecessor, the 3rd Mergen Gegen, but in other ways took entirely new directions, especially in engagement with the tumultuous political events of the mid-twentieth century. The Cultural Revolution cut abruptly into his life—as it did for most of the actors in this book—and he died in its aftermath. The violent, destructive acts that took place require us to reflect about the ways in which the Urad people question responsibility, causality, effects, and consequences.

A new idea seems to have arisen to occlude the whole period, *tngri-yin chag* (time of heavenly fate), during which the power of all Buddhas, deities, spirits, and ghosts went into abeyance, banished by the overwhelming force of the Maoist Communist leaders. This meant that normal expectations of occult retribution for sins did not apply and judgment of other's actions was suspended.[2] However, the *tngri-yin chag* was held to have ended when less forceful leaders took over in China. The deities and spirits gradually returned, and now the delayed outcomes of certain incidents could be explained in ways that implied or directly assigned liability. Thus for many local people the idea of an era "fated by heaven" marked no more than an extended pause in accus-

1. Mergen Gegen in fact lived just outside his courtyard in his *labrang* ("palace"). This building is ancient in appearance, but it was one of the few houses in the monastery to have the advantage of under-floor heating. External ovens led smoke and heat through pipes to warm the raised platform bed.

2. See Charlene Makley (2005) for a thoughtful discussion of the memories of the Cultural Revolution in the Tibetan monastery of Labrang. Mackley's respondents personified the Maoist state in patriarchal fashion, but unlike many people at Mergen they did not attribute the state with supernatural, ghost-banishing power.

tomed forms of consequential thinking. But for others, and above all the new generation, there was a radical epistemological break: the gods of their parents had not gone into retreat, they never existed in the first place. Educated in radical socialist atheism, such people, including even at least one prominent lama in the monastery as we discuss in Chapter 8, saw the 8th Mergen Gegen as a religious functionary whose influence needed to be strictly controlled. By the time of our fieldwork another shift in truth claims was taking place. The Maoist years were already being seen as an era of madness and barbarism, replaced by the contemporary world of scientific objectivity, rational governance and economic calculation (Liu 2009, 16). Such a regime of truth also has no space to account for the holiness of a figure like Mergen Gegen. Yet when local people were remembering and forgetting in our presence, their earlier habitual modes of thinking constantly resurfaced[3]—both Maoist and the more ancient religious ideas. They made no attempt to join up memories of events as a historical process; rather, it was as though they were hopping between separate epistemological islands, aware of (yet having nothing to say about) the distances between them. In this chapter, we document the prevailing "religious" mode of thinking about truth and responsibility in times of violence, while bearing in mind that it coexists and implicitly contests with alternatives.

What is interesting is that local imputations of responsibility do not fall where they would be anticipated according to either Buddhist teachings or Western thought (Williams 1993), i.e., squarely with the intention of an individual human actor to perform the given act. Mostly people continued to refrain from judgment. They were silent when Europeans might see responsibility, but sometimes they assigned blame in unexpected ways, drawing on a range of "causal" processes and determinant agents both seen and invisible. These included the agency of artifacts substituting for persons, the efficacy of touch, synchronous or parallel effects, and the notion of temporally delayed consequences that reveal a previously obscured fault. The result of an action in the world was often considered more important than the intention lying behind it, and it was the former that was subject to most scrutiny. Winding among these narratives was the supreme value given to social—especially hierarchical—relationships. Similarly to the situation described by Duranti in the case of Samoa (1993, 26), interpretation of others' actions was primarily a way to determine what the meaning of a given act was for the people conversing, not for the actor,

3. See discussion by Xin Liu of comparable habits of memory in rural China (2009, 136–38).

and such judgments became a means of publicly understanding and controlling relationships. Enacting human relations in the wrong way was seen not just as morally reprehensible but as agentive in the wide relational cosmos and therefore bound to have occult consequences. It is because these ways of thinking were involved in the "after presence" of the 8th Mergen Gegen that we discuss them in this chapter—in particular the ideas concerning his transformation from a deceased person into several different objects of worship, one of which was attributed with deadly power. We preface that discussion with an account of the great lama's life and times, and we then try to convey the variety of such "causal" ideas through the narratives about other people in the violent period through which he lived.

The Early Activities of the 8th Mergen Gegen

After he returned to Mergen from training at Kumbum Monastery, the 8th Mergen Gegen, Galsangdambijalsan (b. 1898), had thrown himself into religious good works: he ordered the sculpting of the giant Maidar statue, built a tall temple to house it, and also replaced the great Chogchin Temple burned down in 1913. But soon a political bent began to reveal itself: in the late 1920s he supported a brief revolutionary takeover of the Banner, perhaps more impressed by its leader's youthful enthusiasm for an independent socialist Mongolia than anything else (Atwood 2002, 767–73). However with the rise of the Inner Mongol National Autonomy Movement in the 1930s, Mergen Gegen ended up siding with its leader, Prince De, who was in many ways a social conservative. This brought him into conflict with the ruler of the Banner, Duke Shirabdorji, who was supported by the Chinese nationalist party Guomindang (GMD)—and after the duke's death in 1936 with his young widow, the regent, who is known by her Chinese name as Queen Qi Junfeng. The Banner was rent by a bitter civil war. Across southern Inner Mongolia certain prominent reincarnations now appropriated practical as well as spiritual power.[4] Mergen Gegen maintained a troop of soldiers,[5] but to little avail—the monastery was invaded and

4. These kinds of power could be indistinguishable, as when, for example, a Mongolian reincarnation granted a written safe conduct to English missionaries in the Alasha region, assuring them that only his authority would enable them to cross lands infested with bandits and rebel troops (Cable and French 1933, 155).

5. The militia numbered seventy to eighty men with an officer commander but under the overall direction of Mergen Gegen.

ransacked by GMD troops and abandoned by the lamas. Mergen Gegen, along with the local chieftain, Administrator (*tusalagchi*) Erhedorji, was forced to flee for two years to Prince De's stronghold at Batuhagalga Monastery (C. Bailing Miao). Prince De had little alternative but to ally with the Japanese, whose invasion of Inner Mongolia soon reached close to the West Banner. With Japanese backing, the prince's forces took the Banner in 1938, Queen Qi was ousted, Erhedorji reinstalled in power, and Mergen Gegen was able to return. Once again, he restored the monastery, rebuilding his courtyard in elegant metropolitan style.

Mergen Gegen had become a nationally conscious "politicized" lama (Hyer and Jagchid 1983, 179). In 1938 he was chosen by Prince De to take part in a delegation to Japan, followed by another visit in 1942. In the same year he was appointed as one of the two deputy leaders of the autonomous government's long planned *Lama-yin Tamaga*, an organization set up to regularize and unite Chinese and Mongolian Buddhism in Inner Mongolia (Jagchid 1999, 296–97). The high lamas who went to Japan returned unconvinced by the religious merits of Japanese Buddhism, but they did appreciate the modern institutions and technologically advanced society, and they proposed to reform Inner Mongolian Buddhism. Li Narangoa suggests that the proposed reforms were superficial (1998, 238–39), but, taken together, they amount to a significant alteration in ethos, perhaps influenced by strong criticism of clerical obscurantism from both educated Mongols and Chinese secularists (Tuttle 2005, 75). The key ideas during the debates in the *Lama-yin Tamaga* may well have been Mergen Gegen's, since they amount to propagation of "Mongolian Buddhism" along with an opening of monastic life to the outside world: namely, to use Mongolian language texts for teaching, with Tibetan only as a supplement; to establish a school in every monastery and teach young monks literature, mathematics, and other subjects; to establish handcraft production in every monastery; and to conduct examinations of young lamas and send those who failed back to lay life. Perhaps the 3rd Mergen Gegen, with his zeal for education, was an exemplar for the reformist lamas of the 1940s. The plans were hotly debated, with monks becoming red in the face, jumping up and clapping their hands as if in a philosophical *choir* debate (Jagchid 1999, 297).

Mergen Gegen set up a hospital and school of medicine for the whole Banner, staffed by both modern and traditional doctors; a small workshop made and sold medicines. He made a list of over a thousand medicinal plants, trees, and minerals to be found in the Muna Mountains and had it translated into Tibetan and Chinese (Galluu 2003, 142). The

Gegen also established schools for lamas at the Mergen and Güng Monasteries, with plans to extend to eleven of the smaller monasteries in the Banner.[6] The discipline was strict and students paid fees, but they were not charged for exercise books, textbooks, lama clothing, or soap, towels and toothpaste (the last items representing modern hygiene). Mergen gave each lama the duty of planting ten trees each spring and keeping them alive. He himself was the exemplar in planting activity; his *sang* yard and the Labrang Palace next to it had flourishing flowers and fruit trees, a few of which still have a straggling existence today. He also revived the garden planted by the 7th Mergen Gegen in 1865 behind the Temple of Relics and repaired the warm spring that watered it. After he came back from Japan he laid out another garden to the west of his *sang* with apple, apricot, lychee, and other fruit trees (Galluu 2003, 143–45). Both of these gardens were later destroyed.

If these activities can be seen as meritorious religious acts in the footsteps of his predecessors, Mergen's next venture was new. He set up a wool enterprise, with cleaning, dyeing, spinning, and weaving workshops, to make blankets and carpets to "supply the commoners' needs." Another atelier made black leather boots and sold them to people in the Banner. Lamas and lay youth worked in these two enterprises. Galluu remarks that this created a new style of Buddhist lama, someone who worked at a productive trade as well as studying (ibid, 147) and he told us that he was proud to have been among their number. Yet this whole idea of lamas working "in the world" and producing their own sustenance cut across the classical idea that the monks should be supported by the laity in order to devote themselves to their own and other people's enlightenment (see Chapter 2). Similar labor cooperatives had been tried out by Buryat reformist lamas in Russia the 1920s with the hope of convincing the Bolsheviks of their socialist credentials. The 8th Mergen Gegen had certainly heard about the tragic fate of these experiments,[7] but in his case the innovations were, it seems, less inspired by socialism than by a desire to improve the situation of the Mongolian nation.

After the Japanese retreat at the end of the Second World War, the GMD shut down Mergen's workshops as the activities of a "Japanese

6. The subjects taught were Mongol language, Buddhist doctrine, translation from Tibetan and Japanese, mathematics, astrology, and painting.

7. Buryat refugees from Communism had reached Inner Mongolia and their situation was well known to the Kanjurwa Gegen, who was an associate of Mergen Gegen (Hyer and Jagchid 1983, 148–49). Russian Communist policy turned radically against religion in 1928, the reformists were arrested, and all monasteries were closed in the 1930s (Humphrey 1986, 418–19).

collaborator." At this point Queen Qi supported by the GMD returned to rule the Banner, with her young son as duke-in-waiting. In turbulent tides of local enmity, they were both assassinated in 1947. After this, Administrator Erhedorji resumed power and his young protégé, Amurjana, was installed as duke—the last duke of the Urad West Banner. Despite Mergen Gegen's association with these nobles, the Communists, when they came to power in 1949, accepted him; not only did he appear to be a progressive figure, but, given his opposition to the GMD, the logic of "my enemy's enemy is my friend" positioned him on their own side.

The Early Communist Years

The twenty-year history of the Banner from 1949 up to the Cultural Revolution in 1966–1972 indicates that the people living around Mergen Monastery were incorporated ever more firmly into communist political-economic structures, but only partially into those ways of thinking. In the higher structure of Inner Mongolia, the relation between Buddhism and politics had fundamentally changed. For the first time in centuries, sovereign rule was conceived in a way that did not need religion for its own vindication; now it required only the quiescence of religious people. Yet in some inner local recesses, people undertook actions that show that earlier ideas were still what mattered to them.

In 1949 the southwestern part of Inner Mongolia experienced a peaceful transfer of power to the Communists in Suiyuan. At first not many changes were made in local administration, so although the Dukedom was abolished and young Duke Amurjana sent away to the countryside, the local strong man Erhedorji was reconfirmed as ruler of the West Banner.[8] However, before long Erhedorji retired and went away to a region beyond the mountains belonging to the Middle Banner. It seems that he was part of a widespread migration set in motion by the development of the steel industry in Baotou. The city suddenly expanded and appropriated great tracts of land for development, including pasture used by the Urads of West Banner. Large numbers of households melted away to find grazing in the north, never to return. At first no land reform or expropriations of the wealthy were carried

8. The Banner headquarters, formerly called *Yamun*, was renamed the Government House (*jasag-un ordun*) in 1949. A large three-roomed brick building at Halgai (later renamed Bayanhua), it later became a school in 1958, and the Banner administration was moved to Xi Shan Zui town, known colloquially as Qianqi, an abbreviated form of the Chinese for Urad West (Front) Banner.

out as happened elsewhere in Inner Mongolia (Bulag 2002b, 114–34). It was not until 1955 that collectives were introduced and herders were forced to "sell" most of their livestock to them, leaving only a few head for subsistence (M. *ideshi*, "for eating").

Two administrative reforms took place in 1958–1960. The three Urad Banners[9] were separated from the Ulanchab League and organized into the new Bayannuur League, and the expanding Baotou Municipality took over an area of land from the league, including Mergen. From this time onward, the monastery was incorporated just inside the municipality, thereby being cut off administratively from the lands of its previous congregation. The religious-political realm of the 3rd Mergen Gegen's "country" was now divided—the monastery no longer belongs to the West (Front) Banner. As will be shown in later chapters this has had significant political and economic consequences for the monastery.

The huge People's Communes created in 1958 took over the earlier small collectives and also drafted in much new agricultural labor from Chinese regions. The communes were divided into large brigades (*da dui*), which in turn were made up of small brigades (*xiao dui*). These brigades increasingly became the effective units of production and administration. After the Anti-Rightist Campaign of 1957,[10] the region experienced the disastrous "Great Leap Forward" from 1958. The commune became the center of every activity, all adults were marshaled for work, almost all property was collectivized, and people ate in public dining halls. By this time almost all of the lamas had left the monastery, heavily pressured by the Party to transfer from the status of "yellow" (*shira*) to "black" (*hara*, laity). The Chorji reincarnation, a young boy, was removed by his father and sent to state school. Jongrai became a herder, Sengge got a job as a cadre in the Middle Banner, Heshigdelger became a doctor, the Western Great reincarnation also took outside work—all of them married and set up households. They renamed themselves, using the lay names given in childhood, rather than lama names or titles. The anti-lama campaign intensified in 1959 with the

9. After 1949 there were only two Urad Banners, the West and the combined Middle and East Banners. Three Banners were reconstituted in 1958. They had earlier (in 1949) been renamed: the West (*Baragun*) Banner had become the Front (*Emüne*) Banner, the Middle (*Dund*) Banner had remained the Middle Banner, and the former East (*Zegün*) Banner had been redesignated the North (*Hoitu*) Banner.

10. In the "Anti-Rightist Campaign" in the Urad West Banner, 147 people were "classified" as rightists (Compilation Committee 1994, 36). These were mostly teachers, Communist Party, and collective cadres. The party leadership had encouraged criticism of its own lower officials, and then soon afterward used the information about who had been an active critic to pick off the "rightists."

Buddhist resistance in Tibet and Qinghai and the escape of the Dalai Lama. Buyan, whose family had worshipped a picture of the Dalai Lama, remembers brigade officials coming to each house to confiscate such portraits. Though most monasteries were closed by now, people kept Buddhist altars in their homes up until 1966. A brief description of Sagadag Commune will give an impression of the general situation. The commune was located to the north, behind the mountains, and it made its headquarters in the Sagadag Monastery, which had been one of the largest of the subject monasteries of Mergen. A sewing workshop was set up there, staffed by women brought in from Hebei province. The entire precinct was taken over except for the main temple. One monk was left, the Shirege Lama, a fierce angry man, who had his own room and one fruit tree. The Shirege Lama used to unlock the temple in the morning, make an offering all by himself, and then lock the door again. In 1960 the Sagadag Commune was divided into two and the headquarters was moved. The monastery became a school. By this time not a single lama was left. Nevertheless, the *oboo* rituals continued.[11]

The Great Leap Forward brought famine and millions of deaths to large parts of China; the Urad people also suffered hunger. However, because this was a herding area there was some food, and children could obtain a little meat when they went home at holidays. Southwest Inner Mongolia was thus relatively well off, and people remember seeing tractor-loads of famine refugees being brought in from the Inner Land (China). Hungry people collected *goyo* tubers and the seeds of a plant called *chülher*, ground them up, fried, and ate them. But this last food swelled inside the stomach, and many people died as a result.

The 8th Mergen Gegen managed to negotiate this difficult period up to the Cultural Revolution with craft and fortitude. Somehow he managed to persuade the authorities that he sympathized with the communists and to present his earlier modernizing activities in a socialist light. He was not forced to leave monastic life, nor did he suffer in the anti-rightist and anti-Buddhist campaigns. He became, rather, the Buddhist leader who cooperates with the authorities—and perhaps, like the kings of old, they even valued the authenticity of his religious stance, for he did not (or was allowed not to) renounce his vows, nor did he marry. The official line on the Mergen Gegen was that he "developed his nation and its culture," and in this role he was designated as a rep-

11. The Beheli Brigade of Sagadag Commune carried out sacrifices on a nearby mountain. Because the people here were part of the Urad Middle Banner, some of them also made the long trek through the Muna Mountains to sacrifice annually at the Suburgan Rock, rites which continued until the Cultural Revolution in 1966, despite official disapproval.

resentative of Buddhism "an important part of the minority's national front" (Galluu 2003, 148). In this period the Gegen moved from his monastery to Höhhot city. Sometime in the early 1950s he was made president of the Inner Mongolia Buddhist Association, the organization that acted as liaison between the government and Buddhist monks. A crucial event was Mergen Gegen's participation in one of the most popular national ventures of the political leader of Inner Mongolia, Chairman Ulaganhüü (Ulanhu, C. Yun Ze), when in 1954 a grand expedition brought back the Chinggis Khan relics to Inner Mongolia (they had been removed from Ordos earlier to prevent their capture by the Japanese). After this the Gegen was promoted even higher, being appointed in 1956 as a member of the Committee of the All-China Buddhist Association, which had an international as well as a national role. Later he was elected a permanent member of the Inner Mongolian Political Consultative Committee and representative of IM People's Congress.[12] The Mergen Gegen must have been trusted indeed, for he was allowed to visit India and Burma when Buddhists from those countries invited Chinese representatives.

Loyalty to China and Mao became the name of the game in Inner Mongolia. In 1963 the few remaining lamas in Mergen Monastery formed a work team (*lama duguilang*) under the authority of the local brigade. But that was swept away during the Cultural Revolution and no single lama was left. The Sino-Soviet confrontation in the early 1960s directed China's military attention northward to Mongolia, where large Soviet armies were stationed.[13] The Inner Mongols were increasingly seen as potentially unreliable citizens who might be tempted to join with their compatriots across the border. Using his high rank in Chinese politics, Ulaganhüü had managed to carve out and establish somewhat advantageous conditions for the Mongols in the extensive Inner Mongolia Autonomous Region (Bulag 2002b, 114–16; Sneath 2000, 99–101). But suspicions about Mongol loyalty were never far off and they surfaced with a vengeance during the Cultural Revolution and its aftermath from 1966 to 1975. Inner Mongolia was soon to be placed under military rule and Mergen Monastery occupied by the PLA.

12. It was hinted to us that Mergen Gegen was judged suitable for these high positions because the non-prestigious Mongolian chanting tradition separated him from the powerful alliances among the other monasteries. As an outsider to these factions he was more easily controlled.

13. Among the many factors leading up to the Sino-Soviet rift were Khrushchev's speech in 1956 denouncing Stalin, Soviet support for India in its border clashes with China, the withdrawal of an offered atomic bomb, and lack of aid after the disaster of the Great Leap Forward (Spence 1999, 553–59).

The Cultural Revolution

Now everything changed for the highly placed Mergen Gegen and his political protector Ulaganhüü. We do not attempt a full discussion of the Cultural Revolution here (see also Chapters 7 and 8), but confine ourselves to what witnesses of the time told us, since it is just such narratives that reveal their thinking about responsibility and consequentiality. Following an attack on religion as a "vestigial poison,"[14] Mao launched the Cultural Revolution to regain the unswerving loyalty and revolutionary fervor of earlier times and to enhance his own political position after the failure of the Great Leap Forward (Spence 1999, 565–69). Clearing the way by first purging leaders suspected of disloyalty, Mao had Ulaganhüü accused in August 1966 of plotting to split Inner Mongolia from China.[15] In the resulting turmoil, which amounted almost to a regional civil war, the Mergen Gegen was left exposed.

In September 1966 Buyan, aged fourteen, had just entered the first class of a new Mongolian language middle school in Bayanhua, the former center of the West Banner, where he shared a desk with Möngghebatu (Chorji Lama), also in his teens. On his second day the class of around fifty students together with their three teachers set out to smash monasteries. This was in line with the first aim of the campaign to destroy the "four olds": old customs, old habits, old culture, and old thinking. All schools had been turned over to revolution in August and the students organized into Red Guard detachments. In the same month around 220 previously aristocratic, wealthy, or religious people of the West Banner were arrested and their houses searched (Compilation Committee 1994, 39). Later targets were to include the Mergen Gegen in Höhhot, see below, and the former Duke Amurjana, who was dug out of rural obscurity and "struggled" (*temechehü*). In the Mergen area, however, the young participants, if Buyan's memories are anything to go by, knew little of the wider scene, nor even who was organizing the attacks.

Empty monasteries were easy targets. The students of the Mongol

14. The Panchen Lama was attacked and demoted in 1964, and the Chinese Buddhist Association (and following it the Inner Mongolian) became more or less defunct in 1965. For a number of reasons—the inability to pacify Tibet, China's deteriorating relations with Asian Buddhist countries, and the growing impatience of the regime to implement a radical re-education campaign—the structure of religious organizations set up by the government since 1953 was to collapse (Welch 1969, 128–29).

15. The central party authorities stripped him of his major positions, although he was allowed to remain nominally Chairman of Inner Mongolia for a time and was not severely punished (Bulag 2002b, 226–27).

school, joining with the larger Chinese school in Bayanhua and members of the brigade,[16] marched off for destruction arrayed in ranks according to school class. Dressed in uniform, they sang Maoist songs and chanted slogans in Chinese, to the beat of drums and clash of cymbals. As one of the youngest in the bottom class, Buyan was at the end of the procession. He remembers boys breaking off to play, being severely reprimanded, and herded back into the column. Mönghebatu marched along with everyone else. A classmate beat the drum so enthusiastically that his hands bled.

The closest monastery to Bayanhua was Urtu Goul, a few kilometers away. It took only two hours to smash the contents. "Not many texts came out,"[17] said Buyan, briefly slipping into the way of talking of those days. "But I remember one small statue. It was a naked woman, lying under a bull. Now I guess this may have been a statue of Erlig Khan. But at the time, we Mongol school-kids did not know what it was, and we were mocked by the Chinese students. They held up the statue and shouted, 'This your Cow Tatars! This how your Mongols originated!' The taunt was hurtful, as the slogan we had all just been chanting was, 'Knock down the cow-ghost snake-spirit' (C. *niugui sheshen*)."

Buyan remembers his confusion at other signals of the time. "In the morning we were not allowed to wash and we had to eat soup of decayed cabbage. Why? Because peasants in the past lived that way and we had to do the same as a memorial. I remember our teacher. She was so loyal. She drank two bowls of this horrible soup and she was crying. I laughed because I thought she was crying because it was so disgusting. But later I found that was not the reason—she was crying because she was thinking how sad life used to be, how happy we are." People were caught up in the swirling current of action. Buyan said that he felt the whole tide sweeping him along came from somewhere outside, far beyond his own sphere of action. He is someone who is "not religious" and has considerable skepticism about "superstition," and he spoke without a trace of shame about what happened next.

As the column set off from Urtu Goul to wreck the next monastery, Jirgaltu, which was some twenty kilometers away, the word went down

16. Sengge Lama was head of the East Section of the brigade at the time. He remembers that a meeting was held with the party secretary and it was decided to take members of the section to attack the Urtu Goul and Jirgaltu Monasteries the next day. He found an excuse not participate himself.

17. The chanting texts of Urtu Gol had been removed earlier as a precaution. Mergenbagatur, a local literary figure, managed to collect and save many texts in the area. He put them in the library of his institute in Höhhot, which later became the Academy of Social Sciences.

the line, "Tüngsenchecheg has an *ataga*! Let's struggle her!" Tüngsenchecheg was a formerly wealthy herdswoman whose homestead lay on the way. *Ataga* means "jealousy" or "vengeance" in Mongolian and is also the name for a sky god (Ataga Tngri). As an artifact, an *ataga* consists of a bundle of ritual scarves into which a deceased relative breathed his or her last breath and which are knotted to a stick of magic red tamarisk wood. Akin to the shamanic vessels for spirits called *onggud*,[18] an *ataga* was first made to ward off enemies, but once introduced in a family it had to be worshipped and given offerings over the generations for it not to turn on its hosts. It is a dangerous tabooed thing (*cheger baina*), Buyan told us, but he refrained from any speculation about the intentions with which Tüngsenchecheg might have employed it.[19]

It is must have been a kinsman who provided the information about Tüngsenchecheg, as people with an *ataga* keep them hidden even from neighbors and no Chinese could have known about her secret. The Red Guards ordered the woman to give up her *ataga*, but she refused to say where it was. They "struggled" her: made her bow down, undress, and beat her back with nettles. They hung a heavy weight by a thin wire from her neck, and made her hold her arms behind her back, which was extremely painful. Shouted at and humiliated for a whole day, she refused to give in. At night she was taken stumbling to the brigade headquarters. Buyan guessed she must have been tortured during the night, for the next morning the *ataga* was found and burned. The procession set off for Jirgaltu monastery, with Tüngsenchecheg at its head, her body bowed, her arms held out behind her, the weight hanging from her neck. The Red Guards were angry with her for delaying their rampage. People threw things and hit her and shouted in Chinese, "Put your head down and recognize your sin honestly!"

The delay to "struggle" Tüngsenchecheg was fortunate for Jirgaltu Monastery, allowing the remaining lamas to hide the battle standard and possibly some sacred books (which have never been found). The Red Guards shouted at the lamas to bring out the statues and paintings. Two lamas timidly emerged. They were ordered take off their lama clothes, given axes, and forced to smash the statues themselves, to the laughter of the throng. The clay Buddhas were easy to break. One large statue about shoulder height could not be broken, however. The two

18. See Even 1988–1989, 114–19; Pedersen 2007, 155–56. Sengge Lama recalled only two shamans in Urad in the 1950s. They were not good at chanting, but families with *ataga* would invite them when offerings were made to the *ataga*.

19. He said only that an *ataga* was held to be so powerful that if a bird flew over the house where it was kept, the bird would drop dead.

lamas hit it repeatedly. Finally, it split in two and a human corpse was revealed. With a scream, the two lamas dropped their axes and ran off. "I saw it with my own eyes," said Buyan. "There was a skull and rib bones, not much flesh. This was like the preserved corpse of the Panchen Lama."[20] Dried tea and juniper scattered out from the statue casing. An older Chinese student took an axe and smashed the ribs, to the shouting of the crowd. Later, Buyan inquired who this mummified saint could have been, but Chorji denied all memory of the horrifying incident. Now two tractors arrived, delivering good hot food for the guards—meat broth and steamed bread. Buyan gave an embarrassed grin at this memory of such privileges in a world of hunger. After a rest, the youths ransacked the temples for holy books. "The books were in Mongolian," said Buyan, "so we could read them." A huge bonfire was made, in which the closely packed pages burned with difficulty. Many were wrapped with cloth tied with a string with a coin at its end. Some Guards began to take the coins, but others—Mongols—shouted, "Do not take the coins!" This was not from revolutionary honesty but out of fear, the precautionary sense that misfortune would befall those who took such coins. Many books were inside wooden covers. The texts were burned but the covers were saved—they were loaded on the tractors and taken away for firewood. After this successful day the Red Guards marched back, singing Mao's song, "Sunset in the West."

By this time Mergen Monastery, now located in the Baotou district, must also have been ransacked, as Buyan remembers people from Baotou saying, "We have finished our monasteries." Buyan's Red Guards hastened the next day to smash the Suburgan Monastery, where Queen Qi had met her death twenty years earlier. "We ruined it," said Buyan. "And then we thought, where next? Where are other monasteries?" He laughed. "There were no more."

Such episodes are narrated in several different ways. Some broad explanations insulate actors from shame or the need to probe individuals' actions: the idea that everything was fated by heaven, or that the campaign was instigated and led by external others. Part of the notion of the *tngri-yin chag* was that it brought atheists sweeping into power over the land and it was said that such nonbelievers were immune not

20. The Panchen Lamas are famous in Inner Mongolia for having been mummified after death and then worshipped (see Kozlov 1923, 32, for a description of Mongolian embalmment techniques). The 3rd Mergen Gegen's corpse had been similarly enshrined, but was destroyed by the Guomindang before the Second World War. The mummified body of the 6th Neichi Toin was kept in the Güng Monastery.

only to dread but also to actual supernatural punishment: "Those with no apprehension [of supernatural misfortune] will not be affected" (*sejig ügei bol, ajig ügei*). Yet the people who said this could still hold that damaging sacred artifacts, such as the mummified statue, the *ataga*, or the coins attached to holy sutras, would bring disaster in some indefinite future. Intention is almost absent from such narratives; no one seemed interested in why Tüngsenchecheg had an *ataga*, nor even in the reasons for smashing the Buddhas. Yet it is precisely such objects that are mentioned when people talk about the Cultural Revolution, even more than attacks on people, and it seemed to us that this was because these substitute objects distilled the essence of occult powers that in living people were dispersed and fluctuating; it was from the smashed artifacts that the long-term consequences, the more dreadful retribution, could be expected. Still, what most morally enraged those who talked to us was acts that would endanger the entire local community, as will be seen in the following episode.

The Fate of Tulga, a Red Guard

The destroyer of the Banner *oboo* was a local man, Tulga, who was a teacher. In the words of Sengge Lama, "At that time I was a 'power holder' (*dang quan pai*—cadres who were attacked during the Cultural Revolution). Tulga was the man from our district who led the Red Guards and made the rebellion (*zaofan*) to the *oboo*. He came and asked me to go and pull it down. I made an excuse—I said I felt ill." Traditionally, Sengge continued, a brown stallion had always been offered and consecrated to the *oboo* by saying prayers, tying five-colored ribbons (*seter*) round its neck, and then setting it free from human use.[21] So important was this *seter* horse that when it was decided much later (1985) to rebuild the *oboo*, people said that it could be re-sanctified/enlivened because a local man, Blind Manghan, still preserved the remains of

21. The consecrated animal, known as *seter* (T. *tshe thar*), is a "sacrificed" or liberated domestic animal (domesticated implying that it is a part of one's extended person) dedicated to a deity. In Urad the idea is that this animal will provide a mount to the deity, different species/colors being offered to different gods. The animal should be set free and not be killed, ridden, or used in any way, and this offering of a vital part of one's household is held to bind the god to bring prosperity and fertility back to the family. The rite is popular in Urad and is one of the elements that can be fitted into several longer rituals. Thus, the *oboo* ceremony could include both blood sacrifice (killed animals) and offering of consecrated (live) animals. *Seterlehü* was one of Sengge Lama's most frequent services for laity as a household offering.

the last consecrated stallion. Sengge, who by then had become a lama again, took this horse's skull and put it on the new *oboo*.[22] By this time it seemed that Tulga regretted his earlier actions. In Sengge's words,

> Tulga, who destroyed the *oboo*, had his own thoughts: "I have a black stallion, I want to make it a new *seter* horse for the *oboo*." It was such a big festival, you see. The Middle, West and North Banners were all invited. Agarotai Sumu and the four herding Sumus were all there. So our man [Tulga] made a great show of bringing his black stallion, tied the *seter*, and let the horse go free. It ran away to the north, in the direction of U-Bulag—although it was a riding horse it was frightened by crowds of people. Now normally a consecrated horse is caught each time a sacrifice is made to the *oboo*, every three years, and the *seter* is renewed. But that very winter our man went to the mountains, found his black horse, and sold it! Yes, after he had made his name that is what he did secretly. But people found out. They beat him severely, his brain was damaged, and he was put in the hospital in Baotou. He died after three months.
>
> I was requested, along with the Western Great Lama, to conduct the funeral. Usually, a funeral is done three or four days after death, but his family kept him for only one day. Why? Something was leaking out from the corpse. There was such a terrible smell that the people carrying the body were sick and vomited. We knew nothing like that, even if a corpse is kept for four or five days in summer. And then on his grave. . . . in our region the burial place is heaped up with stones . . . on top of the stones . . . suddenly there were thirteen snakes moving there. A herder saw them. What is the reason? The *oboo* has thirteen cairns, you destroyed the *oboo*, and after you died, now there are thirteen snakes. Ha, ha, ha. This has become something people talk about.

This narrative is an example of the delayed occult retribution for wrongdoing (*burugu yabudal*) so frequently mentioned by Urad people. Sengge's tone showed that adult individuals especially prominent in the destruction were judged culpable if they should have known better (Tulga was a teacher) and they could be expected to repent later. But after twenty years during which no one openly blamed him, Tulga caused moral outrage in the community by selling the horse. This was evidence of his personal greed and bad faith, but more importantly this act flouted the social-cosmological order of relations, in which the *seter* horse offering would appease the land spirits and obtain prosperity for

22. The ancestral hero's weapons that had previously been buried under the *oboo* to give it power were stolen during the Cultural Revolution. Sengge replaced them with sacred Buddhist items (written mantras, seeds, precious stones, etc.). He ordered that these be put inside a Chinese clay horse in memory of Manghan's *seter* horse.

the entire community. The "consequential" thinking at the end of the story is magical and a-chronological: the unnatural nauseous disintegration of Tulga's corpse conflates the god's anger at the loss of its horse with the "revenge" of the thirteen cairns of the *oboo* destroyed twenty years earlier, signaled by the appearance of thirteen writhing snakes.[23]

Buyan told us of an analogous case of moral offense: one of his relatives had been an enthusiastic Red Guard and destroyed a nearby *oboo* for which the mother's brother family (*nagachu*) were the patrons. The demolition was of course highly approved in public, but the family was worried and the women went out secretly at night to rebuild the cairn. They said, "We have to do this, because otherwise misfortune will befall you for touching the *nagachu's* thing." The idea here was that the *nagachu* people are senior to us by definition and it is morally wrong and dangerous to insult them. The offense that concerned the family was not having taken part in the Cultural Revolution, but the occult effect of attacking ("touching") this pillar of the social order.

Let us now mention the fate of Tulga's spirit after death, as this is relevant to the afterlife of the Mergen Gegen. Though he was reckoned to have been a bad person, Tulga's spirit is not thought to have become a ghost-demon (*chitgür* or *bug*). These are the vengeful spirits of people who died inexplicably at an early age, or were unjustly executed, or suicides, and in general people who cannot find rebirth in any form, and therefore restlessly haunt this earth. Ghost-demons are assuaged by ritually transferring the spirit to a realm from which they can be reborn.[24] In Tulga's case two especially powerful lamas were employed to carry out the "leading of the soul" at his funeral—so it was reckoned that his spirit had been safely guided away to an appropriate destination, suitable for a sinful person.

Relations with master spirits in nature are mostly initiated by hu-

23. Normally, snakes are regarded as a good sign, but Sengge said that these snakes represented anger and showed the character of Tulga's heavy sins. In such contexts karma is rather infrequently mentioned by Urad people, perhaps because it is so taken for granted. When we pressed them people said that Tulga would certainly have had karma in mind when he decided to compensate for his sin in destroying the *oboo* by offering it his horse. Although the long-term working out of karmic consequences over many lifetimes is less often referred to than the idea of immediate retribution, Sengge said that the fruit of Tulga's sins would certainly appear in his later (but presently unknown) rebirths.

24. There is a clear theory about what should happen to ancestors, i.e., those whose souls experienced a normal transformation after death. According to their karma, their "souls" take rebirth in one of the six realms of the cycle of transmigrations (*sansar*). Either they enter one of the three good fates: Gods (*tngri*), Demi-Gods (*asuri*), Humans (*hün*), or the three bad fates: Animals (*amitan*), Hungry Ghosts (*birid*), and Hell Beings (*tamu*). From any of these realms they will sooner or later be reborn in another one. Note, however, that a ghost-demon roams in an "in between" state (*jabharahu*) and is not the same as a Hungry Ghost.

mans, through appeal or invitation (*jalahu*), but with ghosts it is the other way around—people try to avoid them and are only made aware of a presence when something uncanny intrudes on their sensations. The experience invariably presages misfortune. The Mergen laity therefore bury the dead a long way away, in unmarked mounds at a place called Olan Dobung, down near the Yellow River, or in some distant cranny in the mountains.[25] For fear of possible haunting spirits they stay well away from graves, and only certain categories of relatives visit once a year to make an offering to ancestors on a day in the spring (*hangshi*). We shall return to the ghost theme but now we examine a different, honored form taken by Mergen Gegen's presence after he died.

The Death of Mergen Gegen

Up to 1967–1968 the Cultural Revolution in Inner Mongolia had been less harsh than in other parts of China and relatively few people lost their lives. Now there began a campaign to root out the followers and "pernicious influence" of Ulaganhüü. The attacks began to have an ethnic character, though this was never admitted. Almost all Mongolian army commanders were dismissed, and urban Red Guards—dominated by Chinese—fanned out to the herding areas of the countryside to uncover "traitors." People were abused and beaten, sometimes to death. Sengge Lama, who had become a local official, was attacked as a "power holder" (Chapter 7). It was around this time that Mönghebatu, the Chorji Lama, was brutally "struggled" by his own classmates (Chapter 8).

Worse was to come. The harsh military regime in Inner Mongolia was responsible for starting a campaign that took the lives of tens of thousands of Mongols and cut across the fragile interethnic relations that were the foundation of the Autonomous Region. Prominent Mongolians, from party leaders to army commanders and intellectuals, were attacked, tortured, imprisoned, and killed. Many people committed suicide (Sneath 2000, 111). The ostensible reason was the existence of a secret traitorous party, the New Inner Mongolian People's Revolutionary Party (MPRP, called in short *Nei Ren Dang*). It was held to be a

25. People who die from accidents, suicides, and other abnormal deaths are cremated rather than buried, as are lamas. The Mongols have had a variety of burial customs including exposure of the corpse. We saw the corpse of a young man exposed on open land to the west of Mergen, but no one would tell us why he had not been buried.

vast ring of anti-China treasonous activity, linked to the enemy Soviet Union and aspiring to Mongol secession and joining up with the Mongolian People's Republic. In vain did the accused insist that the MPRP had dissolved in 1947 and had not been revived. Now, "confessions" were extracted under torture and victims were forced to implicate others in membership of a party that almost certainly did not exist. According to official Communist Party estimates after the end of the campaign in 1979, some 346,000 people of minority nationality (most of whom were Mongolians) were "uprooted" as members of the *Nei Ren Dang*, 16,222 people were killed, 87,188 were crippled, and over a million were punished one way or another (including the party secretary of the region around Mergen).[26]

The smallest display of Mongolian culture became impossible, from wearing Mongolian clothes to singing folksongs. The Mergen Gegen, whose official position had rested on his being a representative of Mongolian culture, was doomed. He was harshly struggled in Höhhot, a public humiliation he bore with aloof dignity. He fell ill, however, and was taken, a sick and silent old man, to be cared for in humble circumstances by his relatives. He died in 1972, "at least ten years before his time," as Mongols told us.

A Lord in the Kingdom of Shambhala

We asked some older lamas what Mergen Gegen was like as a person, and Heshigbayar replied quick as a flash, "He was *dogshin*!" (fierce). The way the conversation continued indicates the train of associations in their minds. Heshigbayar next said that Mergen had been extraordinarily brave when he was struggled—he walked with eyes abstracted, as though he didn't notice the insults being thrown at him, and later he said, "It was just a change of state government, why should I be afraid?" At this, other lamas joined in a tumult of speech and Heshigbayar started chanting in Mongolian, ". . . *dogshin hürdün han* . . . (. . . Fierce Wheel-Turning King . . .)." The other lamas joined in. Evidently, all of them knew by heart this prayer of the Panchen Lama,

26. Bürenbayar was an orphan with only six years primary education, but he rose fast in party ranks and therefore was very loyal. He was party secretary for most of the period from 1960 to 1991, but during the Cultural Revolution he was "broken down" and in the anti–*Nei Ren Dang* campaign he was accused and demoted to run a primary school from 1974 to 1979.

the poem of the King of Shambhala. Another lama then said, "Mergen Gegen, he will sit as a Lord (*noyan*) in Shambhala." [27]

"Yes," confirmed Dalantai. "I tell you there are three Holy Ones (*bogda*) of the universe: the Northern Holy One,[28] the Dalai Lama, and the Panchen Holy One. The Northern Holy One and the Dalai Lama will sit as Khans of this world. But the Panchen Holy One will sit as the Fierce Wheel-Turning King of Shambhala and Mergen Gegen will sit with him as a ruling Lord."

This requires some explanation. The Fierce Wheel-Turning Khan is the name for the king of the notional land of Shambhala, destroyer of the enemies of Buddhism. The present Khan of Shambhala is perhaps the 22nd king, the lamas said. During the reign of the 25th king a war will start against the infidels, those with "wrong wills," usually held to be *Lalu*, Muslims. The *Lalu* will prevail for the first six years of war and for the next six years the Buddhists will be victorious, led by a future Panchen Lama who will rule for a hundred years. What is important for people now is that anyone who takes the Kalachakra initiation from the current Panchen Lama (who is "the same" as a future Panchen Lama) will, in a later rebirth, be enlisted as a soldier when the Shambhala war starts. Any sentient being— including women or animals or even frogs—anyone who fights in the righteous war will gain spiritual liberation. So this is why people want to be a soldier in that war.[29]

Such statements recall the disposition towards future enlightenment mentioned in the Introduction in connection with the coming Buddha, Maidar. But whereas Maidar will reign in a far distant future epoch, the Shambhala war will occur in this present epoch of decline—hence the war against infidels, the militancy, and the urgency. The idea of enlisting in a spiritual army, binding people together as faithful Buddhists, had previously swept through northern China in the 1930s. Ethnicity, nationality, class, even humanity, would be irrel-

27. People say there are five purified lands (*arilugsan orun*) in this human world, and Shambhala is one of them, lying to the north. It exists in reality now, but only extraordinarily empowered lamas can visit it. The last Gegen of Boro Hoshuu Monastery in Jirim is said to have visited Shambhala often. "The watermelons of Shambhala are so sweet!" he used to tell awed followers. The geographical route to Shambhala is described in detail in several widely read Mongolian texts. The purified lands of *this* world are different from "pure land" of Chinese Buddhism, which is equivalent to the Mongol "heaven" called *devajan* (T. *bde ba can*, S. *Sukhāvatī*).

28. The Ard Bogd (Northern Holy One) is the Jebtsundamba Hutugtu of Halha Mongolia.

29. One young man from eastern Inner Mongolia told us of how his grandmother walked for many days, enduring much hardship to take part in such a Kalachakra initiation in a different Banner, to bow to the Panchen Lama, and enlist. The Ganjurwa Gegen describes his own enthusiastic participation in such a ritual, held by the 9th Panchen Lama in 1930 (Hyer and Jagchid 1983, 132).

evant. The great lamas would appear not as monks but as the rulers of a land that is wholly Buddhist. It is significant that the messianic idea of Shambhala inspired people as far away as Halha and Buryatia at this time (Humphrey 1986, 418), and that the Panchen Lama conducted a Kalachakra ritual in Beiping (Beijing) in 1931 attended by thousands of Chinese Buddhists with the aim of "providing protection for the country and eliminating disasters" (Tuttle 2005, 169–71). Gray Tuttle argues that implicit in the practice of Kalachakra initiation was a recognition of Buddhism as a "world religion"—this itself being a modern concept (ibid, 68–103). It is not clear that the 8th Mergen Gegen upheld such an idea—like most other Mongol lamas he was noticeably chilly toward Japanese and Chinese Buddhists—but he certainly knew about it.

The old lamas' instant recall of Shambhala, immediately after their praise of Mergen Gegen for withstanding persecution in the Cultural Revolution, indicates that they saw it not as some never–never land but part of this contemporary world of confrontation. For them, the Maoists had replaced the *Lalu* infidels.[30] As for the 8th Mergen Gegen, his personal attitude to Shambhala is unknown, but we do know that he saw his own life had historical import. His nephew, Sechingge, told us that the Gegen had been deeply impressed when a Japanese advisor told him, "Take control of your monastery. It is not just a religious matter but also important for history." Mergen had replied, "This is our history. We cannot separate from this." The lamas' conviction that he is to rule in Shambhala indicates one mode in which he is held to continue to exist, a vision that recognizes his public career, his life in government, and his fortitude as a Buddhist leader.

Sechingge and the Relics of the 8th Mergen Gegen

However, the 8th Mergen Gegen had other modes of existence after death, notably his presence in his holy remains and relics, which were appropriated by his family. He had no children, but in a practice known elsewhere in the Buddhist monastic world, his brother's son Sechingge took on the role of his closest descendant. The whole family were aristocrats and belonged to the Haranuud clan. They were very rich and in the 1930s, when the monastery was sacked and deserted, they had paid

30. Compare with Makley's discussion of "speaking bitterness" at Labrang Monastery, where Tibetans inverted the state-promoted image of pre-socialist exploitative class relations, maintaining that state cadres were the oppressors and that the "exploiters" (the aristocracy, wealthy, and high lamas) were in fact the oppressed (2005, 69).

for a temporary temple to be built in a nearby valley. It was Sechingge's wife, Nabchingerel, (henceforth Nabchin) who cared for Mergen Gegen in his last months, and it was Sechingge's son, Mönghebatu, who was revealed in early childhood to be the 6th Chorji reincarnation, the present master of the monastery. Thus was constituted a thicket of lay-lama relations, similar to the one we described earlier for the nineteenth century, which will appear again in Chapter 9.

Sechingge, who became a key figure in the history of Mergen Monastery, was an entrepreneurial character. He owned some livestock, but in his youth in the 1940s he also worked as manager of the grain store in nearby Qianqi and taught mathematics in Mergen Gegen's school in the monastery. After "Liberation," Sechingge became a cadre, but he resigned and went back to herding in the mountains when "the red dust became too much," i.e., he could no longer stomach the politicking. During the Cultural Revolution his civil status was reclassified as a "herd owner" (i.e., an enemy of the state) because he belonged to the family of Mergen Gegen, although, as he indignantly told us, he had fewer than thirty head of livestock and only one donkey. "A herd owner should have herds, no?" Actually, this indignation was less than transparent, as thirty head was already a lot, and he had been doing thriving underground business against the law of the time. Sechingge recounted how he had been "struggled" and how, as soon as it was possible, around 1973 or 1974 he had instituted a lawsuit to have his name cleared. Because of his local contacts he was quickly successful, whereas most people in the "enemy" category were rehabilitated only in 1979. Sechingge then resumed his business activities.

We now retell Sechingge's story of how the sanctified remains (*sharil*) of the 8th Mergen Gegen were pivotal in reviving Buddhism. Not only did the *sharil* of such a holy lama require veneration, but, as it was now clear that the government would not permit a new reincarnation, the relics became the only prolongation of the existence of the Mergen Gegens on this earth. From the earliest times in Buddhism, relics have been held to make the (absent) sacred person present as an object of worship. Among the many scholarly interpretations of the veneration of relics (as indexical icons, as sedimentations of charisma, as memory sites, as "blazing absences," as "alive" and ontologically equivalent to the Buddha), we favor the approach taken by John Strong, who argues that relics should be seen not only as functional equivalents to the departed master but as expressions and extensions of the Buddha's biographical process. "We should remember," he writes, "that in Buddhism it is biography that makes a Buddha and not the Buddha who makes his biography" (Strong 2004, 6). Mergen Gegen's biography in this sense opened in several directions, two of them by means of the extension provided by his relics.

Sechingge attributed to himself the entire step-by-step strategy of reopening the monastery at a time when the open practice of religion was still dangerous. His account has been challenged by other Mergen people, who tried to play down his role and emphasize their own, but the contentiousness of this history, we think, only shows its importance: the heroic glow surrounding his actions, and those of the lamas, is what they really felt. They were perhaps unaware that in other parts of China several monasteries were being reopened at the same period.[31] We provide this detailed account to show the range of edgy relations brought into play by the existence of the remains, spanning family negotiations, lamas' quarrels, and the outwitting of government officials.

The 8th Mergen Gegen was cremated and his ashes were taken to an official ossuary in Höhhot, where the remains of dignitaries are kept. But holy remains should not lie alongside unclean lay ashes, and by the mid-1970s the time had come to extract them. Permission had to be obtained every step of the way—at that time it was impossible even to travel from Mergen to Höhhot without an official permit. On the grounds that "families have to respect the graves of their ancestors" (somewhat spurious for Mongols, but convincing for Chinese officials), consent was obtained to bury the ashes near Sechingge's house. The Western Great Reincarnation was asked to conduct a low-key funeral, and the remains were buried in an open valley according to Mergen Gegen's will: "Put me in a gap of the mountains."[32] Several years later, when the religious policy was changed in 1982 (see note 31), Sechingge

31. The Chinese Buddhist Association had begun to revive as early as 1972 and certain metropolitan monasteries, such as Yonghegong in Beijing, were "open," although no one dared to worship there (Strong and Strong 1973, 321). In 1982 the Central Committee of the Chinese Communist Party issued "Document No. 19," *The Basic Viewpoint and Policy on the Religious Question during Our Country's Socialist Period,* which restored qualified religious freedom in socialist society. Its premise, however, was that religions would die out in the long run and it still asserted the party's right to maintain ultimate control of religious affairs (Slobodnik 2004, 10). Even before this change in policy, certain monasteries had begun to revive religious services from 1979, after lamas were released from prisons and labor camps and rehabilitated. Labrang Monastery, in Gansu, was officially reopened in 1980 (ibid).

32. Nabchin told us that the family had wanted to bury the Mergen Gegen at the gravesite of their ancestors, but neighbors did not agree. "If Mergen Gegen comes," they said, "we would have to stand up." (They would have to act in a visibly worshipful, and therefore dangerous, way.) So the family obeyed Mergen's will and interred his ashes in the hills.

formed the long-term goal of bringing the ashes into the monastery. They would be placed in the Temple of Relics where all the previous Mergen Gegens' remains had been preserved and there they could be the focus for worship. "What is a monastery without an object of worship?" Sechingge said. At the time, of course, Mergen was empty of any such object, being occupied by the army, and the relics of previous Gegens had been destroyed.

The first step was to "invite the *sharil*," meaning to transform the ashes into a sacred object for worship. A preparatory rite was initiated by Boroheshig and Sengge, both former lamas but now cadres of politically dubious status, as they were still "wearing hats" (i.e., marked as enemies of the revolution). They came to Sechingge's house and took away a photograph of the Mergen Gegen, and performed the Lamp Service to it.[33] For the main rite the scattered former lamas had to be gathered and chanting texts and musical instruments found. Sechingge said, "I wanted to gather lamas from autumn 1982, but the political bosses were seriously concerned I was spreading superstition. We did not know what was permitted and what forbidden. Rumors were spreading, and because of this the first lamas I invited were afraid and some did not come."[34] Sechingge and around ten lamas traveled to Badgar Monastery, the only place where musical instruments survived. But many of the lamas had been lay people for thirty years and they had forgotten how to play them. Sechingge gave them two days to practice and insisted they make a recording on the spot, so that the sacred Mongolian liturgy would be saved for posterity, whatever happened next. The lamas chanted some prayers they knew by heart and read others from texts borrowed from Galluu, and some ten cassettes were recorded. These recordings had a great influence, Sechingge said, as they spread among the Urad people. Sechingge went off for business in the south (*nanfang*, i.e., to China) and when he returned the formerly frightened lamas came to him and said, "We have decided to invite the *sharil* of Mergen Gegen." Now they were ready for this transformative act. Permission to turn the ashes into a shrine had to be obtained first.

Sechingge's account gave details of the lamas who dared to go with

33. This is held on the twenty-fifth of the tenth lunar month to celebrate the birthday of Tsongkhapa, though other deities and lamas may also be worshipped at the same time. A thousand lamps should be lit.

34. Sechingge obtained some prayer texts from Galluu—about whom he remarked sarcastically, "His real name is Goose (*galagu*, pronounced *galuu*), but now he calls himself Fire (*gal*) Dragon (*luu*)." Galluu did not join the group that went in the first month of 1983 to Badgar Monastery, having lost his nerve when the Banner officials issued a reprimand. He begged Sechingge to keep quiet about his reason for staying behind, in case other lamas also took fright.

him to Höhhot to obtain permission, the failure of a previous attempt by the reincarnation of Suburgan monastery, the resulting quarrel when the reincarnation wanted to give up, the exact amounts of money contributed by each person for the travel, hotel, and food costs of the expedition, and Sechingge's own generosity in providing funds. "You are dangerous people to me," he said to the Suburgan Lama, "but I am a businessman and I have some money, let's share it now." They went first to Ulagan Gegen, who had succeeded the 8th Mergen as president of the Inner Mongolian Buddhist Association, becoming effective leader of the religion in the region (see Introduction). Ulagan Gegen agreed that to enshrine Mergen Gegen was a duty. The Bureau of the United Front and the Committee of National and Religious Affairs also agreed, perhaps thinking that ancestor worship was all that was at issue. In triumph, the group returned to Urad and asked a prominent Ordos reincarnation to move the ashes from the burial place in the hills.

With the rite of invitation, in Sechingge's words, the ashes changed from being a human relic to a god (*burhan*).[35] Prayers were chanted to animate (*rabnailahu*) the ashes, which were placed in a special room in Sechingge's house. Now it was incumbent on the lamas to worship this god. A shrine was set up of any materials available; no brass or copper offering cups had survived, so handmade cups of hardened clay were used instead. Five lamas organized a rotation for constant worship and Sechingge paid their expenses.

Soon, however, the lamas began to offer excuses and after a few months only two or three were left. Matters came to a crux with the Lamp Service due to take place in the 10th month. The lamas of the area split into two camps. The Western Great Reincarnation headed a group that insisted on holding the service at Suburgan Monastery, while Sengge and others attended the shrine in Sechingge's house. This rift reflected the different monastic origins of the lamas—the Western Great had come to Mergen from Shira Juu, in Ordos, while Sengge was from Jirgaltu Monastery—and perhaps some preferred to worship in a temple rather than a private house. After this, fewer and fewer people came to worship at Mergen Gegen's *sharil*.

The shrine caused Sechingge a domestic problem too, which made him determined to change the situation. It was high time for his son to be married but neighbors were saying, "Oh, that family keeps a dead

35. *Hümün-ü sharil baigsan-eche-ban burhan bolugad hubirachihaba*. The rite was held on the twenty-first of the first month of 1984 in the presence of two reincarnations and over ten other lamas. Ulagan Gegen did not attend, nor did the Western Great Reincarnation.

person in the house—that is unpleasant (*eb ügei*)—we cannot give our daughter to marry into that family." Evidently the new status of the ashes as a god was not sufficiently secure to overcome the taboo against keeping the remains of the dead anywhere near a home of living people.

Sechingge now organized another expedition to Höhhot to obtain permission to move the *sharil* of his uncle Mergen Gegen into the monastery. This demanded courage, as the local Qianqi authorities had been accusing him of "interrupting production by encouraging superstition," a serious matter. He went again to the Committee of National and Religious Affairs, where the chairman was a Hotung Muslim, a strict man by the name of Ma. He refused point blank. Not to be deterred, Sechingge now wielded a crafty mixture of arguments: "You are a Muslim! If you don't care, why did you agree earlier to let us move the ashes from the burial ground?" [i.e., to be consistent you must agree to the second move]. "Ulagan Gegen has agreed to attend the ceremony of placing the ashes in the monastery" [i.e., a senior official has given approval]. "Superstitious people are preventing my son's marriage because we have the burden of these ashes in my house" [i.e., you should regularize the situation—religious things should be kept in a place of religion]. Ma was overwhelmed. Addressing Sechingge politely as "elder," he asked him to wait while he consulted the United Front Committee. For the next few days Ma evaded meeting Sechingge, but at length he came back with an answer. The *sharil* could either be put in Shiregetü Juu Monastery in Höhhot—clearly unacceptable to the Urads—or it could be placed in a public building near Mergen, the monastery itself being still occupied by the army. Sechingge was delighted, but he would not accept only an oral approval. Ma had to put the decision in writing, because the district authorities, the Baotou Municipality, had been averse to any revival of worship in or around Mergen. Ma then wrote the letter. "I did it. I got an official order—by squeezing him!" said Sechingge. Ma also reluctantly paid the cost of the lamas' trip. Sechingge commented, "At that time money was scarce. But I wanted to get money not just for the expenses but for right custom (*yos*), to show that there were two sides and they had come to agreement."

The Baotou officials obeyed the order from the capital, allocated a brigade house in West Plateau village for the shrine, and accompanied the ashes by car when they were ceremonially moved out of Sechingge's house. Not only this, but the officials, seemingly swayed by a certain religious enthusiasm, agreed to pay the rent of the new shrine house—which thus gave them an incentive to plan the removal of the *sharil* to the monastery as soon as possible. They also agreed to have the family-books and living allowance of ten lamas registered on the municipal account, and furthermore to order the making of ten sets of lama clothes.[36] For around a year the *sharil* was worshipped in the brigade house. But the officials' euphoric decision was not carried out: the family-books were not transferred and the clothes not made. "There was no one to follow-up the decision," said Sechingge. "The Mergen lamas are always in discord; they did not press the administration." In particular, the Western Great Lama, the only Mergen reincarnation at the time, was continuing to hold services at Shira Juu, in Ordos, thus dividing the monks.

What next happened is described by almost everyone around Mergen as a miracle. First one of the former lamas had a dream that the gods, banished during the "time of heavenly fate," were streaming back into the monastery from the north. On the eleventh day of the eleventh month in 1984 there was a tremendous storm with a gusting wind. The solid front wall erected by the army simply blew down. This had to be a sign from heaven—the wall fell as though it had been pushed. Holding the precious *sharil* in front of him, Boroheshig Lama rushed through the gap leading a group of lamas, scrambling over the stones. The soldiers could only stand and watch, their duty was to guard the gate. The lamas installed the *sharil* in the Temple of Relics and refused to leave the monastery. They said to the soldiers, "This is a famous Gegen in the world. He is also a high official famous in our country. If you don't agree to put the *sharil* in the monastery, if you want to throw it away—you do it! If you want to beat him—you do it! We will not." The commanding officer was a Mongol and he ordered his soldiers to give way. Subsequently, the army agreed a division of the space: they built a new wall across the middle of the campus, dividing the military area to the front from the religious buildings to the rear. Now that the monastery had a sacred object to worship, religion could start again. From that time to the present, the 8th Mergen Gegen's ashes have been worshipped annually on the day of his death.

However, the heroic success of the retaking of the monastery is one thing. The Gegen's ashes are another. During our many visits to Mer-

36. Each person was, and still is, registered by their "family-book" with the district or city of their birthplace. As a person moves from home to school to work, the family-book moves with him or her. In this case the Mergen ex-lamas lived and worked in the Qianqi district, but because the monastery now administratively belonged to Baotou municipality, officially recognized lamas would have to change their registration from Qianqi to Baotou. With the new religious policy of 1982 registered lamas acquired a right to a small stipend from the state.

gen, the Temple of Relics was always locked. When we did penetrate inside, we found the temple dank and empty, apart from the altar with a small brass stupa containing the *sharil*. We were told that the remains of great lamas should not be installed in the main temple for services—they have to be paid due respect, but Mongols still prefer to keep them at arm's length. Evidently, something obscurely ominous/polluted still clings even to the most holy of such relics.[37]

In other ways, too, the status of the Gegen was not entirely resolved. For one thing, his official civil rehabilitation was never fully confirmed. More germane to our present theme, however, is the equivocal status of another set of relics of the 8th Mergen Gegen.

Nabchingerel's Relics

When the Gegen died, Sechingge's wife, Nabchin, was caring for him, and she was outraged that local officials took away the body for cremation and made a list of all Uncle Lama's domestic items for confiscation. Nabchin stayed according to custom in the Gegen's house for forty-nine days after the death, this being the time during which the soul transmigrates and is reborn. She was offended that the officials told her she could borrow the furniture, pots, and so forth for this period. A furious quarrel now erupted. "I won't 'borrow'—I'll stay here," she said. The officials now said they would take the house too. "So if you want the house, give us the ashes of Uncle Lama!" Nabchin responded. In the end, the officials agreed, "OK, you take the ashes, we'll take the house." In this way Nabchin appropriated to herself some of the glory of the recuperation of the ashes. The officials divided up Mergen's things among themselves. "I didn't want to give them anything, wretches, they even wanted to take his piss-pot! I didn't give it. I kept back several other things too."

While Nabchin was caring for Mergen during his last illness, one of his teeth had fallen out and was lost. People searched for it, as is the normal custom among Mongols, for it is held most important that a body should be buried whole with all parts intact. If some part is missing the soul will search for it and this will delay the soul's transmigration and rebirth. But the tooth was not found until after the cremation.

37. Many monasteries in Inner Mongolia site the Temple of Relics some distance from other buildings. The relics of three reincarnations of Jirgaltu Monastery were placed in pagodas (*suburgan*) in the open steppe, distant from any habitation.

Normally, it should have been put with the ashes, but Nabchin asked a senior Mergen Lama, Oruwa, for permission to keep the tooth separately and worship it. Oruwa agreed and gave her a document with a mantra in Tibetan. With this legitimization, the Gegen's remains were divided into two, on the one hand the ashes, whose history we have recounted, and on the other the three precious items retained by Nabchin that were to form a second *sharil*: the tooth, the Gegen's seal,[38] and a medal he was awarded as a high Congress delegate.

In point of fact Nabchin kept various mementoes of Mergen, including his spectacle case and his watch. But the three jewels (*gurban erdeni*) of the *sharil* were special. The tooth was placed in the mouth of a stone lion, which formed the handle of the seal, and these with the medal were put into a small brass stupa. Packed with juniper powder, tea, grains, and precious stones, the stupa was then closed at the bottom. It is now kept in a cupboard shrine (*günggarba*) for worshipping in Nabchin's house in Qianqi, together with a photograph of Mergen Gegen, oil lamps, prayer beads, a prayer text, images of deities, incense, sweets, and matches. Nabchin's son told us that the "three jewels" had been enlivened for worship by means of the recordings made at Badgar. Now, he said, these items are gods, the "real Mergen Gegen." They are superior to the relics in the monastery, because together they sum up his life achievements. The tooth is important because it "comes from his live body." The seal shows his power (*erhe*) and his *sülde*. The medal represents his religious devotion (*nom*), because of which he achieved such a high position. These three the family had made into a "serious respected god" (*hündü burhan*) for the sake of others. It should be noted that such a tripartite assemblage was fully within the spirit of early Buddhism. Not only is the tooth the archetypal relic of the Buddha, but the structure of its various identities in ritual—it can be treated as a god, a king, and a monk—established a similar tripartite biography of the Buddha (Strong 2004, 200).

Nor is the separation of Mergen Gegen's *sharil* into two shrines strange or anomalous in the context of Buddhist history, the exemplar being the dispersal of the Sakyamuni Buddha's relics after his death, which enabled the meritorious spread of the religion into areas where Buddhism had previously not existed (ibid, 231). We shall return to this theme in the last chapter. As for the Mergen case, the idea of reincarnation introduces complexity not present in early Buddhism. In the regu-

38. The seal reads "Galsangdambijalsan," the Gegen's lama name, in archaic Mongolian and Tibetan letters.

lar life of the monastery the succession of reincarnations results in the accumulation of sacred *sharil* shrines, and all of these coexist as objects of worship with the current incarnation, who is alive. Mongols say the live human vessel is more potent than the animated remains, but still, all are to be worshipped. Yet bodily relics are also the remains of a deceased human being. An unfathomable gap exists between the positive notion of the division of relics as extending the holy Buddhist presence and the Mongolian folk notion that the corpse must remain whole and complete in order to be reborn in perfect human form and not provoke the presence of a ghost searching for missing elements.

Local opinion was that Nabchin should have returned her relics to the monastery and not set up a new *sharil*. That she did not was attributed to a certain distance between Nabchin's family and the Chorji Lama, the present master of Mergen. For although Chorji is the son of Sechingge, he is not the son of Nabchin but of Sechingge's previous wife, and this family divorce led to tensions (see Chapter 8). Nabchin had never learned to write but she was a strong-willed and creative person, a master of artistic embroidery, and she went her own way concerning the Gegen and his relics. However strongly people felt about "Mongol custom," the point here is that individuals sometimes take pleasure in flouting local conventions and pointing out how the 3rd Mergen Gegen had done so too.

So perhaps it is not by chance that it was Nabchin who told us about the 8th Mergen Gegen's ring, a story that explained a mysterious allusion in the legend of "Mergen Gegen and the Emperor" (see p 170). Uncle Gegen had worn a large and special ring every day until, at some point in his old age it disappeared. Nabchin thought he might have secretly sold it, because he was very poor at this time. The narrative of this ring links the generations of the Mergen Gegens in a most unorthodox way. It was handed down from reincarnation to reincarnation, she said. What happened was that when the 3rd Mergen Gegen was called to Peking to be the worshipped lama of the emperor, he was so impressive that not only did the sovereign wish to retain him but the emperor's daughter fell in love with him. The emperor noticed the affair and had to ask Mergen to leave. Just as he was about to depart, the princess came out to bid him farewell and she gave him this ring. This romantic story goes against several conventions of Buddhist and Mongolian morality: no lama should get involved in love affairs and certainly should not keep a memento of such an occasion. A lama, furthermore, should avoid property and should not wear a showy, precious object like this ring. And finally the close personal possession of any person approaching death should be disposed of, in order to prepare the soul for the separation from the world of the living (Humphrey 2002). Only the few objects with a strictly religious function, like the alms bowl[39] or prayer beads, are handed down from one reincarnation to the next. The story of the ring fits well, on the other hand, with the present-day ideas of the poetic, music-loving, and possibly amorous 3rd Mergen Gegen.

Mergen Gegen as Ghost

By the time we met Nabchin and her family in 2005, Sechingge had passed away. The relics were brought to our attention, but we were not allowed to photograph them. Buyan visited the family on another occasion and was also forbidden to go near, photograph, or look closely at the shrine. For a long time the family simply refused access. In the end they allowed Buyan to look at the relics if he made offerings, lit a lamp, and gave proper respect to the *sharil*, and would also do them a favor. But what Nabchin said during these protracted discussions was significant. She tried to scare Buyan, who is not a religious person, with the idea that it would be too dangerous for him to open the stupa and touch (*hündühü*) the relics. She said that the Western Great Lama had handled the relics—four months later he died. Sengge Lama had also come to visit, had touched them—and then what happened to him? Nabchin herself was not subject to this danger. She carried out elaborate rites of respect, and furthermore because she had cared for Mergen Gegen during his old age he was already accustomed to her physical closeness and so he would not harm her now. What she said to Buyan when he asked "innocently" why the relics were dangerous was: "This is a fierce god (*dogshin burhan*)," but he concluded that Mergen Gegen had become in effect something like a ghost-demon.

Now in Buddhist theory this would be a horrifying idea and could not possibly be true: a reincarnation could not become a ghost-demon. His initial bodhisattva nature was utterly pure. Normally Mongols regard a reincarnation's physical relics as powerful in a benignly transformational, magical, or curative way. Discussing this with us, Buyan contrasted the 8th Mergen Gegen with various saintly cases, including that of a reincarnation who had recently died and been cremated in

39. Mongolian monks keep a *badar ayaga* (alms bowl) even if they do not go out to collect alms.

Höhhot. Among the ashes of such a highly learned lama's body are tiny shining pieces called *peldeng*. These are different in quality from the ashes, being transfigured physical items imbued with vitality and the potential to increase miraculously; they should be found, worshipped, and distributed to worthy people. But it had not been possible to make such a search in the case of Mergen Gegen, and the regenerative potential of his remains was unfulfilled.[40]

It is now time to draw these various strands together. For it must have been a possible explanation for Nabchin to interpret death and misfortune to the spirit of Mergen Gegen, even if few people would openly use the term *chitgür* (demonic ghost) for an eminent lama. On one level, by this impressive image she was upholding her husband's Sechingge's combative vision of Mergen Gegen as the crucial spiritual presence of the area, a spirit revealing its holy magic (*ubadis*) more after death than it had in life. At the same time, perhaps she was feeling the general Mongol revulsion at living in the same space as the remains of the deceased (she and her sons were engaged in lengthy negotiations to obtain new housing with a separate shrine room). But neither this nor the fact that the 8th Mergen Gegen in life had been *dogshin* (fierce, frightening) was a convincing explanation of his continuing deadly power, since *dogshin* can be an admirable, or at least necessary, quality and does not in itself lead to a unfortunate afterlife as a ghost. Perhaps the main reason why these relics had become so powerful and dangerous as to cause deaths was that—unlike the case of Tulga—the spirit of Mergen Gegen had been left in limbo. The normal processes of reincarnation and regeneration had been terminally blocked. In other words his situation conformed to the structural position of the unsettled ghost. That his other *sharil* at the monastery was attributed with no such startling power can perhaps be explained by the fact that it was properly placed and worshipped, and yet sidelined. The monastery had its own reasons for not drawing special attention to the last Mergen Gegen, since it had been accepted that no new—and possibly challenging—reincarnation would appear to disturb the status quo. Nabchin's *sharil* can be seen as defiance of this inertia and sequestration, not to speak of the indifference in the wider society beyond. Essentially, it was a claim that Mergen Gegen's biography-of-lifetimes was not over—

40. For discussion of such jewel-like beads in early Buddhism see Martin (1994) and Strong (2004, 10–11). In Inner Mongolia, lama adepts consider *peldeng* to be produced as a result of a meditation process involving control of semen, whereby it is transformed, heats, and rises up the body to become a generative source of compassion, wisdom, and *bodi sedhil* (enlightenment).

for an active ghost can only be transformed into a positive presence by finding a new site in which to be reborn.

In this way of thinking, intention does appear as part of the causal chain, the presumption of the great lama's will be to be reborn. But this intention is not judged responsible for the misfortune brought about by Nabchin's *sharil*. On the contrary, as Buyan understood perfectly well, it was the two Mergen lamas who were at fault for having wantonly, if inadvertently, touched the relics, and the sin lay in the fact that both of them were "lower" than the Gegen. Only two kinds of person are entitled to touch the remains of a high lama: a still higher lama in the religious hierarchy and someone whose astrological birth year corresponds with that of the deceased. According to this prescription, violation of the priority given to spiritual seniority was just as likely to provoke retribution as contravening the occult correspondences of astrology. In the social milieu of these discussions, Nabchin's causal reasoning was a way of showing (by "proof") that the Mergen Gegen *was* incomparably the senior of all these lamas and that not to recognize this was dangerous. In effect she was stating the crucial importance of the series of relations that reflect religious seniority itself—a hierarchy that was under question at the time in the monastery (Chapters 8 and 9), just as its underlying premises were disregarded by the rationalizing and economistic epistemology of modern China.

It seems that for Nabchin the dangerousness of the *sharil* was an effect of ontologically conceived power. As in the case of Tulga who sold the *seter* horse, the danger to transgressors was manifested through the anger (*agur*, literally breath or steam) of the person (god, reincarnation) offended, but that anger was seen not so much as an intentional psychological state as a cosmic and inevitable effect of the offended one having a beyond-human existence. The 8th Megen Gegen could be seen as angry in this sense at the whole society that had blocked his rebirth and was treating his *sharil* without the appropriate devotion.

In the main Chogchin Temple at the monastery, Mergen Gegen's throne is kept empty. Such a chair, particularly *someone's* chair, is an artifact that puts forward a tension between presence and absence—like a pillow or a mirror it is an object that appears to hold a potential, an implied subjectivity. It waits to be reunited with the subject, if only fleetingly (Wu 2012). Mergen's throne had a desolate air, amplified by the surrounding unheeding activities. What happens, however, when a new reincarnation *is* anticipated? Let us end this chapter in a different monastery, where the lamas were still hoping, however despairingly, that their Gegen would be reincarnated in human form. Rather than focusing on relics, their attention was directed to other questions: where was the Gegen if he has yet to return to us, and could we recognize his presence when he comes?

Awaiting the Düinghor Gegen

The last 7th Düinghor Gegen of Badgar Monastery died in 1955 at the age of twelve. Old Dampil Lama had been attending him, and in 2000 recounted his memories to Hürelbaatar. The boy had fallen ill. His beloved younger sister had to live outside the monastery boundary (*goriya*), but one day she appeared outside his window and called, "How are you my older brother?" "Not so bad. But now it is enough. You will also go. It is better for us to go. I am leaving now." He was not seriously ill, but suddenly the young Gegen shouted, "Teacher, teacher," and he departed this life. Almost immediately his younger sister died too.

A golden rainbow appeared from the Gegen's body, a silver one from his sister's, said Dampil. The golden rainbow circled above the main hall of Badgar and then went to the northwest direction.[41] "You see, our Gegen can transform into several forms. One is visible (*ile*) and obvious [the physical human being], the others are concealed (*dalda*), and people cannot perceive them. The previous, 6th Düinghor Gegen was invisible—he was sitting alongside at the deathbed of our 7th, but people did not see him. When light and the rainbow appeared, people became aware, and we bitterly regretted that we had not noticed he had been in front of us because we couldn't recognize him."

Dampil Lama was obsessed with the next reincarnation. Hürelbaatar asked whether, since fifty years had passed since the death of the last Düinghor Gegen, the lamas would look for a child, skipping a generation to the 9th Gegen, rather than finding the now middle-aged man in whom the Gegen had presumably been reborn shortly after he died. Dampil hesitated, "Ay-a, for a person like me, that is too difficult a question." Then he thought a bit and said, "How can he come when our monastery and *goriya* is in ruins like this? There's no way to speak about it. We couldn't recognize him even if he came. Last year he became known at the door. It happened in the sixth month when I was in the temple. The door was opening and closing—what kind of person was there? I saw no one. There had just been talk about the new rein-

41. This direction is an indication of where the next birth is to be found.

carnation being officially allowed, so I thought maybe this was a sign of the Gegen visiting his monastery.[42] But because I couldn't see him, I couldn't be sure. You see, I didn't keep my vows; they were burned and passed over. What am I now? I'm just sitting looking like a lama. Living this way, of course I couldn't see him. The doctrine created by the Lord Buddha, we did not act by the rule of holy doctrine. That is why we did not succeed [upset, almost crying]. But there is a teaching: if you regret (*gemshibel*) by yourself and enter into a great regret, if you beg (*guyubal*) by yourself, your breaking of your vow will be a little lighter."

Later in this conversation Dampil Lama said the last Düinghor Gegen had died by his own will at an early age because he was in a hurry. He was preparing the helmets and arms for the Shambhala war. He needed to go.[43] "But could the Gegen then also return to Badgar?" we wondered. "Of course," Dampil responded, "because a reincarnation can have several directions (*jüg*)." He explained that the Gegen this last fifty years had probably "gone to *lus*" (*lus* are the reptilian water spirits):

> You see, our Düinghor has always been indebted to the *lus*. In his first body he was suffering with the task of building a vast monastery with many stupas. There was no wood to build with. The *lus* were so powerful they just blew on the trees and they became stupas for the shrine. Next morning, when dawn came, there was a smell as if the trees had been pulled out, and the lamas just stood and received the stupas and carried them in procession to the temple. In ancient times there were such wooden stupas at Badgar. We make the lamas chant this history. This is why our Gegens must go to return the beneficial deed of the *lus*. Now I think our 7th Gegen must have gone to preach doctrine to the *lus*.

This account of the Badgar reincarnation and the forces of nature would seem to have little to do with the 8th Mergen Gegen. But in this part of the world, themes wind round, disappear, and return. Readers may recall the story of the 3rd Mergen Gegen who entertained the Green Snake—also called the King of *Lus*—on his bed (Chapter 3). A later reincarnation is supposed to be able to remember and reenact episodes in the life of his predecessor. Naranbatu recalled how he had met the 8th Mergen Gegen many times, and had received his lama's ini-

42. Some years later official permission was given for the recognition of a new Düinghor Gegen.

43. The Düinghör reincarnation has been associated for generations with mustering troops by means of his *Wang* initiation-empowerment to fight the Shambhala war (Hyer and Jagchid 1983, 162).

tiation from him in the 1940s. Once he rode over and Mergen Gegen gave the young boy a pear from the monastery garden. And Naranbatu could not forget what he saw: "The Gegen Teacher was looking after a snake—a long one, which lay coiled on his bed. He fed it milk every day. A lama person loves living creatures after all, even harmful ones."

Thus, through the addition of further pages, a Gegen's biography gets filled out. But these extensions are not random: the more we thought about them, the more they began to seem reiterative, even exemplary. One quality of a Gegen, which is not true of ordinary people, is that his impending return as the same person dislodges the notion of the chronologically linear life story. Like the Buddha (Strong 2004, 200), an incarnation may appear in many guises in his lifetime(s), but his heterogeneous presence is also thinkable synchronically, perhaps most powerfully in the mysterious state(s) he enters after death and before rebirth.

SEVEN

Sengge: A Lama's Knowledge and Its Vicissitudes

Introduction 2002

One lama above all stood for the Mergen tradition, knew the texts, ardently performed the chants, and tried to insist on correct procedures. This was Sengge Lama, a man who had spent almost thirty years of his life as a cadre under the communists. In many ways his talents and his life suited him very well to the particular character of the Mergen tradition, its language and music, its localization in cults of mountains, springs, and trees, its openness to the preoccupations of the herders. Sengge embodied, the Mongolness of the tradition. It was he who rediscovered the evil Rolling Stone sent by the Tibetans (Chapter 1), placed it in a prominent spot, and ordered lamas to say prayers to control it, thereby reminding all those who cared to listen that Mongolian Buddhists are not mere followers of forms made elsewhere (Elverskog 2007, 63).

Sengge saw himself as a strict traditionalist, yet as a twentieth-century "man of the people" he could not but be an active mediator in interpreting the tradition. We suggest that Sengge's political experience and scientific training was an influence on what he took to be the central teaching—that Buddhism should be concerned with what speakers of English would call "knowledge" more than "belief." In this chapter we shall try to unpack such a statement, bearing in mind that Mongolian language and practice does not operate with categories directly corresponding to either "knowledge" or "belief." This will involve trying to understand a lama's vision of Buddhism in his terms, but also setting his narratives within their historical situation—that is, as they were related to us after the Cultural Revolution had destroyed practically everything; after lamas like Sengge had been forced to decide what in the vast previous edifice they would, or could, revive; and after a tide of new economic and career opportunities for youth had washed even into rural Urad, leaving the tradition looking as though it could well be a lost cause.

This chapter quotes extensively from Sengge, and we would like to convey thereby something of the range of ways of speaking available to people like him in China today. Communist cadres were frequently called to account for themselves to party secretaries, so Sengge would have been used to relating his life story in official circumstances. We recognize that a dialogical approach reveals how meanings are constructed in interactional processes, and although we are not able to document this fully it should be noted that Sengge interacted differently with each of us: Caroline was a "respected professor," and yet the one who needed patient explanation about matters he assumed Hürelbaatar already understood; on the other hand she was also a foreigner from whom sensitive issues should be hidden. Hürelbaatar was treated to another kind of wariness, that obtaining in the familiar milieu where people are presumed to be party to local intrigues. Finally, Sengge was a leading protagonist in a monastic conflict, which undoubtedly created occasions on which sharp opinions could (or could not) be expressed. We begin our chapter with this dispute. Though it was personal, it also reflected splits felt throughout Inner Mongolian society.

The Rift

Sengge Lama used to live in the house on the east side of the yard of the Temple of Relics. When he was in residence the wooden doors in the gate were left hospitably open and juniper branches would be smoking in the censer opposite the entrance. Visitors ignored the locked temple and turned right to Sengge's dwelling. His house was divided into three rooms: left of the central entrance hall was a kitchen that also served to house Sengge's disciple Norbu. To the right was Sengge's room, half of which was taken up by a high brick platform (*hanju*) serving as his bed and sitting space. A small cupboard shrine (*günggarba*) was placed against the wall opposite the door. Sengge told us that his personal deity amongst the gods in this shrine was Öhin Tngri, the goddess of learning and music, the same as that of the 3rd Mergen Gegen. He would sit cross-legged on the *hanju*, smiling, chatting, taking pinches of snuff, and holding court to a stream of supplicants who stood or perched on stools in the space below him. Respected visitors would be invited to sit with him on the brick bed to converse in more intimate fashion.

Here over the years many of our conversations took place. But when we arrived in 2002 the monastery was dark and almost deserted. Chorji arrived from his home in Baotou and told us that Sengge was rarely in residence. A quarrel had taken place. Sengge was no longer cantor (*umjad*) and undisputed leader of chanting. By 2005 the east house in the Temple of Relics had been allocated to another lama, and Sengge stayed there only as a rare visitor.

In 2001, a year when we did not visit, events took place that forced the latent hostility between Sengge Lama and the Chorji reincarnation into the open. Everyone knew that the monastery would have to recruit some young monks: many senior lamas had died, others had been sidelined, and the Western Great (Barugun Da) Reincarnation was now old. Furthermore, there had been a tragedy—Jongrai, the cheerful manager of practical affairs (*ombu*) had been killed in a motorcycle accident. Minggan was the only younger lama permanently attached to the monastery. Chorji was able to apply successfully to Baotou for a large grant to train young lamas, following the government change of policy toward religion. Eight boys were recruited from various places around Urad. The obvious person to take charge of their education was Sengge. However, according to Chorji, Sengge Lama "caused trouble" and was often away from the monastery conducting rituals for laypeople for money. According to Sengge, Chorji squandered most of the grant, allocated far too little to the upkeep of the young pupils, and paid him as teacher only a pittance, which he did not receive regularly or in full. In the end there was no money even to pay for the boys' food and they were sent home. The young lamas left, in tears. Although Sengge's close disciple Norbu and one other young lama subsequently returned, they too shortly departed after Chorji insulted Sengge, who now left in anger. Sengge and Chorji blamed one another for this debacle, but nevertheless they separately each told us how difficult it is these days to find and retain young lamas. The boys disliked the stark conditions of the barracks, getting up early to start services before dawn, the sheer discipline of constant chanting, and some of them were unsuited to the intensive learning involved. If their families lived not too far away, the temptation was simply to strike for home.

We shall return later to the difficulties of renewing the supply of young lamas. The issue we address now is the deeper roots of the split between the two main lamas of Mergen—a fatal division that threatened the monastery's very existence. This was not just a matter of different personalities, but lay in the intersection of fault lines in Inner Mongolian Buddhist society already mentioned in previous chapters. For a start, the families of the two lamas were separated by the political schism that had rent Urad society in the civil war: Sengge's father had been a Guomindang supporter, while Chorji was great-nephew of the 8th Mergen Gegen, who was on the Mongol nationalist/Japanese side. For another thing the distinctive traditions upheld by different monasteries came between them: Sengge was a partisan upholder of the Jirgaltu monastery customs, such as worship of the battle standard, while Chorji's loyalty was to Mergen, and for him the Jirgaltu lamas were incomers who had already caused trouble to his father Sechingge. Sengge was from a "working class" (herder) background, while Chorji was of noble birth. Crucially, the two lamas embodied different ways of being a Buddhist lama, that of the reincarnation (Chorji) and that of the "clerical" monk who advances by diligence in learning and skilled performance (Sengge). These existing sources of dissonance were wrenched into further almost unbearable tension by the Cultural Revolution. In that period of prolonged suffering, the two kinds of lama—and these two people—were both punished and mistreated, but in different ways and for different reasons. These were not just hurtful events, but deeply transformative experiences, and they not only exacerbated different attitudes towards Buddhism but also quickened these men's differences in personality, turning them into new "politically conditioned" kinds of person. In this chapter, we discuss Sengge Lama and in the following chapter we address the experiences of Chorji Lama.

An Outline of Sengge Lama's Early Life

Sengge was born at Bayan Bulag in 1931 in a poor herding family of the West Banner. When he was three his father left home to fight for the Guomindang and never returned. His mother was unlettered, but she loved singing and taught her son to sing. Sengge was the only one of her ten children to survive. To provide the vigor of *sülde* for his life his mother prayed and lit a butter lamp to Jirgal Bagatur's battle standard at Jirgaltu Monastery, and promised to send her son as a lama. When we discovered that Sengge's very life had been placed under the protection of the battle standard it became clear to us why he was so devoted to this object of worship.

At the age of seven he entered Jirgaltu Monastery. "It was difficult to make your only son a lama," said Sengge, "and my mother moved near the monastery with her livestock to look after me." Sengge excelled at his studies. There were over a hundred lamas in Jirgaltu at the time, more than at Mergen, and around forty of them were young. There were several learned senior lamas, and the monastery was famous for the high standard of its chanting and music. Discipline was strict. Studies were formally organized into three levels of chanting, the "Small Chanting" (*baga ungshilga*), "Great Chanting" (*yehe ungshilga*), and "Roots" (*ündüsü*), including texts of the four tantric empowerments (*wang*) that survived in the Mergen tradition.[1]

In my case, I finished all three levels between the ages of seven and fifteen. Some kids finished it later at 18. It was different for different people. Some spent ten years, eighteen years, and they still couldn't do it. Some were fast—they only took seven years.

If one studied and memorized by heart the four *ündüsü*, it was like graduating from university. Among them, the one we found was the most important was Yamantaka Wang.[2] The second was Biruzana [Vairocana] Wang. That was among the texts brought back from England, but with the prayer section (*jalbaril*) to Biruzana lacking. Oh, it shouldn't have been left behind. It is full of powerful and symbolic *shagja* (hand gestures). Now, no one knows about them. It is such a tough, difficult [text] and so important to us.

The third *ündüsü* is Wachirbani Wang. The number of pages is not many, about twenty. But it is very complicated. From here read a middle page, then go to there, backward and forward, a person can lose their mind in that. It is not easy. That book is also missing and has not been found yet. The fourth one was Ayushi Wang

1. Tantric empowerments (T. *dbang*, "kingly power") initiated disciples with the "seeds" of the attributes of a *yidam* and entitled them to "generate" the given deity through meditation. Other monasteries in Inner Mongolia had different, sometimes more extensive, repertoires of *wang* than in the Mergen tradition.

2. Here Sengge was referring to the chanted service called *wang*, rather than the empowerment given by a high lama to his disciples, which was also called *wang* or *abishig*. With the latter type of *wang* a lasting relation is established between a disciple, the guru, and the given god; a secret vow is made to the guru, and thereafter the mantra received becomes powerful and efficacious. Tantric coinitiates call one another "brothers" and "sisters." See Mills 2003, 122–26, on the Yamantaka Wang empowerment in Ladakh as a rite of passage, and Mair 2007, 53–57, on the *abishig*/*wang* rite as performed recently in Ordos.

is the god that makes life longer. That text is also lost. All of the *ündüsü* must be memorized by heart. After that a lama can study by reading other texts.

Sengge's first guru-lama was Ishi-Hairub. He was learned and intelligent, and also practiced as a doctor and performed rituals in laypeople's homes. He used to take Sengge with him to do this work. A severe teacher and disciplinarian, he used to criticize Sengge publicly for looking at girls. "Ai-ya, that was not easy. His face became really red. Ha, ha, ha. Later, our teacher died, and after that I carried on his ritual work, as well as independently studying the sutras by myself."

Sengge's energy and talent were quickly recognized: at fourteen he became the *gonir* (temple keeper); at fifteen the *dormachi*, the maker of ritual artifacts like dough offerings (*baling*). By the age of sixteen he was a full-fledged monk, allowed to go on his own to conduct rituals at the duke's palace and already starting to chant texts for the general laity such as the *Altan Gerel*.[3] Soon he was offered the post of *garaiba*, a position reserved for a lama capable of memorizing the *Biruzana* text, with its complex rhythms and dozens of hand gestures.

After the communists came to power, the young lamas came under heavy pressure to leave the monastery and take up socially useful lives. It is not quite clear when Sengge left the monastery, but sometime in the early 1950s most of the young lamas left together. Aged around twenty-two Sengge, returned to his mother, and after six months entered the Mongolian Ethnic Cadres School in Höhhot. He became a member of the Communist Youth League and around 1955 was sent to the Urad Middle Banner as a cadre (C. *ganbu*). He did further studies at an agricultural college and then worked as a relatively high official in the Bureau of Livestock Husbandry. During this period he married and had three children. He was sent for a further two years of scientific training to Zhalantun in Hulun Buir, and when he returned to the Middle Banner in 1964 he was appointed to the important position of Director of the Bureau at League level. He commented in an aside to us that he held this post only in name, and never really did the work of organizing livestock husbandry. On his appointment he had decided bring his mother to join him in the Middle Banner, but she refused. ("I have become old. Even if I die, I won't go.")

3. *Altan Gerel* (Golden Light) is a compendious text giving guidance about how to purify the mind, and also used to address the guardian deities, to obtain protection against thieves and disease, and help in getting rich. It was translated several times into Mongolian and is widely popular among the laity as a book to be worshipped as well as read.

My mother brought me up, and now I was an adult, how could I leave her alone at home while I was a cadre? I only became a person because of my mother's *achi* (favor). My mind was not at rest. So I stopped being a cadre and came back to the West Banner. I became the headman of the U-Bulag Brigade of Bayanhua Commune and did that job until the Cultural Revolution.

I always missed the lama life. I knew everything, I didn't stop chanting, and that is why I did not forget the texts. Even when I was a cadre, I chanted inside myself. Only at night, by myself, so no one could hear. I chanted *Chagan Shihürtü* [text of a *yidam* deity of wisdom and knowledge].[4] I memorized everything, all doctrine (*nom*).

I did not offer to gods; that was not possible. [But] I did not destroy my deity images. I put them away in a hole in the rocks.

So returning from his high position in the Middle Banner in 1965, Sengge took up the one of the main leadership posts in his home area. This was a difficult time for him: almost as soon as he returned his wife died in childbirth and his mother also died. It was in this role of local administrator, rather than as a former lama, that he was attacked during the Cultural Revolution, as we describe later.

It is clear that Sengge's energy, expressive speech, and good memory were recognized not only in the monastery but also in regional government, where it enabled him to rise to a high rank. Most, however, although his lama's modesty would prevent him saying so, he prided himself on his knowledge of the sacred doctrine (*nom*), and we now discuss what this means in a Buddhist context.

Knowledge, Competence, and Practice

Two interrelated questions arise: what is "known" when people say that they know the sacred texts, and how important is knowledge as distinct from other desirable religious states such as faith?

At one point in 2005 we asked Sengge which was more important in Buddhism, *erdem* (erudition, learning, skill, knowledge, wisdom, virtue) or *bishirel* (faith, belief, trust). Quick as a flash, he replied:

4. *Chagan Shihürtü* (The God with the White Umbrella, S. Sitātapatrā) is the text for a peaceful tutelary deity of the same name, one of the most popular of the Tantric gods. The deity has a thousand heads, arms, and eyes and it holds a white umbrella. This god is said to manifest "the pure *erdem* (knowledge, erudition, wisdom) that covers all living beings" (Sodubilig 1996, 392), and especially in degenerate times it provides blessed protection from inner and outer enemies to the sentient beings beneath its canopy.

Erdem is more important. Just devotion, without studying *erdem*, is not right. First one must study the sutras; just bowing to deities with knowing the meaning, that is superstition, empty veneration (*hogusun bishirel*). If you are literate and understand the sense, if you study the inner part, there is meaning (*uchir*, the meaning of something or reason for it). After you understand the meaning, on that basis, your mind (*sedhil*) may reach the real Buddha's (*burhan*) stage. This idea is in the Buddha's teaching about fake and real piety. Fake devotion (*hagurmag süjig*) is when you are prostrating without understanding the meaning.

Sengge thus relegated both veneration/admiration (*bishirel*) and devotion/piety (*süjig*)—two aspects of "belief" (Hamayon 2005, 15–41)—in favor of "knowledge" (*erdem*). His scorn for "superstition" followed Communist teachings. Nevertheless, his idea of knowledge was distinctive, concerned not so much with factual truth as with the meaning or reason for things. "The essential meaning (*udha*) lies behind the beautiful and precise words composed with meter by Mergen Gegen. Our Gegen made the meaning complete. The reason (*uchir*) is the meaning, isn't it?" Sengge once said.

Sengge's idea of general worldly competence included knowing a large number of facts. He distinguished information he classified as belonging to the contemporary world (*medlege*) from religious matters (*nom*) and he was aware of nuances of vocabulary appropriate for each.[5] These were two kinds of reality, as Caroline discovered when Sengge mentioned the thread (*utas*) that connected Öhin Tngri, the monastery and the *oboo* built by Mergen Gegen to counteract the tears of the departing proctor (p 144). As first confused, Caroline asked, "Was it a real thread? Or some kind of road?" and Sengge replied, "Of course it is a real *utas*. Mergen Gegen did not do things the way they done now, scientifically, using materials and measurements. But our lama created that connection." The thread was notional, but for him it was real. Yet unlike most people at Mergen, Sengge did not ignore the difference between epistemic worlds; on the contrary, he would bring them up and worry at them, as we discuss further at the end of this chapter. Whenever possible he would seek to explain the religious view in terms that would be acceptable to a contemporary lay understanding.

Sengge's account of the world started with the eon (*galab*), which changes over time (*chag*) and generation (*üye*): winds and moisture

5. For example, when relating the story of the proctor who criticized Mergen Gegen (pp 144–45), Sengge paused to say he should not have used the term *silgümjilehü* (criticize, debate) which came in after Liberation, but words related to breaking rules (*jayag*) that would have been used in the eighteenth century.

gradually produced specks of matter, then dust, sand and earth appeared, then microbes, worms and plants, followed by human beings and animals and with them religion. He emphasized that Sakyamuni, the first Buddha, and indeed the subsequent Buddhas (*burhan*, including Padmasambhava, Tsongkhapa, and Neichi Toin) were not "empty things" but real human beings. They were heroes or victors who became *burhan*. Sakyamuni Buddha achieved supernatural power (*shidi*) though meditation, after he realized the suffering of ordinary human life. Sengge was quite careful to distinguish "what people generally think" from "what the sutras say," and both of these from what he felt he really knew. Caroline once asked him, when he was talking about his own life and death, whether, when an ordinary lama died, their soul would take rebirth? "Ha, ha, who knows?" he replied with his usual deprecating laugh.

About the human soul, what is said in the sutras (*nom*) is that one who accumulates many good deeds and does no sins will take birth in the Land of Buddhas. Someone who is just good and didn't do many heavy sins will take rebirth as a human being. A person who does poisonous, sinful deeds will be reborn in hell. Then it is difficult to get human birth. But because [I] did not see them with my own eyes, how can I speak about them [these three kinds of birth]?

Perhaps however this was the kind of reply Sengge had adopted for a non-Buddhist. In other contexts, among Mongols, he would stress the powerful nature of specifically religious knowledge (*erdem*), which existed in a dynamical relation with ignorance. Let us now delve further into this idea of *erdem* by investigating how the monks felt it could be attained amongst the range of their religious practices. Sengge often mentioned how much has dropped out of monastic curriculum as compared with the pre-1949 period. The elderly monks knew about far more than they practice today. Yet as we shall show they had ways to cope expediently with many of the rituals, such that they were not entirely lost, and by these means they could ensure that some quantum of *erdem* could still be attained.

Sengge and the other monks knew that meditation was the supreme practice of achieving enlightenment in Buddhism, that the highest "knowledge" (*erdem*) was acquired this way, and that some of the great initiating figures of the Mergen tradition had practiced lengthy meditation (*diyan, bishilgal*) in caves. However, we found only traces —several abandoned meditation caves high in the mountains—of what had evidently been a crucial practice in earlier times. One Mergen lama,

Heshigbayar, who died around 2000, had tried to complete the lengthy *sharid* meditation[6] for Yamantaka. But he did not succeed—he was too young at the time to carry out such a difficult practice to the end. This kind of meditation was central for personal spiritual advancement, but successful completion also qualified a lama to carry out dangerous and powerful rituals on behalf of the monastery as a whole. Aged monks told us that only a lama who had completed the Yamantaka *sharid* had the right to throw out the *sor*, thereby purifying the community. In the mid–1990s no such lama was available, and to cast the *sor* the monastery had recourse to the Western Great Lama, who was not qualified. Readers may recall the story in Chapter 3, in which the 3rd Mergen Gegen's "heavenly eye" was opened by virtue of having completed the meditation for Green Yamantaka and he was then able to accomplish magical feats. Putting all this together it is evident that acquiring *erdem* is about power as much as knowledge. This is why the practice of getting knowledge is regulated: a disciple needs to have received a *wang* "empowerment" (T. *wang*, M. *abishig* from S. *abhiṣeka*) even to start the *sharid* meditation, and to read advanced sutras he should have a *rung* (order, permission).

The lamas were also aware of the possibility of visionary direct transmission of teaching (Gyatso 1992a, 96), and that the 3rd Mergen Gegen had experienced such an event in his mystical encounter with the goddess Ökin Tngri (see p 154). But no one today claims to have had such an experience. Certain ascetic practices[7] and the general summer retreat (*hailang*) have also died out in Mergen. Elderly lamas described the retreat as a period of different "summer existence" (*jun-u orusil*), a strict regime of prayer, reflection, and fasting that took place each year for six weeks (see also Galluu 2003, 292). The practice went back to ancient Indian communities of monks, who, when the heat was at its height and numerous tiny sentient beings multiplied, would retreat

6. This *sharid* meditation was a particularly exacting form of the visualization and generation in the self of a tutelary deity (*yidam*). Visualization in this case involves the adept "seeing the face" of the deity with his own eyes, and then transforming the self to become (have the same nature as) the deity. It takes many years of training and austerity to acquire the vision firmly such that it becomes a stable presence, and the practitioner may not succeed.

7. Old lamas told us that certain types of constant communal chanting were also forms of ascetic meditation. The main example was the complex Mani service, which was continued throughout the year in the form of "*nungnai* duty" Twelve monks called "meditating lamas" would take these chanting duties, each for one month, so the service never ceased. "Meditation" in this case involved a range of ascetic practices also found in the classic meditation in a cave: fasting (*machag*), "existence without sound" (*nungnai*), and the endlessly repeated chanting of a mantra (in this case the *mani* mantra, *on ma ni pad me hum*). "Fasting" meant strictly limited food and drink, and "existence without sound" meant no conversation.

to a quiet place and avoid traveling in order not to harm them. In the Urad area, each monastery would send groups of some twenty lamas in turn to conduct the retreat, supplied by laity who would bring them food and water. Larger institutions, including Mergen, had outposts located far in the mountains called Gempi hermitages, which were used for such summer retreats. But they have long since ceased to exist.

The present-day lamas do not continue these parts of the inheritance of Mergen Gegen. As Jacques Derrida writes, an inheritance from the past ". . . is never one with itself. Its presumed unity, if there is one, can consist only in the injunction to reaffirm by choosing. [. . .] The injunction [. . .] can only be one by dividing itself, tearing itself apart, differing/deferring itself, by speaking at the same time several times—and in several voices" (2005, 16). Such critical divisiveness must always be part of reproducing a tradition, as we discuss in Chapter 10 for the monastery as an institution. Here we focus on the techniques whereby Sengge's extensive and detailed knowledge from his youth was distilled into condensed practices that could be used in the reduced circumstances of the present day. We take the example of the *wang* and *mandala* service, through which empowerment was received to evoke a *yidam* deity and to invite it to reside.

Sengge described in detail how he had participated in these rites at Jirgaltu, and his appreciation of the empowerments he had received. The seven-day-long *wang* rituals culminated in the construction of a beautiful symbolic diagram (*mandala*) made of colored sands and ash, which Sengge called "city" (*hota*)—the residence or placing of the *yidam* being evoked and at the same time the spiritual domain into which disciples would be initiated. After the deity had been invited to depart, the *mandala* was finally "poured" with melted butter, dough figures, and other precious foods and set alight, an act of purification. The complete series of Yamantaka *wang* rituals took place over four years, each year being addressed to a different gate (east, south, west, and north) of the pure realms (*dewseng*)[8] of four Buddhas representing qualities such as wisdom or compassion. "The teacher guides you," said Sengge, "to these four gates. It is like building a city, building Yamantaka's city. Oh, many people gathered for that." Guided in this terrain, the student should meditate on the emptiness of their own identity,[9] and thereafter he attains the blessing of knowledge. Sengge told us that

8. Probably Sengge's pronunciation of T. *dewachen* (S. *sukhāvatī*), usually known as the paradise realm of Amitabha (see Mills 2003, 95).

9. Meditation on emptiness is in principle the whole point, but Sengge hardly mentioned it (for extended discussion of the practice in a functioning monastery, see Mills 2003, 100–124).

receiving *erdem* through such services in the monastery temple was "the same as," though actually far less respected than the *mandala* rite that marked the completion of an individual *sharid* meditation that might last for years. Yet the temple version too conferred the empowerment of the Yamantaka *wang*, and a lama could thereafter, if his teacher gave him permission, engage in *sharid* meditation by himself in his cell or in some other place. For Sengge such lone meditation involved recitation of mantras in vast numbers.[10] The mantras (*tarni*) are agentive: they generate blessings or benign energies from each syllable, and these act to ameliorate suffering, repel destructive forces, and so forth. It can be seen from this that the lama does not just "attend services" but over time with successive empowerments becomes a person able to have remarkable effect in the world. As Mills aptly remarks, *mandalas* act not as objects but as events that produce ritual authority (ibid, 129). It is significant that Sengge often talked not of being a lama but of "doing lama" (e.g., "After Liberation, I stopped doing lama [*lama-ban hihü-ben bolichihagad*] and I became a cadre").

Hürelbaatar was present at a *mandala* ritual of this kind in 1992 but after that, as far as we know, it was not performed again at Mergen. Sengge said that even if the old monks today know how to construct a full *mandala* they are too poor to do so. It involves many precious elements such as jewels, silver, and gold, and should be poured with expensive items such as butter· But there were radically condensed versions of *mandala* construction. The leading lama during the *wang* service would hold a platter in one hand, a *wachir* (S. *vajra*)[11] in the other. On a disc on the platter he would make, sweep away, and remake *mandala* shapes in sand, according to instructions in the chanted text. If even this could not be done, there was a two-handed gesture representing the *mandala*. This was a pyramid shape in which the two upstanding central fingers represented Mount Sumeru, while the remaining fingers were pleated together to form four points symbolizing the four continents. The practitioner should chant a short simple mantra, offering this "treasure *mandala*" to Lord Buddha, the *yidam*, and guru. If the

10. Sengge said that a monk might meditate for four hours every day, and *sharid* would be completed when the *tarni* had been recited one billion times (on another occasion he said a hundred thousand times). His teacher told him that on completion—which Sengge himself never reached—the monk would see Buddha's hands thrust through his window. "You would be meditating all by yourself at night . . . in those days our windows were made of paper. Suddenly Buddha's hands broke through. Prr! Were you scared or not? But now you know your meditation is successful! That's what we were told."

11. A sacred instrument used in ritual as a symbol of the indestructible element, "diamond" or "thunderbolt."

gesture is offered with sincerity it is "the same as" making the elaborate *mandala* diagram. How can this "the same as" be understood? Clearly the collective, expensive, and long-drawn out ritual was judged to be more widely effective. Yet the power-knowledge received in the simple rite was of the same kind; it gave a jot of experience of divine presence, and as we noted in the case of the "instant" (*agshan*) discussed in the Introduction, what we have here called a "jot" is not something measurable.

Such techniques of making shortcuts were certainly not new, nor unique to Mongolian Buddhism, but in Mergen rather than being simply practical alternatives they had become the only option and therefore crucial for Sengge. For him the abilities acquired through such rituals are not separated from the "knowledge" of the lama. Through these rites, he said, "the monk becomes a learned person (*erdemten*). If you complete the *sharid* you can do merit for a dead person, you can sit as senior lama of the service, you can make libations from the skull bowl (*gabala*)."[12] Knowledge and practice are completely integrated.

It is consonant with this that Sengge said perfect performance of a prayer had to be accompanied by comprehension of its meaning. This statement was probably an implied criticism of the use of Tibetan by Mongols,[13] but it also meant something different from simply understanding the propositions of the sentences. The process of learning by monks tied understanding with person-to-person oral transmission and memorization by heart. The Mongolian language, like English, localizes "by heart" in the body, but more emphatically melds it with physicality: the word *chegeji* means both "chest" (breast, bosom) and the faculty of memory; to know something by heart is to "breast" it. Learning from the teacher then consisted of receiving the text orally into oneself, as if it were a power or energy. Knowing it meant being able to appear before the teacher, the book tucked under one arm, and recite it perfectly. The perfect ideal was the ability attributed to Mergen Gegen in the legend of his performance of the fire ritual before the Manchu emperor (see p 170): the great lama knew by heart with such interiority that he could in effect compose (*jokiyahu*) the prayers.

12. The bowl made of a human skull is dangerous; people normally avoid any human remains (Chapter 6). Therefore, special tantric empowerment is needed to use such a bowl; at the same time, the sinister power of the bowl adds to the lama's efficacy.

13. Sengge's exposition of the Mergen tradition thus differed from that more common in Buddhism across the world, where use of a sacred non-comprehensible language (e.g. Pali in Thailand, Tibetan in Mongolia) allows participants to cut off their religious activities from everyday action (see discussion in Cook 2010, 113–14).

4 Sengge Lama chanting, 1998. (Caroline Humphrey)

As the legend also describes, *reading* that same text was a quite different and inferior operation. Among the monks at Mergen, reading was secondary, and learned later.[14] All of the aspects of performance that Sengge cared so much about—the metered rhythms, the chanting melodies, and the hand gestures—were transmitted orally and not marked

14. For a description of teaching methods in Tibetan language monasteries in Inner Mongolia, see Hyer and Jagchid (1983, 8–9). Even in these monasteries young lamas first memorized basic texts in Mongolian, to make sure they fully took them in, before learning the Tibetan versions.

on written texts. Musical notation was not used at all in the Mergen tradition.[15] Furthermore, just as the chanting should be in smooth unison, all of this aural, physical, and intellectual productivity was (or should be) indissolubly united. One day Sengge asked us rhetorically, referring to an uncertain service sung by some novices: "I have a question to ask. Even if the words are by Mergen Gegen, but they can't sing the melody properly, what can you think about it? Is it *the same thing*?"

In the previous chapter we suggested that in discussions of past events Urad people often make judgments about the effects of actions, while passing over the actors' intentions. Our conversations with Sengge enabled us to see that in religious contexts this structure does not imply an absence of interiority. On the contrary, inner thoughts and feelings are extremely important, but they are seen as an active movement—away from individual reasoning (which is indeed disparaged) and toward common or generic religious states of mind. The most important state of mind emphasized by Sengge was sincerity (*ünenchü*). He said that only with this attitude/feeling would chanting enhance the lamas' merit (*buyan*) and bring blessings and protection from misfortune to all sentient beings in the vicinity. Such a statement implies an orientation from an inner state outward to others, and it applied to lamas' activities in general, not just the services. Cultivating the morally correct state of mind and humbleness are central to the right practice of "giving and receiving" for example. As Sengge put it:

> . . . for example, if a giver wants to give their own money to you, saying "*ma*" (take), you should not think "it's my due" (as a lama). You should not think, "this is my payment" (for a religious service). You should think, "I didn't intend to take your money." You should venerate him that he from his own mind gave his money. You can't be a person who just takes money. When you chant, in your mind you should think about this giver, "Yes, this person's sins will be cleared, may his vital force (*hei mori sülde*) flourish." There must be this kind of deed (*jabudal*), . . . this is merit (*buyan*).

It is in line with this sense of the lama's duty to others that Sengge used to dispense general knowledge, though it could appear almost as an outflow of his personality. It was not just to us as privileged visitors that he spoke so willingly. Our Mongolian colleagues were present at lengthy conversations between Sengge and herding people, and

15. Musical notation was used in some Mongolian monasteries.

we also witnessed numerous occasions when people came to him for advice or simply to mull over old times. For laypeople, especially children, Sengge taught ethics by means of didactic stories and parables (*üliger*). Kindly, anxious to be clear and informative, he was rarely at a loss for an answer. He would tell young lamas the characteristics of various deities, about how to perform the next day's service, joke about curious events, complain about mistakes in the present-day liturgy at Mergen, or recount stories about deities, ghosts, and retribution. As far as we could tell, the people who came to Sengge for knowledge did not feel the relation placed them in the status of "the ignorant," but rather as people who had now learned a little more. And in fact, since some of "the laity" were former lamas, and very many were members of lamas' families, they were already informed about Buddhism (a point to which we shall return in Chapter 10).

To an outsider many of Sengge's accounts would seem like legends, but for him they were seamlessly part of the necessary and practically important explanation of reality—why things are as they are and how we must therefore act. Sengge was intolerant of mistakes, lapses in concentration, and vagueness. Especially in monastic ritual, there was a right way to do things, a clear hierarchy of roles, a definite sequence, and spatial-directional order in ritual actions. Woe to the inattentive lama or disrespectful pupil—Sengge described with a laugh how he used to give them a slap. He cared about the melodious and beautiful effect of singing, which he called "flower tone" (*huwartai ayalgu*), saying this was the legacy of Mergen Gegen. Yet it was his respect for inherited and unchangeable correctness, rather than beauty, that made him criticize a painting of Muna Khan that Minggan Lama did for us. This was an imaginative rendering of the deity, including Chinese-style landscape, monastic buildings, and animals not to be seen in the worshipped prototype. However, we noticed that the younger lama was not cowed by this criticism. Sengge's authority was impaired after the break with Chorji, and he often had to bear what he saw as the lapses of the monks in silence. Sengge was a tall man and always noticeable in the ranks of lamas. At services, his affronted visage could sometimes be seen looming like a tortured specter over the raggedly chanting lamas.

Sengge Lama Decodes the Mantras

In summer 2002, offended and having stalked out of the monastery, Sengge Lama was living mostly at his house in a village near Bayanhua town. He only came to Mergen for the great services and otherwise spent his time conducting rituals for laypeople in the countryside around. His house is an ordinary brick dwelling, with two storehouses on either side forming a yard. Here children, dogs, and chickens roam. Sengge lives with one of his adult daughters, her husband, and their children, with the more sporadic presence of other relatives, young grandchildren, and the occasional disciple. When we visited him that year Sengge was affectionately trying to take charge of his grandson Nasunbayar, the boy who had accompanied him to the Shara Oroi sacrifice in 1998. Nasunbayar had no interest in becoming a lama, however. Sengge, at ease in these domestic surroundings, sat cross-legged on the *hanju*, waited on by his family, gently shushing the young children, and discoursing on anything anyone cared to ask him. From time to time someone would ring up, evidently asking for a divination. Sengge would riffle through his astrology manual, and sometimes he would give the divination out of his head, without consulting his book. Towering above the house was a pole flying a wind-horse flag and we asked him what it meant.

Such *hei mori* flags are flown by practically all Mongolian families in the area. Densely printed on cotton is a horse surrounded by numerous Tibetan mantras and sundry symbolic animals, numbers, and signs. Flown so high that no one can read it and faded by wind and rain, the flag is a thing that seems to point to absent meaning. However, Sengge disabused us of any such idea when he said that Mergen Monastery had created two wooden blocks for printing its own wind-horse, that the *tarnis* on these were in Mongolian, and the whole flag was understandable.

Still, what did Sengge mean by "understandable"? He had an explanation for the whole flag in terms of its function ("it makes the human body light as air, raising the spirit," see Chapter 5). This is meaning conceived as the ontology of the wind-horse, i.e., the immanent spiritual presence that has effect by virtue of it having been written.[16] Sengge also told us the name and religious meaning of each symbol: the four powerful animals, the fifteen auspicious signs, the sun and moon, the decorative letter at the top, the eight trigrams, and so forth. From all this, the crucial elements for him were two inconspicuous Sanskrit mantras written in the Mongolian alphabet specially designed

16. The conviction that the salvific power of writing out the words of the Buddha is an end in itself was given ultimate form in the practice of printing on water. This was a Tibetan practice of slapping down a printed charm on streams and rivers, held to momentarily imprint the water with the Buddha's word and thus distribute blessings (Schaeffer 2009, 19).

for writing Sanskrit. To each of them he again gave a "meaning" that was in fact a purpose: one kept misfortune at bay and another quietened the land and water spirits. The prominent lettering in Tibetan was something he ignored entirely, as if it did not exist.

For Sengge handing out such meanings was, however, only a first step in enabling people to engage in practice that would dispel ignorance. This characteristic of having layers of meaning (and furthermore meaning of different kinds) was found in many objects at Mergen; Sengge would expound such further steps only to people who specially and sincerely sought him out. He gave us the example of the famous six-syllable Mani mantra, *Om Ma Ni Pad Me Hum,* for which the initial meaning is that it is the Heart Mantra of Ariyabalo,[17] which if chanted a minimum seven hundred thousand times will bring rebirth in Ariyalbalo's heaven. The further meaning of the syllables was a key to one elementary step toward self-transformation. They denote, Sengge said, the six types of existence of sentient beings. "Om" stands for those in heaven (*tngri orun*); "ma" is those in the *asuri* region of demi-gods; "ni" is human beings; "bad/pad" is livestock (*mal adugusun*); "me" is *birid,* which are worms and microbes;[18] and "hum" is hell (*tamu*). After death the human soul may be reborn in any of these realms, and what a devotee has to contemplate by sounding each syllable, he said, are the implications of the fact that only human beings have the chance to become conscious of their transience and hence one stage closer to enlightenment and escape from the cycle of rebirths altogether. In such mindful meditation each utterance of the *tarni* is both the mark, and the experience, of cutting attachment to the self that is the true goal of religion.

Most of the time, however, Sengge and the other elderly lamas were occupied with the magically effective aspects of *tarnis*. If we think about decoding mantras what might at first seem obvious—that the sequence "first unread, then read" maps invariably onto the sequence "first ignorance, then knowledge"—is by no means always clear in practice. For example, old lama Galsangochir told us about the *migjim* prayer, which expresses devotion to Tsongkhapa. This consists of five lines in Tibetan, converted by Mergen Gegen into four lines in Mongolian, which are perfectly understandable to lamas and laity alike. However, a common ritual use of the prayer destroys the quality of readability, so only an

17. From S. *arya bala* "possessing the noble powers," Ariyabalo is a Mongolian name for the bodhisattva Avalokiteshvara, the deity of mercy.

18. This was Sengge's idiosyncratic interpretation. *Birid* normally means "hungry ghost."

ontological "effect-meaning" remains. A conversation between lamas indicates how this is done:

Galsangochir: We call it "drinking *sayig*"[19] when you write the *migjim* on paper, burn it, and then put the ashes in water and drink it. This will cure disease and misfortune. It must be done on yellow paper with red ink . . .
Heshigbayar (interrupting): Sometimes you don't even need to write it on the paper, you just chant it in Tibetan and blow it on the paper.
Galsangochir: But only a person who has chanted *migjim* a billion times does not need to write it out.
Heshigbayar: Ah, a million times is also all right!

What this shows is the convertibility, backward and forward, of text into magically powerful ingredient, and of occult receptacles like flags into text. Such written objects are poised in a reversible nexus of the read and the unread, and we see that they can have different realms of operation (devotion to Tsongkhapa, curing disease). Yet for all this multiple character of the text-as-object, the possibility of understanding it (sometime, before, or afterward) is always there, and the person who can comprehend it—or more of it—will always be an authority in relation to the one who cannot. Sengge gave priority to oral over written forms, and in either case he wanted to be the one who knew, but he could not be a miser of knowledge:

Our lamas when they chant, they do it just how our folk speak; they chant *uul*, not *agula* [i.e., the spoken, not the written, pronunciation]. Then people hear it immediately and understand straight away. This is our *dharma*. It is absolutely necessary that the multitude of people and worshippers understand. Our 3rd Mergen Gegen said, "The book I composed—let those people hear by ears, understand in their minds, and worship in their hearts—that is how it must be done." It must be made clear, chant clearly, speak the words clearly. La, la, la is not OK.

His zeal for the spreading of knowledge and his determined assumption of the role of its authoritative arbiter can be related, we think, not only to the Mergen tradition but also to his life as a cadre and his experiences in the Cultural Revolution.

19. *Sayig* is any short text, drawing, or paper cut-out that is burned and the ashes drunk ritually. The rite is not exclusively Buddhist. In the Jirim region the paper cut-out represents a ghost-like spirit called *eliye*, has a human shape and is used to dispel nightmares. This shows that what is imbibed is pure effectiveness, whether that power is beneficent like the *migjim* or troublesome and frightening like the *eliye*.

From "Power Holder" to Knowledgeable Lama

Shortly after returning to his homeland in a leadership position, Sengge was attacked as a "power holder" (*erhe barigchi*), not as a former lama. He explained:

There were several power holders in the village and brigade and we were labeled "black things" (spoken *hara-yum-ud*). But I argued with them [the Red Guards]. I said I had become a cadre when the revolution arrived, but I didn't "exterminate" or "gnaw" [the weak, like other power holders]. Therefore, nothing really bad happened to me till 1968. Earlier there had been "the three don'ts' policy, don't divide, don't struggle, don't classify by class, so there was no (class) division in Urad, and anyway by distribution of land I was a poor agriculturalist. But in 1968 they invented a division into two categories and I was accused of being a herd lord. I had built myself a better house, so they accused me of being a family with property (*yum-tai ail*). I had . . . just two horses, and they called me a herd lord! But again the accusation didn't stick. However in 1969 . . . in late 1968, in the campaign against the *Nei Ren Dang* [the Inner Mongolia People's Party], because I was a cadre and member of the Communist Youth they wanted to squeeze me into it. Then I was continuously struggled. I was beaten, insulted. But that also turned into nothing. Later, they rehabilitated me. I was not punished as a lama, because although I was a lama I wasn't a 'power-holder lama.'" Ha. Ha, ha. That was people above the rank of *gebhüi*. They were beaten.

If the Communist era had transformed Sengge from a talented young lama into an authoritative local leader, the anti–*Nei Ren Dang* campaign undid any coherence his leadership might have had. By pushing him into the artificial category of "herd lord" and above all by punishing him as a "power holder," it confirmed him as an important man while alienating him from the very authority, the state, that had defined him in these ways. He was replaced in the brigade by a new generation of radical leaders (themselves soon supplanted as the waves of political reform hit Urad), but he did not lose the ability—almost perhaps the habit—of taking charge in local events. Yet, he was unnerved politically by this experience. Sengge never spoke against the government and if any such likelihood came up in our conversations he would change the subject. His vocabulary was shot through with communist language.[20]

20. For example, before his quarrel with Chorji, Sengge would say that some endeavor in the monastery had been undertaken "under the leadership of Chorji Teacher" (*Chorji Bagshi-yin*

However, if he had ever been a convinced communist, his demotion and above all the decision to become a lama again cut him off from that massive and collective power-praxis. His reversion to his earlier religious convictions also made the China-wide transformation of value after the mid-1990s into the rationalized, monetized, and computable (Liu 2009, 180) anathema to him. In a life that had spanned from the embattled dukes to mobile-phone toting monks, many diverse ways of thinking had been laid before him, and perhaps in all this he was aware first of all of his responsibility to himself. About his secret chanting of the prayer of the Deity of the White Umbrella, he said to us, "I don't know if it was effective. But other people committed suicide by hanging, or slit their throats, and at least I did not reach that point."

The kind of loss that tortured Sengge as the years went by was not just the destruction of his monastery and its sacred objects and books, but also the fear that memory (his own and that of the other lamas) would not hold out. This is why the crucial recording of the Mergen liturgy at Badgar Monastery in 1983 (see p 246), felt to be so dangerous at the time, was for Sengge something necessary if the tradition was to survive at all. For him this was a heroic and foundational feat. With the precious chanting secure on tape, it was possible to ask: "How can we do the lama's work again?" For the lay patron Sechingge, the ashes of his uncle the 8th Mergen Gegen had been central to his campaign to outwit the officials and reestablish the monastery. For Sengge Lama the ashes were also important, but they paled before the sign from Heaven-Sky (the blowing down of the army wall) and the lamas' re-mastery of the sacred chants—for these were techniques of power. They gave a beaten people, and he himself, a means of being able to have effect in the world.

Sengge had an acute sense that there should be a *complete* range of powerful interjections from the monastery generated by the services through the year. This is why he was upset by the continued absence of certain lost texts that no one had perfectly in their memory, both those missing from Mergen Gegen's published *Bum Jarlig* and others. The prayers should benefit the whole and actual world around, spreading out to include the nonbelievers. Sengge was therefore pleased at one process that happened over the years of our fieldwork, the rediscovery or return of objects that had disappeared during the Cultural

---

uduridalga dor), using the communist expression for "leadership." Sengge often duplicated Chinese and Mongol expressions as a way of making himself clear, as if it had become a habit to talk this way to dim subordinates.

Revolution. In general scraps of sacred texts and broken parts of statues retain some power and protective function. We were told that in earlier times they had been put inside the shrines (*sach*) built by Mergen Gegen at the four corners of the monastery and the *sach* to guard again the Human Stone. Soon there was a plenitude of such relics. No one knew what to do with them, as Mergen Gegen's shrines had not been rebuilt. In one corner of the Officers' Mess lay a heap of delicately carved plaster ears, arms, and drapery. Jongrai Lama made another cache in a hole in a cliff by the Mergen riverbed. Here the broken statues shared space with scorpions, which Jongrai lifted away gently, for a lama would not kill any creature. All such remnants were in a kind of limbo.

More visible were piles of old wooden lattice window frames, gray bricks, and decorated beams that had been part of destroyed buildings. The piles got bigger each time we visited Mergen, and some *oboos* in the region were also piled high with such objects. These were items returned by people who had looted the abandoned monastery for building materials. When misfortune happened in such families, it was attributed to spiritual retribution for having committed the sin of stealing from a monastery. The pieces were returned as a sign of regret. Lamas were asked to pray for these repentant families to avert future misfortunes, and of course the elderly monks were rather pleased that the aggression against them was acknowledged by at least some people. True, they said, it is likely that such returns were made when people were rebuilding their houses and the items were no longer useful—such as when new glass windows made the old lattice frames redundant. Nevertheless, Sengge said, it would have been easier to burn the old frames than to transport them to the monastery, and so there was evidence of genuine repentance. The returned pieces lay abandoned and open to view. Nothing was done with them, and yet for the lamas they were visible proof of the religious feeling raised by their prayers among the lay population.

Factions and Divergent Orientations

After the storming of the fallen wall in 1986, some thirty-four lamas from different monasteries became Mergen monks. The Western Great Lama was the only *hubilgan* (reincarnation) left, but he had been trained with the Tibetan liturgy in Ordos and had little influence. So it was decided to recall Mönghebatu, the Chorji reincarnation, who had been recognized shortly before the government policy changed in 1958. Although now living a lay life, he *was* still a reincarnation. When Mönghebatu took up this invitation he was a comparatively young man and had not yet acquired total control of the monastery.

The lamas salted into three major factions based on their previous affiliations at Mergen, Güng, Jirgaltu, or other monasteries. The issue was (as in the "orchestra" we discussed in the Introduction): which group's selective vision of the tradition could prevail in how services were to be done? By the beginning of the 1990s the leader of the Mergen group was Boroheshig, who was the Da Lama, but his mild character and weakness at chanting reduced his authority. The influential and knowledgeable Oruwa Lama was also in the Mergen group (though he soon died); as briefly was Galluu, whose education, musical talent, and theatrical flair made him stand out. The Jirgaltu group was led by Heshigdalai, who became Leader of Chanting (*umjad*). His ability, advanced age and Buddhist learning made him respected by everyone. Meanwhile, the Güng Monastery lamas thought they were the best qualified of all, as their monastery had supported a faculty (*rasang*) studying the Lam-Rim in Tibetan, a facility that was present at neither Mergen nor Jirgaltu. The knowledgeable, energetic Galsangochir led the Güng group in its competition with the Jirgaltu lamas.

Sengge was rather senior among the Jirgaltu lamas, being a disciple and also the nephew of their leader Heshigdalai. This guru apparently criticized Sengge for not living quietly in the monastery but taking time off to conduct rituals for the laity and more generally for saying and doing what he wanted. As very few of the lamas lived full time in the monastery—almost all had households elsewhere—and few of them were either able or willing to carry out laypeople's rituals, these accusations are difficult to explain except in terms of different values and kinds of authority. Sengge's idea of the "the Mergen tradition" was more extensive than that of the other lamas. Whether it was the Communist experience or his own herding background, Sengge respected and was at ease with humble, non-literate people. At the same time, his career as a cadre had made him accustomed to taking charge; his relatively successful confrontations in the Cultural Revolution made him argumentative. He had become independent, not capable of buckling down to rigid monastic discipline, even to the authority of his teacher and uncle. This should not be thought of as a mere incident of personality—but a particular kind of character formation of the times.

The rivalry between the three groups eventuated in the exclusion of the energetic Galluu in the early 1990s along with his talented nephew

Sodnom, pretender to the throne of Mergen Gegen.[21] The dominating Chorji took charge among the Mergen lamas, as we discuss in the next chapter. Soon the elderly Güng lamas faded in significance and their leaders died. This left two groups: Mergen and Jirgaltu. The former had the advantage: this was their home monastery and furthermore they had indisputable higher sanctity on their side, the Western Great and Chorji Reincarnations. The Jirgaltu lamas, on the other hand, now led by Sengge, were definitely better at chanting the tradition.

Sengge, a non-reincarnate lama, was ambivalent about the preexisting sanctity of the *hubilgan*, and he hardly mentioned the powers and blessings the reincarnations are able to dispense. This attitude may be related to the fact that throughout his life he had never been a disciple of a reincarnation and in any case had been tempered by his internal rejection of fiats of any kind. But because the reproducing of old custom was his guiding principle, the stand-off with the Chorji Reincarnation put him in a difficult situation.[22] Often he downplayed the single defining feature of the reincarnation, which is that the *hubilgan* is born with the "soul"(*sünesü*) of an earlier holy being. When asked how the *hubilgan* is different from an ordinary lama he replied only that he has higher rank ("he sits on a higher seat") and when pressed further he said:

> Yes, the ordinary disciple prostrates before the reincarnated lama . . . when he is sitting in his chair in the temple, and when he comes back from a journey. You cannot *not* call him "teacher," even if you are more learned than him. Our Chorji Bagshi knows absolutely nothing about the meaning of Buddhism—but I who know and chant the doctrine, I cannot not call him "teacher." That is the custom.

Sengge said later that ignorant lamas, including reincarnations, are called wild (*jerlig*, like wild animals). And they are dangerous, because just as their good deeds spread merit, their careless or stupid words disperse sin. There are more sins of the tongue than sins of the body, he said.

One day as we sat talking with Sengge there was a telephone call from the mother of one of the young lamas dismissed the year before.

21. Galluu's pulling out of the expedition to Badgar to record the Mergen liturgy (see p 246) was a reason given by Sengge and Chorji for their antipathy toward him, while both would also have been challenged by the fact that Galluu combined talent at chanting with membership of Mergen Gegen's *sang*.

22. Sengge told us once that the 5th Chorji had saved his life when he was a young lama and that he therefore still respected the present life of the Chorji as 6th Chorji, but not as Mönghebatu the man.

Her son wanted to come back to Mergen and study to be a lama. Sengge told her that he was no longer living at the monastery. "In that case I will not go there," was evidently the reply. Sengge, who was not rich, said that if the boy came to live with him in the village there would be a problem about upkeep. "I am willing to pay for my son's food and expenses," the mother declared. Sengge then replied that he would still have to think about whether to accept the disciple. "You see," he said to the mother, "Mergen Monastery also needs lamas. I should not take pupils at the expense of the monastery. I would be accused, and I should not do it." Evidently, Sengge was still half-loyal to Mergen Monastery.

The Past and the Abyss of Future Time

Let us contrast here the attitudes to the past of Sengge Lama and Professor Naranbatu, who is a former lama of Güng Monastery. We shall suggest that Sengge felt loss, to be sure, but he was not nostalgic for the past, whereas Naranbatu frequently expresses the epitome of Inner Mongolian sadness for what has passed away. The monasteries of their youth are no more: Sengge's Jirgaltu is a jumble of stones; Naranbatu's Güng was erased from the face of the earth. Some army barracks were built nearby using the bricks.

Marilyn Ivy defines nostalgia as "an ambivalent longing to erase the temporal difference between subject and the object of desire, shot through with not only the impossibility but also the ultimate unwillingness to reinstate what was lost" (1995, 10). Such a longing and unwillingness, we feel, was foreign to Sengge: he was not concerned to draw closer to the past but rather tried with all his might to turn the contemporary into a present that encompassed past occurrences as integral to itself. Cyclical recurrence was dominant in his thinking and his life. The sacrifice to the Jirgaltu battle standard had to happen on the prescribed date because that was the date it had always happened, and it had to be done in the same way as before because that was the right way to do it. For Sengge, the ongoing present should have this repetitive character, and therefore new happenings whatever they might be (a death, building a new temple, a drought) were to be fitted into sequences and explained ultimately by the same kinds of causes as previous happenings.[23] The present had to be dealt with, battled, its jag-

23. It was characteristic of Sengge that he reckoned months and years in the twelve-year animal lunar cycle and did not bother to keep common linear time firmly in his grasp. When we

ged edges brought into fitting shape by bringing about holy protection and excluding further disaster. This was done first of all by chanting but also by the array of daily-life rituals and techniques at Sengge's command.

Sengge, as best he could, produced these endlessly necessary spiritual adjustments for the people around Mergen. His ritual services for the laity were provided at the district level (for example the annual Shira Oroi sacrifice), at the valley level (the local offerings to Muna and sacred springs), and for individual households. The main services for households were: divination, funerals, *gürim* (a variety of rites to avert, repel, or exorcise misfortune), sacrifices and animal consecrations, *namanchilal* (confession of sins, begging forgiveness), incense offerings (*sang*) and purifications. These rituals for laity simply cannot be done without a lama, and in the Mergen region Sengge was that essential person. He traveled tirelessly from place to place, on buses, walking, taking a lift, sometimes collected by the households in borrowed car, his bag of texts on his back. Managing all these activities together with attending the services at the monastery was Sengge's life. Jirgaltu was a distant memory. What was important was the capacity to keep this whole range of services going for the people who needed them, and the loss that was important was the absence of any given technique or text that should have been put to the task.

Over the years, we became aware that Sengge had a deep anxiety, the sense that he might not be able to pass on what he knew. The ideas we described earlier, that contemplation of different kinds of rebirth would lead to awareness and understanding, that knowledge could be converted to efficacy and back again, and the necessity of cyclical recurrence of ritual actions to reiterate Buddhist goodness, all predicate articulations between knowledge and time. Now for Sengge along with other Buddhists this current era is acknowledged to be a "time of decline" in which it would be unlikely for great truths to be discovered. But he seems also to have sensed something more disturbing than that standard Buddhist notion, the unnerving thought that time (*chag*) was not replacing itself. The following incident illustrates this.

One evening in 2005 Hürelbaatar had asked some laypeople who had come for the Mani service if he could record them singing the songs of Mergen Gegen. Sengge wandered in, sat down, and said about one favorite song, "In the summer evenings everyone used to gather

asked him which year something happened, he would reply, "It was in the Horse Year—work it out for yourself."

outside their houses and the women came out and sang [this song] to the moon." At this remark, everyone swung into the song loudly and heartily. Now this may sound like typical nostalgia, but we suggest that in this case it was not. No sad distance from the past was being expressed; that night the moon *was* shining at Mergen and the villagers were singing as people had previously sung on such evenings. Then, the talk turned to teaching morality through such songs, and suddenly everyone realized that *this* was not now happening. The song's message could not be passed on.

"Present-day children drink, and speak lewd words in front of their parents."

"When we were small, we could not even look at our parents. If you did, they called you up and said, 'Come here. What are you looking at? Get out!'"

"They would twist your ear!"

"Cuff you." Everyone laughed.

'"Press a thumb on the vein in the neck! Then the children can't speak, can't move," Sengge joined in.

"That's a trick they use in martial arts," someone said. "You can kill someone that way." More pealing laughter.

"A joke?" said Sengge. "But it's true."

"So, Sengge, now you can conquer them all with your martial arts!" someone called out, and the whole room now collapsed in laughter. Sengge admitted, "Well, you have to laugh." But then in response to this vision of the older generation almost killing their children in order to make them listen obediently, he suddenly said something that is very difficult to translate: "The present time-generation (*chag üye*) does not fit the time-generation."[24] The phrase *chag üye* is not a standard one in Mongol[25] and by this pairing Sengge seems to been trying to express the idea of time (*chag*) as a series of generations (*üye*, period, joint, generations of people). In effect what he was saying was that the present cycle of (physical, human) generations jars against the metaphysically defined cycles of time—an intimation even, that cyclical time itself can no longer be presumed.

Derrida's *Specters of Marx* notes that Hamlet says "The time is out of joint" precisely at the moment when the prince becomes aware of the injunction from the father (the ghost) and his own unreadiness

24. *Odu chini chag üy-e chag üye-tei-ben tagarahu ügei.*

25. It may however have been Sengge's translation of the Chinese *shi dai* (era, literally time generation).

to carry it out ("Oh cursed spite/That ever I was born to set it right!") (Derrida 2006, 24). In Hamlet, the son regrets acquiring the father's mantle of repressive authority. But Sengge, even with his partial knowledge (but what knowledge is ever other than partial) and his incomplete empowerments further docked by loss, was like the father in Mergen's familial polity of knowledge. This conversation brought him up sharp to the abyss—that in the passing on of everything he held most valuable there might be no one to receive, no heir. To make them ready to receive the children would have to be punished almost to death. But this was already impossible, which was why everyone laughed so heartily—a laughter in which Sengge's voice could be heard distinctly saying, "A joke? But it's true!"

Sengge was "mindful of death," and at least in what he said to us this was less a concern about his own rebirth than a sad anticipation that merged his own death with that of the Mergen tradition.

I don't know much, but the lamas are very few now. Not many know the doctrine. Not many can chant adequately. It is a pity, what our Mergen Gegen translated, put so much great effort into, composed, all those things are dwindling away. They [the heroic lamas of the past] died in battle; they have become absent. Even the trace (*oru mür*—footprint track) of what they did—it is good. But I too, how long will I live? I am over seventy years old. Ha, ha, ha. [We] must die. . . . A person who becomes old must place his history in safekeeping (*teühe-ben hadagalana*).

Meanwhile, Sengge was making practical plans. Having left Mergen, he addressed the officials of the Qianqi Bureau of Religious Affairs with the request that they provide him and the other elderly lamas with a monastery and upkeep in the West Banner.[26] They had apparently been willing. In 2001 Sengge was mulling over the possibilities. He was planning to take his worshipped objects from Mergen and establish them somewhere else. But where? There was a temple left at the small Urta Goul Monastery, but it was abandoned, had no living accommodation and no lamas attached to it. Then there was Deveseg, but it is located far into the mountains and reachable only by a rocky track that becomes impassable whenever it rains. Furthermore, two reincarnations were attached there, which would put Sengge again in the situation of

26. After the reorganization of 1958, Mergen found itself in the Baotou municipality which paid for the upkeep of Mergen monastery and the salaries of the original Mergen lamas only. This excluded people like Sengge, who were registered where their family houses were located, in the West Banner. Chorji therefore had an official reason not to pay Sengge and others for their services.

having to prostrate before people of higher rank. Both of these alternatives were unattractive for an elderly monk: the monasteries were decrepit, without heating, and Deveseg with no laity apart from a few shepherds in the vicinity would be difficult to supply with food. The final possibility was more speculative. A Chan Buddhist monk now living in America had secured himself land to build a temple at Qianqi town, and it was rumored that a Mongol temple would be built alongside. Perhaps in a year or two Sengge could settle there.

In the meantime Sengge was occupying himself with his legacy. "The most important thing," he said, "is fidelity (*ünenchü*) to Buddha. . . . I may not live long. Before I die, I must bequeath my share (*hubi*) [of my knowledge]. What am I doing now? I am recording cassettes." We have mentioned that Mongol reincarnate lamas often felt the need to "vow" how and where their next incarnation would take place. Sengge's equivalent projection into the future was the bequeathing of his knowledge. He had no choice but to act as if there would be an appropriate receiver, as if the abyss did not exist. By now he knew his knowledge and skill had a value, as he had been asked several times to make recordings by lamas and academics. But he did not have these tapes, and, most importantly, the precious Badgar recordings had disappeared into the keeping of Sechingge and his family. Now Sengge would create his legacy for himself. He told us, "I have already recorded over twenty cassettes, and another fifty or sixty at least will be needed. The lama's whole liturgy, chanting method, rhythms, melodies, how to sing tunes, I am chanting it there, I am describing how to make all the hand gestures that even Galluu doesn't know. Today, I'm fine. Maybe tomorrow, I'll be gone. If I leave this life, I'll bequeath this small thing to my grandson (pointing to Nasunbayar), telling him: 'Don't give it just anyhow to lamas! In the future, if scholars come, you may show them these recordings—take them out and play them and let them listen. And make them understand what it really means.'"

What is a bequest? If we make a comparison with money, which changes its character when it is conceived not as something liquid and generally available but as "a legacy," we can see a similar transformation with knowledge. Sengge's knowledge was no longer something to be spent, to be given away to anyone. It would become a bequest, defined and guarded, that must be handed intact to *someone* in the next generation, someone who must also keep it as an entity. The entire character of such knowledge changes when it is set in such a new relation to the surrounding social world.

Sengge was planning to take the Jirgaltu and other non-Mergen lamas with him to his new establishment. When we left in 2002, it looked as though Mergen Monastery was about to split apart. However, this did not quite happen. Chorji's interest was involved here: he needed a leading lama to keep the services going, for otherwise the Baotou government was quite capable of closing the monastery and converting it to some other purpose. He even briefly resorted to a plan, he told us, to bring back Galluu, despite the challenge this might present to his own leadership. In the end Chorji swallowed his pride and begged Sengge to return, offering him the title of Da Lama. Sengge agreed, and what happened next will become clear in the following chapters.

EIGHT

The Chorji Lama: Inheriting from the Past in a New World

Introduction 2002

One way the notion of tradition can be understood is through successive acts of endowing and inheriting. This chapter attempts to deepen understanding of the actor caught between irreconcilable demands from the past by conceptualizing such an actor as an heir. In moving from Sengge to Chorji, we move from the person who bequeaths to the one who inherits. Sengge had made himself into someone who had something to endow, but he had not been born into a patrimony; he did not know his father, and from his mother he received only her love of singing. Matters were quite otherwise with Mönghebatu, the Chorji Lama. From early childhood he was singled out as an heir, and furthermore in at least two different ways: he was the eldest son of Sechingge, born in the noble family that had become Mergen Monastery's most important patron, and he was the 6th incarnation of the lineage of Chorji Lamas.

Anthropology has classically addressed inheritance by examining the rights of successors in different cultures: who can inherit and what property they receive, and how this relates to the reproduction of social institutions (Goody 1973, 3–20). More recent work has pointed out that questions of inheritance reflect and generate complex moral as well as material interests.[1] As Michael Gilsenan writes, "Inheritance practices are one means of sustaining (or denying) what are regarded as proper relations between the living, and between the living and the community of the dead" (2011, 356). Along with these themes, this chapter will address the more psychological question of *what it means* to be an heir for a Mongolian Buddhist. In Indic-Buddhist traditions heritage is not an idea limited to material property or social status; ancient Pali usage is concerned also with being the heir to one's own deeds (karma) and the heir to a spiritual tradition. These early Buddhist ideas thus raise the question of the heir's relation to the past in a more general way, a past that not only changes from each perspective of the present,[2] but also suggests that each action in the present—becoming immediately the past—should be oriented to its consequences (the future). There is thus a future for the past (Shrimali 1998, 26–30).

These ideas, so central to Buddhism, find a distant echo in the work of Derrida (2006), who reminds us that to inherit is always to shoulder a responsibility of some kind. This means that the heir's orientation toward the future is always caught up (dragged back) into the entanglements of the past. For the duty taken on stems from the will—the willing—of those whose legacy one inherits ("the injunction"). Enigmatically Derrida remarks, "One never inherits without coming to terms with some specter, and therefore with more than one. With the fault but also the injunction of more than one" (ibid, 24). The "more than one" here seems to refer to the opaqueness of any inheritance, the difficulty of knowing what the injunction really was, who and where it came from, and the need for the heir to sort out several different possible lines of action that inhabit the same legacy. Derrida's generalization can be concretized in the following question. How, in effect, should that plurality be narrowed and divided in order to make it actable by heirs ("to carry out the duty") *now,* in a time different from the past? In the last chapter we referred to the lamas of Mergen filtering the possibilities of the legacy of "Mergen Gegen," choosing in effect what to reproduce as the tradition of the monastery. Here we address the dilemmas of inheritance as they fell upon one individual, Chorji Lama.

1. For a subtle extended analysis of the noble heir in relation to ethical technologies of the self, see Faubion 2011, 122–202.

2. "The Buddha, in his numerous discourses, never failed to underline the varied moveable voices of the past. At one given moment in time, the past is one thing; at the next moment, it is another. In that space between any two moments, things have been added to and deleted from the past" (Shrimali 1998, 29).

Derrida, alluding to Hamlet and his father's ghost, calls the necessity of coming to terms with the specter "the originary wrong, the birth wound from which he [the heir] suffers, [. . .] an irreparable tragedy, the indefinite malediction that marks the history of the law or history as law. That "time is out of joint" is what is also attested by birth itself when it dooms someone to be the man of right and law only by becoming an inheritor, redresser of wrongs, that is, only by castigating, punishing, killing." (2006, 24–25). Now Derrida's pronouncement stems from quite different preoccupations from ours, notably the Judaic kernel of the father-son relation projected and expanded through the idea of Marxism as the heritage of a political idea that lingers on in the twentieth century. Yet Derrida's merging of the personal and the social-political is illuminating here. In the case of Mönghebatu, the current Chorji, he inherited not so much an injunction to redress one singular wrong in the past, but rather a curdled mass of disturbed and truncated legacies from several sources: those of his father, Sechingge, of his predecessor the 5th Chorji Lama, and of his great-uncle the 8th Mergen Gegen. Mönghebatu has had to choose among these—though "choose" seems somehow a word too light, too suggestive of freedom, for the decisions he has had to make. The "irreparable tragedy" in his case was that his early life during the Cultural Revolution cut him off from a Buddhist education. Born some twenty years after Sengge Lama and after the Communist Liberation of Inner Mongolia, he belonged to a different, socialist-educated, generation. In other words, not only was he heir to diverse legacies that were difficult to reconcile, but he was cut adrift from what mattered most in his monastery: the Mergen liturgy, which he never managed to master.

Incompatible demands have almost torn Mönghebatu apart as a person. His youth saw him reduced in the Cultural Revolution to a piteous "red bloodsucker"[3] excluded from society as a member of a formerly privileged family and a high lama. In later years, but only after having been ground through the harsh machine of socialist punishment, he was restored to local prominence and became the master (*ejen*) of Mergen Monastery. Today, Chorji has a realm under his control, a certain power to exercise, the possibility of carrying out responsibilities, of redressing wrongs. Yet the world around the monastery is utterly changed from that of his youth: the reviling of religion and the stark,

3. *Ulagan horuhai* "red worm," a type of bloodsucking insect; used as an insult during the Cultural Revolution to refer to Buddhist lamas, alluding both to their living off the work of others and the red color of their garments.

hungry communes have been replaced by commercialism, urbanization, migrating populations, changing laws, shifting administrative boundaries, rapid ecological degradation of the land around Mergen, as well as a government prepared to support approved kinds of religion as promoting harmony in society. Even the contours of marriage and seniority within families have changed in significant ways. In this chapter we trace Chorji's sometimes tortured, sometimes triumphant, path amid these uncertainties.

Derrida's suggestion that the inheritor is doomed to be the man of "right and law" suggests certain lines of enquiry. Centrally, one needs to ask: what kind of "law" might this be? We shall argue that Chorji, and the people around Mergen in general, had no alternative in the historical turbulence of modern China but to take action in their own way—"action," that is, not as a colorless abstract but imbued throughout, soaked, in their own Mongol ideas of justice, fate and fortune. The political and ideological changes have been too contradictory and too rapid for external ideas of law or rights (from China or elsewhere in the world) to eliminate these Mongol values. Rather, the latter persist as threads contributing to the practical operation of diverse kinds of modern laws and discourses. Schein has written about the modern as a structure of feeling within China: "People not only position themselves vis-à-vis modernity through multifarious practices, but also struggle to reposition themselves, sometimes through deploying the very codes of the modern that have framed them as its others" (1999, 363–64). Another way to put this is to say that lying within any "modern" public action vis-à-vis the outside world there are both ancient and recent personal or collective ideas and feelings that, from an inchoate mixture, are channeled in a particular direction in order to achieve success. What was always present in our fieldwork was the idea of the non-neutrality of any act. People were not referring only to Buddhist ideas of *karma*, but through intimations of vengeance, shame, punishment, as so forth, to some other, deeper, inherited, and less explicit notions of what is right and just. It is because Chorji so often invoked his responsibility, "what he had to do," as an explanation for what he in fact did, and its frequently bruising character, that Derrida's musings about the duty of the heir are so relevant. It seems to us that in Chorji's view, he is fated to be such a man, an heir, and wielder of right and law. Mergen Monastery has not ceased to be a place of passion and intrigue and Chorji's "castigating and punishing" made his subjects often absent themselves, sometimes even flee in droves. Yet we surmise that, in tacit acknowledgement of that elusive sense of justice just referred to, while people in Urad railed against him they understood and did not utterly condemn him.

Sechingge's legacy to his son was contradictory; but let us first indicate to readers its main thrust as told to us by his wife Nabchin and her sons:

> He [Sechingge] had a special valor (*gabiya*) and zeal (*jidgül*). He showed great ardor, for Mergen Monastery. He played a great role for the revival of the lama religion, he stood up to the army, he raised an official suit with the Baotou government. He spent such a lot of money and he did much for the inviting of the Chorji. The whole onward progress of the monastery was initiated by our father. These things he did in faith as his lot (*hubi*). He was anxious about the disappearance of Mongol Buddhism; he wanted success in continuing this Mongolian tradition, which is so beautiful. He wanted to keep Mongolian history.

The Familial Nexus

Had social relations remained as they were before Liberation, Mönghebatu would have been the heir in a rich and noble (*taiji*) family. His great-grandfather in the male line was the wealthy Erhimmanglai, deputy administrator (*tusalagchi*) in the Urad West Banner. Erhimmanglai had two sons by his senior wife: the eldest was recognized to be the 8th Mergen Gegen, did not marry, and had no descendants. The second was Chagan Lama, Mönghebatu's grandfather. "Chagan Lama" was his personal name; he was not a lama and "his whole life was hunting," we were told. Chagan Lama's only son was Sechingge, and Mönghebatu is the eldest son of Sechingge's first wife. So by traditional criteria Mönghebatu is indisputable heir of Sechingge's social status.[4] This skeleton of descent does not, however, reveal the changed social meaning of these relations brought about in twentieth-century history.

Erhimmanglai must have been a devout person: an elder of the Haranuud clan, which had its own *oboo* near Mergen, he was not only head of the birth family (*törhüm*) of a reincarnation, but his other sons

4. In Mongolian *öb jalgamijlagchi* is the successor or inheritor, a slightly formal word that applies to both material and immaterial assets. In kinship contexts people talk of a legacy or share of household property as *öb*, a will or testament as *geriyesü*, and the inheritor of a domestic household as *gal golumta-yin ejen* (fire hearth master, usually the youngest son). The successor to inherited political office, however, was the eldest son, a principle only by-passed if this son was incapable. In that case the succession could pass to a younger brother or to a second son (Jagchid and Hyer 1979, 253–54).

were also called Lama—his third and fourth sons, who were born of his second wife, were named Shira Lama and Ulagan Lama. The *törhüm* relation, as mentioned in Chapter 3, put the whole family in a lasting alliance with Mergen Monastery—and in particular with the Mergen Gegen *sang,* which paid Erhimmanglai a "bride price" (the "nine whites" referred to earlier) to acquire the young 8th Mergen Gegen around 1903. As nephew of a Gegen, Sechingge might well have been expected to follow his uncle's footsteps into the monastery, an established practice in Urad as it was elsewhere in the monastic world of Inner Asia. However, Sechingge was also the only son and heir, and fathers of political position frequently resisted giving up their only sons to the monastery. As described earlier, Sechingge was to become patriarch of a large family and the chief lay patron of Mergen Monastery.

Sometime in the early 1950s Sechingge left his first wife, mother of Mönghebatu and his younger brother and sister, and married Nabchin, who already had two sons of her own. Sechingge and Nabchin then had three sons. This made a wonderful large family of eight children, as Nabchin told us. But she was thinking in terms of an older patriarchal pattern in which polygamy and the ranking of first and subsequent wives was accepted. After the Communist takeover, marriage laws changed.[5] According to this law, Sechingge *divorced* his first wife and legally married his second. This put Mönghebatu and his siblings in an uncertain position, caught between earlier Mongol norms and the new law. They were doubly bereft when their mother remarried—they were brought up in effect by their grandmother (Sechingge's mother). Meanwhile, Mönghebatu was recognized as the Chorji Lama.

At this time in the early 1950s monks were flooding out of the monastery, the 8th Mergen Gegen was mostly absent on official duty, and most of the *sangs* could not afford to bring in new reincarnations. The 5th Chorji died in 1950, and his *sang* being in relatively good shape, a search was instituted for the next incumbent. In 1953 the monks collected the names of thirteen boys, all born in the Hare Year along the Muna Mountain chain. With two other lamas, Boroheshig, who was

5. The Marriage Law of 1950 forbade polygamy and concubinage, and the Marriage Registration Regulations of 1955 stipulated that couples must register their marriages legally. Buyan told us that Urad Mongols accepted the change in law with enthusiasm. There was a "fashion" for divorce and remarriage in the 1950s. During the Great Leap Forward and the Cultural Revolution the family was attacked as an institution inappropriate to socialist society. However, this project was rapidly abandoned and a series of laws in the 1980s and 1990s have regulated marriage, inheritance, adoption, divorce, women's rights, the single-child policy, etc. (see Palmer 1995, 110–34).

the *soibong* of the Chorji *sang*, the lama charged with taking care of the reincarnation, took the sealed names to Kumbum Monastery in Qinghai. Here prayers were chanted for the whole winter of 1953–1954, and finally a single name was selected by the Kumbum high lamas by means of drawing sticks from the Golden Vessel (*Altan Bumba*). When the three lamas came back to Mergen they opened the sealed package and it was revealed that Mönghebatu was the next Chorji. Sechingge, however, had already become a cadre and refused to give his son. He was persuaded by Communist officials, who told him, "If you do not hand over your son you are not following state religious policy."[6] Evidently Sechingge (although he had remarried or was about to remarry) considered Mönghebatu to be his heir, and he made three stipulations: that if he had no other son, Mönghebatu would leave the monastery and inherit the family property; that at the age of eight he would cease studying Buddhist sutras and learn "[communist] party texts" (*Eb Hamtu Nam-un bichig*), and when he reached eighteen he would be given the choice whether to become a cadre or return to be a lama. This history, told us by Chorji as a firmly established explanation, was an entirely appropriate response from a party cadre. Chorji himself fully approves of his father's stipulations. "You see, becoming a reincarnate lama is like a girl who leaves her own family and is given to another one," he once said with a hint that this was not the manly path he would have personally chosen. Meanwhile, a vague suspicion that his selection as a *hubilgan* was not entirely god-given hovered around in the way people talked. And knowing the history of Mergen, where the duke's kin had so regularly provided reincarnations over the centuries, the fact that one family should be *törhüm* to two reincarnations fits the pattern.

Still, whatever the hidden agendas, the situation should have been clear: Mönghebatu was handed over from the realm of one master, his father, to that of another, the 8th Mergen Gegen who was master (*ejen*) of the monastery. But Sechingge's stipulations muddied the water. By insisting that his son was both recallable to heirship in the family and had his own opt out he undermined the rights of the monastery and Mönghebatu's identity as Chorji Lama. This bifurcation of iden-

6. The United Front Policy was aimed at integrating preexisting political and religious elites, allowing some expression of national minority interests while co-opting representatives selected for their loyalty. For discussion of this policy as it affected the Tibetan female reincarnation Dorje Phagmo, whose experiences in many ways paralleled those of Chorji, see Diemberger (2008, 154–62).

tity would have been a difficult enough situation for any young boy to manage, but Sechingge's remarriage complicated matters further. If Mönghebatu did decide on a lay career it was far from certain that he would become *the* heir, since his traditional rights as first son of the first wife were soon compromised by the birth of three younger half-brothers to whom the new state law might give precedence. The domestic impasse was soon (in the 1960s) to be rendered almost irrelevant by the eradication of all familial property. But Mönghebatu could not simply turn to the Chorji role as an alternative, for that was shortly to be blocked off too.

Mönghebatu as Young Chorji Reincarnation

No occult signs attended the birth of Mönghebatu; nor was he tested for miraculous recognition of holy items belonging to the previous Chorji, as had once been common in such situations. We were told only one curious fact that linked the earlier incarnation to Mönghebatu. It seems that the 5th Chorji had been a singularly ugly man with a dark face pitted with smallpox scars. He was also a drinker. Toward the end of his life he made a will (*irügel*) that his next incarnation would be a well-favored person with the regular beautiful face of a Buddha. Mönghebatu, as everyone around Mergen recognizes, is a handsome man and fulfills this injunction splendidly. This reincarnation link of physical *opposites*, via the will of the 5th Chorji, contrasts with the inheritance by the heir of physical traits within the family. Mönghebatu, like it or not, had a very similar shape of head, body weight, and voice to his formidable father Sechingge. Even his intonation and flashes of charm are similar. Because of this, whatever the relations between father and son, he could not escape being the heir of his father in the eyes of all those who knew them both.

Mönghebatu was given the lama name Ishiperenleijamsu when he entered the monastery at the age of five. He was cared for by the *soibong* Boroheshig whom he remembers with fondness. "When I think about it now, Boroheshig Lama really loved me; he went everywhere with me, he fed me, he used to carry me on his shoulders." Chorji lived at Mergen for three years. He "sat in services" and he remembers blessing devotees by touching their heads with an implement with a dragon's head handle, but he learned little from his three teachers ("I was too young"). He left at the age of eight, as his father had ordered, to go to a state school. Referring to his lack of knowledge of Buddhism, he once said, "If I had studied *nom* (doctrine) at the time, I would not now have to rely on Sengge, go begging to him."

After his return to the monastery Chorji had little interest in his previous incarnations and could not remember what Boroheshig told him about them. It was from other people that we learned about the 5th Chorji and the miraculous effects generated by his meditation.[7] Chorji said about the discovery of himself as *hubilgan* that he did not know what it would look like from a religious point of view, but speaking simply it was just a matter of whose child was hit upon. About the future, he told us he had no idea whether he would be reincarnated or not:

> Ha, ha, if you ask Galluu or Sengge, they'll always have something to say. If religion develops, then the people themselves will choose someone and the party and government will see to it. If I see any relation between the reincarnation and religion, it is that the *hubilgan* is worshipped. The Chinese call him "Living Buddha," but that is a lie. It's a fake. In reality it is just a title. They give you this name and elevate you and make you mysterious. In Tibet the one chosen as Living Buddha is trained, so the *hubilgan* is a person with really good knowledge of Buddhism and he becomes a true servant of religion. Apart from that, there's nothing.

Chorji—though remember he was speaking to a foreigner—was a reincarnation who was unsure whether he believed in reincarnation or not. Later chapters will show that this was not the entire picture. Meanwhile, we can get some idea about the conditions that led to the expression of such ideas from looking at his life history after he left the monastery.

Seared and Expelled in the Cultural Revolution

Re-entering lay life Chorji became a schoolboy at the Bayanhua state school not far from Mergen. He was a thin, silent, peaceable boy, his schoolmate Buyan recalls, very different from the man he has become.

7. Ishichoimpel, the 5th Chorji, took part in the summer retreat meditations in the mountains (Mönghe 1996, 60). He was also good at divination. An elderly Chinese man, Fu, told us that the 5th Chorji used to worship an elm tree near the Öhin Tngri hill and sat there for days chanting. One day, looking from afar, Fu saw a large flock of sheep surrounding the lama. Thinking these might be his own sheep, he hastened over—but when he arrived there were no sheep at all. Fu regarded this as a holy miracle.

Religion receded from his life: he hardly knew his distant great-uncle Mergen Gegen who was living in Höhhot, and he went back to the monastery only once on a visit for the Hare Year ritual dance (*cham*) in 1963. The other pupils used to tease him for being a lama, but this seemed hardly important among the various insults they bandied among themselves. Indeed, when the Cultural Revolution started in autumn 1966, Mönghebatu took part in destroying monasteries along with the other boys.

It was not until the May 4, 1967, a date he cannot forget, that Mönghebatu was attacked. He was at home in the countryside chopping wood, when a tractor arrived bearing his Red Guard classmates, including Buyan. His hands and feet were tied, he was beaten, then taken to Halgai. He could not stand up, and a teacher's husband dared to ask, "What are you doing beating this child?" But the protest was to no avail: Mönghebatu was hit with a steel door-spring, blood poured from his wounds, and one of his eyes was permanently damaged. The tall conical paper hat they had put on his head was pulped. Over the next few terrible days he was given three kinds of hat to mark his disgrace. One labeled him in Chinese "Turtle's Egg,"[8] another proclaimed him one of the "Four Types of Non-Humans," and a third "Feudal Aristocracy." Chorji now blames only two of the people who beat him, and says each have experienced supernatural retribution. One developed an incurable ulcer on his mouth; another died not long ago.

Mönghebatu was sentenced to seventy-three days "transformation through labor," which he had to perform at his school.[9] While his friends attended political meetings, he had to clean latrines, make mud bricks, and feed pigs, animals the Mongols hold to be unclean. He was then sent home to his family, this now being Sechingge's household with Nabchin. For the next ten years he was ordered to do nothing but manual labor. The whole family suffered: Sechingge was demoted, accused of being a herd owner, and both he and Nabchin were horribly "struggled."[10] Later, after experiencing constant pain, a rusty needle

8. In Chinese *wang ba dan* (turtle's egg) an insult similar to "bastard."

9. Some teachers at the school were also sentenced to "transformation by labor," but none of the other pupils. The "six articles of public security" (C. *gongan liu tiao*) condemned a wide variety of people as "bad members of society," "feudal aristocracy," "landlords," "anti-revolutionaries," "rightists," and "careless speakers," etc. Chorji told us that he scarcely thought about being a lama at this time, as he would have been condemned under one or another heading anyway.

10. Sechingge was struggled as a "power holder" in the same group as Sengge Lama, who remembers: "All of us were taken into a meeting, our heads were forced down, the mass of people were sitting, we were in front, and they made us bow. The person who was most hard and determined (*jorig*) was Sechingge. He and I, we two did not bend. We had acted as cadres under Communist Party leadership, we didn't do the wrong things of past society. So why do you struggle

was found inside Nabchin's bladder—broken off it seems during one of these torture sessions. Mönghebatu was periodically called up to public meetings, where, wearing one of the hats, he was humiliated before the whole community. Stuck out in the countryside, unable to make even a simple journey unless ordered to do so, he lost all contact with his school friends. "There are no words to talk about it," he said about that time.

In mid–1976 Mönghebatu's family was among a group of people whose "hats were removed," and by the end of the year all of the "rightists" were also returned to common citizenship. He was now able to marry. Before this time, no one would have wanted to have a relation with a pariah "person with a hat" (*malagaitai hümün*). Still under a shadow, Mönghebatu married a woman from a similar class enemy family; no politically approved boy would have wanted to marry her either. He decided to leave the Banner, unable to bear living with the people who had tormented him for so long. True, there had been occasional kindnesses—his schoolmate Buyan had given him some camel fat[11]—but Mönghebatu's main memory is of abandonment. "There was no one," he says.

Reentering the Monastery as a Person of Experience

Mönghebatu's next ten years or so were spent moving from place to place outside the Banner, working in a variety of low-status jobs: from 1977 he worked in a mine, then as a primary school teacher, and then as a jack-of-all-trades at a radio station. He first got a "real post" (i.e., politically approved) in 1981, when he became an assistant in a social security office, and in 1983 he was made accountant of Öljei Sumu. Having thus battled his way up the ladder of employment, in 1986 he was at last able to get some education. He entered the Department of Mongolian Language and Literature at the Inner Mongolia University, where he took his degree in 1988. With this qualification, Mönghebatu finally obtained a cadre-like post in the Political Consultative Committee (PCC) of Chog Banner.

The PCC is an institution that operates, like the Communist Party,

us? Those young people carrying the red badge came and pressed our heads down with their hands. As soon as they took off their hands, we stood up again. We straightened up even more. For that we were beaten quite a lot. After 1968 for a full four years we 'wore hats.'"

11. This was the best possible gift in those days, "when a human life was worth no more than that of a tree," as Buyan says.

at all levels, from that of the Chinese state, through the provinces and leagues down to local district level. Designed to give a certain limited political expression to non-Communist social forces, especially those of previous society such as formerly wealthy, high-status, and religious personnel, the PCC ensures that potential opposition is defused and contributes to overall Party goals. It is among a variety of institutions in China that has aimed to reintegrate former "enemies of the people" into their own local society, rather than eradicate or expel them as happened in the USSR (Humphrey 1999). The PCC includes both delegates, who attend meetings but otherwise work elsewhere, and its own salaried employees. Mönghebatu has been in this latter category since 1988, and it is as an official of the PCC that he now manages Mergen Monastery.

How and why did his return take place? In Mönghebatu's account it came about as a result of a chance meeting. On his way to work he ran across Sharatanaa, a former Mergen lama and now a state official, who suggested: "I can get a high position (*noyon*[12]) for you, if you agree to do something for the Communist Party. Why don't you go back to manage the monastery—that will be a nice job." Mönghebatu would be eligible for such a position because he was not a member of the party—he had several times applied for membership but been refused—which forbade members to work in religious institutions. Yet it was now again state policy to support religion, in a strictly limited way, of course. After this conversation, Mönghebatu wrote a letter to Baotou officials asking to return, and the Baotou city United Front committee[13] then wrote to the party secretary's office suggesting appointing Mönghebatu to manage Mergen. The monastery was lacking a master (*ejen*) and it needed someone to continuously and reliably carry out party policy. The party bosses agreed and Mönghebatu was offered the post—"you make a nice religious life there and we'll provide you with some funds to support four or five lamas." Mönghebatu did not immediately accept, but he was planning to return to his homeland in any case and first took another administrative position near Mergen.

Sengge Lama remembers differently that he and Boroheshig, who

12. The word *noyon*, earlier used for "feudal lords" like the Dukes of Urad, was seamlessly transferred to high communist officials. *Darga* (leader, literally "one who presses") and *ejen* (master) are other ancient words that Mongols have moved from one social formation to another.

13. The United Front representing non-Communists from many backgrounds also exists at all levels from the state to the district. It is a more advisory body than the PCC and includes members living internationally.

had become the Da Lama, took the initiative. "That Old Man Lama and I together went to Sechingge and said, 'Tell Mönghebatu not to become a member of the Communist Party. If he does he cannot become head of the monastery. We are starting lama work at Mergen and therefore we need to find our reincarnation. After all Sechingge was the father—we got him to explain this to his son. When Mönghebatu came back home, his father had a lot of persuading to do." By this time Sechingge had already played an important role in retrieving the Gegen's ashes and reopening the monastery, so it is possible that the initiative to re-install his son as Chorji came as much from him as the elderly lamas.

Whatever the advantages of the job and changes in the party line, Mönghebatu may have felt pushed around by the elders of his family and the monastery. What complicated the matter was that there was a rift with his father. Sechingge in the 1980s had engaged in various business deals, among which was a project to set up a tourist riding camp. He had ordered his son, who was then working as a lowly radio presenter near the Mongolian border, to buy some camels, horses and saddles for the camp. But the camp went bankrupt, and Sechingge legally transferred all its debts to Mönghebatu, claiming that his purchase of the camels had been too expensive, causing the whole project to fail. Mönghebatu was deeply angered. He was only able to pay off the debts years later after he had taken the post at Mergen.

Both father and son must have realized that in this precarious world it would be best to paste over their differences. However, there was another hurdle before the position of Chorji could be taken up. The officials at Baotou required some gifts. The monastery sent some beef, some tea. But still the final go-ahead was not issued. At this point, the monks were lucky. Chogbüren, son of Erhedorji the big-man leader of the West Banner in the 1930s–1940s (see p 227), came forward with a donation of a whole ox for the sacrifice to Jirgal Bagatur's battle standard. No one at Mergen thinks this reiterative act, as if the whole revolutionary era had never happened, was in the least surprising. The lamas seized the chance, had the ox diverted straight to Baotou, killed, and the meat given bit by bit to the officials. "No way would Chorji have been installed otherwise," said Sengge triumphantly.

Mönghebatu accepted the PCC post and returned to the monastery without ceremony in 1990. His reasons, as he explained them to us, were as follows: "I'd spent two years at university studying that culture stuff (*soyul-moyul*). We had been taught about history and such, and

I thought that doing something about religion was part of work for the nation. Religion is part of Mongol culture, isn't it? I took the job because the party's religious policy had improved and because it was a kind of cultural work."

With his new post approved by Ulagan Gegen, Mönghebatu moved into the role of Chorji Lama. It was not easy for him, however, to be the master of Mergen. Already in place were the senior lamas, some revered for their quiet knowledge, others vying to demonstrate brilliance at chanting. In particular, there loomed Sengge Lama, old enough to be his father, who had been a leading cadre in the very state apparatus that had brought about Mönghebatu's own disgrace and exile. Faced with them, Mönghebatu did not take the religious lama path, and he signaled this by not shaving his head[14] and rarely donning monks' clothing.

Instead, Mönghebatu/Chorji chose to become heir to the managerial-political legacy of his great-uncle the 8th Mergen Gegen. He was appointed to administer the whole monastery, as the lamas evidently desired at the time, though according to earlier notions he would have had charge only of the Chorji *sang*. This distinction was later to have repercussions (see next chapter). Receiving an annual sum for upkeep of the monastery and grants for particular projects,[15] he had the Maidar statue rebuilt and thus began the series of public celebrations we have described in this book. So here was a paradox: a man formed agonistically within the communist *dispositif*, with little knowledge of Buddhism, a would-be party member and official, who transformed his colors into those of a reincarnation. Chorji did not study under a lama teacher, nor did he take another higher vow when he re-entered the lama's state. "I would have had to give up my wife," he said with a laugh. But he says that he had intimations that this was his destiny. Significant dreams are taken seriously in Mongolia as revealing a truth, and he said, "There was a dream . . . a long time ago, just after I came back as Chorji . . . I saw a monastery, there was a holy book, and I was doing something . . . If I hadn't had that experience in a past life, how could I have had this dream?" This dream, it seems, marked a turning point. Mönghebatu felt he had inherited a thread of Chorji identity, even if it was not the only identity he had.

14. Mongolian monks have their heads shaved every month or so. Chorji adopted a compromise hairstyle that could just be imagined as a tonsure that had grown out.

15. Chorji compared these grants unfavorably to those received by Badgar Monastery as a "centrally protected unit."

The "Cumulative Person," Duty, and Individuality

One way a person may be created discursively as an individual is by attributing to him or her ever more distinctive actions, signs, and effects: the more added on, the more *different* the person becomes from anyone else. Chorji is someone who exemplifies this way of being a person, by talking in this way about his life. He is in some ways a very modest man, deprecating about his abilities, referring often to his lack of knowledge of Buddhism, and he does not claim to be a man of faith (*süjügtei*). However, he does talk about his actions as *üile*, a Mongol word that in such a context means more than just an act but rather a task or duty. Chorji often used to list all the things he had done, like a demonstration that needed no further explanation in the face of all those who had previously rejected him. We suggest that the distinction between act and task was given in his case by his teleological identity as heir to the mastership of the monastery. He was not only right but bound to act in this capacity, he implied. The things he set himself to do *were* his duties. We do not think he was trying to be individualistic,[16] but the more extravagant, varied, and remarkable were these duties, the more completely in effect he would become the person he felt he ought to be.

What these duties were, Chorji understood in his own way. He was too honest to play the role of the reincarnation by making himself the object of worship, prostrations (*mörgül*), and offerings, as we described in the Introduction for Ulagan Gegen. A corollary was that he very rarely gave out blessings or empowered amulets, the usual response by a Gegen to veneration and offerings. If the worshipped Gegen is in principle an attractant, drawing people to his monastery, the abdication of this activity by the chief lama at Mergen was more than just a lack; it became a centrifugal effect, as people turned elsewhere for these things (Chapter 11). Chorji did not study the texts, or meditate,

16. Yunxiang Yan has argued, against the assumption that socialism invariably increased collectivism, that in China its effect was to increase individualism. This happened because a prime act of the communists had been to destroy the familial and local systems that had imposed Confucian and other conformity on individuals. Subsequently, the state privatized the family by detaching it from communal structures and bringing it into a capitalist environment. The resulting retreat of the state from everyday life led to the development of ultra-utilitarian individualism (Yan 2003, 229–35). Some parts of this argument certainly apply in the case of the Mongols of China, but we suggested (see Chapter 1) that the Mongols, perhaps more than the Chinese, had other ways of asserting individuality and constructing others as individuals even in "traditional society."

nor could he give empowerments (*wang* or *abishig*). He did not conduct household rituals for the laity. He did not act as a guru teacher to young lamas ('How could I when I do not know the texts myself?'). He did sit in temple services, but chanting little, and often with an abstracted or bemused expression. The only religious ceremony he really enjoyed and insisted on continuing was the annual sacrifice to Yellow Peak, the energetic and inspiring ritual we described in Chapter 5.

Forgoing the aloof authority of the reincarnation and guru roles, Chorji gained in freedom for practical activity. His performance of the *ejen's* managerial tasks was determined. He inherited a rambling realm of decrepit buildings, rubble, and barracks built by the army. The trees of Mergen were mostly stumps, the lake had been filled in, and the only water came from a spring channeled through a leaking tap. Chorji made repairs his first priority. Obtaining the funding and permissions involved complex and constant negotiations with local officials—neither the money nor the permits came for free. Even after the army finally left in 1996, he had to keep the military sweet, for they did not allow him to forget that they were owners of the campus. To his annoyance, officers would occasionally swoop down and order the monastery to provide them with a banquet. Furthermore, he had no alternative but to keep up good relations with the various organizations that subsequently rented the Officers' Mess building. Meanwhile, Chorji took a series of official posts: vice chairman of the PCC of Jiuyuan district of Baotou, president of the Buddhist Association of Baotou, and vice director of the Taiwan and Expatriate Association of Baotou. After it was reopened, Mergen, like all monasteries in Inner Mongolia, was put under a Management Committee to regulate all administrative, economic, and ideological activities. The members are approved by the district Religious Affairs Bureau and include certain lay representatives of the locality. Chorji became its chairman. Providing support to Chorji in all this was his lay patron, a high official in Baotou.[17]

Chorji's close familial relations fell into the background. Maintaining a distance from his stepmother, Nabchin, and her sons, who lived in Qianqi, he set up home in Baotou with his wife and two daughters, thus effectively ending any pretensions to the family-heir position in the West [Front] Banner (that identity was taken up by his younger half-brothers, as we describe in the next chapter). Chorji lived in a spa-

17. We were not surprised to discover that this person—continuing a well-worn tradition—was related to Erhimmanglai, and hence was a kinsman of the 8th Mergen Gegen and of Chorji himself.

cious apartment in a pleasant quarter of the city. Replete with expensive furniture and modern appliances, this was the comfortable life of the Chinese middle class. His home was a world away from the monastery and contained few if any signs that he was a Buddhist lama. Not only does Chorji have no interest in relics; with no prominent *güng-garba* shrine his apartment also did not provide the usual honorable place for photographs of ancestors and family members.[18] This invisibility did not mean, however, that the legacy-injunction of his father had evaporated—far from it.

Worldly Struggles

For all his bursts of managerial energy, Chorji ran into opposition among the monks. One episode concerned his support for "Mergen Gegen Studies." This academic enterprise chimed well with Chorji's modern vision of religion as part of Mongolian history and culture and he became vice chair of the studies association. Not only that, but he used money allocated to the monastery to support the republication of Mergen Gegen's *Collected Works*, the five-volume facsimile and tape recordings in handsome golden boxes that appeared in 1998. But the older lamas complained this did not "make religion": the texts, printed small and without performance instructions, could not be used by them for chanting efficacious prayers. A rift appeared between different views of the primordial religious act of chanting, which we discuss in Chapter 10.

At the end of the 1990s certain lamas joined together and wrote a letter of complaint against Chorji: he did not act like a reincarnated lama, he did not live in the monastery, and he had repaired only his own *sang*, neglecting others, requiring elderly monks to live in quarters with leaking roofs, etc. All this, along with the quarrel with Sengge, was taken by local people as infringements of the right order of things, and therefore certain to result in misfortune, along the lines of the unspoken sense of justice mentioned earlier. Subsequent deaths and illnesses were interpreted as the consequences to be expected. We discuss in the next chapter how the laity attempted to rectify this situation.

Chorji's great endeavor of this period, indeed a vindication and continuation of Sechingge's zeal, was his lawsuit taken out against the army to recover ownership of the entire Mergen campus. This was

18. Maybe Chorji thought of the whole monastery as his shrine.

a most daring act for a mere lama and only Chorji's several political posts made it feasible. Nevertheless, he was convinced he would lose. He told us in 2002 that he risked everything, including being dismissed from his posts if he failed. In that case, if he was left with nothing, he planned to go to Lhasa to learn about true philosophical Buddhism, unlike the "thoughtless chanting" that went on at Mergen. He might even be punished and imprisoned. The PCC was angry with him. The other members of the committee, all of whom were Chinese, were saying, "You are a committee member, why are you causing problems for the government?" Imagining the worst, Chorji said, "If I am thrown in jail, no Mongols would come to see me."

One thing that lay behind this despairing statement was Chorji's dispute with the lay herders living around the monastery. They told us they had donated money and livestock for rituals but those gifts had been diverted to other purposes such as giving banquets for officials. A more severe confrontation then occurred. While the law case was being pursued, in the expectation of losing, Chorji gave all the housing in the monastery to the herders. He wanted to have Mongols on site to prevent the army, should it win, acquiring empty dwellings that they would then fill with their own enterprises. However, to his annoyance the herders "did not trust me"; they did not move into the houses, but simply put locks on the doors and left them empty. To everyone's surprise, Chorji then won the case—meaning that the lawsuit moved from lower to higher courts, and finally in Beijing came to be resolved in Chorji's favor (as a consequence of the central government policy to redress the wrongs of the Cultural Revolution). Rejoicing at his success, Chorji had a polished marble stone inscribed and set up in front of the main temple. But he also abruptly terminated the herders' rights and began to rent the buildings to various outsiders. "What could I do?" he commented, "I cannot let the houses fall into disrepair and the monastery has to have some income from somewhere." Most of the laity turned against him for this sequence of events. In 2002 they boycotted the monastery. And gradually, it turned out that although Chorji had "won" the lawsuit, the decision of the higher court was left in limbo; the officials at the municipality level did not ratify it and ownership of the land was left still unclear.

Chorji had now quarreled with virtually everyone. The Western Great Incarnation was offended because Chorji had left his house in disrepair, and he retreated to his village home. Bayanbilig was lying low, but he was on Sengge's side. Minggan also kept well out of sight. In summer 2002 Chorji also turned on us, furious that we had the incorrect documentation on our research permits, which on this occasion did not mention his name nor that of the monastery. He was deeply insulted by the disrespectful demeanor of a person from Höhhot who had arrived with us, did not greet him, and "did not treat me as a person" (*hümün-iyer üjegsen ügei*). These were violations of his honor as master of the monastery. Finally, flailing in an incoherent series of alcohol-fueled farewell rites, he lashed out at one and all. He had the gates locked so that no one could leave and insisted on repeated groveling apologies. A couple of frightened lamas obeyed his every demand. Finally, we had to abandon Chorji, sitting alone in his palace, staring down at the vista of empty buildings.

It seemed to us that with almost all the lamas gone the monastery might have to close down. But over the two next years, Chorji made efforts to retrieve the situation. Young lamas were urgently needed, as well as someone to take the lead in chanting and training them. Sengge Lama agreed to take the post of Da Lama, but then thought better of it, accusing Chorji of "telling him off like a child." Still, Chorji went ahead and made repeated efforts to recruit a second group of young monks, a story we tell in later chapters. Meanwhile, relations with us were repaired and we invited him on a visit to England.

A Visit to Britain and Religious Innovations

In 1998 and 2000 Sengge and Chorji had raised the question of the "lost texts" of Mergen Gegen, which they maintained were those held in the British Library that had not been copied and republished in Inner Mongolia in 1997.[19] We mention this visit to England as it reveals

19. Despite the local intellectuals' opinion that Mergen Gegen's works had been stolen as booty by British imperialists during the attacks on Beijing in the late nineteenth century (Ba. Mönghe 2004, 23), both lamas separately said to us that they were glad the *Bum Jarlig* had been acquired by the British; otherwise it would have been destroyed—no other copy had survived in China. In fact the *Bum Jarlig* and other texts by Mergen Gegen were purchased in the early nineteenth century in Beijing by Edward Stallybrass, a missionary, and subsequently given to the British Museum (later British Library). On the English missionaries studies of Mongolian Buddhist texts, see Bawden (1985, 157,199, 268, 279–80). The three unpublished texts are numbers nine, ten, and eleven from the second volume of the *Bum Jarlig* printed in 1770–1773. It was only when we examined the collected works in London that we realized that the texts most missed by Sengge Lama (parts of the "four root" sutras, see p 263) were not the same as the three unpublished texts. The Mergen lamas did not seem to know that Professor Naranbatu had a facsimile of the whole *Bum Jarlig*—hence their appeals to us to retrieve them.

something of Chorji's religious, but not specifically Buddhist, sensibility: we began to see that religion for him was not just a matter of "Mongol culture," despite what he himself had said.

Chorji duly visited the British Library, for which occasion he dressed in his lama's clothes and prostrated to the *Bum Jarlig*, the collected works of Mergen Gegen. He was sincere in his homage, but we had the impression that his religious feelings were also aroused in other ways. Chorji was taken along the Thames from the Tower to Parliament, then to Buckingham Palace, all the way being told about the places and buildings, what happened in them, what the symbols meant and who had lived in there. He kept saying, "The city is unnecessary, the countryside is good." Then, sitting in St. James' Park with a picnic lunch, he was transformed. He was particularly taken with a beautiful tree and he took many photographs of it.[20] The next year at Mergen we discovered how serious a photographer Chorji had become. He had set up an exhibition of large prints in his palace, and all of the subjects he had chosen were rocks, trees, and springs in the Muna Mountains. These were sacred sites, and he had lovingly—religiously—captured their originality and beauty.

Returning to the monastery Chorji started innovating in the style of the 8th Mergen Gegen's reforms: earlier he had proposed setting up a dairy farm, though this plan was rejected by local officials on the grounds that religious institutions should not run businesses. Now he pulled down an army wall and made a new entrance so that worshippers would not have to enter via the Officers' Mess. Next he proposed reviving the monastery's medical faculty and medicine dispensary, to be located on the site of the old Emchi ("doctor") *sang*. And in an impressive achievement he installed a glittering series of eight large bodhisattva statues in the main Chogchin temple and eight fierce gods in the Janghan Temple. This was new—the temples had not contained these deities earlier, at least not in this prominent form. Their appearance completely altered the layout of the inner sanctum in Janghan temple—the brilliantly painted statues filled the space. No room was left for Jirgal Bagatur's battle standard, clothing, and armor, which to Sengge's dismay, were taken out and propped up in a dusty corner of the outer room. Gone was the secrecy and sanctity that had surrounded these objects in previous years. Furthermore, Chorji came up with a

20. Later, Chorji visited a farm in Devon. He said he had never expected that English people led "real lives," he admired the "advanced" farming and the orderliness; he went into the village church and bowed before the altar. In his lama's robes he also respectfully attended a service in King's College Chapel, Cambridge.

different story about them, one that eradicated the Jirgaltu Monastery connection and fitted well with wider Chinese versions of history. No longer the attributes of a specifically Urad ancestor, the relics belonged to "a Mongol hero" who defeated the Hotong Muslim aggressors—these being terrible people who had invaded nearby regions in the nineteenth century and strung up three-year-old children as a warning of their ferocity.

Chorji and the Chinese Presence

During our early visits to Mergen the only intimations that there were Chinese Buddhists in the vicinity was the awed stories people told about a barefoot monk who had meditated in the "Daoist cave" (*daoren wopu*) in the mountains and his disciple who had returned from emigration in America to find and bury his bones (see also Chapter 9).[21] The nearby Chinese villages and small towns had no Buddhist temple—in fact they had few temples of any kind.[22] In 1998–2005 a few Chinese villagers occasionally attended Mergen ceremonies as worshippers, but more came as bystanders or traders of souvenirs and drinks. A misconceived Chinese tourist camp in front of the Officers' Mess had gone bankrupt and was deserted, to the lamas' relief (see Evans and Humphrey 2002, 189–210). Otherwise, life at Mergen continued almost as though the place was not located at the edge of dense Chinese settlement.

Chorji, however, no doubt following the new Party policy that designated religion as a harmonizing factor in interethnic relations, initiated certain joint rituals with Chinese Buddhists from Baotou. This was regarded by the other lamas as a great and unwelcome innovation, though they could understand that Chorji was following party policy. The fact was that most of the local Mongols—including Chorji himself—continued to regard the influx of Chinese in the region as a threat facing their way of life. "Goats are good in the cliffs, Chinese are good at the table," people said, implying that while the Mongols had been pushed back into the mountains, the Chinese were gorging themselves

21. People said that this greatly admired monk lived in extreme asceticism, drinking water collected drop by drop as it dripped off a rock. He was rumored to have killed himself after being forced out and beaten during the Cultural Revolution (see also Crane 2001).

22. Before the Cultural Revolution there had been a Dragon King (*Long Wang Miao*) temple in a village close to Mergen; there were also several small "land shrines" in the neighborhood mostly dedicated to prayers for rain.

on rich food. A sharp symbolic boundary had been erected against the Chinese. They were said to be dirty and committed sins like killing and eating snakes. They could not possibly be employed as cooks for the lamas. Certain habits, foods, utensils, and even ways of walking were avoided for the reason that they were "Chinese." In the past the monks did not even use blankets or matches because the Chinese used them (when one rich educated man slept under a blanket people said, "He is using a Chinese blanket, soon his luck will finish," and indeed the man died poor). Marriage with Chinese had been disapproved; most people did not speak the Chinese language. Now however people say there is no way out, we have to speak Chinese and there are mixed marriages. Nevertheless, the Han farmers and migrant workers continued to be described as acquisitive and blind to others' interests: they dig deep wells and take all the water; they scour the mountains for anything of value (gold, medicinal herbs, fruit, "hair grass"[23]); they behave provocatively at the *oboo* ceremony.[24] They used to cut the beautiful trees of Muna Mountains for firewood, and now they blast the hillsides for building stone. Particularly objectionable was the cutting of fine stone for sale from a rock outcrop near the stupas containing the relics of the reincarnations of Jirgaltu Monastery. Indeed, during our visits from 2005 onward the days and far into the night resounded to heavy booms like thunder or warfare—this came from the quarrying in the Valley of the Caves and the way up to Debeseg Monastery. People said the dynamiting of the mountains was the cause of the droughts of recent years—the absence of rain was the retribution for damaging the land. Stories of the punishments heaped on the heads of the Chinese were uncountable: they were said to suffer misfortune after misfortune for killing snakes, for polluting springs, for stealing monastery property. Yet nothing kept them at bay.

Nevertheless, for all the vitriol attached to "the Chinese" as a category, day-to-day relations were amicable, if distant. Thus the monks were polite when Chorji twice invited Chinese Buddhists from Baotou to the inauguration rituals for the new statues. Significantly, however, the Mergen monks held the ritual by themselves first, while the Chinese attended only a joint second performance. On one such occasion the two groups of monks lined up separately outside the temple and each in turn chanted prayers. Facing the small group of Mongol lamas

23. "Hair grass" (*fa cai*) is said to be highly nutritious and is used by the Chinese as a vegetable for special dinner parties.

24. In 2005 a Chinese dance troupe with "naked women" performed near the Banner *oboo* festivities, arousing much criticism from elders.

5 Chorji Reincarnation, surrounded by lamas chanting on occasion of visit by Chinese Buddhists, 2005. (Hürelbaatar Ujeed)

was a large mass of Chinese Buddhists (*heshang*) from Baotou city, the monks dressed in gray robes, along with around fifty men and women lay devotees neatly clothed in identical brown robes, singing fervently and expertly playing gourd and percussion instruments.

More aggravating to the few remaining monks than this dutiful performance of inter-ethnic harmony was that Chorji rented out the main house of the Güüshi *sang* to Chinese Buddhists. True, they rarely made use of it, but an alien shrine was established there and this was felt to be an intrusive outpost within the very heart of Mergen Monastery.

In 2005 the massive motorway linking Beijing to Baotou and Lanzhou was being constructed in the plains just south of the monastery, and a new tourist camp with a Chinese manager had been built in the upper valley of the Mergen River. Unlike the earlier failed camp with its crude concrete imitations of Mongol tents, this complex was a well-built multi-story structure with three restaurants and several European-style chalets. It stands on the way to the Bird Gulley, where the elusive silver coveted by Mergen Gegen (pp 153–54) was held to be located, and local people said that the presence of careless Chinese tourists had finally eliminated any sanctity that place had. They minded about that and were also conscious of the geography—the location of this camp above Mergen, with the motorway taking up former pasture below, meant that the monastery was surrounded. "Our Mongols have now lost the upper land," one man burst out. "Sooner or later this precious three hundred *mu* of land will just be Chinese food"—a thought that reflected the fact that the more commercialized China was becoming, the more the monastery became valuable as property ripe for development.

Chorji tried to maintain friendly relations with the tourist-camp manager, but he did not encourage the tourism that was so prevalent elsewhere in Inner Mongolia. His attitude was made clear by the road he made for tourists going to the camp, which took a detour round the monastery on three sides, rather than proceeding through it. Visitor's tickets were no longer sold at the entry to the precinct, as they briefly had been, and a notice forbade trade without special permission. Tourists could pause and enter Mergen, but there was little to encourage them. The first thing they saw inside the precinct was a notice in Mongolian pointing left to a path that seemingly led nowhere, saying "Praying this way." Chorji, thus unwelcoming, was well aware that by taking this stance he was forgoing a substantial income like that reaped by other monasteries such as Badgar. "Our monastery is different. If the tourist road came straight through here, the religious things would be destroyed. Things would get worse, that is really true," said Chorji.

Meanwhile it was impossible not be aware of simultaneous disjunctive activities at this one place. Was this absurd, inimical, or merely the way things had to be in the increasingly dense inhabitation of the land? It was evident above all aurally. Over the crump of blasting from distant quarries, other sounds rang out clearly in the morning air: from the Chogchin Temple the wail of the conch shell and the clashing of cymbals, and from the most recent occupants of the Officers' Mess, a military training camp for a Baotou middle school, shouts "One! Two! Three! Four! Quick march!," and the stamp of hundreds of trainers. These two groups of people, the lamas and the schoolchildren, had nothing to do with one another. At night, the lamas joked and told stories in one former barrack. The military teachers stayed in a barrack next door, focused with fierce cries on their games of mahjong. Chorji, living in his *sang* courtyard, sat with neither group.

Conducting without a Score

Chorji's broken education (a few years of Maoist dogma, a couple of years of Mongolian literary studies) cut him off from two prime sources of authority in the monastery: serene performance of the reincarnation role and command of the liturgy. Through his own efforts he had been able to clamber some way up the ladder of external political positions, and thus armored he could be the *ejen* with some resolution. Chorji in fact achieved many things. But one of the common words in his conversations was *arga-ügei*: "There's nothing to be done, no way out"—a wretched contrast with the mastery of *arga* (skillful means) attributed to the 3rd Mergen Gegen (Chapter 2). Chorji saw plots and hindrances at every turn and he was easily angered with anyone, including his own lamas:

> What are you doing? Today, two mistakes happened. The things people offered should be announced in the prayer hall. Why didn't you do that? How will those people come to the next service? You want to divide it up yourselves! If you want to do things, do them in the right way, or just go! How can you act in this way? And the consecrated things should be distributed to the congregation—but what happened? If you don't know how to do it, you can look how others do it! . . .

The lamas would mumble some reply, for it was in Chorji's power to destroy their livelihoods and disrupt what they held dear. They could dislike his rough tone, so jarring to monkish dispassionateness, and still understand that he was acting as master. We are reminded here of what Latour wrote about the orchestral conductor, an idea that stands for any coordinator of a "society," who, although he distributes the roles to the players, has no means whereby he could "possess" the whole performance. Indeed, he cannot perform any single part beautifully. His property is to pay attention to the passages, the transitions, to be neither fully in, nor fully out. In fact his role is to break the routines of all the others and to compel each to pay attention to the playing of all the others (Latour 2010, 16). If Chorji saw his task as managing the transitions and the activities *between* the efficacious chants, he was hindered at every point by the fact that the lamas, and he himself, had no score. The 3rd Mergen Gegen's statutes lay unread, and in any case would not have provided a model for coordination. In other words, there was a crisis of non-agreement about what to pay attention to in others' actions. The conditions for not disintegrating, let alone achieving harmony, were more exacting than those of Latour's "conductor in despair." As Chorji said to us:

> You can't blame the children [i.e., the boy lamas], they only arrived the other day. What can they know? It was only because I was sitting there . . . otherwise the senior lamas would have scared them off. Because I was there, they couldn't run away. If you give them [the senior lamas] just a little gap, they'll do their own thing, they'll ruin you.

Chorji was to make attempt after attempt to re-launch Mongolian Buddhism at Mergen. We have suggested that it would be incorrect to attribute this directly to his patrimony, for an inheritance is always something that must be acted upon anew—if not, it would be as if Chorji were affected by it like a physical cause. Was not his idea of adopting the boy lama as his heir (Chapter 1) evidence of his awareness that inheritance must be projected into the future in new ways? Unlike his great-uncle, the 8th Mergen Gegen, who was a monk who went out into the political world, Chorji brought that world into the monastery. He thus found himself at that point of tension between the limits negotiated within a tradition and "the forces that push the tradition onto new terrain, where part or all of the tradition ceases to make sense and so needs a new beginning" (Asad 2006, 289). We shall discuss this new terrain further in Chapter 10, but we would like to end here on a different note—the winding inner intimations that nevertheless persist within a tradition. For beyond Chorji's immediate triple legacies there was also the earlier, fervent specter of the 3rd Mergen Gegen's fabulation of a people yet to come (Chapter 2).

Writing of specters, Derrida observes that the young people of the Left in 1960s France had rejected Stalinism, Soviet bureaucracy, etc., but they still had to ask themselves the question that had been asked earlier, "Whither Marxism?" A "since Marx" continues to designate the place of assignation from which we are *pledged*. But if there is a pledge or assignation, injunction, or promise, the "since" marks a place and a time that doubtless precedes us, but so as to be as much *in front of us* and *before* us. [. . .] If "since Marx" names a future time-to-come as much as a past, the past of a proper name, it is because the proper of a proper name will always remain to come" (Derrida 2006, 19, emphasis in original).

Perhaps it is appropriate then to not to ignore naming. We point out therefore that the *batu* (strength, firmness) central to Mergen Gegen's grand schema is the same word as the name chosen by Sechingge for his son, Mönghe ("eternal") Batu.

NINE

Regroupings of Laity

Introduction 2005

When we left in 2002 the monastery seemed on the point of abandonment as a place of religious activity. Almost all of the lamas, including Chorji, had gone to their homes. Sengge and other elderly monks were planning to move to a new monastery. Of the few lamas left amid the deserted courtyards, only Minggan, the dreamy painter, had any mastery of the liturgy.

Returning to Mergen in 2005 we found an amazing transformation. The old temples had been expertly painted and colored flags were flying. A fine new temple in Chinese style had been constructed for the four Maharanza guardian deities. And most important of all a year earlier Chorji had brought in a new group of twelve young lamas from northeastern Inner Mongolia. With their participation the Shira Oroi sacrifice had just taken place and preparations for the Mani services were in full swing. Chorji met us and said with a smile about the absence of Sengge, "The sun still rose after Mao died." We were equally surprised by the transformation of Minggan. He was now the proctor (*gebhüi*), teaching and supervising the young monks and was to be seen in full regalia, with crested hat and stick of discipline, stalking with a frown between the rows of chanting youths. Furthermore, Chorji had at last given him a house inside the monastery walls.

The flags were flying in preparation for another great celebration, to which we had been summoned by elegant printed invitations. The occasion was the 300th anniversary of the founding of Mergen Monastery and was to include a public offering of donations by laity. Dignitaries, including officials from the capital and other cities and foreign professors from Russia and Mongolia, had been invited. This essentially nonreligious event had been attached to a popular religious service in order to ensure the presence of a considerable body of worshippers. Recalling the similar celebration of "Mergen Gegen Studies" in 1995 (Chapter 1), we were reminded of the monastery as a site of *performance*, that of "Buddhist monastery" put on largely for the government in response to the state's own demand for manifestations of proper ethnic-cultural loyalty.

This was a renewed signal to us that Mergen Monastery was more than one nexus of relations, some of which were disconnected from the earlier ensembles described in earlier chapters. With different "audiences" a shifting of elements took place; parts of Mergen were now connected to new environs and at the same time they disengaged from earlier publics. It was not only that the formerly crucial patronage of the duke's family had long since disappeared, but Mergen's earlier "congregation" had been excised while a new one was not fully established. Many local herders were taking up new occupations, the lamas no longer came from the vicinity, and the monastic hierarchy was challenged. All this was taking place amid seismic changes in the region and in China. Evident also was the permeable nature of "holding together" at Mergen. By this we refer not only to the dispersed and partial character of any location (Strathern 2004; Candea 2009) but also to the sometimes shockingly new and sometimes reiterative temporal processes whereby a tradition is made. This chapter shows how the agency pushing internal changes came not only from "inside" but also from "outside," in particular from the laity, whose earlier relative passivity could no longer be assumed. "Mergen Monastery" as we conceive it is not a preexisting core held together by its resistance and accommodation to external systems, but a dynamic configuration that swallows penetrating elements, which are "dealt with" (digested, regurgitated, excreted . . .) as will be shown in this and the following chapter.

Occasions like the 300th anniversary were demonstrations of the monastery's public importance, and thus had to establish their place among the other mass festivities (*nair*) in the area. The anniversary event, with speeches by officials, banquets, wrestling matches, local pop group, folk singers, a fair with stalls selling drinks, food, clothes, etc., and even the presence of Chorji's successful lawyers, was distinguished by two spectacular gifts to the monastery from new lay patrons. The Darhan pop group from Höhhot gave a huge pile of books in Mongolian "to develop Mongolian culture" among the lamas[1]; and a commercial company donated a magnificent set of volumes of the *Ganjur* in Tibetan. The latter were borne under a ceremonial umbrella to the platform outside the Chogchin temple, and then one by one, the heads of regional organizations, along with herders dressed in their finest clothes, and we too, came up to make offerings of money. The names and sums gifted were announced by loudspeaker to the throng and thus a new trans-regional constellation of donors was made known.

Liu describes the contemporary Chinese middle classes as absorbed in economic and consumer activity, ignoring history and being left consequently with a dispiriting absence of any direction from the past that would lead to a future (Liu 2002, 171–72). The Urad herding households had also benefited from increased prosperity. Many of the people we met however did not seem oriented to the wide world but obstinately drew lines to chosen pasts: always selective, always contentious, these narrative choices became the arteries of their own changed ensembles and new sensibilities. Veena Das (2007) shows insightfully how temporalities associated with the past are experienced as affect, and how this impinges on the present circumstances in which memories are evoked. We describe the temporal complexity attending public events of different scales, and in so doing we document a contrast. The more the history mentioned at large communal occasions is boxed off and relegated to a completely irrecoverable "past-time" (Anagnost 1997, 7), the more optimistic, carefree, and festive the public affect—yet this is a quickly exhausted collective cheerfulness. By contrast people meeting in small encounters find it more difficult to ignore the ongoing penetration of hurtful past actualities into the present. Even if referred to only in allusions or attempts to explain extraordinary events, their conversations invoke duration, accident, and destiny. These narratives often seem imbued with sadness and affront—yet such fate-laden accounts are causally alive and can provoke new self-understanding. All these interventions, from "'outside" but also from "the past," are loaded in to the conglomerate we have been calling the tradition.

Political Economic Conditions

How had Chorji Lama been able to achieve his miracles? Undoubtedly the main political-economic factor was the long-term effects of the

1. The Darhan pop group celebrates Mongolian culture, and the musicians said they gave the books to Mergen because this is the only monastery to chant in the Mongolian language.

boundary change of 1958 that had brought Mergen just inside the territory of Baotou municipality (C. *shi*), enabling the monastery to seek funding from this wealthy industrial city. Baotou's stunning economic success after the late 1990s resulted in a stream of funds to the monastery that its earlier "parish" would have been ill able to afford. The Urad West Banner (the former "parish") had been linked with the other two Urad Banners to form the Bayannuur League (C. *meng*, M. *aimag*).[2] This entity remains far poorer than Baotou with its long-established steel plants and burgeoning commerce. Despite its predominantly rural and extractive economy, the League was later also named a municipality, a move aimed to enhance urban control of hinterlands.

This situation was to set in motion deep and subtle changes that may alter the character of Mergen Monastery forever. By cutting the monastery off from almost all of its previous lay community and surrounding territory (the Urad West Duke Banner of yore), the boundary changes—always important in China—had radically altered its sociopolitical role. Mergen is now deprived of its previous constellation of local benefactors that might have provided an alternative to state support. It is no longer the recognized religious center of a polity, as it had been when it was the Banner monastery. Moreover, there is now no such figure as the duke to act as main patron. The monastery is marooned in the distant fringe of a Chinese-dominated industrial municipality that in general is hardly aware of its existence. The "congregation" to benefit from the blessings of the monastery had been reduced to a few immediate neighbors. Yet to play a resounding role Mergen would have to attract both worshippers and patrons from afar.

The situation requires us to rethink anthropologically the archetypal Buddhist monastic-lay "gift-economy" relation whereby a community of householders provides the material conditions for the monks' pursuit of spiritual goals, and the monks provide religious guidance and blessings to the households (Yü 2008, 210–11). In Mongolia, even before Liberation the situation was best understood not as a duality (monks and householders) but as a three-cornered relation in which political authorities took on much of the responsibility for monasteries (Chapters 3 and 4). These days the great majority of Mergen's funding comes from state grants from Baotou. The new situation may not seem very different from that under the Qing, but in fact it is profound. For previously the West Banner nobles who gave Banner funds did so amid an

2. The center of Bayannuur is the small city of Linhe. The center of the Urad Front Banner (formerly the West Banner) is the smaller town commonly known as Qianqi.

ethic of donating, an eager willingness to give, enabling them to make merit as well as receiving blessings from supremely respected monks. This no longer the case, and the state grants (*jing fei*) are considered to be boons, which are difficult to extract, conditional, and sporadic. Mergen, along with other Inner Mongolian monasteries, is engaged in a competitive economy of supplication[3] to the municipal authorities. "Asking is difficult," Chorji used to groan, "you have to give a banquet, give gifts. . . ."

What does it mean for Mergen to be attached to Baotou municipality rather than the Banner of old? The representations of contemporary administrative jurisdictions have an imaginative-affective quality no less than the "past-times" recalled from history. Baotou exudes the atmosphere first of the heroic socialist modernism of the 1950s–1960s (evident in its massive steel plants and Soviet-style city planning) and more recently of scientific investment-oriented connectivity to the global economy. The slogans on its website read: "Baotou national rare-earth[4] high-tech industrial development zone," "One-hour direct flights to Beijing," "Rich in minerals such as iron, niobium, gold, magnesium, copper and coal," and "well-trained human resources."

To appreciate what "the Banner" brings to mind in contrast to Baotou, let us quote the development aims of the mayor of Bayanhua, the township close to the West Banner center, Qianqi, and the home of Sengge Lama.

> If we can grasp six words, we can understand the way forward. 1) *Soft.* This is goat's wool, the basic resource; we must increase the quality and decrease the quantity to protect the mountains. 2) *Hard.* This is the mountains, which have much granite stone to be quarried. 3) *Flow.* Our aim to produce ten brands of pure water from mountain springs. The water is there, but we need to process it. 4) *White.* This refers to plastic bags for sugar. We will support four factories with 88 webbing-machines and import the oil from Höhhot. 5) *Restaurants.* They are being built along all three main roads of our town—with dancing too. 6) *Green.* This word means vegetables, and production of fodder for the goats.

For local people this was an altogether more understandable formula of development than the high-tech aura of Baotou. Not that the Mon-

3. To apply for something is called *guyuchilahu*, the polite form, but in fact people say the monastery has to beg (*guyuhu*) for favors.

4. China is home to seventy percent of the world's production of rare earth elements; ninety percent of that is located in Baotou municipality. See http://www.rev.cn/en/int.htm

gols liked it—especially the idea, which the mayor emphasized, that goats are harmful to the environment and should be fed agriculturally produced fodder instead of grazing on grass and trees—but they certainly saw its rationale and some of them were prepared to accede to his slogan, "If we can't protect the mountains, the forest will become a stone forest." The sturdy, self-help aura of the Banner had a certain familiarity and attainability—from which the monastery was now separated.

A second theme concerns the official designation of the monastery and the funding directed to it. The monastery is conceptualized as a "cultural relic" (C. *wenwu*) of the Mongolian people, and coincidentally as a place of religious activity (C. *zongjiao huodong changsuo*). This designation, under the IMAR 2003 development policy, "Let Us Construct Inner Mongolia as a Great National Cultural Region," had the effect of aligning Mergen with all other objects identified as cultural relics or heritage, and hence meshes its fate with the cultural politics ongoing in Inner Mongolia as a whole. In particular, it has prescribed the "cultural" character of the developments that can take place at Mergen, thus limiting economic options for the lamas. On the one hand, monks must be registered at Baotou and monthly salaries are then allocated to them, at a low level equivalent to that of a manual worker. On the other hand, they are not permitted to set up "non-cultural" ventures at the monastery, hence the refusal of Chorji's plan to start a dairy farm. The cultural heritage designation has also affected planning decisions around the monastery, for ethnic culture in undeveloped areas of China is an opportunity for commercialization (Schein 2000). What could be more natural, as local planning officials would see it, for a cultural relic than to have a tourist camp built next door?

Finally, in line with central government environment protection policy, the most drastic measure to affect the local people was the decision to close the Muna Mountains to pasturing. It was held that overgrazing across most pasturelands of Inner Mongolia was a crucial cause of desertification and the sandstorms that increasingly swept over North China. In 2002 the closure of the mountains was beginning, and herders around Mergen had sent a delegation to Baotou to protest. Erhimbayar, a leader of the group, said to us in 2003:

> We were thinking, even if it is a government policy, they must let us survive. If they don't let us live, everything will be extinguished. If you want to close the mountains, you must arrange our lives in a suitable way. Otherwise, we will be thrown

away on the steppe—but there is no land for us there. They have been squeezing us from the south, they have pushed right up to the foothills, so there is nowhere for us to go.

However, the mountains were soon definitively placed off bounds, a pattern reproduced over vast areas of pastureland across Inner Mongolia. Urad herders had either to quit the area to find work or sell most of their stock and raise the remainder in pens with fodder. It was apparent that the old free grazing life had gone forever—a devastating blow that people have yet to come to terms with.

These powerful directives—the expansion of urban zones, the designation of religion as a cultural relic, and the prohibition on open pasturing—affect Mongol populations to a much greater extent than Chinese, and yet governmental structures were carefully crafted to disallow or negate specifically national objections. An important factor was the absence of a specifically Mongolian political authority in the area. Baotou city with its massively predominant Chinese population has relatively few Mongolian officials and they, with the exception perhaps of Mongol members of the relatively powerless Political Consultative Committee, do not represent ethnic interests but rather sectional party and government functions. As for the adjacent Banner (formerly West now renamed the Front Banner) the pattern is long established whereby, while the head of the Banner is a Mongol, the party secretary is a Chinese and has far greater power at his disposal. In this situation there is no authority legitimated and able to take up and alter policies that affect one nationality more than another.

This double lack—both political and economic—could not but be reflected in the emasculation of *sülde* and the land deity cults,[5] as we now briefly describe in the case of the Urad Front (West) Banner *Oboo*. Formerly the main site of the cult of military victory in the region, it was the lowland counterpart of the sacrifice on Yellow Peak (Chapter 5). It had been a prime site of the dukes' parading of noble ancestry, the place of occasionally dramatic blood sacrifice (rumored to have included human victims), symbolic demonstration of communal unity (signified by a leather rope wound round the stones and branches contributed by participants), exclusion of women, displays of masculine

5. For the contrasting situation in Tibetan regions of Amdo, see Makley (2007, 241), who describes mountain and land rituals as active generators of lay masculinity and aggression in contemporary confrontations.

prowess (wrestling, horse races, archery), and regular confabulations of officials, lamas, and aristocrats. When it was revived in 1985 the *oboo* still languished under these highly dubious associations from a communist point of view, but soon the umbrella of "supporting ethnic culture" allowed it to flourish again in a transformed and officially approved manner. The rebuilt *oboo* no longer contained ancestral military weapons as before—Sengge Lama had placed pacific Buddhist items beneath it (Chapter 6).

The Banner *oboo* has by far the widest radius of attraction of all the sacred cairns in the area, and a large gathering is an opportunity for officials to demonstrate their execution of cultural policy. In so doing, they have to refer to the history of the *oboo*—but this is relegated to "what our ancestors used to do" and described on a recently erected stele, as if it were so distant from present affairs that people need to be informed about it, like tourists visiting their own past. Banner festivities, now designed for families and local organizations, with minimal respect given to the prayers chanted by the Mergen lamas, are an example of the ephemeral jollity referred to earlier. Just one aspect of the past social relations of the *oboo* has wound itself into the present like an underground chain. This is the fact that patrons are required to supply the offerings, and that these days a manager, known as "master" (*ejen*) of the *oboo*, is necessary to organize the ceremonies.[6] Major *oboos* today bring about some of the largest regular Mongol gatherings in Inner Mongolia, and the questions of what to make of the roles of patron and manager—and who should take up these positions—can be important matters of negotiation. Such tangles of relations tell us much about how matters are really arranged among the Mongols. It turned out that after the Banner *oboo* was taken up by officialdom, Manghan's family (the owners of the horse skull that served as the initiatory offering) had no further male descendants, and a daughter took over the role of manager. Meanwhile Chorji's half-brother Chinggelbatu, became the main patron-sponsor of the event. Chinggelbatu as an official in the Banner was able to obtain lavish funding that the other family could never have managed. He soon joined in the master role and assimilated it to that of patron. On the marble stele detailing the history of the *oboo*, the two masters legitimated their position in way that would

6. The master-manager of an *oboo* is commonly allocated some land from which to make a living while he organizes the seasonal rites, provision of ritual items, the schedule of donations and attendance, engages the lamas to chant, manages the games, and oversees the periodic rebuilding of the cairn (Hürelbaatar 2006).

have had meaning only to local Mongols—by genealogy, as daughter of Manghan and son of Sechingge.[7]

In more ways than one the monastery was now separated from the *oboo*, the main lay gathering of the region. But close to Mergen there emerged other lay groupings that had various close interests in the monastery. Before describing them, we briefly discuss the ways in which the lay population can be said to be religious at all.

Ambiguities of Lay Religiosity

The immediate neighborhood of Mergen Monastery consists of three hamlets: the Mergen settlement at the gates, and West Plateau and East Plateau villages, along with some straggling construction along the main road. Almost all of the people living in the three hamlets are Mongols, while to the south the houses along the main road are mostly Chinese. It is difficult to pin down descriptively the ways these people are religious. We mentioned earlier that the laity feels they have little responsibility for providing for the monastery economically, although they do give donations from time to time, for they are aware of the subsidies, grants, and lamas' salaries paid by the Baotou government. Just as important, the custom that the lamas would be sons of local families praying for their own community was lost after the group of mostly Urad boy lamas was dispersed in 2001. These two features have distanced the monastery from the neighboring laity.

Some local people, especially Chinese, say they do not have faith. And yet, what they do suggests something more complex, and is further differentiated by class, state service, and education. One day we met a middle-aged, evidently poor Chinese woman making the trek to Mergen on foot in blazing sun. "I don't believe in Buddha," she said

7. The inscription on the back of the Banner *oboo* stele read as follows: "The banner of *oboo* of Urad Front Banner was first established between 1650 and 1670. This *oboo* was also named the General's (*Jangjun*) *Oboo*. The Mongols of the Urad region construct a worshiping *oboo* with stones, earth, trees and willows in a shape of a stupa. Before [they] go to war [they] kill cattle and anoint their spears, and battle standards with blood to predict and pray for victory in battle. In ordinary times, [they] worship heaven and earth and the mountain master at the *oboo*, and pray for avoidance of drought, disaster, and the sufferings of misfortune. Everyone from princes, dukes, and officials to the commoners participated in this important ritual. For offering to the *oboo*, a bull was killed and its skin was cut into strings and encircled round the *oboo*. Because meat was offered to the *oboo* and eaten by all participants, this was called a red offering. Along with the offering, the three manly games—horse-racing, wrestling and archery—took place. Erected with reverence by the youngest son of Sechingge and the third daughter of Manghan. 2005–08–08"

at one point. "So why do you come here?" we asked. "Why shouldn't I come, even if I don't believe?" she flashed back. We have no idea why she was making the visit, but plenty of "nonbelievers" come because they have been hit by a misfortune, which the lamas may help them counteract. No complicated Buddhists ideas of sin or karma are involved, simply the thought that "something I do not understand" has caused me to have this trouble and the lamas have spiritual powers to remove or suppress it.[8] Such an apprehension was attributed even to the Chinese soldiers based at Mergen, who are credited by lamas for having stopped the rampages of the Red Guards: "Good boys. Maybe they are Buddhists, maybe the ghosts touch them and they know fear" (Crane 2001, 171). Many of the elderly people in these parts can neither read nor write, and yet it is not because the services are in Mongolian that they attend—some people told us they do not try to understand the chanting. The greatest numbers come to the big annual gatherings at New Year, Mani, and the Maidar circumambulation, for those are occasions on which people can fulfill the most common goals: making holy wishes (*irügel*), "gathering merit-fortune" (*buyan hurahu*) and blessings (*adis*), or collecting empowered items like *utlaga* and *mani ürel* to enhance one's religious state.[9] Often humble objects of a person's life are directly inserted into these religious acts; we met a young woman who gave a gift of needles and thread to Minggan for him to read a prayer-wish (*irügel*) for her deceased father.

Others attend because they are caught up in layered histories that cannot be ignored. An old Chinese farmer arrived one day with a bulky gift of watermelons, saying he had discovered the remains of a stupa while plowing and wanted advice about whether he should perform a rite there. "If you destroy a stupa it is a sin. If you rebuild it that is a merit," he said. Later, it turned out that he had briefly been a monk at

8. For poetic descriptions of such feelings among the Chinese of this region see Crane 2001. In 1996 George Crane visited the region with a disciple of the Chinese ascetic known as the "barefoot monk" who had meditated in the *daoren wopu* cave in the mountains above Mergen and died in the Cultural Revolution. The purpose of their journey: to find and give a proper internment to the bones of the master. Crane describes sadness, attempts to appease ghosts, lingering hatred of the Japanese occupiers, and Chinese who "became at least partially Mongols" (2001, 211).

9. *Adis* (from S. Adhiṣṭhāna) is a blessing bestowed by a reincarnation or guru (see Introduction). *Mani ürel* are "seeds" produced through rituals in the *mani* service that are held to increase in number of their own accord, thus increasing the merit (*buyan*) and fortune of the recipients. *Utlaga* is made of dried powdered juniper and other substances according to recipes devised by individual lamas. It is regarded as more, or less, effective depending on the power of the lama and the *tarni* he whispered into it. The smoke of *utlaga* can drive away small demons, such as those causing ill health or crying in infants, and it can also be used to purify polluted objects and people.

Mergen in his youth. The discovery of the stupa had set his imagination going: he said that it had been built during the Qing Dynasty as a memorial for the 3rd Mergen Gegen, who had drunk water at this place (now his farm) and consequently died. The attendance of a lama is needed for this kind of disturbance from the past to be resolved, the anxiety to be at least temporarily allayed.

During the past decades many Urad people have abandoned herding and taken up professions; many of the children of the herders living round Mergen have received higher education and taken jobs in Chinese-speaking environments (factories, administration, banking, teaching, business, etc.) in cities in Inner Mongolia. Educated people may see themselves as good Buddhists but they seldom visit a monastery. One such woman, who only went to Mergen twice in her life, said, "I don't know what kind of people go to the monastery. Are they sinful (*nigültei*) or do they have faith (*süjigtei*)?" She was implying that people went there *because they needed to*, in order to atone for their wrongful deeds, and she cited a saying popular during the Cultural Revolution: "For a religious person, Buddha is with you anywhere, anytime." Such people are concerned with the ethical aspects of Buddhism: they read books about it, often maintain a personal deity and shrine at home, and might attend a teaching by a famous lama. But they go to the monastery infrequently and are quite critical of the local lamas.

Our concern in this book, however, is with the ordinary working people of the locality, some of whom are relatively wealthy, but not highly educated. These are people whose lives are tangled up with the monastery, as the examples given in this chapter will explain. Martin Mills has argued that anthropologists of Buddhism have made too absolute a divide between laity and monks, ignoring the many networks, abilities and activities that cross the boundary. He describes, for example, how householders in Ladakh own property inside monasteries as dwellings for their monk-relatives, and how monks leave the precinct regularly to take part in agricultural and other duties. Because of these ties the ordinary monk, as distinct from scholars and reincarnations, has a "profoundly ambiguous status" (Mills 2003, 66; see also Goldstein 1998, 21–22). The same is undoubtedly the case for Mergen. Here people of hybrid status were more numerous than those seen unambiguously as monks. We have mentioned Jongrai, with his thriving village household and primarily bursarial function in the monastery. There were also a fair number of former monks living in the vicinity, people who had never returned to monastic life, or who had done so but subsequently left the monastery. Furthermore, a few of the laity had taken the basic *ubashi* vows, the first in the series taken by monks. They shaved their heads, wore approximations of lama's clothing, and devoted themselves to religious activity. There were few men in this category, but at Mergen and Badgar Monasteries there were several such elderly women, who are called *chibaganchu*. Some large monasteries in China issue such devotees with registration documents that allow them to become preferential worshippers at Buddhist institutions throughout the country, evidence of the increasing mobility of lay devotees.[10]

In Inner Mongolia the laity/monk relation has been subject to a quite different history than the case described by Mills. In Ladakh the issue is the mutual interpenetration of what Mills calls "the chthonic productive consciousness" of villagers with religious goals and rituals, wherein the latter takes up and spiritually transforms the former. The result is a clear, one-way superiority of Buddhist ideals over those seen as this-worldly (Mills 2003, 66, 344–47). In Inner Mongolia a quite different ideology intervened. Since the 1950s the Communist Party has proclaimed the very reverse: productive, wealth-creating life is to be embraced and religion is outmoded superstition. This means that when a monk simultaneously maintains a lay household, it is the latter that is more highly valued in an all-China state perspective, while the role in the monastery is seen as a lowly paid service.[11] Of course many lamas do not accept this view, especially when they are in the monastery, but nevertheless it is available to all of them. Hence their identity is subject to perspectival swings, now seeing "the monastery" from the point of view of civic life and now the other way around.

Baruun Da's *Sang* and the Unauthorized Stupa

The elderly lamas remembered the old division of the monastery according to the estates (*sang*) of the reincarnations described in Chapter 3, but it seemed redundant in any practical sense after Chorji Lama took charge of the whole place. Actually, the old *sang* idea was not quite dead

10. *Guiyi zhengshu* is a document issued by some Buddhist institutions verifying the religious credentials of the person. A number of vows have to be taken to get such a pass. With it, as one *chibaganchu* said, you can go to any monastery, show the document, and be welcomed as a true subject [of Buddhism].

11. Some middle-class people told us they were Buddhists, but on no account would they allow their son to become a lama, so inferior and limited has that status become. They conceded that people who could no longer contribute to worldly life, like elderly women, might appropriately devote themselves to religion.

and we shall show how it became the germ that delineated new lay constituencies that inserted their own elements into the monastery.

By 2005 evidently any claims based on a reincarnation's *sang* would have to take account of changed circumstances. In the past the reincarnations' estates had been economic institutions; but now with their serfs and livestock long since gone, there were few resources with which to gainsay Chorji's sovereignty and he hardly recognized the identity even of his own *sang*. It became no more than a courtyard he could lock up: the entire Mergen precinct was his area of operation. This was a signal that the whole idea of the holy hierarchy of reincarnations might be dislodged (for although Chorji was a reincarnation he had not made this the basis for his activities). In this situation, where management of the whole site was what counted, any claims made on behalf of a *sang* would have to jostle with incomers, who had made separate contracts with Chorji.

The ups and downs of Chorji's endless lawsuit with the army were the backdrop to his renting of the former Officer's Mess to a succession of Baotou institutions. By 2005 the latest of these, military training for schoolchildren, had assumed mass proportions with hundreds of trainees and numerous instructors. Meanwhile, since religious personnel were permitted to produce subsistence food, in another part of the precinct the Chinese lay Buddhists who had rented the former Güüshi *sang* employed a team of peasants to cultivate vegetables for sale. Soon Chorji too, with the help of Sechen, a former schoolteacher, organized the young lamas into vegetable gardening squads. The products were used for the lamas' own food, and also sold to the restaurant. In fact the history of restaurants at Mergen is a good example of the burgeoning of external entrepreneurship in the monastery.

In 1998 the restaurant consisted of a Chinese couple who had rented a corner of a barrack to cook modest dishes for the relatively rare visitors at the Officers' Mess such as ourselves. Meals were eaten outside in the shade of two willows. By 2000 these cheerful cooks, who worked only in the summer, had disappeared. A new restaurant opened in a different barrack, and by 2005 this operation had expanded to a couple of canteens with a numerous staff. These cooks and waiters cultivated a large plot of land in the east of the precinct for their vegetable supplies. By 2007 another restaurant operation had opened, organized seasonally by the military training people, who had signed a ten-year contract with the monastery. They made substantial investments, demolished some barracks, built eight pleasant dormitories, and constructed a spacious modern building labeled with large gold characters Civilized

Dining Hall (*wenming canting*). The agreement was that this enterprise could run the training business rent free for ten years, but after that all the improved buildings would revert to monastery ownership.

It is in this context of construction at Mergen that we should consider the stand taken by the family of the Western Great (Baragun Da) Reincarnation. Long before the elderly lama died in 2003, relations with Chorji had soured. This was a long-running conflict over status and religious traditions going back to the days of Sechingge. The Baragun Da as a reincarnation was equal to Chorji, but in age and learning he was by far the senior. A mild man, he was not given due respect and the other lamas also tended to disregard him on account of his inability to chant the Mongolian liturgy fluently. He was from Ordos, had been educated there in the Tibetan liturgy at Shira Juu Monastery, and arrived at Mergen already set in Tibetan ways.[12] Nevertheless he acquired lay followers in greater numbers than the other senior lamas of Mergen, for he was a reincarnation who gave blessings, had medical expertise, and contacts in wealthy Ordos. Distinctly popular with the laity, streams of people would visit him in preference to other lamas and bring offerings and gifts.

Baragun Da was someone for whom *sang* identity was important. When we visited his village home he was distant and unwelcoming; ill at ease with foreigners, he had dressed, even in 2002, in severe Mao uniform. He faced away from us and disclaimed any knowledge of his previous incarnations. Nevertheless, on the subject of the three *sang* estates remaining from the days of his youth he thawed into relative volubility. We well remember the shiver of disdain that crossed his face when he had to remind Chorji, who was present during this visit, which was the worshipped deity of the Chorji *sang* (Mahakala).

After the Baragun Da Reincarnation died, his family claimed ownership of the property (furniture, etc.) in his *sang* and wanted to move it out. But Chorji refused. He allowed them to take only a few items recently brought in by the old lama; the rest he said belonged to the monastery. The bad feeling created by this disagreement was compounded when the Lama was cremated within his own *sang*. This went against former practice whereby senior Mergen lamas had been cremated outside the precinct, in the hollow of an ancient ruined fort north of the monastery, and their ashes then placed in the Temple of Relics. Taking

12. When the Baruun Da was recognized as a young boy in Ordos his *sang* had been unable to afford to "invite" him to Mergen (they could not find the wherewithal to pay the "nine whites" price). During the Japanese occupation Ordos was cut off from Mergen and the reincarnation could not cross the battle lines until late in his education.

advantage of Chorji's absence a new grouping emerged: the relatives rapidly gathered money from lay supporters and built a large elegant white stupa (*suburgan*) for the Baragun Da's ashes. What was most defiant about this monument was its dominating site, for it was placed inside the monastic precinct directly to the north—that is "above"—the main Chogchin Temple. As we mentioned in Chapter 3 (see also Mills 2003, 48–52) all monastic and indeed much lay-built space is hierarchically marked by the different values given to the cardinal directions; the space behind, i.e., to the north of an object should be occupied by a senior and protective structure.[13]

That the building of this new stupa was seen by some as provocative is shown by the hostile rumors that then circulated: the remains of a bonfire were pointed out, in which some large bones could be seen, and it was said that these were the remains of the Lama's cremation. "Look how those relatives respect their ancestor when they leave his bones lying in the open!" said one accuser. This was disingenuous and must have been a deliberate slander, for such carelessness was unbelievable: any Mongolian family would remove and reverence the bones, if only because of the danger and pollution bound to arise from leaving them in the open.

The new white stupa is a pointed memorial to the idea of the holy reincarnation. It both holds the consecrated power-relic (*sharil*) of the last life, and is an accusatory reminder of a particular instance of temporality and personhood, distributed back through the eight incarnations of the Baragun Da. The form of the memorial stupa copies the proportions of those erected for exceptionally revered lamas throughout northern Buddhist history. Nevertheless, if we look at this case as a decision, it cannot be seen as the execution of a timeless "cultural schema" (Ortner 1989); previous reincarnate lamas, even the 8th Mergen Gegen, had not been accorded the honor of a built stupa. Erecting this particular structure was a choice to deviate from accepted practice. The stupa's very grandness stands as a mute reproof for the disregard with which the lama was treated in his last lifetime.

Thus, the two most recent constructions at Mergen manifest incompatible chronotopes. The monument of Baragun Da's stupa is an example of laypeople creating the latest layer in a palimpsest defined by stacking up links from the past. In contrast, the Civilized Dining

13. In the past a number of stupas, long since demolished, had stood where Baruun Da's family placed his memorial. They had been placed to guard from occult forces emanating from the mountains and were not memorials for individual lamas.

Hall is a reproof to the monastery in a quite different way: implying by means of its prominent label that it (alone) is civilized. Without history, the dining hall stands as the implantation of a present-future time of Chinese civility.

The Oboo of the Community of Monks: Remaking the Diagonal

Monks have clear precedence over laypeople attending monastery services,[14] but the balance has become debatable at the worshipping rituals for *oboos*, springs, rocks, etc., outside. Whereas in the past, even noble patrons used to prostrate to the lamas, in recent years the role of patron initiator has become dominant. The larger and more public the rite, the more the lamas appear as hired religious specialists, mere adjuncts to the festivities (see description of the Jirgaltu *Oboo* rites in Hürelbaatar 2006). In the absence of other manifestations of "civil society" any large-scale "revival" of this kind potentially has the aspect of a spontaneous public gathering,[15] and to a lesser degree so do minor local rites such as the Muna cults in the valleys around Mergen. This situation is highly dynamic—hence alive with the possibility of challenging established hierarchies. The landscape around Mergen is bestrewn with defunct *oboos* and ruined shrines,[16] each of them capable of eliciting some hitherto dormant association. Therefore, which sites people choose to neglect and which a lay initiator decides to activate is significant.

Only one *oboo* was re-activated close to Mergen, apart from the mountain peak of Shira Orui. The Oboo of the Community of Monks (*Olan Huwarag-un Oboo*) was rebuilt just outside the western wall in 1999. This was the cairn that had first been constructed in the eighteenth century by the 3rd Mergen Gegen in order to keep at bay the

14. Occasionally, however, even humble laypeople may claim abilities normally attributed only to lamas. Jonathan Mair talked for a while with a tiny, frail old Mongol woman who had come to the Mani service. She liked him and gave him some prayer beads in the form of a bracelet. "Should I ask the lamas to enliven (*amilagulhu*) it?" he asked. "No, there is no need," she assured him. "[I have] told these beads with my own hand, chanting *mani*, and [I have] completed it (*bütügegsen*)." The old lady was saying she had enlivened the beads herself.

15. See Diemberger (2007a) for the case in a Tibeto-Mongol area of Henan.

16. The Lamahai-yin Oboo to the north of Mergen, which had been worshipped by the Hubilgan Lama's *sang*, still exists as a pile of stones, but after this line of reincarnations died out, its cult was discontinued and has not been revived. The Dain-u Tohai (War Marker) Oboo to the east of Mergen has also not been revived, and the Gurban Chindamani (Three Jewels) Oboo was destroyed when the railway was built. The Haranuud noble clan has not revived its family *oboo*. A ruined Geser Temple on the east bank of the Mergen River has also not been revived.

curse of the tears of the rebellious proctor (Chapter 3). It had been leveled when the army used its stones to build the wall of the compound. During our first visits it was barely distinguishable from other rocky outcrops in the plateaus around Mergen, but we arrived in 2000 to discover an elegant dry-stone construction of three stories topped with a trident and willow branches, surrounded by thirteen smaller cairns. Lay people told us proudly that offering rites are now held annually to the *oboo* and that most of the households living nearby attend (Evans and Humphrey 2003).

Why was this *oboo* revived? Lamas at the monastery had died "abnormally," illnesses were coming in, and there was discord among the monks. Also, accidents and a murder had happened among the people of West and East Plateau villages. To discover the cause of all this misfortune, the elderly herder Erhimbayar had taken action: together with the Western Great Reincarnation he journeyed to Kumbum, the great monastery in Qinghai. There, senior monks told them that something terrible (*sürhei yaguma*) was making obstacles to the wellbeing of the monastery and the homeland. You must make a "correction" (*jasalga*) by repairing your *oboo*. In fact this was the third time the Kumbum lamas had made this suggestion and nothing had been done. Now Chorji acceded to the request of the old families of the area and allowed them to rebuild the *oboo*, saying he knew nothing about such rites and that the monastery had no resources to support them.

This was the go-ahead Erhimbayar needed. The lay families appointed him to organize the rebuilding and become the master of the *oboo*. Erhimbayar is the dignified elder with a sweet smile, mentioned earlier in the context of the herders' attempts to defer the closure of the mountains. Prior to that, he had mobilized local people in a protest at the implications of administrative boundary changes on rights to land. In this case his ability to gather and lead was channeled by the "pasttime" of monastic *sang* estates to create a new grouping. Erhimbayar's father had been chief horse herder for the 8th Mergen Gegen's *sang* and he himself had served in the monastery's militia and later became a respected herder. A patriarch with several upstanding sons, he told us why he had agreed to the task. "It is because the *oboo* was built by Mergen Gegen and continuously worshipped by his Gegen *Sang*. I am a Gegen *Sang* man, a true servant (*bogul*) of Gegen *Sang*. And everyone knows this—the *oboo* is your affair, they told me. So I moved (i.e., rallied) all the previous subject (*shabi*) households of Gegen *Sang*. Also all the other old families round here. And my eldest son moved the young people."

So the social relations of a long time ago—the quasi-feudal organization existing before the Communist takeover in the late 1940s—did not die completely when they stopped being an organizational principle of political-economic life. This point is worth making again in relation to Latour's statement "If a dancer stops dancing, the dance is finished" (2005a, 37). Evidently, something here was not finished. It lived on in a ghostly jealousy between the Chorji *sang* and the Gegen *sang*. In the 1940s the 5th Chorji and the 8th Mergen Gegen had clashed over a wrestling match between their lamas, and as a result the Chorji had stormed out of the monastery; he went to meditate near Debeseg. This confrontation was actually about precedence.[17] According to Sengge the ill feeling filtered into the next generation, when the current Chorji kept the Gegen *Sang* locked and uninhabited. And it lingered among the complex of elements that forms Erhimbayar's identity ("I am a Gegen *Sang* man"). The event of the rebuilding of the *oboo*, which was important to him, enabled the reshuffling and refocusing of Erhimbayar's ideas of what he is as a person. His years as a cadre were now cast into the background, his activism on behalf of herders also rendered secondary, the startlingly obsolete identity as a Gegen *Sang* man enabled him to assert a new individuality as the moral rectifier of the community.

This assembling of laity attached to his previous incarnation's monastic rivals was not warmly welcomed by Chorji, who washed his hands of the affair. In fact, lay relations with the monastery did not proceed smoothly. Erhimbayar is a man with a strong sense of what is appropriate for the good life of a Buddhist layman. So, although he is also a ritual specialist who regularly makes divination of house sites, lucky days for weddings and so forth, he thought that this ability was not sufficient for divining the right date for offering to the *oboo*—that should be done by the lamas.[18] The date chosen was immediately con-

17. Sengge was sent from Jargaltu Monastery, which was subject to the Chorji *sang*, to take part in this wrestling tournament at a festival after the raising of the *sülde* at Mergen. Young men like Sengge were expected to be fall-guys (*idesi* – "food") for the crafty older wrestlers, but on the other hand according to custom (*yosu*) the senior lama's wrestler should in general win. On this occasion Chorji, although he was a reincarnation junior to Mergen, expected his chief wrestler to prevail, as the man was an experienced champion known across the region; but he was upended unceremoniously by Mergen Gegen's young boy. Mergen Gegen's sarcastic crowing with delight so angered Chorji that he walked out, even though there was a background expectation that the fighter of the senior lama (Mergen Gegen) should win.

18. Erhimbayar said that the correct date would be found in the lost *Yellow History*, which according to him was not destroyed in the Cultural Revolution after all but had been kept hidden by one of the Mergen lamas. If the history was really consulted, this was an unusual case of referring to historical documents and it did not happen when rebuilding the *oboo* itself. The 3rd

tradicted by Sengge Lama, who, with his wider regional concerns, objected that it clashed with the date of sacrifice to the Banner *oboo*, and he refused to attend. The main grudge, however, was about why only the laity gave money for the offerings and not the monastery. After all, this *oboo* was re-consecrated primarily to ensure the wellbeing of the monks as a body. But inside the monastery there were no Gegen *Sang* monks left to take responsibility. In the second year, irritation arose about what had happened to a goat and some money left over from last year in the hands of a lama—this incident stood for the unreliability and corruption suspected among the monks.

Finally, there was dismay about the ascetic character of the offerings insisted upon by Erhimbayar and the subsequent feast—no meat, no alcohol. He had no theological argument for a "white" (milk products) rather than a "red" (blood) offering. He told us several times that he had no idea who the god in the *oboo* was—that was a matter for the lamas.[19] Rather, he was insisting on a Buddhist ethic, the injunction on nonviolence. He was angry when, on one occasion, the feast was held in the monastery, "animals were killed," alcohol supplied and the event ended up with everyone quarrelling—a sign, he thought, that the offended spirit of the *oboo* had seen people eating meat and drinking and made them fall out as a kind of punishment. Thereafter Erhimbayar held the dinner at his own home, preparing dishes with butter, cream, and sugar at his own expense. This displeased both the lamas invited to chant and the lay participants. Could we not have a good meal with meat afterward, they pleaded, even if we offer only milk products to the *oboo*?

We asked Erhimbayar if matters in the monastery and village had improved after the rebuilding of the *oboo*:

"They certainly have," he replied.

"How so?" we enquired.

"The hooting of the owls disappeared."

Hürelbaatar understood immediately what this meant. Owls calling are a bad omen. "Ai-yaa!" said Erhimbayar. "There were a lot of them before, sometimes laughing, sometimes crying. The whole thing is always bad. This bird calls at the door of the family, the window, the chimney."

Mergen Gegen's detailed instructions for the construction of *oboos* (*BJ* 1780–1783, vol. 4, text 16) were not consulted and the Community of Monks *Oboo* was rebuilt according to memory.

19. The lamas disagreed about the identity of the god. Erhimbayar knew, however, which sacred items had been buried under it, or placed in its "stomach": the five kinds of grain, tiny pieces of gold, silver, and pearls, *tarni* mantras written on paper, and relics from Kumbum.

We asked if anything else good had happened: "The clearest thing is the disappearance of the calling of the birds. Quarrelling, bad words (*hara hele ama*) about other people, that kind of thing . . . have all lessened. That is why people attend the *oboo* rituals."

Erhimbayar was quietly pleased that he had acted rightly, but still, managing the *oboo* was expensive and time-consuming and he wished in 2002 to hand over the responsibility to the monastery. Chorji declined. For this and other reasons Erhimbayar was contemplating resigning from the Monastery Management Committee (C. *miao guan hui*).[20] This body hardly ever met in any case. "The meetings, well, Chorji doesn't hold them. He doesn't inform us and he pays no attention to what other people say. So I won't go there much anymore," said the elder. By 2005 he had resigned from the committee, thus removing the only representation of the lay community.

Soon it became clear that the old story of the Cursing Proctor—the initial *raison d'etre* of the Oboo of the Community of Monks—could produce a further corrective innovation. A new ritual site suddenly appeared at a point along the transverse line of the diagonal, and revived with it was the memory of the line of righteous flight from the monastery. One of Chorji's improvements, while we had been away, was to tear down some old army workshops near the Temple of Fierce Deities (Janghan Dugan). This revealed a small straggling, but somehow elegant, elm tree. No one now remembers who it was, lamas or laity, but some individuals decided to worship it. A brief rite with a mantra was sufficient to consecrate (*seterlehü*) and put life into (*ami talbihu*) the tree, after which people tied colored ribbons on it and made prayer-pledges (*dagatgal*) there. We were told that this tree is not just any tree but grows at the site of an earlier water-spirit (*lus*) shrine long ago destroyed. Sengge Lama said this shrine had been set up where the rebellious proctor *first* dropped his tears on being expelled from the monastery, before crying a second time when he looked back at the monastery from the place where the *oboo* was founded. Thus the water spirit/elm tree shrine was on the direct line of spiritually empowered places that led from the Öhin Tngri hill in the northeast, through the doors of the Janghan and Maharanza Temples to the Oboo of the Community of Monks, and onward to another *oboo* far away in the southwest. The newly worshipped tree was a visual reminder at once of the

20. The Monastery Management Committee in 2002 had four members, Chorji, the Baragun Da, Jongrai, and Erhimbayar. After the deaths of Baragun Da and Jongrai, Minggan took Jongrai's place. For a description of the more elaborate Management Committee of Labrang Monastery, see Slobodnik (2004, 13).

righteous proctor's concern about irreligious behavior and also of the constant effort required to negate his ancient curse. In fact while walking around in the Mergen precinct it is impossible to see—and easy to forget—the Oboo of the Community of Monks, which is hidden by the high army wall. The new Sacred Tree, on the other hand, is close and in full view.

If we return to the master of Mergen and picture to ourselves his relations with surrounding laity, he was the monastery's link to the resources of the outer world (Baotou) but at the same time he was challenged by the emergence of several new local assemblages. One, that of the followers of Baragun Da, asserted the singular charisma of the reincarnation, which could simply insert itself as a force, dislodging hierarchy; another, called up around the Oboo of the Community of Monks and the Sacred Tree, was a ritual "correction" to the misfortune and discord that dogged the monastery; and the third, rallied at the Banner Oboo, asserted control over the lost lowland parish of the monastery. All three, we think, were the product of laities made anxious, but also emboldened, by the momentous upheavals in their lives. If the monastery authorities would not, or could not, provide what they wanted, the laity could summon old precedents, or dissonant histories of moral principle, and—in different ways—take action themselves.

It is with the subjectivity of a layman that we end this chapter, in order to attempt to convey the volatile perspectives of someone who was rejected person in the networks around Mergen. So far in this chapter we have been discussing successful men. Sainjirgal was the very opposite, and he challenged other discourses through his very embodiment of misery. He was poor in the sense of being dispossessed, without much of a household, but, more poignantly, he was oppressed by *who he was*: the descendant of Togtoh, a black negative ancestor of the place, accused not only of assassinating Queen Qi, regent of the Banner in the 1940s, but of later rebelling against the early Communist government and subsequently being executed as a counterrevolutionary.

Sainjirgal's Lament

When we first met him in 1998, Sainjirgal was working as the ticket seller for the tourist camp located in front of the monastery. The camp went bankrupt and he took up occasional work as a guide, and by 2005 he was working for the new tourist camp in the mountains. He was shunned by most of the neighbors, who warned us that he spoke lies and nonsense. Over the years we knew him, he became a shambling, incoherent figure, but he was eager to talk.

Sainjirgal was a true native of the Mergen land—he had an extensive repertoire of Mergen Gegen's songs and would burst into voice at any small association. He knew every valley in the mountains, all the stories about rocks, crannies, and waterfalls. These were more than triggers of memory; he saw them as having a purpose, as being memorials or reminders (*durashal*) of Buddhist striving. For example, he said the human footprint on a rock in the mountains was that of the legendary Tangsug Lama (from whose story *The Journey to the West* flowed many parables, see Atwood [1992] 2004); and he told us about his treasured prayer beads (*erihe*) given him as a *durashal* by his father-in-law, a reincarnation from the Middle Banner. The 108 beads called to his mind Mergen Gegen's song beginning, "Our hundred and eight disciples stopped and prayed," and immediately he started to sing it.

Sainjirgal maintained the innocence of his ancestor Togtoh: he had not found a human sacrifice for the Banner *oboo* (though asked to do so) and he had not killed Queen Qi. Furthermore, Sainjirgal said that although his family had been aristocrats they had of their own accord let all their serfs go free, and he proclaimed himself extra-loyal to the party and government. He had served eight years in the army as a young man ("I fought in battles, my blood ran out, I broke my bones") and what was his reward? He had been put in prison for ten years. The reason for his imprisonment, if there was one, never became clear to us. He blamed local officials, rather than the State. Sainjirgal often showed us the scars on his head and arms—his physical existence had become a bodily memorial of endurance.

We summarize Sainjirgal's rambling laments, spoken in a mixture of Mongol and Chinese, as follows:

"The most fortunate thing for me is that thanks to the Communist Party I became a person (*hümün bolugsan*). I'll tell you about my history—it could be written as a novel or a TV series. My life includes some dirty things (*bujar burtag yaguma*), but I must also tell you that I received the party's education. When our state is so good, when they care for us just like the Chinese, why have our Mongols changed? Now they do not fit their own name and inner nature. Mongolian people were honest in the past, weren't they? When Liberation came I was nine years old. Officials of that time were like Li Feng, they were true Mongols, concerned about the people's well-being, their prosperity, and food and clothes. Our leader then did not drink or eat the property of the people. A local leader should do something good, so people can see what he is doing, but now the Mongol leaders are selling their homeland, the herders have no space, no pasture.

"I am the poorest man. My future has all gone. In the Middle Banner, the younger brother of the director of the prosecutor's office knifed someone, but he was not punished. I protected the country for the Communist Party, but as a return I got ten years jail. I cursed them, and my curse is right. My wife is slow-minded. Other people's tears burst out suddenly, but my tears are in my chest. There's no way out! When I shout to heaven, there's no reply. When I shout to earth, no reply. Whatever I have inside, there's no place to speak it out. For me, there are many things I cannot look at. When we talk about Mongols we say they are 'heroic' (*erelheg bagaturlig*), but where are those heroic ones now? Chinggis Khan had the ability to turn history, but can our Mongols now turn history? Our Mongol people have done little. Now there has been a change in the party and government, but what are the traces left on me? This scar on my head, this bullet wound, these hard things are my marks of old man Mao Zedong's achievements.

"In the past I didn't believe in ghosts and gods. I wasn't afraid of them. When I remember. . . . I was fifteen when my father burned our family god. Ever since that we did not prosper. In the end, we became exhausted, depleted. Because I didn't believe [in religion] I joined the army. When I came back I went into the Janghan Temple and sitting there was the god made of copper. I stole its two eyes and sold them. After that I went ever further downhill. There was that great snake at Dargai near Bayanhua railway station, it had two eyes like the lamps of a car, it could swallow a whole sheep. Not afraid of people. [I] killed that big snake and carried it on horseback to sell to a restaurant, and it was so long its head and tail touched the ground on either side. Since then my household went right down—we had three hundred animals dying, disease, wolves, a flood, thieves, everything.

"Then what happened? There was a platoon sergeant called Li in Two Wells and his son said something to me, 'You are not a filial son. You are a son who can't find the ashes (*sharil*) of your father.' It was true. I could not find my father's grave. Just before *hangshi* [the day Chinese annually refurbish ancestral graves] that boy helped me find it . . . we went looking. . . . there were so many graves . . . a low place, you couldn't imagine a tomb was there, but I found the place. And I couldn't speak—tears were dropping. My father died so many years ago. Maybe because I burned *hengshigüü*[21] at the grave, or because I built up a tomb, or because I made a blood offering to the valley—since that moment whatever I did became successful. Now many people are not religious, but I am devoted.

"I am brave. I will not regret doing something for my Mongol people even if I die—I really won't regret it. What do our Mongols care about our Mongol nation-

21. *Hengshigüü* is the vapor of sacrificed cooked fat and meat, which is imbibed by deities and spirit beings.

ality? They say they care, but they do nothing. Our Mongols are angered inside, but they are afraid of speaking . . . here in China whatever the *shizhang* (military command) says it's like Buddha's *abural* (salvation). Whatever the Gegen Lama says, that's what happens. I don't think in that way. You may conquer the country, but if you can't construct it that shows your weakness, isn't it so? We are citizens of the Chinese Republic. As citizens we know about these things. We carried out our duty. If you [leaders] construct wrongly, I'll criticize you. I don't agree. I don't accept. I, at least, had my blood run out. I feel pity for myself for this. The mass of people don't speak about these things because they are afraid, but I am not afraid."

The pathos of Sainjirgal was that, disheveled and sodden, he was shunned by everyone. He was the only person to speak to us in such frank terms. For him, the heroic spirit of *sülde* could not be sidelined safely as texts and rituals. Rather, its demise was real, and to be truly and physically felt. His uncomfortable message reminded us that people do not always form into solidary groups, there are political discourses that do not work, that organize nothing and even drive people away.

In this way the centrifugal impulse of Sainjirgal's laments was like the opposite of the cheerful, multitudinous attraction of the Banner *oboo*. Of all the laypeople we met at Mergen, Sainjirgal was the one whose hard life had made him ponder the reason (*uchir*) for the existence of holy and strange things. He had little time for the monastery, but talked instead of the mountains, saying that it is not easy to climb up the Valley of the Birds.

"Right in a cranny, in the past, there was a big Gold Ox. Not stone, genuine gold. It had a history, because the 2nd, 3rd, and 4th Mergen Gegens brought it out by chanting *tarni* and fed it with grass. Yes, that was magic (*fa shu*). I didn't see it with my own eyes, but when I was fifteen or sixteen I saw its light (*gerel*). The rays came out from the eyes of the Golden Ox like the light comes out from the steel-making furnace in Baotou. That kind of light streamed out. I saw that with my eyes," he said.

On another occasion, Sainjirgal said that the Gold Ox was Mergen Gegen, in the form he took during his nightly meditation away from the monastery. What is interesting is how Sainjirgal groped for understanding: the vision of the golden light became something like an alternating beacon that posed the question of where reality lies, in the seen or in the seer.

"What I know is that five people died in the Valley of the Birds in recent years, right in the land of the Golden Ox. They were ignorant university students. In early times, because of the eyes, no one touched it.

But those boys did not do good things and they all died in a mountain torrent. Nature (*baigal*) operates that way. As long as you worship the holy thing (*burhan*), the *burhan* will be inside you. If you think there is a *burhan*, then there is. If you don't exist (*chi baihu ügei*), the *burhan* also does not exist. Not everyone can see the Golden Ox, nor see the shining eyes, because they don't have faith.

"Society is the same. If you glorify the Communist Party, holding it up, if the mass of people do this, then the party will be built up. If you don't elevate it, the mass of people won't respect it, and then the party will stagnate. This . . . it's the same in Buddhism. If you worship it and elevate it and repair it, then it will get better and better. This is what I can see. Usually I don't worship *burhan*, and I'm not afraid of ghosts, but from my true feelings (*ünen sedhil*) I am afraid and I worship (*shitüne*) [them]. They make me see with my real genuine eyes (*yag jinhini namayi nidü-ber üjegüljee*)."

Most of this chapter has described certain regroupings of laypeople living around the monastery as their concerns broke into monastic arrangements during the period of our fieldwork. They remind us that it is not only the members of an institution but also external people who care for what that institution stands for, will intervene and insist, and will place a stake (an *oboo*, a sacred tree, a stupa) to make sure that their concern is symbolically and physically evident. We ended, however, with an isolated individual, because it is important to point out that among the shifting configurations there are also processes of degrouping or anticoagulation. It would be a mistake, we think, to write off someone like Sainjirgal merely as "untypical." The more interesting observation is that despite living in the same landscape and inheriting the same ideas as other people, the twists and turns of drastic personal histories can have a progressively differentiating and singularizing effect. Each fateful "wrong step" is an event that isolates such a person further in social oblivion, and yet these steps (the acts that count as sins, the remorseful rites, the redeeming visions) are not something new, but all are locally understandable elements of that assemblage we could call "society"—which consists of means for undoing as well as reforming relations.

TEN

Tradition and Archivization

Introduction 2007

Two powerful external directives—the inclusion of Mergen in an urban municipality and the designation of the monastery as a cultural relic—called for a response. The place had to be made intelligible to outsiders: to officials and patrons, urban people, visitors interested in history, Chinese worshippers, and even casual tourists. At the same time, a new intake of young monks and a break in the old teaching practices subtly altered the inner workings of the monastery. We discuss these changes as a present day process of "archivization."

The aim was to refit the monastery for the contemporary: new technologies were introduced that defined what could be picked out and conserved in written form, and thus made consonant with—and available to—modern people. Of course the making of archives of one kind or another had been present since the beginning of the monastery's history; it was always in tension with—and usually swamped by—the fertile, capricious currents of the oral tradition. But in recent years the balance has swung in favor of new homogenizing techniques, which have shouldered aside the largely unspoken understandings and improvisations of the monks. Indeed that has been, in part, their aim—to deliver a definitive, writing-based form of authenticity. Yet we noticed at the same time that some acts of archive making had a different character: they were still acts of definition by writing, but were individual, performative, and eventual in ways that recalled earlier decisive actions. Unlike the other archival process happening at the same time, which was mainly concerned with regularizing and labeling Mongolian Buddhism as an adjunct of "Mongolian culture," these were direct and proud *acts of declaration*—designed to effect a state of affairs, to mark or institute a change in the situation. The overall archivization of Mergen was thus an arena of complex, emergent, and contradictory activities.

Before broaching the several connotations of the archive, we first describe the recruitment of young monks and the situation in the monastery since our previous visit in 2002, since this was a direct spur to *using* archives, as distinct from making archives that are then set aside. We then discuss the vagaries of the spontaneous production of tradition at Mergen—the mercurial decisions that for some people seemed to call for replacement by authoritative documentation/archives—giving the example of the ritual consecration of the new guardian deities in 2005. This may have been one of the last important rituals to take place at Mergen in the pre-archived fashion. For shortly after we left that autumn a series of dramatic events were to close the monastery once again. It was however quite soon to reopen, and when we arrived in 2007 it was to find the monastery in more or less fully archived mode.

A New Generation of Young Monks

It was difficult to recruit young monks in the Urad area. There was other work available and the life of a lama had little prestige. The law now stipulated that young children could no longer be sent to monasteries by their parents; the choice could only be made after education. Local herders told us that only someone from a poor family with few prospects and weak school results would find the simple provision of food, lodging, and a strict life at a monastery an attractive proposition. We knew also that it had been hard to retain young monks from families living near Mergen: if they were lonely or found the life too hard, they could easily escape home. So Chorji scoured the distant regions of Jirim and Hinggan for recruits. At length one of his classmates with a high post in Chifeng was persuaded to "give" some boys, provided they and their parents agreed, from his jurisdiction to that of the monastery. Chorji managed to sign up around eight youths of various ages in 2004 and soon made a trip to recruit a further four. In fact they disproved the herders' negative comments, as the novices were mostly able boys from relatively prosperous families. Two were returnees, previously taught by Sengge. Tümen—charming, charismatic, and forceful—was the leader. He became a supporter of Chorji. The talented and expressive Darjai had been close to Sengge Lama, living in his rooms at Mergen and attending to his needs when he visited the monastery.

Chorji appointed Minggan the proctor responsible for discipline, Tümen and Darjai were the leaders of chanting (*umjad*), while two old lamas had the lesser posts of steward-storekeeper (*nirba*) and preparer of ritual utensils (*gonir*). A former schoolteacher called Sechen was employed to look after the domestic affairs of the monastery.[1] However, the question of who would teach the boys Mergen-style chanting had been more difficult to resolve. Sengge Lama was the only person still alive who really mastered the liturgy and the hand gestures. Chorji told us that he had gone three times to Sengge's village house to beg him to return to the monastery to teach. On the last occasion, he had offered a ritual scarf and even bowed to the ground three times. Sengge had said "yes," but he came only once or twice. In the end, the novices were taught by a makeshift team. Between them, Minggan, Sechen, and Rashisereng, a professor from Höhhot, taught Mongolian and Tibetan chanting, Mongolian writing, and practical subjects. The boys praised Minggan's lessons, but there was much that was unsatisfactory in the arrangement. Rashisereng, an expert in Buddhist theory, did not know the Mongolian liturgy, while Minggan who had a relatively good knowledge of liturgy through attending services at Mergen, had after all been initially trained in Tibetan chanting at Badgar. Further, according to Chorji he was hopelessly unreliable. The boys told us that they had learned most texts of the first level (*baga ungshilga*) from Minggan but although they had not completed it they were already attempting the Middle Chanting (*dumda ungshilga*), as this was required for the important services for the fierce deities.

The young lamas lived in one of the army barracks, where they cooked for themselves at a wood-fired stove and ate together at a long table. After lessons had ceased for the summer they spent their free time lounging and playing. They wore T-shirts and army fatigues—not that this upset the lay worshippers who now began to reappear and were glad to see any lamas at all. Chorji, following the custom of bosses, treated the boys as his personal following and would order to them to

1. In 2005 after the death of the Baragun Da, five old lamas, including Sengge, were still attached to the monastery. With Chorji, Minggan, and the twelve young recruits, Mergen Monastery could draw upon nineteen of its own lamas for great services, along with visiting lamas invited from other places.

clear the precinct, work in the vegetable gardens, or prepare for the anniversary celebration. Soon elderly invited lamas began to arrive in twos and threes to take part in the services, including Sengge Lama who stayed with his close disciple Darjai in his old rooms. We observed the young lamas chanting alongside the visitors and were amazed at their ability, for most of them had had only one year of training. Their fresh voices, even that of one solemn-faced boy who looked no more than ten years old, rang out clearly and surely. It seemed almost like old times.

There were signs of trouble, however. Chorji and Sengge were barely speaking to one another. As a result, although Sengge had arrived to take part in the Mani rites, he was not informed of the times of the services. He would turn up late or hover at the edge, although he did not complain openly. He brought his small dog to the monastery, which he used to carry under his arm as though for comfort. Chorji's suspicion that plots were afoot against him was justified. A group of four elderly lamas was still planning to join Sengge and set up a new monastery. These four stubbornly absented themselves from a main part of the Mani service. Meanwhile Chorji was planning to dismiss the steward. Rows were brewing over the choice of texts for some services, and an embarrassing lapse occurred during a Yamantaka chant. On this occasion we saw Chorji sitting on his throne being shown the page by Minggan. The elderly Bayanbilig Lama was chanting something that was clearly different to everyone else, and matters proceeded that way for half an hour or so, but suddenly another of the old lamas shouted out his version. Everyone fell silent in consternation, for chanting is supposed to happen in smooth unison. The chanting soon started again; it was noticeably more ragged and uncertain.

In the middle of another service some young lamas set up a strong and simple chant of their own, "Om Mani Pad Me Hum." For a time, their rhythmic song drowned the weaker voices of the elders, but after a while it died away and something like unanimity reasserted itself. After this service the young lamas were joking and trying out wrestling holds in the yard. Tümen said, "What chaos that was! Oh my throat is sore. I tried . . . I really tried to pull the other lamas after me, chanted as strongly as I could. But I did not manage it." It was not clear to us whether Tümen, earlier taught by Sengge, had tried to steer the chanting as his former master had instructed, or whether the young monks as a group had got stuck and resorted to the simple chant in order to have anything to sing at all. That evening Chorji held a meeting of the novices and told them to follow his line or they would be punished.

In the evenings one or two of the young lamas would secretly slip over to Sengge's room to ask him how next day's service should be conducted. But he could not describe every detail. One day we saw a group of lamas anxiously preparing for the following morning's ritual, setting out numerous butter lamps, bowls with grains, and dough figures in front of the great Maidar statue. No one came to aid them. They were peering at an "archive," an old photograph of a quite different ritual setting, the layout at the altar for Mergen Gegen's ashes, and trying to copy it.

Documents and Spontaneity in the Mergen Tradition

The 3rd Mergen Gegen left indications in his collected writings both about the deities to be worshipped and the services to be performed during the year. Among them is a history of the Temple of Fierce Deities (Janghan Dugan), the only extant temple in the monastery built during his lifetime as far as we can tell. A brief résumé of the changes in this temple indicates how the replication involved in performing tradition in fact produces variation.

The 3rd Mergen Gegen describes how when the monastery was founded the wrathful deity Damjin Dorlig, mounted on a lion "descended into the bodies of human beings and showed them the rules of accepting and rejecting." This god was the first to be made as a statue at Mergen. Soon a group of wealthy lay patrons offered much silver, and Erlig Khan the King of the Underworld was installed as the main deity in the Janghan Temple, along with five wrathful gods including Damjin Dorlig on the left side and five Khans—of Duty, Wisdom, Rule, Wealth, and Feeling—on the right. This array was complemented with statues of Padmasambhava, Tsongkhapa, and two other eminent teachers (*BJ* 1780–1783, vol. 1, no. 14, p. 88). This series of gods of the Janghan Temple did not survive into the late twentieth century, for when we first arrived, although the temple was still dedicated to worship of various wrathful deities, its main function was to house the sacred battle standard and other relics of the Urad ancestor Jirgal Bagatur. After the break with Sengge in 2001, Chorji moved the battle standard out and installed a row of different wrathful gods of tantric character. This was an act entirely in the spontaneous tradition, accompanied as it was by an innovative borrowing from Chinese temples directed towards external sensibilities ("so as not to arouse the laity to improper thoughts"): the sexual acts going on in the lower parts of the statues were covered with a curtain. For Sengge, worship of the battle standard *was* part of the "tradition" (even though it had been installed at Mergen only after the Cultural Revolution). For Chorji, the standard was an interloper from another monastery. Yet when he sought to replace it, he did not consult the writings of Mergen Gegen, which he could have done, for by then they had been republished by the "Mergen Gegen Studies" scholars. Instead he ordered a series of gods from Tibetan sculptors on the advice of senior Mergen lamas. One of these gods was Erlig Khan, but he was not placed in the central position and it is doubtful whether the lamas even know of the eminence accorded him by Mergen Gegen. Damjin Dorlig and the five Khans were nowhere to be seen. The lamas had advised that the wrathful god Yamantaka be given the place of honor, based on what they remembered of pre–Cultural Revolution times and what they thought was most important for their own worship.

This sequence of events shows that the Janghan Temple did indeed come to house a spontaneous or living tradition. By this we refer to the reproduction of a given activity (worship of fierce and martial gods) under the assumption of doing "the same" ontologically, even if the actions are in fact different (see also discussion in Chapter 5). The performance of tradition in this way destroys what had gone before even as it assembles its own version. It is at work in silence about what it accomplishes and is not concerned to leave a record or an authoritative account for future reference. Rather than use the abstract and generic word "tradition" (*ulamjilal*) the lamas talk of the specific things they do, such as following a particular guru's teaching. Such a sure-handed, piecemeal performance is at variance with, and opposes, any attempt to categorize, pin down or preserve the correct or original version. Thus although *nothing* now remains of Mergen Gegen's original set-up in the eighteenth century, each generation bore in mind the idea that the Janghan Temple is for the worship of fierce protectors and installed the particular objects they thought most powerful.

The writings that we can think of as early archives, such as Mergen Gegen's collected works (*Bum Jarlig*), were almost entirely ignored by the lamas. Precisely because their own texts were supposed be exact copies of prayers in the *Bum Jarlig* they did not use the republished facsimile of the 1780–1783 edition, because its small print and archaic cutting of letters made it so difficult to read. It seems no accident that today none of the lamas knows when the monastery's copy of the *Bum Jarlig* was lost or destroyed, and similarly the whereabouts of the *Yellow* and *Brown Histories*, even whether they still exist, remains a mystery.

For at bottom, the old lamas did not care very much. Their working prayers were in their memories. The texts they used at services were handwritten or Xeroxed versions of what they had been taught by their guru teachers, including several prayers not in the *Bum Jarlig*, and their pride was to chant heads up, barely glancing at the texts in front of them.

A similar process of transformative reproduction took place with the services held through the year, again despite the fact that a schedule was written down and enshrined in the works of Mergen Gegen. We have access to Mergen Gegen's detailed sequence of daily, periodic and annual services for the mid-eighteenth century (*BJ* vol. 1, text 9, see Ujeed 2009,154–60), the equally long list made by Galluu referring to the 1930–1940s period before the Communists came to power, the much shorter sequence followed in the late 1990s, and the drastically reduced list of services carried out in 2005. It is true that there are some continuities—in other words the lamas filled certain time slots with the "same" activities. Through the entire period, the incense offering rite (*sang*) for the spirit of victory (*sülde*), the expulsion of sins (*sor gargahu*) and the ritual dance (*cham*) for Maidar have been carried out in the first lunar month. The Mani services have always been held in summer, in the sixth month (Mergen Gegen) or seventh month (twentieth century), and the Lamp Service in honor of Tsongkhapa in the tenth month (discontinued only recently). However, many other great services mentioned by Mergen Gegen had either stopped altogether by the 1930s–1940s (e.g., an offering to the Master of Three Worlds), or changed in timing (the summer retreat, the Nigucha Huriyanggui "secret summary" service, the Ganjur service and others), or altered in the prominence given to them. For instance, Mergen Gegen mentions a service called the reading of holy will-wishes (*irügel*) for the benefit of sentient beings in the first month, but by the period described by Galluu this had developed into a prominent sequence where Mergen Gegen gave his *irügel* on one day, followed by those of the Hubilgan, Western Great and Chorji Reincarnations on the next days (Galluu 2003, 247). By the 1980s, in keeping with the reduced role of reincarnations at Mergen, none of these rites were performed.

On the other hand, rituals mentioned in lists of services given us by the present day monks do not appear in the 3rd Mergen Gegen's eighteenth-century sequence. These include of course worship of the 8th Mergen Gegen and otherwise consist of the rites of a popular kind, such as the *oboo* offerings, the sacrifices to the battle standard and Yellow Peak, and fire worship. We know because the 3rd Mergen Gegen wrote the texts, that these popular rites took place during his lifetime, so their omission from his list of services indicates that he did not consider them proper for the monastery. The tradition, however, incorporated them as integral to the Mergen schedule. By the period of our fieldwork, the vastly elaborate array of services prescribed by Mergen Gegen had shrunk to a few, and among the latter the inserted folk rites formed a rather large proportion. Nevertheless, the monks at Mergen assured us that their performances were a continuation of what had gone before.

Enlivening the Four Guardian Deities

Shortly after we arrived in 2005 we were participants in the ritual to consecrate (*rabnailahu*) the four guardian deities (*Dörben Maharanza*) in the new entrance temple.[2] This enabled us to get some understanding of how individual actors combine in the making of a live tradition. One general feature of services at Mergen (unlike at Badgar), the greater frequency of lay participation in temple ritual, can be attributed to the distant influence of 3rd Mergen Gegen—that is to the interest he is said to have had in the popular appeal of Buddhism (see Chapter 2). In this spirit, at the conclusion of the rites for the four Maharanza deities, we laypeople were told to take part by throwing holy rice into the air. Minggan said this was to spread the gods' blessing while another lama told us it was for the purification of the space, but no matter—both interpretations amounted to the same thing—the tradition was for laity to be involved in vital, physical, and empowering acts. It had been Chorji's decision to reconstruct the entrance temple with guardian gods. The sequence of chants and rituals was decided by Minggan. He made his choice according to a precedent improvised a couple of years earlier by the Baragun Da. As Sengge Lama resented all the Chorji's innovations and had absented himself from the earlier initiation of the glossy new gods in the Janghan and Chogchin Temples, it had been left to the Baragun Da to put together such consecration rites in a way that conformed, as he saw it, to Mergen ways. The Baragun Da had now died, but Minggan told us he faithfully followed his elder, especially in two rites: "Opening the Eyes" of the new deities by anointing them

2. The temple was built according to elderly lamas' memories and it contained the same four guardian gods as found in temples throughout Mongol lands. Laypeople treated these gods as a quartet, their names unknown. But lamas said that the guardian gods represent the four cardinal directions and that most lamas would know their names and different powers.

with honey and "Washing the Face" by bathing the images in holy water infused with specific ingredients. Since no one was able to reach the heads of these towering statues, the anointing was done by flicking honey with a paintbrush up into the dim heights of the temple and the washing was carried out on the reflection of the face of each god in a mirror laid on a table. Lamps were lit, holy water scattered. These actions, performed while the lamas were ardently chanting the *Rabnai* text, accomplished the enlivening. Before this there had been no need to bow to the gods because they could not see you. Now, people and deities were in communication and inert offerings, such as the rice we threw in the air, were transformed into blessed things. The rite at Mergen was thus a version of the consecration known so well from Indic cases, which accord primacy to sight, the direct engagement and return of vision, and the bodily performances in front of the images (Pinney 2001, 168).

The point of this illustration is to show how performance of each ritual was a concatenation of individual decisions in the light of mental images of the right way to do things that were created on the basis of—again idiosyncratically inflected —communications among the lamas. No doubt details would have been different if Sengge had been in charge. Sniffily he told us that Minggan's version was "too Tibetan." It was difficult to know quite what he meant. Perhaps he was referring to some ineffable aesthetic quality; perhaps to the choice of texts, which had to accommodate to what the young lamas had learned, which was derived from what their teacher Minggan knew, and he had been first trained at Tibetan-chanting Badgar monastery.[3] It is not that the potential for different versions was seen as unproblematic—the lamas adhered to the notion that there was a right way. But controversy did not shake self-confidence. Self-effacing Minggan, who now had to take decisions, was sure that his way was just fine.

One could contrast the lamas' concern with "what works" with that of the professional scholars, for whom ancient items are valued not for their efficacy but as witnesses to what will never happen again; such relics are precious and should be kept out of circulation and stored in libraries. These days it could almost be true to say that there are

3. Minggan planned the sequence of chants very carefully. He took into account not only Baragun Da's precedent, but also the knowledge of the young lamas and the number of minutes each chant takes to perform. The sequence he chose consisted of nine texts, *Bilig Baramid*, *Itegel*, *Lama Yoga*, *Sakyamuni Magtagal*, Long-life prayer (*dangshig*) for Mergen Gegen, *Blue-Gowned Wachirbani*, *Rabnai*, *White Dara Ehe*, and *Shajin Badaranggui*, all said to have been written by Mergen Gegen. The *Rabnai* is the only one of these texts directly related to the enlivening of deities.

as many professional scholars engaged in "Mergen Gegen Studies" as there are lamas in the monastery. This observation requires us to think more seriously about the archiving process.

Working Texts and Archives

In using the word "archive," we are referring to Derrida's musings on this idea, though we use only certain aspects of his work. His book *Archive Fever* ([1995] 2005), responding to the turning of Freud's house into a museum, has very different preoccupations from our own, and yet certain of Derrida's ruminations are illuminating. From his elliptical writings, we have extracted the following ideas: that archives are instituted by authorities, they are controlled and owned; that items are "consigned" as a corpus[4] and set aside in archives such that the archive becomes an auxiliary prosthetic for another activity (archives are "domiciled" in "house arrest," ibid, 2); that archiving is an insistent ongoing process, which is not an action of spontaneous memory but of inscription, of pinning-down a trace; that there is something destructive about our contemporary *"mal d'archive,"* the fever for the old and original, the compulsion exactly to repeat, which menaces spontaneity and introduces forgetfulness;[5] that the archive is not just a recording of the past but is also an act, a promise (or instruction or covenant) for the future, and finally that the new material and technical forms taken by archives feed back into the structures of the content to be archived.[6] Thus, the process of archivization is not one of closure, but of transformation.

A living tradition, especially in a hierarchical literate culture, is al-

4. "By consignation we do not only mean, in the ordinary sense of the word, the act of assigning residence or of entrusting so as to put into reserve (to consign, to deposit) in a place and on a substrate, but the act of *con*signing through *gathering together signs*. [. . .] Consignation aims to coordinate a single corpus, in a system or a synchrony in which as the elements articulate the unity of an ideal configuration" (Derrida [1995] 2005, 3).

5. The archive "will never be either memory or anamnesis as spontaneous, alive and internal experience. On the contrary: the archive takes place at the place of originary and structural breakdown of the said memory" (ibid, 11). The archive thus always works *a priori* against itself (ibid, 12).

6. Writing about the advent of telephone credit cards, tape recorders, computers, printers, faxes, E-mail, etc., Derrida observes that this "archival earthquake" does not limit its effects to the secondary recording of the history of psychoanalysis, but would have transformed, had it occurred during Freud's lifetime, the initial inside of its production and its events. The archive is not just the place for stocking a content *of the past*, but its technical apparatus also "determines the structure of the *archivable* content even in its coming into existence and in its relationship to the future. Archivization produces as much as it records the event" (1995, 16–17).

ways likely to be accompanied by the creation of internal archives by people in authority—archives that are given greater or lesser importance in ongoing activity. The 3rd Mergen Gegen clearly valued his compositions not as documentation but as powerful *working texts*—as a technique (like a gear) of producing new spiritual, blessed, or purified states. His liturgy was always composed for vocal rendition. Even his medical texts were in verse because this made them easier to remember (Galluu 2003, 117) and we are reminded that from ancient times Mongolian working instructions, such as battle orders, were rhymed for the same reason (Heissig 1966, 35). "Heard by great numbers, may it become famous in the world," Mergen Gegen wrote in his colophon to the ethical parables *Subashita,* "You disciples, understand it in your minds! May there be merit!" However, the printing of his collected works *Bum Jarlig,* selected by lamas after he had died, had a more archive-like character, namely the coordination of a single authoritative corpus. The name *Jarlig,* which means order or command, suggests something unalterable, to be obeyed, while the colophon insists above all on the sanctioned accreditation of the collection, which was certified and blessed by the famous 3rd Jangjiya Gegen Rolbidorji. It is difficult to be certain, but even at that early period the printing of the collected works in the capital city may not have been intended for *practical chanting,* but rather as a meritorious spin-off from the active tradition. The fact of printing alone would accrue merit to the sponsors, counterbalance their sins, or even be "a passport to paradise" (Heissig 1966, 159–63), since it constituted a "spreading of the teachings," irrespective of the extent to which the book was read. It seems very possible that even at Mergen Monastery face-to-face guru-disciple teaching was done not by using the Beijing print but by employing handwritten manuscripts or local prints.[7]

This situation is complicated by the fact that the holy book in North Asian Buddhism was in fact often not read at all, but kept bound up in its covers and periodically paraded as a divine object in a circumambulation of sacred space. True, this practice was not in the spirit of the 3rd Mergen Gegen's endeavors, but this aspect of the book—the notion that it has its own holy effect as an object—could not be entirely gainsaid. In this spirit, Chorji prostrated to the *Bum Jarlig* in the British Library, and the lamas accepted gladly—although they could not use it—the 108 volumes of the Tibetan *Ganjur* gifted by the commercial

7. According to Ba. Mönghe (personal communication) there was a small printing shop at Mergen, but it had ceased to exist by the early twentieth century.

company. At Mergen the importance accorded any object of veneration, including the "book as holy object," depended almost entirely on its genealogy of worship: which holy person gave it, how it was given, the depth of rites of veneration it had received before, and from whom. We discuss this further in the next chapter, but meanwhile illustrate this point by reference to Minggan's paintings. Caroline had wondered about them: the young lama painted several beautiful and correctly iconic deities, so why were none of them worshipped at Mergen, while the altars held mass-produced statues and photographs? The answer is that all of these objects, however uninspiring their appearance, had genealogies of worship, whereas Minggan's paintings, fresh off the easel, did not. The consequence of these various factors was that the Tibetan *Ganjur*, which is in any case not part of the Mergen tradition, languishes in a cupboard; the new brightly painted gods, so recently initiated, were not the objects of the deepest devotion; while Minggan's paintings were seen as "merely artistic," items for sale and not gods at all.[8]

Naming and Labeling

Even after the clear out of the inner room of the Janghan Temple, in corners, alongside walls and nestling under the main statues of the monastery there was a proliferation of deities and objects of worship. Sechen set about labeling them. He was someone with no Buddhist education at all, having first come to Mergen as an itinerant schoolteacher in 2004–2005 to earn some money. Sechen had not moved his family to the area and was planning to return home when he had earned enough. However, soon he became Chorji's right-hand man. Perhaps his schoolmasterly instincts were affronted by the unspoken, nameless confusion of deities at Mergen, or perhaps both he and Chorji had been infected with an enthusiasm for documentation as a result of the energetic production of "Mergen Gegen Studies." Chorji was preparing to publish an album of his photographs of the sacred and beautiful places around the monastery, "A World Through a Chorji's Eyes" (Menghebatu 2006). His book would do for the landscape what Sechen

8. Laity experiencing some problem would go to monks to ask for advice about which god would put things right, and they would then request a small image to be painted and consecrated for domestic worship. Such images were given, not sold. Minggan's paintings as far as we know were not taken up in this way for religious worship at Mergen.

was attempting for the gods: to use modern technology to name and provide interpretative captions for chosen objects.

Whatever the reason, by summer 2007 Sechen was busily engaged in making labels in Chinese and Mongolian for each god. This was by no means an easy task, for the elderly lamas who might have helped were either deceased or staying away from the monastery, while the master artisans who had made the new statues were Tibetans hired by Chorji from distant monasteries in previous years, and they could not be consulted either. Sechen pored over scholarly books. Soon he had produced labels for several of Chorji's new gods and two lengthy placard inscriptions, placed on either side of the entrance doors to the Chogchin Temple. He introduced a computer to the monastery and with it was able to make identical labels for every item. This produced one effect of "consignment," the *gathering together of signs*, coordinating the elements in a single corpus, in a system or a synchrony, and articulating the unity of an ideal configuration (Derrida [1995] 2005, 3).

At issue here is a radical divergence in ways of naming. In Mongolian religious practice the identity of a worshipped deity is important, because different gods have different powers. A worshipper must have some kind of name in mind, however unspecific, whereby to conceptualize the being he/she is honoring. Yet, as Derrida writes in *Acts of Religion*, in a *thinking of the name*, "the name does not have the grammatical value of the substantive; it signifies the power of naming, of calling in general. [. . .] The magical power of the name produces effects said to be real and over which we are not in command. [. . .] The name is transcendent and more powerful than we are." By secularizing a sacred language, Derrida continues, we are playing with ghosts, denying that at stake are very grave matters. "By writing [. . .] we believe that it does not matter. Writing dissimulates the gravity of the matter; it neutralizes a fatality, the proper place of which is the name in speech" (2002, 213–14). Earlier at Mergen, as we observed, none of the statues, paintings, pagodas, or relics worshipped by local people had a name in writing.[9] The word people had in mind could be an unspecific as *burhan* (any worshipped deity) or as redolent of a whole history as

9. When the 8th Mergen Gegen rebuilt the Chogchin Temple in the 1920s, he inserted high up on its outside walls a large number of stone plaques of carved deities, each named in Chinese; these plaques may have been rescued from the earlier temple, dating perhaps from the eighteenth century. This series can be seen as an earlier essay in archivization, akin to the splendid illustrated books that provide images of hundreds of deities from the *Ganjur* (e.g., Rashisereng 2001). In both cases, the aim was to provide a conspectus of gods, rather than specific objects of worship.

"Mahakala"; they knew for themselves to whom they were praying and what specific powers that god had.

In religious practice the spoken names of gods are speech acts, so people do not speak them casually. Along with the name, the mantra (*tarni*) of the god[10] is a spell that brings into being the particular power of the deity. This is why one of Sechen's acts was significant. He erased the Maidar Buddha's mantras in Sanskrit on the doorposts of the Maidar temple and replaced them with a name label and an explanatory placard in Mongolian and Chinese. In essence Sechen was replacing a sacred invocation with propositional information. One of his two placards was like a brief encyclopedia entry about Maidar. However, Sechen's activity was fraught with anxiety, like Derrida's *mal d'archive*. Not only was he untutored in Buddhism and therefore worried about getting the facts right, but having started the enterprise he said he must finish it and label every single god in the entire precinct. The diverse, disagreeing (therefore "inaccurate") sources in Mongolian, Chinese, Tibetan, and Sanskrit became a minefield for him. That summer Sechen was to be seen anxiously consulting Professor Naranbatu. He said, "The Chinese source says that Namsarai Burhan should be holding a white prosperity-bringing rat, but what am I to do? Those Tibetans masters for some reason made a black rat." Naranbatu may be a professor but he is also a former lama. His reaction was a religious one. Responding perhaps to Sechen's speaking aloud of the name "Namsarai," he replied, "First let me bow to this god."

Christopher Pinney has written in the context of popular deity worship in India of a "profound orientation within societies", when attention is directed either to a precise interpretative closure or alternatively to the figural and an ongoing performative productivity, a differential accentuation that "mo[u]lds different models of causality. In the one it is language which constrains the image, and in the other it is the image that appropriates language" (2001, 166). The great Maidar statue with its mantras (necessary, yet unintelligible signs of words) was exactly the image that absorbs language into the figural and performative. Perhaps halfway between the two modes was Chorji's photograph album, so expressive of his visual veneration of places, yet labeling and interpreting them too.[11] Sechen, on the other hand, was doing his best to install a straightforwardly semiotic and linguistic closure.

10. Lamas said that the mantra often spells out the name of the god in disguised form.

11. An example of Chorji's pointed captions is "A pity" in Mongolian, Chinese, and English, set beneath a photograph of a hacked-off tree stump. This is an interpretative move, a procedure that is inevitable when a book is intended to explain an understanding of a subject to an outside

The Textbook for Lamas

By absenting himself from the monastery, Sengge only added to the problem that made archives of various kinds seem necessary. Perhaps Sengge Lama subconsciously perceived this dilemma—this is our explanation of what many local intellectuals saw as his obstinacy. Professors in Höhhot had conceived the idea of collaborating with him to produce a textbook of the Mergen liturgy for young monks. Instead of the scrappy handwritten *aides-memoire* the lamas had been using, this publication would set out in legible Mongolian script an authoritative text containing not only the words of the prayers but the ritual instructions ("repeat three times," etc.), thus eliminating all the vital quandaries—about timing, cutting short, replacing, and so forth—that exercised the leading lamas when they were planning services. Sengge went to Höhhot to take part, but later—he never explained why—withdrew from the project. It was not that he disapproved of professors of Buddhist studies as such; he told us that he had a high opinion of their knowledge. Perhaps what he truly objected to, but did not formulate as an explicit idea, was the archival form of the textbook—the set template with its imprimatur from outside, laying down once and for all what should happen in the future.

Minggan was not so happy at having been left to carry out the teaching, and he once complained to us that Sengge was "mean" in not sharing his knowledge with the new recruits. Sengge's attitude can be linked to his dislike of the classroom teaching that would come with the new textbook. He clung to what one might call the "kinship mode" of instruction: the intimate life together of guru and disciple, the oral transmission not just of "knowledge," but of habits, tone, gesture, and care for performance. We described Sengge in Chapter 7 as happily discoursing on all kinds of topics. What we now realized was that this was general knowledge and morality for the laity. The intensive teaching of lamas was another matter. The gurus of his youth had never dispensed this religious kind of teaching, which was efficacy and power, to large groups, and especially not to "just anyone" recruited by someone else.

---

readership. Our book does this too. We acknowledge that, however much we have tried to expose Urad and not our own values (which as two authors are not identical in any case), we have also interpreted practices, revealed elements the Mergen people do not talk about, and named things they do not name. This is a reminder that instituting any kind of archive is not just making a record but, like it or not, exercises an authority—that of having the word (if not the last word). This is something Chorji well understood, and he laughed that he would write his own book if he did not like ours.

During the dispute with the monastery Sengge had one or two disciples, but they lived with him at home in the village. Here beset by villagers who needed his services, conditions were not conducive to intensive Buddhist teaching, but at least the close one-to-one relation could be maintained.[12] Readers may remember that Sengge had created what was in effect his own archive: his precious tape recordings of the whole Mergen liturgy. It is significant, therefore, that Sengge said this legacy should be shown only to professors and not to lamas—he must have understood that even his own recordings could become authoritative auxiliary inscriptions; that they would be removed from his voice and hand, no longer sounds taught through imitative-interpretative interaction to a trusted disciple, and therefore not the means whereby the religious tradition as he understood it would stay alive.

Authoritative Proclamations

Let us now consider a different kind of archiving activity at the monastery. The archive can imply the inscription of a law (in the broad sense), and it proceeds from the institution of a right, or the assertion of the legitimacy of a "consignment" (see note 4). Whether this involves family or state law, land and property, conferring a name or hitherto unwritten rights, the right to make an archive has an analyzable history (Derrida 2005, 4). We observed just such a process of "law-inscription" in the last few years at Mergen. We are referring here not of course to the cosmic "law" of replacement and retribution discussed earlier, but to the conjunctions of state law and local rights by which particular people seek to define, implement and display archives as material items (name plates, inscribed stele, exhibited official letters, and so forth). During the Qing Dynasty Mongolian monasteries proudly displayed gold-painted insignia boards with the names and ranks bestowed on them by Emperors. Now the Mergen landscape is

12. One of Sengge's disciples was Altanbagana, who chafed against his guru's combination of strict discipline and frequent distraction to perform rites for laity. Yet in a conversation with Hürelbaatar Altanbagana mentioned how the teacher Marpa had tested his disciple Mila by harsh treatment, and he retold the story of the guru whose disciple decided to leave because the daily chores of looking after the master gave him no time for meditation. The disciple went off one snowy day. He lived by himself. But one winter day he looked round and thought, "whose are all these footprints in the snow? They are mine!" He realized how much time he had wasted getting water, firewood, etc., for himself. So went back to lama teacher and apologized, "I blamed you, but then I realized I needed just as much time to look after myself." Altanbagana was moved by these stories and did not leave Sengge until he had learned enough to operate on his own.

increasingly implanted with similar official notices, each of which declares what this place or object is and thus lays a subtle or not so subtle claim on the future. We are reminded that archives are—in intention at least—*institutive* as well as conservative. Different kinds of archives may be political in different ways.

To document the recent history of such institutive acts we examine three stele—two polished marble slabs and one plastered brick wall monument—erected recently at Mergen. The first, set up by the Baotou People's Municipal Government in 2000 in front of the Janghan Temple, is made of white marble and inscribed entirely in Chinese. This stele is a claim of jurisdiction over the monastery and a declaration of its nature. The front announces:

Cultural Heritage Preservation Object of Baotou Municipality
MERGEN MONASTERY

The back is inscribed with a brief history, beginning: *Construction of the monastery started to in the 16th year of Kangxi of Qing Dynasty (1766),* and ending: *The area within the wall is protected as cultural heritage (wenwu).*

Announced by Baotou People's Municipal Government on 16th April 1999
Stone erected by Baotou People's Municipal Government on 20th June 2000.

The second marble slab was erected in 2001 by Chorji, in the name of the Monastery's Management Committee, to proclaim the successful outcome of his law case with the army. Prominently situated between the Chogchin and Janghan Temples, the stele can be seen as the affirmation of a right to property in land. With hindsight, however, knowing that the decision was not fully confirmed, this stone has a propitiatory air, or alternatively the feel of a forlorn hope, depending on how one looks at it. This black marble monument has a Chinese inscription in front:
In June 2001 the government of the Autonomous Region clarified and confirmed the ownership of 1,300,000 square meters of land. For this, thanks to the Party and People's Government.

The back, inscribed in both Mongolian and Chinese, reads:

To the government of the Inner Mongolia Autonomous Region
[In recognition of their] making merit for our people by upholding government by law.
Mergen Monastery Management Committee of Baotou
Dated: 2001.9.8

The third monument, constructed in 2005 beside the main entrance gate, seems to us to have a similarly institutive character as archive, though that is not so obvious at first sight. Again erected by Chorji in the name of the Management Committee, it consists of a plastered wall, like a massive signboard. On one half is painted an idealized scene of the monastery in Chinese style, with the incongruous army buildings left out. The other half is an inscription in Chinese:

Introduction to Mergen Monastery.
Mergen Monastery is a Lamaist (Yellow Religion) monastery. Its construction started in the16th year of Kangxi in the Qing Dynasty, 1677 in the public calendar. It is the only monastery in the world where the chanting is in Mongolian. The architectural type of the three white pagodas is a mixture of Mongolian and Tibetan styles. In the main hall there is the 13.5 m high statue of Maidar. On the two walls alongside this statue there are installed 1,000 statues of bodhisattvas. Over several hundred years many highly learned monks gathered here and the sound of chanting sutras has not been stopped. With its blue-blue Welcoming Guest pine trees and green-green larch trees, Mergen Monastery has already become one of the attractive tourist sites in Inner Mongolia.
Management Committee of Mergen Monastery.

One overt aim of this inscription is to inform visitors and tourists—it is seemingly written not for local actors but outsiders—and as such it "consigns" the monastery as the adjunct of a region (". . . one of the attractive tourist sites of Inner Mongolia"). No matter that the "welcoming guest" larch and pine trees were whittled down to a few struggling specimens, the painted image showed how the monastery was intended to be viewed by visitors. If we consider its site, the placing of this inscription at the main entrance can be considered to effect an archiving of the entire monastery.

Looking more closely, however, we see that this wall also had a dialogical purpose. It can be seen as a response to the Baotou Municipal stele. It corrects the glaring mistake on the Baotou stone (the sixteenth year of Kangxi's reign was 1677, not 1766) and more significantly it counters the "cultural relic" designation by making a claim for the religious nature of Mergen—it mentions Buddhas and bodhisattvas and declares that "the sound of chanting sutras has not been stopped." Its last sentence, which appears to give way to the heritage designation, was a shrewd tactical move by the committee. The monks were highly ambiguous about the commercialization of Mergen, and by declaring that the monastery was "already an attractive tourist site" the message conveyed was—"no more tourist development is needed."

Despite their monumental appearance the three constructed archives are uncompleted in a context that is still dynamic. Set down as tactical moves in regional struggles, they declare a position. Thus, the intent of the first (Baotou) stele is no doubt to *establish* Mergen as a "cultural heritage preservation object," but the fact is that the monastery is not yet only that. It still—just—lives on its own religious terms. Each of these archives thus has the coloring of its historical moment of inception. The pathos of Chorji's black marble slab is that it records a moment of euphoria, while at the same time leaving unclear who now owns the monastery. The information-cum-painting at the entrance gate is already peeling, ready to be repainted if not replaced, and a reminder of the similarly decaying Communist inscriptions on the previous gateposts. As Derrida observed, we must be attentive to "the logic and the semantics of the archive, [. . .] which put into reserve ('store'), accumulate, capitalize, and stock a quasi-infinity of layers, of archival strata that are at once superimposed, overprinted, and enveloped in each other" (2005, 22).

A curious visitor could nevertheless arrive at Mergen, read these inscriptions at the gate, and conclude that the monastery is itself an archive of the Mongolian people. It is a repository for culture including religion, an interesting curiosity, but in actuality no more than an auxiliary to the real life going on elsewhere. The place appears to have all the characteristics of the archive: it has been given a history, seems to be legitimately recognized, has an authority in charge, the Management Committee, and it is placed in a structure, i.e., subordinate to the Baotou Party and People's Government. However, *from inside*, all of this display was still a matter of doubt and disregard. Internal activities were generated separately in accordance with the lamas' own preoccupations. This can be seen from one fact (though there are many others): the founding date of 1677 supplied to outsiders on the wall monument at the gate was frankly ignored when the 300th anniversary was celebrated in 2005. The monastery decided on its own history, thank you very much.

The contemporary monumentalizing by public inscriptions is essentially similar to practices under the Qing and the Communists. However, other archival processes we observed in 2002–2007 were new in an important respect. When the inner surety about what to do next begins to falter, the earlier lighthearted disregard of the archive is reconsidered. The entire balance of spontaneous performance versus archive may swing toward the latter, such that both internally and externally created archives come to guide and even constitute practice. They now appear to the actors to be crucial resources for reproducing the tradition. Archiving techniques in this case not only determine what kind of item can be selected for documentation, but also provide the material for the *content* of the tradition. Both of these moves displace spontaneity. Mergen Monastery was on the cusp of such a swing in favor of the archival.

Archives as Performance Scripts

If matters hung in the balance in summer 2005, events were soon to swing the monastery decisively in the direction of reliance on archives. Shortly after we left the monastery, the cohort of young monks rebelled against the conditions: no visits to the town, no spending money, mostly self-produced food, no television or radio, no female companionship, and a schedule of arid lessons six days a week. Chorji was living in his flat in Baotou, leaving the lamas to keep services going in his absence. The young monks insisted on departing as a body, despite the attempt of a local official to persuade them to stay. Minggan was left alone—to bear the extraordinary wrath of Chorji when he heard the news. As proctor, Minggan was responsible for the monks. Chorji accused him not only of encouraging the boys to leave but also of financial malpractice. Further, Chorji saw a plot: he imagined that Minggan was planning with Sodnom (the pretender to be the next Mergen Gegen) to take over the monastery.[13] After a bitter row, Chorji banished Minggan and forbade him to set foot in Mergen in the future. Once again the monastery was abandoned and it seemed this time could not recover.

News of these sad events reached us in Cambridge and once again we had to rethink the ending of our book. However, only a few months later, messages filtered through that Mergen had reopened. Chorji had managed to recruit yet another group of young lamas, five or six of them, including two from the earlier group trained by Sengge in 2001. Sechen, the former schoolteacher, was brought back to teach secular subjects. Chorji decided to eliminate the troublesome post of proctor—"unreliable," "such people start to reach for power"—and he engaged Professor Naranbatu to provide occasional lessons in the pronunciation of Sanskrit words. Meanwhile, as for the essential matter of how the

13. Both Minggan and Sodnom had been disciples of old Lama Heshigbayar and hence they were friends.

lamas were to learn to chant, the idea was that the archives should enable them to do this by themselves. The two older lamas had some elementary experience from their months with Sengge Lama, but Chorji's main plan now was to ensure that sufficient resources were available for any boy with some schooling to access the liturgy. Anyone who could read could follow the new textbook—the one abandoned by Sengge Lama—which had just been published. For rituals they could copy a film of some Mergen services made in the 1990s, and as for the melodies of the chants, these the young lamas would learn for themselves by listening to the tape recordings made at Badgar in 1987 (see p 246). They were to reproduce the steps of the sacred *cham* dance by imitating those in a video made in the early 1990s.

In summer 2006 the fount of any possible revival of older forms of teaching was cut off—for Sengge Lama, the conscience and living embodiment of "Mongolian Buddhism" as it had evolved till then, suddenly died.

We have described a temporal sequence at Mergen over the period of our fieldwork, a general movement in the direction away from the open riches of diverse, many-layered interpretations and towards the use of set archived resources. We do not, however, wish to suggest that a unidirectional Weberian process of increasing archivization necessarily obtains, and certainly not at Mergen. One can observe that the members of what seem to be similar institutions may entertain law as an optional extra, or devote much attention to basing each action on statutes. In the eighteenth century, when the 3rd Mergen Gegen was alive, he was certainly trying to implement, not least in the statute-writing part of his work, a law-like regime that made his writings both discursive and authoritative archives. It is just that other elements in the situation—the volatile reincarnations, the mobility of lamas, the priority given to memorization over reading, the individualization of teaching, and oral and visual engagement with gods—combined to reduce the archival function and divert practices in open ways. Above all, the power of the liturgical text combined with the lamas' reaching out for spiritual marvel had prioritized the "activation" of the text by diverse means. Think for example about what is implied by the final words in a small ancient book, a common type of text that was the condensed (*Huriyanggui*) version of the 108 volumes of the *Ganjur*.[14] One such text, which was mightily contracted into six pages, ends as

14. Anonymous undated Mongolian handwritten manuscript in personal library of Caroline Humphrey.

was usual for many hand-copied texts: *This [book] will be miraculous (gaihamshig) if you copy it, if you hold it, if you "summon" it (urihu) and if you read it.* Reading is the last priority. Chorji, however, did not have much choice about making the readability of the liturgy central to the continuation of worship. The textbook became an archival script for a different kind of performance. This was aimed less at creating spiritual effectiveness than producing a kind of performance that is characteristic of post-modern, media-conscious China: the tangible yet mirage-like "regurgitation of oneself," as Liu has perceptively observed (2009, 186). The young Mongolian lamas were now enacting "Mongolian lamas." Without a script they could not do it.

But, and it seems ever this way at Mergen, this particular situation continued only for a time. As we shall describe in the epilogue, Chorji too became dissatisfied with a textbook compiled by professors.

Mahmood writing about the notion of "discursive tradition" asks: "The central question privileged by such an understanding of tradition is: how is the present made intelligible through a set of historically sedimented practices and forms of reasoning that are learned and communicated through processes of pedagogy, training, and argumentation?" (2005, 116). At Mergen it was not just that there was now no need to learn anything by heart for an exacting guru—there was no need to take anything to heart either. The crucial absence was the teacher and the guru-disciple form of pedagogy. There was no one now who would take time to explain to each young monk how the Buddhist teachings could "make the present intelligible." As Talal Asad has shown in his work on Islam (1986), however, the sites of engagement with a religious discursive tradition are not limited to professional practitioners—he emphasizes the wider field of relations through which religious truth is established. A parent argues with a child about the correctness of some practice, an aged relative explains the moral import of a didactic story. What are the implications of this insight for Buddhism in China today? And was it not consonant with the earliest habits of the Mergen lamas (Chapter 3) for an expanding web of the tradition to be spun by all those actors who had now diverged away from the monastery? In the final chapter we investigate both dispersal and concentration in the ongoing story of the Mergen tradition.

EPILOGUE

Dispersion and Creation

The recent permutations of Buddhism among Mongols in China are very different from those occurring in other regions of Inner Asia. In Mongolia, Buryatia, Tyva, and Kalmykia a surge of enthusiasm for religion in the 1990s resulted in the creation of numerous "dharma centers" and other Buddhist groups organized for laypeople. These have brought in Buddhism of every stripe. Reaching beyond Gelug orthodoxy they include a range of other schools (Nyingma, Kagyu, etc.) as well as hosting European and American Buddhist teachers. The Tibetan exile community in India has been the main source of a stream of well-educated monks who fan out to these regions, founding new temples, providing inspiration, and a focus for new followings. Teachers patiently explain the main ideas of Buddhism to large lay audiences and the latter are encouraged to take an active part in prayer sessions. Meditation retreats, summer schools, and pilgrimages are organized for new adherents. These new movements are often at odds with the "traditional" monastic establishments (Zhukovskaya 2008, 60; Bakaeva 2008, 181; Mongush 2008, 232–35). Importantly, they offer an active arena for women, unlike the male-dominated monastic institutions, which for the most part have been reluctant to approve the establishment of nunneries.[1] Change sets further changes in

1. In Buryatia a recent study found that, along with young lamas going to India for study, it is devout laywomen who predominate in making international links with Buddhist centers as well as staffing the new organizations in the city of Ulan-Ude. In response to such challenges to its authority, the Buryat

motion. In Mongolia, lamas and ex-lamas are in contact with—even switch roles with—the shamans and other practitioners who have become extraordinarily popular. In Kalmykia, Buddhist monks share a broad religious domain with new cults (the White Father, Unification Church (Moonie) adherents, communication with astral beings, and so on). It is significant that the governments in Buddhist regions of Russia have sometimes encouraged the new religious forms. In Buryatia the president was in conflict with the "traditional sangha" in the 1990s and supplied funds to the new Buddhist institutions (Zhukovskaya 2008, 62), while in Kalmykia, President Ilyumzhinov gave enthusiastic backing to a variety of Buddhist organizations, as well as taking part in the new cults himself (Oglaev 2000).

By contrast with this turbulent diversity, the Mongol Buddhists of Inner Mongolia have perforce been relatively quiescent, their activity mostly contained within highly state-regulated structures. New Age–type cults and shamanism are illegal. The censure of religious innovation, the absolute ban on the Dalai Lama, the tricky bureaucratic controls, and the channeling of approved religious activity toward state ideological goals has led to a general apathy in many regions. Even in areas of greater faith, like Urad, there are no approved public organizations of Mongolian lay Buddhists. Unlike in Mongolia and Buddhist regions of Russia, there are very few publications of Buddhist teachings written in a way that modern people can understand: academic studies are plentiful, but books that would tell people what the tenets are and how to follow them are almost absent. A handful of educated former lamas and spiritually powerful academics give instruction to a few people; but otherwise Buddhism is accessed either by joining in the Chinese "pure land"[2] chanting services, which relatively few Mongols do, or by a more passive attendance at Mongolian monasteries and temples. Virtually all of the latter operate in Tibetan and provide little

"traditional sangha" made innovations of its own, strengthening its position by discovering holy sites for pilgrimage in areas of the country where their influence had been weak (Bernstein 2012).

2. Pure Land Buddhism (C. *jingtuzong*) is a branch of Mahayana Buddhism developed in China and Japan that focuses on Amitabha and his Pure Land of Ultimate Bliss (S. Sukhāvatī). Entry into the Pure Land is attained through concentration of the mind by recitation of mantras and is popularly perceived as achieving the first stage of enlightenment. In Inner Mongolia the rebuilding of Chinese temples has been much less active than Mongol ones, and Pure Land lay devotees (*ju shi*) organize mass collective chanting in meeting halls and occasionally in corners of Mongolian monasteries. There is little contact between these groups and Mongol lamas. Mongols attracted to this realm of Buddhism focus on Ayushi, an emanation of Amitabha held to be the Buddha of long life, and on Aryabalo, the successor of Amitabha, who is worshipped to develop compassion and for the cleansing of bad karma.

opportunity for laypeople to gain greater understanding or express their own religious feelings.

These monasteries try to solve the kind of problems faced at Mergen in their own ways. So there is no such thing as a "typical" monastery. But certain difficulties are omnipresent: the unpredictable patronage and funding, the dearth of young monks, a disconnection with laity, the pressure to become a tourist attraction, and the general uncertainty of life when economic prospects keep changing, people are mobile, and pent-up sufferings remain below the surface. In these same conditions, but with its own concatenation of personalities, we have shown how the people of Mergen scattered apart; the monastery had to close down several times, and it has attained what seems to be a steady state only in a reduced and made-over form. However, as we document in this Epilogue, the pruned offshoots may take root and blossom.

There are many ways that a social ensemble may disintegrate, but the process at Mergen resembles neither the fractal model (self-similar patterns appearing at different scales) described by Marilyn Strathern (2004) nor the multidimensional chameleon rhizome metaphor evoked by Deleuze and Guattari (1998). We have argued that Mergen Monastery never was a monolith; and we suggested the analogy with the symphony orchestra in order to emphasize that the components of the ensemble were clearly identifiable yet dissimilar elements. Another kind of dissolution can be envisaged in the light of the fragility of achieving harmony in such an assemblage. The bassoonist, as it were, may play his part perfectly, and so may the cellist, but if each does not attend to all the others, each from their perspective on the whole piece of music, the result is disjointed sounds—or breakdown (Latour 2010, 4). The question we address in this epilogue is what the shards of such a breakdown turn into, bearing in mind that the breakaway violinists and the secessionist flautists each have their own priorities as well as a positional view of what the "whole" (the Mongolian Buddhist tradition) might be. This situation cannot be fractal, not only because the starting points are different from one another, but also because the process of splitting / growth occurs over time and in distinct places, and both conditions introduce "nonlinear" changes. A notion of creative dis-integration may be more appropriate, if by creative we imply qualitative, not quantitative, change. As will be shown each separate line of transformation had its own arc of intention, implying also a distinctive notion of a "whole" to be reproduced.

Certain features of Tibeto-Mongolian practice have long energized such a dynamic process. They concern exceptional sacred items, or concentrations of people and things, that historically have been mobile, not tied to any one place. They are drawn in to institutions and spin out of them again. Such objects can be referred to and treated according to ordinary causality and scientific probabilities; they can also be seen as members of the class of sacred things. But, over and above that, such a rare item shines out with a pointed singularity that allows a series of events to be synthesized in a living present; thus rather than suggesting a "horizontal" comparison with like and unlike objects, these items are singular in the way they both contract and extend past and future series.[3] Temporarily placed in any one social environment they may bring about a temporary readjustment of the ensemble, but the very "heat" of their power makes them apt focal points for branching schemes and centrifugal increments to their histories. One such object was part of the ensemble at Güng Monastery and then at Mergen, only to be excluded in 2006. Its ongoing story is the first of our examples in the more general argument we wish to make: that processes that at first look like dispersion and disintegration can also be seen, from a wider vantage point, as expansion and renewal. This is the case with Dalantai's Mahakala.

Chosen by a Deity

Erdenichimeg was an elderly laywoman who had taken *ubashi* vows from Baragun Da, and she was allowed to live in the lower courtyard of the Gegen *sang* as a *chibagancha* who would also take care of her companion, Galsangochir, one of the most aged of the lamas. She spent considerably more time in religious pursuits than most of the lamas. Devoted to the fierce, flame-ringed protector deity Mahakala, she passed the day in telling her prayer beads and circumambulations of the oldest stupa of Mergen. In particular she worshipped the "heart stone" (*jirühen chilagu*) of a particular statue of Mahakala, the one said to have demonstrated its power by conquering Muna Khan and rescuing the Panchen Lama in the 1930s (Chapter 5).

The cult that has recently gathered around this stone points to its

3. This idea was suggested by Deleuze's metaphysical theory of the "soul," which is a way to conceptualize the singularity of each thing; no two grains of wheat or sand are the same. The soul is associated with the process of individuation implied in Deleuze's theory of repetition, which is always a repetition of difference. See discussion in Williams 2011, 42. The singular worshipped object can be seen as a cognized, amplified case of this temporal, differentiating quality of "soul."

singularity as an object of worship: a tiny triangular black stone painted with Mahakala's image,[4] it is said to be a *süng*, a sacred and powerful enlivening object.[5] We now describe the genealogy of this stone, showing how it wound its way from hand to hand, crossing countries, monasteries and the lay-lama divide. Its power both accreted people to it like a magnet and also acted like a negative charge, causing people to shun it. This stone or deity, for the two are regarded as the same and both called Mahakala, made its human-like feelings known, and indeed chose its owner (*ejen*), as revealed by seers (*üjegechi*) twice during its history. This is a "person-object" as a single entity.

First we should point out that an image of Mahakala has had this quality of history-laden singularity before. A corpus of legends grew up around the idea that a powerful statue of the god was made at the time of Emperor Hubilai, that the emperor received a tantric initiation from 'Phags-pa Lama conferring on him the fierce intelligence of this god, and that the "three-fold intellect" of Mahakala enabled Hubilai to rule his vast empire. When the Mongols aligned with the Manchu state, they handed over the famous statue to the new rulers who placed it in a specially built temple in Mukden (Shenyang) (Grupper 1980, 47–63).[6]

In the Mergen case, a doctor called Dalantai, a well-educated and urban person who lives in Qianqi, is the present keeper of the Mahakala "heart stone" and he told us its story. The power of the stone lay in its origin in the holy Western Land (Tibet). An old lama from our homeland who was visiting Lhasa "invited" it from Tibet to Güng Monastery in Urad. It was the time of the final rebuilding of Güng; the lamas were constructing a statue of Mahakala, had reached the chest, and now they were searching for an enlivening object to place inside. A Tibetan lama caretaker brought the stone to Inner Mongolia, and it was duly used to enliven the new statue at Güng. This Tibetan became a good friend of Dalantai's uncle, a lama who later took over as *choyag* of

4. Mahakala is characteristically depicted as black, multi-armed, and wearing a crown of five skulls (represented the negative afflictions to be transformed into the five virtues). His blackness indicates the absorption of all color, signaling the deity's all-embracing and comprehensive nature.

5. *Süng* is possibly a Mongol rendering of the Tibetan *gzungs*—mantra, mystic formulas, memory, memorization; power, "that which holds." In general *gzungs* are empowering words but, in practice, may include empowering objects or substances.

6. A statue believed to be the same one is still worshipped now for its magical power: a grandmother from Shenyang who fell ill a few years ago, vowed to this Mahakala that if she recovered she would dedicate her granddaughter to its worship. She got better and forgot about her promise. Later, her relatives tried to get her to convert to Christianity. But the old woman found herself resisting. She was disturbed by a series of dreams, remembered her vow, and took the granddaughter to the temple to begin the worship that would continue into the future.

the Mahakala, i.e., the monastery official dedicated to the special care of this object of worship.[7] In the 1930s the Mahakala demonstrated its power through the episode of Muna Khan and the Panchen Lama's car. Well into the 1960s the Tibetan lama and Dalantai's uncle made sure the Mahakala was given respectful worship and offerings. Worship had to cease in 1965 and the statue was demolished in 1966. Uncle Lama, who had knowledge of medicine, left the monastery and became a doctor cadre. The Tibetan lama, who had stayed in the vicinity, searched for the stone in the ruins, and secretly took it. Unable to return to his homeland, he took refuge in the country house of his friend, the doctor cadre. It was not until 1971 that he told the family what he had done, quietly saying, "I have the Mahakala." Dalantai, who was also living at his uncle's place, recalled, "At that time we were afraid. So we made a hole in the wall of the house and we worshipped it there secretly." The fear was mainly political, but it was also fear of what the Mahakala would do if it were not worshipped or given offerings.

By 1976, Dalantai continued, our uncle doctor came down with a serious illness. He was a drinker, and he had cancer of the throat. We asked a Chinese diviner (*shen guan*) for the reason, and he said: "Your god (*burhan*) is staying in a tiny house and because of this he is sweating." In other words, the god was angry. Then we took the Mahakala out from the wall and worshipped it in the mountains for two years, hidden in the rocks.

However, the uncle did not survive and responsibility for the wrathful Mahakala passed to his younger brother, another Güng ex-lama, Shiraotgon. Perhaps because the god was a black Mahakala and "too hot to handle,"[8] the family now passed it to a powerful reincarnated lama, the Shabrang Bagshi of Shira Juu Monastery in Ordos—he was already a devotee of Mahakala and he placed the stone in an amulet case (*guu*) worn around his neck. In 1986 Dalantai went to Qianqi to take up a post as director of a hospital, and an inexplicable illness made him visit a Mongolian seer (*üjegechi*). The seer revealed, "An important worshipping object (*shitügen*) is following you—it demands to return to you." So Dalantai knew his illness was caused by the god/stone, which had chosen him. To recover he had to get the Mahakala back from the Ordos Reincarnation. But he did not dare ask such a high lama for it

7. In larger Mongolian monasteries there were several *choyag*, each dedicated to the care of a particular deity or worshipped lama.

8. Mahakala is surrounded by blazing fire demonstrating his amazing energy. Lamas said that the black form of the deity is the fiercest (*dogshin*), with great tantric power to repel evil spirits and curses; by the same token it is also capable of causing great harm if angered.

directly. He remembers begging a senior relative to make the request formally. Sitting outside the audience room he overhead the conversation because the old men were deaf and shouting to one another. "It must be given back to its owner," the Shabrang Bagshi yelled, agreeing. He took the amulet from his neck, and handed it together with a ritual scarf, money, and sugar lumps to Dalantai.

However Dalantai, as a layman, still felt some hesitation in taking charge of the god. He returned it to his uncle Shiraotgon, who was one of the band of lamas that restarted worship at Mergen in 1987. Shiraotgon Lama installed the Mahakala for worship in the West room of the Mergen Gegen's *sang*, while he lived in the East room. During this period, the deity-stone was a prominent part of the Mergen ensemble and many people, including Galsangochir Lama and his *chibagancha* companion, worshipped it. When Shiraotgon died, several lamas tried to get hold of the precious object, but Dalantai would not give it away. However, he wanted the stone maintained at Mergen, where regular prayers would keep it content, and he donated a sum of money for offerings and worship in proper conditions.

We were present in 2005 when Dalantai organized the worship of Mahakala with a "red meat" offering on the seventeenth of the seventh lunar month, the day of the annual offering to the god ordered by the Panchen Lama in the 1930s. The amulet containing the stone was hung on a finger of the new Mahakala statue in the Janghan Temple while a group of the older lamas headed by Sengge carried out the chanting. Chorji was absent, and his recently recruited young lamas only dared creep into the ceremony as it was ending. Later Chorji expressed his anger that this ritual had been carried out: "It will tire out my lamas. And it's pointless—we have already worshipped my Mahakala statue." But in making this protest he was ignoring a key fact about the practice of Mongolian Buddhism—not all lamas are equal, and not all Mahakalas are equal either. People worship *singular* objects and singular lamas.[9] In this rationale, rather than people selecting among an array of gods to worship, the sacred object is the active agent that makes the link between people. The "history" of the object constitutes its temporality, which is not a steady accumulation but rather punctual, a way of concentrating the effectiveness of past events into moments and abrupt demonstrations of power.

9. The singularity of objects of special worship is established in several ways, by which high lama initially blessed it, by its origin in a holy place, by the material it is made of (e.g., gold, sandalwood), or by some miracle it had performed.

The upshot of the disagreement with Chorji was that Dalantai was unable to leave his Mahakala for worship at Mergen. He took it to his home in Qianqi and vacated the northwest room in his house to make a shrine for it. By 2007 the "heart stone" had become the center of a small cult, with over thirty people regularly attending the rites of worship.

The moments when people experience the power of such an object are arbitrary and naked—and they can only be assuaged by worship. This way of thinking is extremely widespread in Mongolian cultural regions and it implies, especially in the case of fearsome deities, not only illness or misfortune but also an affliction of an affective kind, a sense of doom, and then the release that follows worship. Dalantai's story shows why he was so ambivalent about keeping the god, but he told us that having at last accepted it, the accomplishment of the ritual "relieved his feelings" (*sedhil*). He was entirely sincere in his worship of this god and he attributed many good things that had recently happened in his life to the presence of the Mahakala stone.

It is significant that the duty of worship is inherited within families. Some of the people present at the Dalantai's 2005 rite were "not religious"; they had no altar at home, did not attend monastic services, and came only to the Mahakala rite. One woman gave as her reason for attending, "because my father's older brother worshipped this god," the implication being that misfortune would befall her if the worship were not continued.[10] Among the growing circle of the cult were the two daughters of the last Duke Amurjana, now elderly women. They gladly came to Dalantai's rites in Qianqi because this deity had belonged to the Güng ("Duke's") Monastery, which of course had been the monastery maintained by their father's family, and its precious Mahakala had been his main worshipping deity. Lest it be thought that such inherited worship is purely formal let us briefly say something about Udbalchecheg (henceforth Udbal), one of these daughters. Udbal was among those who had had to abandon the pastoral herding way of life with the closure of the mountains.[11] In 2007 she was living with

10. Often a deity-image is created for someone if a seer divines that the person is in danger. For example, one old woman told us that when she was a child it was divined that she would die in her teens. So an image of Ayush (the god of long life) was made for her. She chanted its mantra and said that because of this she had lived to an old age. Although the physical image was destroyed in the Cultural Revolution, she continued to chant the mantra secretly. The flipside of the same thinking is that not only is it dangerous to discontinue worship, but that unusually extravagant offerings should be avoided—otherwise similarly expensive gifts would have to be continued regularly for fear of offending the god.

11. During their history Mongols have adapted to different kinds of farming, and considerable areas of Inner Mongolia have been given over to mixed herding with cultivating for decades (Hürelbaatar 1997, 69–89). The problem in Urad was not so much inability to adopt new methods

her husband in a Chinese suburb of Qianqi in a house next to a brick factory. They used their small yard for their milk business. Here, several cows slumped against a wall were fed with manufactured fodder purchased at the market, milked by hand, and with no access to a field. Udbal did not complain about these conditions. She had long ago been cowed into the wretched status of "bad misfit" (*magu eteged*) during the Cultural Revolution. She had roughened her speech and turned herself from aristocrat's daughter to a woman worker.

Professor Naranbatu came along when Hürelbaatar met Udbal, and he started with the memories:

> I remember when I was a young lama at Güng Monastery, your mother brought you to worship the gods. You were only five or six. Do you remember that? You were already quite tall, but people carried you in their arms, because you were the daughter of the duke. On the second day of every New Year the Güng came to the monastery to greet the lamas, to worship. He came with a whole suite of followers. When the duke dismounted, a red carpet was laid out for him to walk on. A Güng's foot shouldn't step on earth. First, the duke bowed to the god (*burhan*), after that he bowed to the Da Lama.

Naranbatu's mention of her mother brought bitter tears to Udbal's eyes. Her mother had been terribly "struggled" in the Cultural Revolution and so was Udbal separately.[12] It was clear to everyone in this conversation why the family had been specially punished. They had been singled out not long after the Communists took over. Her father, Duke Amurjana, was mild and inoffensive, Udbal told us, but he was accused, beaten, and forced to do hard labor. It happened because he had taken a fateful decision. When the Communist General Biligbagatur arrived in the area, the previous leaders had a choice: to go to Ulaanchab to submit to him or to hold out. Erhedorji and the 8th Mergen Gegen went to submit. Duke Amurjana hesitated, but he did not go. Urad people said that the duke had not only failed to "turn East" (to the communists) but had sent an envoy to the West, to defeated Prince De who

---

of livestock rearing as the immediate practical problems: building pens, lack of farming land for fodder, and above all switching from the lucrative goats to other types of livestock more suited to intensive farming, such as cattle. Some Urad herders simply moved to the towns, others sought space in grassland regions such as Chahar (without success; all the land was taken up), but most sold some of their herds and switched to the "modern" methods, while also taking up casual labor to make ends meet.

12. Udbal's mother was made to drink a concoction of hot chili, suffered internal burns, and before long she died. Udbal was not allowed to see her all that time. The brigade did not even allow her to attend her mother's deathbed.

had retreated to Alasha.[13] This decision sealed the fate of Amurjana's family, who were persecuted for decades afterward. "Yes," said Naranbatu, "your father made a real historical mistake (*teühen aldaga*). The history of your family was broken by that turning point." Udbal replied that her mother, who was educated and could read Chinese, had tried to persuade Amurjana to "go East," but he did not agree.

We mention this sad conversation not to go over again the suffering of that period, but to show how the long strands of history mentioned in earlier chapters are shaped into branching structures in people's memories (such as "go East/go West"), forming alignments that they draw upon today. Udbal's devotion to Mahakala was the way she could be loyal to her beloved father, gainsaying his "historical mistake" by cherishing the god who could protect the future of their souls.

The inheritance of the duty of worship rests on an intimate relation with a deity and this individualized devotion is stronger than the general idea of attending a monastery and praying to all the gods there. Yet, to return to the ideas mentioned at the beginning of this chapter, Dalantai was not someone who simply extracted his own precious element ignoring the idea of a whole—for he was planning to use the heart stone to revive the Güng Monastery as a replication of his vision of Mongolian Buddhism. At that time, 2008, Mergen had been modified by the departure of virtually all of the older lamas.[14] The Mahakala stone was one vital shard among the elements scattered; yet, in the potential of the reconstituted Güng Monastery it could also draw certain strands together.

Rebuilding Güng Monastery: "The Time Has Come"

The Urad Front [i.e., the former West] Banner had been left without any large functioning monastery. But several initiatives were stirring. Earlier, as we mentioned, Sengge had hoped to take the older lamas from Mergen and revive Urta Goul Monastery over in the Banner. After Sengge died, a local elder Batuchilagu, who was also an ardent devotee of his own local Muna Khan cult,[15] received permission to rebuild the

13. Udbal, however, denied her father had any relation with Prince De.

14. Mergen would still spring sporadically to life: large numbers of Chinese would come from Baotou for big occasions. But very few, or no, locals attended the daily services.

15. The Muna worshipping sites dispersed around Mergen included Batuchilagu's standing stone, venerated annually by the men of the clan-like Goul Sumu, the sacred tree of Öljei Goul, worshipped annually, and the holy birch tree of Husutai Goul, worshipped by a rotation of house-

small Dabagan Monastery and started collecting funds. Meanwhile, there was a move to revive Suburgan Monastery, and behind the Muna Mountains the small Shirege Monastery had acquired a reincarnation. Among these various projects, Dalantai's plan to reopen Güng Monastery was the most important for the former worshippers at Mergen.

It began with a stroke of fortune. After Güng Monastery was razed to the ground, the army used the bricks to build a camp there. The troops left and the barracks gradually turned into roofless ruins. Then something strange happened—people saw a truck with lifting gear trundling up the valley, and two large white statues were raised out and deposited in the ruins. It turned out they were the gifts of two local Chinese men, who wanted to build a temple on a holy site. The Banner refused permission. But Dalantai saw his chance: as a Mongol he could well be allowed to revive a Mongolian cultural institution. For him this was not only the ideal opportunity to find a proper housing for his Mahakala stone; the unexpected gift from the Chinese was an auspicious sign, a mark of destiny, an indication that "the time has come," as he repeatedly almost sang to us over the telephone.

Over the months we learned by phone of the tortuous process of obtaining permission. Finally the highest level, the Inner Mongolian government, gave the go-ahead. Full of enthusiasm, Dalantai recalled the superiority of Güng Monastery—how it had been founded before Mergen Monastery, how the 3rd Mergen Gegen had decreed that his closest disciples were to be bequeathed to it, how the chanting at Güng was more accomplished than at Mergen and the lamas more learned. It is significant that Dalantai was planning to rebuild Güng Monastery not on the basis of government grants as Chorji had done at Mergen, but by donations "from society, from the mass of people."[16] It is worth considering this further, for Dalantai's venture has a different character from the lamas' teaching in the impoverished northeast, which we describe later. His cult shows an aspect of "Mongolian Buddhism" that appeals to the middle class. Dalantai is a graduate in modern medicine with many years of experience working in the main hospital of Qianqi. Now that he has retired he lives in a comfortable modern house and

holds, and other Muna shrines in the Middle and East [Back] Banners. These rites drew large numbers of people from near and far, including many who had moved away to live in towns, and at this time they were more popular than the ordinary services in Mergen Monastery.

16. Dalantai was planning to borrow money to repair one of the barracks at Güng, build a temple, and start services there. A grand opening ceremony would bring a fine influx of donations, and these would repay the loan and enable him gradually to enlarge the monastery. A neighboring farmer and the two Chinese donors of the statues would help him.

runs a private clinic and dispensary for both standard and Mongolian medicines. An active, kindly, straightforward man, he is well placed in many influential urban networks in the town. He knows that there are both Mongols and Chinese here who are well disposed to the "giving" aspect of Buddhism, people who can afford to gather merit by making donations. These people tend to be well educated and to value Buddhism for its high culture, its attainments in philosophy, medicine, sculpture, and so on, and for its historical role in China. That there is a *Mongolian* Buddhism has become a matter of pride, evidence of Mongolian civilization over and above that of Buddhism in general, and certainly a marker of superiority over ordinary irreligious folk.

Dalantai performs divinations and helps bereaved families with funerals, but he never undertakes duties that only a lama can perform. He is very scrupulous about this and indeed he is unlike the publicity-seeking "fake" religious specialists who attempt to make a living from the gullible (see Yü in Zhang and Ong 2008 for an interesting discussion of Tibetan "Living Buddhas" who appeal to urban Chinese). Nor is he remotely interested in the kind of controlled exhibition of "minority culture" for Chinese eyes encouraged by the government (Nyiri 2010, 172–214). In any case, even in a mostly Chinese town like Qianqi, there are too many networks of sharp-eyed Mongols, alert to even small infringements, to make either of these an unproblematic option. For Dalantai and the worshippers of Mahakala, genuineness and singularity are the crucial qualities they seek. The "heart stone" is genuine (*jinghini*) because its power had been proved by its magical interventions. There is nothing like it in the region. A similar attitude is held about Güng Monastery. Otherwise it would be difficult to explain why the group of townspeople did not decide to build a temple in the town, but instead went to the trouble of rebuilding a ruin in a distant valley accessible only by dirt road. Güng Monastery is the unique place where it is right for the heart stone to take up residence and from there radiate its power—because it was here that this same Mahakala stone had overcome the power of the mountain god Muna Khan and enabled the Panchen Lama to proceed on his religion-spreading journey.[17]

Dalantai drew together many strands for the opening: he invited the West Reincarnation from Debeseg and three elderly former Mergen lamas to chant; he asked Sengge's grandson for the Mahakala text, and

17. Interestingly, both kinds of power are worshipped. A makeshift shrine was created on the exact spot of Muna Khan's appearance: three metal *sülde* tridents hung with ritual scarves and a table for offerings alongside a majestic juniper tree.

when this was refused according to the old lama's will, obtained a Xerox copy from one of Sengge's disciples. A painted image of Mahakala was acquired, along with oil lamps, hangings, temple furnishings, and Buddhist symbols for the roof. Donations poured in, all carefully listed on a red silk banner. Clearly, Dalantai could not aim at reconstituting anything truly ambitious like the repository built for Mahakala in the seventeenth century at the Chahar court, still less the magnificent mandala complex of temples centered on Mahakala at the Manchu imperial sanctuary at Mukden (Grupper 1980, 90–149). Still, he produced a gigantic banner depicting the brightly colored scene of the beautiful buildings planned for the future. Meanwhile, Dalantai's new monastery would have to be a modest, made-up hybrid—the Mahakala would sit in a rebuilt barrack-temple alongside the two Chinese statues of unknown Buddhist gods. Nevertheless, in his vision of the "whole," which is different from the multi-deity assemblage at Mergen, the holy object would be a radiant center, like a spreading patch of sunlight appearing from the clouds. At the opening ceremony dozens of cars drove up the dusty track to the mountain valley; state dignitaries, Professor Naranbatu, and academics from "Mergen Gegen Studies" were present; flags and balloons were flying. A multitudinous and cheerful crowd feasted in a great marquee. All shared in Dalantai's happiness that the heart stone would be able to radiate its powerful protection from the core of a new manifestation of Mongolian Buddhism.

"Aim Entirely for Ultimate Compassion for the Sake of Living Beings"[18]

The idea that at least some lamas should serve the ritual needs of the lay community was a different part of the Mergen tradition. Sengge Lama had been tireless in this work. The young monks at Mergen cannot follow him (they do not know these texts, do not have the necessary empowerments, and in any case Chorji would not allow them to leave the precincts and travel to households). The elderly lamas have neither the energy nor the inclination, so after Sengge's death there was an unfulfilled need in the region.

When he was "thrown out of Mergen like rubbish," Minggan retreated with his family to the suburbs of Baotou and made a living by

18. *Amitan-u tusa dur bodi-yin tüil-dür ogugata jorimu* (Mergen Gegen's *itegel* text, Galluu and Jirantai 1986, 870), a sentence quoted to us by Minggan Lama.

doing some trading. But the laity called on him to perform their rituals and he began to live from this occupation. He traveled all over Ordos and Bayannuur regions. He told us he would prefer to be back in the monastery. "You are free now," we said to him encouragingly. "Well, I have no choice," he replied. "It is much better to live permanently in a monastery. Gathering for holy services happens in a monastery. It is calm and easy There is no need for endless traveling."[19] In a low voice he told us about the "black cauldron laid on my back," his expression for the accusation made against him and spread among the people of the Mergen area.

It was in the context of such complex feelings that Minggan expressed his way of projecting Buddhism—both spatially and temporally—through the notion of *badaragulhu* ("to make flourish"):

> I almost never get angry. Things have happened and they are past. We are struggling for the true right way of doing things (*ünen yosu*), not for personal matters. We are fighting (*temechehü*) for Buddhism. [voice louder] Not for our benefit and not to get money. I am struggling for our religion to flourish, our Mongol doctrine. [. . .] If only the religion and the monastery had spread prosperously. Now we don't have worshippers [at Mergen], the services can't be done properly, what's that? When laypeople go into the service the lamas stare angrily, they aren't given food or tea, there is no place for them to sit. When I was living there I tried to discuss this many times. [. . .] Chorji replied, "The worshippers just come to eat and drink." I said, "You cannot take that attitude. If they eat once or twice, next time they will bring something. The human heart is nourished by meat, not with iron." He swore at me and replied, "If that's what you think, then you do it." On my side I was speaking for true custom and for his own sake.

Minggan has a friendship with Sodnom, his co-disciple, who had been rejected by the monastery after the rumor had spread that he was the reincarnation of Mergen Gegen. "We did have the idea of returning to Mergen some time," said Minggan. "If we went back and took disciples, the conflict could have been be ended. It did not have to go on forever." But the continuing ban from the monastery made their plan impossible, and they gave up on the idea of returning to Mergen. The two lamas became busy elsewhere, constantly on the road, conducting

19. Minggan had gone back to Mergen to pray, but a phone call had been made to young lamas telling them not to allow him to enter the Chogchin Temple. He was sad and angry. "Even just as a pilgrim they should have allowed me to pray." One year he was invited by some households to chant at the Shira Orui ritual and he went to Mergen to borrow the great drum, cymbals, and other implements, but was not allowed to take them.

rituals for households: first, to block (*horiglahu*) the decline of the pastoral economy, and second, to suppress demons and ghosts. They were also invited for divinations, for moving into a new house, for purification rites, *oboo* ceremonies, offerings to Muna Khan, curing from illness, ensuring long life, and rituals to raise good fortune.[20] Funerals and "leading the soul" were an important part of their work, which also involved inventing new rites when clients demanded it.[21]

Soon, these two lamas together with Sodnom's uncle Galluu were to carry "Mongolian Buddhism" far and wide. Galluu had been invited earlier, together with three Mergen lamas, to Shira Mören Monastery in the city of Tongliao, in Jirim (East Inner Mongolia), to teach the Mergen chanting tradition. Attempts to introduce Mongolian chanting are not always successful: in Tongliao there was conflict with older lamas, and the monastery reverted to chanting in Tibetan. A plan of Minggan and Sodnom to revive Suburgan Monastery also came to nothing. However, in other places elements of the Mergen tradition are taking root. Minggan was constantly invited to the impoverished regions of the northeast. He traveled to Liaoning, where he trained thirteen or fourteen disciples in Mongol chanting, including at least one of the boys who had left Mergen earlier. The main area of enthusiasm for "Mongolian Buddhism" however is Hinggan League. This region is the poorest in Inner Mongolia, infertile, rural, and overpopulated. Here, Minggan was invited to Hotala Bilig-tu Monastery in Ulagan-Hota (Ulaanhot), formerly known as Wang-un Süme. Its able and entrepreneurial patron was Bao Tianhu, who was not a lama but an expert bonesetter and attributed with certain spiritual powers. He recruited over thirty lamas. Minggan first taught them Mergen's *Small Chanting* with the melodies, and after a year or two moved on to teach the Fierce Gods liturgy. Minggan even said that he was planning to teach the *sülde* and Muna Khan texts.[22] The young lamas were happy to change over from

20. Minggan also still paints in his spare time. He did paintings for two monasteries in Eastern Inner Mongolia "in a new style," which pleased the local lamas.

21. The Mongolian bodyguard of a mafia-boss from Shenzhen, in south China, wanted to make a private offering at the Urad West Banner *Oboo* and asked Minggan to chant. The boss had made a lot of money and given some to this bodyguard, who started his own business and in the process killed several people. The offering was to "cleanse sins" and thus protect against the supernatural retribution to be expected. "The *oboo* was not enough for him," laughed Minggan. "He had us chant *nom* (doctrine) at the Yellow River too. We went out by boat and threw a lot of money and food into the river—ha, ha, the old prayer [Mergen Gegen's] was not strong enough. We had to invent something new."

22. Minggan did not clarify whether the lamas of far Hinggan would chant these texts when worshipping their own local mountain, or whether they would worship the Muna Mountains from a distance.

Tibetan to Mongolian: "They didn't know what doctrine they were chanting, they had no way of understanding it, there was no translation. They said that only after I taught in Mongolian did they see their road (*jam*) and begin to understand the meaning of Buddhism and doctrine." As for the master, Bao Tianhu, who had been reading Buddhist texts in an awkward translation from Tibetan made by a young local lama, he particularly welcomed the beautiful Mergen prayers. We asked Minggan if there was anyone who objected to the switch to Mongolian. "Not a single person," he replied. "Ordinary laypeople come asking me to teach Mongolian Buddhism. What I am doing is like holding a lantern in the night." This statement is like a distant affirmation of the age-old notion of the light that issued forth from the mouth of the enlightened Buddha sitting silent under the tree, beams that had to be translated into human language by advanced disciples, filtered first through their bodies before they became audible to human beings (Abé 2005, 295).

What made the Mongols of this region eager to receive the Mergen version of Buddhism? Though Hinggan League is economically less prosperous than Urad, the Mongols there had stronger exposure to "modernity" in its Japanese form. The city of Wang-un Süme, named after its main monastery, had been a key center for the Japanese-backed Manchukuo [Manzhouguo] government. Sited amid a relatively dense Mongolian population, the town briefly became the base for the East Mongolian Autonomous Government after the Japanese retreat—above all a Mongolian national government. Soon taken over by the Communist leader Ulaganhüü, Wang-un Süme then became the capital of the Inner Mongolia Autonomous Region and was renamed Red City (Ulagan Hota). Later Ulaganhüü, who had never gotten along with the Eastern Mongols, moved the capital twice, ending up in his home town of Höhhot. This history made the Mongols of Hinggan very conscious of ethnicity and also accustomed to competing with other regions. These factors may have inclined them to accept the Mongolian vernacular form of Buddhism. But also at work must have been the far older historical traces of Neichi Toin's teaching in Mongolian to laypeople. Present-day Hinggan is the region of Neichi Toin's most famous exploits and it is where the monastery built for him at Bayan Hoshigu was located (Chapters 2 and 3).[23] The diverse activities of Minggan,

23. At present Bayan Hoshigu monastery no longer exists, but some laypeople planned to rebuild it, and furthermore to use Mergen as the prototype. They therefore made a visit to Urad to sketch the architecture and consult with "Mergen Gegen Studies" experts.

Sodnom, Galluu, and Sengge's disciple Altanbagana[24] can thus be seen as "spreading" the faith. The dynamic of such movement comes not only from the lamas; Minggan's story shows that it harkens to earlier missionizing that was energized as much (if not more) by initiatives from the laity.

To look at these processes another way and return to the orchestra analogy, Dalantai's new cult is an example of taking one part (the "heart stone") out of an ensemble in which it had "played" for a time, and inserting it in a different ensemble; here its tune could be dominant in a specific grouping. Minggan, on the other hand, with his affection for monastic life, sought to reconstitute his idea of the "whole" (the body of trained lamas, the full liturgy, the lay rites, even the Muna Khan cult) in a new place. Nothing could "remain the same" in either case, for both ventures were mediated by new actors and a different time. Still, we were not prepared for the curious transformations of the Mergen tradition that were to take place in Ulaanbaatar, in Mongolia.

Uprightness

Lamas at Mergen had told us that some people from Mongolia had come and Xeroxed all of their chanting texts in order to set up Mongol-language Buddhism in their country. We did not succeed in making contact with these people, [25] but Galluu's activity was more evident. From the early 2000s, he had spent much of his time in Ulaanbaatar, where he studied for a higher degree in Buddhism. In 2003 he was invited to consecrate the Mongol Buddhist Mergen Gegen Mongol Scripture Center, an NGO with official accreditation, set up and managed by a nun, whose ordination name is Bayanchimeg.[26] The center is housed

24. Altanbagana had first trained in Tibetan, but he was impressed when he met Sengge and Chorji in Chengde, and he came to Mergen to learn Mongol chanting as Sengge's disciple (Chapter 10). When he left Sengge, he went back to Chengde and took charge of a small monastery nearby. Minggan visited him there and described a mixed, innovative form of Mongol-language practice with a largely Chinese congregation.

25. In 2009 Caroline did however meet Ganbaatar (Gangbagatur), a former disciple of Sengge Lama, who was practicing the Mergen chanting tradition in Ulaanbaatar. A quiet, sincere young man, he and one other lama had set up a temple in a yurt alongside some apartment blocks. In these modest surroundings he chanted his own selection of Mergen Gegen's texts for the benefit of lay clients. He published a book in Cyrillic and Mongol scripts of short versions of these texts, along with a CD of his own chanting and clear explanations of each object of worship (Ganbaatar 2010).

26. Bayanchimeg was keeping a low profile in the city due to hostility from other religious (shamanist) movements. We are very grateful to Chuluunbat for finding Bayanchimeg and carrying out an interview with her.

in an ordinary apartment with occasional hired halls elsewhere. It is not a monastery but a teaching place, from which the thirty or so disciples produced over the last five years have branched out all over Mongolia. Familiar as we were with the intense local detail of incarnations, rites, dates, monastic regulations, legends, and so forth, of Galluu's volumes on Mergen, we had not expected the elements that he was to take from that tradition and transform in the new city environment.

Bayanchimeg launched into a rhapsody of the spiritual inspiration of the vertical Mongol script itself—it has to be remembered that Mongolia, by contrast, has been using the horizontal Cyrillic script since the 1940s: "It was not me," she said, "who laid the foundations of Mongol chanting; the entire Mongol people have the vertical Mongol script transmitted to them, we are upright-Mongol-writing people, the nation with upright wind-horse fortune." The word she kept repeating, *bosuga* (vertical, upright), is related to the verb *boshu* to rise, stand up, or revolt. In Inner Mongolia, where the Mongol script is in everyday use, few people would make such an association, but it was a reminder to us that uprightness, with connotations of vigor, fortune, and auspiciousness, did have deep resonance in the Mergen tradition, for instance in the texts Mergen Gegen wrote to celebrate the *sülde* with its erection of a (vertical) pole on the mountaintop, and his text for the wind-horse itself.

Next Bayanchimeg extolled "our teacher" Galluu who, as an old man, had "Mongolized himself" and taken a new name, Lubsangrashi. He was the heart disciple of Mergen Gegen, who wrote a sutra called "Chinggis Khan"; he was the teacher who hid and preserved the holy books of secret teachings originally written in Mongolian. "Our teacher is utterly necessary because it is not sufficient just to give the disciples a Mongol text to read. That will not reach them. The roots of the words must be brought out, each sentence must be discovered, the mantras must be explained, and then a person can be reached by uniting these meanings with their own innate wisdom, the Mongol person's pure talent; otherwise the whole thing just becomes something raw. And the teaching must be in Mongolian not Tibetan, because this makes it understandable and truthful, as only in this way can you heal yourself, isn't that so? Not by going with others' language, thinking with another's head, walking with another's legs."

If all this sounds like the direct transmission of the Mergen teaching ethos, what Bayanchimeg said next emphasized a difference from the old passive collectivity of the laity. She was asked if "the faithful" (*itegegchid*) help financially. She replied: "We do not have 'the faithful.'

We are not a monastery or a temple. People who are led by their hearts, by their own feelings, veneration, and convictions (*ünemshil bishire-liyer*), that kind of person comes here of their own accord. So we do not preach to a congregation, because each Mongol person is a Buddha (*burhan*), and each one comes singly, bringing their own body. They only come together, about a hundred people, during fasting and Buddha's birthday to light butter lamps since that is a Mongol custom." In effect, it seems that what has happened in Ulaanbaatar is the reproduction of the crucial guru-disciple relation, but without many other features of the Mergen ensemble: without a monastic institution, with no hierarchy of offices,[27] reincarnations, or the great chanting services. Each person who appears is a potential disciple, teaching is done intensively, face-to-face, and then these disciples take off to repeat this process elsewhere.

One of Bayanchimeg's remarks was that her Scripture Center had no need of help from Mergen Monastery. Why should she go there when the real, main teacher was in Ulaanbaatar? In any case, on her way to the Chinggis Khan shrine she had visited Mergen: the place was not working, it had broken up, and she had seen its ruins. But Mergen was not finished, as we now recount.

Samtan Lama and the Mantras

We have described how the dispersed offshoots from Mergen took different forms according to the actors' perspectives and their practical possibilities of prolonging "the tradition." The divergent visions of the tradition could be seen as virtual "wholes" in the sense that they consisted of conceptual elements that the actors were working to integrate and complete. Now we discovered that Chorji too had such a vision for Mergen. In their re-vindication of the much criticized concept of holism, Rane Willerslev and Morten Pedersen proposed an idea of "proportional holism" that explains beautifully what we think Chorji was trying to do. "To study holism anthropologically," they write, "is to explore the culturally specific work actors do for their cosmos to retain its proportions" (2010, 262). The work of holistic practice consists of creating a balance, but also necessary distances, between systems that

27. Bayanchimeg stressed individual choice and ability: people attending the Center have different educational levels. They can take a range of vows and also specialize, choosing from astrology, curing, making spells, and so forth as they see fit.

otherwise would appear singular and disjunctive. We suggest that the mantras (*tarni*) and the texts read in Mongolian were two such systems, that archivization at Mergen had left them adrift, and that a religious sensibility required them to be put in a correct relation again.

Chorji made visits to Lhasa. He was mellowing with time: he made up with his half-brothers and invited them to Mergen, and he set up an elaborate shrine in his new apartment in Baotou. As a culmination of the archival project he was planning to publish a complete compendium of all documentation of the Mergen tradition, including a facsimile of all Mergen Gegen's works and all audio and video recordings, as well as other old Mongolian Buddhist texts.[28] He said he would distribute the digital materials for free in order to spread Mongolian Buddhism. But with his new idea of "the whole" he felt something was missing.

Now a graying and abstemious figure, he saw his overland journeys to Lhasa as a pilgrimage. He could also visit his daughter who was studying medicine there, and on the way he could open himself to experience majestic landscapes and photograph them. On one occasion, during the long trek home, he borrowed a desert vehicle and set off into the sands around Alasha. This was real Gobi land, a sea of rippling golden dunes reaching to the horizon. Struggling over one crest, he saw a small blue lake. At its corner, surrounded by bushes and a few trees, was a white temple. He photographed this scene (Menghebatu 2009, 76–77). The building was the monastery of Badain Jaran, and living there was a single monk, Samtan Lama.

Talking with Samtan, Chorji was excited because he understood that this talented and experienced lama[29] could solve what he now realized was a great problem at Mergen: the pronunciation of the sacred mantras. It was as though a magical coincidence had taken place: the discovery of visual beauty and a religious realization of aural authenticity. Samtan Lama had received from his guru, and that guru from his teacher, and so back into the mists of time, the sounds that were the means to enlightenment.

At Mergen the young lamas had been struggling with a particularly

28. The facsimile will be based on the British Library holdings. Chorji generously organized a magnificent festive public occasion at Mergen when Caroline brought the digitized materials to the monastery.

29. Samtan Lama knew both Tibetan and Mongolian liturgies; he had studied at the great Labrang Monastery, had been invited to interpret and teach at the College for the Advanced Study of Buddhism in Beijing, had translated the *Moon Cuckoo* story into Mongolian, and had been the guru for two well-known reincarnations.

intractable problem of reading, since the mantras (*tarni*) that are densely present especially in the most serious prayers, are written in *galig*, the special Mongolian alphabet designed to render the sounds of Sanskrit and Tibetan. Professor Naranbatu had been called in to explain the pronunciation to be attached to each strange written letter. But should the lamas be following a lay intellectual who had left monastic life so early? Chorji had thought so until he met Samtan Lama. But now he realized that just as with venerated images and holy objects, the power of mantras lies in the ritual sacralization of their transmission.

In his essay on "word" in Buddhism, Ryuichi Abé writes that the authority of religious teachers rests ultimately on their ability to verbalize the dharma, ideally as skillfully as the Buddha, and that "the most important goal of the Buddhist teaching appears to be to produce heirs of the dharma, enlightened teachers whose lineage succession assures the sustenance of Buddhism as a living religious tradition" (2005, 299–300). If the word is an expedient means,[30] it is also nevertheless a necessary means, and Mahayana traditions value the various kinds of textual presence (chanting, memorizing, copying out, printing, furling in the wind, etc.) so highly because, following the Buddha's entering into Nirvana, his body is preserved *in* and *as* the sacred words. This idea of textual presence, expounded for example in the canonical *Lotus Sutra*, encompasses what Abé terms the physiological dimension of words, whereby the words that issued from the Buddha's mouth, his life breath, become integral to the readers' beings through their work of studying and speaking the text. As the speech acts of divinities, mantras integrate the physical and mental aspects of such action into forms of meditation. They carry meanings that are necessarily different from the expedient use of words, even those in prayers. For example, the deity may manifest itself linguistically in the single syllable *ah*, which however has five forms that are sonic manifestations of stages in the awakening of the practitioner to emptiness (ibid, 306).

The five stages in the meditative sequence are examples of the "meaning" of mantras that are taught by the guru and conferred by the *wang* ritual empowerment to an advanced disciple (see p 276 for Sengge Lama's exposition of a common, in principle not dissimilar

30. Some scholars argue that Buddhism is generally skeptical about language because, denoting things of this world, it obscures the awakening experience. Abé argues to the contrary that while meditative silence may have brought the Buddha's enlightenment experience, his act of preaching gave rise to the Buddhist religion. "The supreme truth cannot even be known to us, not to mention realized, unless it is first spelled out as words—in the order of the worldly truth" (ibid, 297).

kind of meaning for the *mani* mantra). Mantras are an efficient and precise means intended to remind the serious practitioner of profound philosophical ideas.[31] However, because in the ritual context mantra sounds not only denote but *create* reality by emulating experientially the body, speech, and mind of enlightened beings, a lesser but still potent effect is created even if very little of the esoteric meaning has been taught.

It was renewal of this central practice of Buddhism that Samtan Lama could bring to Mergen in its devitalized state. He was invited and went for a month in early 2009. He began with the basics: he transliterated all the mantras in Mergen Gegen's *Small Chanting* into ordinary Mongolian script, thus rendering them at least readable and pronounceable by the neophyte lamas in services. Chorji was happy and hoped to be able to persuade Samtan to return to do the same for the mantras in Mergen Gegen's more advanced texts. But who is to say—and we end our book on this note—that in the future Samtan could not also revive among the more receptive and talented of the lamas, the meditative potential of the mantras? What would this mean? The Sanskrit mantras (*tarnis*) are reproduced in Mergen Gegen's texts, but they issued from divinities and thus were not—and could not have been—composed by him. Uttering them in meditation, taught by a lineal guru, would open up for the disciples experiential access to ultimate truth.[32] To "bring out" the *tarni* is entirely consonant with Mergen Gegen's intentions, since it means the appropriate combining of the Mongolian liturgy with the great historical chain of Buddhist *tarni* practice. For Chorji, by working to secure the active presence of an authentic guru, he could re-create a proper proportional relation between these two kinds of practice.

Final Words

This book has traced two histories: that of the tradition of Mongolian Buddhism at Mergen and that of our own encounters with the people upholding this tradition. In terms of simple fact neither of these histories could ever be finished: as Caroline is writing these words, Hürelbaatar is in Inner Mongolia trying to find out whether Samtan Lama

31. See Gyatso, 1992c, 175–77, on the various kinds of memory involved in the practice of *dhāraṇī*.

32 See Cook, 2010, 97–104 and 113–14, for discussion of the comparable use of Pali words in meditation by Thai Buddhist devotees.

has agreed to return to Mergen. We learned during the research that the enterprise of tracking a tradition means somehow accounting for both the lamas' understandings of the identity of the tradition through time and for constant, restless, and unpredictable change. If it seemed to us that the religious potentiality of the Mongolian language lay at the heart of this identity, our researches showed that in fact the actors drew many other diverse strands from the assemblage that held together briefly during the first years of fieldwork. Looking at the *longue durée* we have shown that seemingly robust ensembles appeared in the Urad region—such as the great morality-infused structure in Mergen Gegen's *Altan Tobchi*, the nobles' cult of *sülde*, the mausoleums of heroic ancestors, or the relics of the 8th Mergen Gegen—only to change their colors or slip into obscurity and be replaced by others. Individual people too could not but change and transform themselves, and by introducing details of their lives we hope to have shown how each of them, even at one moment, is more complex than the idea of the institution to which they have only ever lent some of their attention and energy. The institution (the monastery) and the tradition (the recognized and replicated parts of Mergen Gegen's works) consist only in those elements of the actors' worlds that can be communicated between them and are taken for the whole. Such a conjunction has a genealogy but it is always in process, forever in the making. The story of Mergen has shown how it is preferable to regard individuals and institutions not as *beings* but as *movements* (Latour 2003, 11); they are always "on their way" not just to another place but also to becoming something else.

Such an understanding is, we think, consonant with Buddhist thought. John Strong writes, for example, of the understanding of the bodhisattva as being defined *prospectively*, by what he will become, his future Buddhahood, and how this implies that his relics are seen to be "pre-present," thus challenging the European notion that relics are always remnants (Strong 2004, 232–33). We hope we have been able to show that something of this prospectiveness is intrinsic to people who are Buddhists in their understanding of themselves, and also to worshipped objects such as the *sharil* of the 8th Mergen Gegen and the "heart stone" of Mahakala. It is true that the Mergen stories have also shown how dynamic trajectories do not always work positively. In diverse forms we have seen what Greenblatt calls "attempted cultural murder" (2010, 14): from the legend of the killer rolling stone to the conflicts of the Cultural Revolution that devastated the main characters of our book, Sengge and Chorji, setting them on conflicting paths that can be seen as almost symmetrically opposite to one another. It is not by chance that repeated incidents of exclusion and tears were taken by the people of Mergen to produce the curse that beset their monastery. In the broader political-religious circumstances of Inner Asia, the Mergen lamas' denial of Tibetan Buddhist forms in favor of Mongolian and Sanskrit might be seen as self-defeating in respect of power and influence in society from the eighteenth century to the present. But who is to know what may happen in future decades? The movements we have documented are not to be imagined as generalized unidirectional flow, but rather as episodic—crystallizing or flipping over into a new form with particular events or creative acts. If the common tenor of Buddhism has always been a creative tension between dispersion and centralizing acts of concentration, the events we witnessed in the several histories of Mergen perfectly manifest this very Buddhist way of being in time.

Bibliography

Works by Mergen Gegen

Abbreviations

BJ *Bum Jarlig,* Mergen Gegen collected works
AT Mergen Gegen's history *Altan Tobchi*
S Mergen Gegen's moral teachings *Surgagal*

Mergen Gegen Lubsangdambijalsan. *Wchir Dhara Mergen Diyanchi Blama- yin Gegen-ber Öljei Badaragsan Süme-dür Hural-un Ungshilg-a Togtagagsan.* [Readings for the Öljei Badaragsan Monastery Assigned by the Reincarnation of Vajradhara Mergen Diyanchi Lama.] Peking wooden block print. British Library. 1774.

BJ Mergen Gegen Lubsangdambijalsan. *Wchir Dhara Mergen Diyanchi Blama-yin Gegen-ü 'Bum Jarlig Hemegdehü Orushiba.* [Collected Works of the Reincarnation of Vajradhara Mergen Diyanchi Lama.] Peking wooden block print. British Library. 1780–1783.

BJ Mergen Gegen Lubsangdambijalsan. *Wchir Dhara Mergen Diyanchi Blama-yin Gegen-ü 'Bum Jarlig Hemegdehü Orushiba.* Five boxed volumes (Vols. 1–4 are a reprint of 1780–83; vol. 5 is a compilation of other texts by Mergen Gegen along with musical notation for numerous chanting melodies. A sixth box contains four cassettes of chanting). With introduction and commentary by Naranbatu. Höhhot: Inner Mongolian Educational Press, 1998.

Mergen Gegen Lubsangdambijalsan (trs.) *Sayin Ügetü Erdeni-yin Sang Subhasida Hemegdehü Shastir.* (Subhashitaratnanidhi) [Precious Treasury of Aphoristic Sayings.] Attributed to

Sakya Pandita Kunga Gyaltsen. Peking wooden block print. British Library, n.d.

Mergen Gegen Lubsangdambijalsan. *Mergen Gegen Lubsangdambijalsan-u 'Bum Jarlig hemegdehü orushiba*. Edited by S. Galluu and G. Jirantai. Beijing: Nationalities Press, 1986. (See also under Galluu and Jirantai, eds.)

AT1 Mergen Gegen Lubsangdambijalsan. *Altan Tobchi. Mongol'skaya Letopis' XVIIIv.* Facsimile of manuscript, translation into Russian, with notes and commentary by P.B. Baldanzhapov. Ulan-Ude: Akademiya Nauk SSSR, [1765] 1970.

AT2 Lubsangdambijalsan [Mergen Gegen]. *Altan Tobchi*. Transliterated in roman script by Chimiddorji and Mönghebuyan. Translated into Chinese by Gerel. Hailar: Inner Mongolian Cultural Press, [1765] 1998b.

AT3 Mergen Gegeen Lubsandambizhaltsan. *Ikh Mongol Ulsyn Ündsen Altan Tovch Tuuzh Orshivoi*. Transliterated into Cyrillic and with notes by D. Bürnee. Edited by A. Tsanzhid and Sh. Choimaa. Ulaanbaatar: Mongol Ulsyn Ikh Surgul, [1765] 2006.

Unpublished manuscripts

Mergen Gegen. (Handwritten manuscript.) *Haguchin daguu shilüg-üüd*. Library of Inner Mongolian Institute of Language and Literature, n.d.

S1 Mergen Gegen. (Handwritten manuscript.) *Mergen Juu-yin Gegegen johiyagsan surgal shilüglel-ün debter bulai*. Library of Inner Mongolian Institute of Language and Literature, n.d.

S2 Mergen Gegen. (Handwritten manuscript.) *Mergen Gegen-ü surgal orushibai*, n.d. Acquired in Ulaanbaatar, 2006.

Anonymous Mongolian texts

Hutugtu hormusta tngri-yin heühen kang chung ma-ber arigun tngri-yin orun-eche baguju balbu-yin merhiten hemehü orun-dur amugulang hemegchi ehe-ner bolon hubilun mandugad baigulugsan ihe suburgan-u taguji orishiba. [History of the Great Stupa which was Built by Kang Chung Ma, the Girl of Holy Hormusta Sky God, who Came Down from the Pure Heaven Land to the Place called Merhitan of Nepal and was Reincarnated as a Woman called Amugulang.], n.d.

Gazar-un shinji [Characteristics of Land] Manuscript Mo 16. Kongelige Bibliotek: Copenhagen, n.d.

Sources in English and other languages

Abé, Ryuichi. "Word." *Critical Terms for the Study of Buddhism*. Edited by Donald S. Lopez, Jr., 291–310. Chicago and London: University of Chicago Press, 2005.

Agamben, Giorgio. *Qu'est-ce qu'un dispositif?* Translated by Martin Rueff. Paris: Rivages Poche/Petite Biblioteque, 2007.

———. *La Règne et la Gloire*. Translated by Joel Gayraud and Martin Rueff. Paris: Seuil, 2008a.

———. *Signatura Rerum: Sur la Méthode*. Translated by Joel Gayraud. Paris: Librairie Philosophique J. Vri, 2008b.

———. *The Kingdom and the Glory: For a Theological Genealogy of Economy and Government*. Translated by Lorenzo Chiesa with Matteo Mandarini. Stanford University Press, 2011.

Altanorgil, ed. *Höhe Hota-yin Teühen Monggul Surbulji Bichig*. Vols. 1–6. Hailar: Inner Mongolia Cultural Press, 1998–1999.

Anagnost, Ann. "The politics of ritual displacement." *Asian Visions of Authority*. Edited by Charles Keyes, Lauren Kendall, and Helen Hardachre, 221–54. Honolulu: University of Hawaii Press, 1994.

———. *National Past-times: Narrative, Representation, and Power in Modern China*. Durham, NC: Duke University Press, 1997.

Anderson, Amanda. *The Way We Argue Now*. Princeton University Press, 2006.

Appadurai, Arjun. "The Past as a Scarce Resource." *Man* 16 (2), (1981): 201–19.

Arbinbayar and Somun. *Otug-un obug-a orud*. [The Places of the Otug Oboos.] Höhhot: Inner Mongolia Press, 2001.

Asad, Talal. "The Idea of an Anthropology of Islam." *Occasional Papers Series*. Washington DC: Center for Contemporary Arab Studies, Georgetown University, 1986.

———. "Interview with David Scott." *Powers of the Secular Modern: Tala Asad and His Interlocutors*. Edited by David Scott and Charles Hirschkind, 243–304. Stanford University Press, 2006.

Atwood, Christopher. [1992] 2006. "The Marvellous Lama in Mongolia: The Phenomenology of a Cultural Borrowing." *Acta Orientalia* (Hung.) XLVA (1), (2006): 3–30.

———. "Buddhism and Popular Ritual in Mongolian Religion: A Reexamination of the Fire Cult." *History of Religions* 36 (2), (1996): 112–39.

———."'Worshipping Grace': The Language of Loyalty in Qing Mongolia." *Late Imperial China* 21 (2), (2000): 86–139.

———. *Young Mongols and Vigilantes in Inner Mongolia's Interregnum Decades, 1911–1931*, vols. 1 and 2. Leiden: Brill, 2002.

———. *Encyclopedia of Mongolia and the Mongol Empire*. New York: Facts on File, 2004.

———. "Validation by Holiness or Sovereignty: Religious Toleration as Political Theology in the Mongol World Empire of the Thirteenth Century." *The International History Review* XXVI (2), (2004b): 237–56.

———. "How the Mongols Rejected the *Secret History*." Paper given in Ulaanbaatar, 2006.

Ayusheeva, M.V. "Predvaritel'noe opisanie 'sobraniya sochinenii' Mergen-Gegena Lubsandambizhalsana (1717–1766)." *Pis'mennoe nasledie mongol'skikh narodov*. (Materialy mezhdunarodnogo seminara 2–6 avgusta 2004.) Edited by B.V. Bazarov, et al. Ulan-Ude: BNTs SO RAN, (2005): 99–106.

Badiou, Alain. *Ethics: An Essay on the Understanding of Evil*. Translated and with an introduction by Peter Hallward. London: Verso, 2001.

Bakaeva, E.P. "Kalmytskii buddizm: istoriya i sovremennost'." *Religiya v istorii i kul'ture mongoloyazychnykh narodov rossii*. Edited by N.L. Zhukovskaya, 161–200 . Moscow: Vostochnaya Literatura RAN, 2008.

Bakhtin, M.M. *Speech Genres and Other Late Essays*. Translated by Vern W. McGee. Austin: University of Texas Press, 1986.

Ba Jingyuan. "Wulate Qianqi kangri nü siling Qi Junfeng." *Baotou Wenshi Ziliao Xuanbian* 13, (1991): 102–12.

Ba Jingyuan, and Yun Changxiu. "Riben huazhuang lama zai Wudangzhao." *Baotou Wenshi Ziliao Xuanbian* 7, (1982): 168–73.

Baldanzhapov, P.B. *Altan Tobchi: Mongol'skaya letopis' XVIII v*. Akademiya Nauk SSSR, BION: Ulan-Ude, 1970.

Baldanzhapov, P.B., and Ts.P. Vanchikova. *Čaγan Teüke—"Belaya Istoriya": mongol'skii istoriko-pravovoi pamyatnik XIII–XVI vv*. Ulan-Ude: Izdatel'stvo Buryatskogo Nauchnogo Tsentra SO RAN, 2001.

Banzarov, Dorzhi. *Sobranie sochinenii*. Moscow: Izdatel'stvo Akademii Nauk SSSR, (1891) 1955.

Bao, Saijirahu. *Hasar-un chadig*. Höhhot: Inner Mongolian People's Press, 1999.

Barnstone, Willis. *The Poetics of Translation: History, Theory, Practice*. New Haven and Boston: Yale University Press, 1993.

Bauman, Brian G. *Divine Knowledge: Buddhist Mathematics According to the Anonymous Manual of Mongolian Astrology and Divination*. Leiden: Brill, 2008.

Bawden, Charles R. *The Mongol Chronicle Altan Tobci*. Wiesbaden: Otto Harrassowitz, 1955.

———. *The Jebtsundamba Khutukhtus of Urga: Text, Translation, and Notes*. Wiesbaden: O. Harrassowitz, 1961.

———. "Mongol notes II: Some 'Shamanist' Hunting Rituals from Mongolia." *Central Asiatic Journal* 12 (2), (1968): 101–43.

———. *Shamans, Lamas, and Evangelicals: The English Missionaries in Siberia*. London: Routledge and Kegan Paul, 1985.

———. *Tales of an Old Lama*. Translated by C.R. Bawden from a Mongolian text *Övgön Jamabalyn Yaria*. Recorded and edited by Ts. Damdinsüren. Tring, UK: Institute of Buddhist Studies, 1997.

Belka, Lubos. "The Myth of Shambhala: Visions, Visualisation, and the Myth's Resurrection in the Twentieth Century in Buryatia." *Archiv Orientalni* 71 (3), (2003): 247–62.

Berger, Patricia. *Empire of Emptiness: Buddhist Art and Political Authority in Qing China*. Honolulu: University of Hawaii Press, 2003.

Bernstein, Anya. *Religious Bodies Politic: Rituals of Sovereignty in Buryat Buddhism*. Unpublished manuscript, 2012.

Berounsky, Daniel. "Tibetan Ritual Texts Concerning the Local Deities of the Aga Buryat Autonomous Region, Part 1." *Mongolica Pragensia '06*, (2006): 191–240.

Binsteed, G.C. "Life in a Khalkha Steppe Lamasery." *Journal of the Royal Asiatic Society* 23, (1914): 847–900.

Bira, Sh. *Mongolian Historical Literature of the XVII–XIX Centuries, Written in Tibetan*. Edited by Ts. Damdinsüren, translated by Stanley N. Frye. Bloomington, Indiana: The Mongolia Society Occasional Papers, 1970.

———. *Mongolyn tüükh, soyol, tüükh bichlegiin sudalgaa*. Tokyo: Institute for Languages and Cultures of Asia and Africa, 1994.

———. "Khubilai Khan and Phags-pa Bla-ma." *Mongolyn tüükh soyol tüükh bichelgiin sudalgaa*, vol. 3. Ulan-Bator: International Association of Mongolian Studies, 2001.

Bjerken, Zeff. "Hall of Mirrors: Tibetan Religious Histories as Mimetic Narratives." *Acta Orientalia* (Denmark) 64, (2002): 177–223.

Bloch, Maurice. *Ritual, History, Power: Selected Papers in Anthropology*. London: The Athlone Press, 1989.

Bogue, Ronald. "Minority, Territory, Music." *An Introduction to the Philosophy of Gilles Deleuze*. Edited by Jean Khalfa, 1996. London: Continuum, 2003.

———. *Deleuze's Way: Essays in Transverse Ethics and Aesthetics*. Aldershot, UK: Ashgate, 2007.

Borjigin, Uranchimeg. "Circulating Prophetic Texts." *Time, Causality, and Prophecy in the Mongolian Cultural Region*. Edited by Rebecca Empson, 21–60. Folkestone: Global Oriental, 2006. (See also Ujeed, Uranchimeg.)

Bulag, Uradyn E. *Nationalism and Hybridity in Mongolia*. Oxford: Oxford University Press, 1998.

———. "From Yeke-juu League to Ordos Municipality: Settler Colonialism and Alternative Urbanization in Inner Mongolia." *Provincial China* 7 (2), (2002a): 196–234.

———. *The Mongols at China's Edge: History and the Politics of Unity*. London and Boulder: Rowman and Littlefield, 2002b.

———. "Going imperial: Tibeto-Mongolian Buddhism and Nationalisms in China and Inner Asia." *Empire to Nation: Historical Perspectives on the Making of the Modern World*. Edited by Joseph Esherick, Hasan Kayah, and Eric Van Young, 260–95. London: Rowman and Littlefield, 2006.

———. *Collaborative Nationalism: The Politics of Friendship on China's Mongolian Frontier*. Latham, MA: Roman & Littlefield, 2010.

Bühechilagu, G. *Urad Teühe-yin Nourag*. Hailar: Inner Mongolian Cultural Press, 2007.

Bürintegüs, ed. *Monggol Jang Üyile-yin Nebterhei Toli*. (Oyun-u boti.) Chifeng: Inner Mongolian Scientific and Technical Press, 1999.

Buyanbadarahu, S. *Urad-un Gurban Güng-ün Hoshigun-u Tobchi Teühe*. Qianqi: Urad North Banner: Combined Committee of Local History and Party History of Urad North Banner, 1987.

Cable, Mildred and Francesca French. *Something Happened*. London: Hodder and Stoughton, 1933.

Cabot, Mabel H. *Vanished Kingdoms: A Woman Explorer in Tibet, China, and Mongolia 1921–1925*. New York: Aperture Foundation, 2003.

Camman, Schuyler. *The Land of the Camel: Tents and Temples of Inner Mongolia*. New York: The Ronald Press Company, 1951.

Candea, Matei. 2007. "Arbitrary Locations: In Defence of the Bounded Field-site." *Journal of the Royal Anthropological Institute*, n.s., 13, (2007): 167–84.

———. "A partial postscript on arbitrariness, 2009." http://www.candea.net/publications/afterword.htm.

Casey, Edward S. "How to Get from Space to Place in a Fairly Short Stretch of Time: Phenomenological Prolegomena." *Senses of Place*. Edited by Steven Feld and Keith H. Basso. Santa Fe, NM: School of American Research Advanced Seminars Series, 1996.

de Certeau, Michel. *The Practice of Everyday Life*. Berkeley: University of California Press, 1984.

Chabros, Krystyna. *Beckoning Fortune: A Study of the Mongol Dalalga Ritual*. Wiesbaden: Otto Harrassowitz, 1992.

Chakrabarty, Dipesh. *Provincializing Europe: Postcolonial Thought and Historical Difference*. Princeton University Press, 2000.

———. *Habitations of Modernity: Essays in the Wake of Subaltern Studies*. University of Chicago Press, 2002.

Charleux, Isabelle. "Padmasambhava's Travel to the North: The Pilgrimage to the Monastery of the Caves and the Old Schools of Tibetan Buddhism in Mongolia." *Central Asiatic Journal*, 46 (2), (2002): 168–232.

———. *Temples et Monastères de Mongolie-Intérieure*. Paris: Institut National d'Histoire de l'Art, 2006.

Chia, Ning. "The Lifanyuan and the Inner Asian Rituals in the Early Qing (1644–1795)." *Late Imperial China* 14 (1), (1993): 60–92.

Chiodo, Elizabetta. "'The Book of the Offerings to the Holy Chinggis Qagan': A Mongolian Ritual Text, Part II." *Zentralasiatische Studien* 23. Wiesbaden: Otto Harrassowitz, 1993.

———. "Yamantaka and the Sülde of Chinggis." *Tractata Tibetica et Mongolica: Festschrift für Klaus Sagaster*. Edited by Karenina Kollmar-Paulenz and Christian Peter 45–60. Wiesbaden: Harrassowitz, 2002.

Choiji. *Nei Menggu Ci Miao*. Höhhot: IM People's Press, 1994.

Clarke, Peter. *New Religions in Global Perspective*. London and New York: Routledge, 2006.

Collins, Steven. *Selfless Persons: Imagery and Thought in Theravada Buddhism*. Cambridge University Press, 1982.

Compilation Committee of Chinggis Khan's Eight White Palaces. *Chinggis Hagan-u Naiman Chagan Ordu*. Hailar: Inner Mongolian Cultural Press, 1998.

Compilation Committee of Inner Mongolian Folklore. *Monggul Arad-un Üliger-ün Chigulgan*, vol. 1. Hailar: Inner Mongolian Cultural Press, 2000.

Compilation Committee of Urad South Banner. *Wulate Qienqi Zhi*. Höhhot: Inner Mongolian People's Press, 1994.

Cook, Joanna. *Meditation in Modern Buddhism: Renunciation and Change in Thai Monastic Life*. Cambridge: Cambridge University Press, 2010.

Cooper, Frederick. *Colonialism in Question: Theory, Knowledge, History*. Berkeley: University of California Press, 2005.

Crane, George. *Bones of the Master: A Journey into Secret Mongolia*. London and New York: Bantam Books, 2001.

Crang, Mike. "Relics, Places, and Unwritten Geographies in the Work of Michel de Certeau (1925–1986)." *Thinking Space*. Edited by M. Crang and N. Thrift, 135–53. London: Routledge, 2000.

Crossley, Pamela Kyle. *A Translucent Mirror: History and Identity in Qing Imperial History*. Berkeley: University of California Press, 1999.

Crossley, Pamela Kyle, and Evelyn S. Rawski. "A Profile of the Manchu Language in Ch'ing History." *Harvard Journal of Asiatic Studies* 53 (1), (1993): 63–102.

da Col, Giovanni. 2007. "The View from Somewhen: Events, Bodies, and the Perspective of Fortune around Khawa Karpo, a Tibetan Sacred Mountain in Yunnan Province." *Inner Asia* 9 (2), (2007): 215–36

Das, Veena. *Life and Words: Violence and the Descent into the Ordinary*. Berkeley: University of California Press, 2007.

David, Armand. "Journal d'un Voyage en Mongolie fait en 1860." *Bulletin des Nouvelles Archives du Musée d'Histoire Naturelle de Paris* 3: 18–96, 1867, and 4: 3–83, 1868.

Dawajamsu, B., and J. Gerelchogtu, eds. *Mohulai-yin Onggun Sülde*. Höhhot: Inner Mongolia People's Press, 2001.

De Lesdain, Count. *From Pekin to Sikkim Through the Ordos, the Gobi Desert, and Tibet*. London: John Murray, 1906.

Deleuze, Gilles. *Difference and Repetition*. Translated by Paul Patten. New York: Columbia University Press, 1994.

Deleuze, Gilles, and Félix Guattari. *Anti-Oedipus*. Translated by Robert Hurley, Mark Seem, and Helen R. Lane. Minneapolis: University of Minnesota Press, 1977.

———. *Kafka: Towards a Minor Literature*. Translated by Dana Polan. Minneapolis: University of Minnesota Press, 1986.

———. *A Thousand Plateaus*. Translated by Brian Massumi. London: Athlone Press, 1998.

Derrida, Jaques. *Acts of Religion*. Edited and with an introduction by Gil Anidjar. New York and London: Routledge, 2002.

———. *Archive Fever: A Freudian Impression*. Translated by Eric Prenowitz. University of Chicago Press, [1995] 2005.

———. *Specters of Marx: The State of the Debt, the Work of Mourning, and the New International*. Translated by Peggy Kamuf. New York and London: Routledge Classics, [1993] 2006.

Dharma Güüshi. *Altan hürdün minggan hegesütü*. Edited by Choiji. Höhhot: Inner Mongolian People's Press, [1739] 2000.

Dharmatala, Damchö Gyatsho. *Rosary of the White Lotuses: Being the Clear Account of How the Precious Teaching of Buddha Appeared and Spread in the Great Hor Country*. Translated by Piotr Klafkowski; supervised by Nyalo Trulka Jampa Kelzang Rinpoche. Wiesbaden: Otto Harrassowitz, [1889] 1987.

Diemberger, Hildegard. "Animal Sacrifices and Mountain Deities in Southern Tibet: Mythology, Rituals, and Politics." *Les Habitants du Toit du Monde: Études Recueillies en Hommage à Alexander W. MacDonald*. Edited by Samten Karmay and Philippe Sagant, 261–81. Nanterre: Société d'ethnologie, 1997.

———. "The Horseman in Red. On Sacred Mountains of La stod lho (Southern Tibet)." *Tibetan Mountain Deities: Their Cults and Representations*. Edited by Anne-Marie Blondeau, 43–56. Vienna: Verlag der Österreichischen Akademie der Wissenschaften, 1998.

———. "Festivals and their Leaders: The Management of Tradition in the Mongolian/Tibetan Borderlands." *The Mongolia-Tibet Interface: Opening New Research Terrains in Inner Asia*. Edited by Hildegard Diemberger and Uradyn Bulag, 109–34. Leiden: Brill, 2007a.

———. *When a Woman Becomes a Religious Dynasty: The Samding Dorje Phagmo of Tibet*. New York: Columbia University Press, 2007b.

———. "The 12th Dorje Phagmo of Tibet, 'Female Living Buddha,' and Cadre: A Political Paradox?" *Inner Asia*, 10 (1), (2008): 153–69.

Dmitriev, S.V. "Sülde: k probleme istorii formirovaniia voenno-politicheskoi terminologii." *Mongolica* 5, (2001): 21–30. Sankt-Peterburg: Russian Academy of Sciences.

Dobu, ed. *Uyigurjin monggul üsüg-ün durasgaltu bichig-üd*. Beijing: Nationalities Press, 1993.

Dorungga, ed. *Chinggis Hagan-u Tahil-un Sudur Orushiba*. Höhhot: Inner Mongolian People's Press, 1998.

Dreyfus, George B.J. *The Sound of Two Hands Clapping: The Education of a Tibetan Buddhist Monk*. Berkeley and Los Angeles: University of California Press, 2003.

Duara, Prasenjit. *Rescuing History from the Nation: Questioning Narratives of Modern China*. University of Chicago Press, 1995.

Duranti, Alessandro. "Intention, Self, and Responsibility: An Essay in Samoan Ethnopragmatics." *Responsibility and Evidence in Oral Discourse.* Edited by Jane H. Hill and Judith T. Irvine, 24–47. Cambridge University Press, 1993.

Eldengtei and Ardajab. *Monggul-un Nigucha Tobchiyan–Seiregülül Tailburi.* Hüh-hot: Inner Mongolian Educational Press, 1986.

Elverskog, Johan. *The Jewel Translucent Sutra: Altan Khan and the Mongols in the Sixteenth Century.* Leiden: Brill, 2003.

———. *Our Great Qing: Mongols, Buddhism, and the State in Late Imperial China.* Honolulu: University of Hawaii Press, 2006a.

———. "The Legend of Muna Mountain." *Inner Asia* 8 (1), (2006b): 99–122.

———. "Tibetocentrism, Religious Conversion, and the Study of Mongolian Buddhism." *The Mongolia-Tibet Interface: Opening New Research Terrains in Inner Asia.* Edited by Uradyn E. Bulag and Hildegard Diemberger, 59–80. Leiden and Boston: Brill, 2007.

Empson, Rebecca. "Enlivened Memories: Recalling Absence and Loss in Mongolia." *Ghosts of Memory: Essays on Remembrance and Relatedness.* Edited by Janet Carsten, 58–83. Oxford: Blackwell, 2007.

———, ed. *Time, Causality, and Prophecy in the Mongolian Cultural Region.* Folkestone: Global Oriental, 2007.

Erdenibayar. "Sumpa Khenpo Ishibaljur: A Great Figure in Mongolian and Tibetan Cultures." *The Mongolia-Tibet Interface: Opening New Research Terrains in Inner Asia.* Edited by Uradyn E. Bulag and Hildegard Diemberger, 303–14. Leiden and Boston: Brill, 2007.

Erdenipel. "Konechnaia prichina religii v Mongolii." *Istoriia v trudakh uchenykh lam.* Edited by A.S. Zheleznyakov and A.D. Tsendina, 155–247. Translated by B. Rinchen and Sambuu. Moscow: Tovarishchestvo nauchnykh izdanii KMK [c.1920s–1930s], 2005.

Evans, Christopher, and Caroline Humphrey. "After-lives of the Mongolian Yurt: The 'Archaeology' of a Chinese Tourist Camp." *Journal of Material Culture* 7 (2), (2002): 189–210.

———. "History, Timelessness, and the Monumental: The Oboos of the Mergen Environs, Inner Mongolia." *Cambridge Archaeological Journal* 13 (2), (2003): 195–211.

Even, Marie-Dominique. *Chants de chamanes Mongols. Études Mongoles . . . et Sibériennes* 19–20. Paris: Université de Paris X and CNRS, 1988–1989.

Fabian, Johannes. *Time and the Other: How Anthropology Makes its Object.* New York: Columbia University Press, 1983.

Farquar, David. "Emperor as Bodhisattva in the Governance of the Ch'ing Empire." *Harvard Journal of Asiatic Studies* 38 (1), (1978): 5–34.

Faubion, James. *An Anthropology of Ethics.* Cambridge University Press, 2011.

Forêt, Philippe. *Mapping Chengde: The Qing Landscape Enterprise.* Honolulu: University of Hawaii Press, 2000.

Foucault, Michel. *The Archaeology of Knowledge.* Translated by A.M. Sheridan Smith. London: Routledge, [1972] 2002.

Futaki, Hiroshi. "'A Prayer for Incense-Offering to the White Old Man' composed by Mergen Gegen." *Bulletin of the Japan Association for Mongolian Studies* 28, (1997): 43–63.

Futaki, Hiroshi. "Klassifikatsiia tekstov o belom startse." Translated by M.P. Petrova. *Mongolica* 5, (2001): 33–37. Sankt-Peterburg: Russian Academy of Sciences.

Gaadamba, M., and D. Tserensodnom. *Mongol Ardyn Aman Zokhiolyn Deezh Bichig*, Ulaanbaatar: Shinzhlekh Ukhaan Akademiin Khevlel, 1967.

Galdanwangchugdorji. *Mergen Heyid-ün Ug Teühe Orushibai*. Edited and with commentary by Ba. Mönghe and Ü. Naranbatu. Hailar: Inner Mongolian Cultural Press, [1846] 1994.

Galluu, S. *Monggul-iyar delgeregülügsen burhan shajin-u nom soyul uralig-un teühe*. Höhhot: Inner Mongolian People's Press, 2 vols., 2003.

Galluu and Jirantai, eds. *Mergen Gegen Lubsangdamijalsan-u 'bum jarlig hemegdehu orushiba*. Beijing: National Press, 1986.

Ganbaatar, D. *Burkhany Nomyn Mongol Unshlagyn Sudar*. Tergüün devter. Ulaanbaatar: Mönkhiin Üseg Grupp. 2010.

Gerasimova, K.M. *Obnovlencheskoe dvizhenie buryatskogo lamaistskogo dukhovenstva*. Ulan-Ude: Siberian Division Academy of Sciences of the USSR, 1964.

Gernet, Jaques. *A History of Chinese Civilization*. Translated by J.R. Foster. Cambridge University Press, 1982.

Gilsenan, Michael. "Translating Colonial Fortunes: Dilemmas of Inheritance in Muslim and English Laws across a Nineteenth-Century Diaspora." *Comparative Studies of South Asia, Africa, and the Middle East* 31 (3), (2011): 355–71.

Ginzburg, Carlo. *Clues, Myths, and the Historical Method*. Translated by John and Anne Tedeschi. Baltimore: Johns Hopkins University Press, 1989.

Goldstein, Melvyn. "The Revival of Monastic Life in Drepung Monastery." *Buddhism in Contemporary Tibet: Religious Revival and Cultural Identity*. Edited by Melvyn C. Goldstein and Matthew T. Kapstein, 15–52. Berkeley: University of California Press, 1998.

Gombojab. *Ganga-yin urushal*. Edited and with an introduction by L.S. Puchkovskii. Moscow: Izdatel'stvo vostochnoi literatury, [1725] 1960.

Gombrich, Richard. *Precept and Practice: Traditional Buddhism in the Rural Highlands of Ceylon*. Oxford: Clarendon Press, 1971.

Gombrich, R., and G. Obeyesekere. *Buddhism Transformed, Religious Change in Sri Lanka*. Princeton University Press, 1988.

Goody, Jack. "Strategies of Heirship." *Comparative Studies in Society and History* 15 (1), (1973): 3–20.

Gordon, Colin, ed. *Michel Foucault: Power/Knowledge: Selected Interviews and Other Writings, 1972–1977*. Translated by Colin Gordon, Leo Marshall, John Mepham, and Kate Soper. New York: Pantheon Books, 1980.

Greenblatt, Stephen. 2010. "Cultural Mobility: An Introduction." *Cultural Mobility: A Manifesto*, edited by Stephen Greenblatt, 1–23. Cambridge University Press, 2010.

Grupper, Samuel Martin. "The Manchu Imperial Cult of the Early Ch'ing Dynasty: Texts and Studies on the Tantric Sanctuary of Mahakala at Mukden." PhD dissertation, Indiana University, 1980.

Gyatso, Janet. "Genre, Authorship, and Transmission in Visionary Buddhism: The Literary Tradition of Thang-stong rGyal-po." *Tibetan Buddhism: Reason and Revelation*. Edited by Steven Goodman and Ronald Davison. Albany, NY: State University of New York Press, 95–106, 1992a.

———. "Introduction." *In the Mirror of Memory*. Edited by Janet Gyatso, 1–20. New York: State University of New York Press, 1992b.

———. "Letter Magic: A Peircean Perspective on the Semiotics of Rdo Grub-chen's *Dhāraṇī* Memory." *In the Mirror of Memory*. Edited by Janet Gyatso, 173–214. New York: State University of New York Press, 1992c.

———. *Apparitions of the Self: The Secret Autobiographies of a Tibetan Visionary*. Princeton University Press, 1998.

Hahn, Cynthia. "The Voices of the Saints: Speaking Reliquaries." *Gesta* 36 (1), (1997): 20–31.

Hamayon, Roberte. "L'anthropologie et la Dualité Paradoxale du 'Croire' Occidental." *Théologiques* 13 (1), (2005): 15–41.

Hansen, Valerie. "Gods on Walls: A Case of Indian Influence on Chinese Lay Religion?" *Religion and Society in T'ang and Sung China*. Edited by Patricia Ebrey and Peter N Gregory, 75–115. Honolulu: University of Hawaii Press, 1993.

Heesterman, J.C. *The Inner Conflict of Tradition: Essays in Indian Ritual, Kinship, and Society*. University of Chicago Press, 1985.

Heissig, Walther. *Die Pekinger Lamaistischen Blockdrucke in Mongolischer Sprache*. Wiesbaden: Otto Harrassowitz, 1954.

———. *Die Familien—Und Kirchengeschichtsschreibung der Mongolen. Teil 1: 16–18. Jahrhundert*. Wiesbaden: Otto Harrassowitz, 1959.

———. *A Lost Civilization: The Mongols Rediscovered*. London: Thames and Hudson, 1966.

———. *The Religions of Mongolia*. Translated by Geoffrey Samuel. London: Routledge and Kegan Paul, 1980.

———. "A Mongolian Source to the Lamaist Suppression of Shamanism in the 17th Century." *Schamanen und Geisterbeschwörer in der Östlichen Mongolei*. Edited by W. Heissig, 61–136. Wiesbaden: Otto Harrassowitz, [1953] 1992.

———. "Zum einfluss des Mergen gegen auf die Cagan Ebügen-Verehrung." *Zentralasiatische Studien*, 30, (2000): 53–67.

Hevia, James. *Cherishing Men from Afar: Qing Guest Ritual and the Macartney Embassy of 1793*. Durham, NC: Duke University Press, 1995.

Heylen, Ann. *Chronique du Toumet-Ortos: Looking Through the Lens of Joseph Van Oost, Missionary in Inner Mongolia (1915–1921).* Leuven Chinese Studies XVI. Leuven University Press, 2004.

Hirsch, Eric, and Charles Stewart. "Introduction: Ethnographies of Historicity." *History and Anthropology,* 16 (3), (2005): 261–74.

Hobsbawm, Eric. "Introduction: Inventing Traditions." *The Invention of Tradition.* Edited by E. Hobsbawm and T. Ranger, 1–14. Cambridge University Press, 1983.

Holbraad, Martin. "Response to Bruno Latour's 'Though shalt not freeze-frame,'" 2004. http://abaete.wikia.com/wiki/Response_to_Bruno_Latour's_"Thou_shall_not_freeze-frame"_(Martin_Holbraad)

Holmberg, David. *Order in Paradox: Myth, Ritual, and Exchange among Nepal's Tamang.* Ithaca, NY: Cornell University Press, 1989.

Horchabagatur, L. and O. Chogtu, eds. *Chinggis Hagan-u Altan Bichig.* Hailar: Inner Mongolian Cultural Press, 2001.

Humphrey, Caroline. *Karl Marx Collective: Economy, Society and Religion in a Siberian Collective Farm.* Cambridge University Press, 1986.

——— "Fairs and Miracles: At the Boundaries of the Jain Community in Rajasthan." *The Assembly of Listeners: Jains in Society.* Edited by Michael Carrithers and Caroline Humphrey, 201–28. Cambridge University Press, 1991.

———. "The Moral Authority of the Past in Post-Socialist Mongolia." *Religion, State, and Society* 20 (3 & 4), (1992): 375–89.

———. "Chiefly and Shamanist Landscapes in Mongolia." *The Anthropology of Landscape.* Edited by E. Hirsch and M. O'Hanlon, 135–62. London: Routledge, 1995.

———. *Shamans and Elders: Experience, Knowledge, and Power among the Daur Mongols.* Oxford: Clarendon Press, 1996.

———. "Genres and Cultural Diversity in Cultural Politics: On Representations of the Goddess Tara in Mongolia." *Inner Asia* 2 (1), (1997a): 24–47.

———. "Exemplars and Rules: Aspects of the Discourse of Moralities in Mongolia." *The Ethnography of Moralities.* Edited by Signe Howell, 25–47. London: Routledge, 1997b.

———. "The Fate of Earlier Social Ranking in the Communist Regimes of Russia and China." *Institutions and Inequalities: Essays in Honour of André Béteille.* Ramachandra Guha and Jonathan Parry, eds., 56–87. Delhi: Oxford University Press, 1999.

———. "Landscape Conflicts in Inner Mongolia." *Contested Landscapes: Landscapes of Movement and Exile.* Edited by Barbara Bender and Margot Winer, 55–68. Oxford and London: Berg Publishers, 2001.

———. "Rituals of Death as a Context for Understanding Personal Property in Socialist Mongolia." *Journal of the Royal Anthropological Institute,* n.s., 8 (1), (2002): 65–87.

———. "Stalin and the Blue Elephant: Paranoia and Complicity in Post-Communist Metahistories." *Transparency and Conspiracy: Ethnographies of*

Suspicion in the New World Order. Edited by Harry West and Todd Sanders, 175–203. Durham, NC: Duke University Press, 2003.

———. "On Being Named and Not Named: Authority, Person, and their Names in Mongolia." *The Anthropology of Names and Naming*. Edited by G. Vom Bruck and B. Bodenhorn, 157–76. Cambridge University Press, 2006b.

———. "Vital Force: The Story of Dugar Jaisang and Popular Views of Mongolian-Tibetan Relations from Mongolian Perspectives." *The Mongolia-Tibet Interface: Opening New Research Terrains in Inner Asia*. Edited by U. Bulag and H. Diemberger, 159–74. Leiden: Brill, 2007.

———. "Reassembling Individual Subjects: Events and Decisions in Troubled Times." *Anthropological Theory* 8 (4), (2008): 357–80.

Humphrey, Caroline, and A. Hürelbaatar. "Kontekstual'noe issledovanie buddizma: istoricheskaya pamyat' ob aginskom datsane." *Mir Buddiiskoi Kul'tury*. Edited by Ts.P. Vanchikova, 183–86. Ulan-Ude-Aginskoe: ZabGPU, 2001.

———. "Regret as a Political Intervention: An Essay in the Historical Anthropology of the Early Mongols." *Past and Present* 186, (2005): 3–45.

Humphrey, Caroline, and Hürelbaatar Ujeed. "Fortune in the Wind: An Impersonal Subjectivity." *Social Analysis* 56(2), (2012): 152–67.

Humphrey, Caroline, and James Laidlaw. *The Archetypal Actions of Ritual: A Theory of Ritual illustrated by the Jain Rite of Worship*. Oxford University Press, 1994.

———. "Sacrifice and Ritualization." *The Archaeology of Ritual*. Edited by Evangelos Kyriakidis, 255–76. Los Angeles: University of California Cotsen Advanced Seminars, 2007.

Hurcha, N. "Attempts to Buddhicise the Cult of Chinggis Khan." *Inner Asia* 1 (1), (1999): 45–58.

Hürelbaatar, A. "Herding with Cultivating in Inner Mongolia." *Inner Asia Occasional Papers* 2 (1), (1997): 69–89.

———. "Contemporary Mongolian Sacrifice and Social Life in Inner Mongolia: The Case of the Jargalt Oboo of Urad." *Inner Asia* 8 (2), (2006): 205–28.

Hyer, Paul, and William Heaton. "The Cultural Revolution in Inner Mongolia." *The China Quarterly* 36, (1968): 114–28

Hyer, Paul, and Sechin Jagchid. *A Mongolian Living Buddha: Biography of the Kanjurwa Khutughtu*. Albany: State University of New York Press, 1983.

Ikels, Charlotte. *The Return of the God of Wealth: The Transition a Market Economy in Urban China*. Stanford University Press, 1996.

Ingold, Tim. *The Perception of the Environment: Essays in Livelihood, Dwelling, and Skill*. London and New York: Routledge, 2000.

Ivy, Marilyn. *Discourses of the Vanishing: Modernity, Phantasm, Japan*. University of Chicago Press, 1995.

Jackson, Roger J. "'Poetry' in Tibet: *Glu, mGur, sNyan ngag* and 'Songs of Experience.'" *Tibetan Literature: Studies in Genre*. Edited by José I. Cabezon and Roger R. Jackson, 368–92. Ithaca, NY: Snow Lion Publications, 1996.

Jagchid, Sechin. *Essays in Mongolian Studies*. Provo, UT: Brigham Young University, 1988.

———. *The Last Mongol Prince: The Life and Times of Demchugdongrub, 1902–1966*. Bellingham, WA: Western Washington University Press, 1999.

Jagchid, Sechin, and Paul Hyer. *Mongolia's Culture and Society*. Boulder: Westview Press, 1979.

James, William. *Pragmatism and the Meaning of Truth*. Cambridge, MA: Harvard University Press, 1975.

Jimbadorji. *Bolur Toli*. Beijing: National Press, [1849] 1984.

Jinpa, Thupten. *Self, Reality, and Reason in Tibetan Philosophy: Tsongkhapa's Quest for the Middle Way*. London: Routledge Curzon, 2002.

Jirantai. "'Muna Khan' ba 'Muna'." Compilation Committee of Oral Literature of China, Inner Mongolia Section, *Monggul Arad-un Üliger-ün Chigulgan*, 107–9. Hailar: Inner Mongolian Cultural Press, 2000.

Jullien, Francois. *La Propension des Choses: Pour une Histoire de L'efficacité en Chine*. Paris: Seuil, 1992.

Jürüngga. *Erdeni Tonumal Neretü Sudur Orushiba*. Beijing: National Press, 1984.

Kaplonski, Christopher. "Exemplars and Heroes: The Individual and the Moral in the Mongolian Political Imagination." *States of Mind: Power, Place, and the Subject in Inner Asia*. Edited by David Sneath, 63–90. Bellingham, WA: Western Washington University Press, 2006.

Kapstein, Matthew T. *The Tibetan Assimilation of Buddhism: Conversion, Contestation, and Memory*. Oxford University Press, 2000.

———. "Just Where on Jambudvipa are We? New Geographical Knowledge and Old Cosmological Schemes in 18th century Tibet." *Forms of Knowledge in Early Modern South Asia*. Edited by Sheldon Pollock, 336–64. Durham: Duke University Press, 2011.

Karmay, Samten G. "The Tibetan Cult of Mountain Deities and its Political Significance." *Reflections of the Mountain: Essays on the History and Social Meaning of the Mountain Cult in Tibet and the Himalaya*. Edited by Anne-Marie Blondeau and Ernst Steinkellner, 59–76. Vienna: Verlag de Österreichischen Akademie der Wissenschaften, 1996.

———. "A Comparative Study of the Yul Lha Cult in Two Bonpo Areas and its Cosmological Aspects." *The Arrow and the Spindle: Studies in History, Myths, Ritual, and Beliefs in Tibet*. Edited by Samten Karmay, 53–72. Kathmandu: Mandala Publications, 2005.

Keane, Webb. "Religious Language." *Annual Reviews of Anthropology* 26, (1997): 47–71.

Khalfa, Jean, ed. *An Introduction to the Philosophy of Gilles Deleuze*. London: Continuum, 2003.

Klein, Anne C. and Khetson Sangpo. "Hail Protection." *Religions of Tibet in Practice*. Edited by Donald S. Lopez, 400–409. Abridged Edition. Princeton University Press, 2009.

Kowalewski, J.E. *Dictionnaire Mongol-Russe-Français*. Kazan': Imprimerie de l'Université,1846.

Kozlov, P.K. *Mongoliya i Amdo i mertvyi gorod Khara-Khoto*. Moscow-Petrograd: Gosudarstvennoe Izdatel'stvo, 1923.

Kracauer, Siegfried. *History: The Last Things Before the Last*. Completed after the death of the author by Paul Kristeller. Princeton: Markus Wiener Publishers, [1969] 1995.

Kragh, Ulrich Timme. "Of Similes and Metaphors in Buddhist Philosophical Literature: Poetic Semblance through Mythic Allusion." *Bulletin of SOAS* 73 (3), (2010): 479–502.

Krahl, Regina. "The Yongzheng Emperor: Art Collector and Patron." *China: The Three Emperors, 1662–1795*. Edited by Evelyn Rawski and Jessica Rawson, 240–69. London: Royal Academy of Arts, 2005.

Kripolska, Marta. "'The Old Man and the Birds' in Mongolian Poetry: Questioning the Authorship of the Song." *Acta Orientalia* (Denmark) 64, (2003): 225–46.

Kuhn, Philip A. *Soulstealers: The Chinese Sorcery Scare of 1768*. Cambridge, MA: Harvard University Press, 1990.

Kwon, Heonik. *Ghosts of War in Vietnam*. Cambridge University Press, 2008.

Lacaze, Gaelle. "Games of Power: State Control, the *Naadam*, and the Cult of Chinggis Khan." *States of Mind: Power, Place, and the Subject in Inner Asia*. Edited by David Sneath, 91–107. Bellingham, WA: Western Washington University Press, 2006.

Laidlaw, James. *Riches and Renunciation: Religion, Economy, and Society among the Jains*. Oxford University Press, 1995.

———. "For an Anthropology of Ethics and Freedom." *Journal of the Royal Anthropological Institute*, n.s., 8, (2002): 311–32.

———. "Ethical Traditions in Question: Diaspora Jainism and the Environmental and Animal Liberation Movements." *Ethical Life in South Asia*. Edited by Anand Pandian and Daud Ali, 61–80. Bloomington: Indiana University Press, 2010.

Latour, Bruno. "What if We Talked Politics a Little?" *Contemporary Political Theory* 2 (2), (2003): 143–64.

———. *Reassembling the Social: An Introduction to Actor-Network Theory*. Oxford University Press, 2005a.

———. "'Thou Shalt not Freeze Frame'—Or How Not to Misunderstand the Science and Religion Debate." *Science, Religion, and the Human Experience*. Edited by James D. Proctor, 27–46. Oxford University Press, 2005b.

———. "La société comme possession—la 'prevue par l'orchestre.'" *Anthologie de la Possession*. Edited by Didier Debaise, 1–12. Dijon: Less Presses du Réel, 2010.

Lattimore, Owen. *The Mongols of Manchuria: Their Tribal Divisions, Geographical Distribution, Historical Relations with Manchus and Chinese, and Present Political Problems*. New York: The John Day Company, 1934.

———. *Mongol Journeys*. London: The Travel Book Club, 1942.

Lattimore, Owen, and Fujiko Isono. *The Diluv Khutaght: Memoirs and Autobiography of a Mongol Buddhist Reincarnation in Religion and Revolution*. Wiesbaden: Otto Harrassowitz, 1982.

Lear, Jonathan. *Radical Hope: Ethics in the Face of Cultural Devastation*. Cambridge, MA, and London: Harvard University Press, 2006.

Lessing, F.D. "The Question of Nicodemus." *Studia Altaica: Festschrift für Nikolaus Poppe*, 95–99. Wiesbaden: Otto Harrassowitz, 1957.

Lessing, Ferdinand, ed. *Mongolian-English Dictionary*. Berkeley and Los Angeles: University of California Press, 1960.

Li Narangoa. *Japanische Religionspolitik in der Mongolei 1932–1945. Reformbestrebungen under Dialog zwischen Japanischem under Mongolischem Buddhismus*. Wiesbaden: Harrassowitz Verlag, 1998.

Liu, Jinsuo. *Arban Buyantu Nom-un Chagan Teüke*. Höhhot: Inner Mongolian People's Press, 1981.

Liu, Xin. *The Otherness of Self: A Genealogy of the Self in Contemporary China*. Ann Arbor: University of Michigan Press, 2002.

Liu, Xin. *The Mirage of China*. New York and Oxford: Berghahn Books, 2009.

Lopez, Donald S., Jr. "Foreigner at the Lama's Feet." *Curators of the Buddha: The Study of Buddhism under Colonialism*. Edited by Donald S. Lopez, Jr., 251–95. University of Chicago Press, 1995.

———. "Mindfulness of Death." *Religions of Tibet in Practice*. Edited by Donald S. Lopez, Jr., 315–35. Abridged Edition. Princeton University Press, 2009.

Lu, Xinyu. "Ruins of the Future: Class and History in Wang Bing's *Tiexi District*." *New Left Review* 31, (2005): 125–36.

Lubsangchültüm [Chahar Gebshi]. *Chahar gebsi-yin sumbum, Monggul teühe-yin surbulji bichig yisün jüil*. Edited by Altanorgil. Höhhot, 1983.

Lyotard, Jean-Francois. *Discours, figure*. Paris: Klinksiek, 1973.

MacIntyre, Alasdair. *Whose Justice? Which Rationality?* University of Notre Dame, 1988.

McLellan, David, ed. *Karl Marx: Selected Writings*. 2nd ed. Oxford University Press, 2000.

Mahmood, Saba. *Politics of Piety: The Islamic Revival and the Feminist Subject*. Princeton University Press, 2005.

Mair, Jonathan. "Faith, Knowledge, and Ignorance in Contemporary Inner Mongolian Buddhism." (unpublished PhD thesis), University of Cambridge, 2007.

Makley, Charlene. "'Speaking Bitterness': Autobiography, History, and Mnemonic Politics on the Sino-Tibetan Frontier." *Comparative Studies in Society and History* 47 (1), (2005): 40–78.

———. *The Violence of Liberation: Gender and Tibetan Buddhist Revival in Post-Mao China*. Berkeley: University of California Press, 2007.

Martin, Dan. "Pearls from Bones: Relics, Chortens, Tertons, and the Signs of Saintly Death in Tibet." *Numen* 41, (1994): 273–324.

Martynov, A.S. and T. Pang. "About Ideology of the Early Qing Dynasty." *Archiv Orientalni* 71 (3), 2003: 385–94.

Massey, Doreen. "Space-Time, 'Science' and the Relationship between Physical Geography and Human Geography." *Transactions of the Institute of British Geographers*, n.s., 24 (3), (1999): 261–76.

———. "Landscape as a Provocation: Reflections on Moving Mountains." *Journal of Material Culture* 11 (1–2), (2006): 33–48.

McCleary, Rachel M. and Leonard W.J. van der Kuijp. "The Market Approach to the Rise of the Geluk School, 1419–1642." *Journal of Asian Studies* 69 (1), (2010): 149–80.

Meillassoux, Quentin. *After Finitude: An Essay on the Necessity of Contingency.* Translated by Ray Brassier. London: Continuum, 2008.

Menghebatu [Mönghebatu], S. *Hubilgan-u Haragan-dehi Yirtinchü* [A World Through a Chorji's Eyes.] Beijing: Nationalities Press, 2006.

Menghebatu [Mönghebatu], S. *Yige bei huofo de shijie.* [The World in the Eyes of a Living Buddha.] Hailar: Inner Mongolian Press, 2009.

Miller, James. *Monasteries and Culture Change in Inner Mongolia.* Wiesbaden: Otto Harrassowitz, 1959.

Mills, Martin. "Vajra Brother, Vajra Sister: Renunciation, Individualism, and the Household in Tibetan Buddhist Monasticism." *Journal of the Royal Anthropological Institute* 6 (1), (2000): 17–34.

———. *Identity, Ritual, and State in Tibetan Buddhism: The Foundations of Authority in Gelukpa Monasticism.* London and New York: Routledge Curzon, 2003.

Mitchell, W.T., ed. *Landscape and Power.* University of Chicago Press, 1994.

Mitter, Rana. *A Bitter Revolution: China's Struggle with the Modern World.* Oxford University Press, 2004.

Mönghe, B. *Mergen Süme.* Hailar: Inner Mongolian Cultural Press, 1996.

Mönghe, B. *Han Muna-yin Següresü.* [The Sigh of Muna Khan.] Hühhot: Inner Mongolian People's Press, 2006.

Mönghe, Ba. *Mergen Gegen Lubsangdambijalsan.* Hailar: Inner Mongolian Cultural Press, 1995.

Mönghe, Ba. "Mergen Gegen-ü Altan Tobchi-dehi Hasar-un düri-yin uchir." *Mergen Gegen Sudulal-un Ögülel-üüd.* Edited by U. Naranbat and B. Mönghe, 204–36. Hailar: Inner Mongolian Cultural Press, 1997.

Mönghe, Ba. *Urad-un mergen gegen-ü utha soyul-un üyile ajillagan-u ulamjilal shinechilel.* Höhhot: Inner Mongolia Cultural Press, 2004.

Mönghe, Ba. *Mergen Gegen Lubsangdambijalsan tan-u nayan nigen ehitü shilüg daguu hemehü orushibai.* Höhhot: Inner Mongolia People's Press, 2010.

Mönghedelger. *Habutu Hasar.* Höhhot: Inner Mongolia People's Press, 1998.

Mongush, M.V. "Religiia v istorii i sovremennoi kul'ture tyvintsev," *Religiia v istorii i kul'ture mongoloyazychnykh narodov rossii.* Edited by N.L. Zhukovskaya, 215–41. Moscow: Vostochnaya Literatura RAN, 2008.

Mostaert, Antoine. "'L'overture du sceau' et les addresses chez les Ordos." *Monumenta Serica* 1, (1935–1936): 315–37. Peiping: Henri Vetch.

Mueggler, Erik. *The Age of Wild Ghosts: Memory, Violence, and Place in Southwest China*. Berkeley, Los Angeles, and London: University of California Press, 2001.

Myagmarsambuu, G. and Ch. Oyunchimeg. *Tseregiin Tüükh Sudlal*. Ulaanbaatar: Mongolyn Tsergiin Tüükhchdiin "Khar Süld" Holboo, 2007.

Nair, Rukmini Bhaya. *Narrative Gravity: Conversation, Cognition, Culture*. New Delhi: Oxford University Press, 2002.

Naquin, Susan, and Evelyn S. Rawski. *Chinese Society in the Eighteenth Century*. New Haven and London: Yale University Press, 1987.

Naranbatu, Ü., and Ba Mönghe, eds. *Mergen Gegen Sudulul-un Ögülel-üüd*. Hailar: Mergen Gegen Studies Committee, Inner Mongolian Cultural Press, 1997.

Narasu and S. Almas. *Urad-un Jang Agali*. Höhhot: Inner Mongolia People's Press, 1993.

Nietupski, Paul Kokot. *Labrang Monastery: A Tibetan Buddhist Community on the Inner Asian Borderlands, 1709–1958*. Lanham, MD, Boulder, CO, New York; Toronto, CN; Plymouth, UK: Lexington Books, 2011.

Ning Chia. "The Lifanyuan and the Inner Asian Rituals in the Early Qing (1644–1795)." *Late Imperial China* 14 (1), (1993): 60–92.

Nyiri, Pal. "Struggling for Mobility: Migration, Tourism, and Cultural Authority in Contemporary China." *Cultural Mobility: A Manifesto*. Edited by Stephen Greenblatt, 172–214. Cambridge University Press, 2010.

Obruchev, V.A. *Ot Kiakhty do Kul'dzhi*. Moscow: Izdatel'stvo Akademii Nauk SSSR, 1950.

Ochi. *Chahar Gebshi Lubsangchültüm*. Hailar: Inner Mongolian Cultural Press, 1996.

Oglaev, Yu. O. *Kirsanovshchina: sbornik publikatsii SMI*. Stavropol': Stavropol'skaia Kraevaia Tipografiia, 2000.

Ong, Aihwa. "Chinese Modernities: Narratives of Nation and Capitalism." *Ungrounded Empires: The Cultural Politics of Modern Chinese Transnationalism*. Edited by Aihwa Ong and Donald Nonini, 171–202. New York: Routledge, 1997.

Onon, Urgunge.. *The Secret History of the Mongols: The Life and Times of Chinggis Khan*. Translated, edited, and with an introduction by Urgunge Onon. London: Curzon, 2001.

Ortner, Sherry B. *High Religion: A Cultural and Political History of Sherpa Buddhism*. Princeton University Press, 1989.

Otgun. "Mergen Juu, Mergen Gegen ba Muna Han." *Mergen Gegen Sudulul-un Ögülel-üüd*. Edited by U. Naranbatu and Ba. Mönghe, 60–72. Hailar: Mergen Gegen Studies Committee, Inner Mongolian Cultural Press, 1997.

Otgonbaatar, R. *Mongol modon baryn nomyn eh garchig*. Tokyo University of Foreign Studies, 1998.

Palmer, Michael. "The Re-emergence of Family Law in Post-Mao China: Marriage, Divorce, and Reproduction." *The China Quarterly* 141, (1995): 110–34.

Pedersen, Morten. "Tame from Within. Landscapes of the Religious Imagination among the Darxads of Northern Mongolia." *The Mongolia-Tibet Interface. Opening New Research Terrains in Inner Asia*. Edited by U. Bulag & H. Diemberger, 175–96: Leiden: Brill, 2007.

Perdue, Peter. *China Marches West: The Qing Conquest of Central Eurasia*. Cambridge: Harvard University Press, 2005.

Perry, Elizabeth J. and Li Xun. *Proletarian Power: Shanghai in the Cultural Revolution*. Boulder, CO: Westview, 1997.

Pietz, William. "Person." *Critical Terms for the Study of Buddhism*. Edited by Donald S. Lopez, 188–230. Chicago and London: University of Press, 2005.

Pinney, Christopher. "Piercing the Skin of the Idol." *Beyond Aesthetics: Art and the Technologies of Enchantment*. Edited by Christopher Pinney and Nicholas Thomas, 157–80. Oxford: Berg, 2001.

———. "Things Happen: or, From which Moment does that Object Come?" *Materiality*. Edited by Daniel Miller, 256–72. Durham and London: Duke University Press. 2005.

Pollock, Sheldon. "Ramayana and Political Imagination in India." *Journal of Asian Studies* 52 (2), (1993): 261–97.

———. "The Cosmopolitan Vernacular." *Journal of Asian Studies* 57 (1), (1998): 6–37.

———. "Cosmopolitan and Vernacular in History." *Public Culture* 12 (3), (2000): 591–625.

———. *The Language of the Gods in the World of Men: Sanskrit, Culture, and Power in Pre-Modern India*. Berkeley and Los Angeles: University of California Press, 2006.

Popov, P., trans. "Dnevnik Fan'-Shao-Kuy'ia: iz puteshestviia na zapad." *Zapiski Imperatorskago Russkago Gegraficheskogo Obshchestva po Obshchei Geografii*. Tom 5, (1875): 143–211.

Potanin, G.N. *Ocherki Severo-Zapadnoi Mongolii*. Vypusk 4. Materialy etnograficheskie. St. Petersburg: Karshbaum, 1883.

Pozdneev, A.M. *Ocherki byta mongol'skikh monastyrei i buddiiskogo dukhovenstva v Mongolii vsvyazi s otnosheniyami sego poslednego k narodu*. Zapiski Imperatorskago Russkago Geograficheskago Obshchestva po Otdeleniyu Etnografii. Tom 16. Sanktpeterburg: Tipografiya Imperatorskoi Akademii Nauk, 1887.

Pozdneev, A.M. *Mongolia and the Mongols*. Translated by John Roger Shaw and Dale Plank. The Hague: Indiana University and Mouton & Co., Uralic and Altaic Series, vol. 61, [1892] 1971.

Przheval'skii, N.M. *Mongoliia i Strana Tangutov*. Moscow: OGIS, [1875] 1946.

Puchkovskii, L.S. "Introduction" to Gombojab *Ganga-yin urushal*. Edited and with an introduction by L.S. Puchkovskii. Pamyatniki literatury narodov vostoka. Teksty, Malaya seriia 10. Moscow: Izdatel'stvo vostochnoi literatury, 1960.

Purbueva, Ts.P. *Biografiia Neidzhi-Toina: istochnik po istorii buddizma v Mongolii.* Novosibirsk: Nauka, 1984.

Purdue, Peter C. *China Marches West: The Qing Conquest of Central Eurasia.* Cambridge, MA: Balknap Press of Harvard University Press, 2005.

Pürevjav, S. *Khuv'sgalyn ömnökh ikh khüree.* Ulaanbaatar: Ulsyn khevleliin khereg erkhlekh khoroo, 1961.

Rachewiltz, Igor de. *The Secret History of the Mongols: A Mongol Epic Chronicle of the Thirteenth Century.* Two volumes. Leiden: Brill, 2004.

Rashi et al. *Horin Nigetü Tailburi Toli.* Höhhot: Inner Mongolian People's Press, [1717] 1979.

Rashipongsug. *Bolur Erihe.* Edited by Hühündür. Höhhot: Inner Mongolian People's Press, 1985.

Rashisereng, G., ed. *Monggul ganjuur-dehi burhan-u bürin iji hürüg jirug.* Höhhot: Inner Mongolian People's Press, 2001.

Rawski, Evelyn S. *The Last Emperors: A Social History of Qing Imperial Institutions.* Berkeley: University of California Press, 1998.

Rawski, Evelyn, and Jessica Rawson, eds. *China: The Three Emperors, 1662–1795,* London: Royal Academy of Arts, 2005.

Richter, Daniel K. *Facing East from Indian Country: A Native History of Early America.* Cambridge, MA, and London: Harvard University Press, 2001.

Rintchen, B. *Matériaux pour l'étude du chamanisme mongol.* 1. Sources litteraires. Wiesbaden: Otto Harrassowitz, 1959.

Robbins, Joel. "Continuity Thinking and the Problem of Christian Culture: Belief, Time, and the Anthropology of Christianity." *Current Anthropology* 48 (1), (2007): 5–38.

Robinson, James Burnell. "The Lives of Indian Buddhist Saints: Biography, Hagiography, and Myth." *Tibetan Literature: Studies in Genre.* Edited by José I. Cabezon and Roger R. Jackson, 57–69. Ithaca, NY: Snow Lion Publications, 1996.

Roerich, George N. *The Blue Annals.* Delhi: Motilal Benarsidas, 1949.

Rubin, Miri. *Corpus Christi: The Eucharist in Late Medieval Culture.* Cambridge University Press, 1991.

Ruegg, D. Seyfort. "The Preceptor-Donor (yon mchod) Relation in Thirteenth Century Tibetan Society and Polity, Its Inner Asian Precursors and Indian Models." *Tibetan Studies.* Edited by H. Krasser, T. Much, E. Steinkellner, and H. Tauscher, 857–72. Vienna: Verlag der Oesterreichischen Akademie der Wissenschaften, 1997.

Sagγang, Sečen. *Erdeni-yin Tobči: A Manuscript from Kentei Ayimaγ.* Edited and commented on by Elisabetta Chiodo, with a study of the Tibetan Glosses by Klaus Sagaster. Wiesbaden: Harrassowitz Verlag, [1662] 1996.

Sainjirgal and Sharaldai. *Altan Ordon-u Tailga.* Beijing: Nationalities Press, 1983.

Samuel, Geoffrey. "Tibet as a Stateless Society and some Islamic Parallels." *The Journal of Asian Studies* 41 (2), (1982): 215–29.

———. *Civilized Shamans*. Washington and London: Smithsonian Institute Press, 1993.

Santha, Istvan, and Tatiana Safonova. "Pokazukha in the House of Culture: The Pattern of Behaviour in Kurumkan, East Buryatia." *Reconstructing the House of Culture: Community, Self, and the Makings of the House of Culture in Russia and Beyond*. Edited by Brian Donahue and Joachim Otto Habeck, 75–96, 2010.

Sardar, Hamid. "Danzan Ravjaa: The Fierce Drunken Lord of the Gobi." *The Mongolia-Tibet Interface*. Edited by U. Bulag and H. Diemberger, 257–94. Leiden: Brill, 2007.

Schaeffer, Kurtis R. *The Culture of the Book in Tibet*. New York: Columbia University Press, 2009.

Schein, Louisa. "Performing Modernity." *Cultural Anthropology* 14 (3), (1999): 361–93.

———. *Minority Rules: The Miao and the Feminine in China's Cultural Politics*. Durham and London: Duke University Press, 2000.

Seigel, Jerrold. *The Idea of the Self: Thought and Experience in Western Europe since the 17th Century*. Cambridge University Press, 2005.

Serruys, Henry. "Early Lamaism in Mongolia." *Oriens Extremus* 10, (1963): 181–216.

———. "A Genre of Oral Literature in Mongolia: The Addresses." *Monumenta Serica* XXXI (1974–1975); (1977): 555–613.

Sharf, Robert H. "Ritual." *Critical Terms for the Study of Buddhism*. Edited by Donald Lopez, 245–70. University of Chicago Press, 2005.

———. "On the Allure of Buddhist Relics." *Representations* 66, (1999): 75–99.

Shastina, N.P., trans. and ed. *Shara Tudzhi: Mongol'skaya letopis' XVII veka*. Svodnyi tekst, perevod, vvedenie i primechaniia N.P.Shastinoi. Moskva-Leningrad: Izdatel'stvo Akademii Nauk SSSR, 1957.

Shrimali, K.M. "A Future for the Past?" *Social Scientist* 26 (9/10), (1998): 26–51.

Siklos, B. "Mongolian Buddhism: A Defensive Account." *Mongolia Today*. Edited by Shirin Akiner, 155–82. London: Kegan Paul International, 1991.

Simmel, Georg. *The Sociology of Georg Simmel*. Translated, edited, and with an introduction by Kurt H. Wolff. Glencoe, IL: The Free Press, 1950.

Skrynnikova, T.T. 1992/3. "Sülde–The Basic Idea of the Chinggis-Khan Cult." *Acta Orientalia Academiae Scientiarum Hung* XLVI (1), (1992/3): 51–59.

Slobodnik, Martin. "Destruction and Revival: The Fate of the Tibetan Buddhist Monastery Labrang in the People's Republic of China." *Religion, State, and Society* 32 (1), (2004): 7–19.

Sneath, David. *Changing Inner Mongolia: Pastoral Mongolian Society and the Chinese State*. Oxford University Press, 2000.

———. "Introduction." *Imperial Statecraft: Political Forms and Techniques of Governance in Inner Asia, Sixth–Twentieth Centuries*. Edited by David Sneath, 1–22. Bellingham: Western Washington University Press, 2006.

———. *The Headless State: Aristocratic Orders, Kinship Society, and Misrepresentations of Nomadic Inner Asia*. New York: Columbia University Press, 2007.

Snellgrove, David. *Indo-Tibetan Buddhism*. Bangkok: Orchid Press, 2004.

Sodubilig. *Shashin-nu toli*. Höhhot: Inner Mongolian Educational Press, 1996.

Sørensen, P. *The Mirror Illuminating the Royal Genealogies*. Wiesbaden: Harrassowitz Verlag, 1994.

Southwold, M. *Buddhism in Life, the Anthropological Study of Religion, and the Sinhalese Practice of Buddhism*. Manchester University Press, 1983.

Spence, Jonathan. *The Search for Modern China*. New York: Norton & Co., 1999.

Spence, Jonathan. *Treason by the Book*, London: Penguin, 2001.

Spiro, Melford E. *Burmese Supernaturalism: A Study in the Explanation and Reduction of Suffering*. Englewood Cliffs, NJ: Prentice-Hall, 1967.

———. *Buddhism and Society: A Great Tradition and its Burmese Vicissitudes*. London: Allen and Unwin, 1971.

Ssorin-Chaikov, Nikolai. "On Heterochrony: Birthday Gifts to Stalin, 1949." *Journal of the Royal Anthropological Institute*, n.s., 12, (2006): 355–75.

Stebetak, Zdenek. "Invocation Formulas and Typical Lexemes of Mongolian Tantras—Case of Mani-yin coka." *Mongolica Pragensia '03*. Edited by Jaroslav Vacek and Alena Oberfalzerova, 155–74, 2003.

———. "Liturgical Communication with Layman Mongols, The Use of the Maitreya Supplication in Alsha Banners." *Mongolica Pragensia '04*. Edited by Jaroslav Vacek and Alena Oberfalzerova, 145–52, 2004.

Strathern, Marilyn. "Disembodied Choice." *Other Intentions: Cultural Contexts and the Attribution of Inner States*. Edited by Lawrence Rosen, 69–90. Santa Fe. NM: School of American Research, 1995.

———. "Cutting the Network." *Journal of the Royal Anthropological Institute* 2 (3), (1996): 517–35.

———. *Partial Connections*. AltaMira Press of Rowman and Littlefield Publishing, Lanham, MD, 2004.

Strong, Sarah, and John Strong. "A Post-Cultural Revolution Look at Buddhism." *The China Quarterly* 54, (1973): 321–30.

Strong, John S. *Relics of the Buddha*. Princeton and Oxford: Princeton University Press, 2004.

Struve, Lynn. "Chimerical Early Modernity: The Case of 'Conquest Generation' Memoirs." *The Qing Formation in World-Historical Time*. Edited by Lynn Struve, 335–80. Cambridge, MA, and London: Harvard University Press, 2004.

Sujata, Victoria. *Tibetan Songs of Realization: Echoes from a Seventeenth Century Scholar and Siddha in Amdo*. Leiden: Brill, 2004.

Syrtypova, Surun-Khanda. *Kul't bogini-khranitel'nitsy Baldan Lkhamo v tibetskom buddizme*. Moscow: Vostochnaia Literatura RAN, 2003.

Tambiah, Stanley J. *Buddhism and the Spirit Cults in Northeast Thailand.* Cambridge University Press, 1970.

———. *World Conqueror and World Renouncer: A Study of Buddhism and Polity in Thailand against a Historical Background.* Cambridge University Press, 1976.

———. *The Buddhist Saints of the Forest and the Cult of Amulets: A Study of Charisma, Hagiography, Sectarianism, and Millenial Buddhism.* Cambridge University Press, 1984.

Taveirne, Patrick. *Han-Mongol Encounters and Missionary Endeavors: A History of Scheut in Ordos (Hetao) 1874–1911.* Leuven University Press, 2004

Tighe, Justin. *Constructing Suiyuan: The Politics of Northwestern Territory and Development in Early Twentieth-Century China.* Leiden: Brill, 2005.

Tsendina, A.D. "Khasar i Chingis v letopisiakh Mergen-gegena i Dzhambadorzhi." *Mongolica* 4, Sankt-Peterburg: Russian Academy of Sciences, 30–35, 1998.

Tserensodnom, D. *Mongolyn Burhany Shashny Uran Zohiol.* Tergüün devter. Ulaanbaatar: Shinzhleh Ukhaany Akademiin Khel Zolhiolyn Khüreelen, 1997.

Tsybikov, G.Ts. *Buddist-palomnik u svyatyn' Tibeta.* Novosibirsk: Izdatel'stvo 'Nauka,' Sibirskoe Otdelenie, [1919] 1981.

Tuttle, Grey. *Tibetan Buddhists in the Making of Modern China.* New York: Columbia University Press, 2005.

———. "The Ninth Panchen Lama, Shambhala, and the Kalacakra Tantra." *L'image du Tibet aux XIXème–XXème Siecles.* [The Image of Tibet in the 19th–20th Centuries.] Edited by Monica Esposito, 303–27. Paris: École Française d' Extrême-Orient, 2008.

Ujeed, Uranchimeg Borjigin. "Indigenous Efforts and Dimensions of Mongolian Buddhism Exemplified by the Mergen Tradition." PhD thesis, School of Oriental and African Studies, University of London, 2009.

———. "Persecuted Practice: Neichi Toyin's Way of Conducting Missionary Work." *Inner Asia* 13 (2), (2011): 265–78.

Ushakin, (Oushakine) Sergei. "Mesto—imeni—ia: sem'ia kak sposob organizatsii zhizni." *Semeinye uzly: Modeli dlia sborki.* Edited by S. Ushakin, 1: 7–54. Moscow: Novoe Literaturnoe Obozrenie, 2004.

Uspensky, Vladimir L. *Catalogue of the Mongolian Manuscripts and Xylographs in the St. Petersburg State University Library.* Tokyo: Institute for the Study of the Languages and Cultures of Asia and Africa, 2001.

Van der Kuijp, Leonard W.J. "The Dalai Lamas and the Origins of the Reincarnate Lamas." *The Dalai Lamas: A Visual History.* Edited by Martin Brauen, 14–31. Chicago: Serindia Publications, 2005.

Valeri, Valerio. "Wild Victims: Hunting as Sacrifice and Sacrifice as Hunting in Huaulu." *History of Religions* 34 (2), (1994): 101–31.

Wagner, Roy. *Symbols that Stand for Themselves.* Chicago and London: University of Chicago Press, 1986.

Waley-Cohen, Joanna. "Commemorating War in 18th century China." *Modern Asian Studies*, 30 (4), (1996): 869–99.

Waquet, Francoise. *Latin, or the Empire of a Sign*. Translated by John Howe. London: Verso, 2001.

Weintraub, Karl Joachim. *The Value of the Individual: Self and Circumstance in Autobiography*. Chicago: University of Chicago Press, 1978.

Weirong, Shen. "The First Dalai Lama Gendün Drup." *The Dalai Lamas: A Visual History*. Edited by Martin Brauen, 33–41. Chicago: Serinidia Publications, 2010.

Welch, Holmes. "Buddhism since the Cultural Revolution." *The China Quarterly* 40, (1969): 127–36.

Whitehead, Alfred North. *Adventures of Ideas*. Cambridge University Press, 1933.

Willerslev, Rane and Morten Axel. "Proportional Holism: Joking the Cosmos into the Right Shape in North Asia." *Experiments in Holism*. Edited by Tom Otto and Nils Bubandt, 262–76. Chichester: Wiley-Blackwell, 2010.

Williams, Bernard. *Shame and Necessity*. Berkeley: University of California Press, 1993.

———. "Making Sense of Humanity." *Making Sense of Humanity and Other Philosophical Essays*. Cambridge University Press, 1995.

Williams, James. *Gilles Deleuze's Philosophy of Time*. Edinburgh University Press, 2011.

Wu, Hung. "Pillow and Mirror: Absence as Subjectivity." Lecture given at the University of Cambridge, 2012.

Wu, Pei-yi. *The Confucian's Progress: Autobiographical Writings in Traditional China*. Princeton University Press, 1990.

Wylie, Turrel V. "Reincarnation: A Political Innovation in Tibetan Buddhism." *Proceedings of the Csoma de Körös Memorial Symposium* (1976). Edited by Louis Ligeti, 579–86. Budapest: Akademiai Kiado, 1978.

Yang, Haiying, and Uradyn E. Bulag. *Janggiya Qutugtu: A Mongolian Missionary for Chinese National Identification*. Cologne: International Society for the Study of the Culture and Economy of the Ordos Mongols, 2003.

Yee, Cordell D.K. "Chinese Maps in Political Culture." *The History of Cartography: Volume 2, Book 2. Cartography in the Traditional East and South East Asian Societies*. Edited by J.B. Hartley and David Woodward, 71–95. University of Chicago Press, 1994.

Yü, Dan Smyer. "Living Buddhas, Netizens, and the Price of Religious Freedom." *Privatizing China: Socialism From Afar*. Edited by Li Zhang and Aihwa Ong, 197–213. Ithaca and London: Cornell University Press, 2008.

Yu, Wansoo. *The Five Hundred Shir-a Darqat Families in Ordos: "People in Eternal Mourning for Chinggis Khan."* Master's Degree dissertation. Department of Uralic and Altaic Studies, Indiana University, 1989.

Yunxiang, Yan. *Private Life Under Socialism: Love, Intimacy, and Family Change in a Chinese Village 1949–1999*. Stanford University Press, 2003.

Zhang Mu. *Menggu youmu ji* [Records of Mongolian Pastoral Life]. Translated into Mongolian by Namyon and Banzaragcha, 1988. *Mongul-un Hoshigu Nutug-un Temdeglel*, 3 vols. Beijing: Nationalities Press, [1867] 1982.

Zhelezniakov, A.S. and A.D. Tsendina, eds. *Istoriya v trudakh uchenykh lam*. Moscow: Tovarishchestvo nauchnykh izdanii KMK, 2005.

Zhukovskaia, N.L. *Lamaizm i rannie formy religii*. Moscow: Nauka, 1977.

———. "Buddizm i shamanism kak factory formirovaniia buryatskogo mentaliteta." *Religiia v istorii i kul'ture mongoloyazychnykh narodov rossii*. Edited by N.L. Zhukovskaia, 9–36. Moscow: Vostochnaya Literatura RAN, 2008.

Zürcher, Erik. "Beyond the Jade Gate: Buddhism in China, Vietnam, and Korea." *The World of Buddhism*. Edited by Heinz Bechert and Richard Gombrich, 193–211. London: Thames and Hudson, 1984.

Zwalf, W., ed. *Buddhism: Art and Faith*. London: British Museum Publications, Ltd., 1985.

Index